DOWNERS GROVE PUBLIC LIBRARY

3 1191 00937 7573

MAY 19 2010

WITH

DOWNERS GRC   _IBRARY

IN SF CAR
Card, Orson Scott.
Ultimate Iron Man ultimate
 collection

Downers Grove Public Library
1050 Curtiss St.
Downers Grove, IL 60515
(630) 960-1200
www.downersgrovelibrary.org

GAYLORD

ULTIMATE

IRON MAN

ULTIMATE COLLECTION

ULTIMATE

IRON MAN

ULTIMATE COLLECTION

WRITER:
ORSON SCOTT CARD

ULTIMATE IRON MAN
PENCILS: ANDY KUBERT
WITH **MARK BAGLEY** (ISSUE #5)
INKS: DANNY MIKI
WITH **BATT, JESSE DELPERDANG, JOHN DELL & SCOTT KOBLISH**
COLORS: RICHARD ISANOVE
WITH **DAVE McCAIG & LAURA MARTIN**
LETTERS: CHRIS ELIOPOULOS
COVER ARTISTS: ANDY KUBERT, BRYAN HITCH,
DANNY MIKI & RICHARD ISANOVE

ASSISTANT EDITOR: SEAN RYAN
EDITOR: NICK LOWE
CONSULTING EDITORS: RALPH MACCHIO & MIKE MARTS

ULTIMATE IRON MAN II
ART: PASQUAL FERRY
WITH LEONARDO MANCO (ISSUE #5)
COLORS: DEAN WHITE
WITH LAURA MARTIN, DAVE McCAIG, PAUL MOUNTS & LARRY MOLINAR
LETTERS: VIRTUAL CALLIGRAPHY'S CORY PETIT
COVER ARTISTS: PASQUAL FERRY, JUSTIN PONSOR & DEAN WHITE

ASSISTANT EDITOR: LAUREN SANKOVITCH
EDITOR: BILL ROSEMANN
SENIOR EDITOR: RALPH MACCHIO

COLLECTION EDITOR:
CORY LEVINE
ASSISTANT EDITOR:
ALEX STARBUCK
ASSOCIATE EDITOR, SPECIAL PROJECTS:
JOHN DENNING
EDITORS, SPECIAL PROJECTS:
JENNIFER GRÜNWALD & MARK D. BEAZLEY
SENIOR EDITOR, SPECIAL PROJECTS:
JEFF YOUNGQUIST
SENIOR VICE PRESIDENT OF SALES:
DAVID GABRIEL

EDITOR IN CHIEF: JOE QUESADA
PUBLISHER: DAN BUCKLEY
EXECUTIVE PRODUCER: ALAN FINE

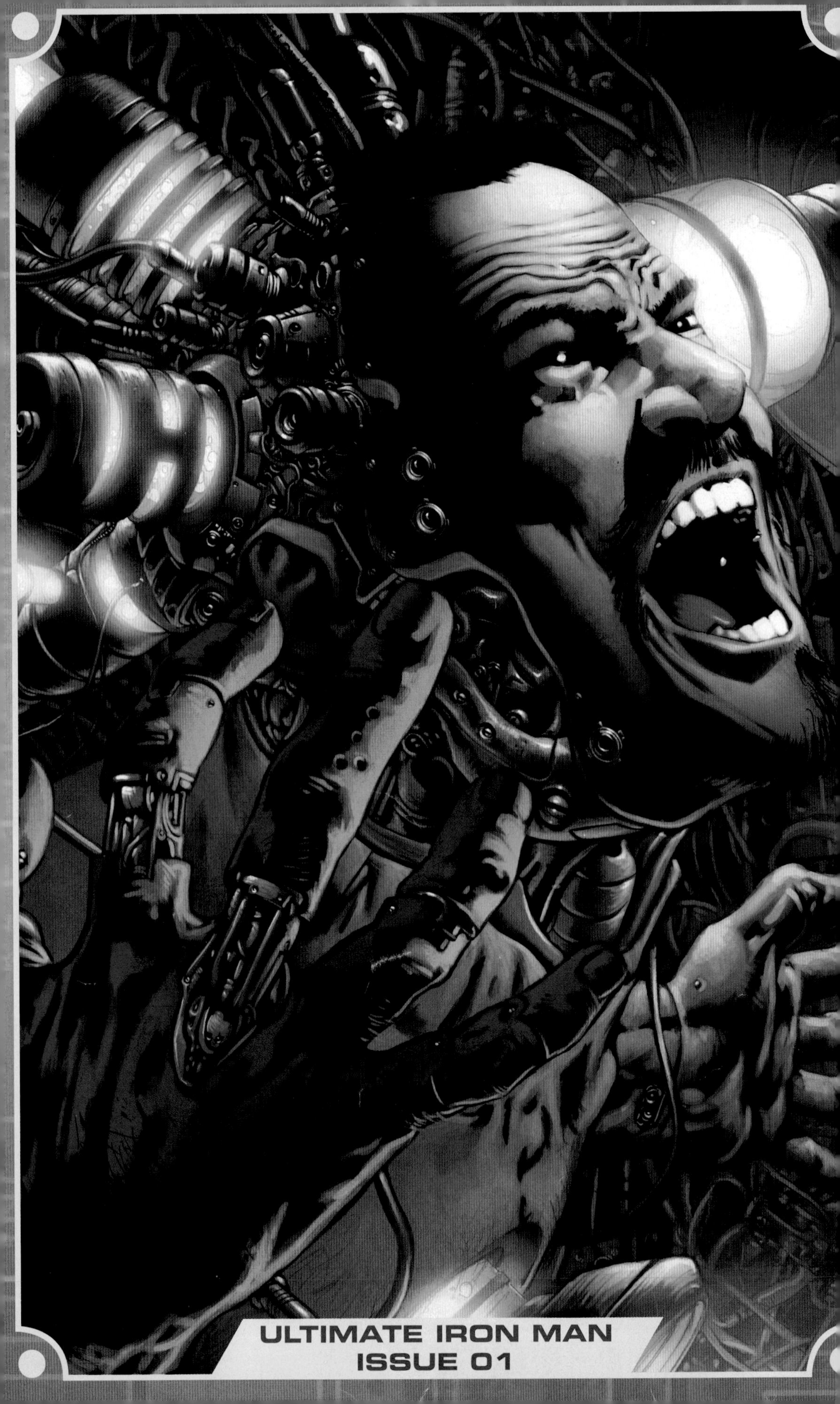
ULTIMATE IRON MAN
ISSUE 01

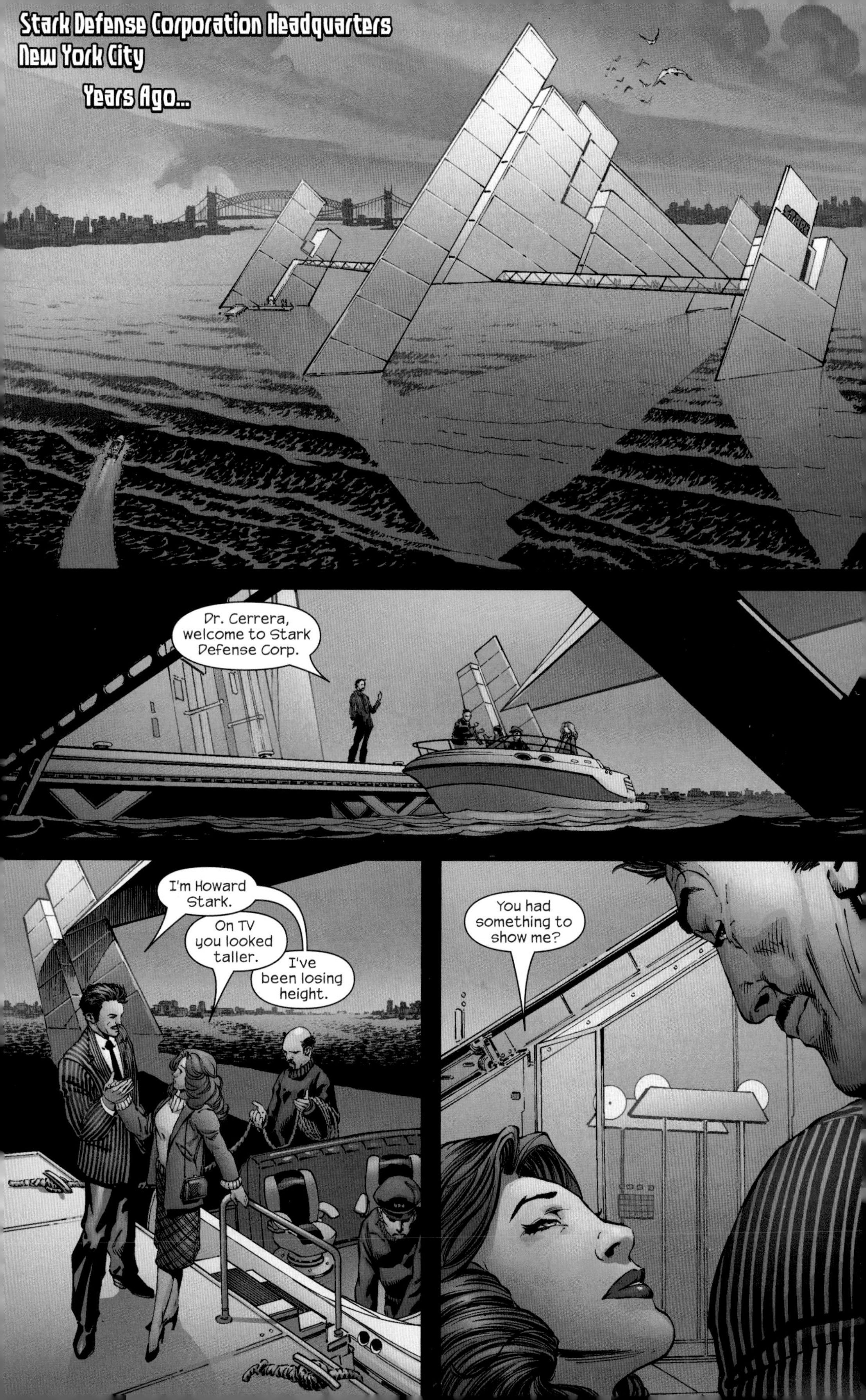
Stark Defense Corporation Headquarters
New York City
Years Ago...
Dr. Cerrera, welcome to Stark Defense Corp.
I'm Howard Stark.
On TV you looked taller.
I've been losing height.
You had something to show me?

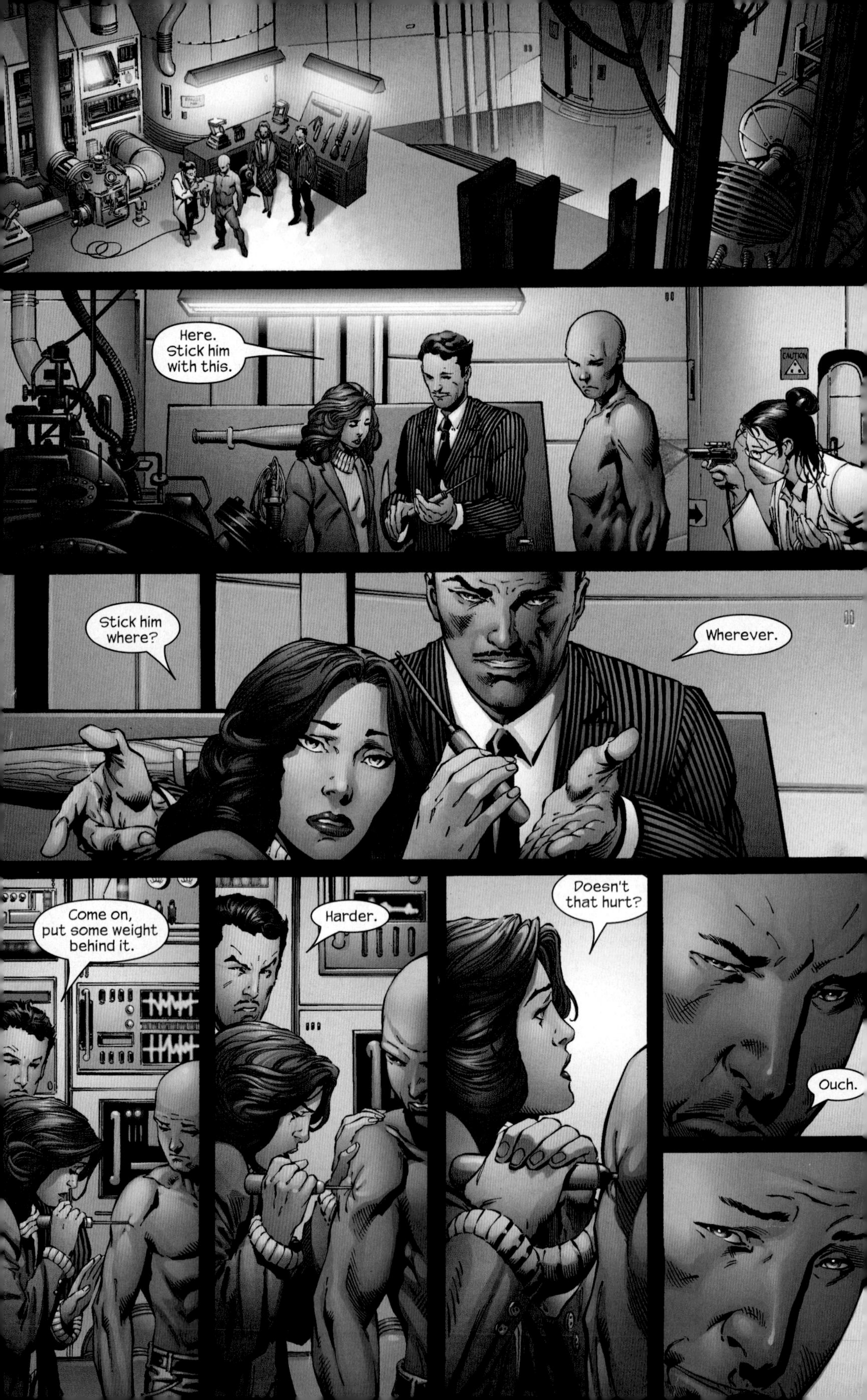
Here. Stick him with this.
Stick him where?
Wherever.
Come on, put some weight behind it.
Harder.
Doesn't that hurt?
Ouch.

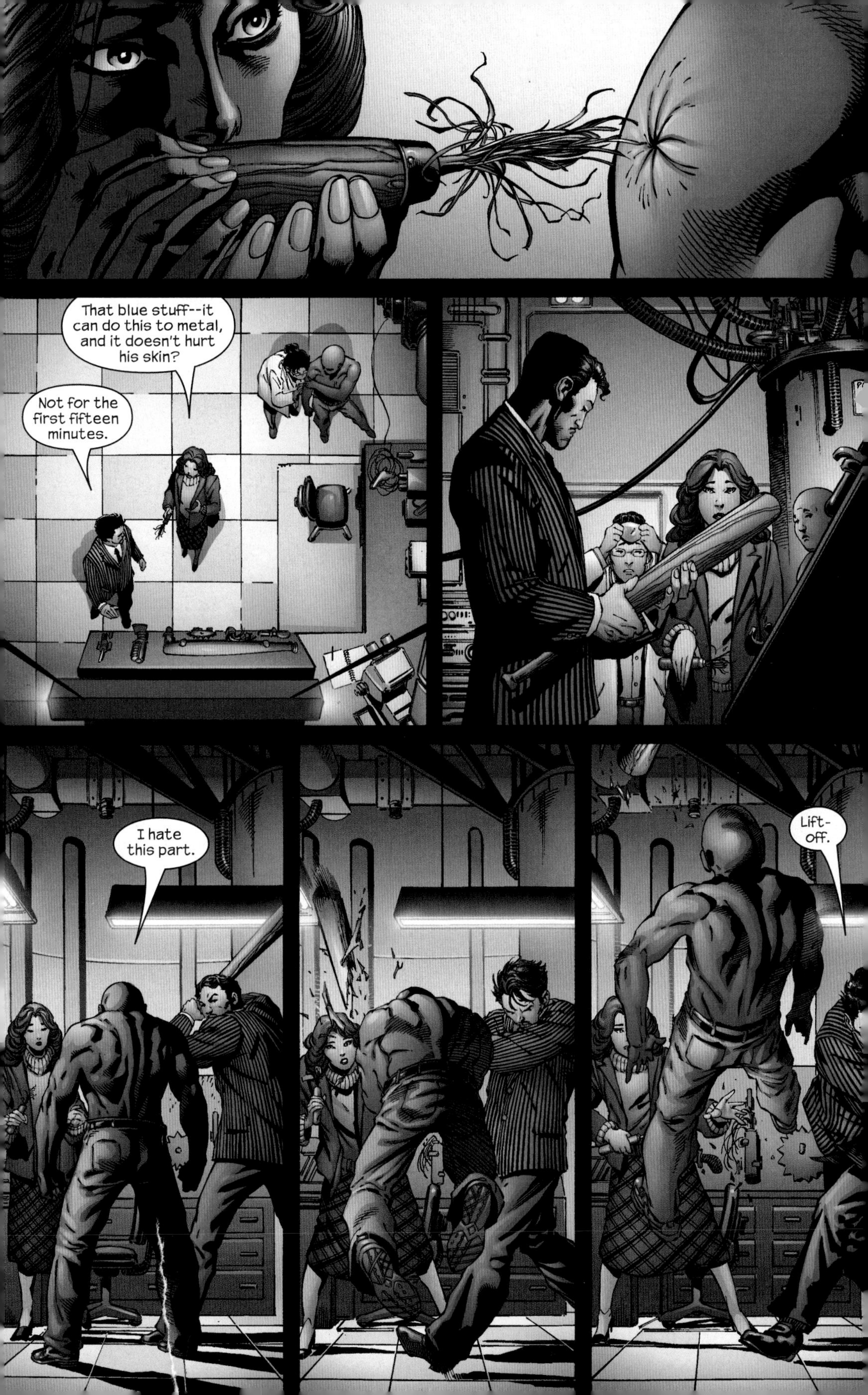
That blue stuff--it can do this to metal, and it doesn't hurt his skin?
Not for the first fifteen minutes.
I hate this part.
Lift-off.

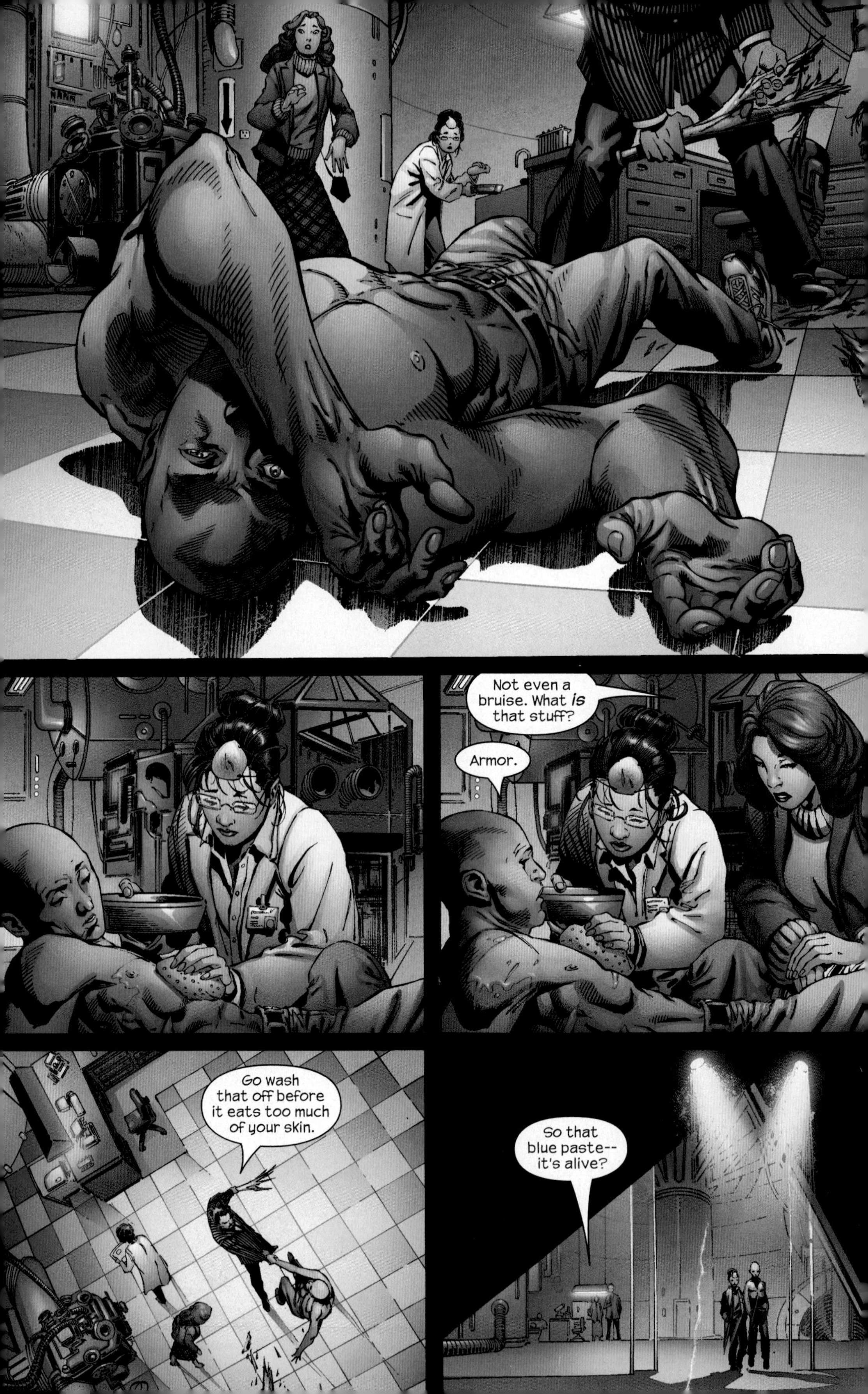
Not even a bruise. What *is* that stuff?
Armor.
Go wash that off before it eats too much of your skin.
So that blue paste-- it's alive?

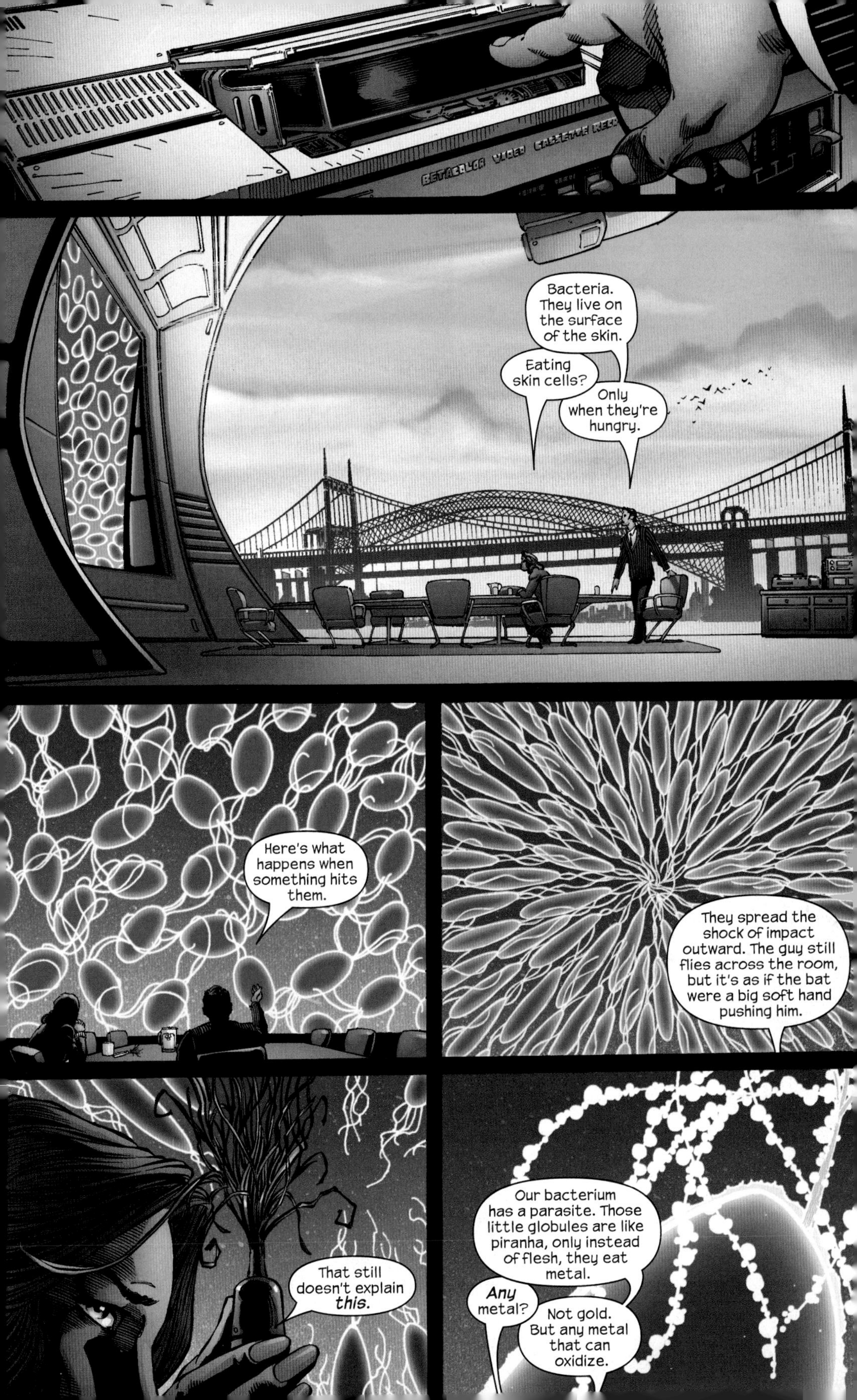
BETACOLOR VIDEO CASSETTE REC
Bacteria. They live on the surface of the skin.
Eating skin cells?
Only when they're hungry.
Here's what happens when something hits them.
They spread the shock of impact outward. The guy still flies across the room, but it's as if the bat were a big soft hand pushing him.
That still doesn't explain *this.*
Our bacterium has a parasite. Those little globules are like piranha, only instead of flesh, they eat metal.
Any metal?
Not gold. But any metal that can oxidize.

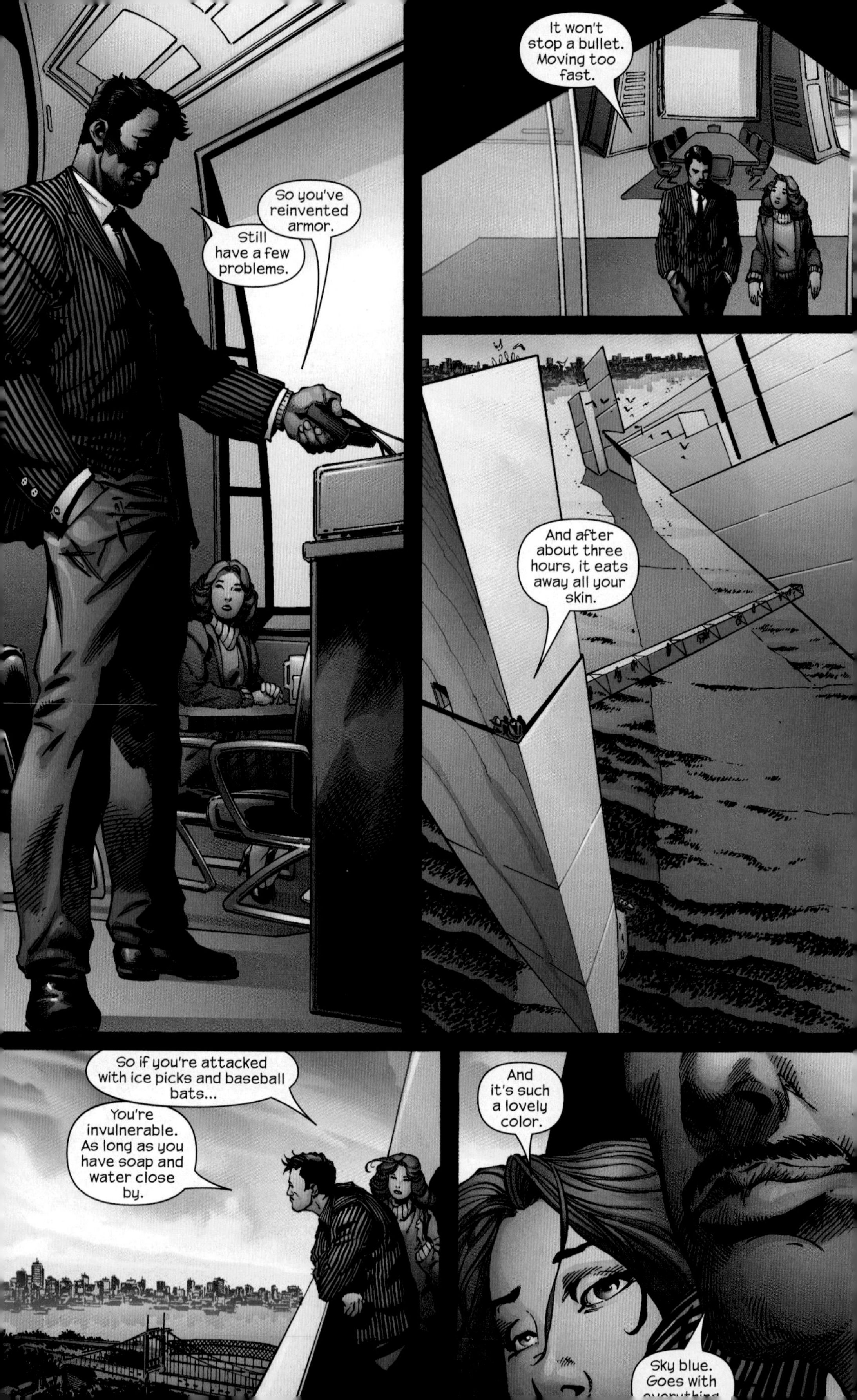
So you've reinvented armor.
Still have a few problems.
It won't stop a bullet. Moving too fast.
And after about three hours, it eats away all your skin.
So if you're attacked with ice picks and baseball bats...
You're invulnerable. As long as you have soap and water close by.
And it's such a lovely color.
Sky blue. Goes with

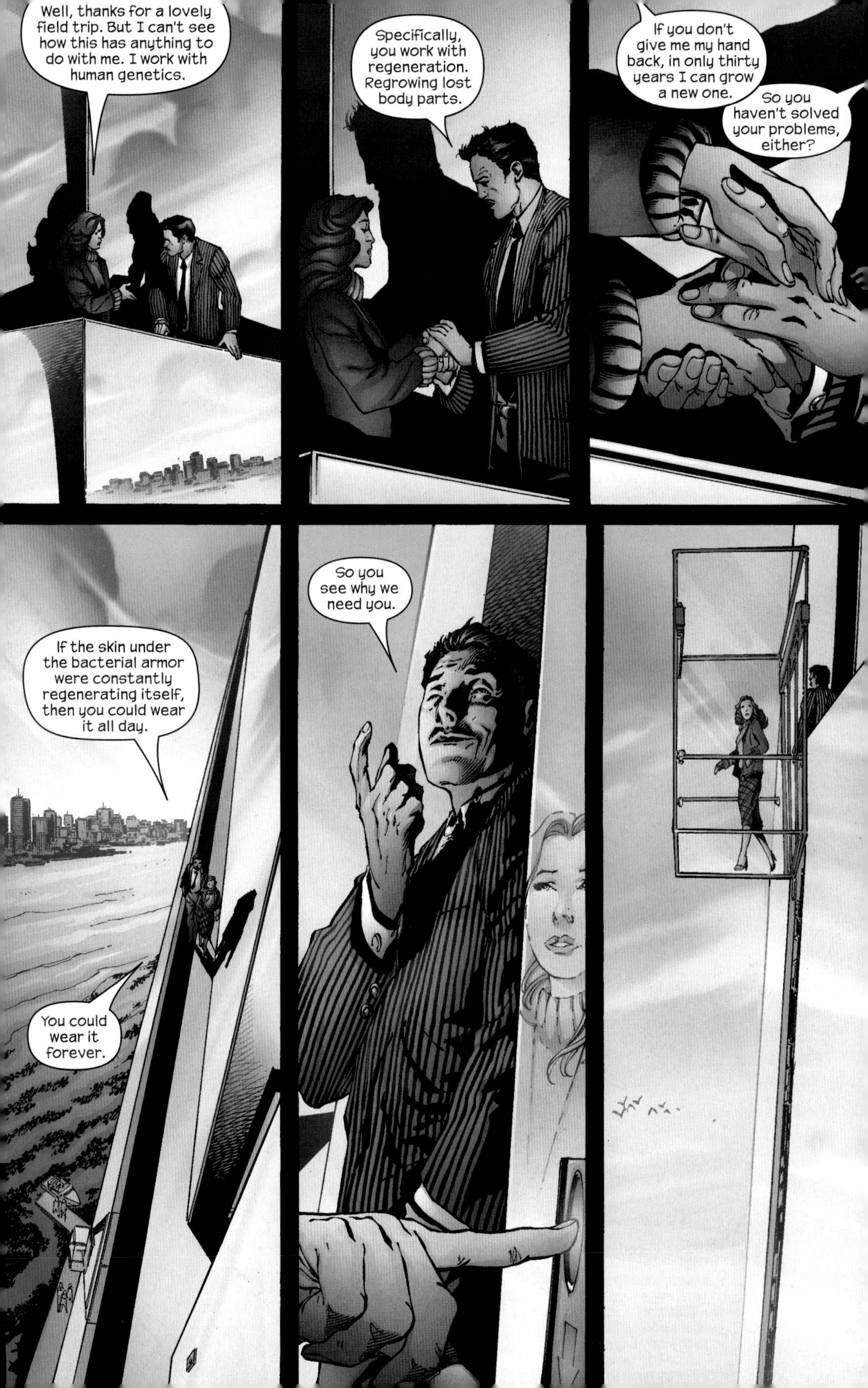
Well, thanks for a lovely field trip. But I can't see how this has anything to do with me. I work with human genetics.
Specifically, you work with regeneration. Regrowing lost body parts.
If you don't give me my hand back, in only thirty years I can grow a new one.
So you haven't solved your problems, either?
If the skin under the bacterial armor were constantly regenerating itself, then you could wear it all day.
You could wear it forever.
So you see why we need you.

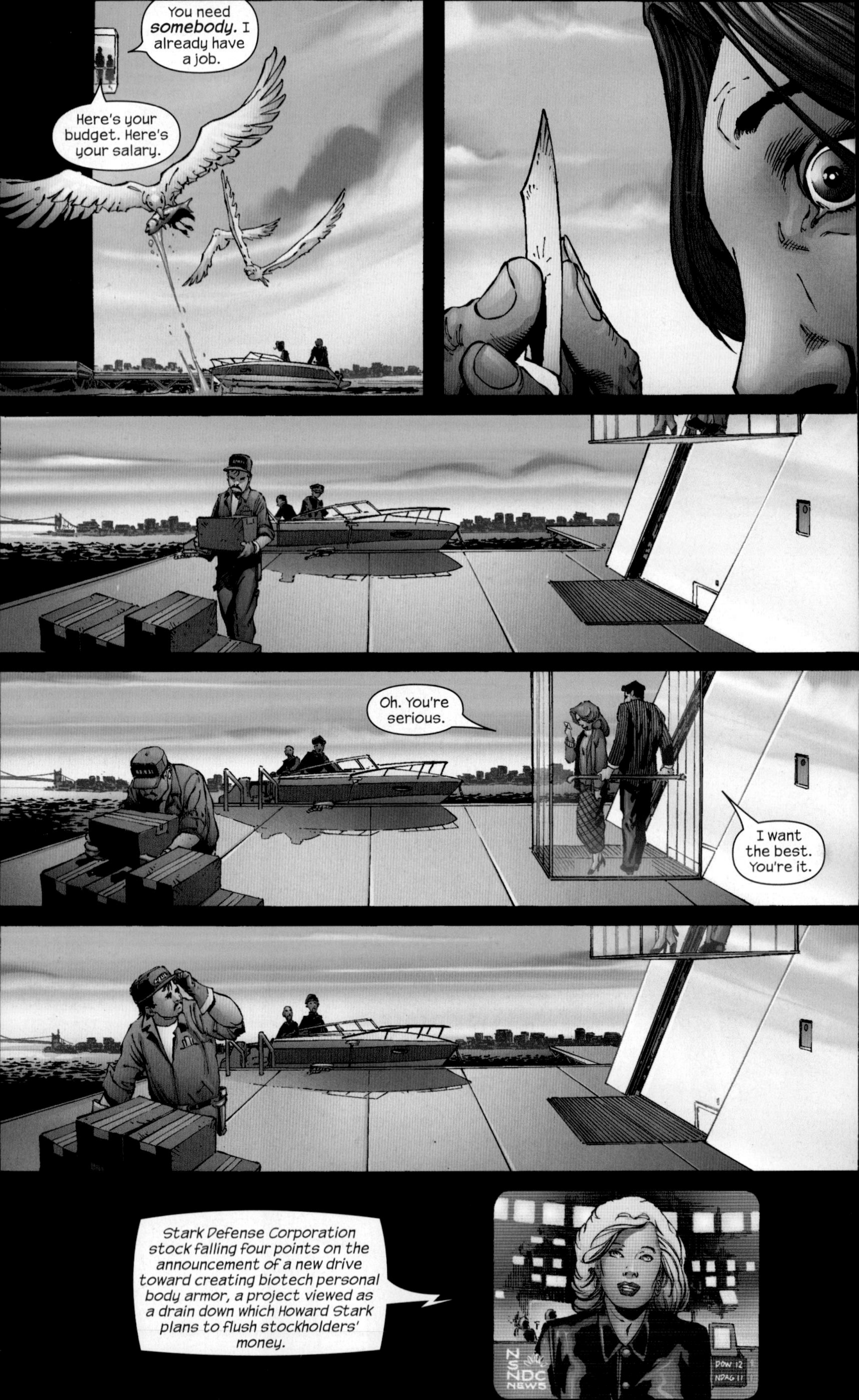
You need somebody. I already have a job.
Here's your budget. Here's your salary.
Oh. You're serious.
I want the best. You're it.
Stark Defense Corporation stock falling four points on the announcement of a new drive toward creating biotech personal body armor, a project viewed as a drain down which Howard Stark plans to flush stockholders' money.
NDC NEWS
DOW 12
NDAQ 11

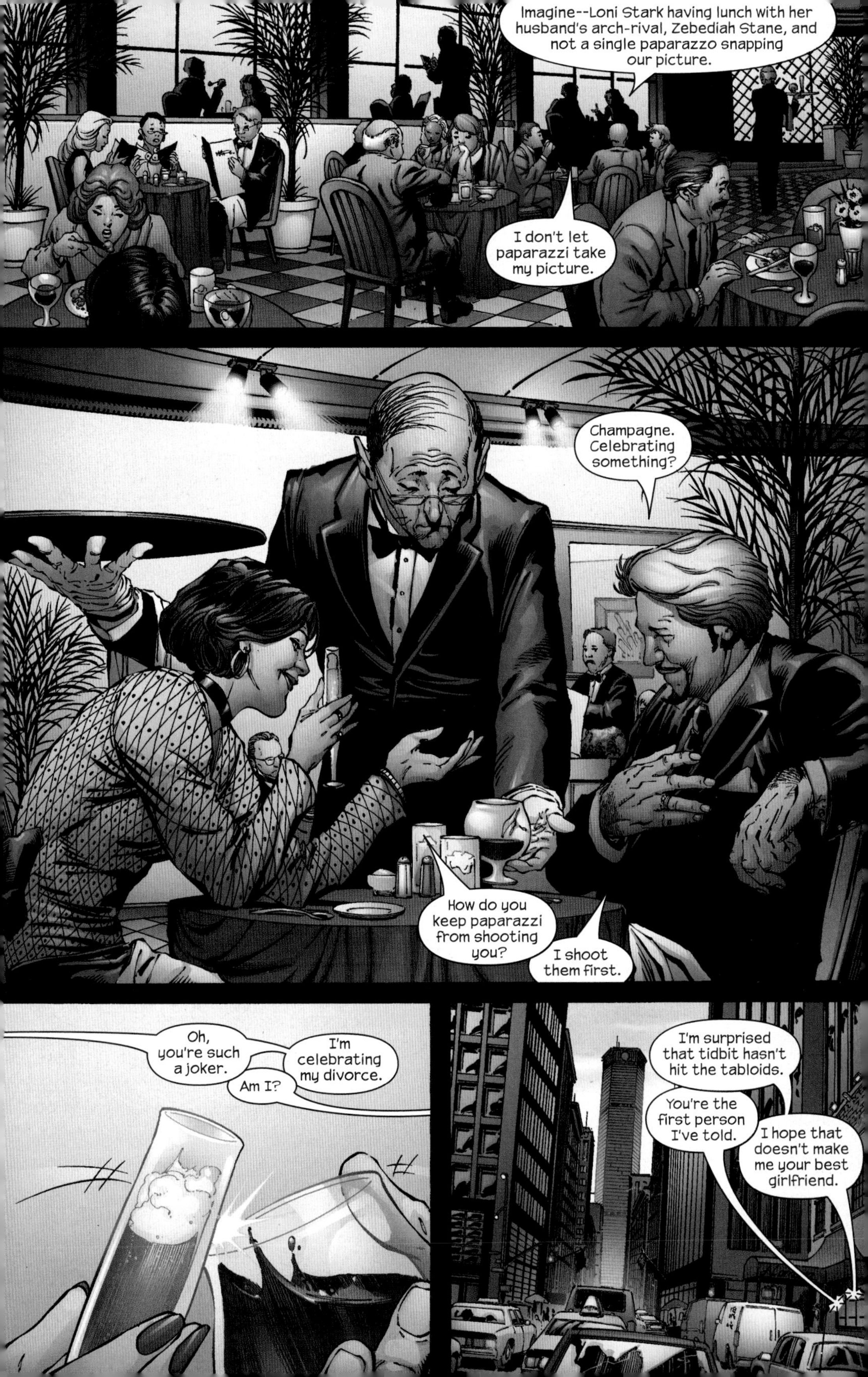
Imagine--Loni Stark having lunch with her husband's arch-rival, Zebediah Stane, and not a single paparazzo snapping our picture.
I don't let paparazzi take my picture.
Champagne. Celebrating something?
How do you keep paparazzi from shooting you?
I shoot them first.
Oh, you're such a joker.
I'm celebrating my divorce.
Am I?
I'm surprised that tidbit hasn't hit the tabloids.
You're the first person I've told.
I hope that doesn't make me your best girlfriend.

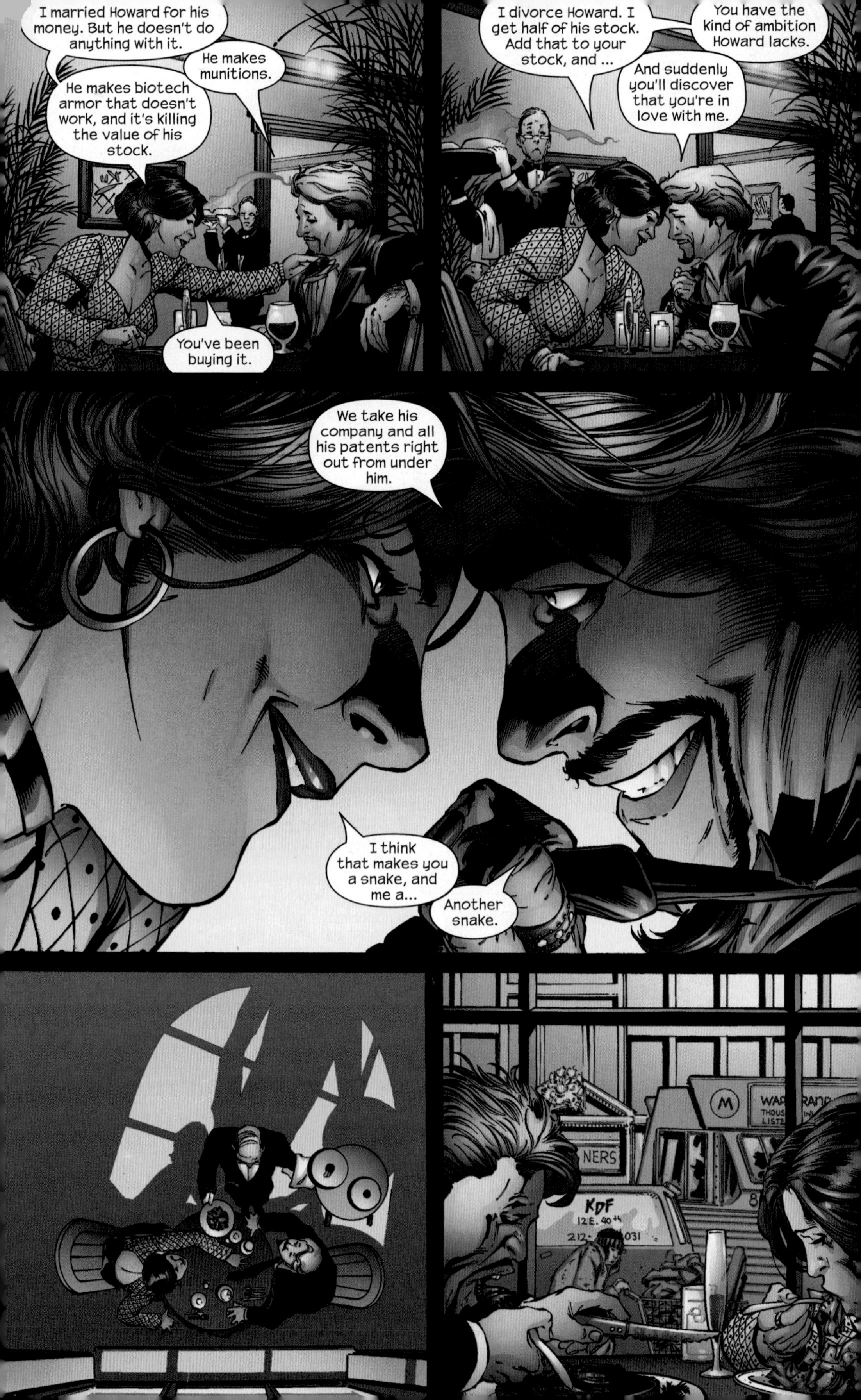
I married Howard for his money. But he doesn't do anything with it.
He makes munitions.
He makes biotech armor that doesn't work, and it's killing the value of his stock.
You've been buying it.
I divorce Howard. I get half of his stock. Add that to your stock, and ...
You have the kind of ambition Howard lacks.
And suddenly you'll discover that you're in love with me.
We take his company and all his patents right out from under him.
I think that makes you a snake, and me a...
Another snake.
NERS
KDF
12 E. 40th

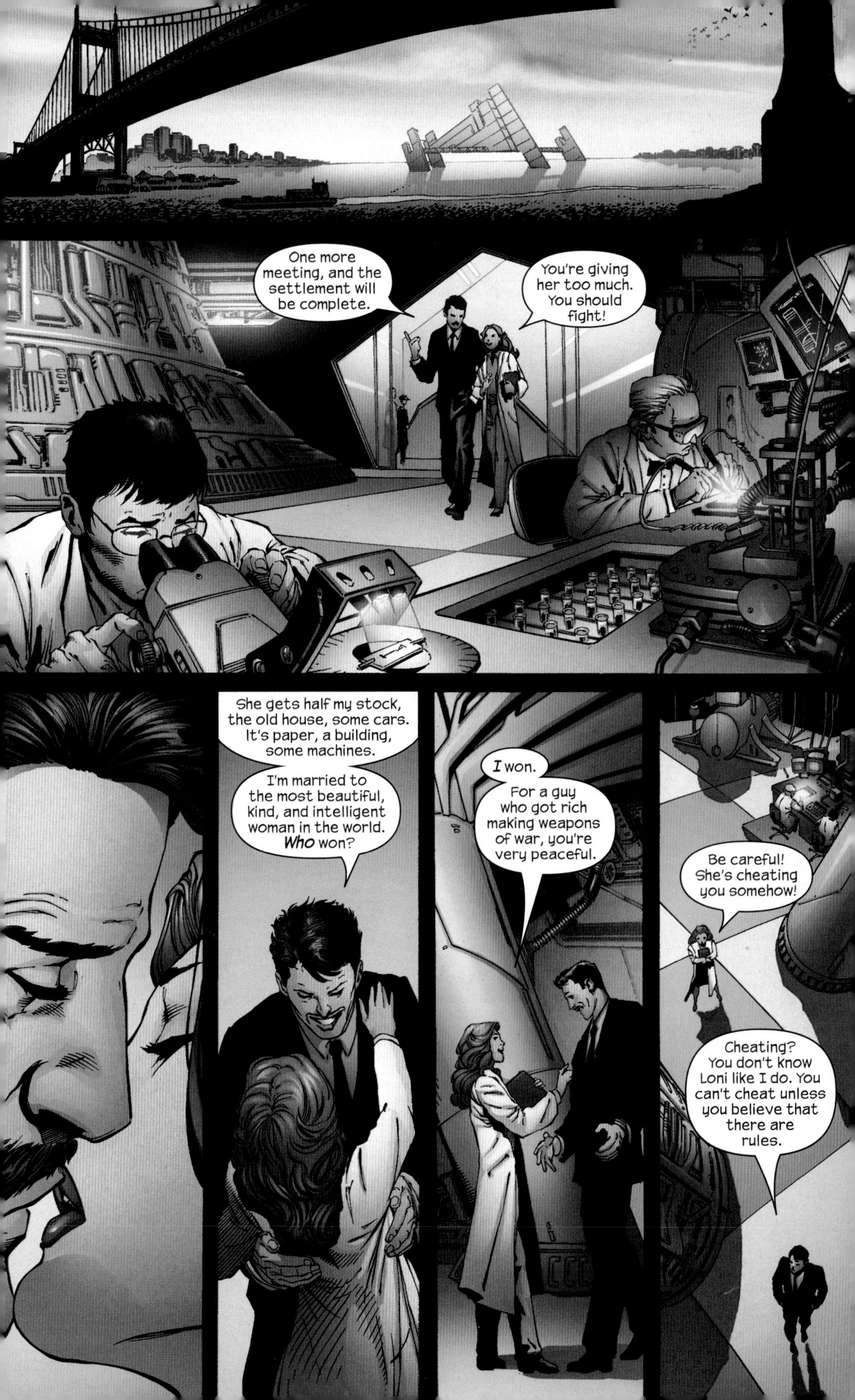
One more meeting, and the settlement will be complete.
You're giving her too much. You should fight!
She gets half my stock, the old house, some cars. It's paper, a building, some machines.
I'm married to the most beautiful, kind, and intelligent woman in the world. *Who* won?
I won.
For a guy who got rich making weapons of war, you're very peaceful.
Be careful! She's cheating you somehow!
Cheating? You don't know Loni like I do. You can't cheat unless you believe that there are rules.

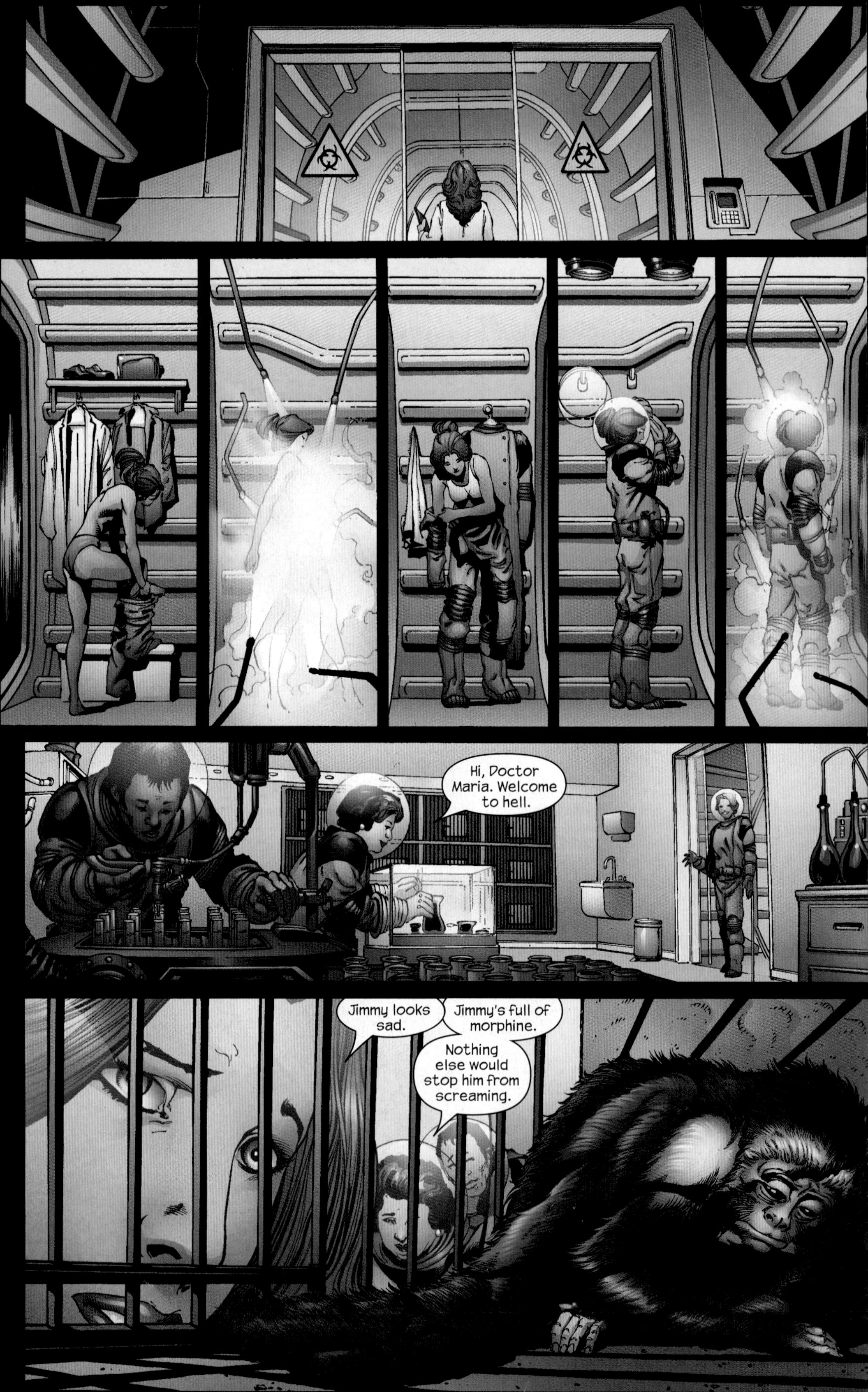
Hi, Doctor Maria. Welcome to hell.
Jimmy looks sad.
Jimmy's full of morphine.
Nothing else would stop him from screaming.

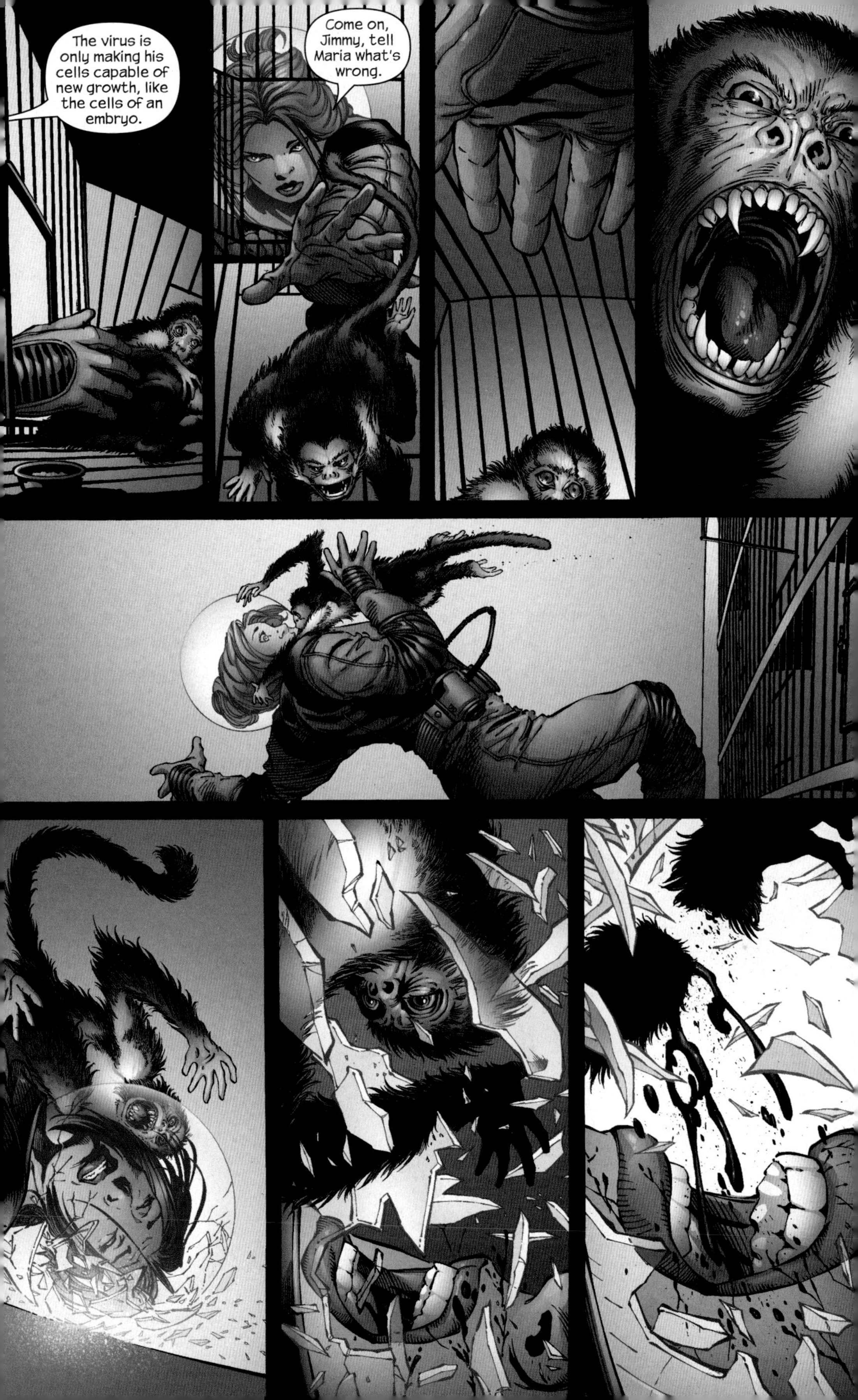
The virus is only making his cells capable of new growth, like the cells of an embryo.
Come on, Jimmy, tell Maria what's wrong.

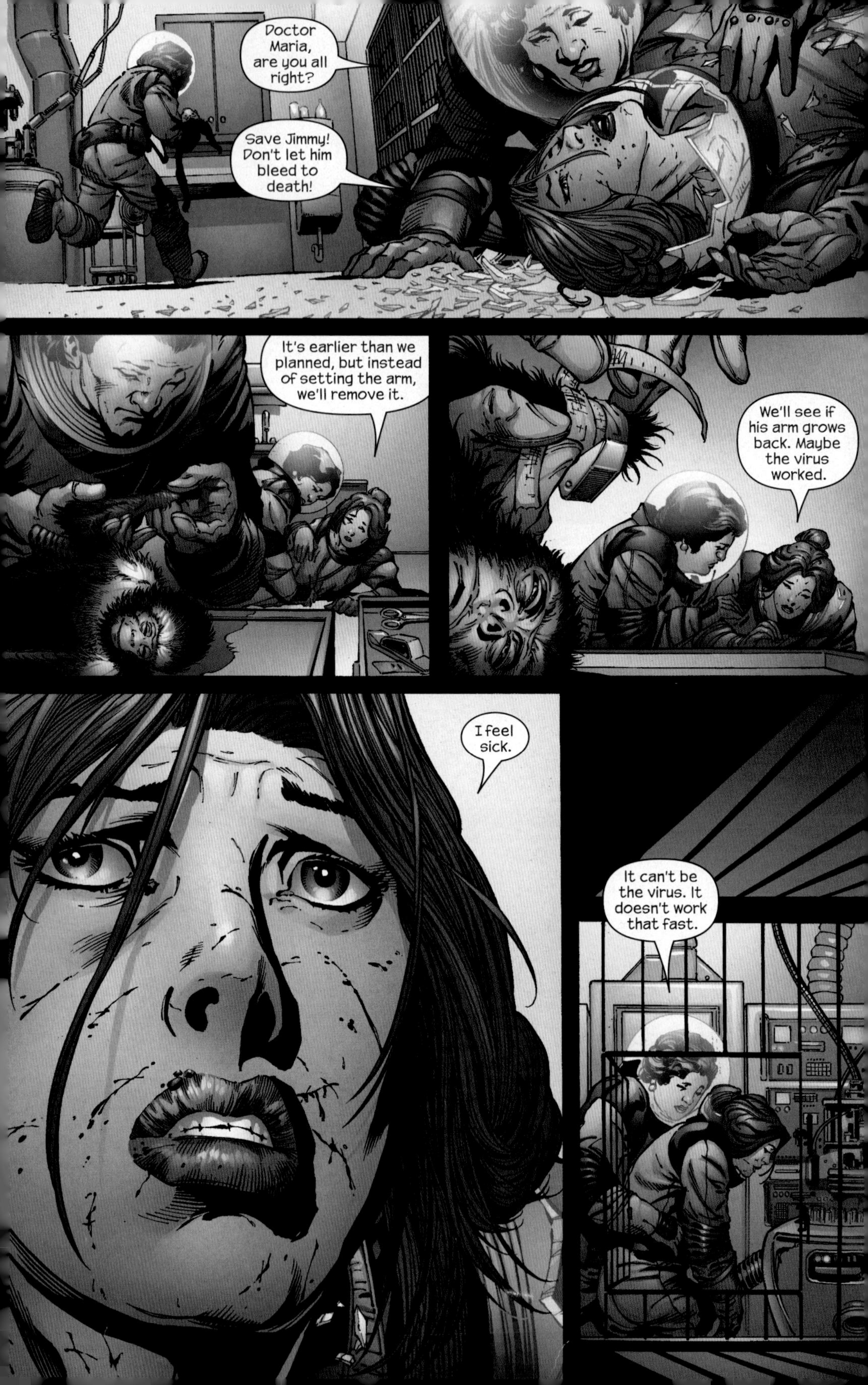
Doctor Maria, are you all right?
Save Jimmy! Don't let him bleed to death!
It's earlier than we planned, but instead of setting the arm, we'll remove it.
We'll see if his arm grows back. Maybe the virus worked.
I feel sick.
It can't be the virus. It doesn't work that fast.

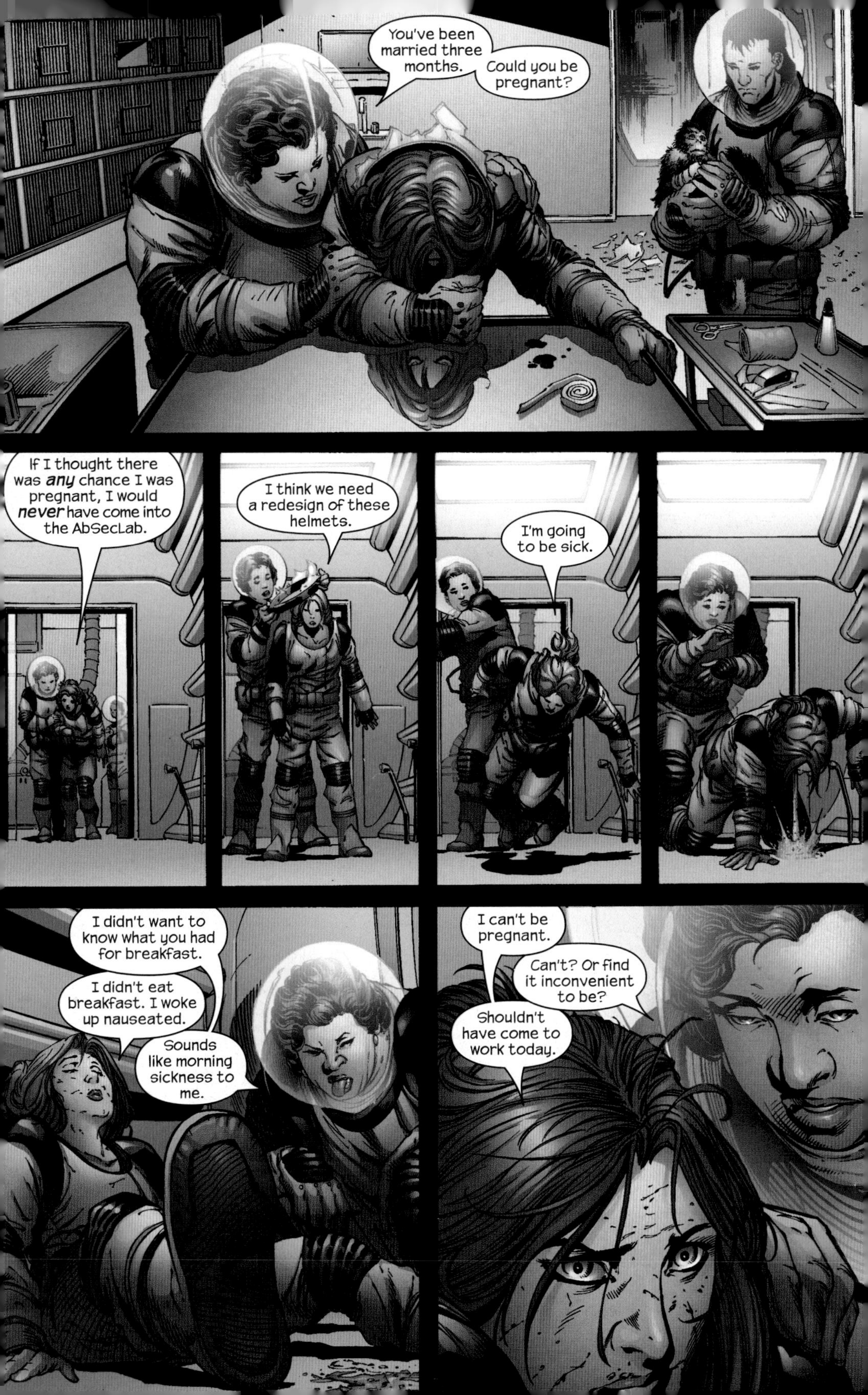
You've been married three months.
Could you be pregnant?
If I thought there was *any* chance I was pregnant, I would *never* have come into the AbSecLab.
I think we need a redesign of these helmets.
I'm going to be sick.
I didn't want to know what you had for breakfast.
I didn't eat breakfast. I woke up nauseated.
Sounds like morning sickness to me.
I can't be pregnant.
Can't? Or find it inconvenient to be?
Shouldn't have come to work today.

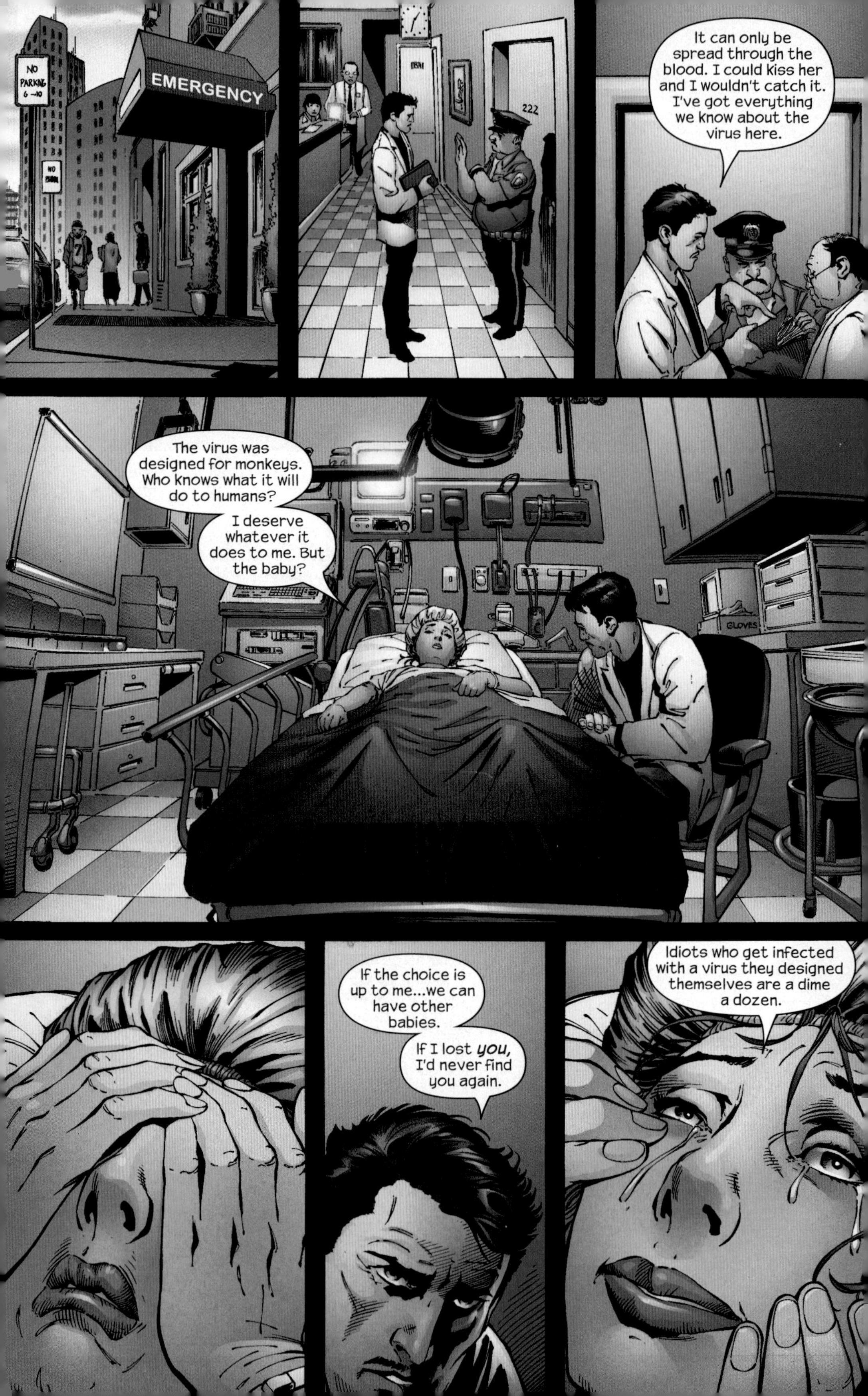
NO PARKING 6 —10
NO PARKING
EMERGENCY
222
It can only be spread through the blood. I could kiss her and I wouldn't catch it. I've got everything we know about the virus here.
The virus was designed for monkeys. Who knows what it will do to humans?
I deserve whatever it does to me. But the baby?
GLOVES
If the choice is up to me...we can have other babies.
If I lost *you*, I'd never find you again.
Idiots who get infected with a virus they designed themselves are a dime a dozen.

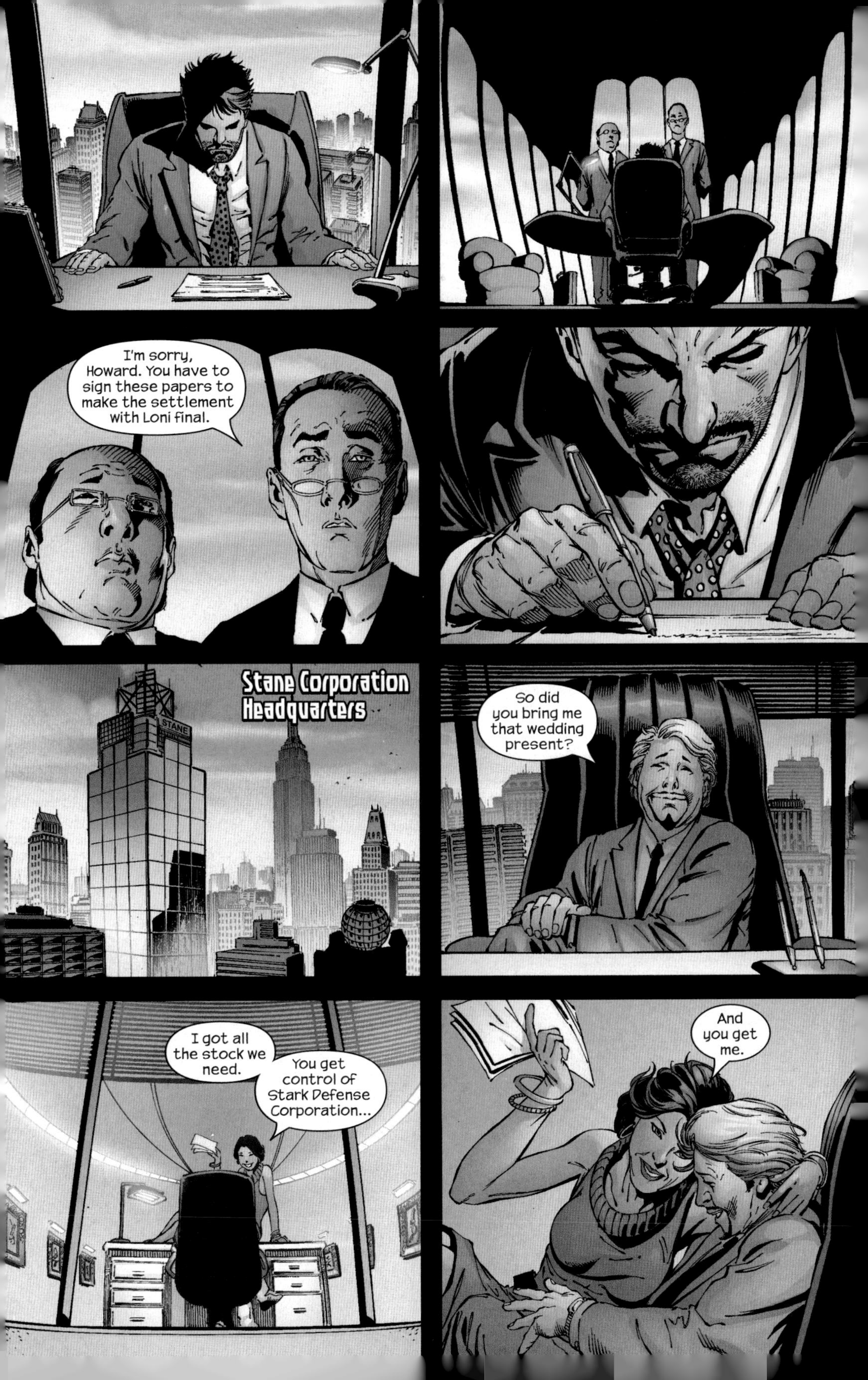
I'm sorry, Howard. You have to sign these papers to make the settlement with Loni final.
Stane Corporation Headquarters
STANE
So did you bring me that wedding present?
I got all the stock we need.
You get control of Stark Defense Corporation...
And you get me.

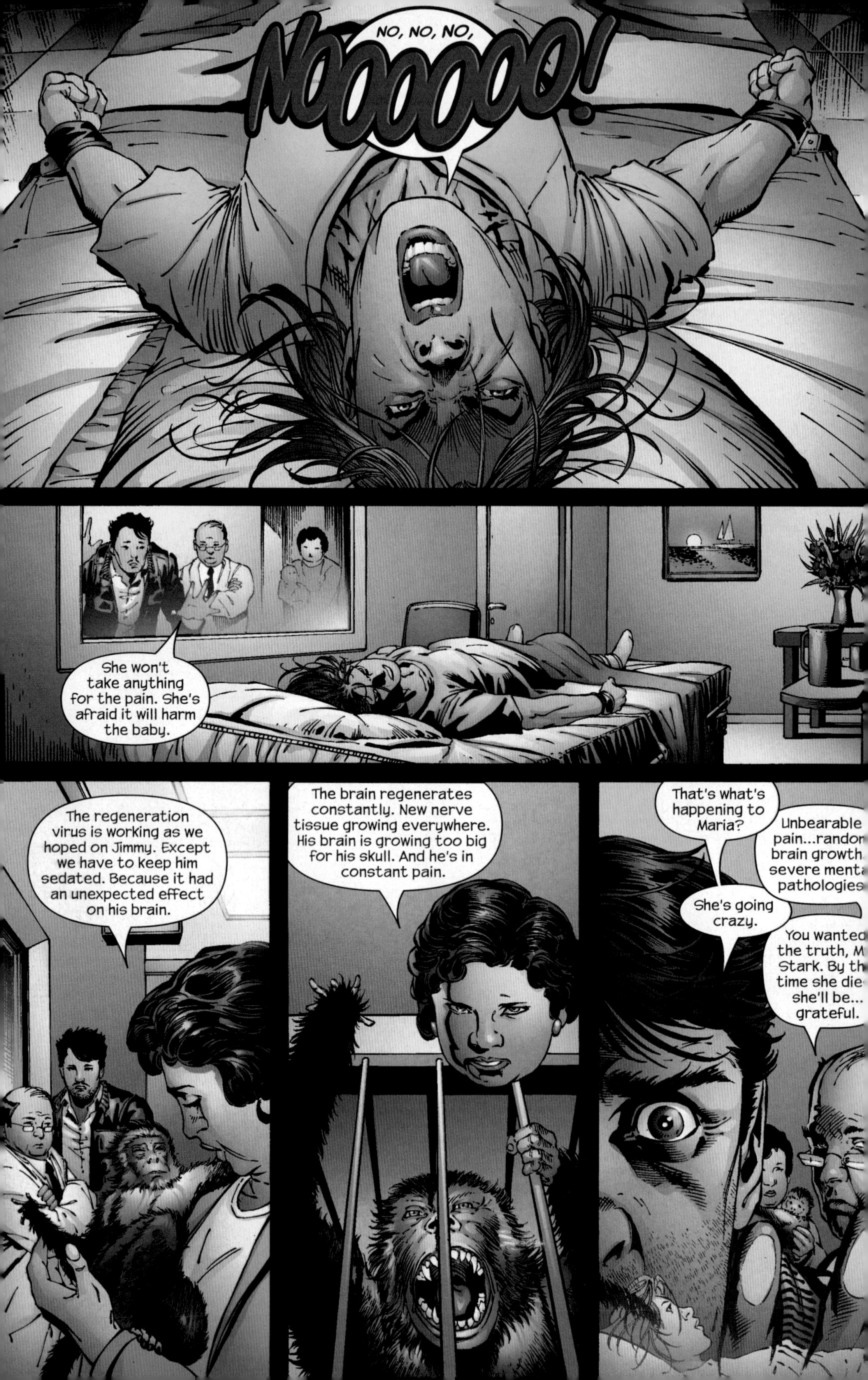
NO, NO, NO,
NOOOOOO!
She won't take anything for the pain. She's afraid it will harm the baby.
The regeneration virus is working as we hoped on Jimmy. Except we have to keep him sedated. Because it had an unexpected effect on his brain.
The brain regenerates constantly. New nerve tissue growing everywhere. His brain is growing too big for his skull. And he's in constant pain.
That's what's happening to Maria?
Unbearable pain...randor brain growth severe menta pathologies
She's going crazy.
You wante the truth, M Stark. By th time she die she'll be... grateful.

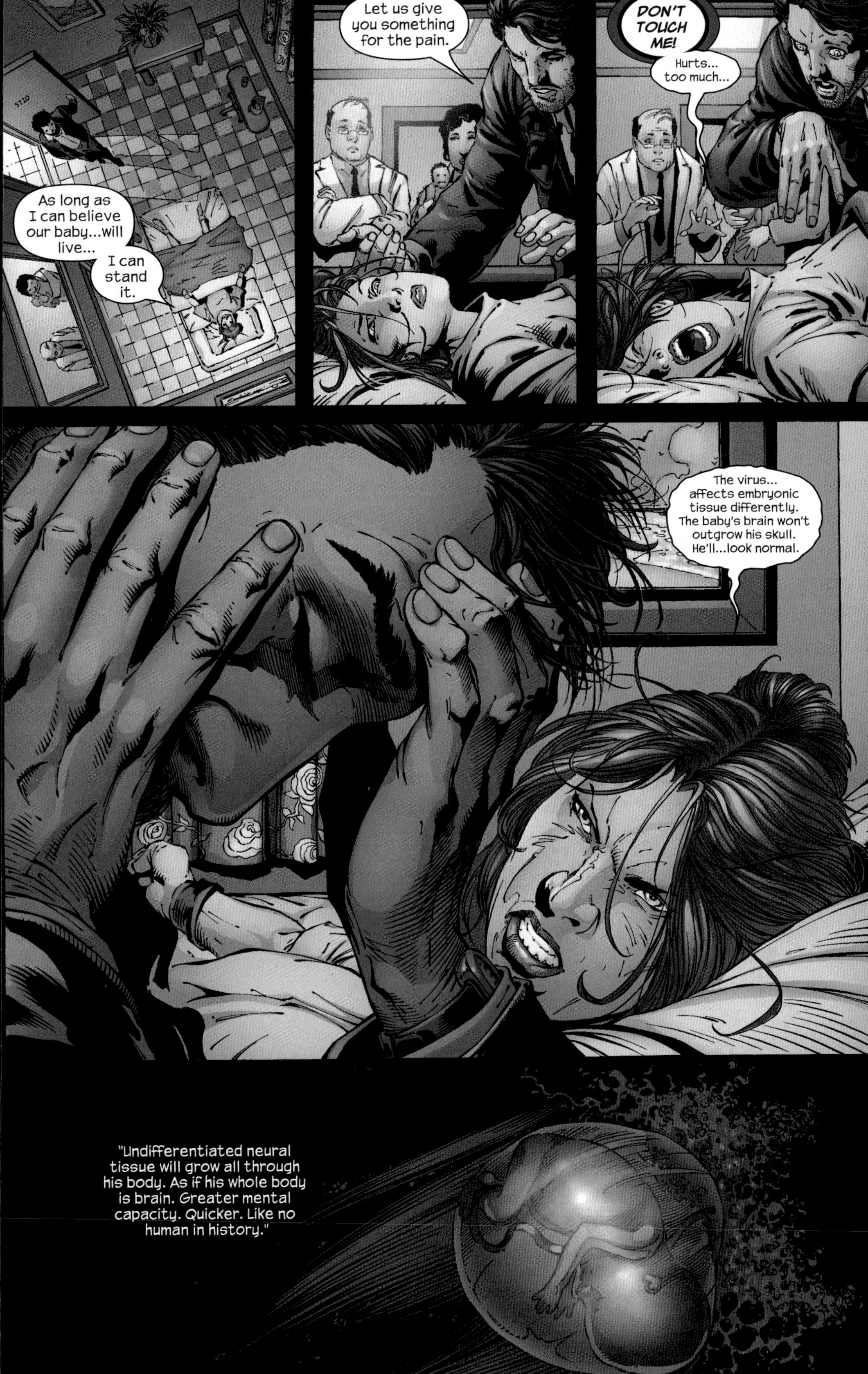
As long as I can believe our baby...will live...
I can stand it.
Let us give you something for the pain.
DON'T TOUCH ME!
Hurts... too much...
The virus... affects embryonic tissue differently. The baby's brain won't outgrow his skull. He'll...look normal.
"Undifferentiated neural tissue will grow all through his body. As if his whole body is brain. Greater mental capacity. Quicker. Like no human in history."

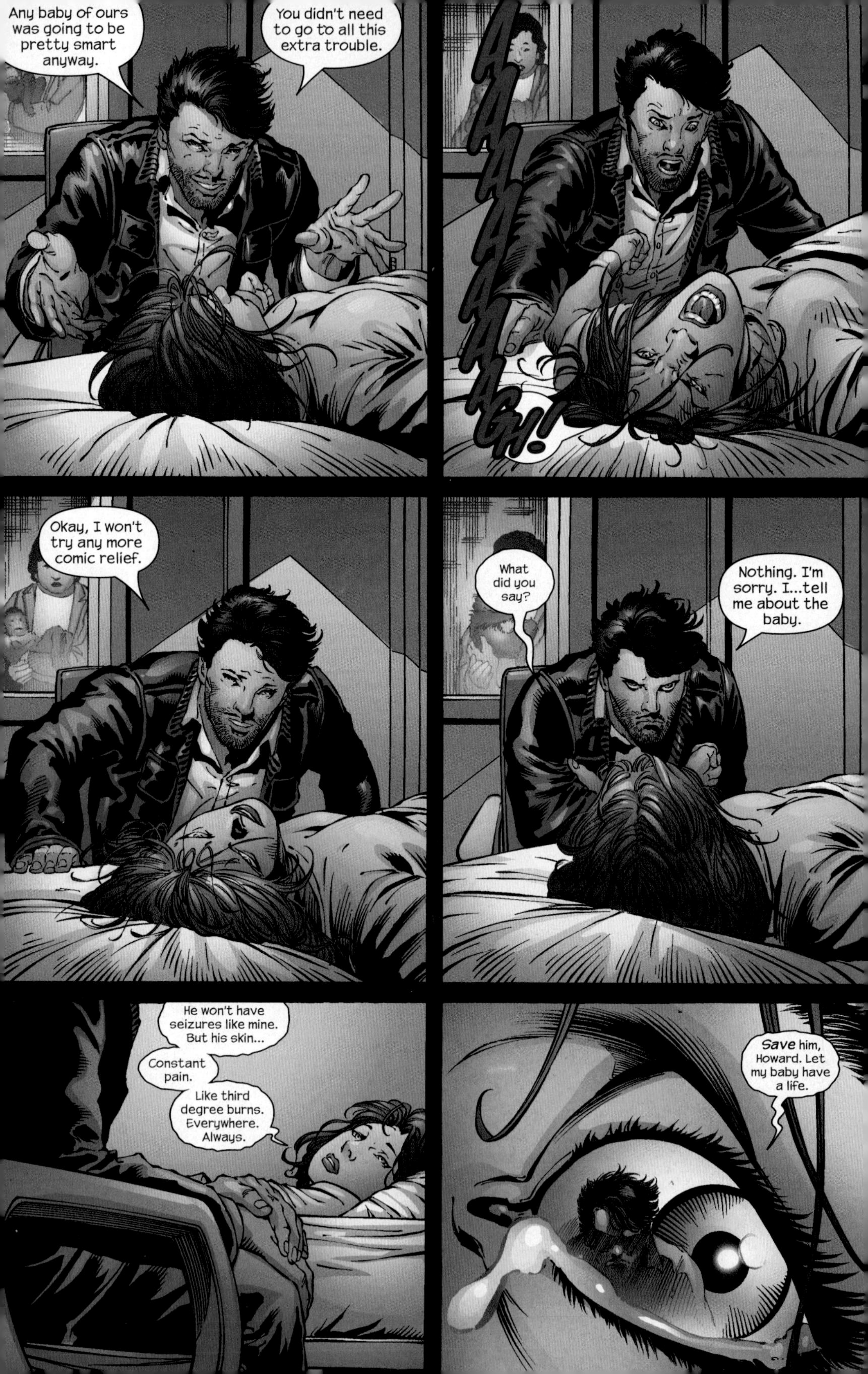
Any baby of ours was going to be pretty smart anyway.
You didn't need to go to all this extra trouble.
AAAAAAAAGH!
Okay, I won't try any more comic relief.
What did you say?
Nothing. I'm sorry. I...tell me about the baby.
He won't have seizures like mine. But his skin...
Constant pain.
Like third degree burns. Everywhere. Always.
Save him, Howard. Let my baby have a life.

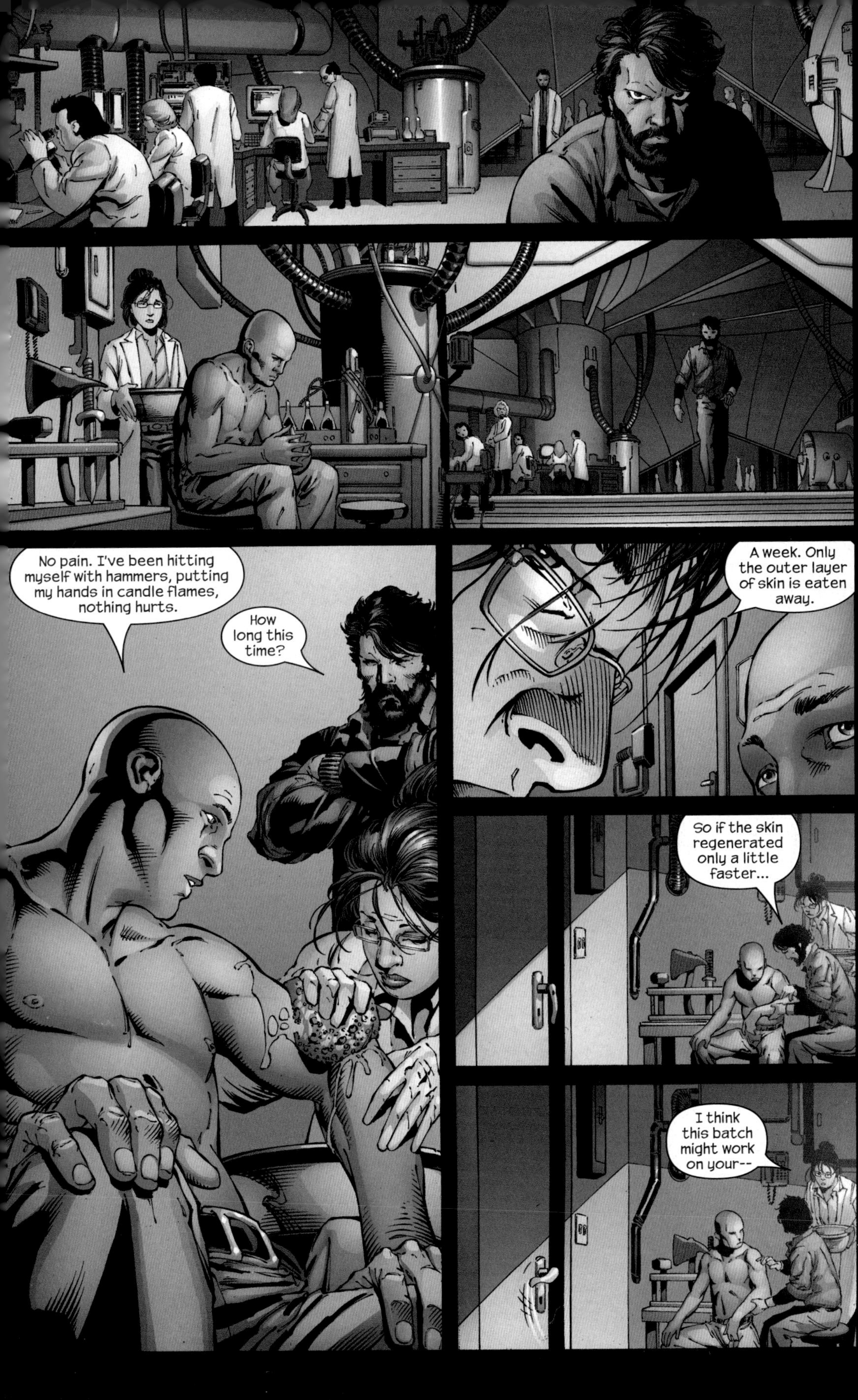
No pain. I've been hitting myself with hammers, putting my hands in candle flames, nothing hurts.
How long this time?
A week. Only the outer layer of skin is eaten away.
So if the skin regenerated only a little faster...
I think this batch might work on your--

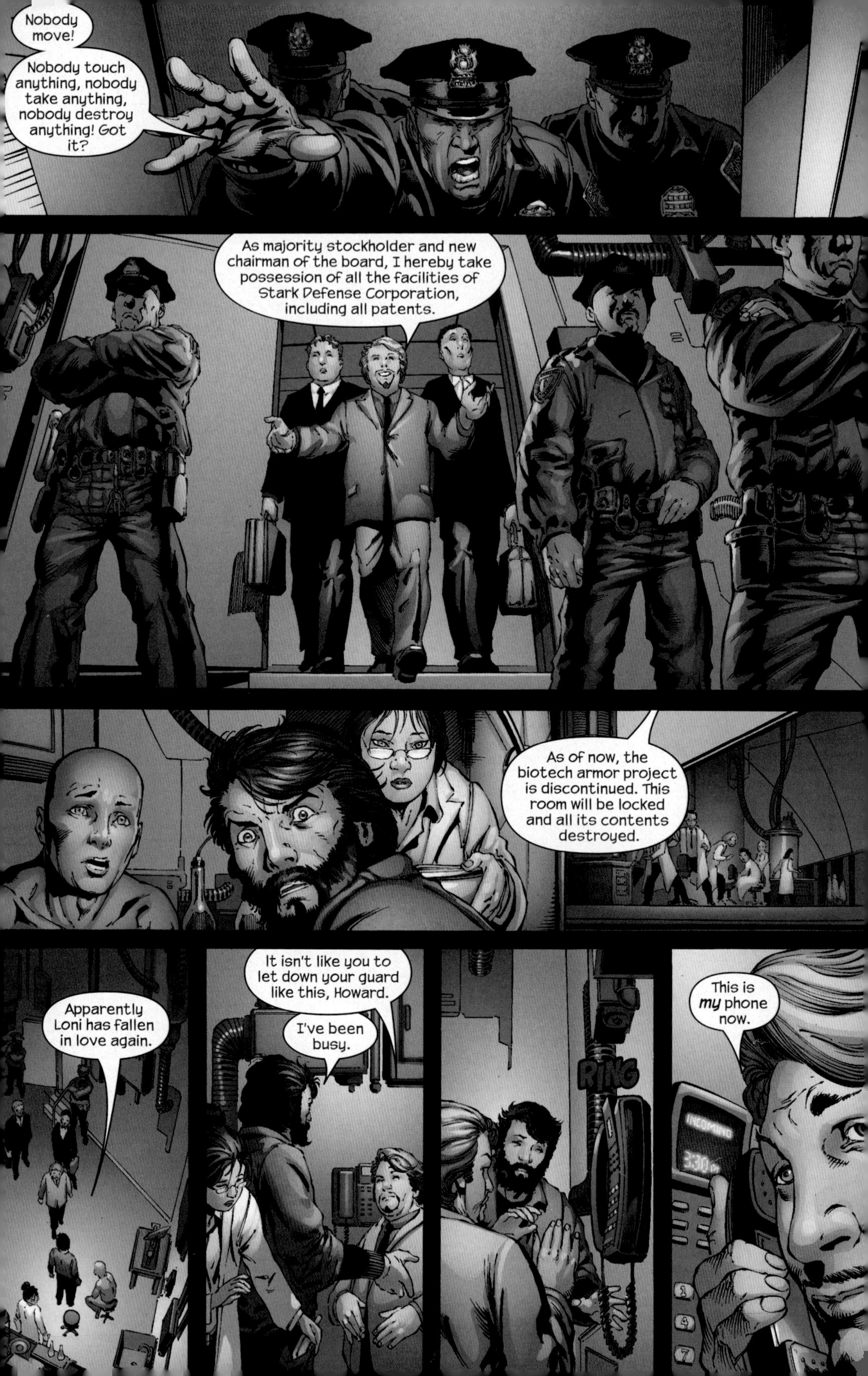
Nobody move!
Nobody touch anything, nobody take anything, nobody destroy anything! Got it?
As majority stockholder and new chairman of the board, I hereby take possession of all the facilities of Stark Defense Corporation, including all patents.
As of now, the biotech armor project is discontinued. This room will be locked and all its contents destroyed.
Apparently Loni has fallen in love again.
It isn't like you to let down your guard like this, Howard.
I've been busy.
RING
INCOMING
This is *my* phone now.

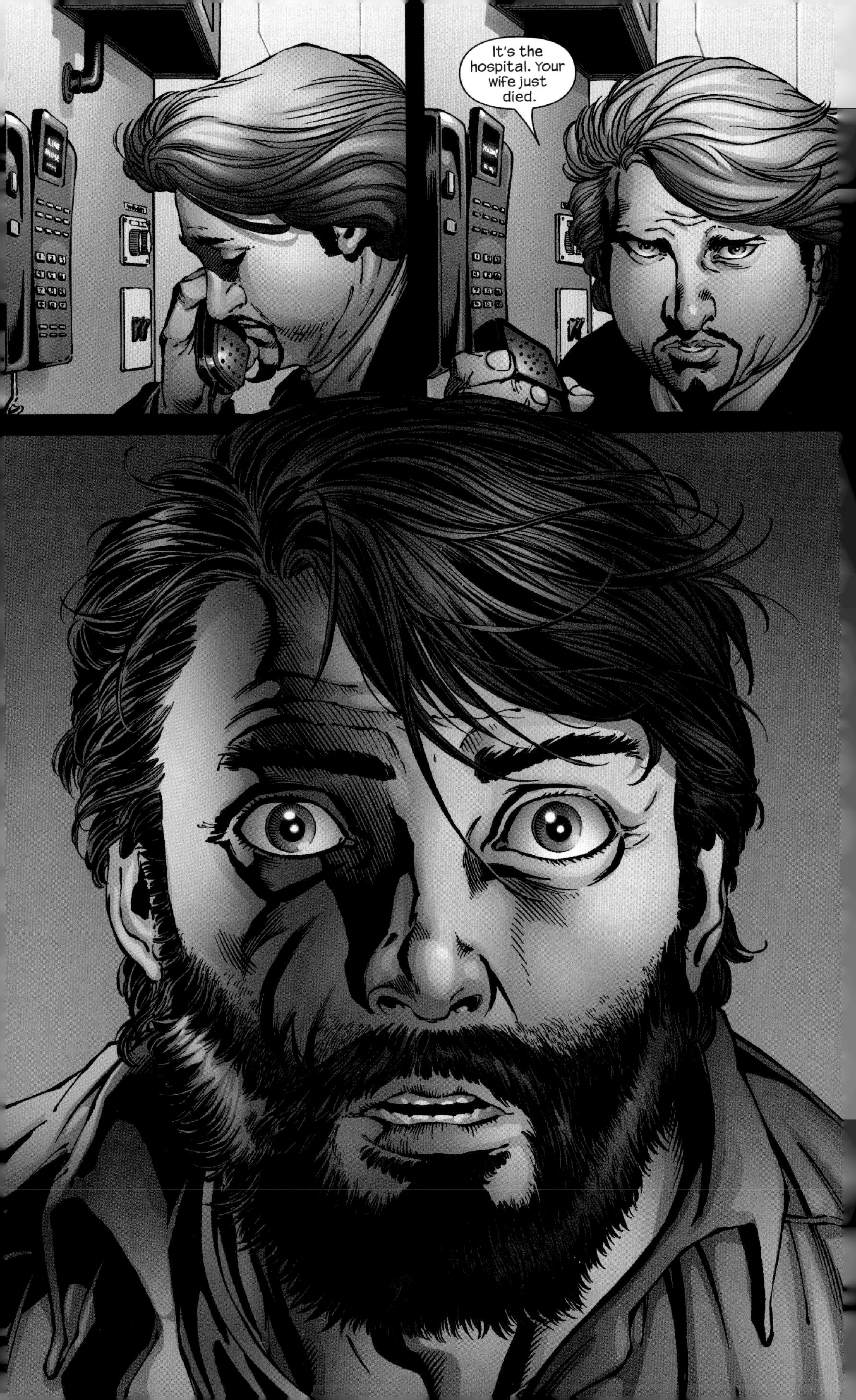
It's the hospital. Your wife just died.

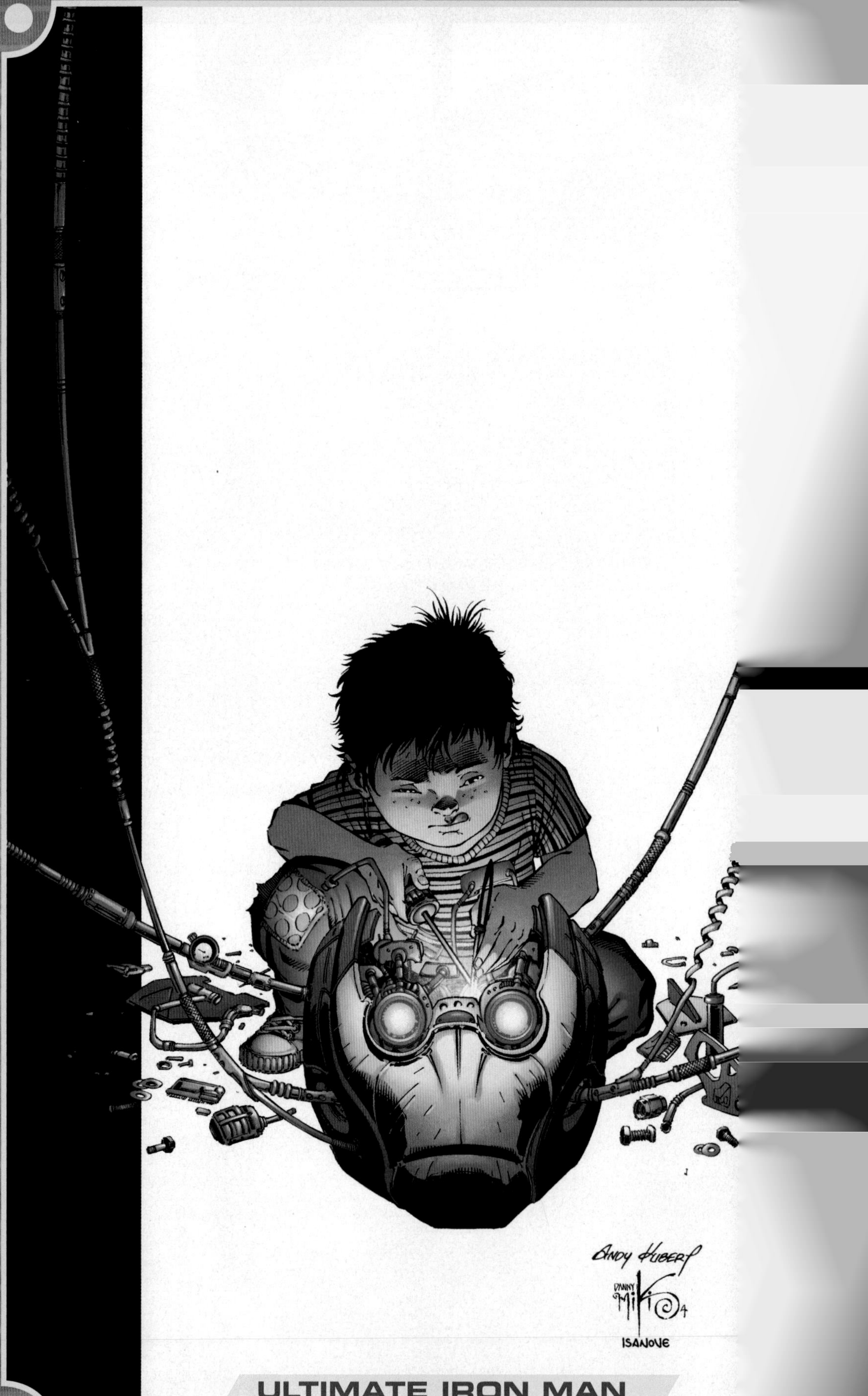
ANDY KUBERT
DANNY MIKI ©4
ISANOVE

ULTIMATE IRON MAN
ISSUE 02

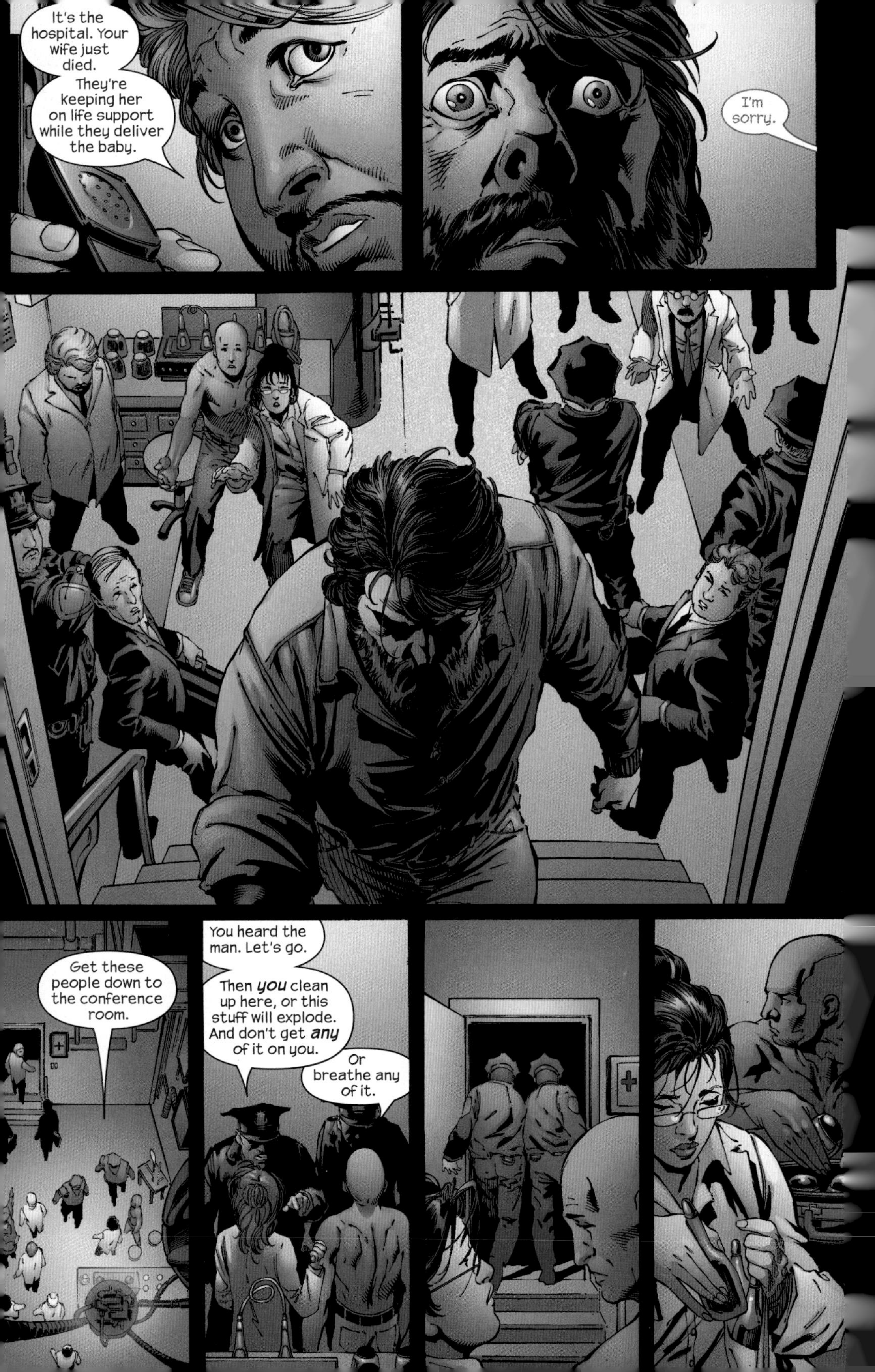
It's the hospital. Your wife just died.
They're keeping her on life support while they deliver the baby.
I'm sorry.
Get these people down to the conference room.
You heard the man. Let's go.
Then *you* clean up here, or this stuff will explode. And don't get *any* of it on you.
Or breathe any of it.

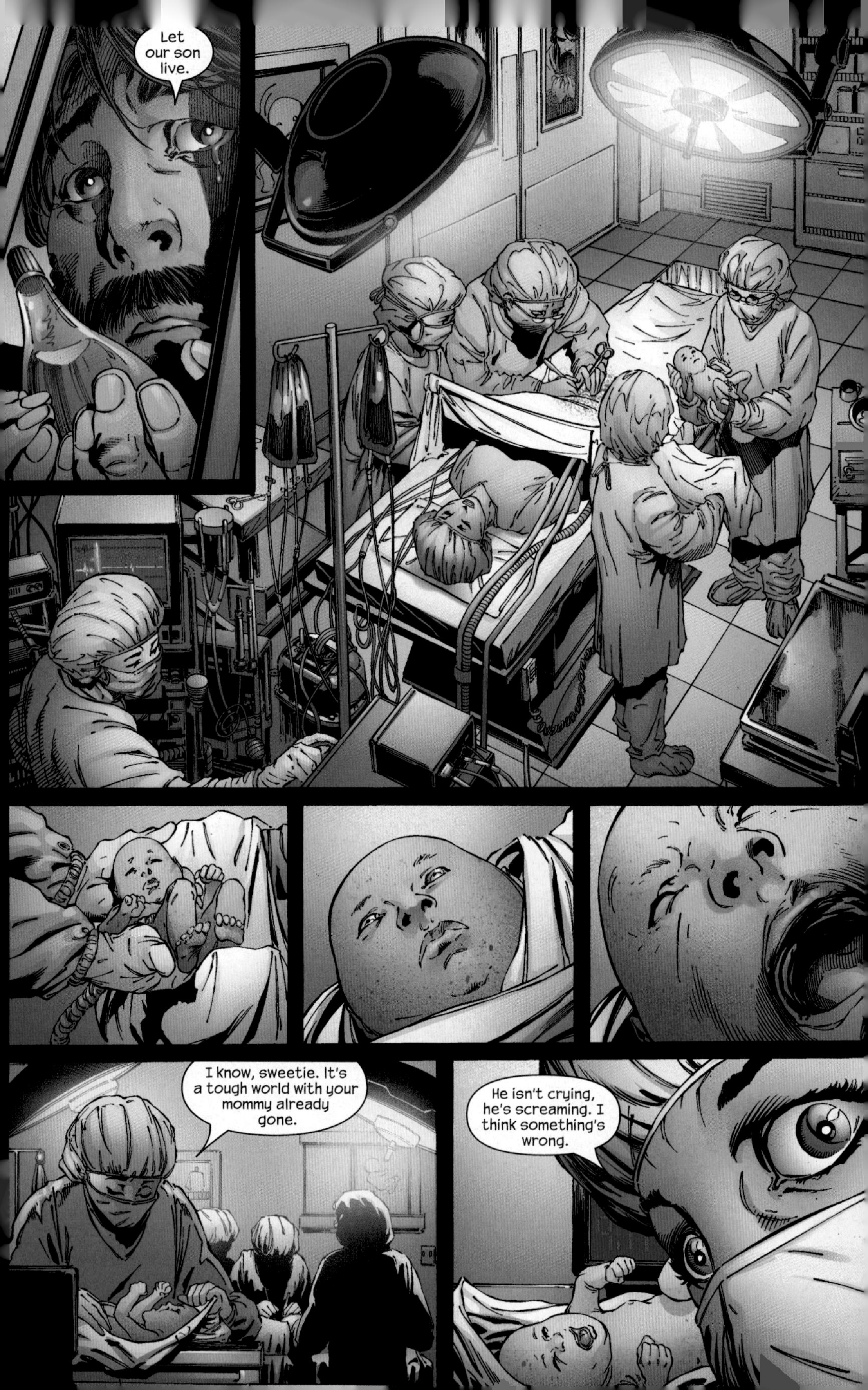
Let our son live.
I know, sweetie. It's a tough world with your mommy already gone.
He isn't crying, he's screaming. I think something's wrong.

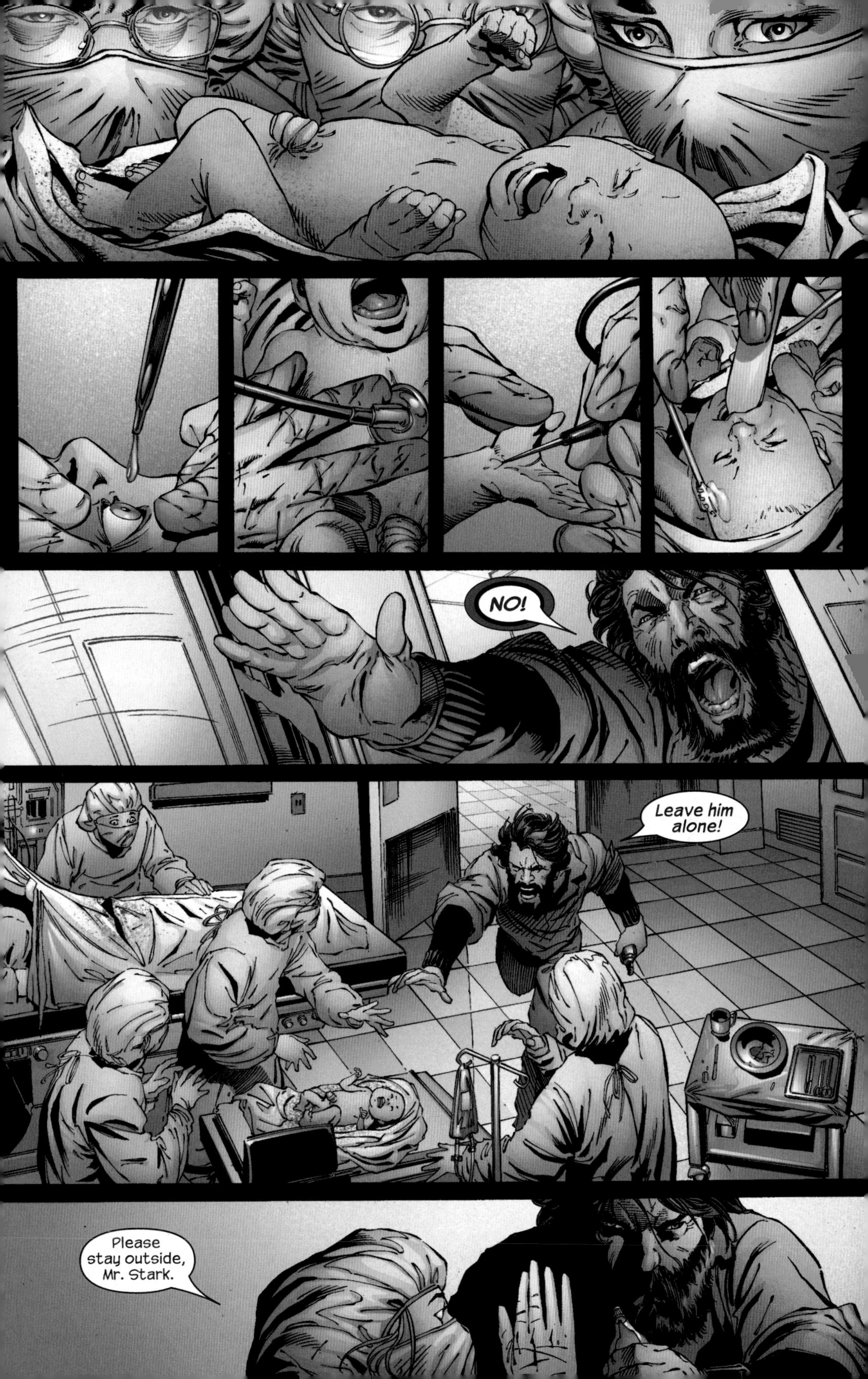
NO!
Leave him alone!
Please stay outside, Mr. Stark.

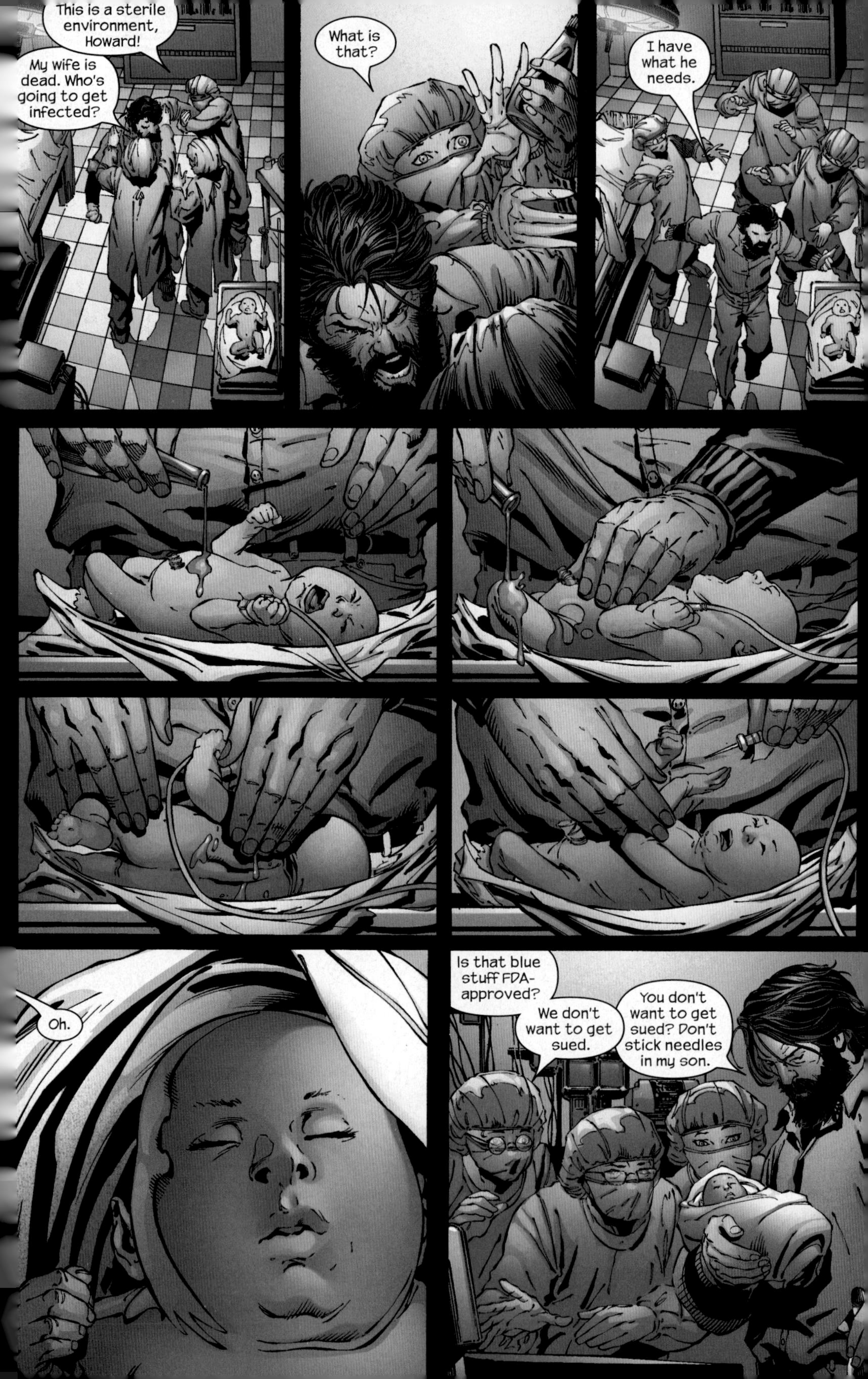
This is a sterile environment, Howard!
My wife is dead. Who's going to get infected?
What is that?
I have what he needs.
Oh.
Is that blue stuff FDA-approved?
We don't want to get sued.
You don't want to get sued? Don't stick needles in my son.

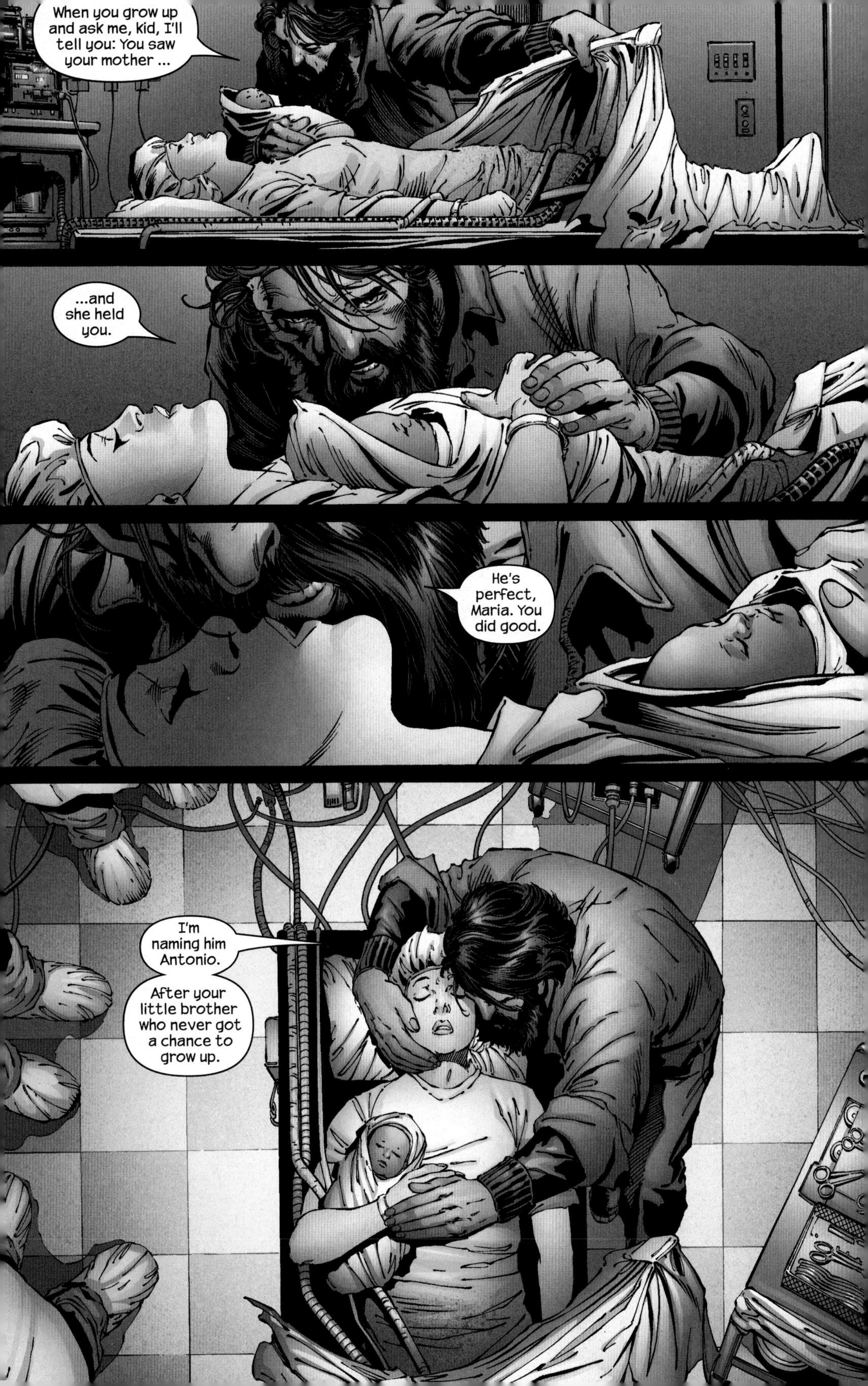
When you grow up and ask me, kid, I'll tell you: You saw your mother ...
...and she held you.
He's perfect, Maria. You did good.
I'm naming him Antonio.
After your little brother who never got a chance to grow up.

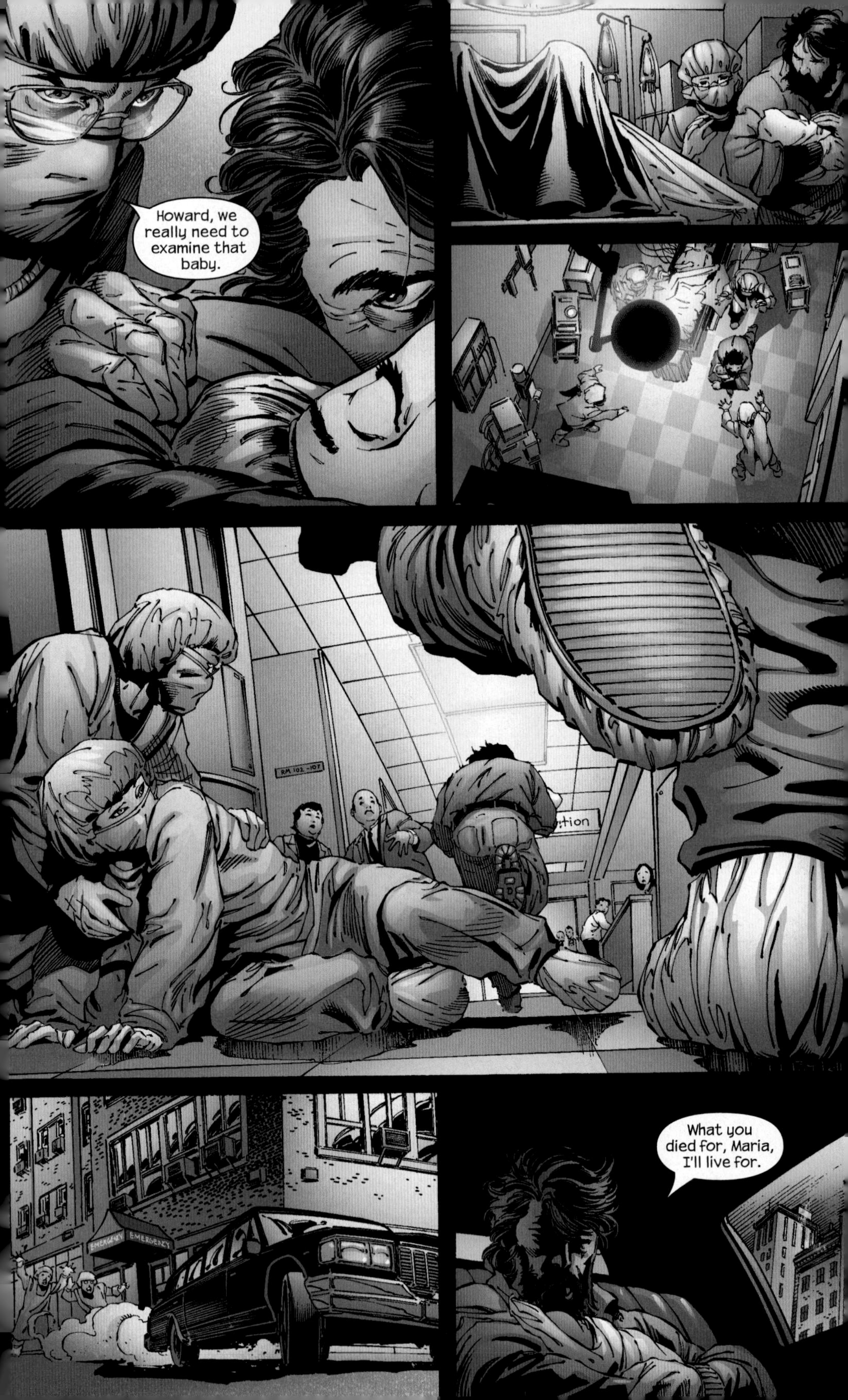
Howard, we really need to examine that baby.
RM 102-107
What you died for, Maria, I'll live for.

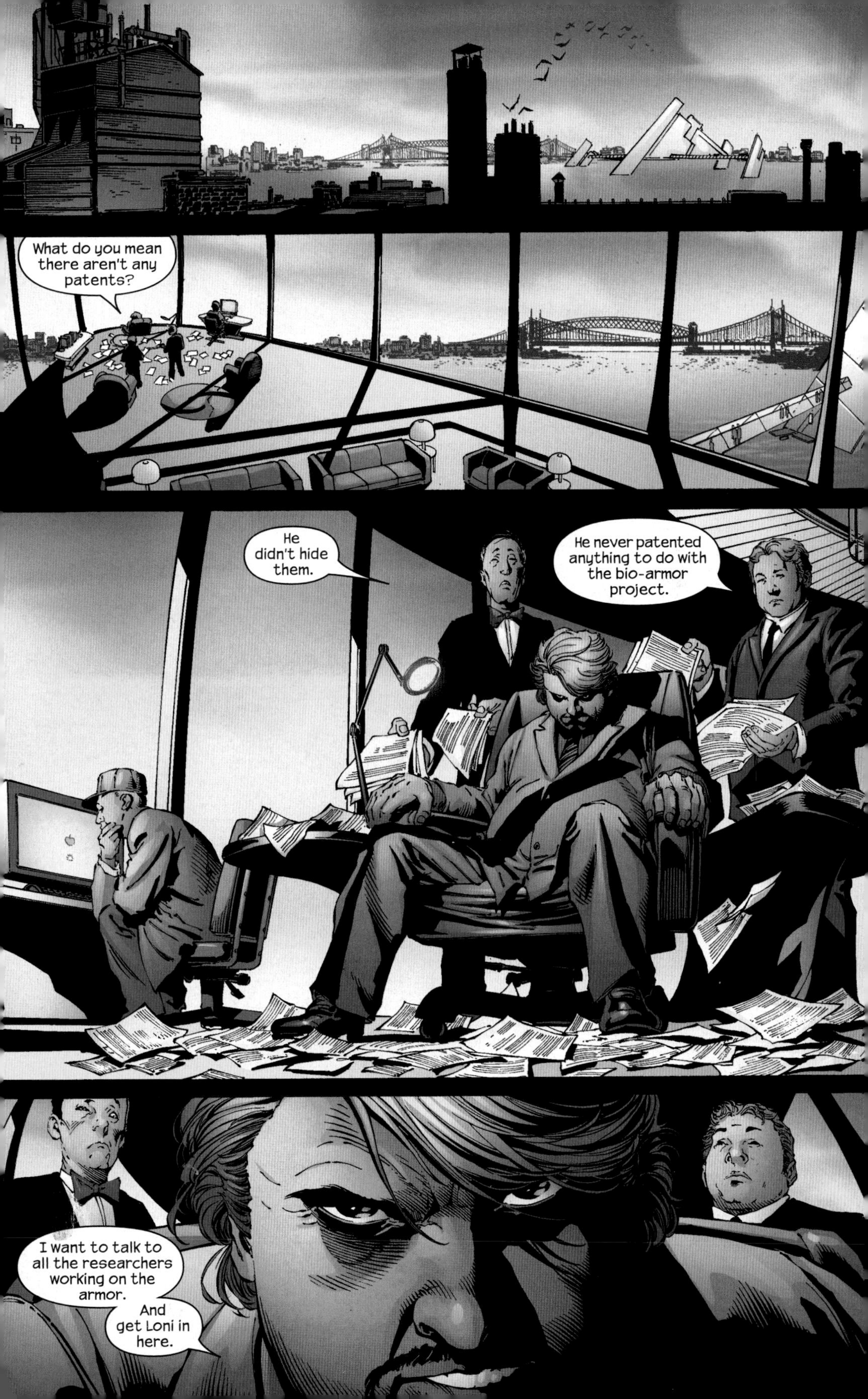
What do you mean there aren't any patents?
He didn't hide them.
He never patented anything to do with the bio-armor project.
I want to talk to all the researchers working on the armor.
And get Loni in here.

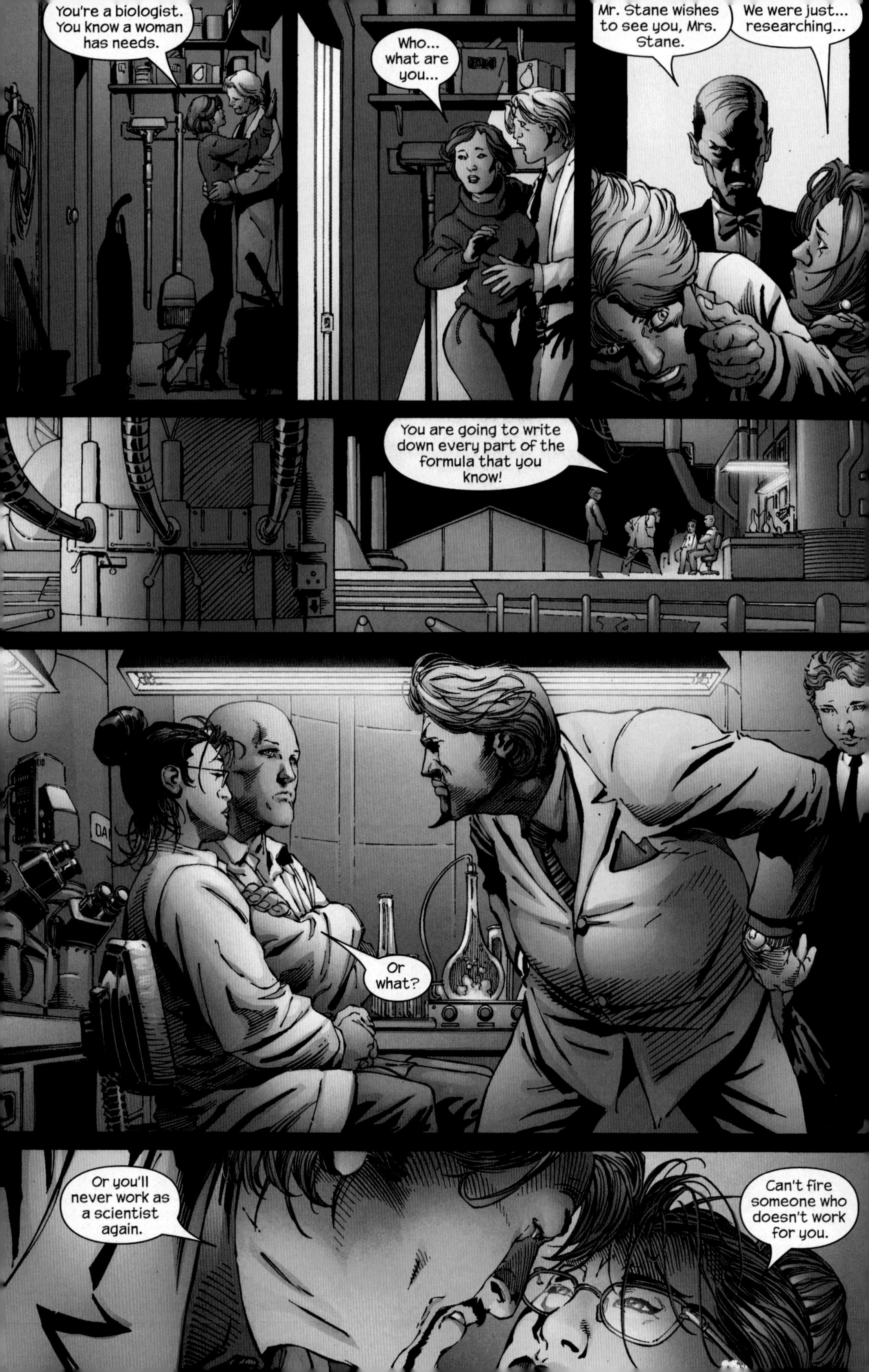

You're a biologist. You know a woman has needs.
Who... what are you...
Mr. Stane wishes to see you, Mrs. Stane.
We were just... researching...
You are going to write down every part of the formula that you know!
Or what?
Or you'll never work as a scientist again.
Can't fire someone who doesn't work for you.

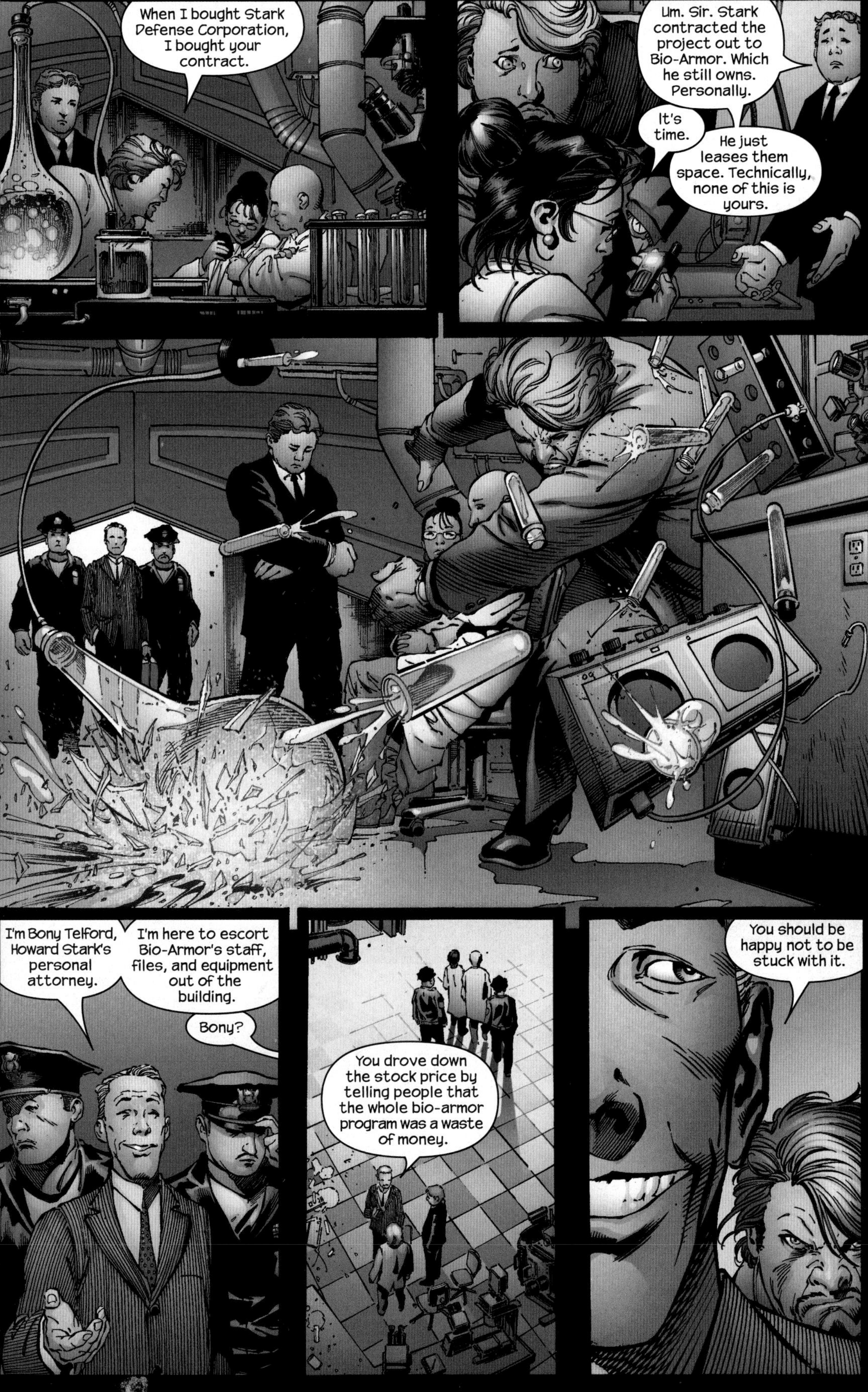
When I bought Stark Defense Corporation, I bought your contract.
Um. Sir. Stark contracted the project out to Bio-Armor. Which he still owns. Personally.
It's time.
He just leases them space. Technically, none of this is yours.
I'm Bony Telford, Howard Stark's personal attorney.
I'm here to escort Bio-Armor's staff, files, and equipment out of the building.
Bony?
You drove down the stock price by telling people that the whole bio-armor program was a waste of money.
You should be happy not to be stuck with it.

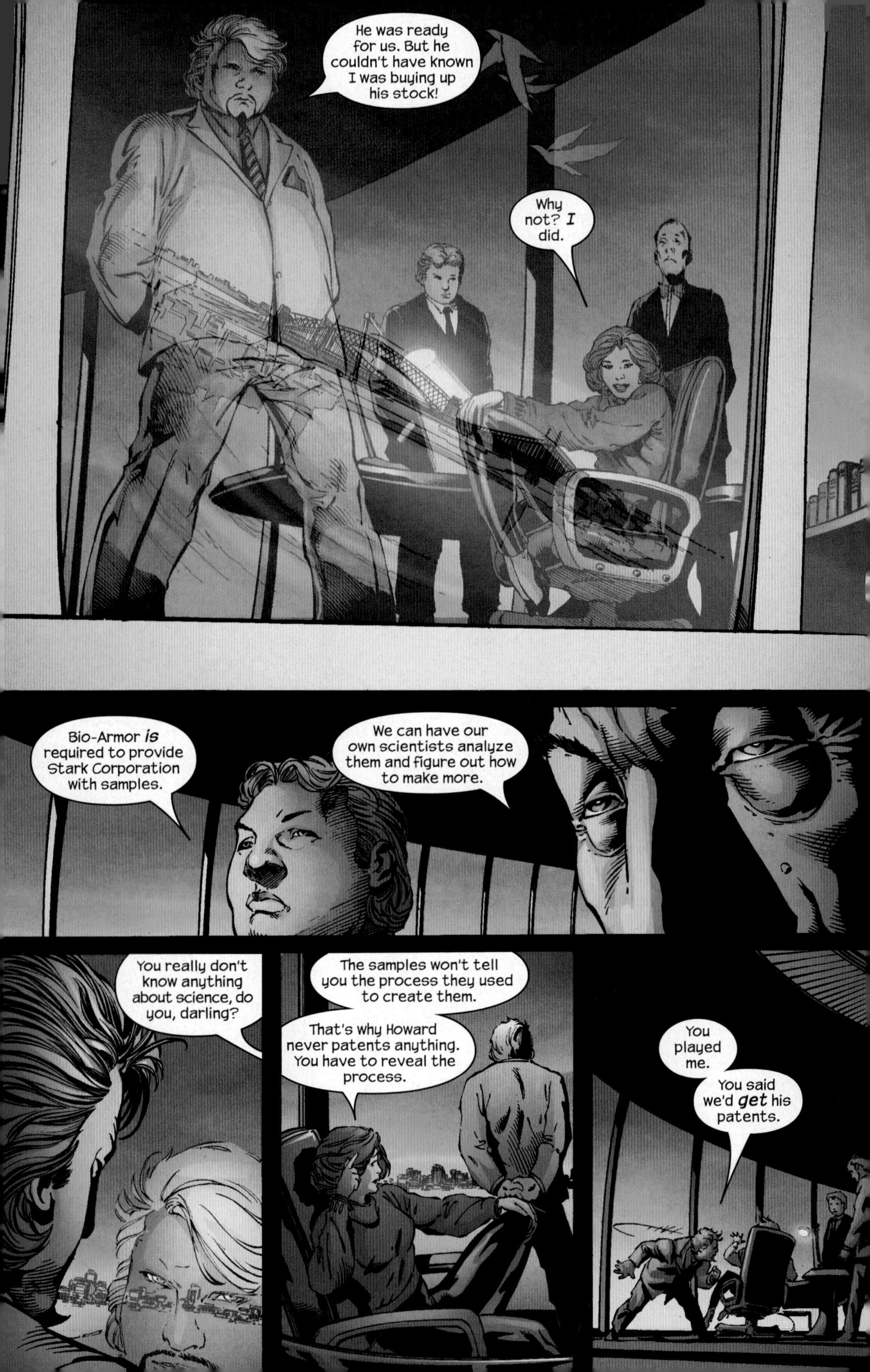
He was ready for us. But he couldn't have known I was buying up his stock!
Why not? *I* did.
Bio-Armor *is* required to provide Stark Corporation with samples.
We can have our own scientists analyze them and figure out how to make more.
You really don't know anything about science, do you, darling?
The samples won't tell you the process they used to create them.
That's why Howard never patents anything. You have to reveal the process.
You played me.
You said we'd *get* his patents.

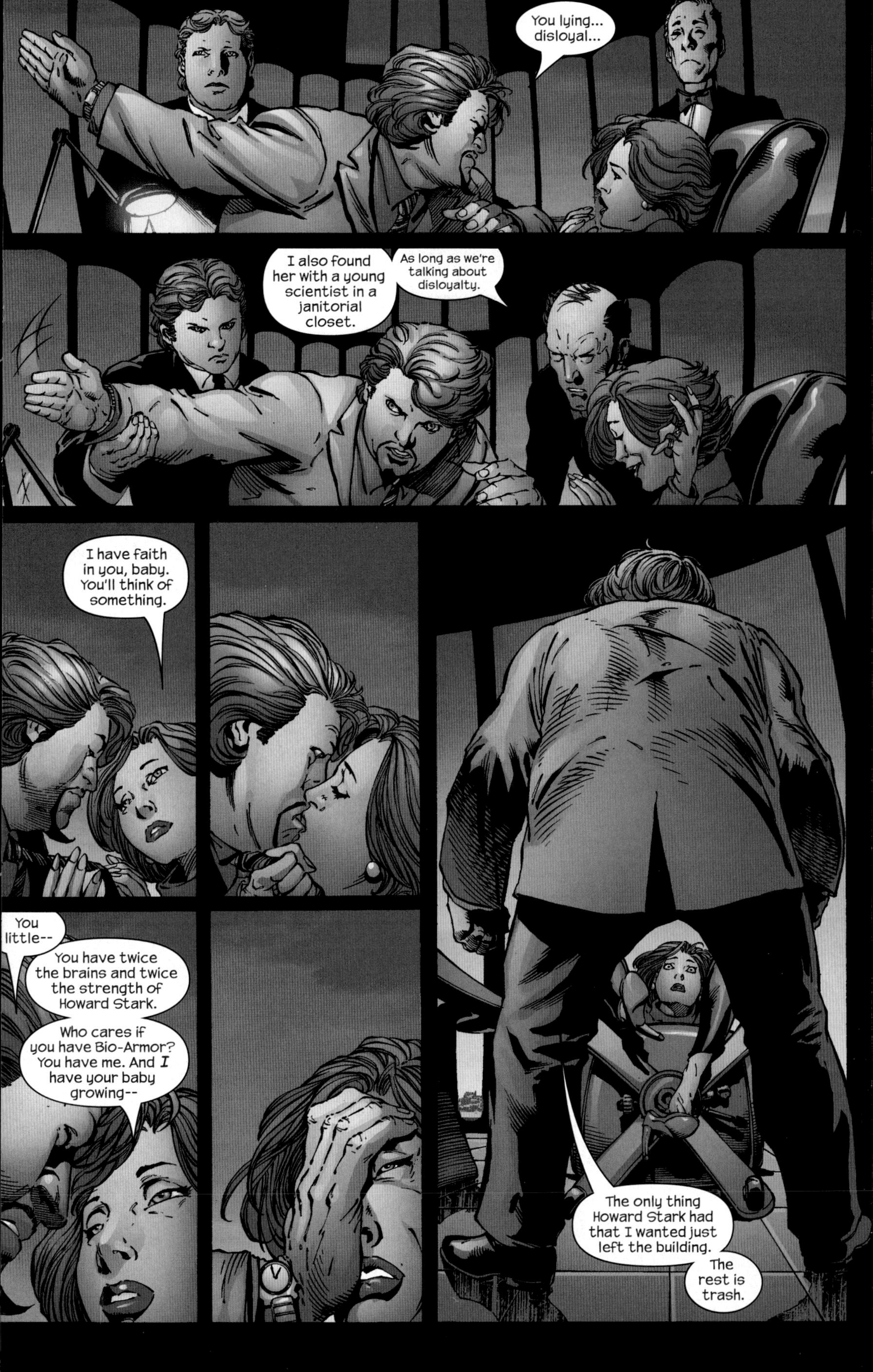
You lying... disloyal...
I also found her with a young scientist in a janitorial closet.
As long as we're talking about disloyalty.
I have faith in you, baby. You'll think of something.
You little--
You have twice the brains and twice the strength of Howard Stark.
Who cares if you have Bio-Armor? You have me. And *I* have your baby growing--
The only thing Howard Stark had that I wanted just left the building.
The rest is trash.

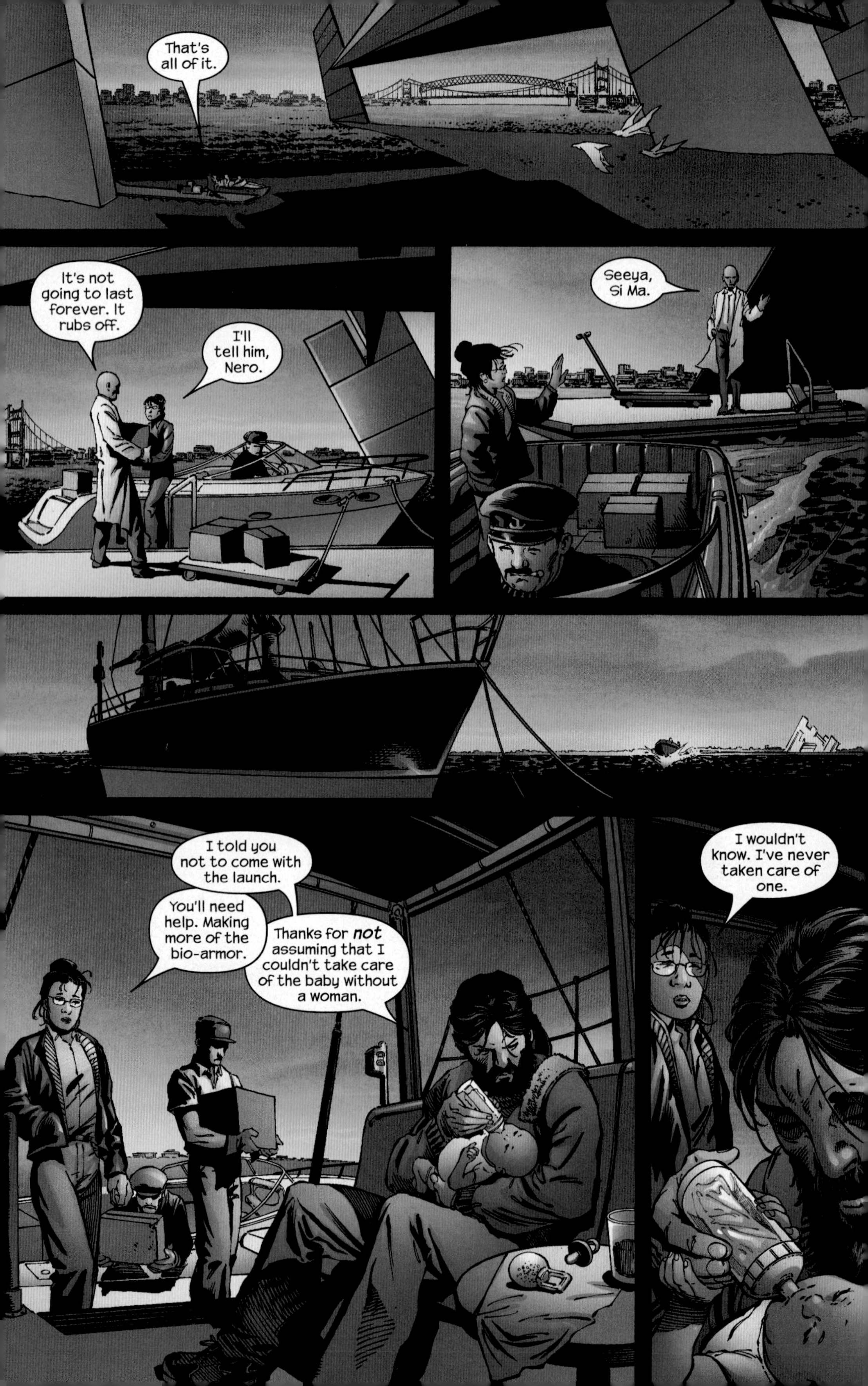
That's all of it.
It's not going to last forever. It rubs off.
I'll tell him, Nero.
Seeya, Si Ma.
I told you not to come with the launch.
You'll need help. Making more of the bio-armor.
Thanks for **not** assuming that I couldn't take care of the baby without a woman.
I wouldn't know. I've never taken care of one.

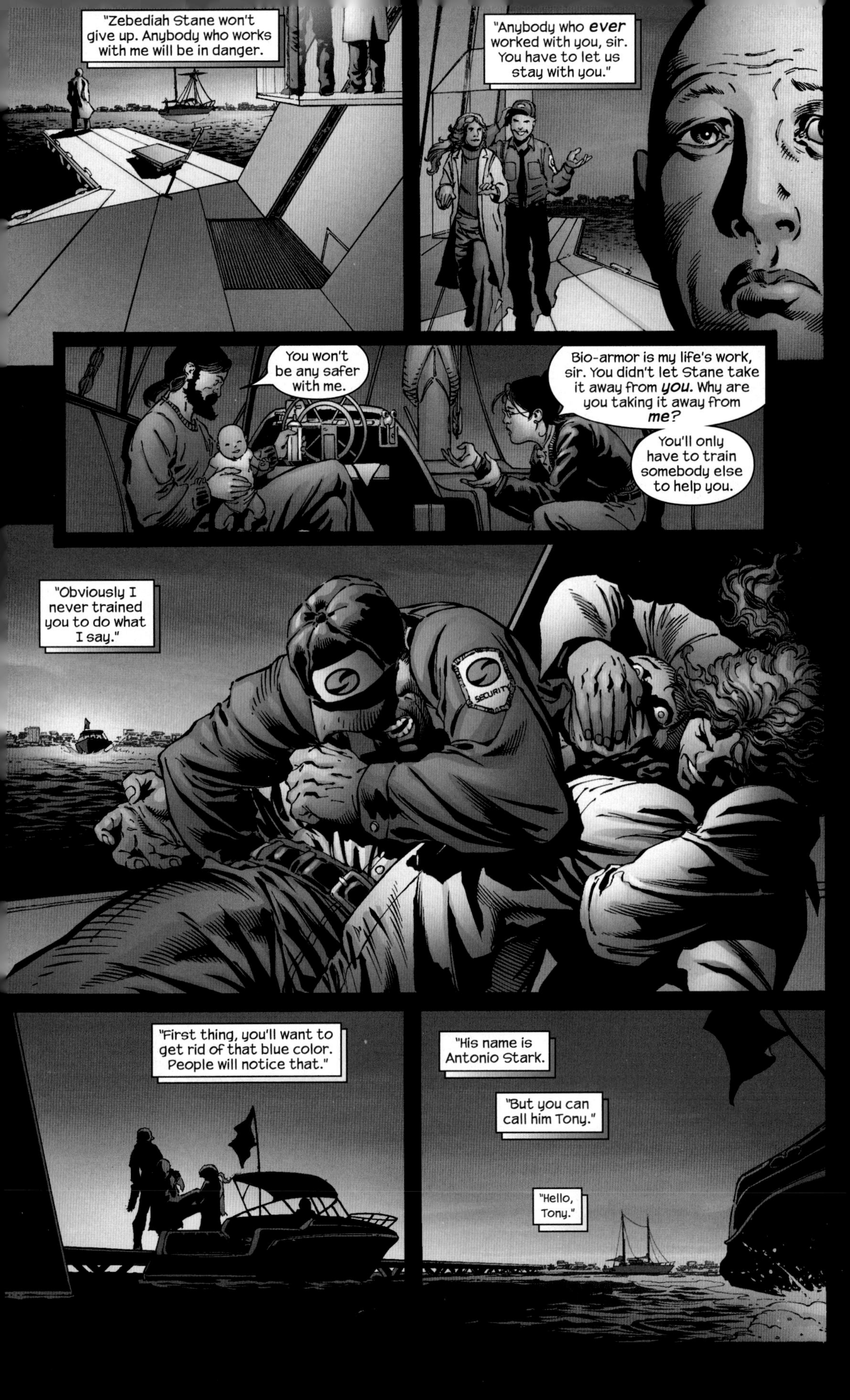
"Zebediah Stane won't give up. Anybody who works with me will be in danger.
"Anybody who ever worked with you, sir. You have to let us stay with you."
You won't be any safer with me.
Bio-armor is my life's work, sir. You didn't let Stane take it away from you. Why are you taking it away from me?
You'll only have to train somebody else to help you.
"Obviously I never trained you to do what I say."
SECURITY
"First thing, you'll want to get rid of that blue color. People will notice that."
"His name is Antonio Stark.
"But you can call him Tony."
"Hello, Tony."

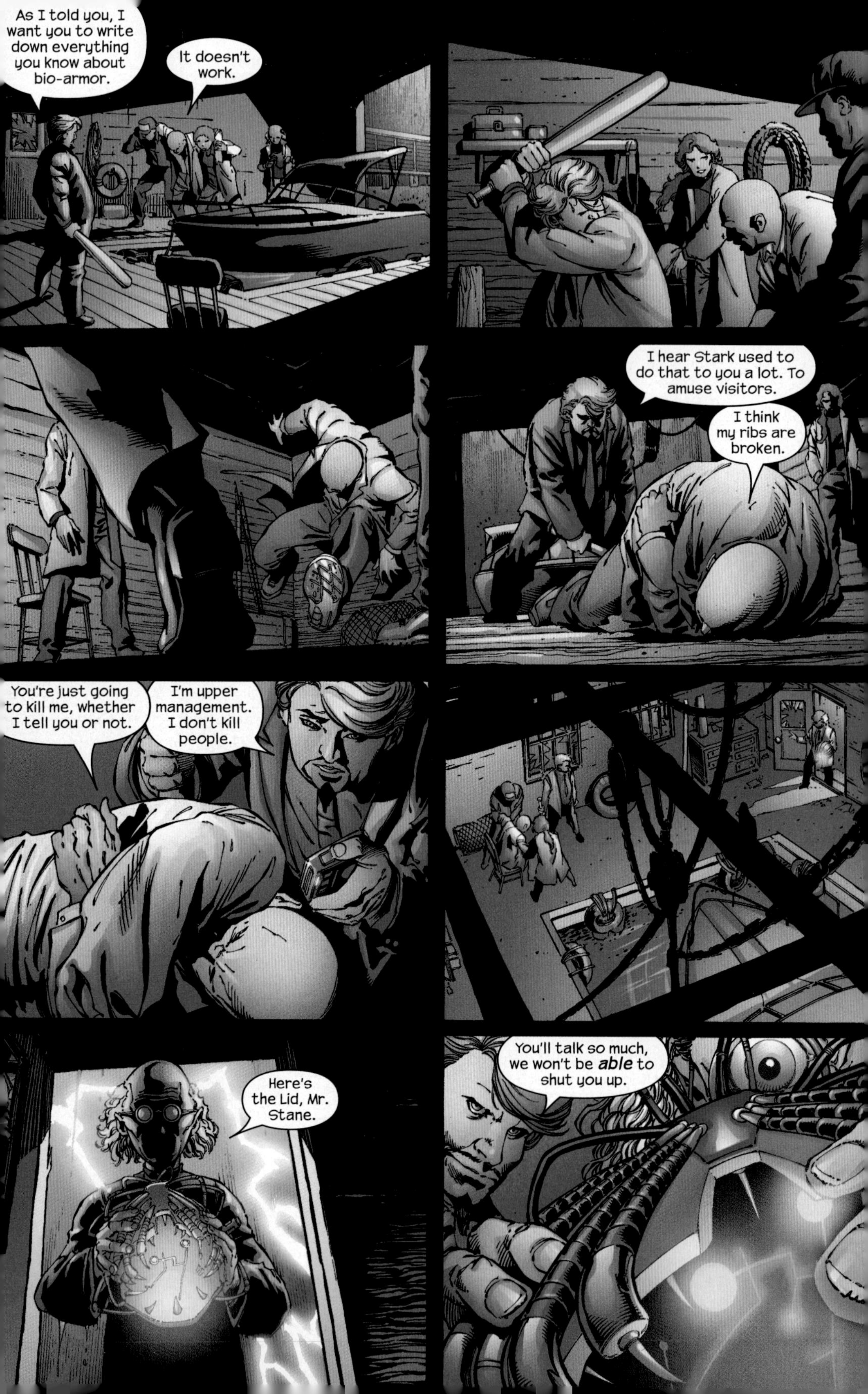
As I told you, I want you to write down everything you know about bio-armor.
It doesn't work.
I hear Stark used to do that to you a lot. To amuse visitors.
I think my ribs are broken.
You're just going to kill me, whether I tell you or not.
I'm upper management. I don't kill people.
Here's the Lid, Mr. Stane.
You'll talk so much, we won't be *able* to shut you up.

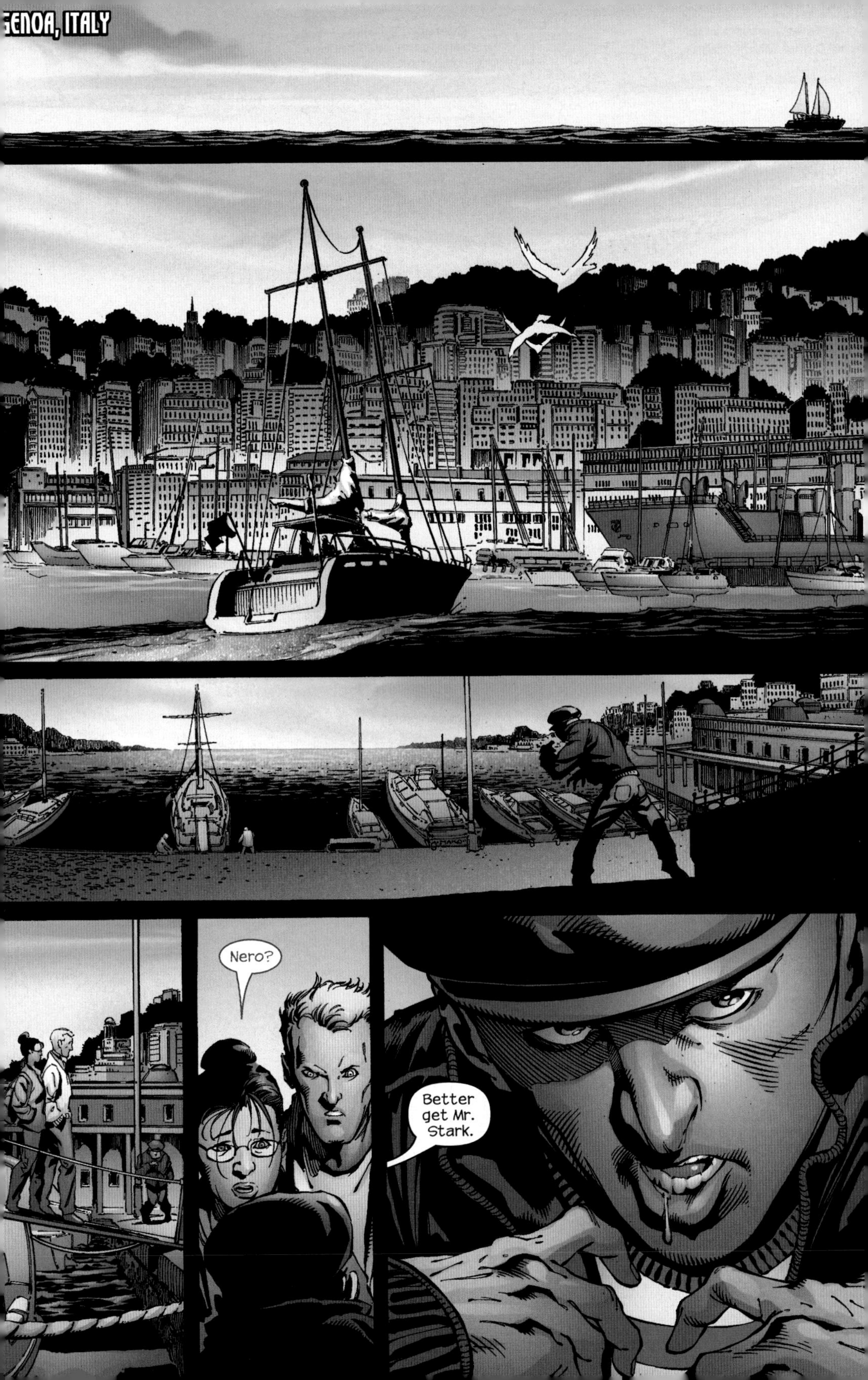
GENOA, ITALY
Nero?
Better get Mr. Stark.

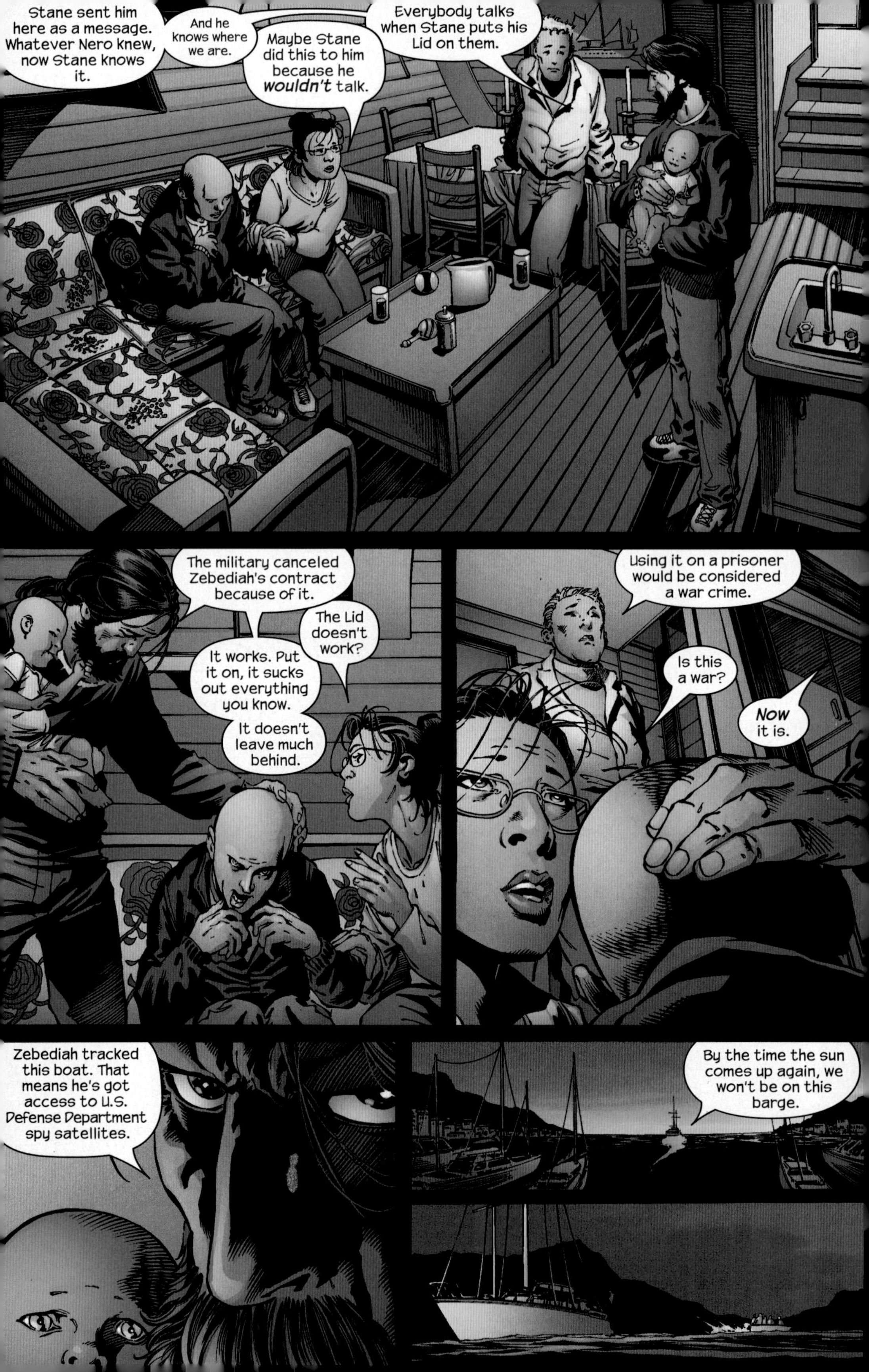
Stane sent him here as a message. Whatever Nero knew, now Stane knows it.
And he knows where we are.
Maybe Stane did this to him because he *wouldn't* talk.
Everybody talks when Stane puts his Lid on them.
The military canceled Zebediah's contract because of it.
The Lid doesn't work?
It works. Put it on, it sucks out everything you know.
It doesn't leave much behind.
Using it on a prisoner would be considered a war crime.
Is this a war?
NOW it is.
Zebediah tracked this boat. That means he's got access to U.S. Defense Department spy satellites.
By the time the sun comes up again, we won't be on this barge.

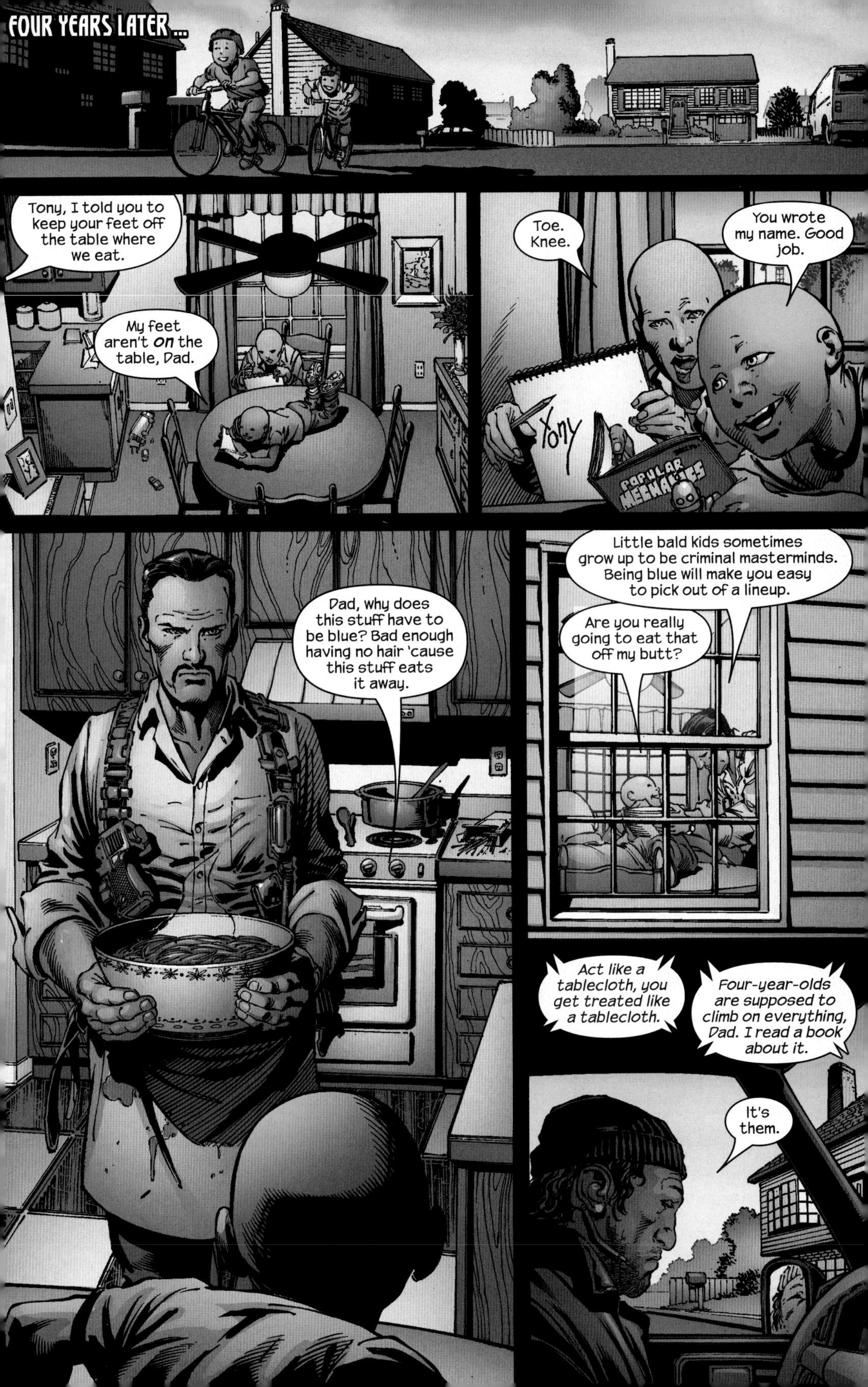
FOUR YEARS LATER ...
Tony, I told you to keep your feet off the table where we eat.
My feet aren't ON the table, Dad.
Toe. Knee.
You wrote my name. Good job.
Tony
POPULAR MECHANICS
Dad, why does this stuff have to be blue? Bad enough having no hair 'cause this stuff eats it away.
Little bald kids sometimes grow up to be criminal masterminds. Being blue will make you easy to pick out of a lineup.
Are you really going to eat that off my butt?
Act like a tablecloth, you get treated like a tablecloth.
Four-year-olds are supposed to climb on everything, Dad. I read a book about it.
It's them.

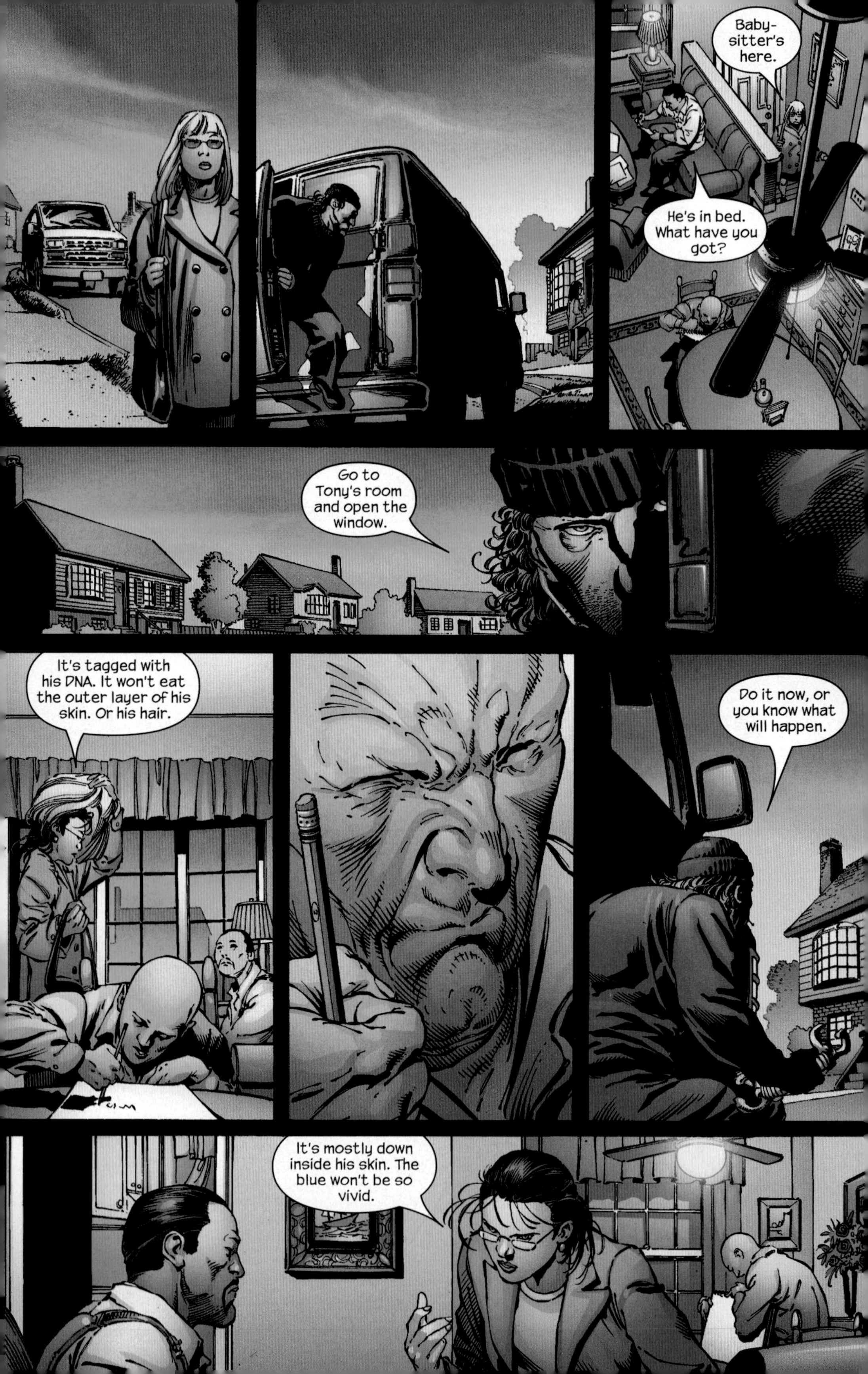

Baby-sitter's here.
He's in bed. What have you got?
Go to Tony's room and open the window.
It's tagged with his DNA. It won't eat the outer layer of his skin. Or his hair.
Do it now, or you know what will happen.
It's mostly down inside his skin. The blue won't be so vivid.

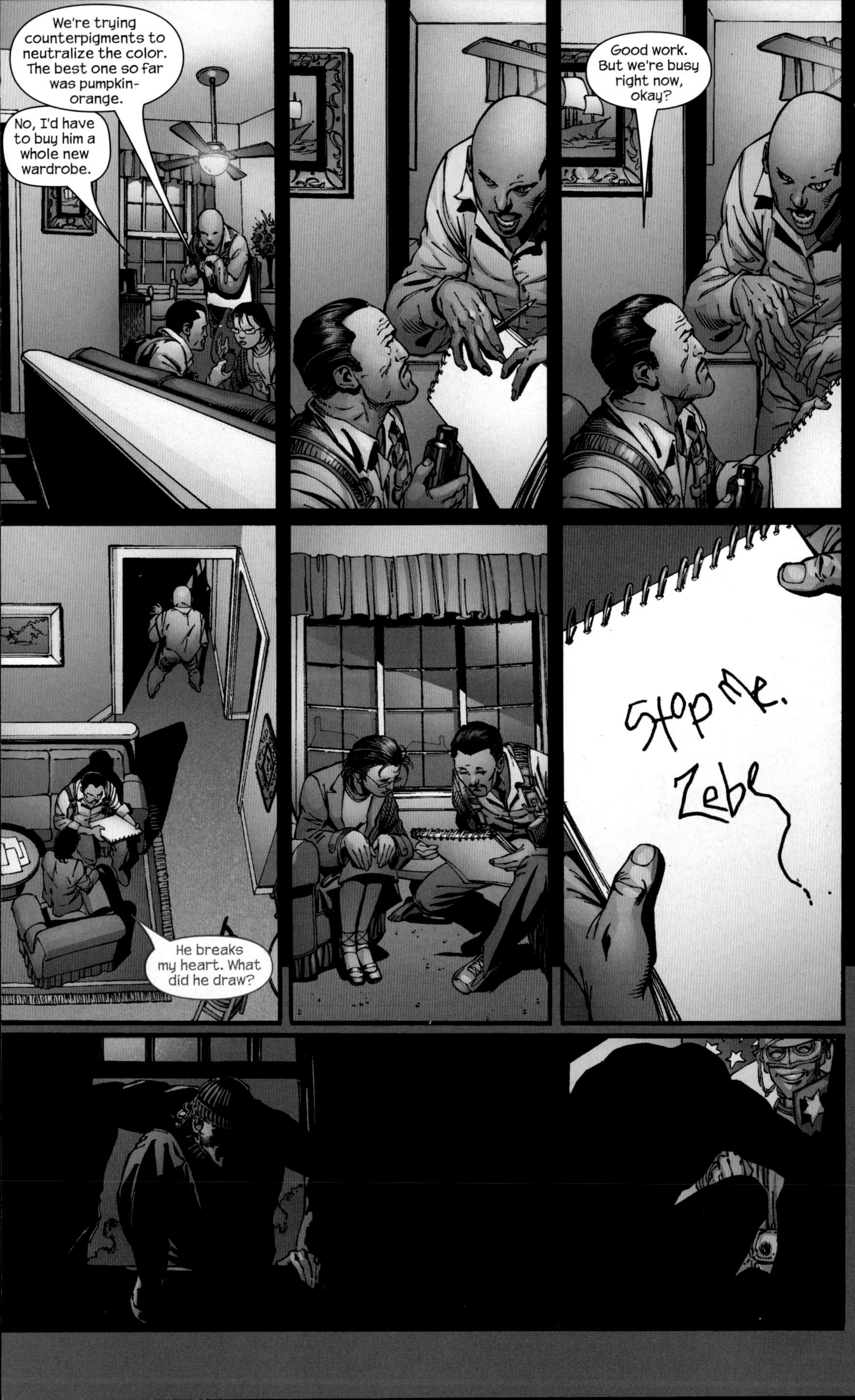

We're trying counterpigments to neutralize the color. The best one so far was pumpkin-orange.
No, I'd have to buy him a whole new wardrobe.
Good work. But we're busy right now, okay?
He breaks my heart. What did he draw?
Stop me.
Zebe

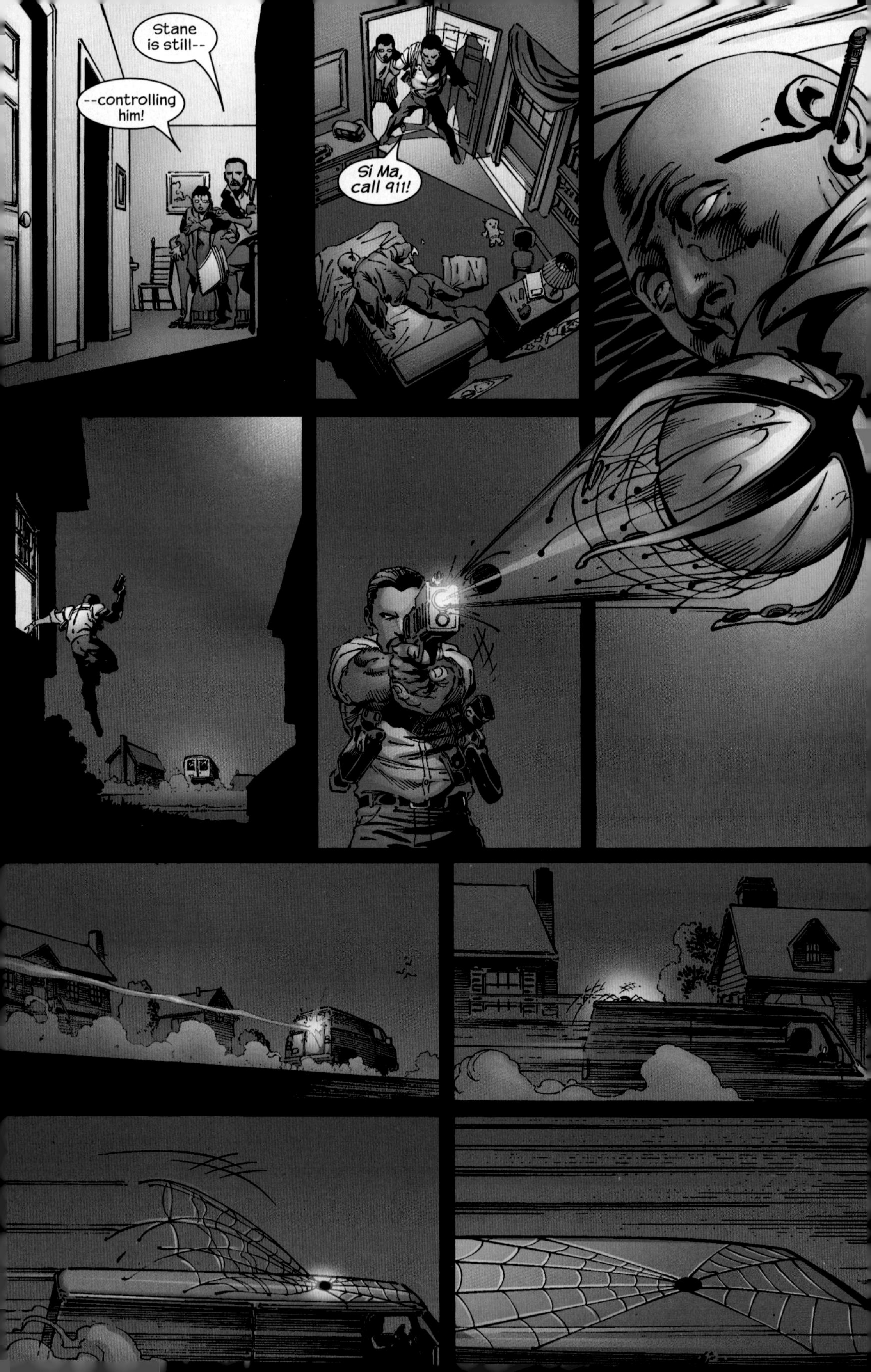
Stane is still--
--controlling him!
Si Ma, call 911!

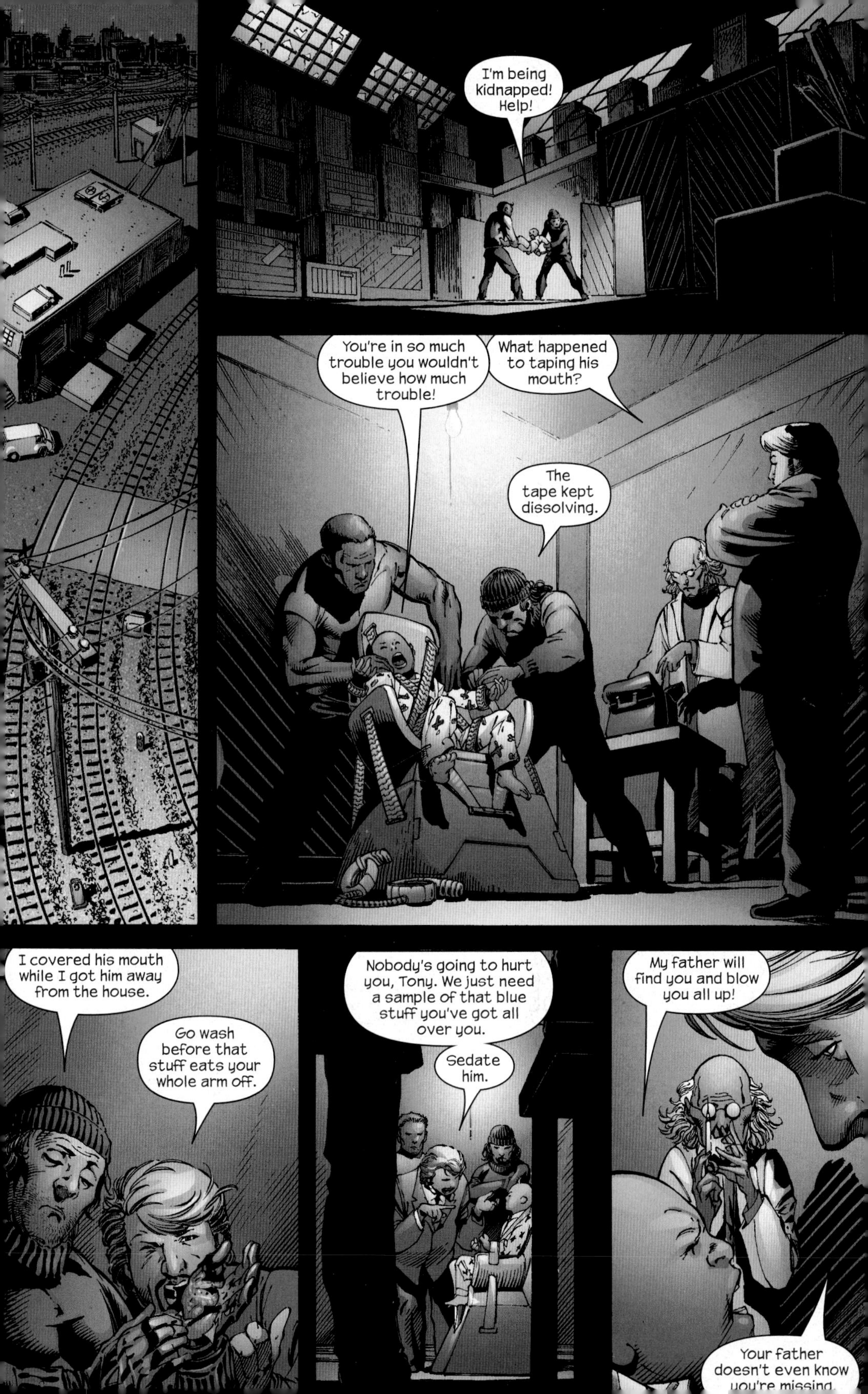
I'm being kidnapped! Help!
You're in so much trouble you wouldn't believe how much trouble!
What happened to taping his mouth?
The tape kept dissolving.
I covered his mouth while I got him away from the house.
Go wash before that stuff eats your whole arm off.
Nobody's going to hurt you, Tony. We just need a sample of that blue stuff you've got all over you.
Sedate him.
My father will find you and blow you all up!
Your father doesn't even know you're missing.

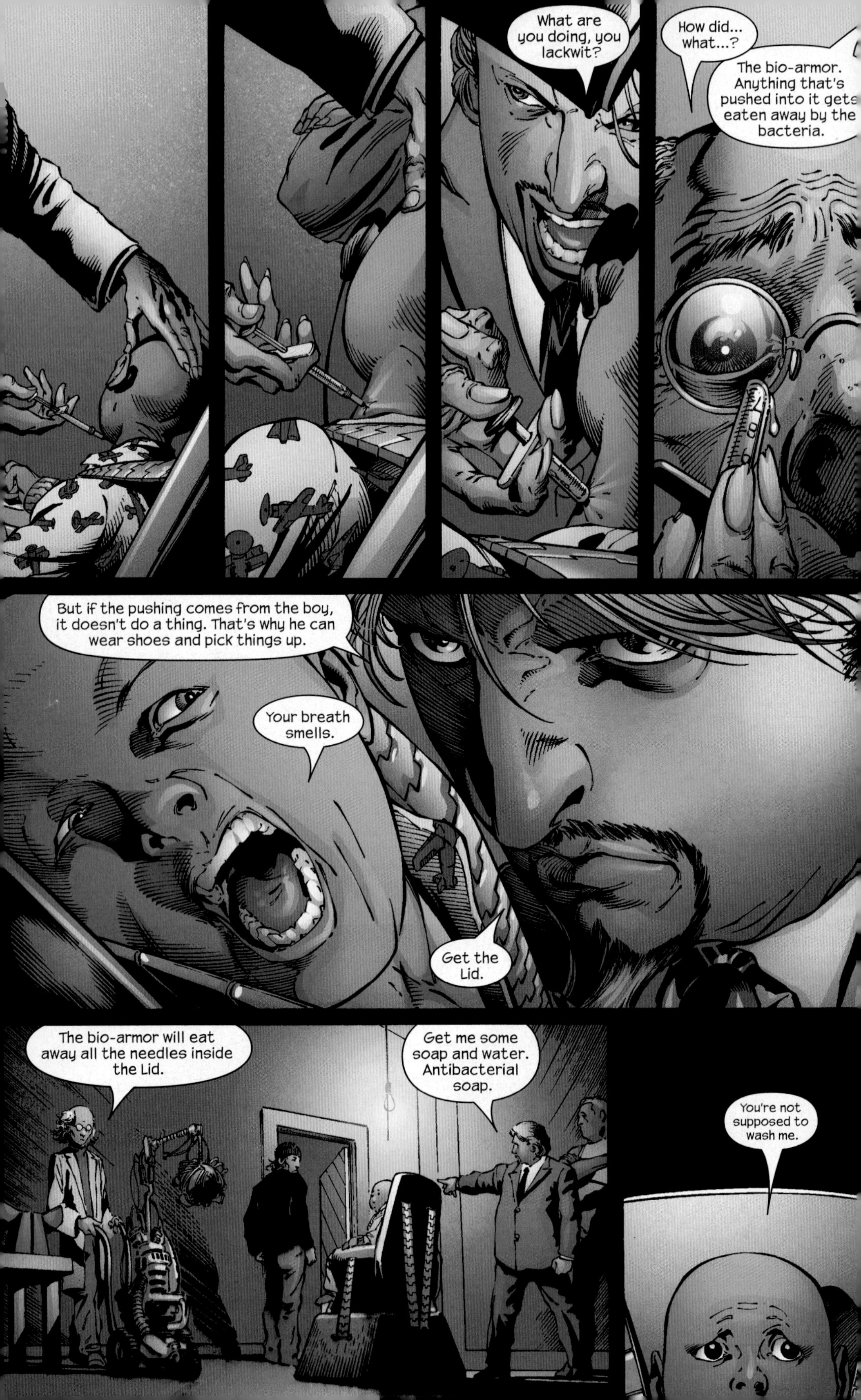
What are you doing, you lackwit?
How did... what...?
The bio-armor. Anything that's pushed into it gets eaten away by the bacteria.
But if the pushing comes from the boy, it doesn't do a thing. That's why he can wear shoes and pick things up.
Your breath smells.
Get the Lid.
The bio-armor will eat away all the needles inside the Lid.
Get me some soap and water. Antibacterial soap.
You're not supposed to wash me.

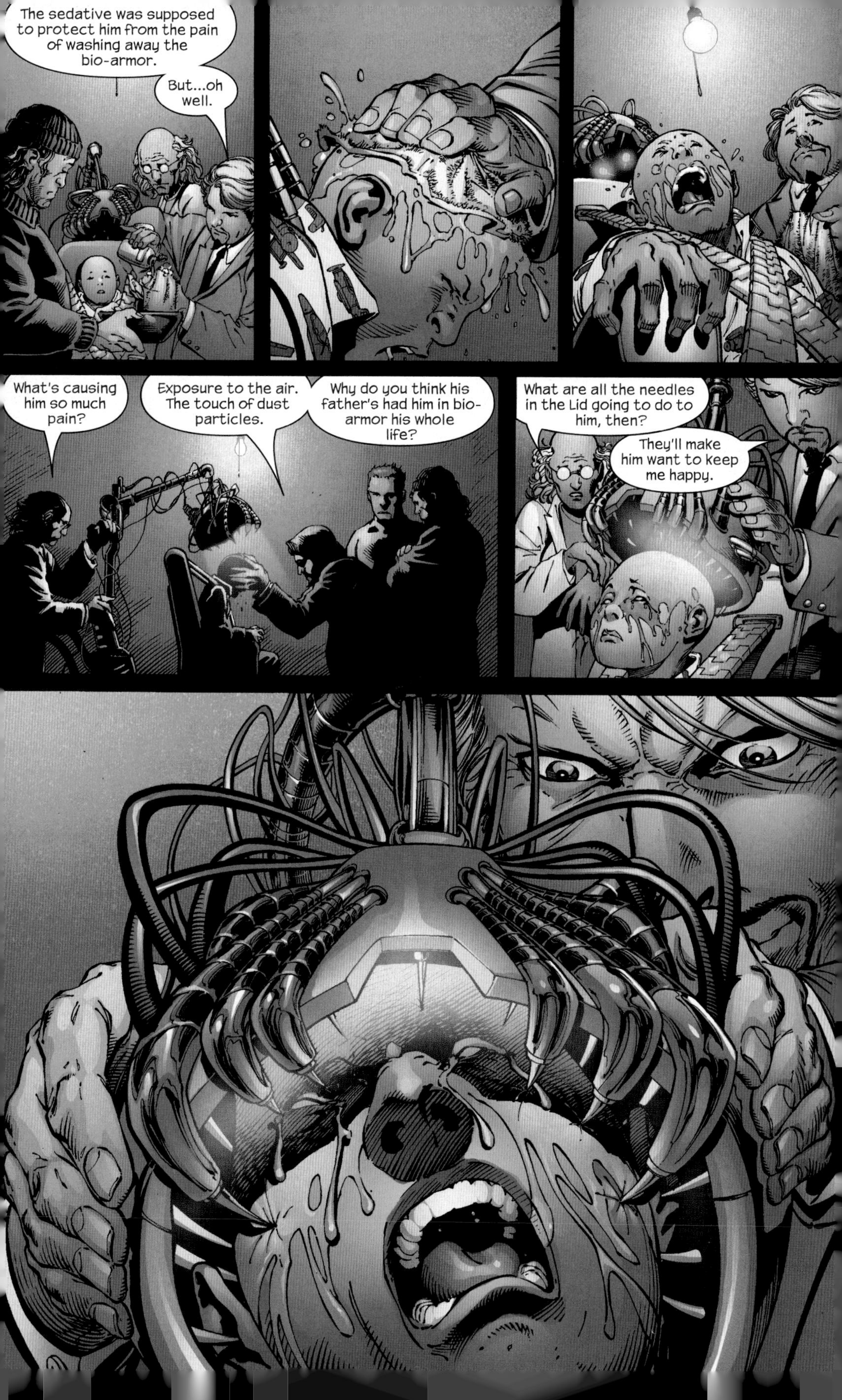
The sedative was supposed to protect him from the pain of washing away the bio-armor.
But...oh well.
What's causing him so much pain?
Exposure to the air. The touch of dust particles.
Why do you think his father's had him in bio-armor his whole life?
What are all the needles in the Lid going to do to him, then?
They'll make him want to keep me happy.

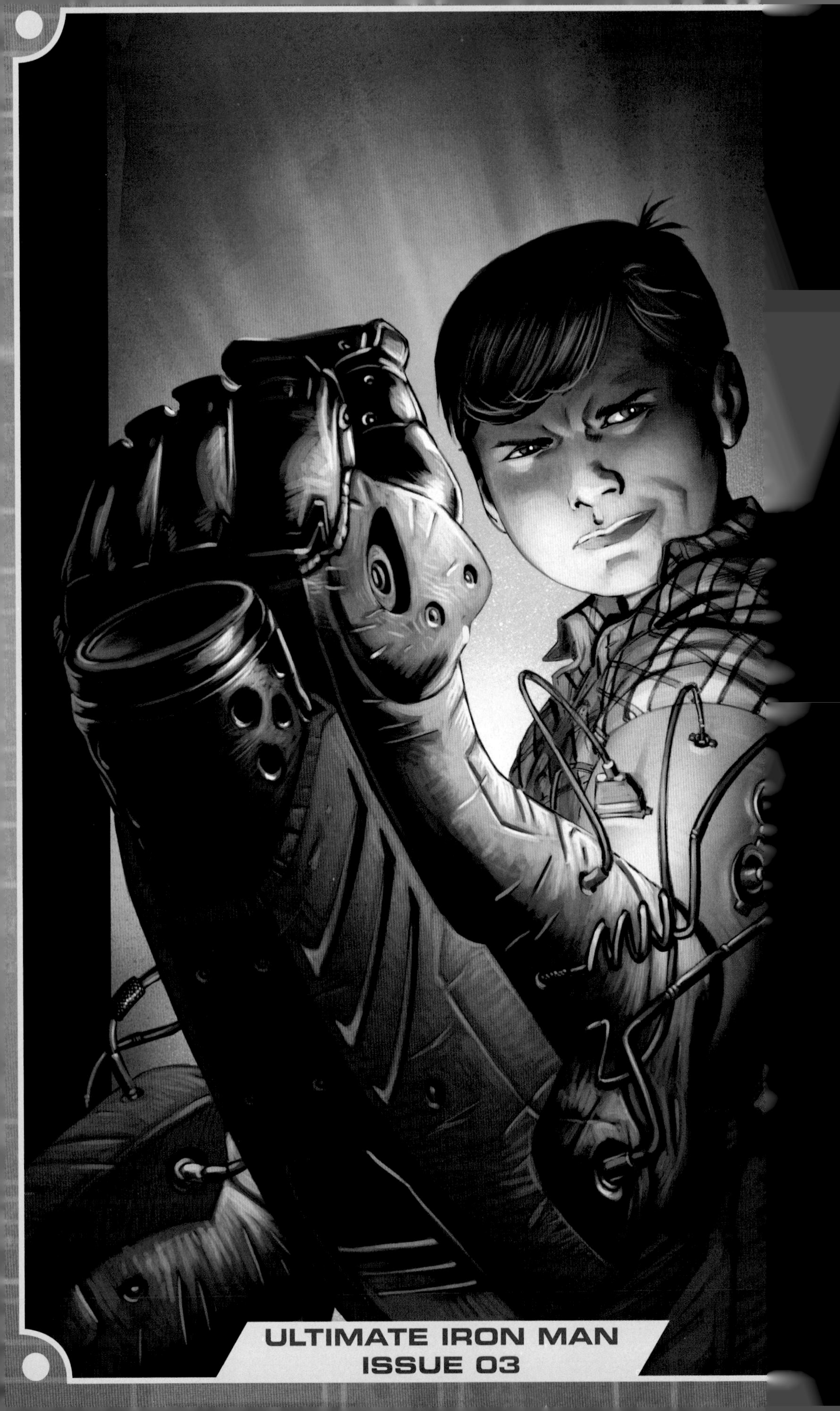
ULTIMATE IRON MAN
ISSUE 03

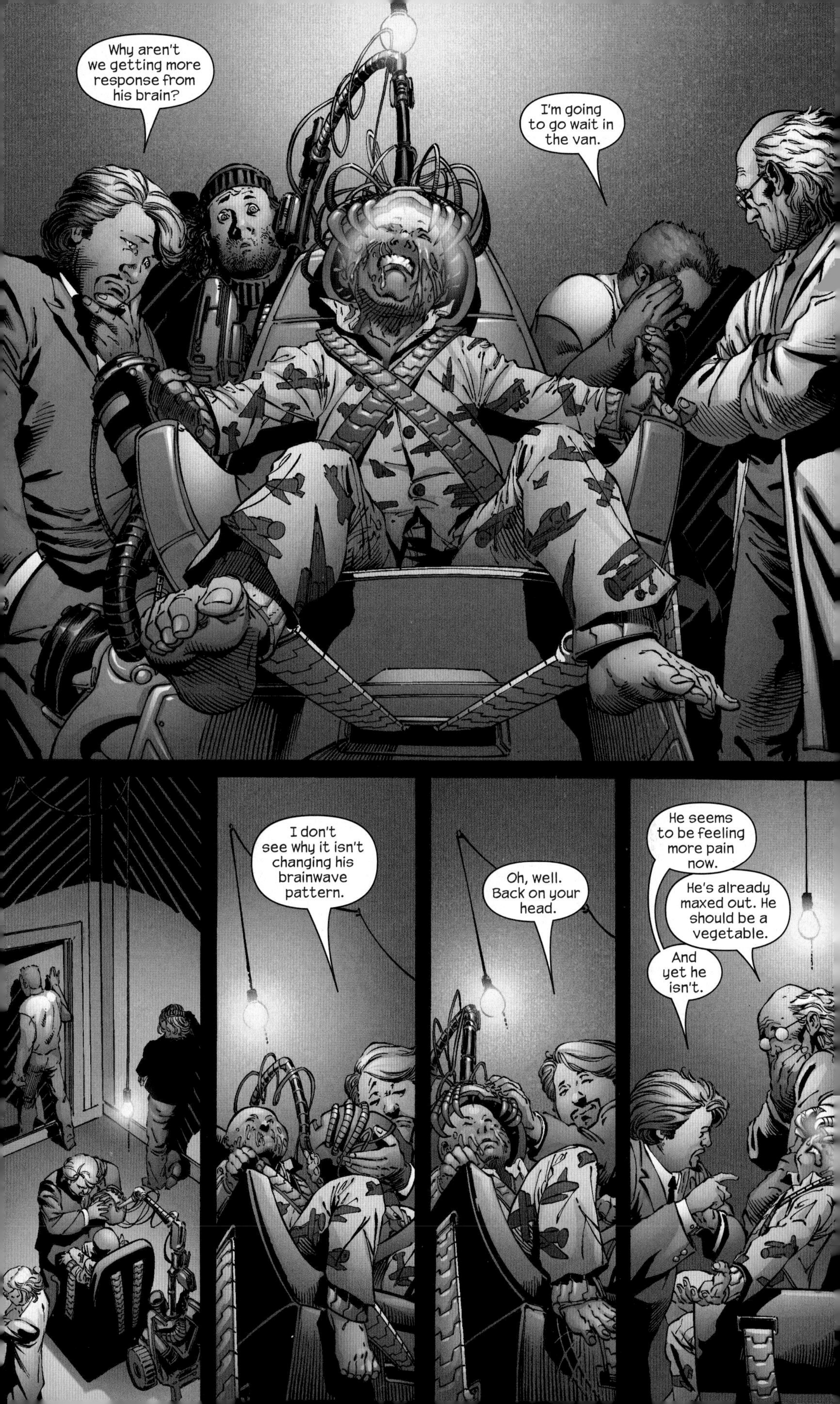
Why aren't we getting more response from his brain?
I'm going to go wait in the van.
I don't see why it isn't changing his brainwave pattern.
Oh, well. Back on your head.
He seems to be feeling more pain now.
He's already maxed out. He should be a vegetable.
And yet he isn't.

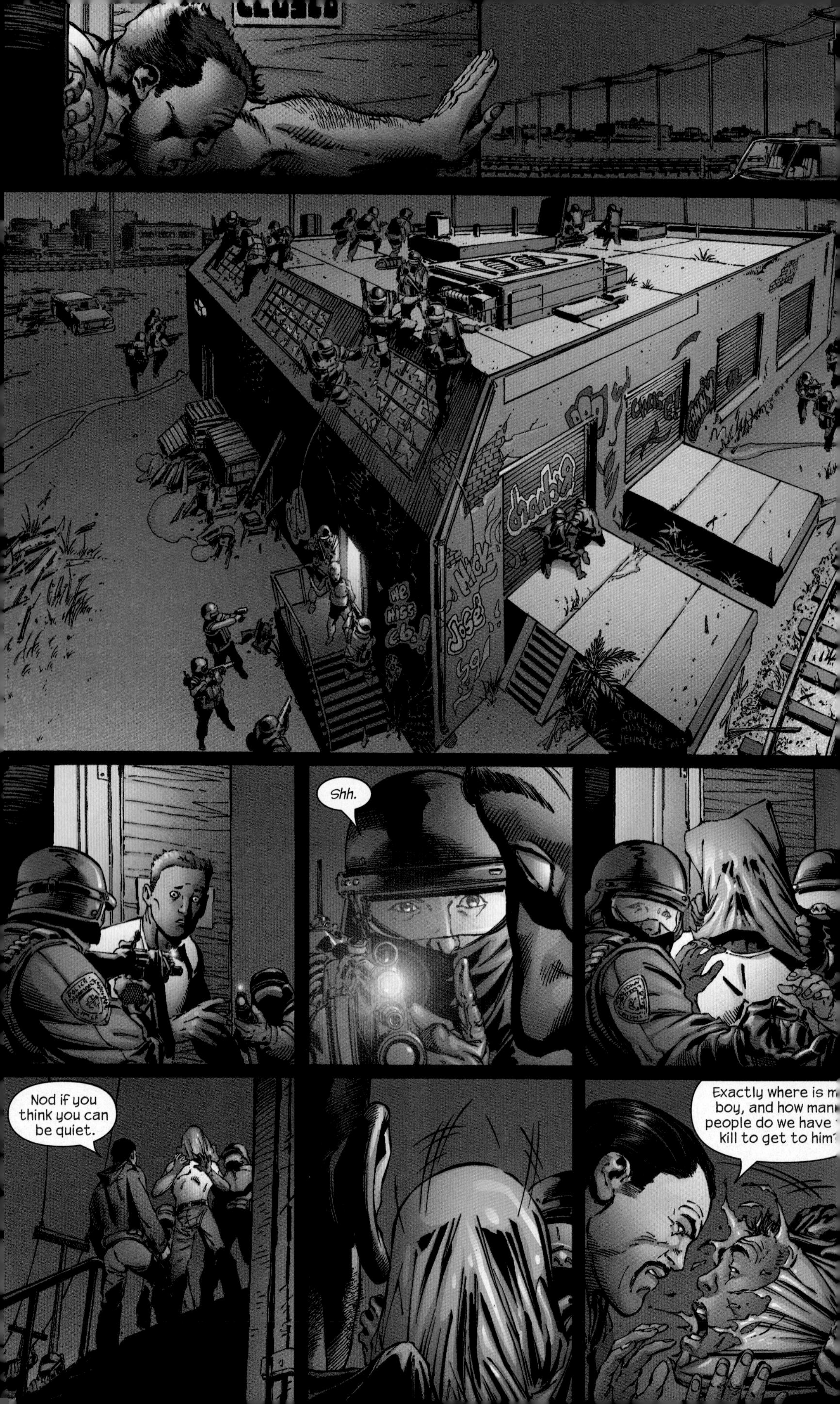

Shh.
Nod if you think you can be quiet.
Exactly where is m boy, and how man people do we have kill to get to him

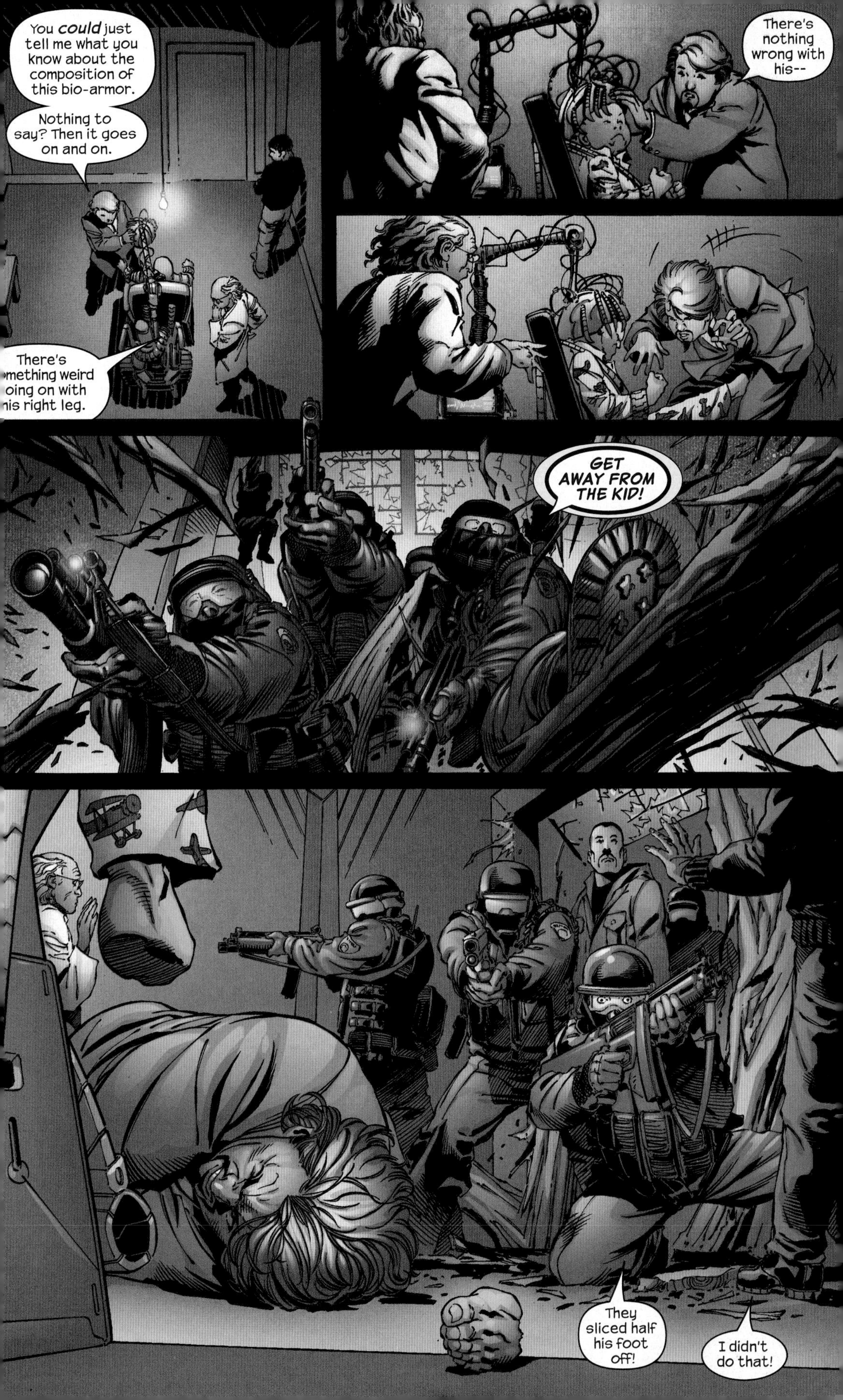
You could just tell me what you know about the composition of this bio-armor.
Nothing to say? Then it goes on and on.
There's
mething weird
oing on with
is right leg.
There's nothing wrong with his--
GET AWAY FROM THE KID!
They sliced half his foot off!
I didn't do that!

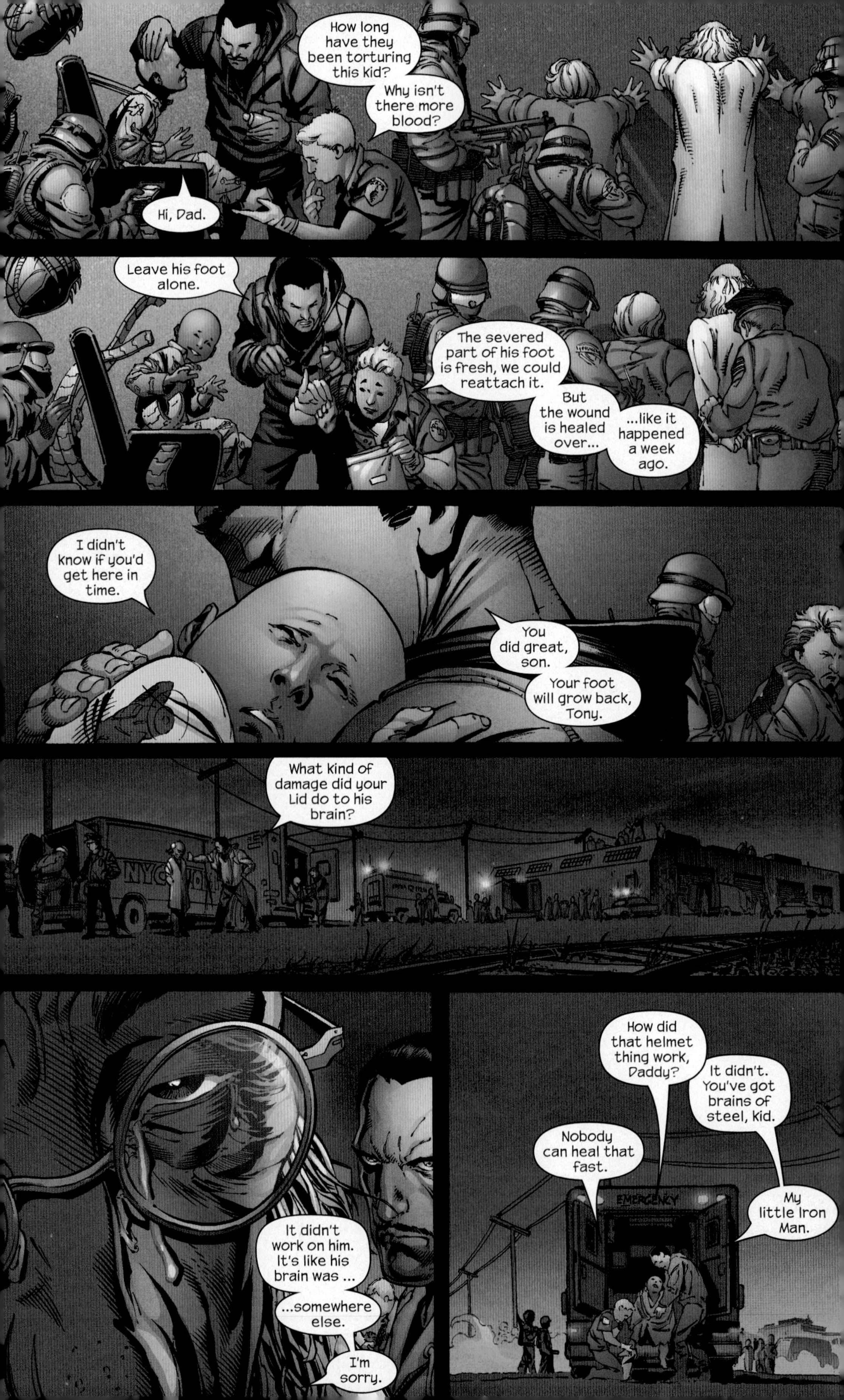
How long have they been torturing this kid?
Why isn't there more blood?
Hi, Dad.
Leave his foot alone.
The severed part of his foot is fresh, we could reattach it.
But the wound is healed over...
...like it happened a week ago.
I didn't know if you'd get here in time.
You did great, son.
Your foot will grow back, Tony.
What kind of damage did your Lid do to his brain?
It didn't work on him. It's like his brain was ...
...somewhere else.
I'm sorry.
How did that helmet thing work, Daddy?
It didn't. You've got brains of steel, kid.
Nobody can heal that fast.
My little Iron Man.

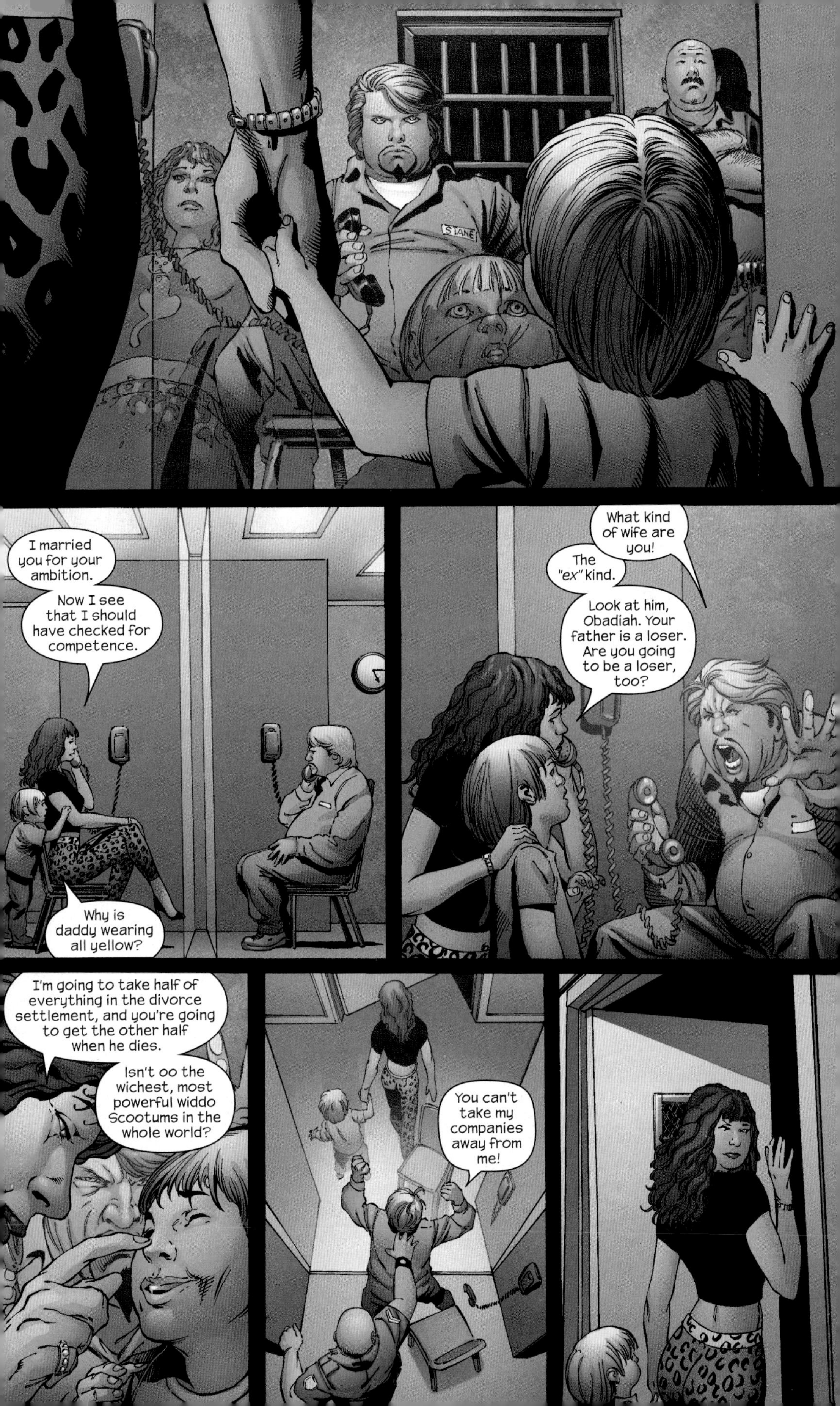

STANE
I married you for your ambition.
Now I see that I should have checked for competence.
Why is daddy wearing all yellow?
What kind of wife are you!
The "ex" kind.
Look at him, Obadiah. Your father is a loser. Are you going to be a loser, too?
I'm going to take half of everything in the divorce settlement, and you're going to get the other half when he dies.
Isn't oo the wichest, most powerful widdo Scootums in the whole world?
You can't take my companies away from me!

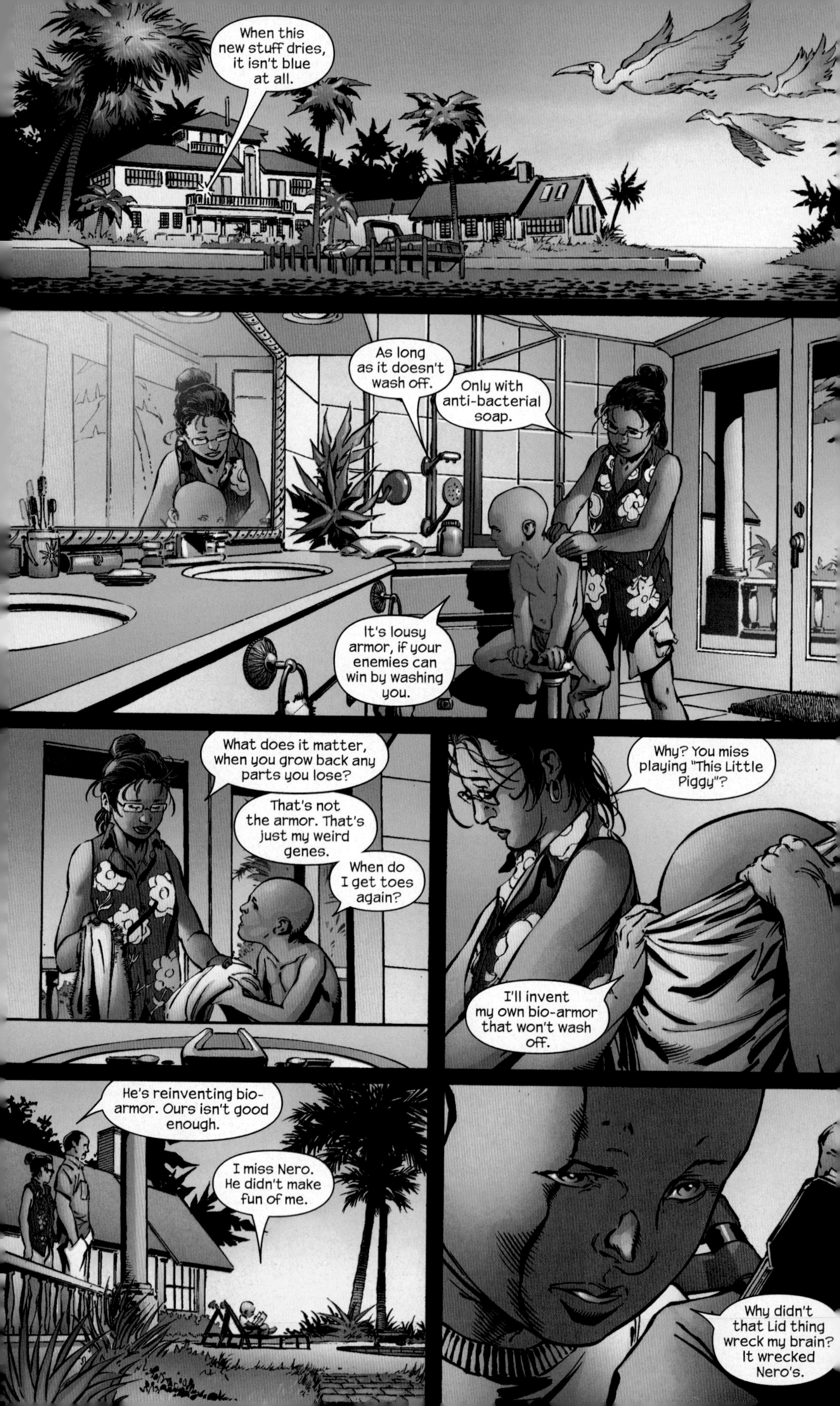
When this new stuff dries, it isn't blue at all.
As long as it doesn't wash off.
Only with anti-bacterial soap.
It's lousy armor, if your enemies can win by washing you.
What does it matter, when you grow back any parts you lose?
That's not the armor. That's just my weird genes.
When do I get toes again?
Why? You miss playing "This Little Piggy"?
I'll invent my own bio-armor that won't wash off.
He's reinventing bio-armor. Ours isn't good enough.
I miss Nero. He didn't make fun of me.
Why didn't that Lid thing wreck my brain? It wrecked Nero's.

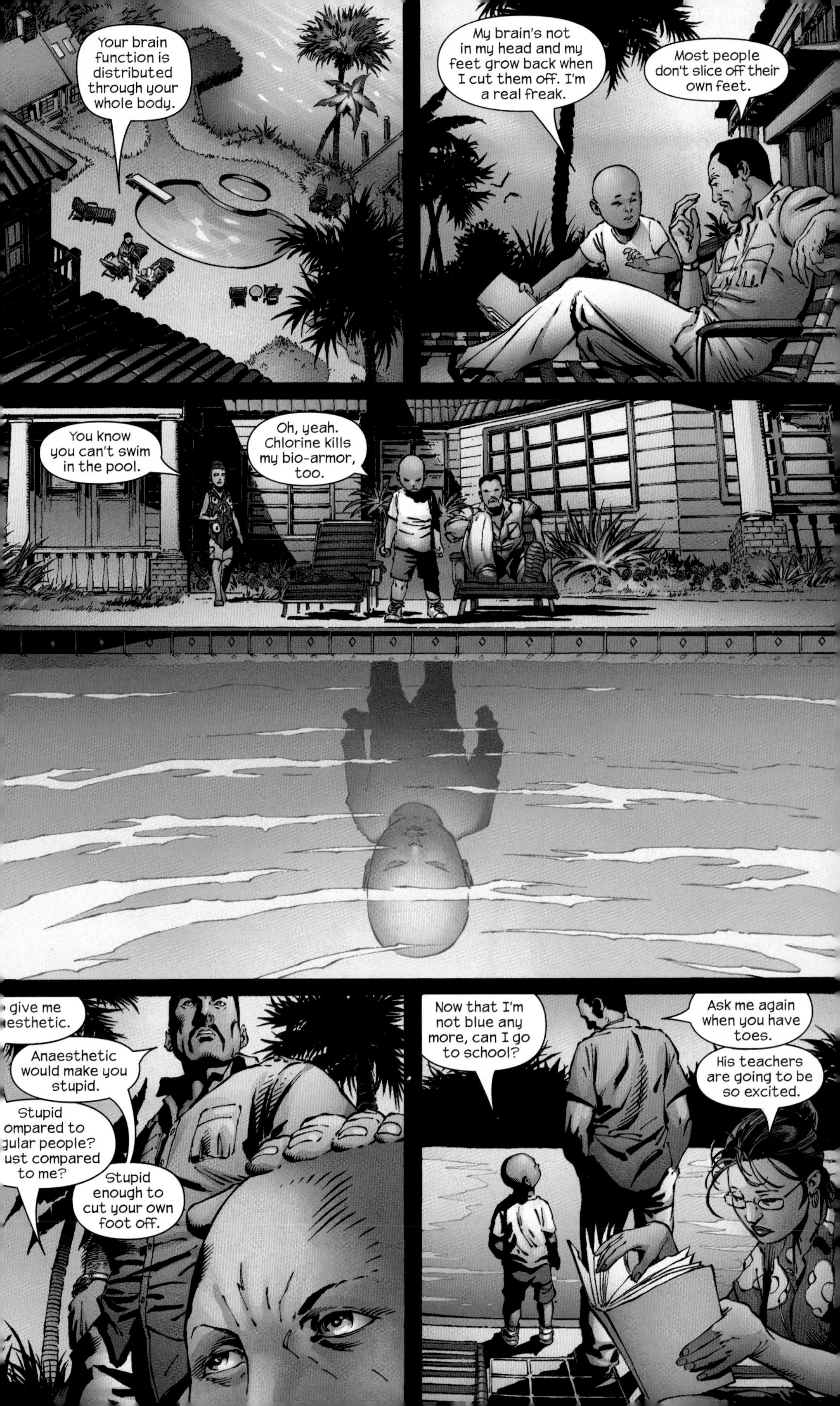
Your brain function is distributed through your whole body.
My brain's not in my head and my feet grow back when I cut them off. I'm a real freak.
Most people don't slice off their own feet.
You know you can't swim in the pool.
Oh, yeah. Chlorine kills my bio-armor, too.
give me esthetic.
Anaesthetic would make you stupid.
Stupid ompared to gular people? ust compared to me?
Stupid enough to cut your own foot off.
Now that I'm not blue any more, can I go to school?
Ask me again when you have toes.
His teachers are going to be so excited.

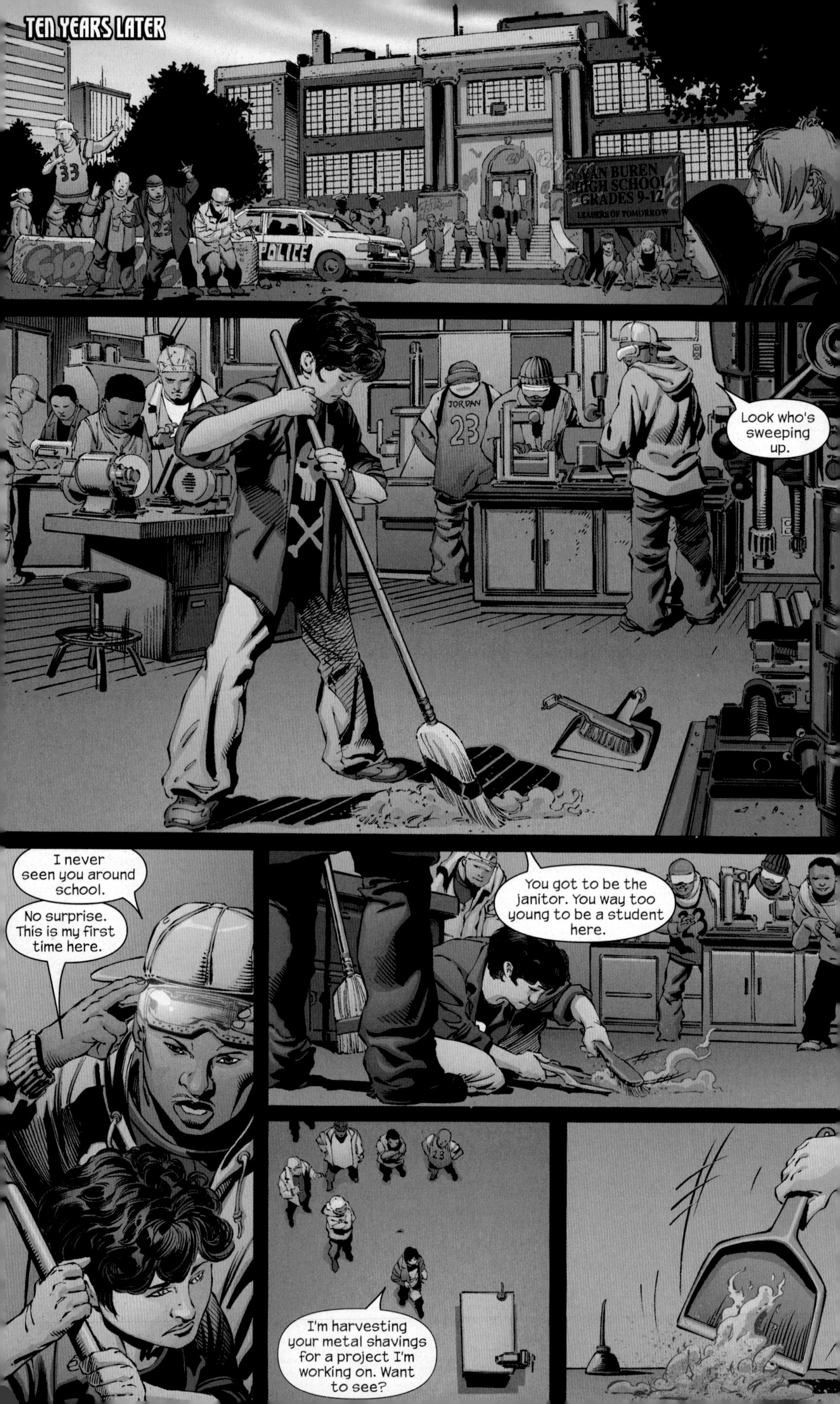

TEN YEARS LATER
VAN BUREN HIGH SCHOOL GRADES 9-12
LEADERS OF TOMORROW
POLICE
JORDAN
Look who's sweeping up.
I never seen you around school.
No surprise. This is my first time here.
You got to be the janitor. You way too young to be a student here.
I'm harvesting your metal shavings for a project I'm working on. Want to see?

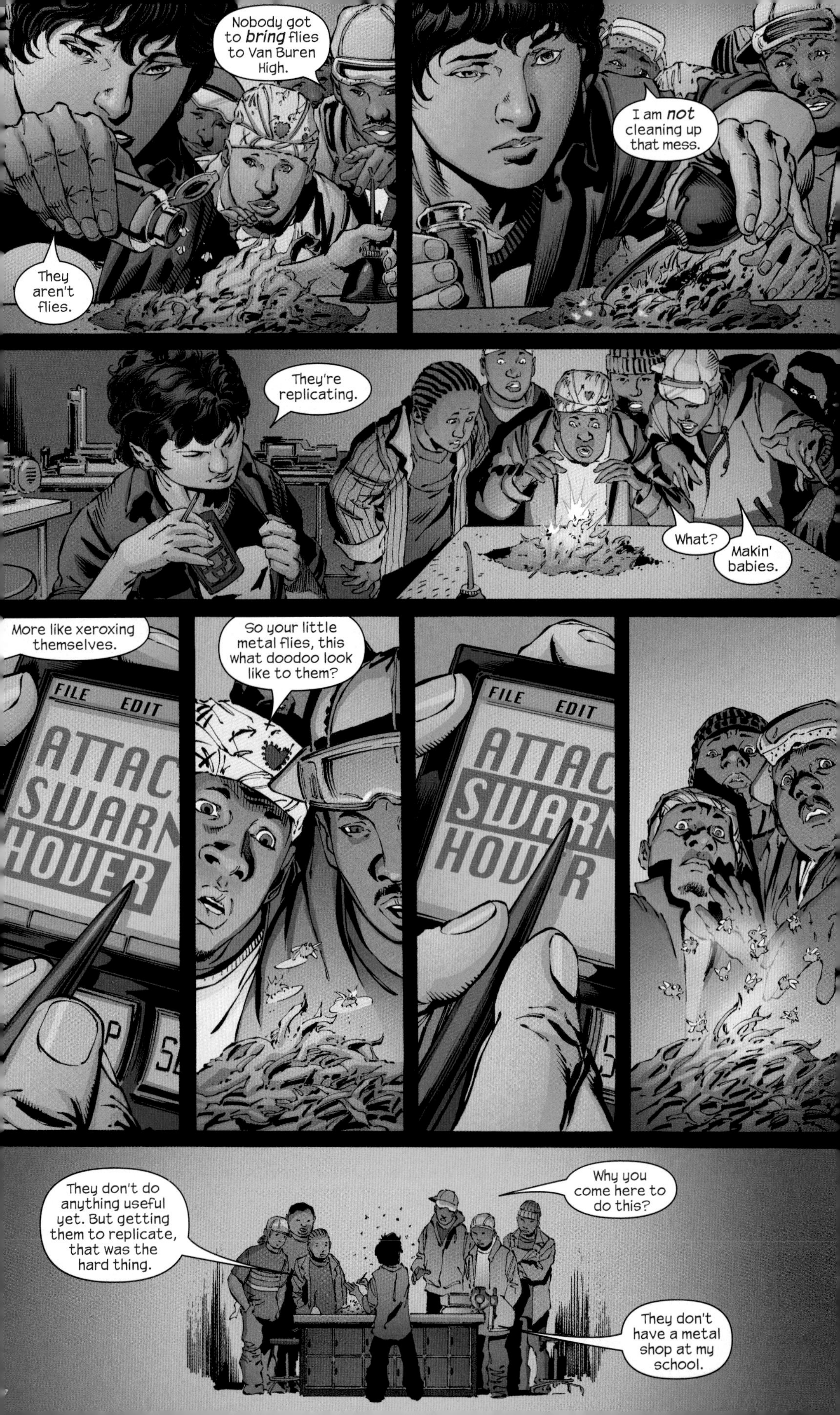
Nobody got to *bring* flies to Van Buren High.
They aren't flies.
I am *not* cleaning up that mess.
They're replicating.
What?
Makin' babies.
More like xeroxing themselves.
FILE EDIT
ATTAC
SWARM
HOVER
So your little metal flies, this what doodoo look like to them?
FILE EDIT
They don't do anything useful yet. But getting them to replicate, that was the hard thing.
Why you come here to do this?
They don't have a metal shop at my school.

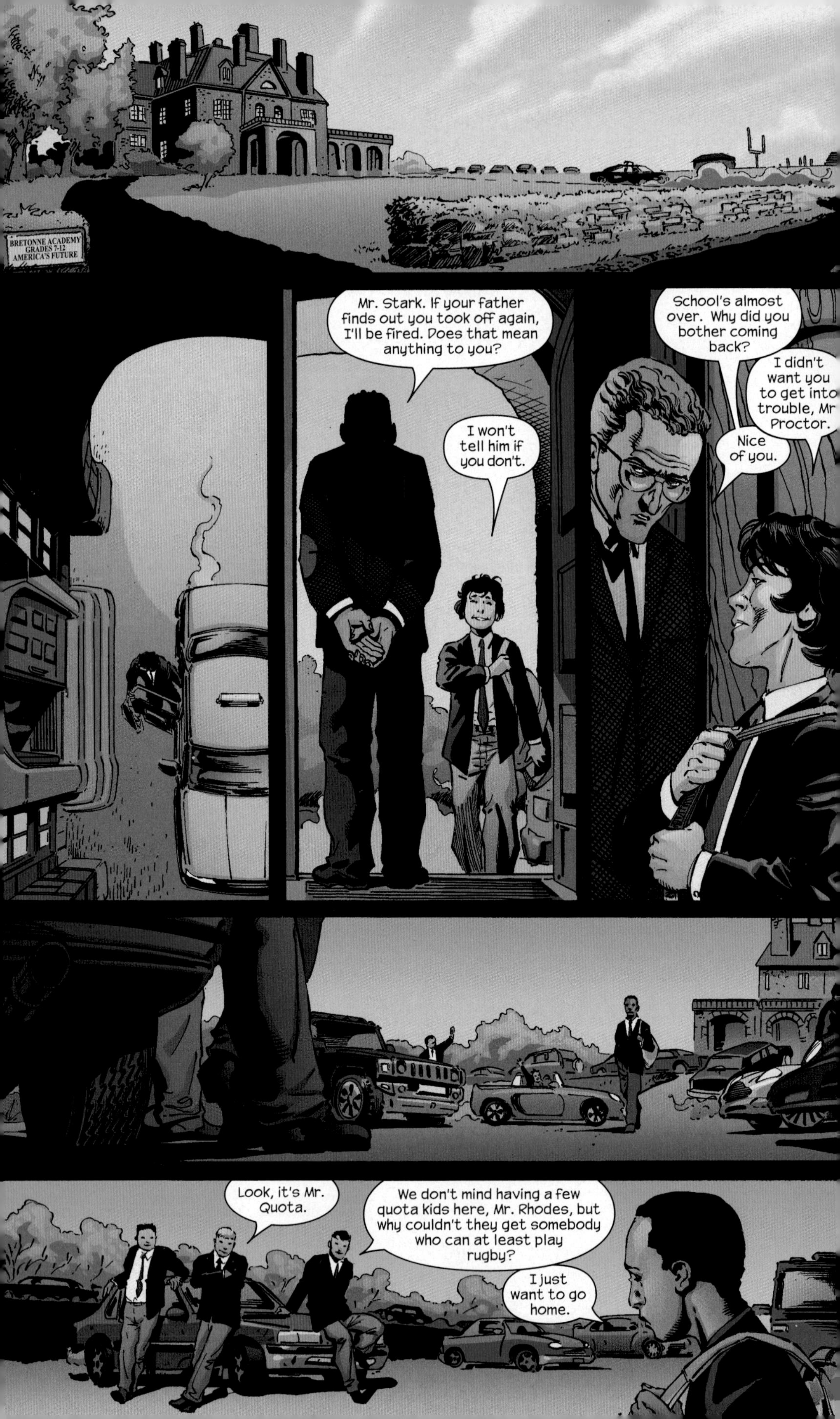
BRETONNE ACADEMY GRADES 7-12 AMERICA'S FUTURE
Mr. Stark. If your father finds out you took off again, I'll be fired. Does that mean anything to you?
I won't tell him if you don't.
School's almost over. Why did you bother coming back?
I didn't want you to get into trouble, Mr Proctor.
Nice of you.
Look, it's Mr. Quota.
We don't mind having a few quota kids here, Mr. Rhodes, but why couldn't they get somebody who can at least play rugby?
I just want to go home.

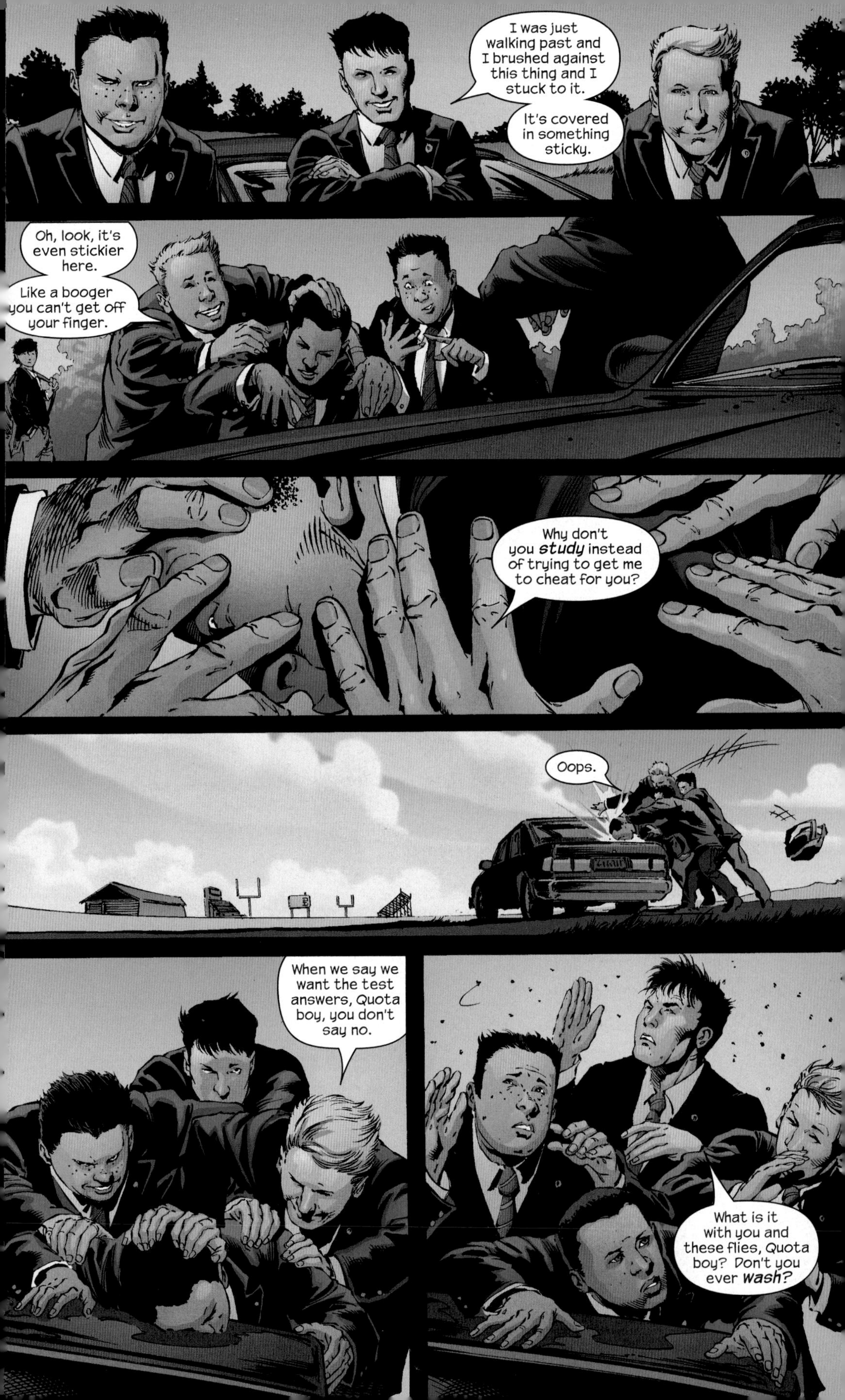
I was just walking past and I brushed against this thing and I stuck to it.
It's covered in something sticky.
Oh, look, it's even stickier here.
Like a booger you can't get off your finger.
Why don't you *study* instead of trying to get me to cheat for you?
Oops.
When we say we want the test answers, Quota boy, you don't say no.
What is it with you and these flies, Quota boy? Don't you ever *wash*?

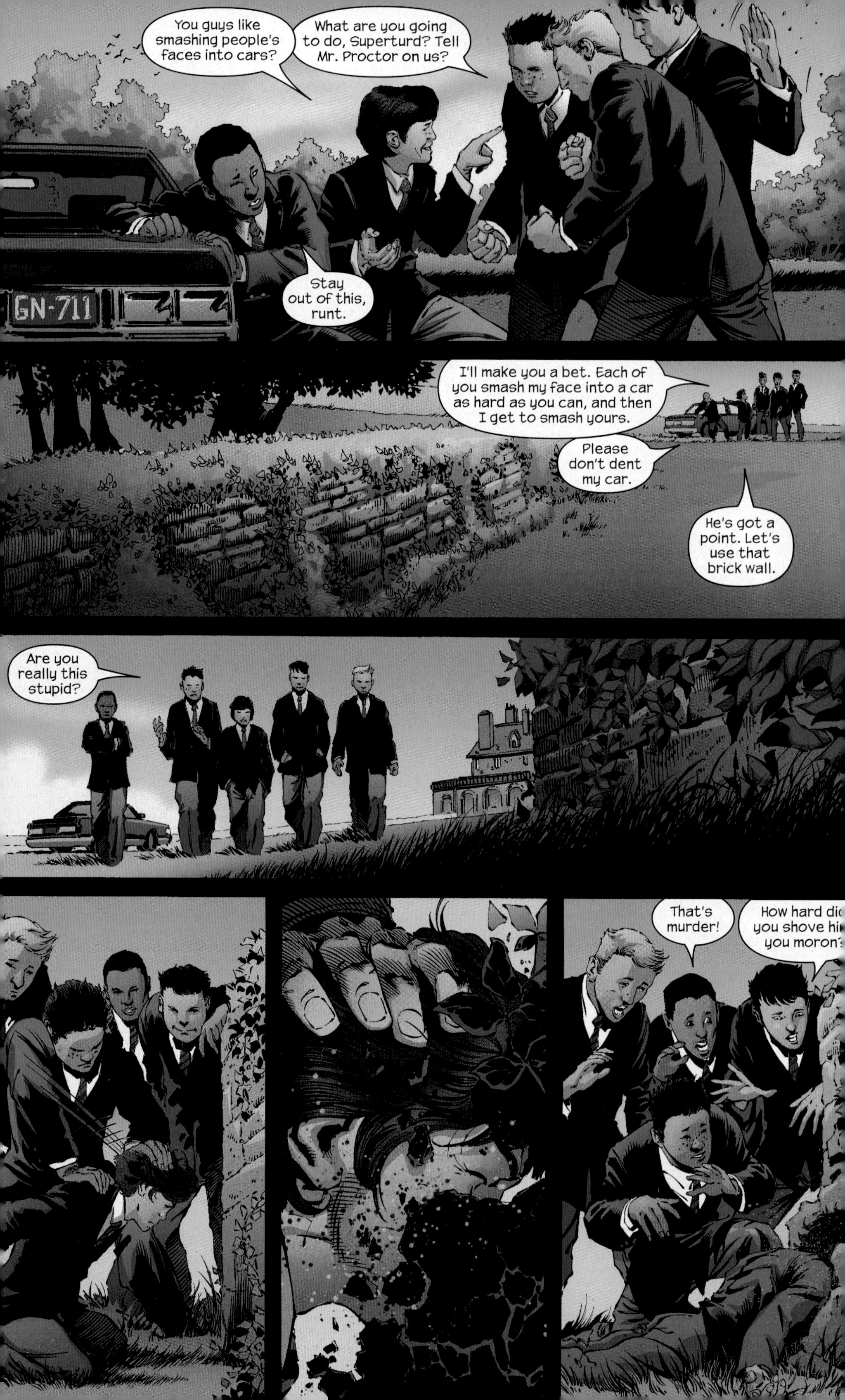

You guys like smashing people's faces into cars?
What are you going to do, Superturd? Tell Mr. Proctor on us?
Stay out of this, runt.
GN-711
I'll make you a bet. Each of you smash my face into a car as hard as you can, and then I get to smash yours.
Please don't dent my car.
He's got a point. Let's use that brick wall.
Are you really this stupid?
That's murder!

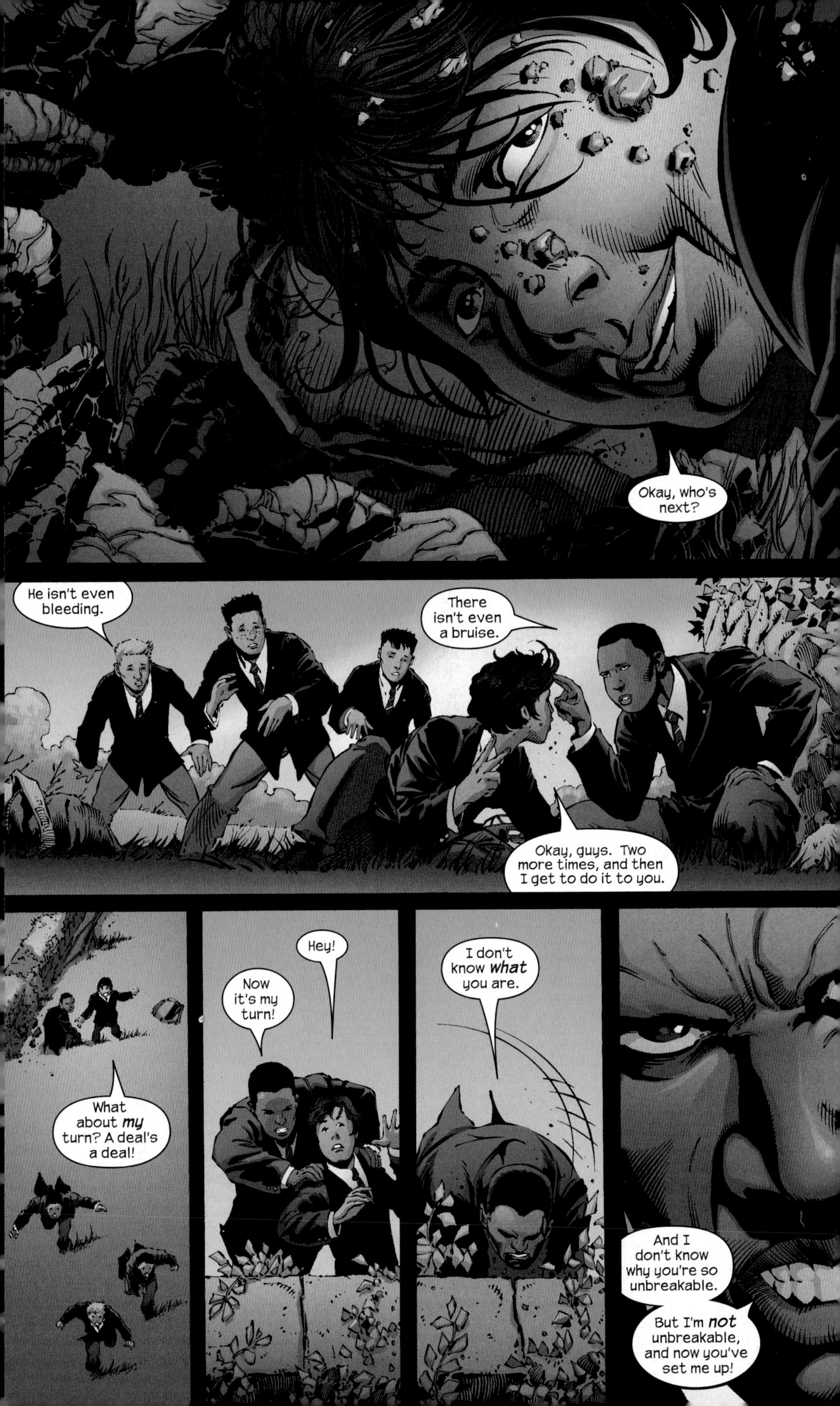
Okay, who's next?
He isn't even bleeding.
There isn't even a bruise.
Okay, guys. Two more times, and then I get to do it to you.
What about *my* turn? A deal's a deal!
Now it's my turn!
Hey!
I don't know *what* you are.
And I don't know why you're so unbreakable.
But I'm *not* unbreakable, and now you've set me up!

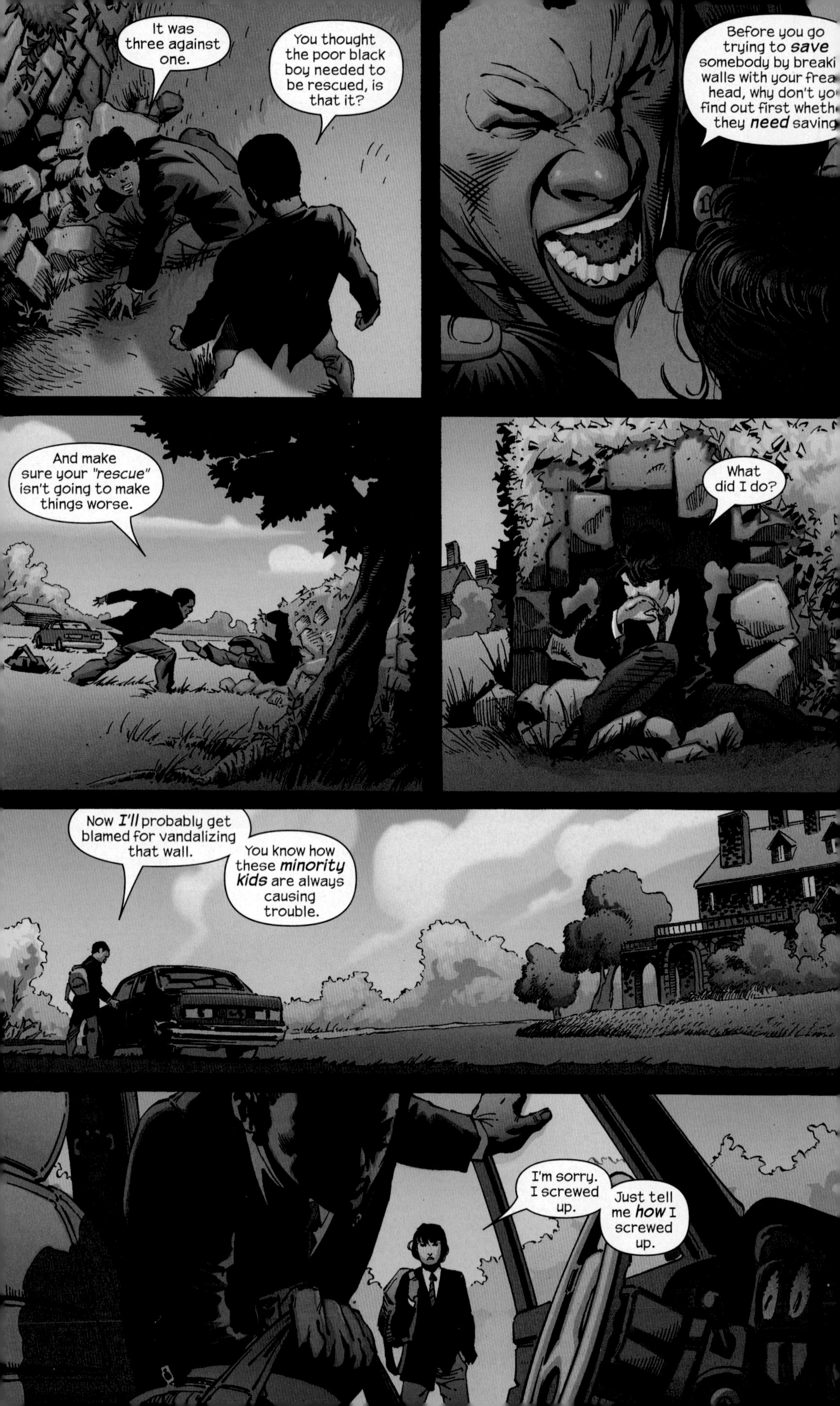

It was three against one.
You thought the poor black boy needed to be rescued, is that it?
Before you go trying to *save* somebody by breaki walls with your frea head, why don't yo find out first wheth they *need* saving
And make sure your "*rescue*" isn't going to make things worse.
What did I do?
Now *I'll* probably get blamed for vandalizing that wall.
You know how these *minority kids* are always causing trouble.
I'm sorry. I screwed up.
Just tell me *how* I screwed up.

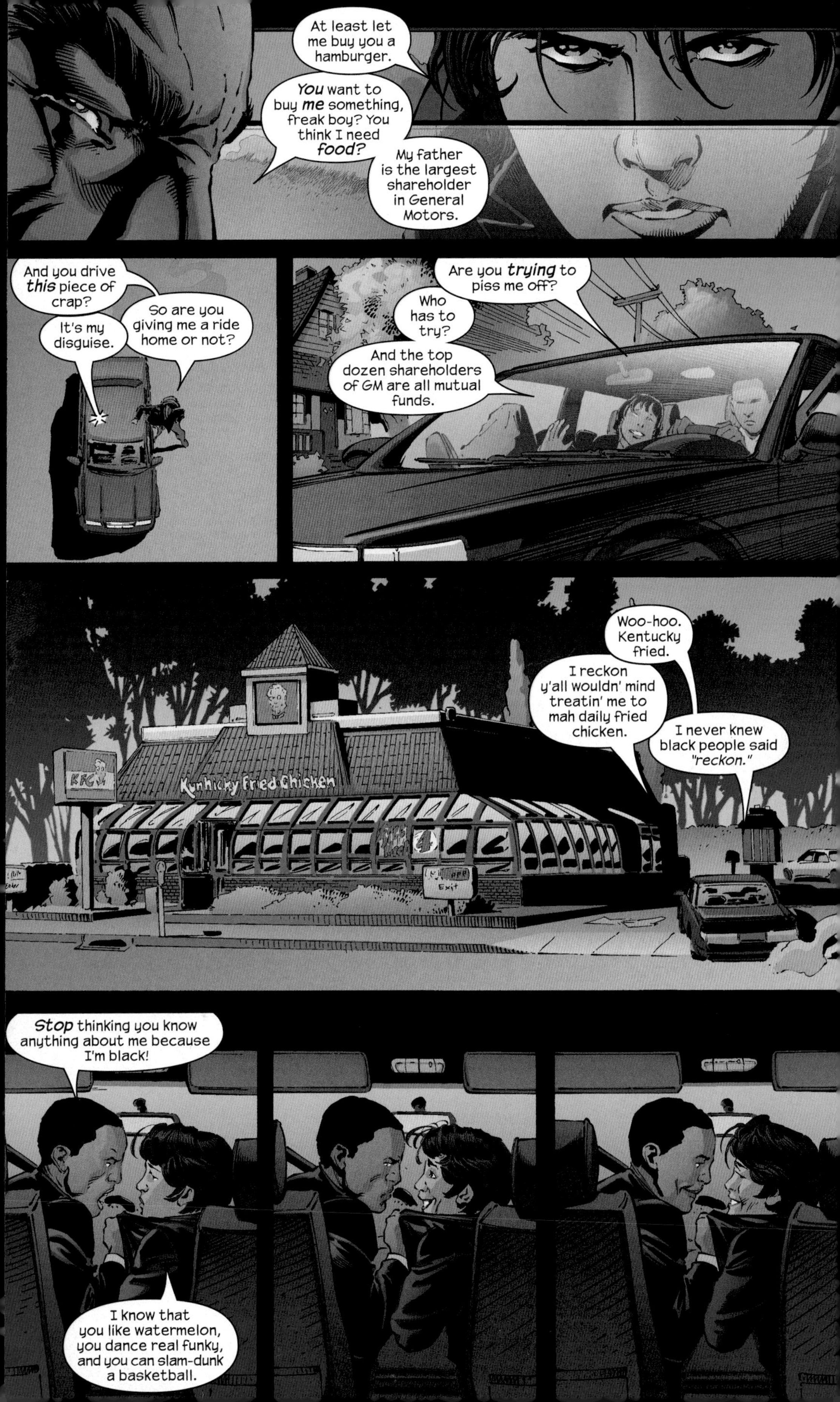
At least let me buy you a hamburger.
You want to buy me something, freak boy? You think I need food?
My father is the largest shareholder in General Motors.
And you drive this piece of crap?
It's my disguise.
So are you giving me a ride home or not?
Are you trying to piss me off?
Who has to try?
And the top dozen shareholders of GM are all mutual funds.
Woo-hoo. Kentucky fried.
I reckon y'all wouldn' mind treatin' me to mah daily fried chicken.
I never knew black people said "reckon."
Kunhicky Fried Chicken
KFC
Exit
Stop thinking you know anything about me because I'm black!
I know that you like watermelon, you dance real funky, and you can slam-dunk a basketball.

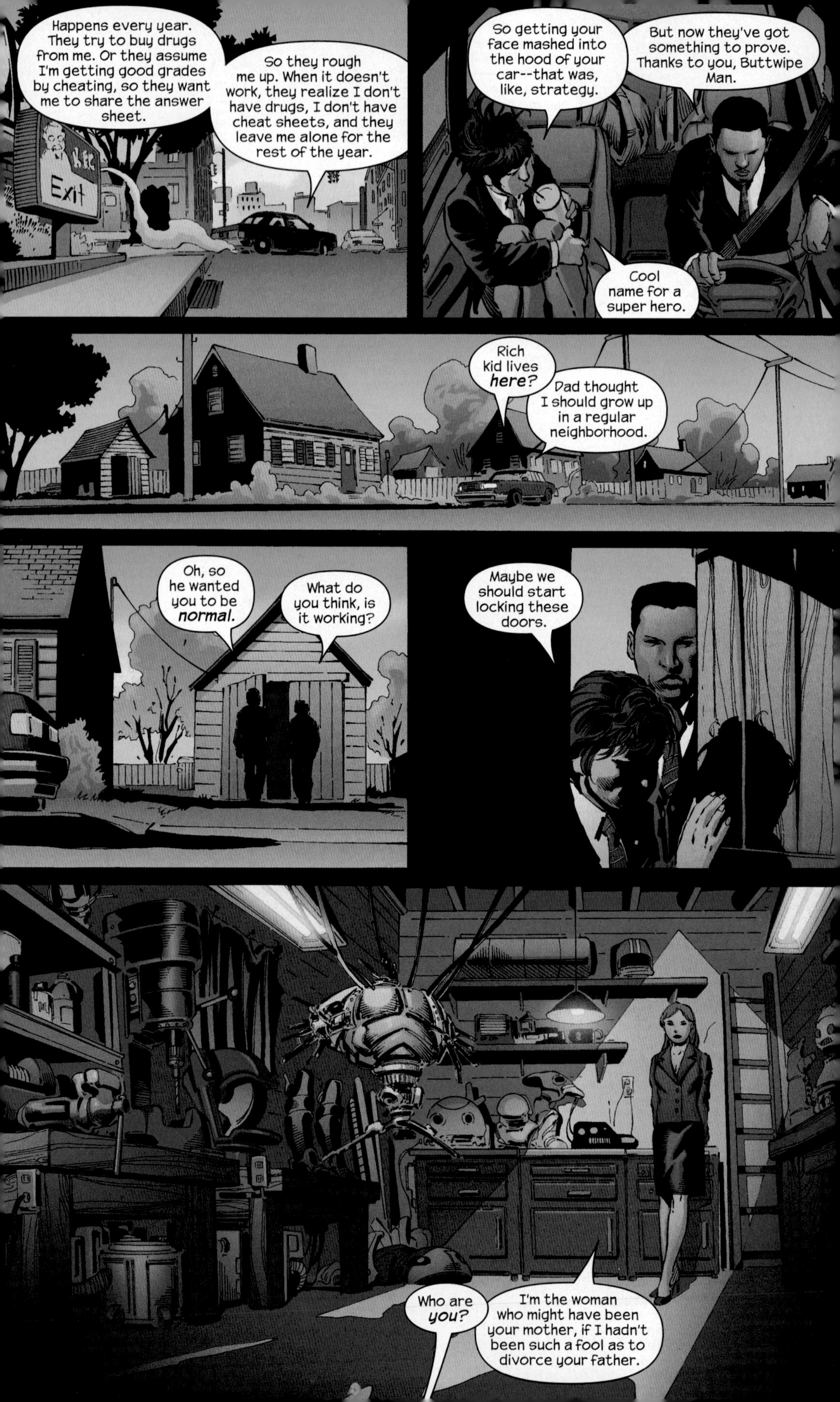
Happens every year. They try to buy drugs from me. Or they assume I'm getting good grades by cheating, so they want me to share the answer sheet.
So they rough me up. When it doesn't work, they realize I don't have drugs, I don't have cheat sheets, and they leave me alone for the rest of the year.
KFC
Exit
So getting your face mashed into the hood of your car--that was, like, strategy.
But now they've got something to prove. Thanks to you, Buttwipe Man.
Cool name for a super hero.
Rich kid lives *here*?
Dad thought I should grow up in a regular neighborhood.
Oh, so he wanted you to be *normal*.
What do you think, is it working?
Maybe we should start locking these doors.
Who are *you*?
I'm the woman who might have been your mother, if I hadn't been such a fool as to divorce your father.

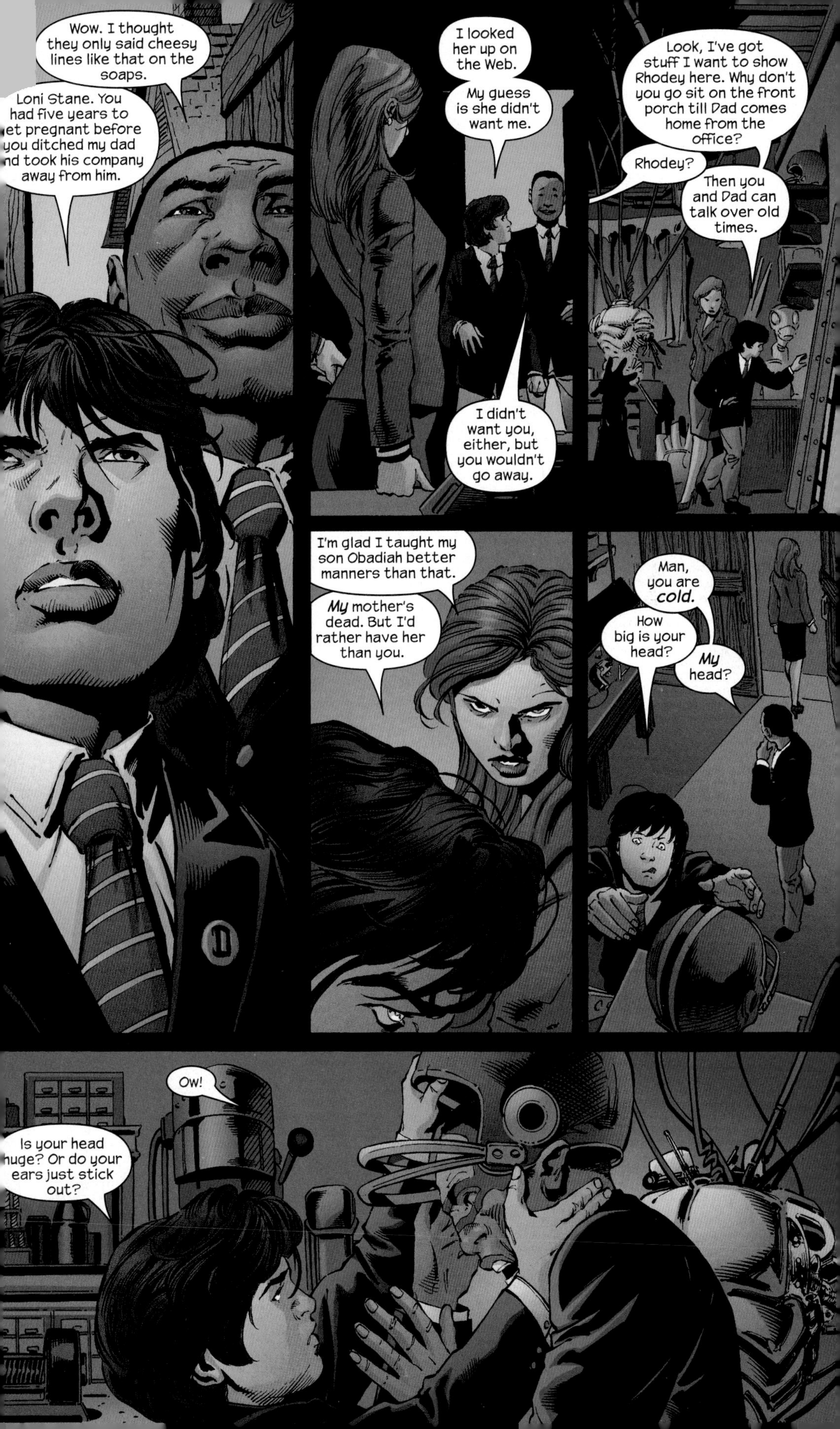
Wow. I thought they only said cheesy lines like that on the soaps.
Loni Stane. You had five years to get pregnant before you ditched my dad and took his company away from him.
I looked her up on the Web.
My guess is she didn't want me.
I didn't want you, either, but you wouldn't go away.
Look, I've got stuff I want to show Rhodey here. Why don't you go sit on the front porch till Dad comes home from the office?
Rhodey?
Then you and Dad can talk over old times.
I'm glad I taught my son Obadiah better manners than that.
My mother's dead. But I'd rather have her than you.
Man, you are ***cold.***
How big is your head?
My head?
Ow!
Is your head huge? Or do your ears just stick out?

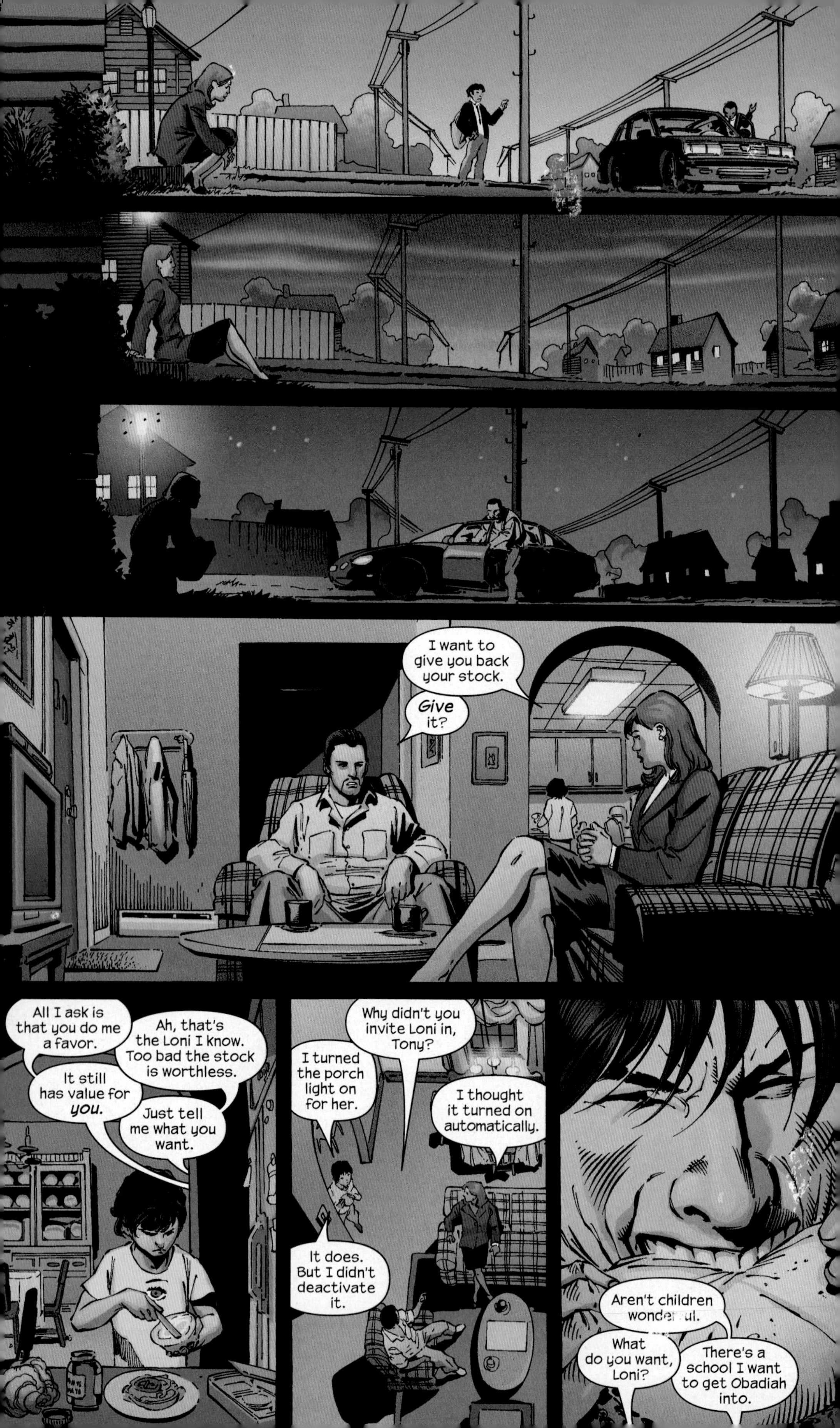
I want to give you back your stock.
Give it?
All I ask is that you do me a favor.
Ah, that's the Loni I know. Too bad the stock is worthless.
It still has value for you.
Just tell me what you want.
Why didn't you invite Loni in, Tony?
I turned the porch light on for her.
I thought it turned on automatically.
It does. But I didn't deactivate it.
Aren't children wonderful.
What do you want, Loni?
There's a school I want to get Obadiah into.

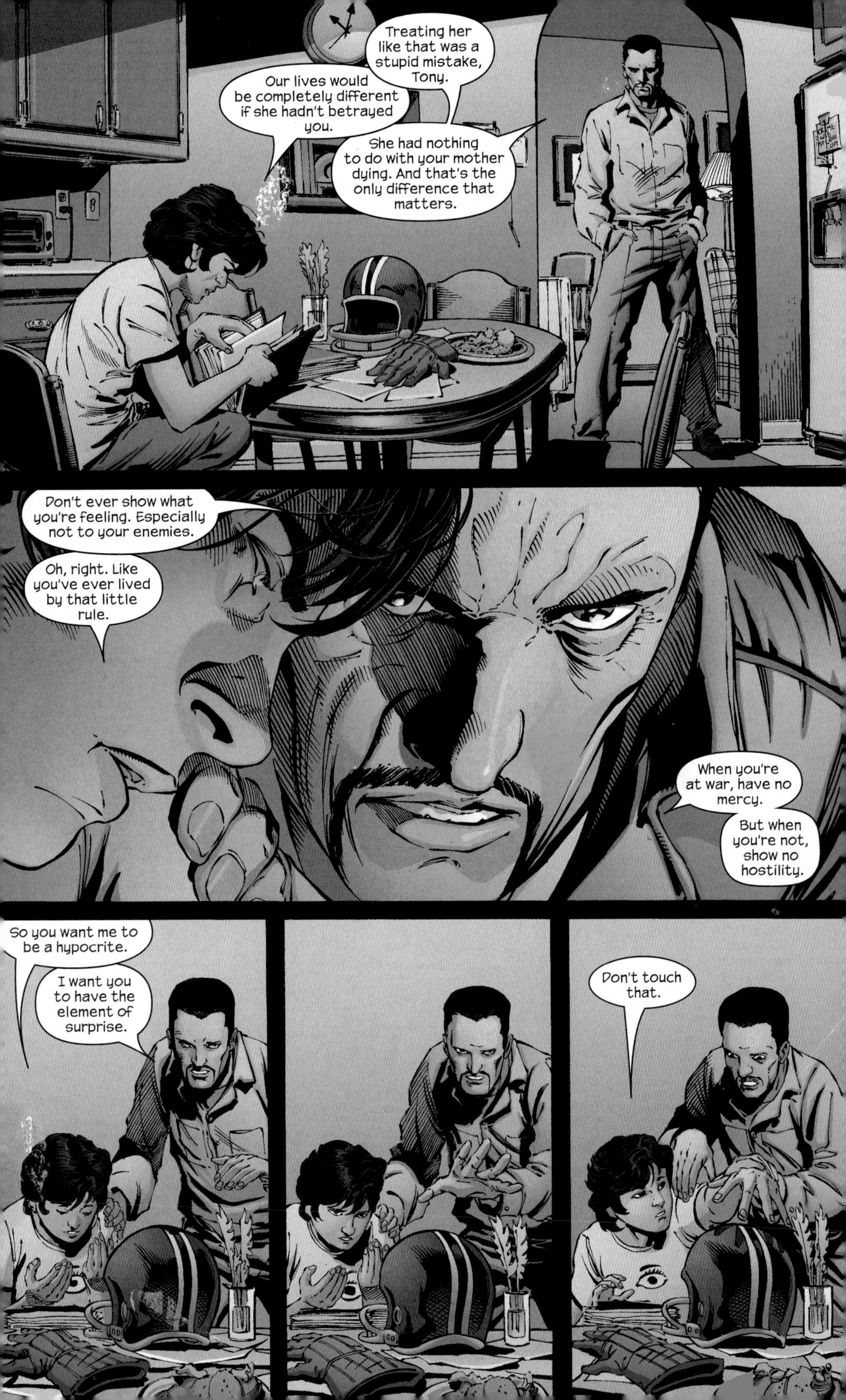
Our lives would be completely different if she hadn't betrayed you.
Treating her like that was a stupid mistake, Tony.
She had nothing to do with your mother dying. And that's the only difference that matters.
Don't ever show what you're feeling. Especially not to your enemies.
Oh, right. Like you've ever lived by that little rule.
When you're at war, have no mercy.
But when you're not, show no hostility.
So you want me to be a hypocrite.
I want you to have the element of surprise.
Don't touch that.

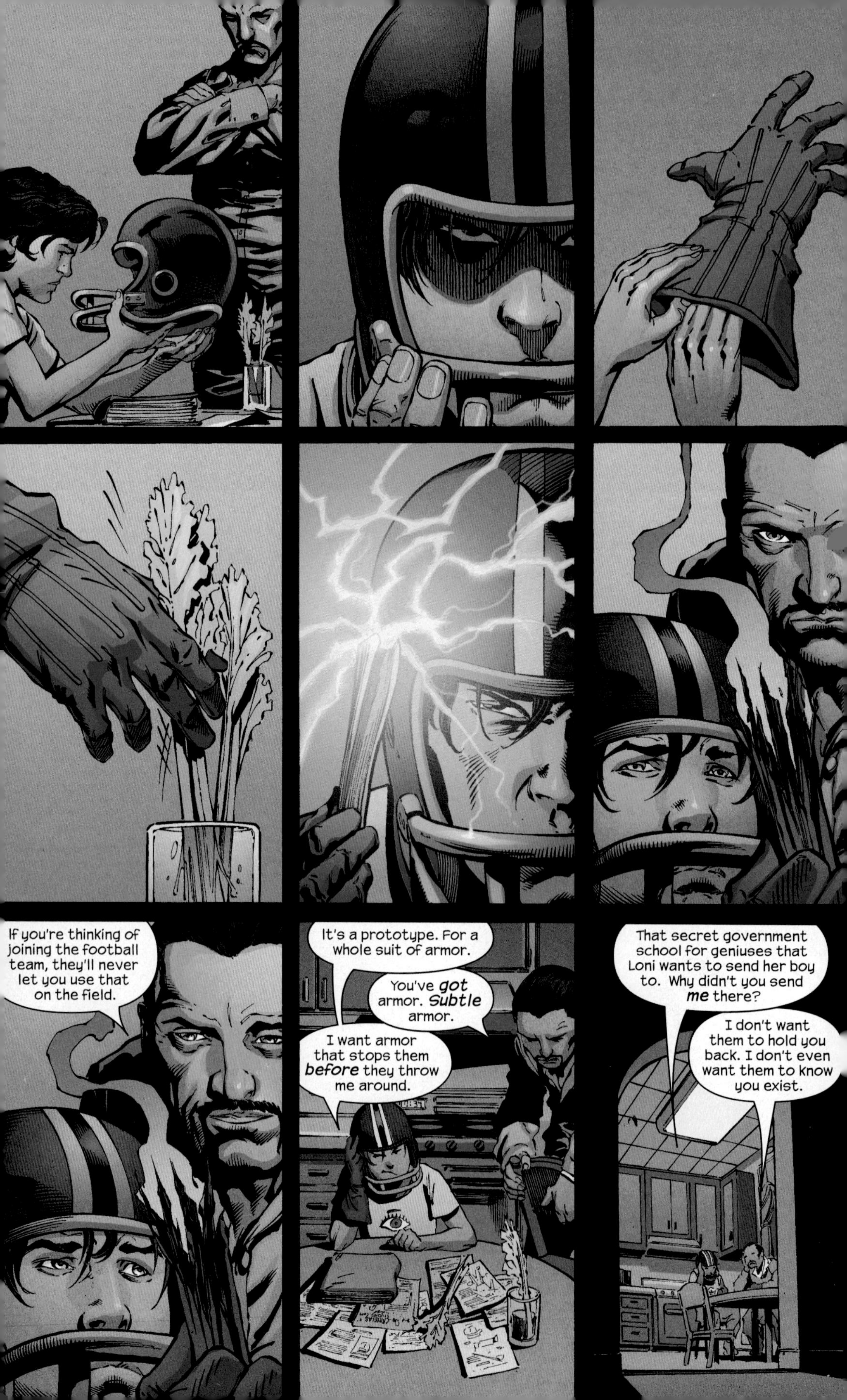

If you're thinking of joining the football team, they'll never let you use that on the field.
It's a prototype. For a whole suit of armor.
You've got armor. Subtle armor.
I want armor that stops them before they throw me around.
That secret government school for geniuses that Loni wants to send her boy to. Why didn't you send me there?
I don't want them to hold you back. I don't even want them to know you exist.

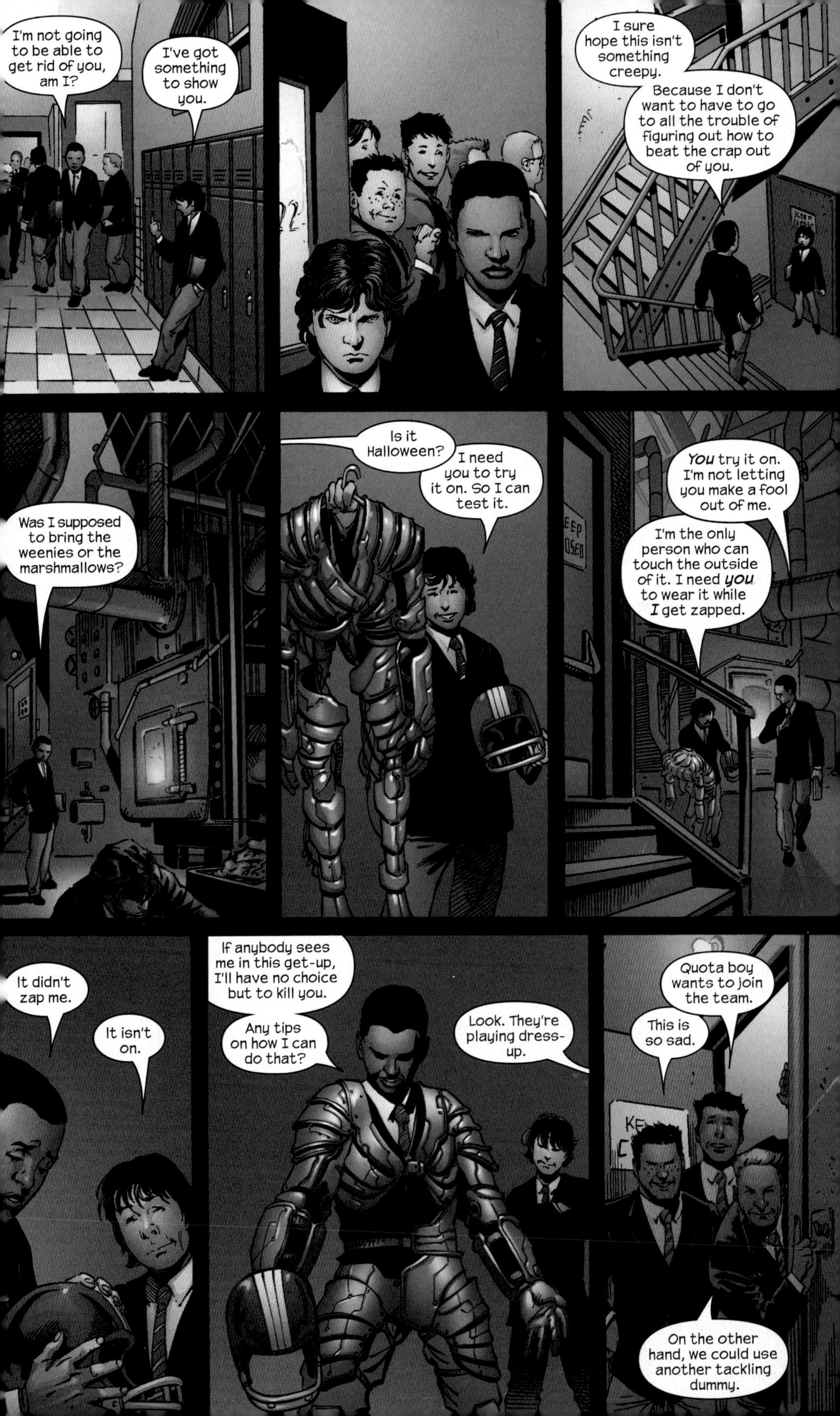
I'm not going to be able to get rid of you, am I?
I've got something to show you.
I sure hope this isn't something creepy.
Because I don't want to have to go to all the trouble of figuring out how to beat the crap out of you.
Was I supposed to bring the weenies or the marshmallows?
Is it Halloween?
I need you to try it on. So I can test it.
YOU try it on. I'm not letting you make a fool out of me.
I'm the only person who can touch the outside of it. I need *YOU* to wear it while *I* get zapped.
It didn't zap me.
It isn't on.
If anybody sees me in this get-up, I'll have no choice but to kill you.
Any tips on how I can do that?
Look. They're playing dress-up.
Quota boy wants to join the team.
This is so sad.
On the other hand, we could use another tackling dummy.

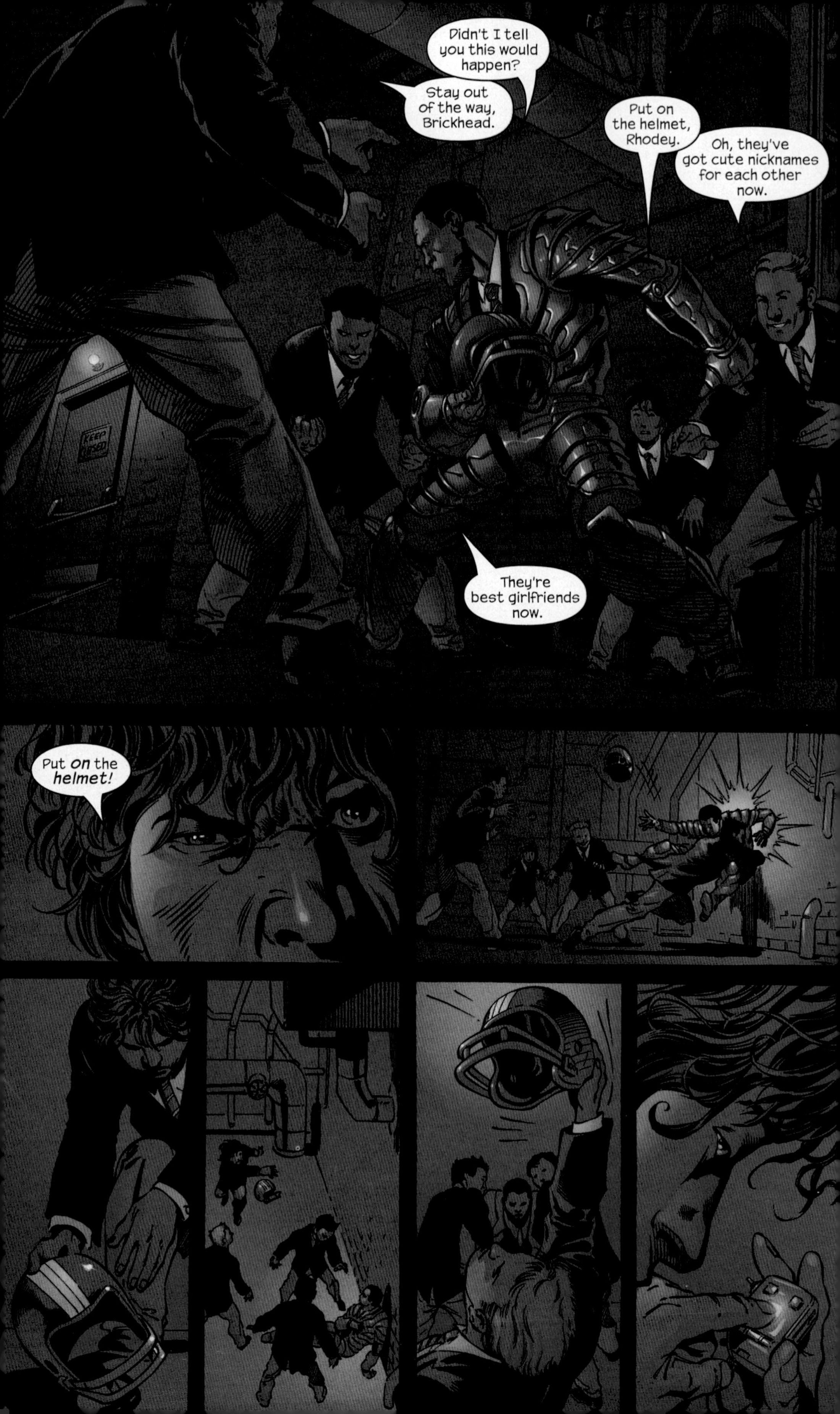
Didn't I tell you this would happen?
Stay out of the way, Brickhead.
Put on the helmet, Rhodey.
Oh, they've got cute nicknames for each other now.
They're best girlfriends now.
Put on the helmet!

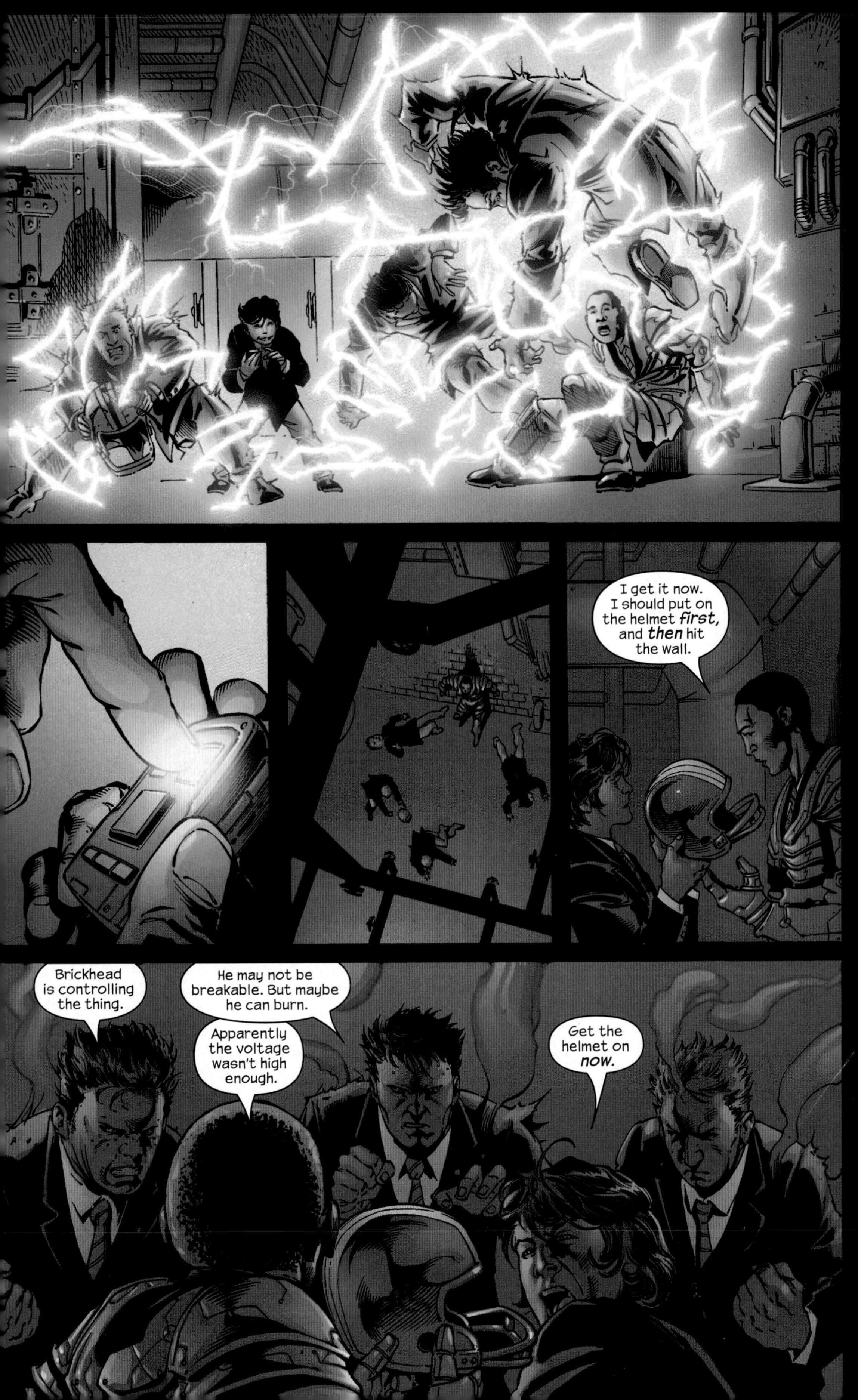
I get it now. I should put on the helmet *first,* and *then* hit the wall.
Brickhead is controlling the thing.
He may not be breakable. But maybe he can burn.
Apparently the voltage wasn't high enough.
Get the helmet on *now.*

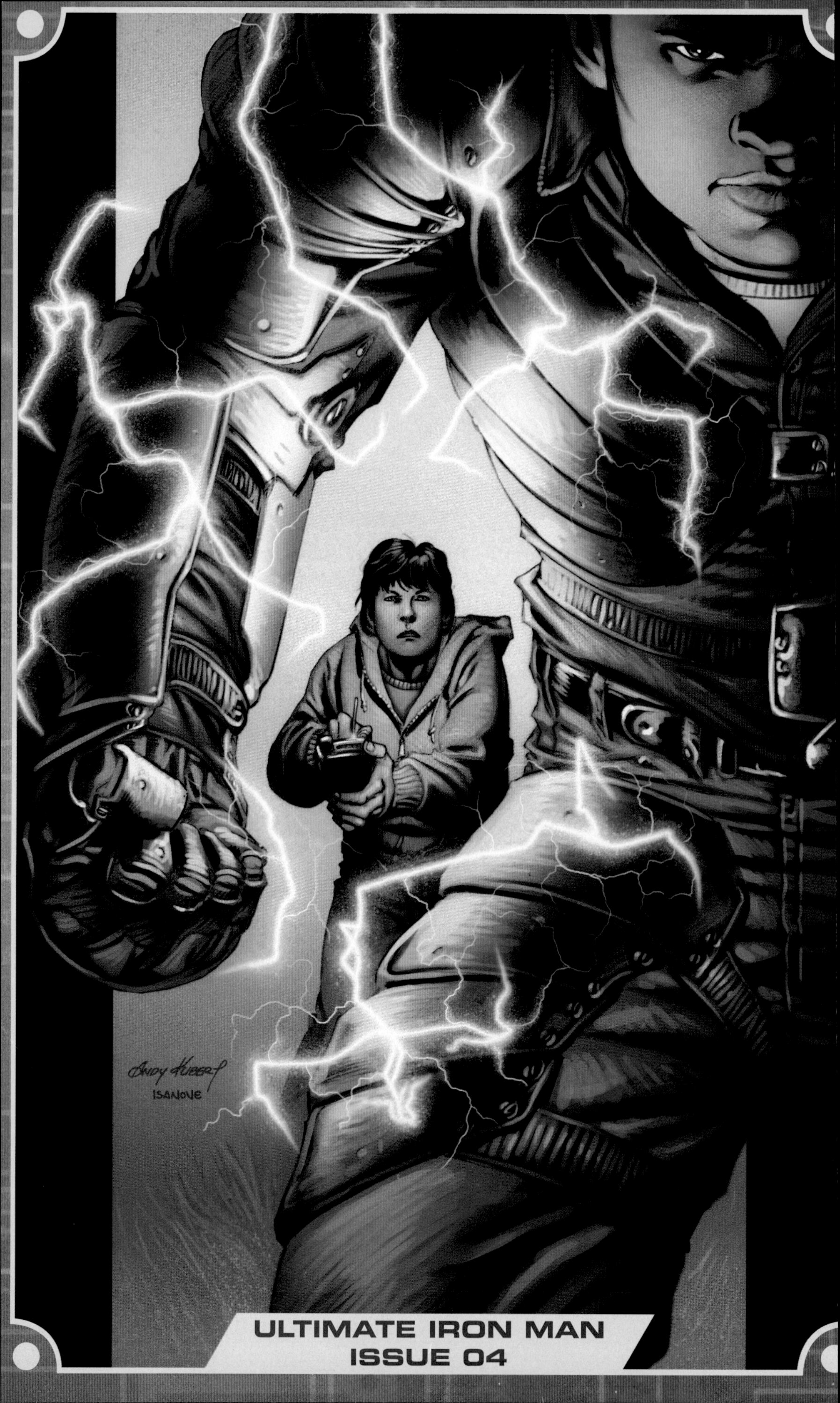
ANDY KUBERT
ISANOVE
ULTIMATE IRON MAN
ISSUE 04

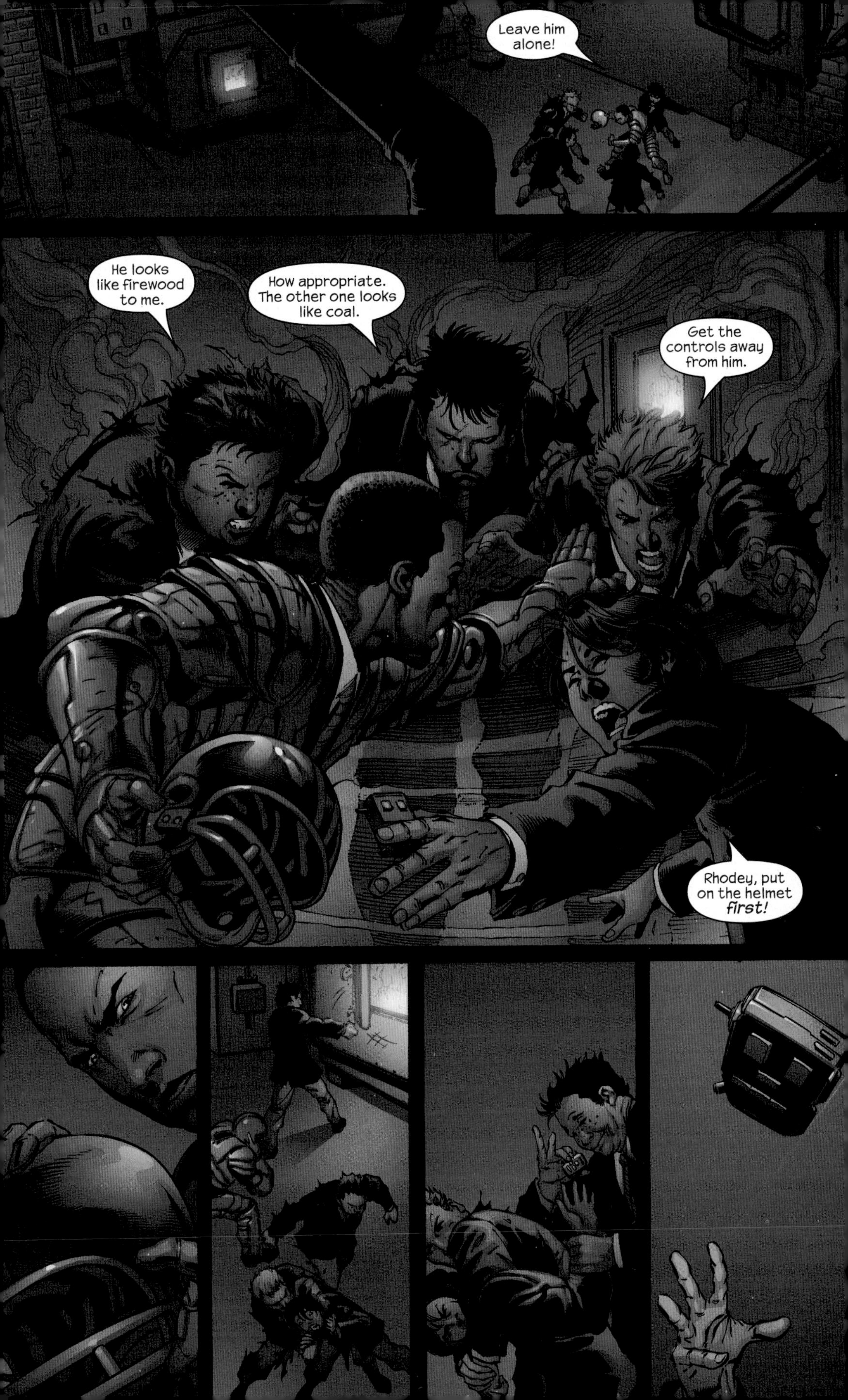
Leave him alone!
He looks like firewood to me.
How appropriate. The other one looks like coal.
Get the controls away from him.
Rhodey, put on the helmet *first!*

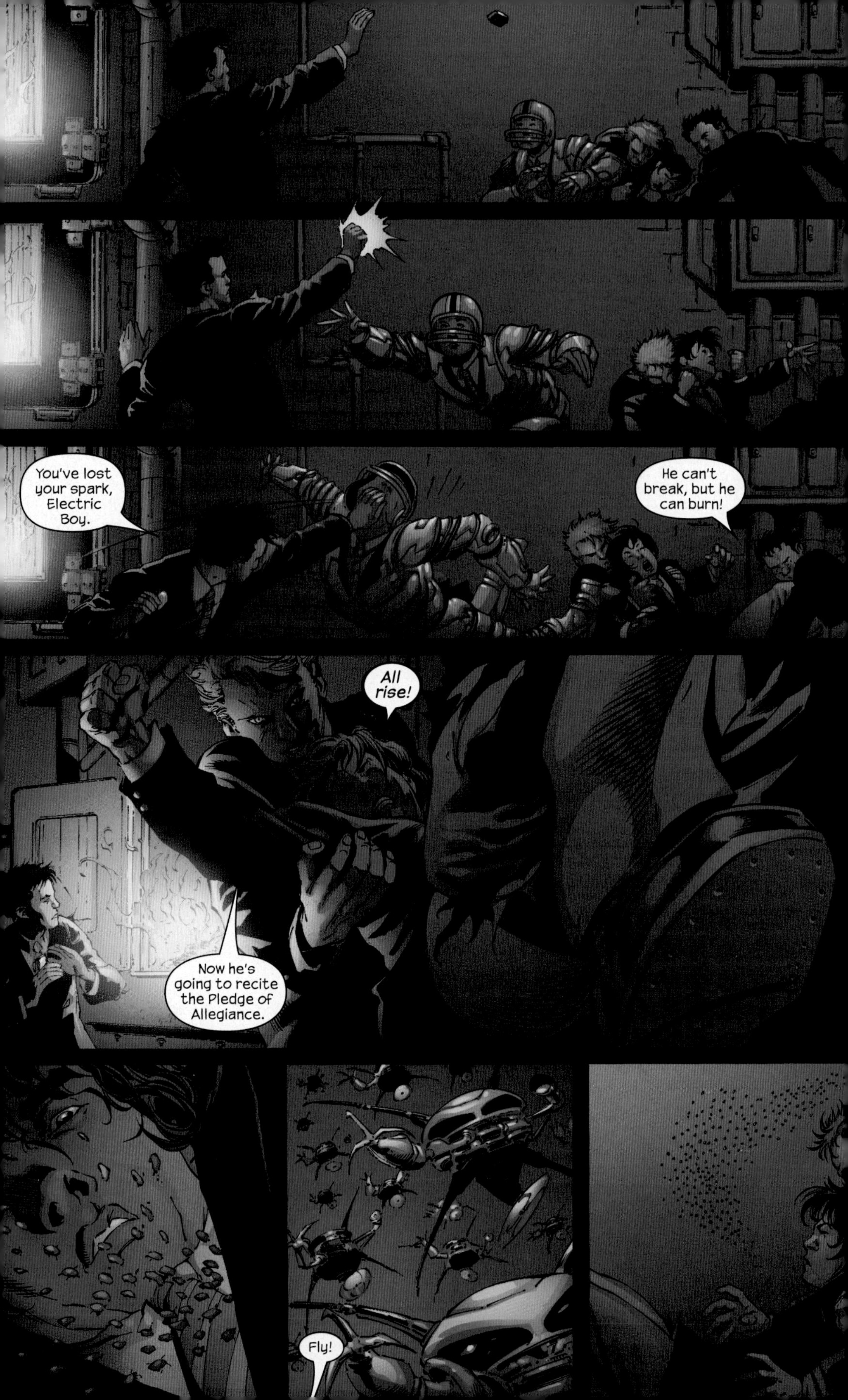
You've lost your spark, Electric Boy.
He can't break, but he can burn!
All rise!
Now he's going to recite the Pledge of Allegiance.
Fly!

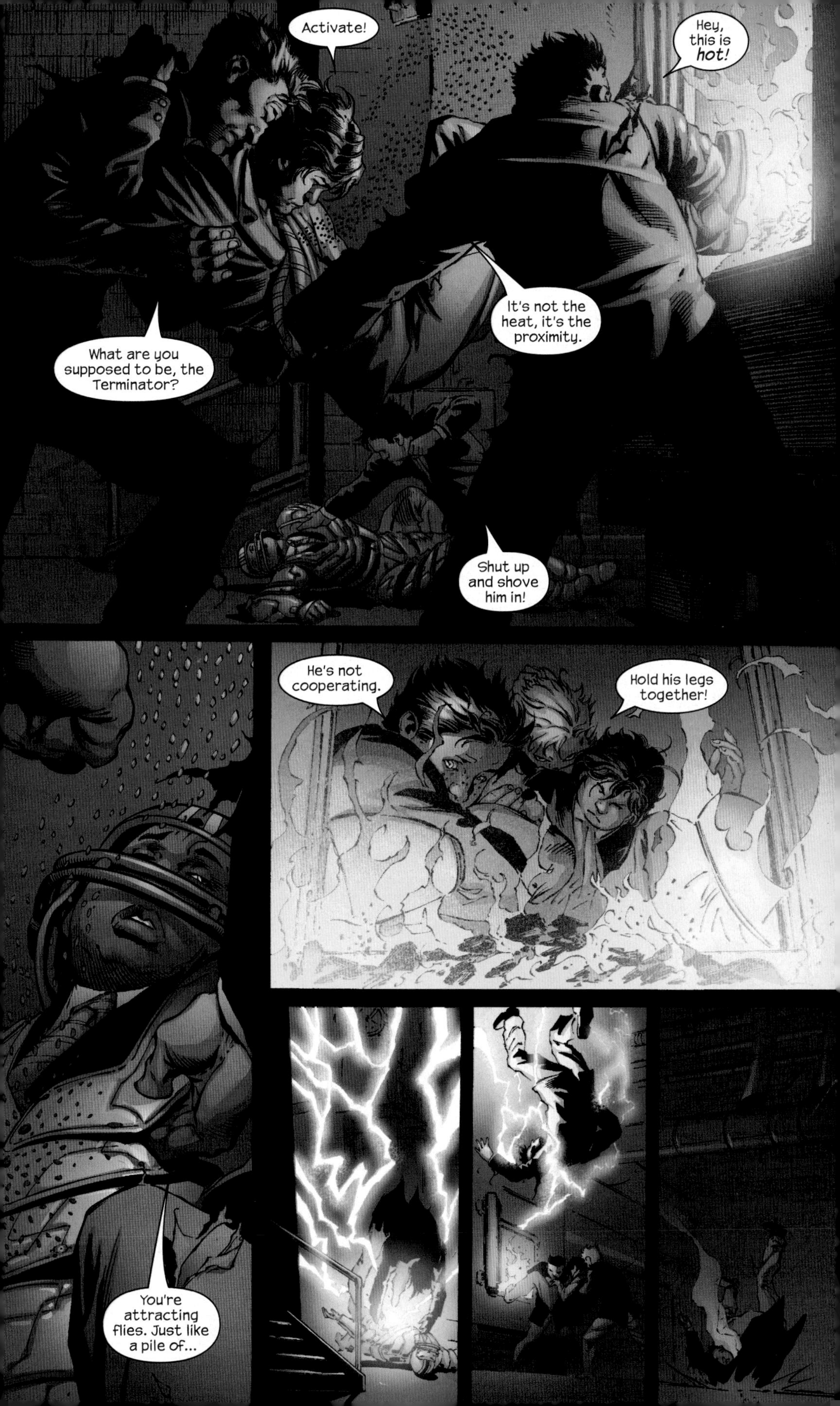
Activate!
Hey, this is *hot!*
What are you supposed to be, the Terminator?
It's not the heat, it's the proximity.
Shut up and shove him in!
He's not cooperating.
Hold his legs together!
You're attracting flies. Just like a pile of...

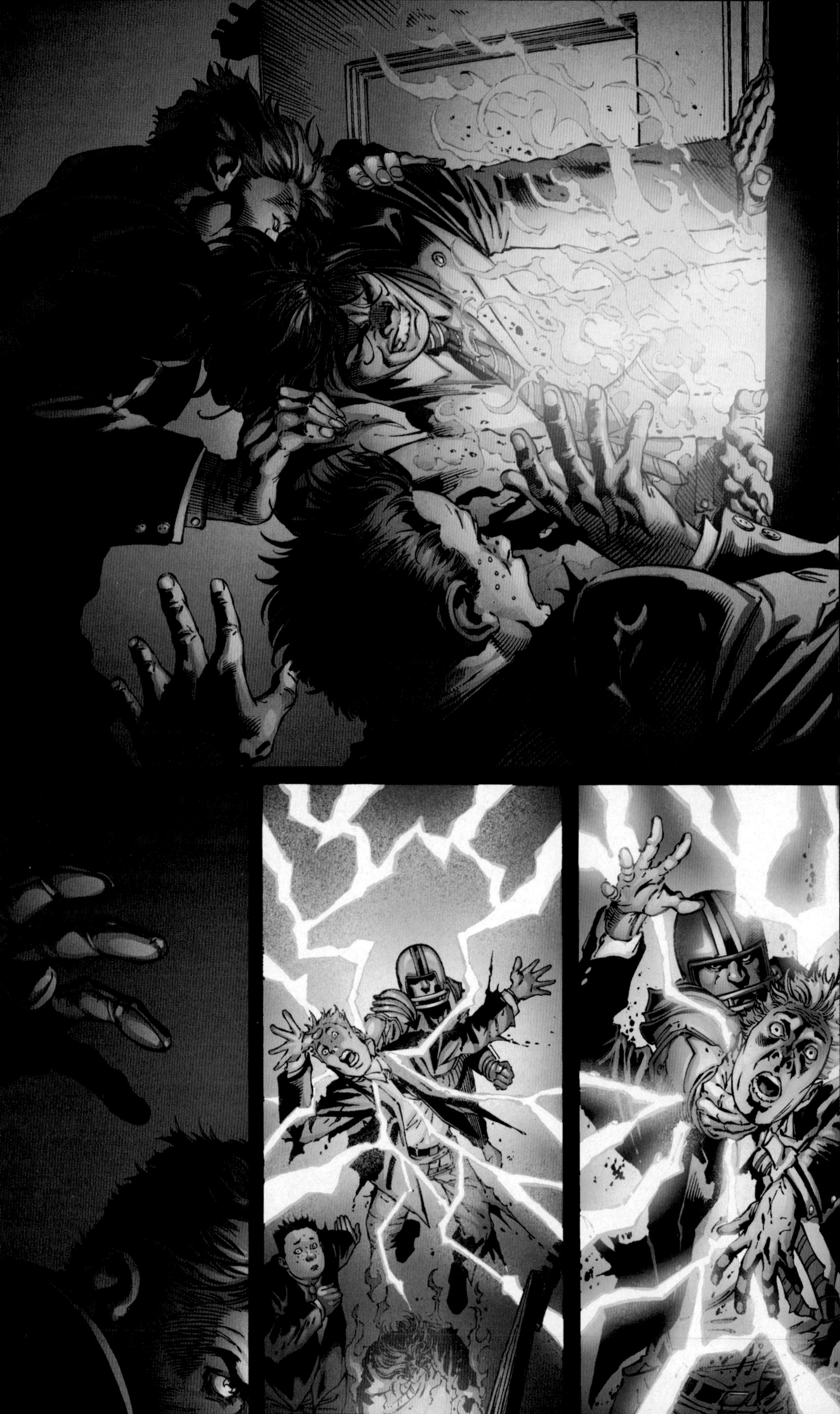

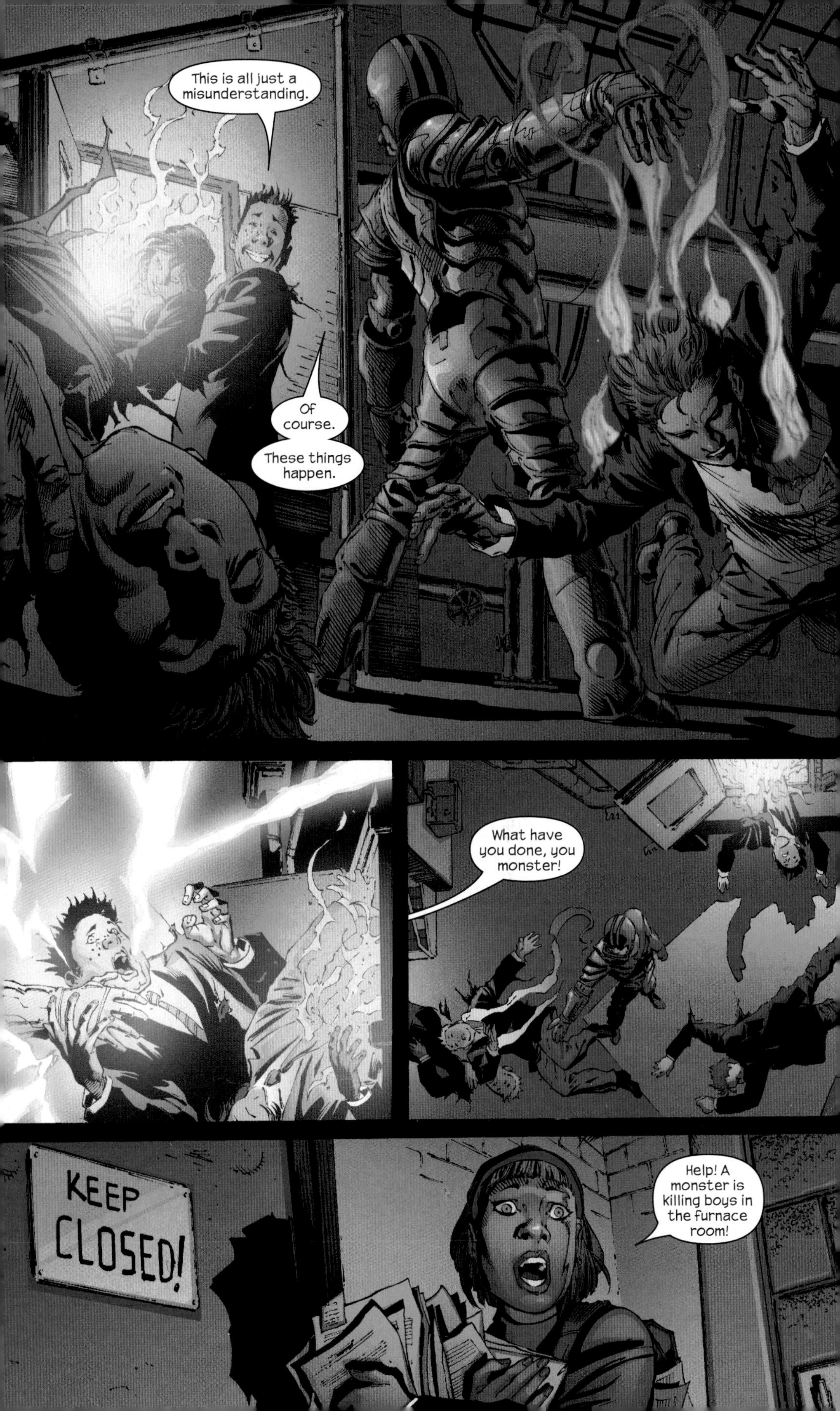
This is all just a misunderstanding.
Of course.
These things happen.
What have you done, you monster!
KEEP CLOSED!
Help! A monster is killing boys in the furnace room!

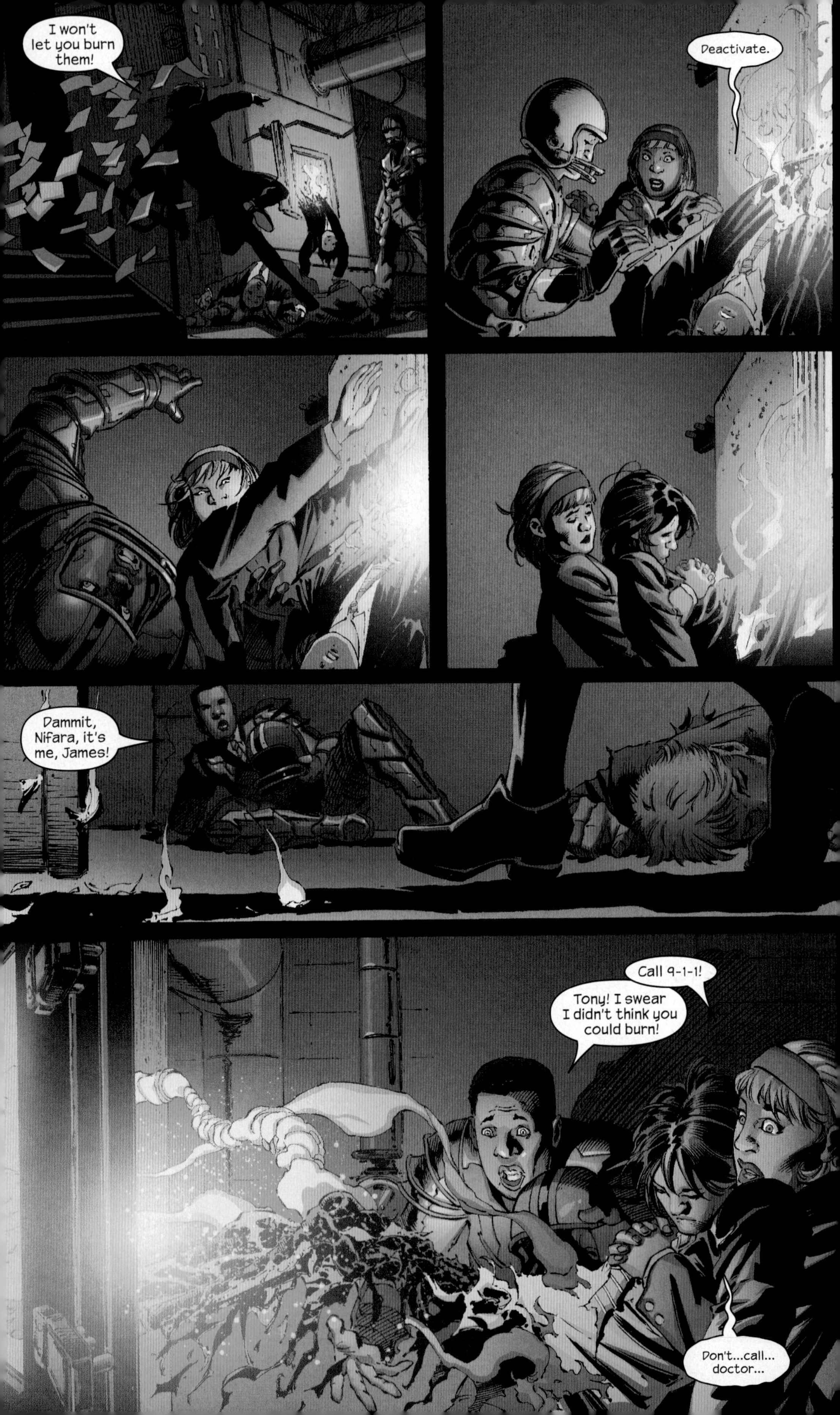
I won't let you burn them!
Deactivate.
Dammit, Nifara, it's me, James!
Call 9-1-1!
Tony! I swear I didn't think you could burn!
Don't...call... doctor...

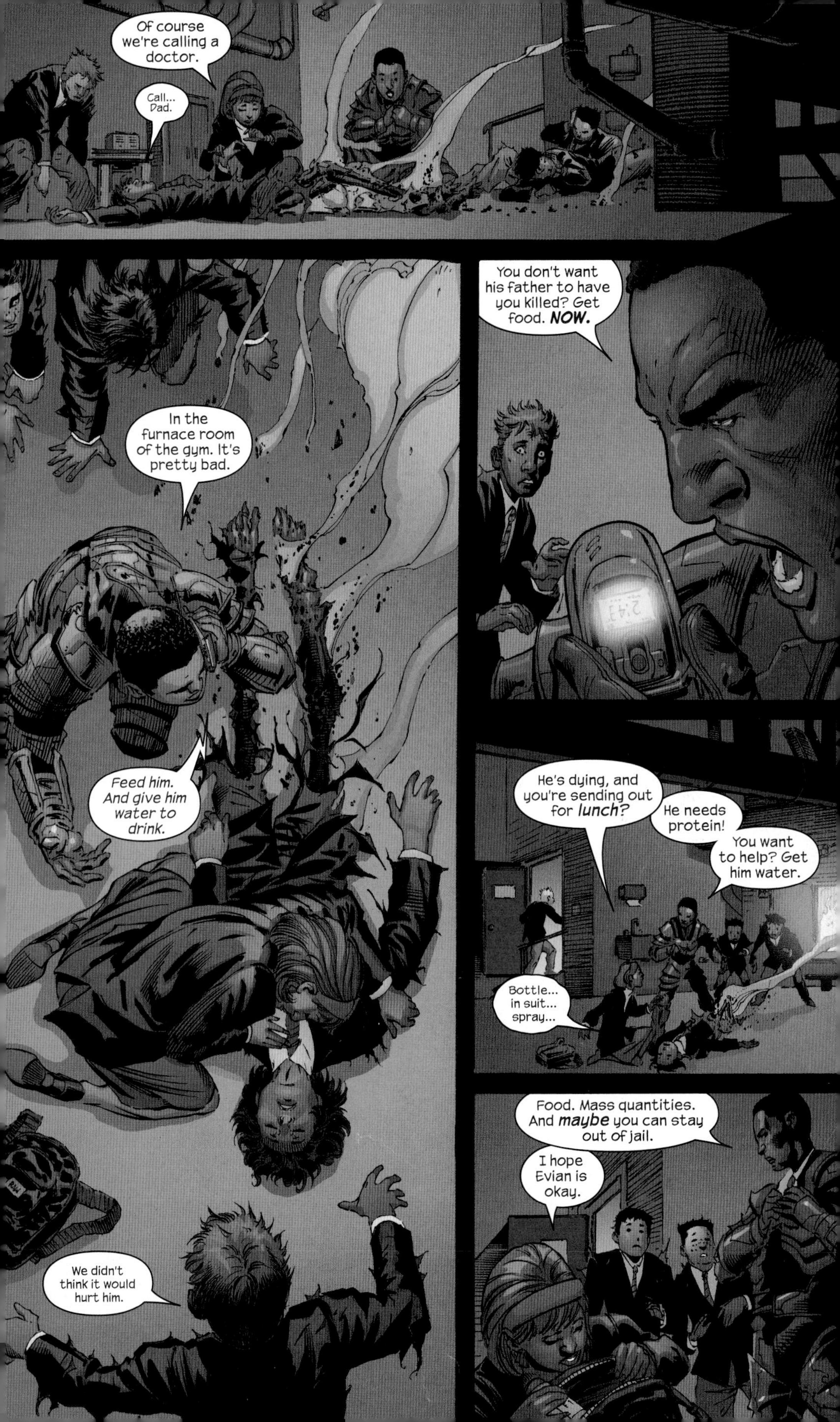
Of course we're calling a doctor.
Call... Dad.
In the furnace room of the gym. It's pretty bad.
Feed him. And give him water to drink.
We didn't think it would hurt him.
You don't want his father to have you killed? Get food. *NOW.*
He's dying, and you're sending out for *lunch?*
He needs protein!
You want to help? Get him water.
Bottle... in suit... spray...
Food. Mass quantities. And *maybe* you can stay out of jail.
I hope Evian is okay.

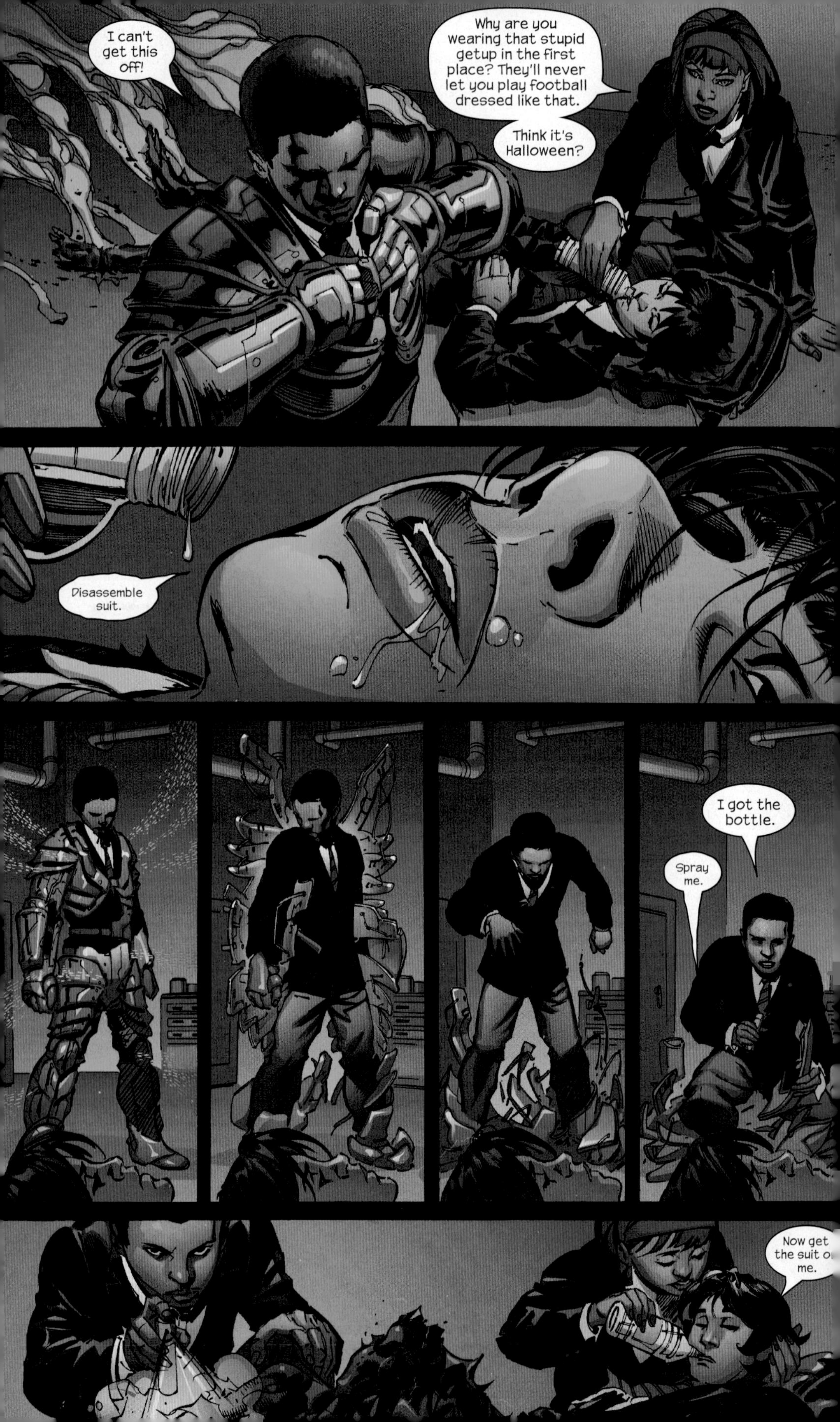
I can't get this off!
Why are you wearing that stupid getup in the first place? They'll never let you play football dressed like that.
Think it's Halloween?
Disassemble suit.
Spray me.
I got the bottle.
Now get the suit o
me.

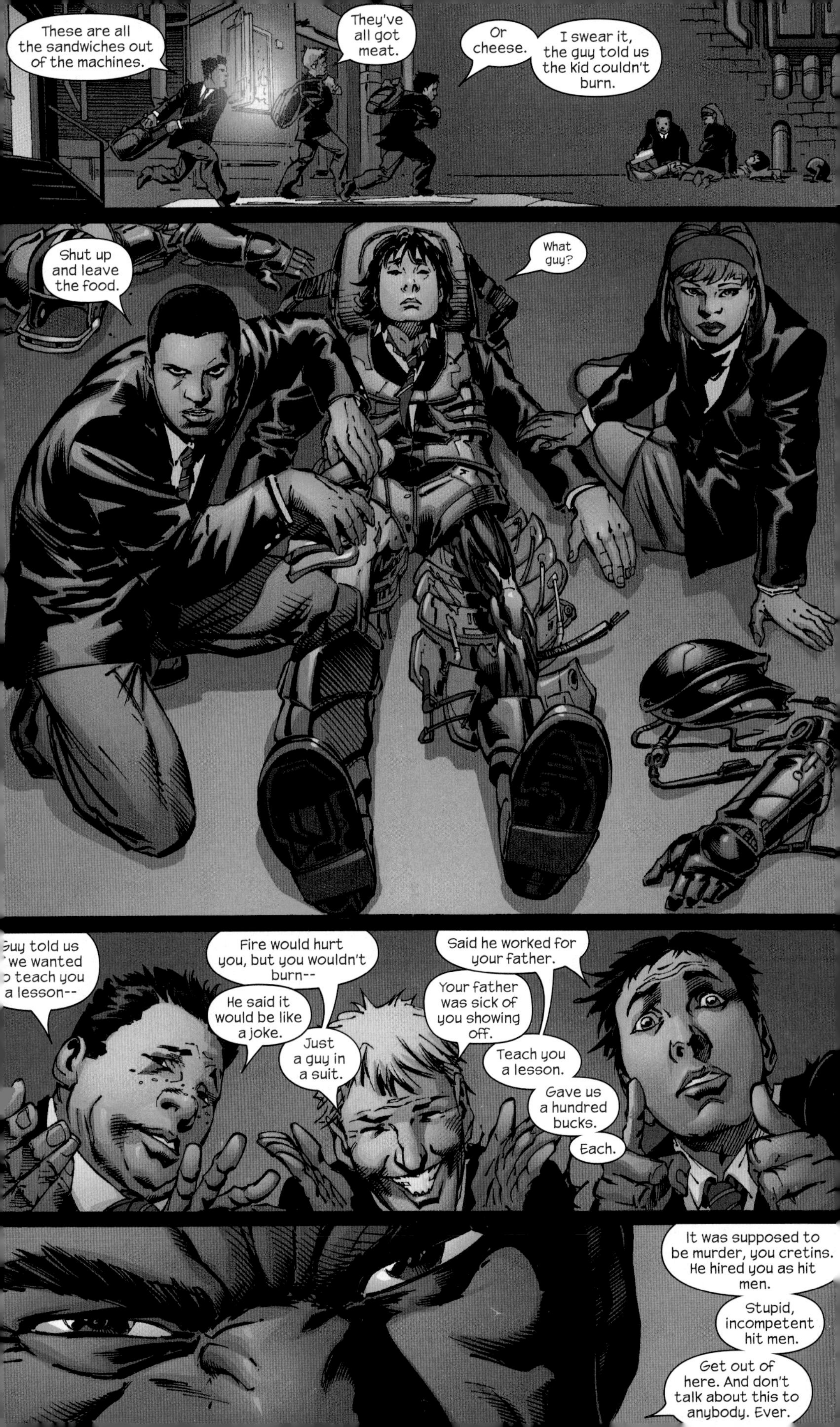

These are all the sandwiches out of the machines.
They've all got meat.
Or cheese.
I swear it, the guy told us the kid couldn't burn.
Shut up and leave the food.
What guy?
Guy told us we wanted to teach you a lesson--
Fire would hurt you, but you wouldn't burn--
He said it would be like a joke.
Just a guy in a suit.
Said he worked for your father.
Your father was sick of you showing off.
Teach you a lesson.
Gave us a hundred bucks.
Each.
It was supposed to be murder, you cretins. He hired you as hit men.
Stupid, incompetent hit men.
Get out of here. And don't talk about this to anybody. Ever.

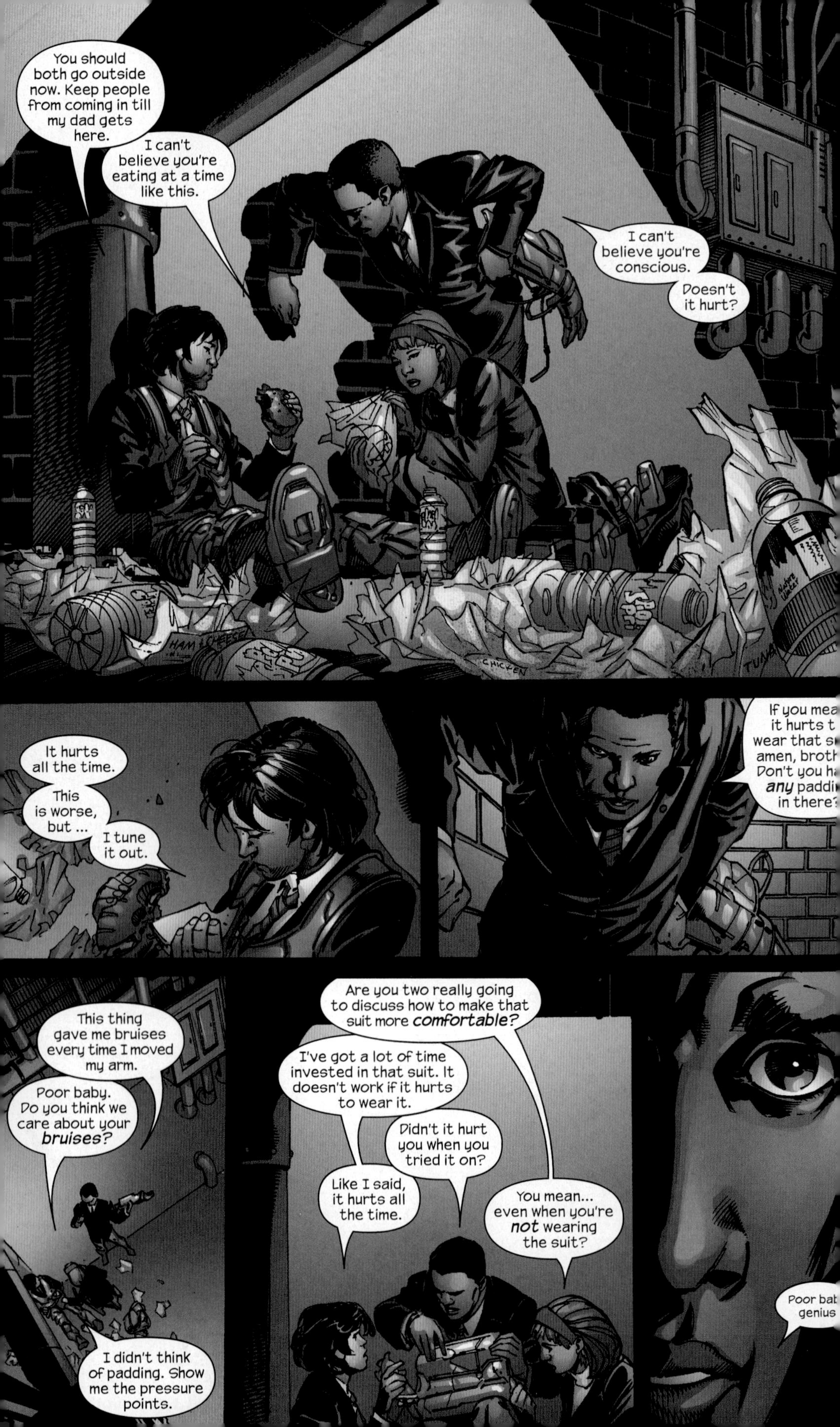
You should both go outside now. Keep people from coming in till my dad gets here.
I can't believe you're eating at a time like this.
I can't believe you're conscious.
Doesn't it hurt?
HAM & CHEESE
CHICKEN
TUNA
It hurts all the time.
This is worse, but ...
I tune it out.
If you mea
it hurts t
wear that s
amen, broth
Don't you h
any paddi
in there
This thing gave me bruises every time I moved my arm.
Poor baby. Do you think we care about your *bruises?*
I didn't think of padding. Show me the pressure points.
Are you two really going to discuss how to make that suit more *comfortable?*
I've got a lot of time invested in that suit. It doesn't work if it hurts to wear it.
Didn't it hurt you when you tried it on?
Like I said, it hurts all the time.
You mean... even when you're *not* wearing the suit?
Poor bab
genius

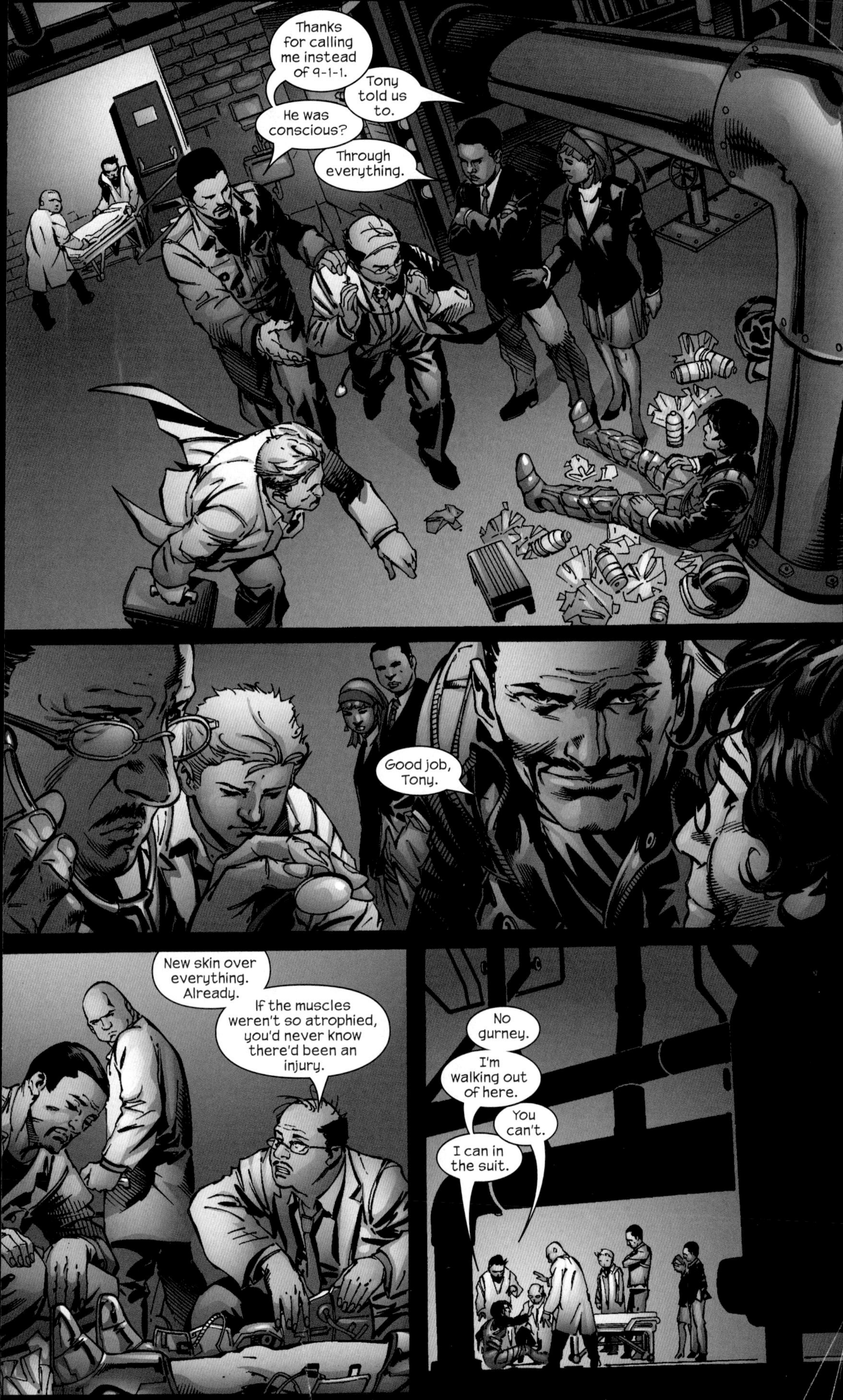
Thanks for calling me instead of 9-1-1.
Tony told us to.
He was conscious?
Through everything.
Good job, Tony.
New skin over everything. Already.
If the muscles weren't so atrophied, you'd never know there'd been an injury.
No gurney.
I'm walking out of here.
You can't.
I can in the suit.

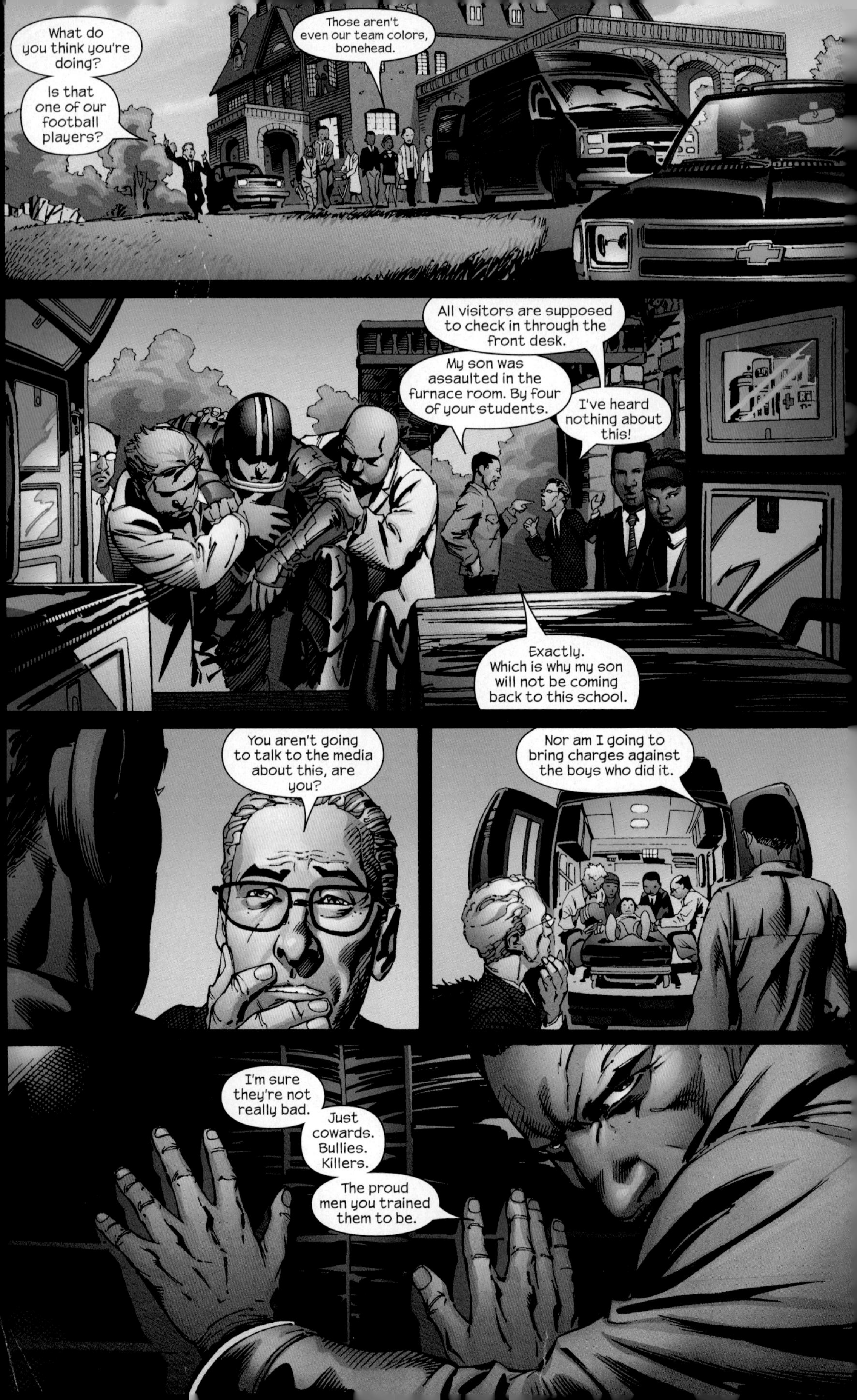
What do you think you're doing?
Is that one of our football players?
Those aren't even our team colors, bonehead.
All visitors are supposed to check in through the front desk.
My son was assaulted in the furnace room. By four of your students.
I've heard nothing about this!
Exactly. Which is why my son will not be coming back to this school.
You aren't going to talk to the media about this, are you?
Nor am I going to bring charges against the boys who did it.
I'm sure they're not really bad.
Just cowards. Bullies. Killers.
The proud men you trained them to be.

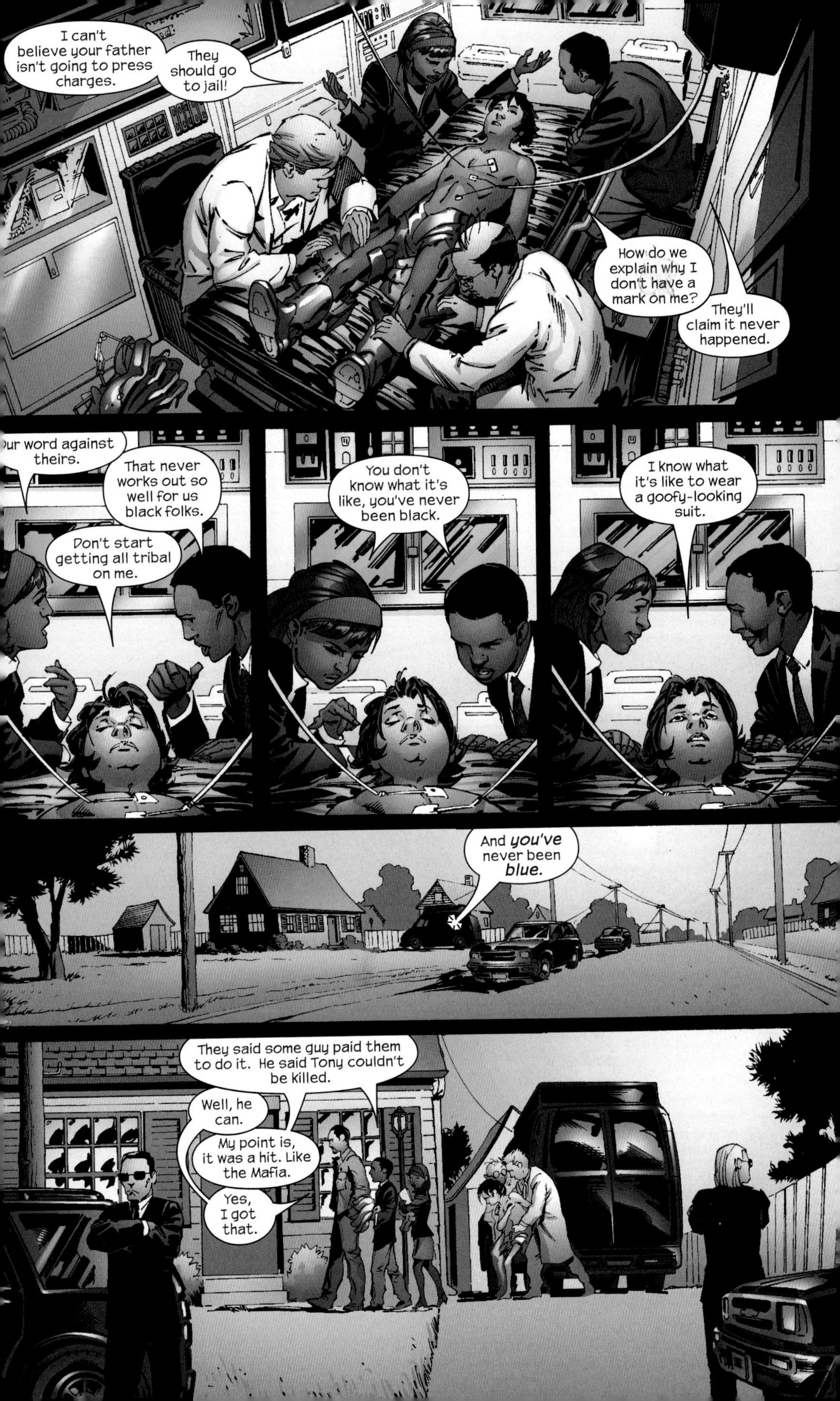

I can't believe your father isn't going to press charges.
They should go to jail!
How do we explain why I don't have a mark on me?
They'll claim it never happened.
ur word against theirs.
That never works out so well for us black folks.
Don't start getting all tribal on me.
You don't know what it's like, you've never been black.
I know what it's like to wear a goofy-looking suit.
And *you've* never been *blue.*
They said some guy paid them to do it. He said Tony couldn't be killed.
Well, he can.
My point is, it was a hit. Like the Mafia.
Yes, I got that.

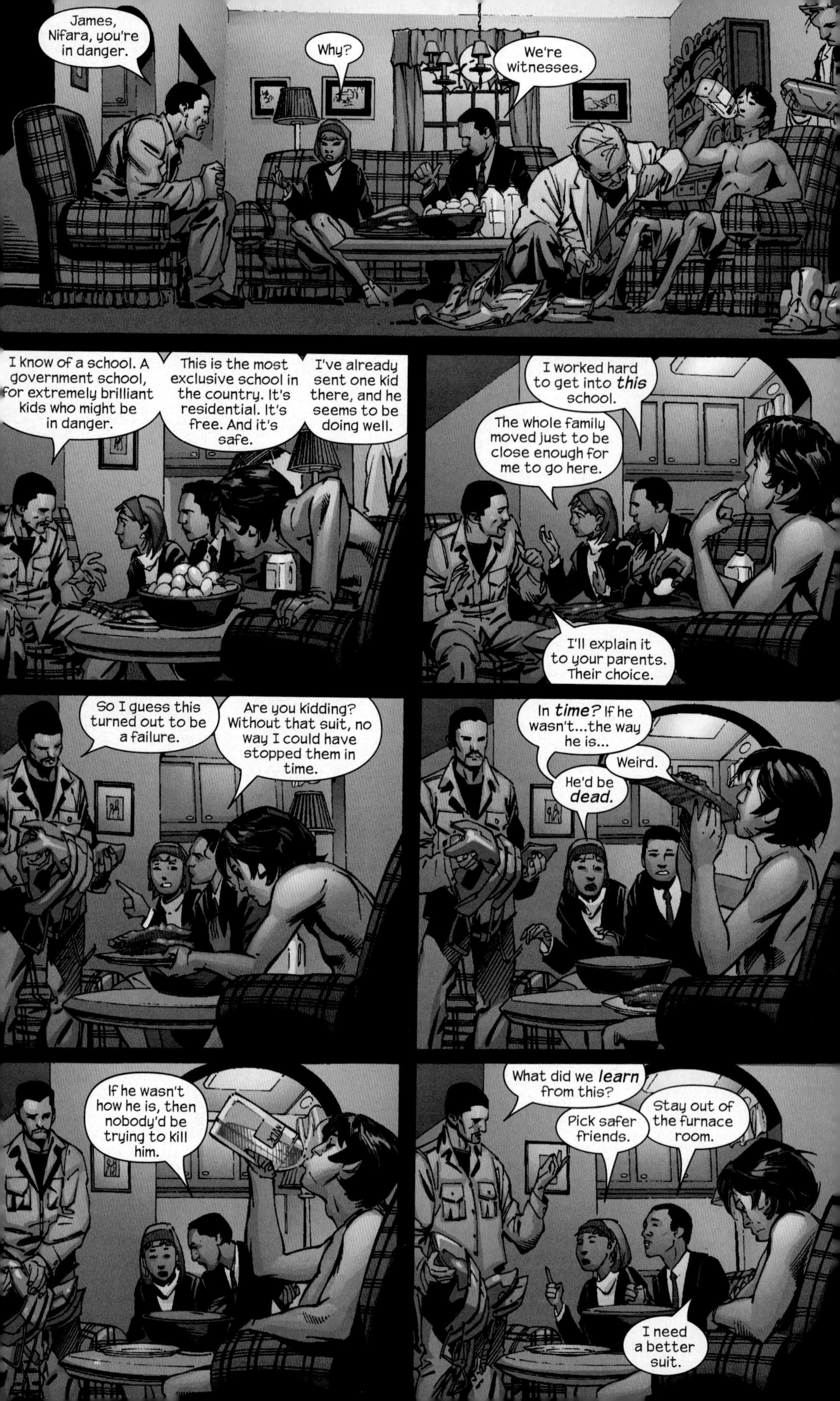
James, Nifara, you're in danger.
Why?
We're witnesses.
I know of a school. A government school, for extremely brilliant kids who might be in danger.
This is the most exclusive school in the country. It's residential. It's free. And it's safe.
I've already sent one kid there, and he seems to be doing well.
I worked hard to get into *this* school.
The whole family moved just to be close enough for me to go here.
I'll explain it to your parents. Their choice.
So I guess this turned out to be a failure.
Are you kidding? Without that suit, no way I could have stopped them in time.
In *time?* If he wasn't...the way he is...
Weird.
He'd be *dead.*
If he wasn't how he is, then nobody'd be trying to kill him.
What did we *learn* from this?
Pick safer friends.
Stay out of the furnace room.
I need a better suit.

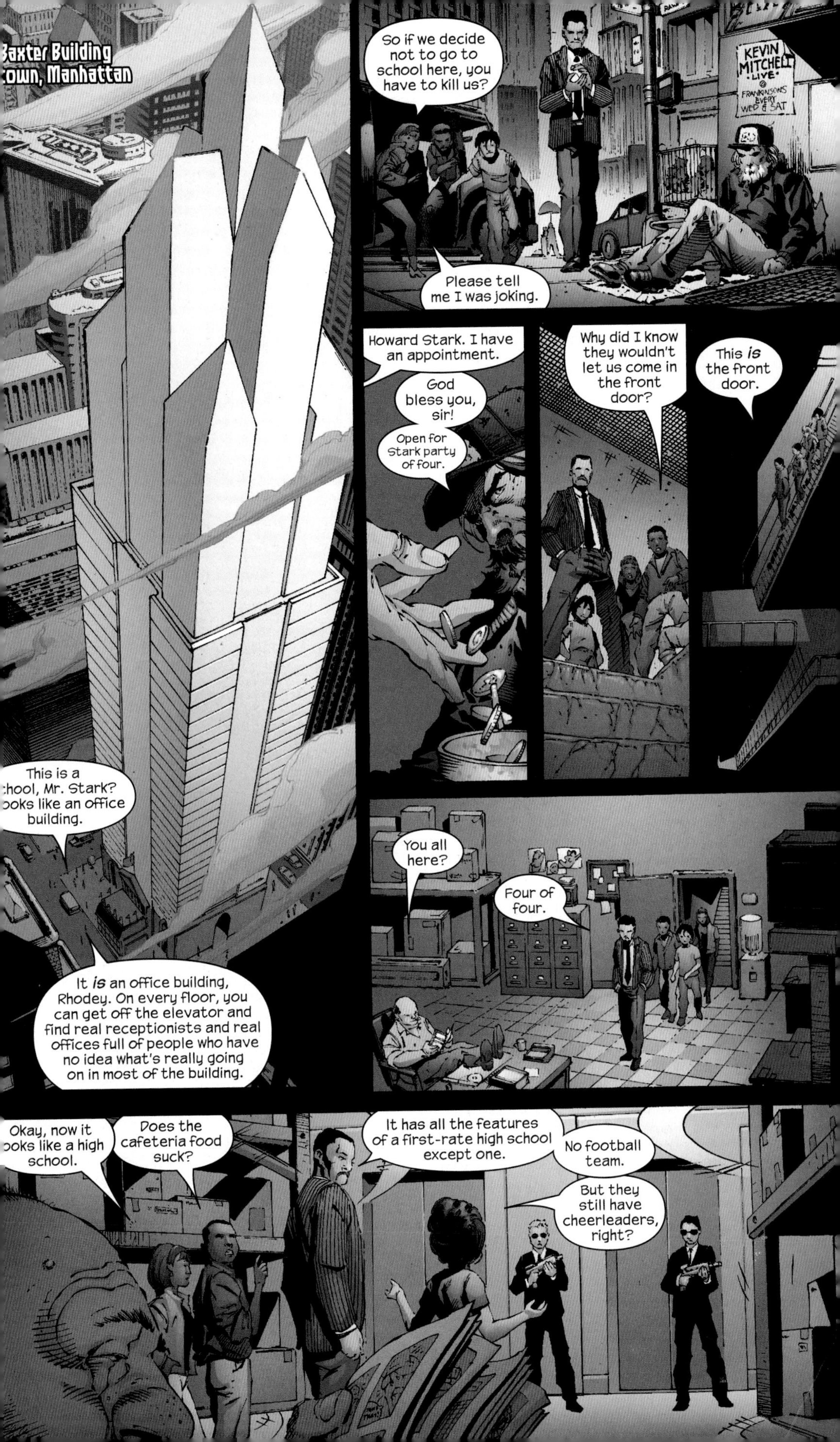
Baxter Building
town, Manhattan
So if we decide not to go to school here, you have to kill us?
Please tell me I was joking.
Howard Stark. I have an appointment.
God bless you, sir!
Open for Stark party of four.
Why did I know they wouldn't let us come in the front door?
This *is* the front door.
KEVIN MITCHELL LIVE @ FRANKINSONS EVERY WED & SAT
This is a chool, Mr. Stark? ooks like an office building.
It *is* an office building, Rhodey. On every floor, you can get off the elevator and find real receptionists and real offices full of people who have no idea what's really going on in most of the building.
You all here?
Four of four.
Okay, now it ooks like a high school.
Does the cafeteria food suck?
It has all the features of a first-rate high school except one.
No football team.
But they still have cheerleaders, right?

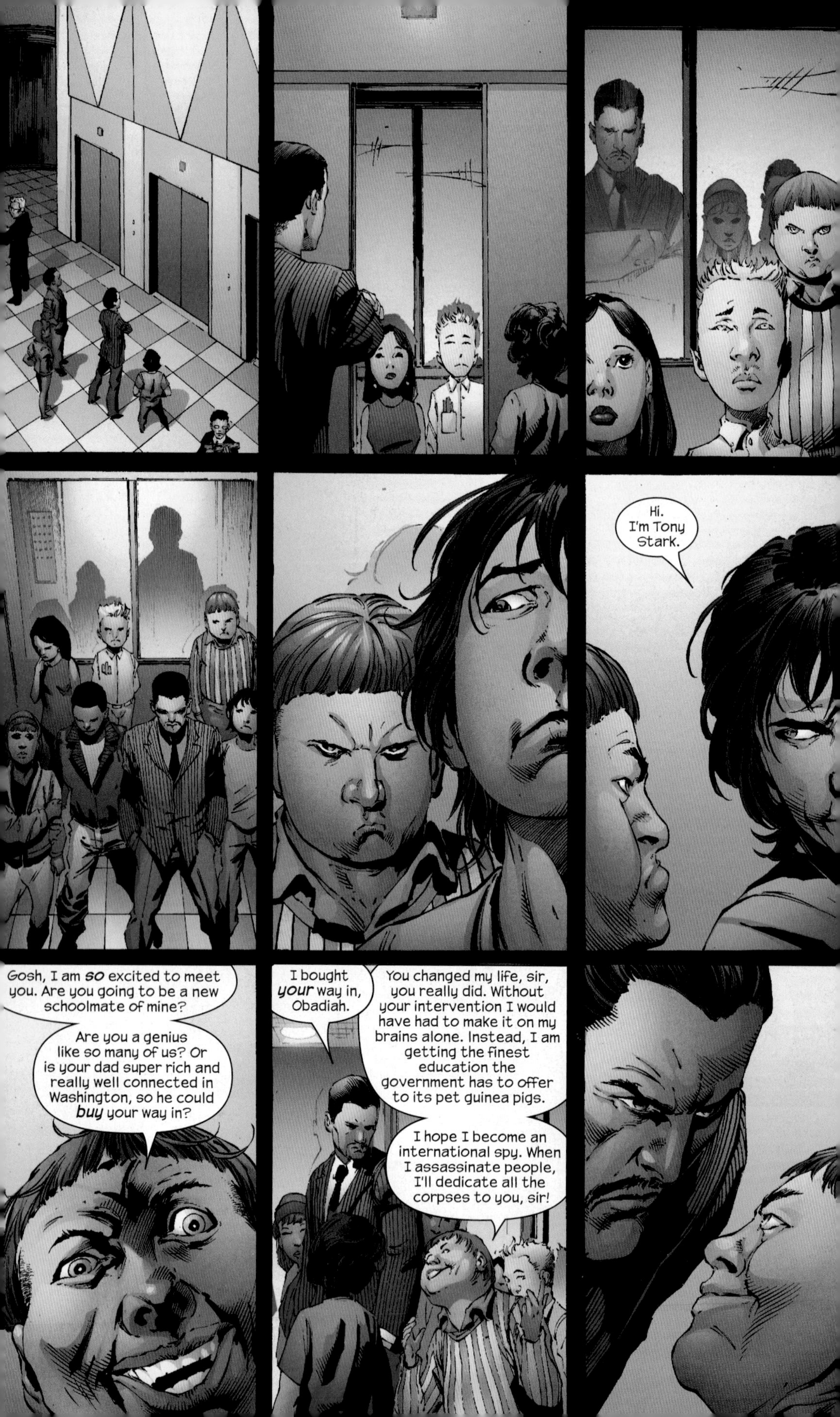
Hi. I'm Tony Stark.
Gosh, I am SO excited to meet you. Are you going to be a new schoolmate of mine?
Are you a genius like so many of us? Or is your dad super rich and really well connected in Washington, so he could buy your way in?
I bought your way in, Obadiah.
You changed my life, sir, you really did. Without your intervention I would have had to make it on my brains alone. Instead, I am getting the finest education the government has to offer to its pet guinea pigs.
I hope I become an international spy. When I assassinate people, I'll dedicate all the corpses to you, sir!

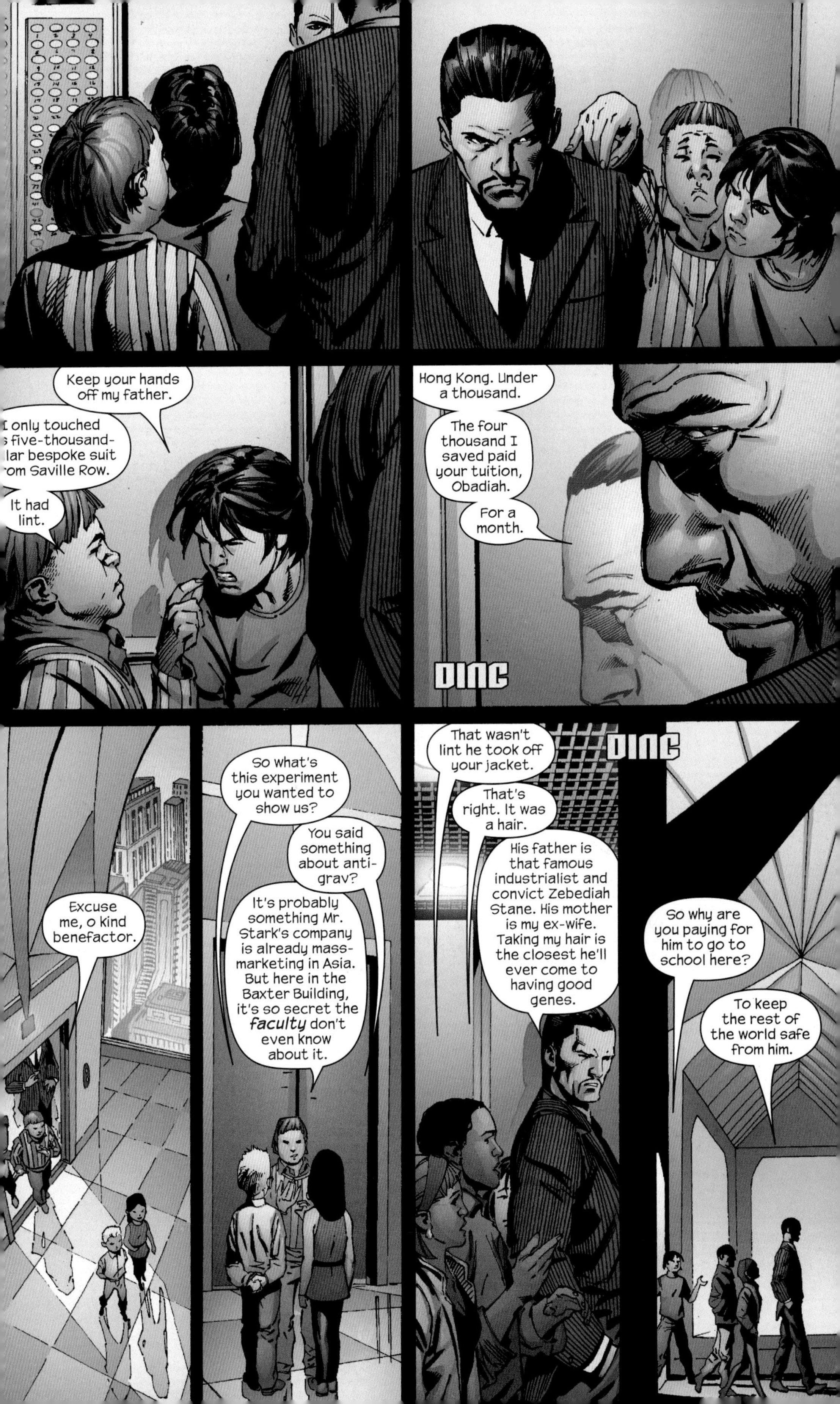

Keep your hands off my father.
I only touched his five-thousand-dollar bespoke suit from Saville Row.
It had lint.
Hong Kong. Under a thousand.
The four thousand I saved paid your tuition, Obadiah.
For a month.
DING
Excuse me, o kind benefactor.
So what's this experiment you wanted to show us?
You said something about anti-grav?
It's probably something Mr. Stark's company is already mass-marketing in Asia. But here in the Baxter Building, it's so secret the *faculty* don't even know about it.
That wasn't lint he took off your jacket.
DING
That's right. It was a hair.
His father is that famous industrialist and convict Zebediah Stane. His mother is my ex-wife. Taking my hair is the closest he'll ever come to having good genes.
So why are you paying for him to go to school here?
To keep the rest of the world safe from him.

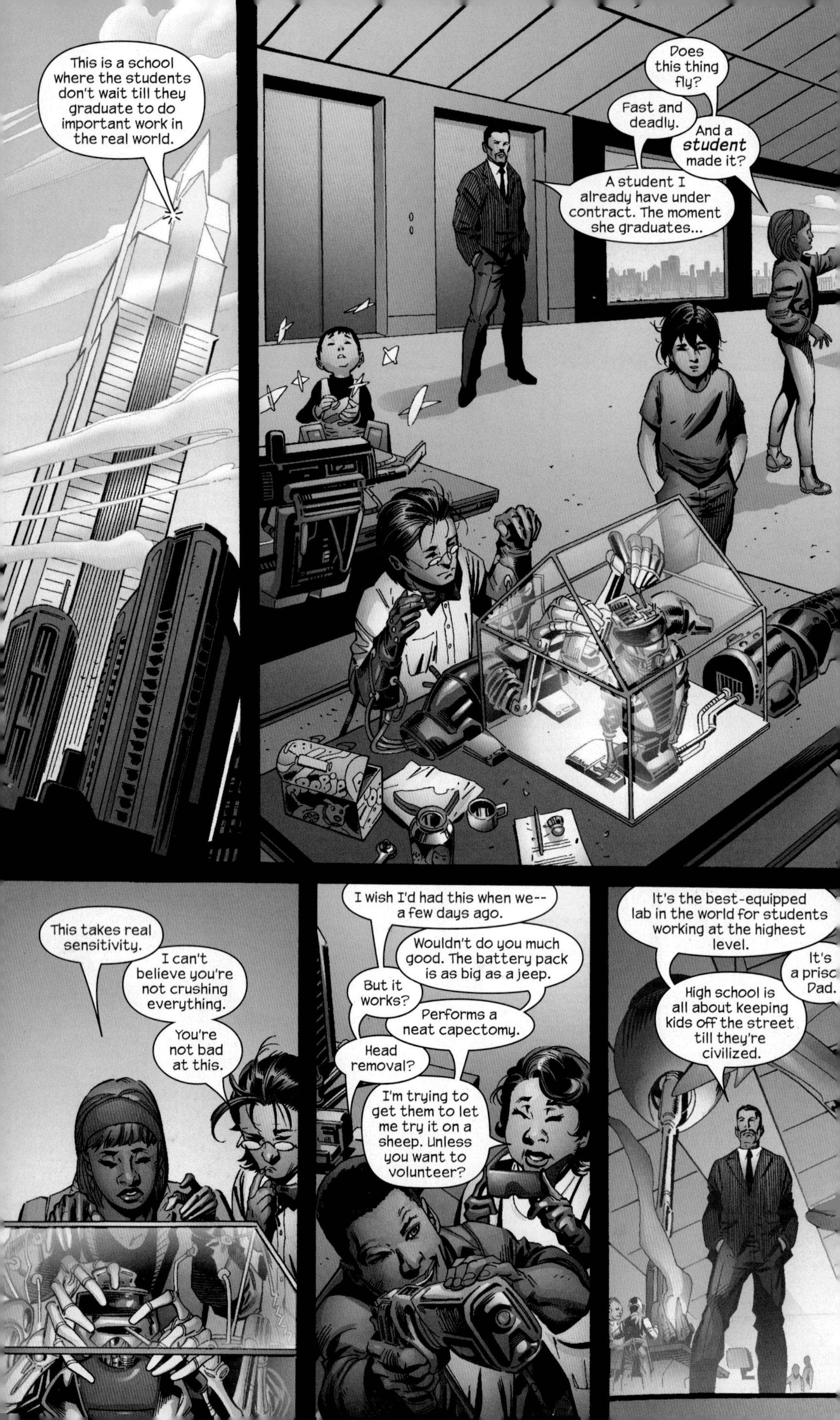
This is a school where the students don't wait till they graduate to do important work in the real world.
Does this thing fly?
Fast and deadly.
And a *student* made it?
A student I already have under contract. The moment she graduates...
This takes real sensitivity.
I can't believe you're not crushing everything.
You're not bad at this.
I wish I'd had this when we-- a few days ago.
Wouldn't do you much good. The battery pack is as big as a jeep.
But it works?
Performs a neat capectomy.
Head removal?
I'm trying to get them to let me try it on a sheep. Unless you want to volunteer?
It's the best-equipped lab in the world for students working at the highest level.
High school is all about keeping kids off the street till they're civilized.

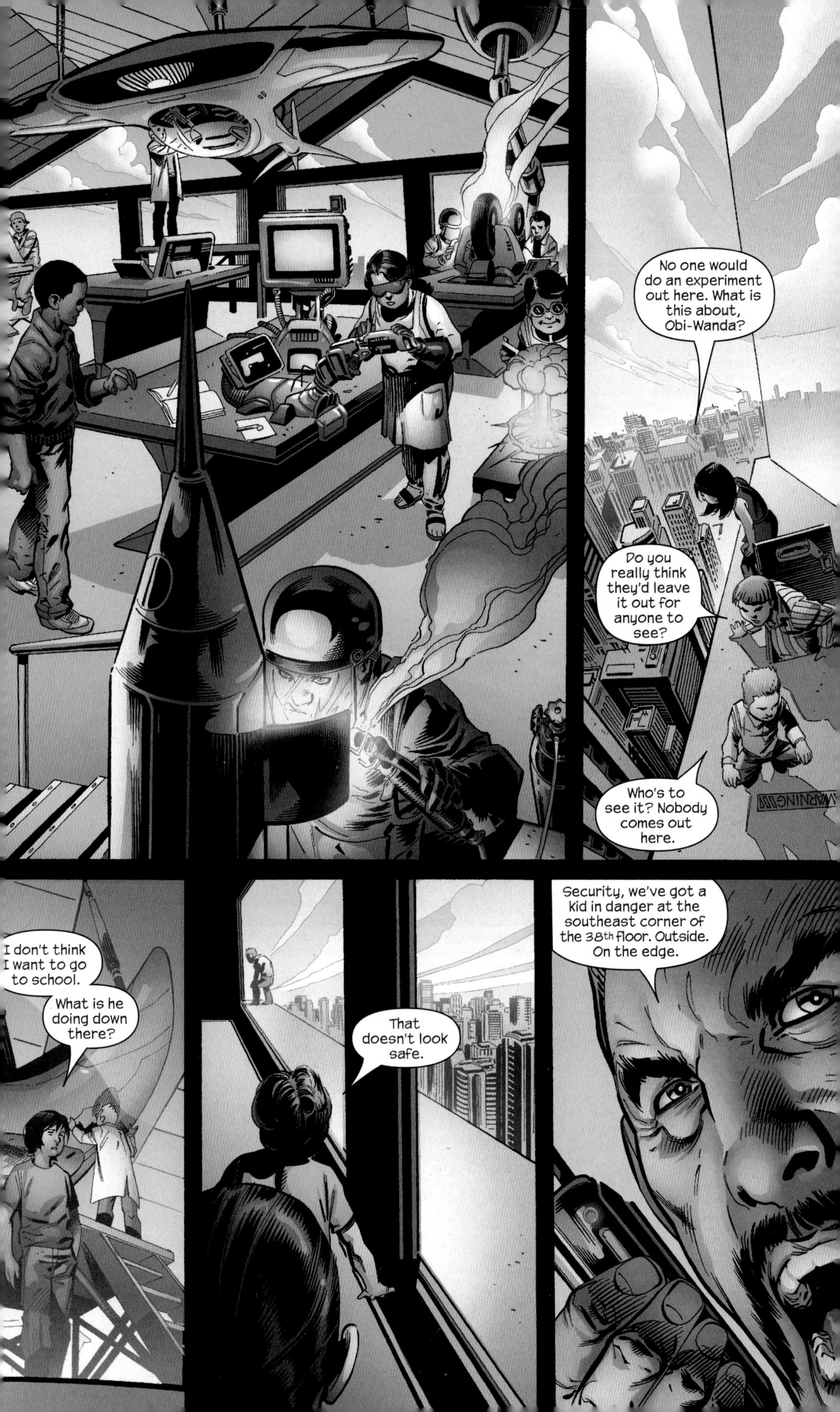
No one would do an experiment out here. What is this about, Obi-Wanda?
Do you really think they'd leave it out for anyone to see?
Who's to see it? Nobody comes out here.
I don't think I want to go to school.
What is he doing down there?
That doesn't look safe.
Security, we've got a kid in danger at the southeast corner of the 38th floor. Outside. On the edge.

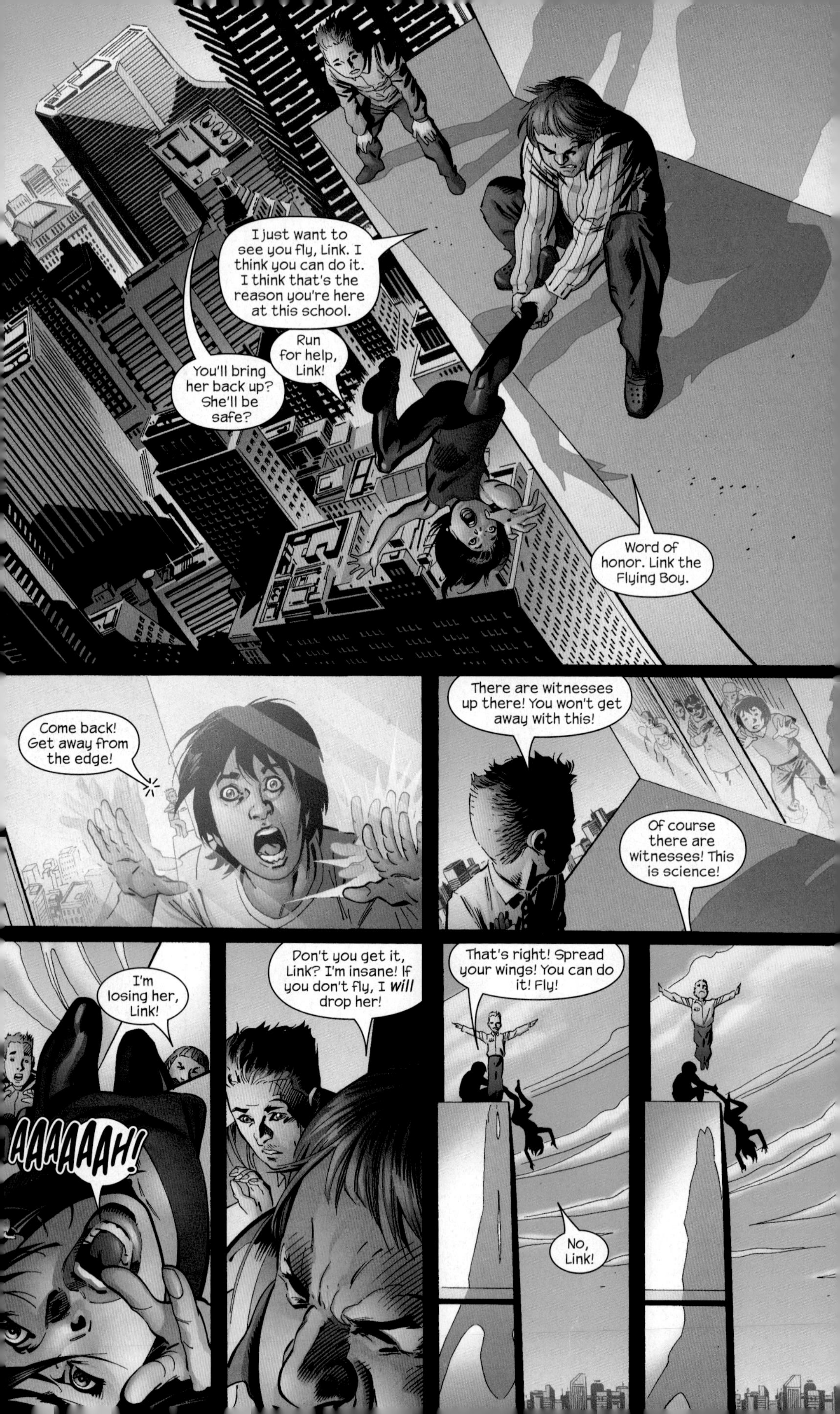
I just want to see you fly, Link. I think you can do it. I think that's the reason you're here at this school.
Run for help, Link!
You'll bring her back up? She'll be safe?
Word of honor. Link the Flying Boy.
Come back! Get away from the edge!
There are witnesses up there! You won't get away with this!
Of course there are witnesses! This is science!
I'm losing her, Link!
AAAAAAH!
Don't you get it, Link? I'm insane! If you don't fly, I *will* drop her!
That's right! Spread your wings! You can do it! Fly!
No, Link!

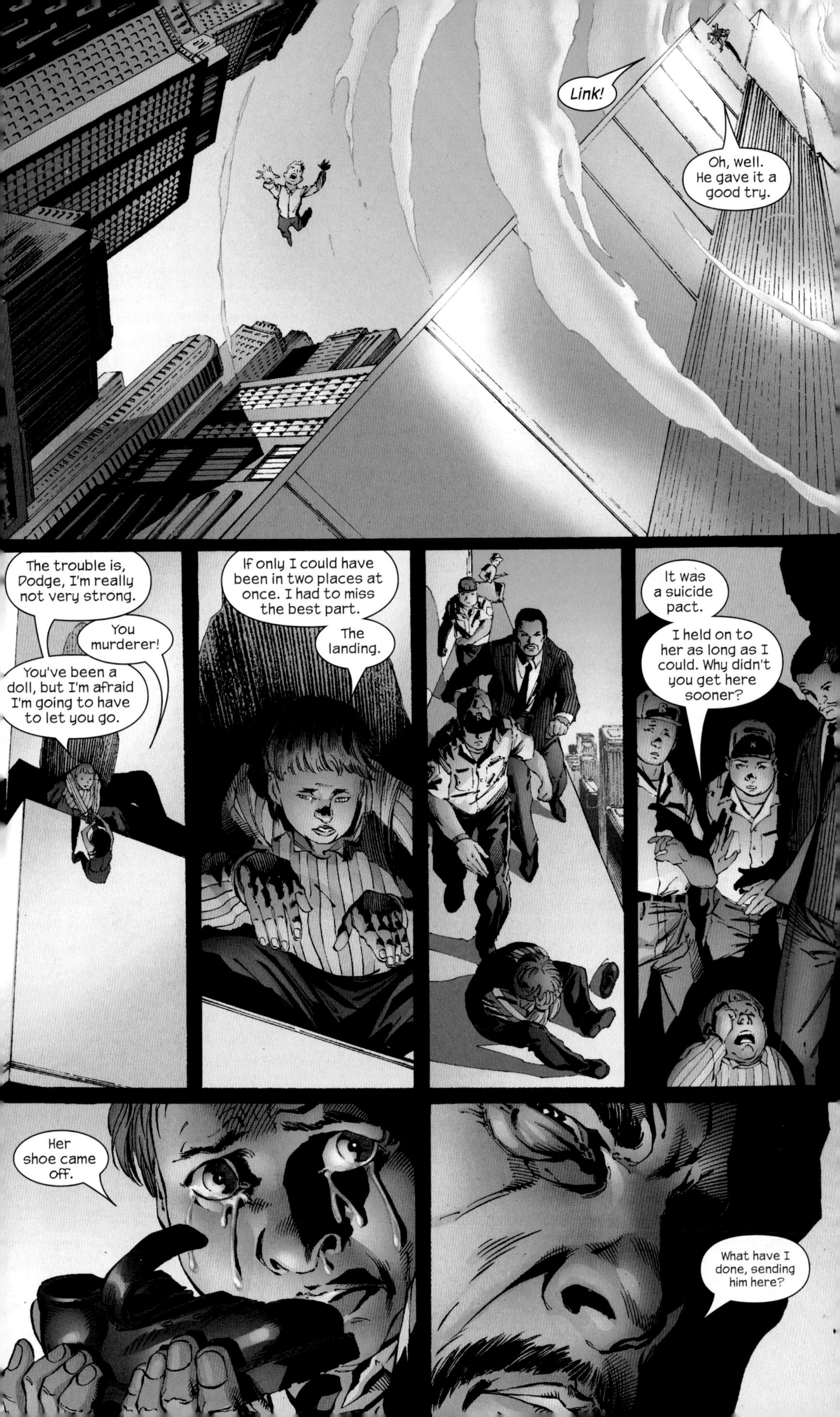
Link!
Oh, well. He gave it a good try.
The trouble is, Dodge, I'm really not very strong.
You murderer!
You've been a doll, but I'm afraid I'm going to have to let you go.
If only I could have been in two places at once. I had to miss the best part.
The landing.
It was a suicide pact.
I held on to her as long as I could. Why didn't you get here sooner?
Her shoe came off.
What have I done, sending him here?

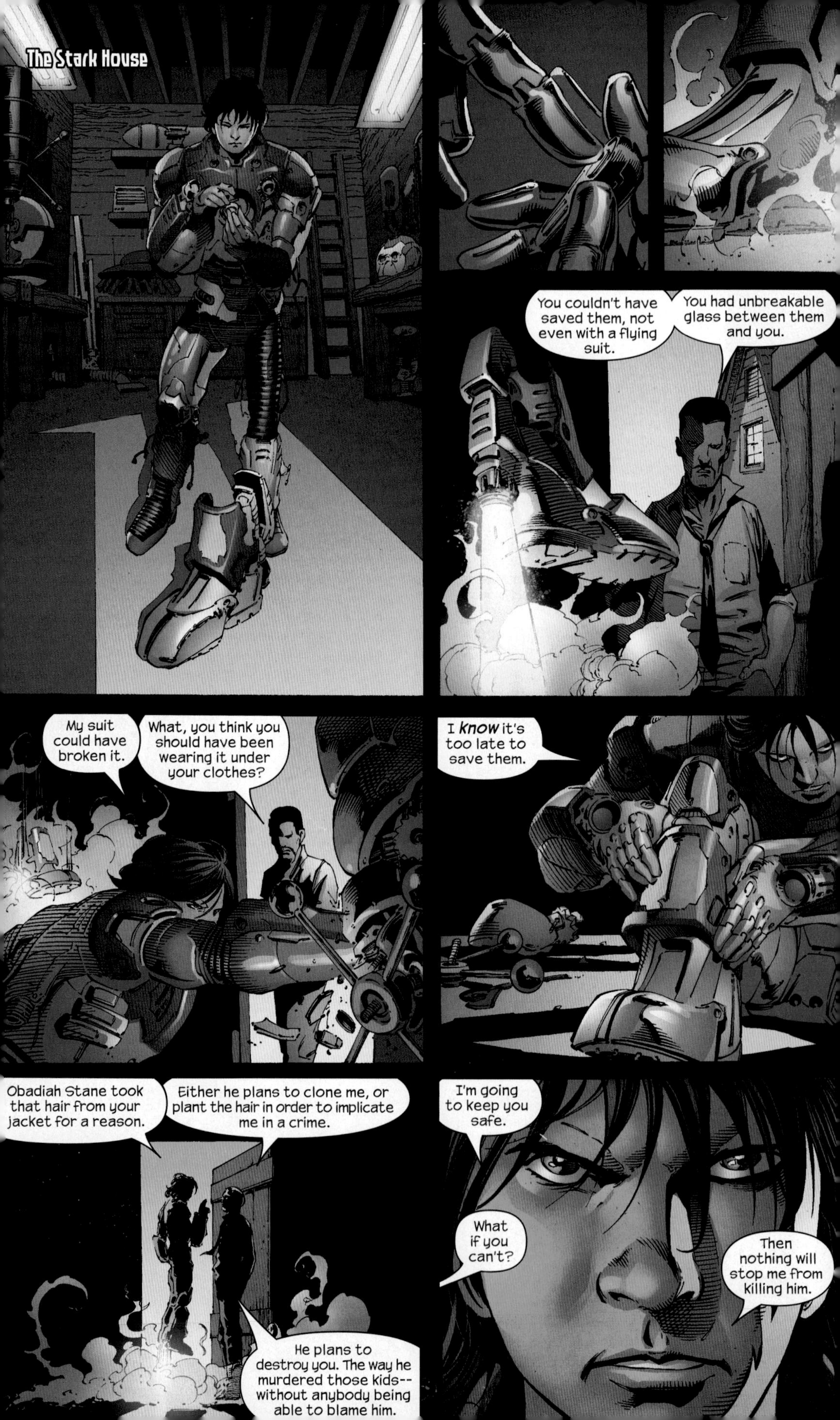
The Stark House
You couldn't have saved them, not even with a flying suit.
You had unbreakable glass between them and you.
My suit could have broken it.
What, you think you should have been wearing it under your clothes?
I *know* it's too late to save them.
Obadiah Stane took that hair from your jacket for a reason.
Either he plans to clone me, or plant the hair in order to implicate me in a crime.
He plans to destroy you. The way he murdered those kids--without anybody being able to blame him.
I'm going to keep you safe.
What if you can't?
Then nothing will stop me from killing him.

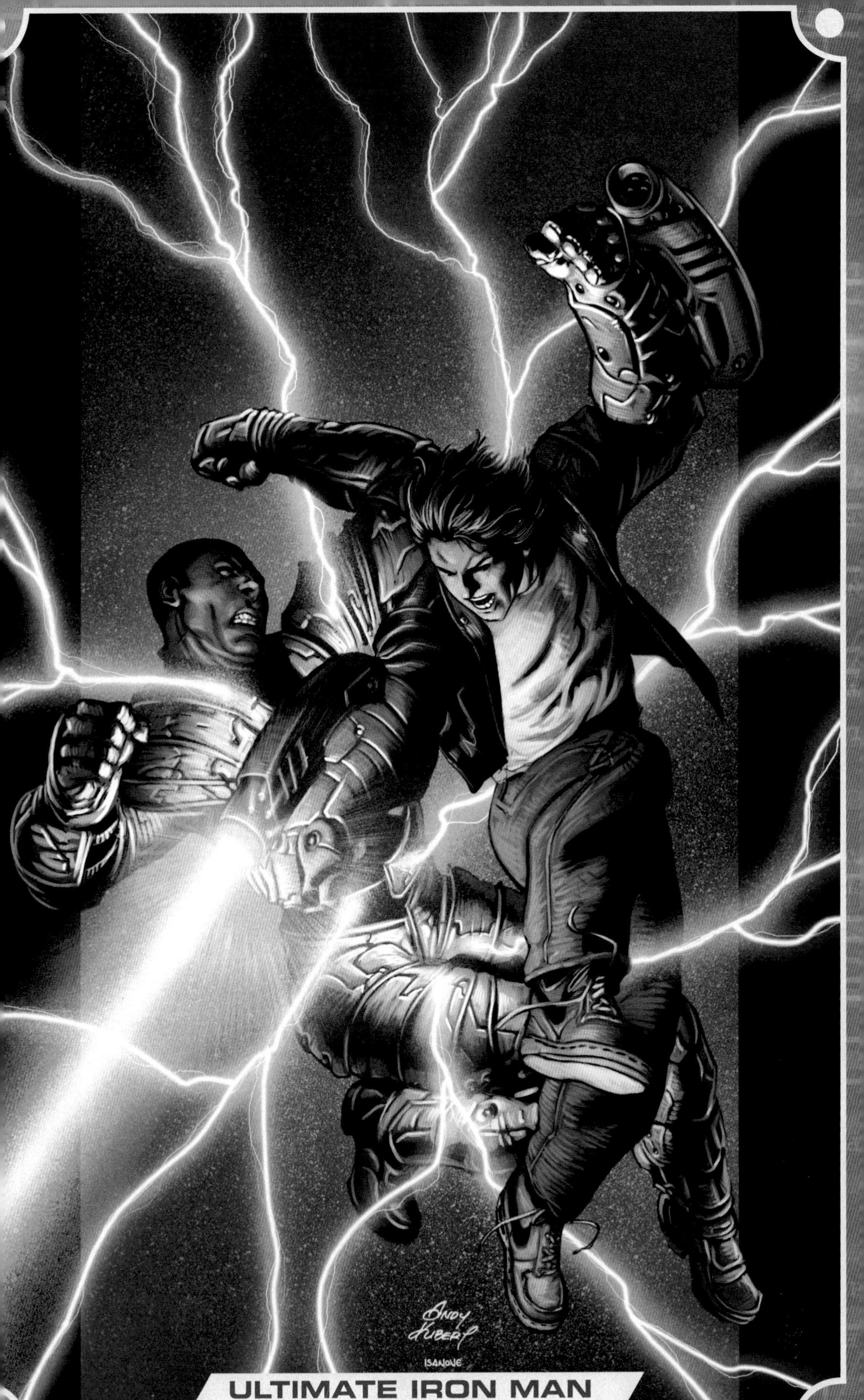
ANDY KUBERT
ISANOVE

ULTIMATE IRON MAN
ISSUE 05

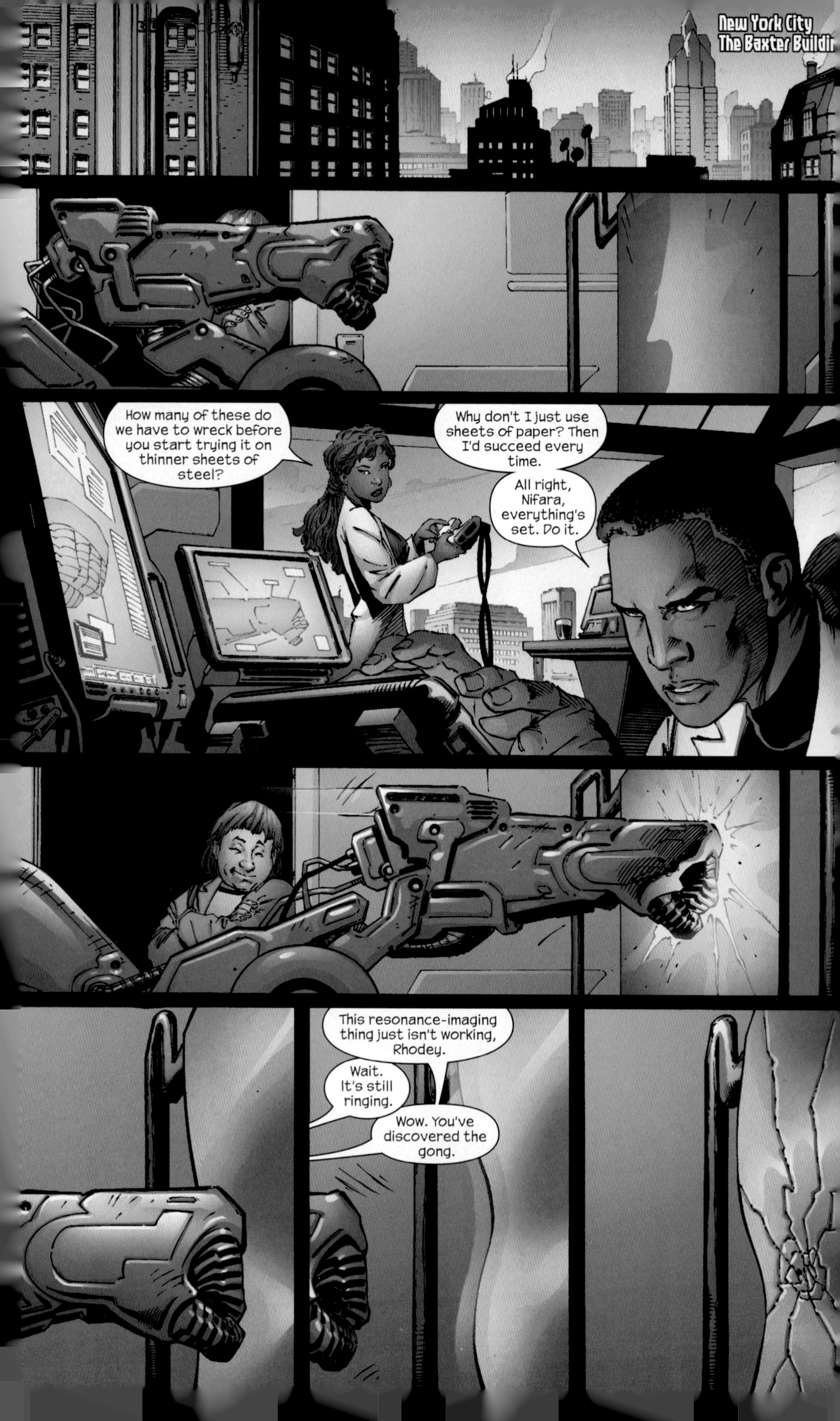
New York City
The Baxter Buildir
How many of these do we have to wreck before you start trying it on thinner sheets of steel?
Why don't I just use sheets of paper? Then I'd succeed every time.
All right, Nifara, everything's set. Do it.
This resonance-imaging thing just isn't working, Rhodey.
Wait. It's still ringing.
Wow. You've discovered the gong.

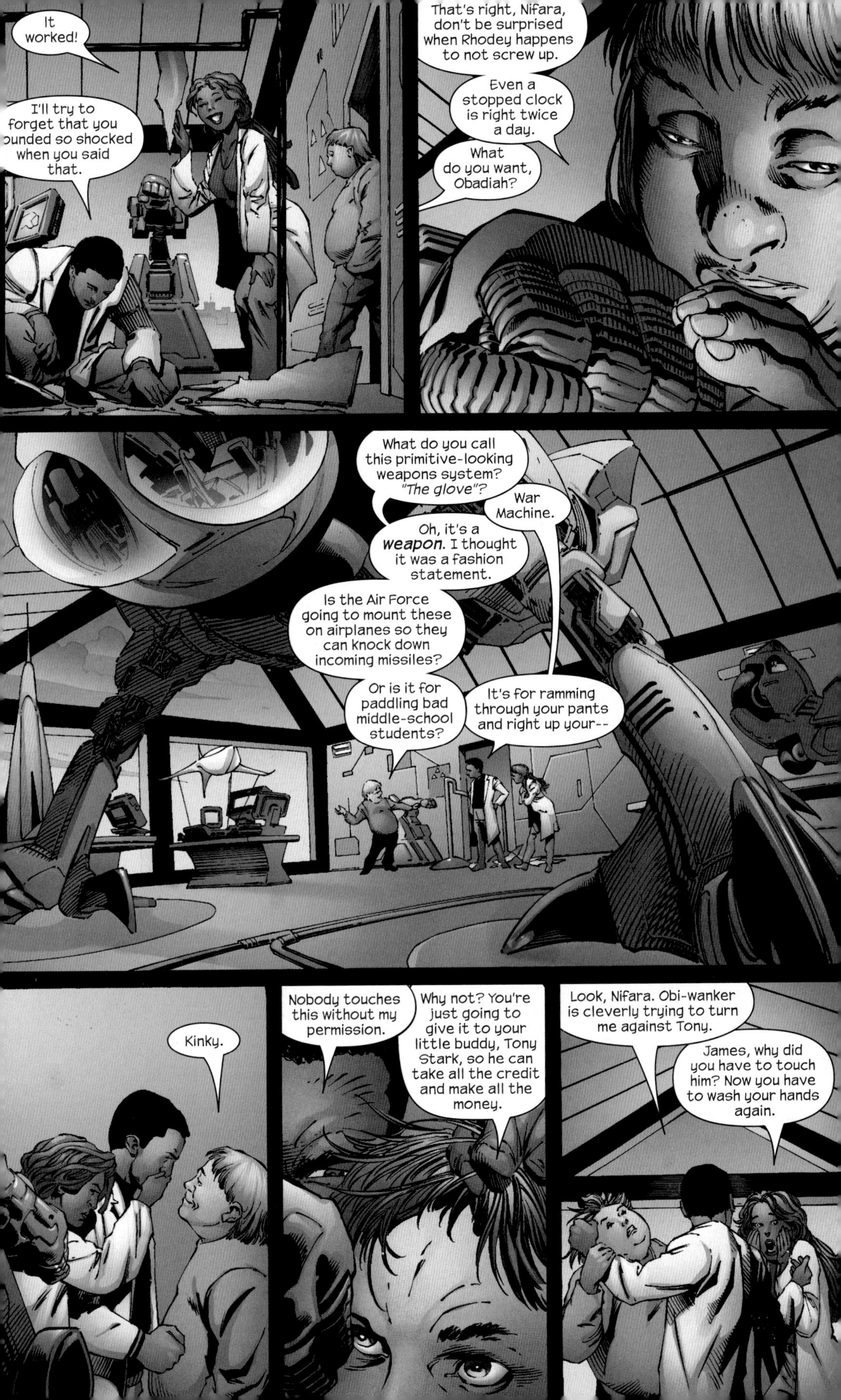

It worked!
I'll try to forget that you ounded so shocked when you said that.
That's right, Nifara, don't be surprised when Rhodey happens to not screw up.
Even a stopped clock is right twice a day.
What do you want, Obadiah?
What do you call this primitive-looking weapons system? *"The glove"?*
War Machine.
Oh, it's a ***weapon***. I thought it was a fashion statement.
Is the Air Force going to mount these on airplanes so they can knock down incoming missiles?
Or is it for paddling bad middle-school students?
It's for ramming through your pants and right up your--
Kinky.
Nobody touches this without my permission.
Why not? You're just going to give it to your little buddy, Tony Stark, so he can take all the credit and make all the money.
Look, Nifara. Obi-wanker is cleverly trying to turn me against Tony.
James, why did you have to touch him? Now you have to wash your hands again.

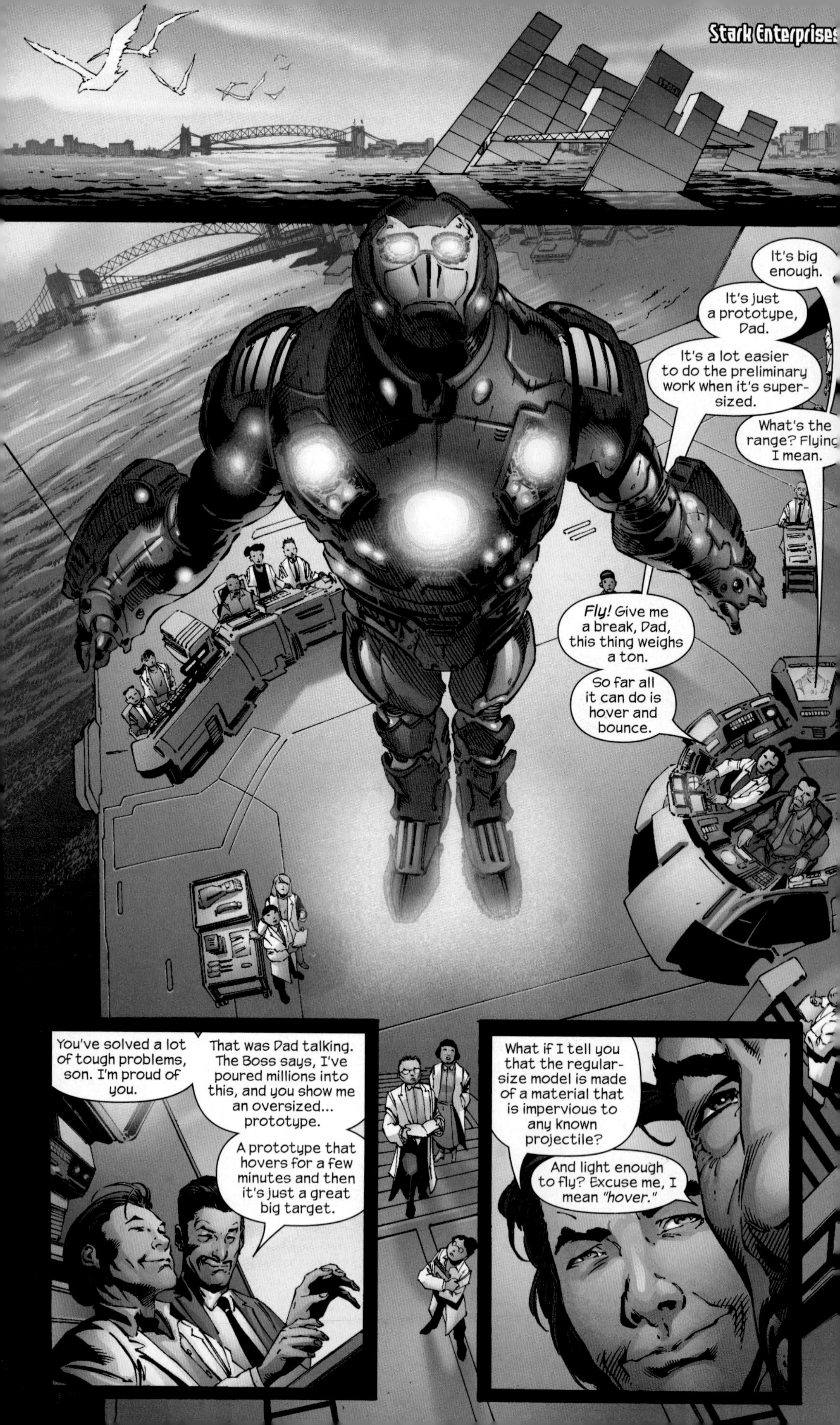
Stark Enterprises
It's big enough.
It's just a prototype, Dad.
It's a lot easier to do the preliminary work when it's super-sized.
What's the range? Flying I mean.
Fly! Give me a break, Dad, this thing weighs a ton.
So far all it can do is hover and bounce.
You've solved a lot of tough problems, son. I'm proud of you.
That was Dad talking. The Boss says, I've poured millions into this, and you show me an oversized... prototype.
A prototype that hovers for a few minutes and then it's just a great big target.
What if I tell you that the regular-size model is made of a material that is impervious to any known projectile?
And light enough to fly? Excuse me, I mean "hover."

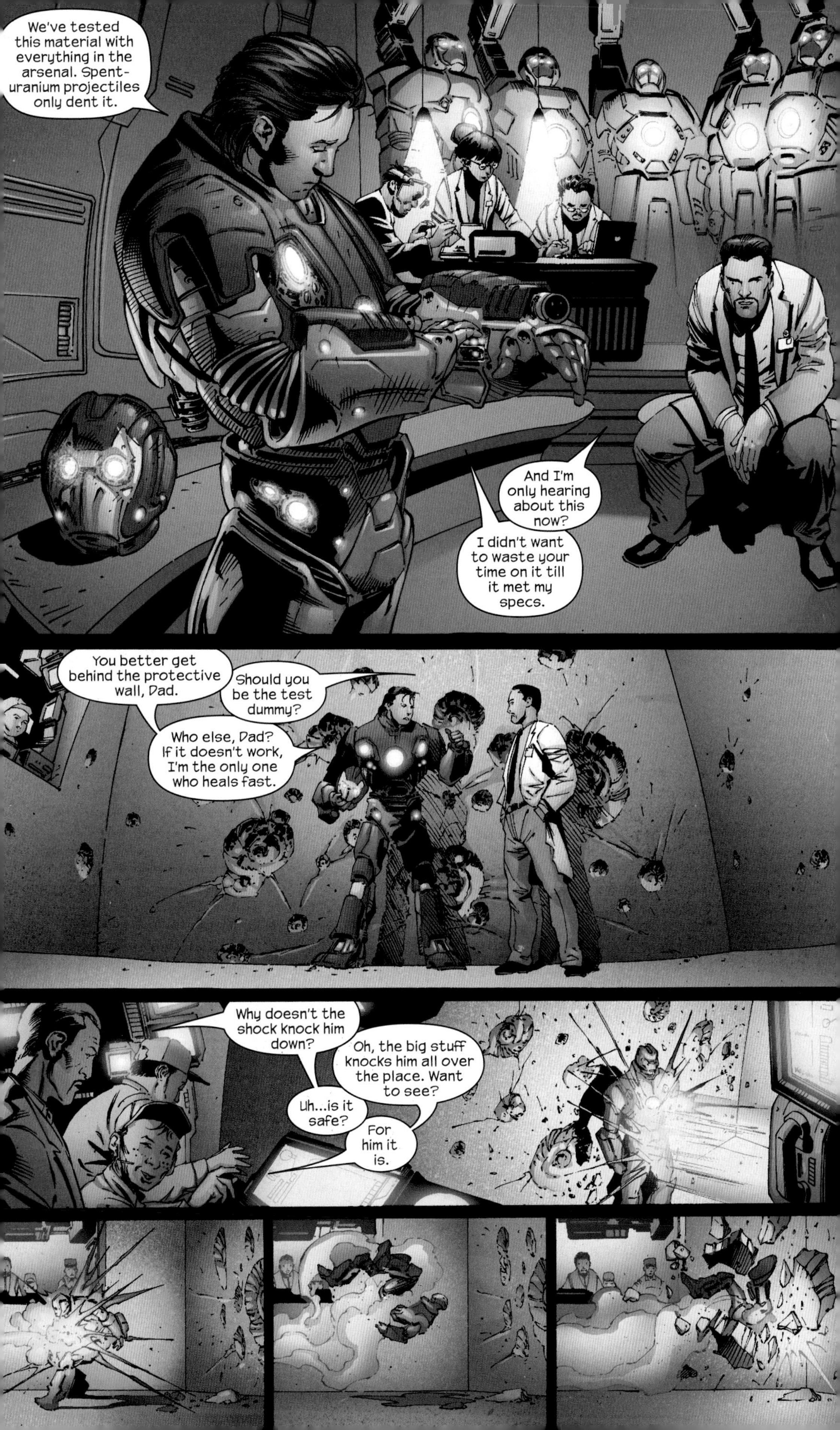
We've tested this material with everything in the arsenal. Spent-uranium projectiles only dent it.
And I'm only hearing about this now?
I didn't want to waste your time on it till it met my specs.
You better get behind the protective wall, Dad.
Should you be the test dummy?
Who else, Dad? If it doesn't work, I'm the only one who heals fast.
Why doesn't the shock knock him down?
Oh, the big stuff knocks him all over the place. Want to see?
Uh...is it safe?
For him it is.

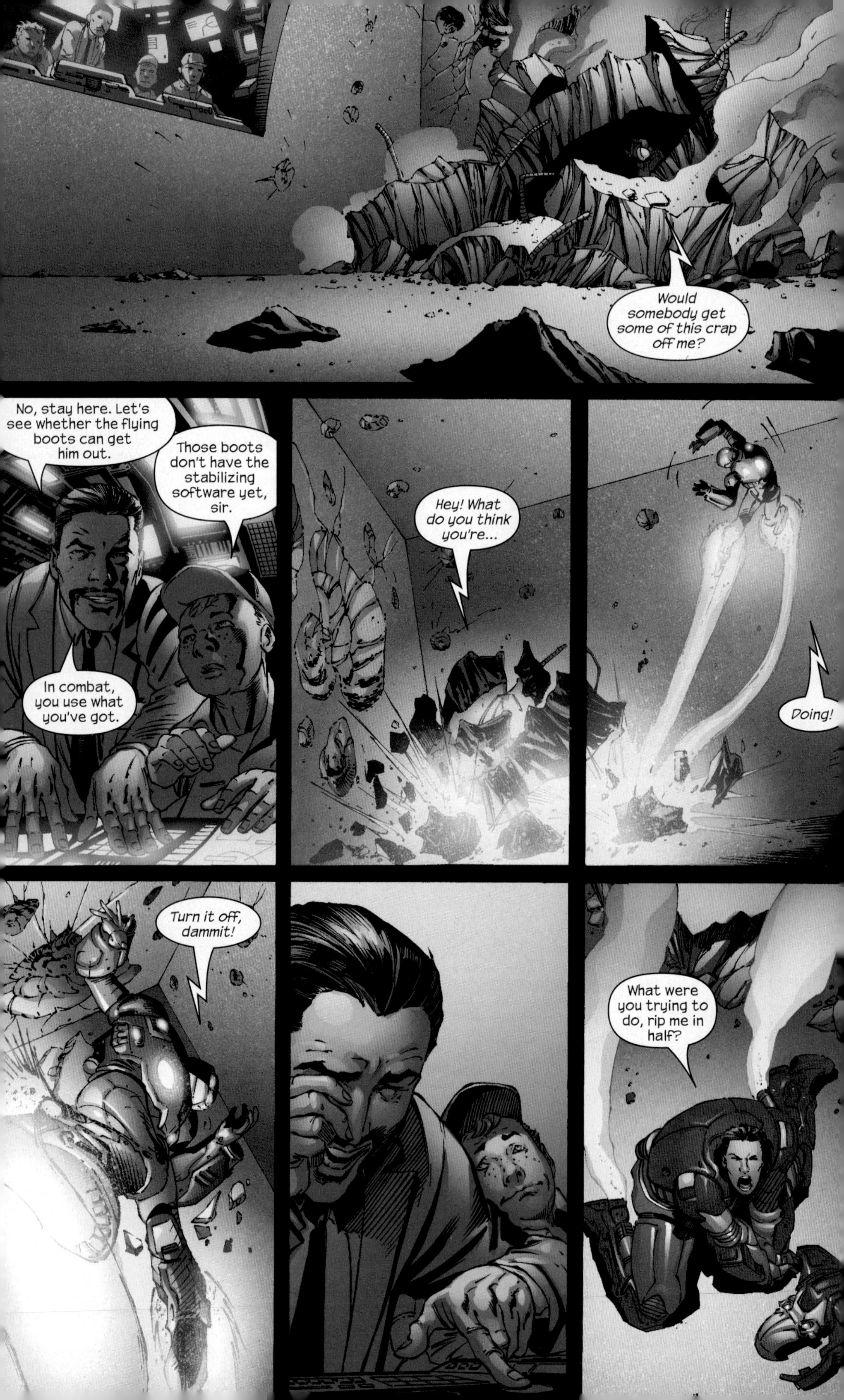

Would somebody get some of this crap off me?
No, stay here. Let's see whether the flying boots can get him out.
Those boots don't have the stabilizing software yet, sir.
In combat, you use what you've got.
Hey! What do you think you're...
Doing!
Turn it off, dammit!
What were you trying to do, rip me in half?

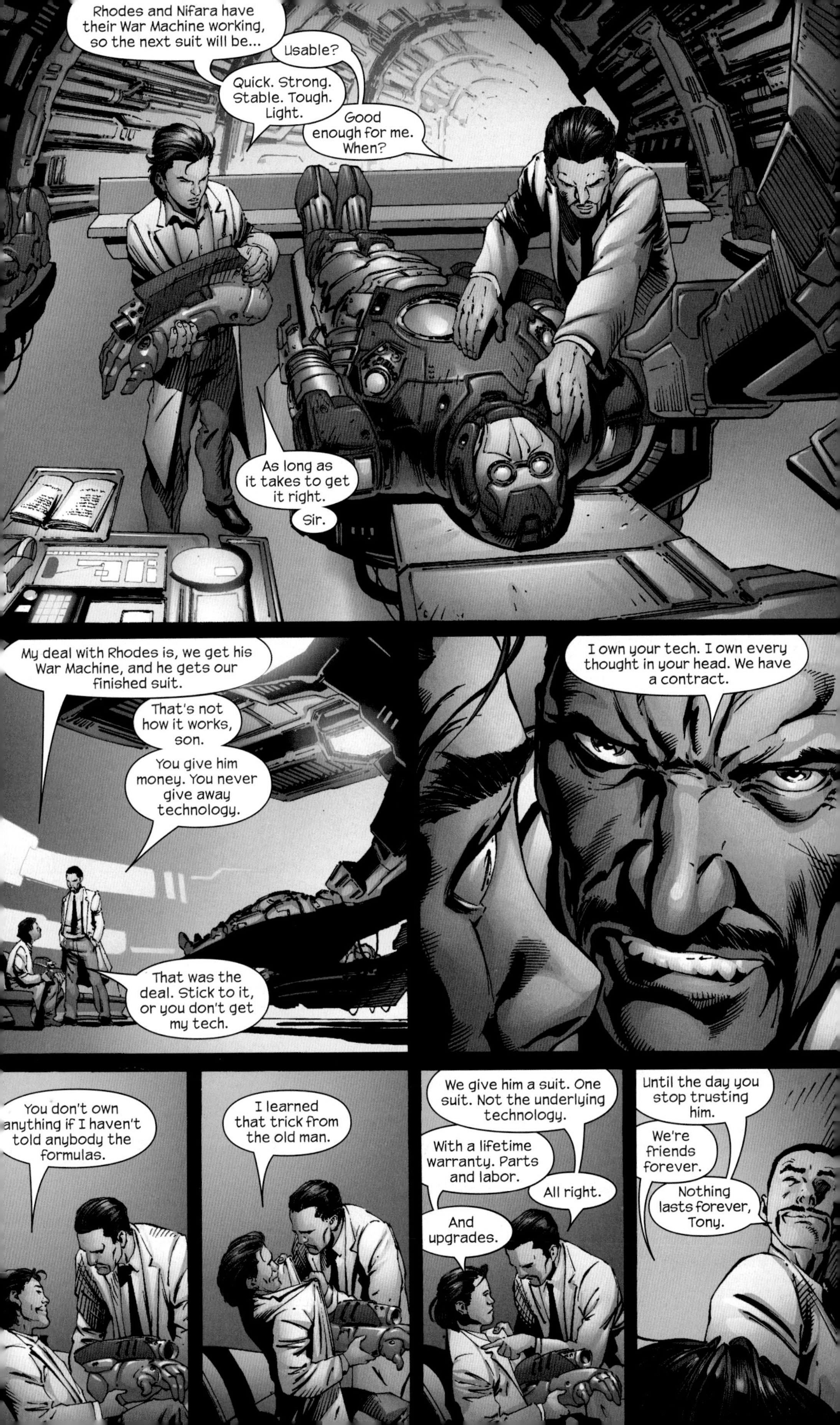
Rhodes and Nifara have their War Machine working, so the next suit will be...
Usable?
Quick. Strong. Stable. Tough. Light.
Good enough for me. When?
As long as it takes to get it right.
Sir.
My deal with Rhodes is, we get his War Machine, and he gets our finished suit.
That's not how it works, son.
You give him money. You never give away technology.
That was the deal. Stick to it, or you don't get my tech.
I own your tech. I own every thought in your head. We have a contract.
You don't own anything if I haven't told anybody the formulas.
I learned that trick from the old man.
We give him a suit. One suit. Not the underlying technology.
With a lifetime warranty. Parts and labor.
All right.
And upgrades.
Until the day you stop trusting him.
We're friends forever.
Nothing lasts forever, Tony.

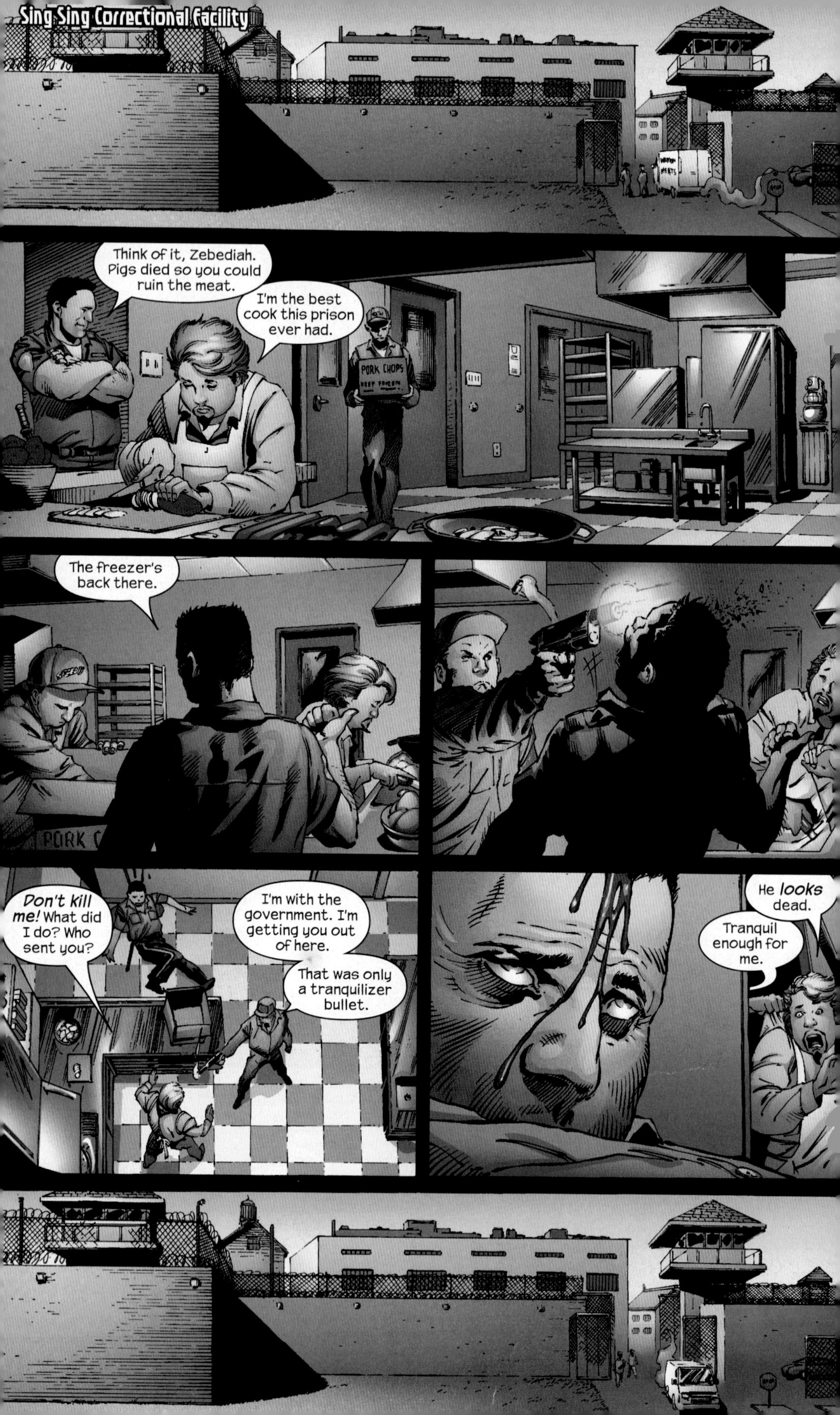
Sing Sing Correctional Facility
Think of it, Zebediah. Pigs died so you could ruin the meat.
I'm the best cook this prison ever had.
PORK CHOPS
The freezer's back there.
Don't kill me! What did I do? Who sent you?
I'm with the government. I'm getting you out of here.
That was only a tranquilizer bullet.
He looks dead.
Tranquil enough for me.

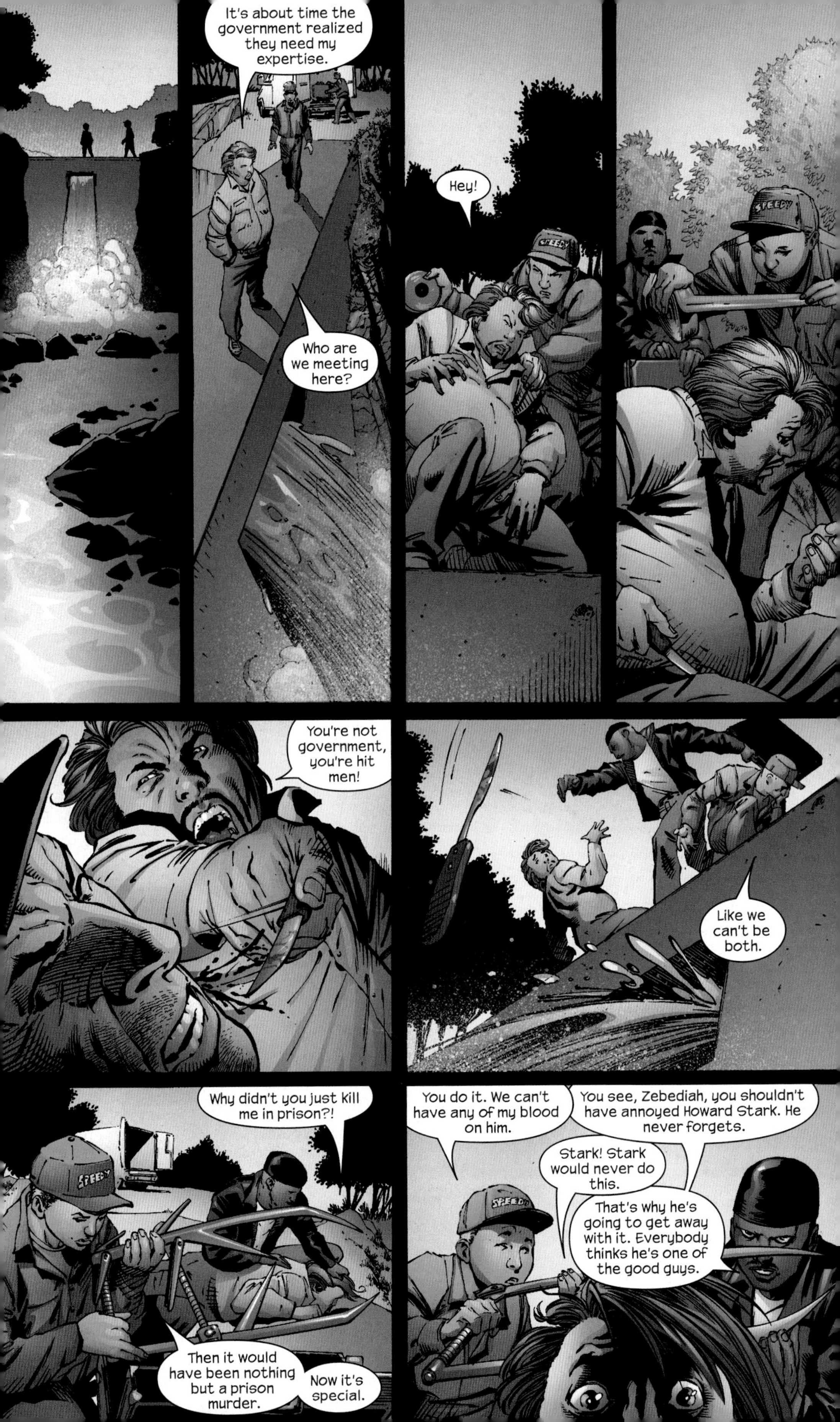
It's about time the government realized they need my expertise.
Who are we meeting here?
Hey!
You're not government, you're hit men!
Like we can't be both.
Why didn't you just kill me in prison?!
Then it would have been nothing but a prison murder.
Now it's special.
You do it. We can't have any of my blood on him.
You see, Zebediah, you shouldn't have annoyed Howard Stark. He never forgets.
Stark! Stark would never do this.
That's why he's going to get away with it. Everybody thinks he's one of the good guys.

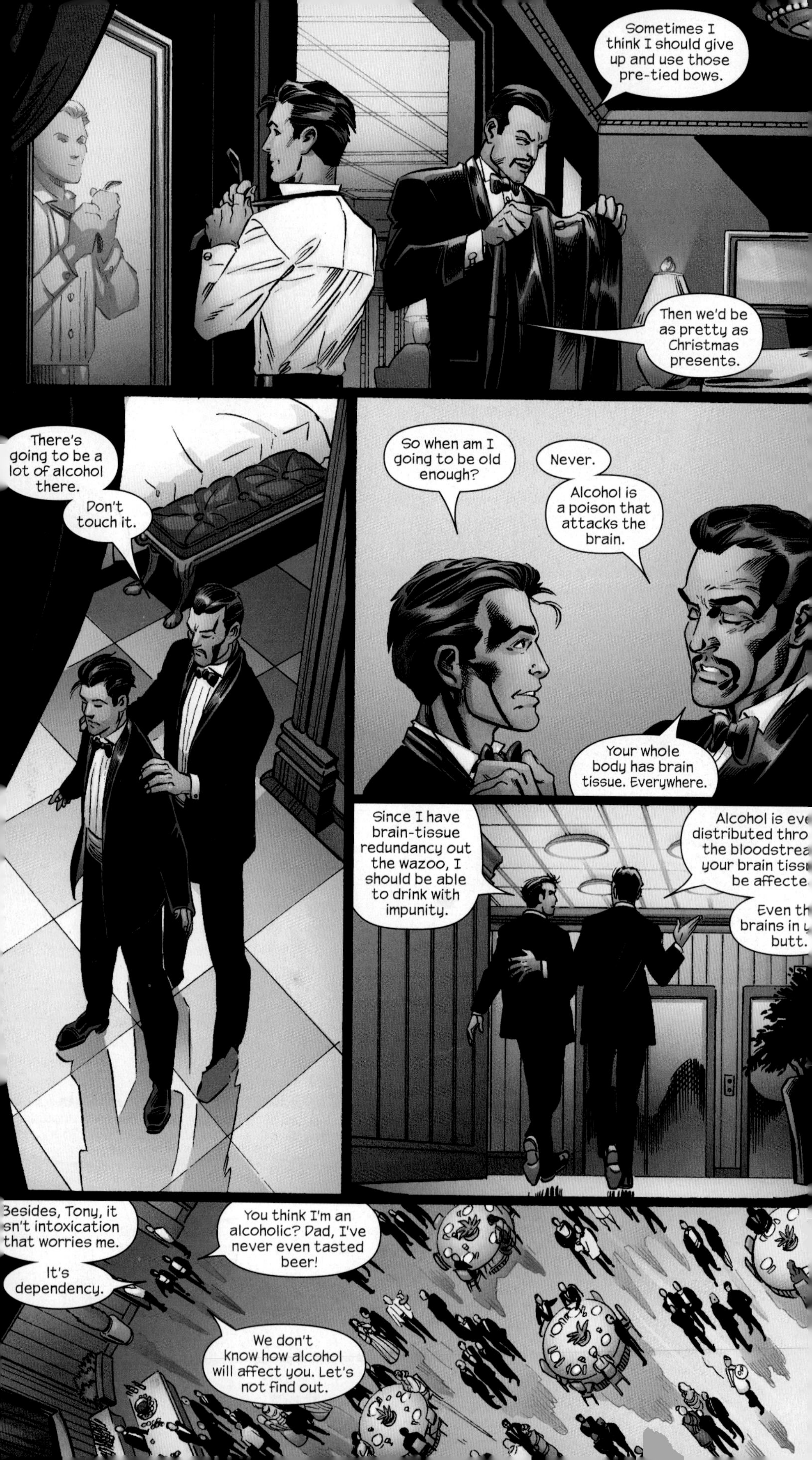
Sometimes I think I should give up and use those pre-tied bows.
Then we'd be as pretty as Christmas presents.
There's going to be a lot of alcohol there.
Don't touch it.
So when am I going to be old enough?
Never.
Alcohol is a poison that attacks the brain.
Your whole body has brain tissue. Everywhere.
Since I have brain-tissue redundancy out the wazoo, I should be able to drink with impunity.
Alcohol is eve distributed thro the bloodstrea your brain tiss be affecte
Even th brains in y butt.
3esides, Tony, it sn't intoxication that worries me.
It's dependency.
You think I'm an alcoholic? Dad, I've never even tasted beer!
We don't know how alcohol will affect you. Let's not find out.

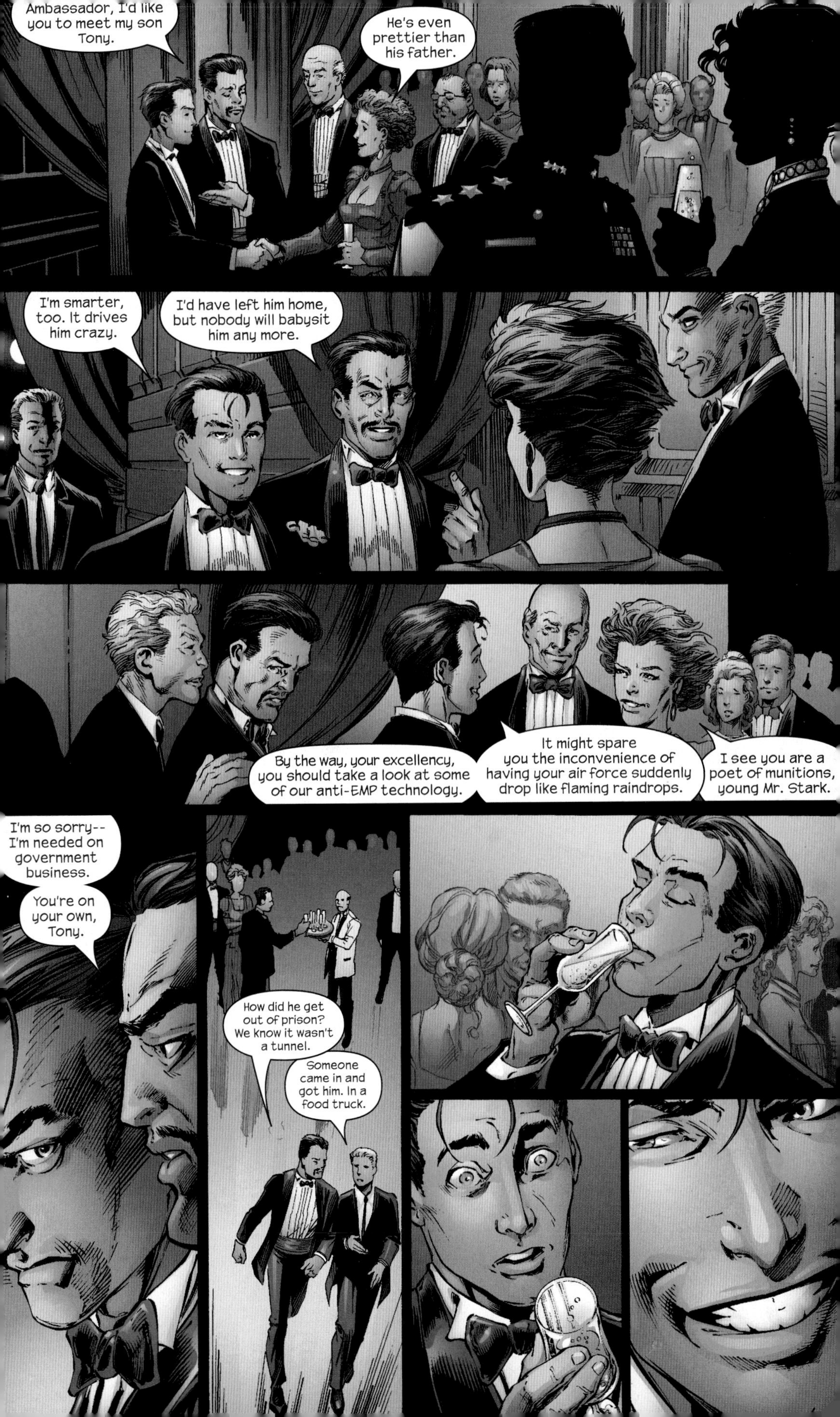
Ambassador, I'd like you to meet my son Tony.
He's even prettier than his father.
I'm smarter, too. It drives him crazy.
I'd have left him home, but nobody will babysit him any more.
By the way, your excellency, you should take a look at some of our anti-EMP technology.
It might spare you the inconvenience of having your air force suddenly drop like flaming raindrops.
I see you are a poet of munitions, young Mr. Stark.
I'm so sorry-- I'm needed on government business.
You're on your own, Tony.
How did he get out of prison? We know it wasn't a tunnel.
Someone came in and got him. In a food truck.

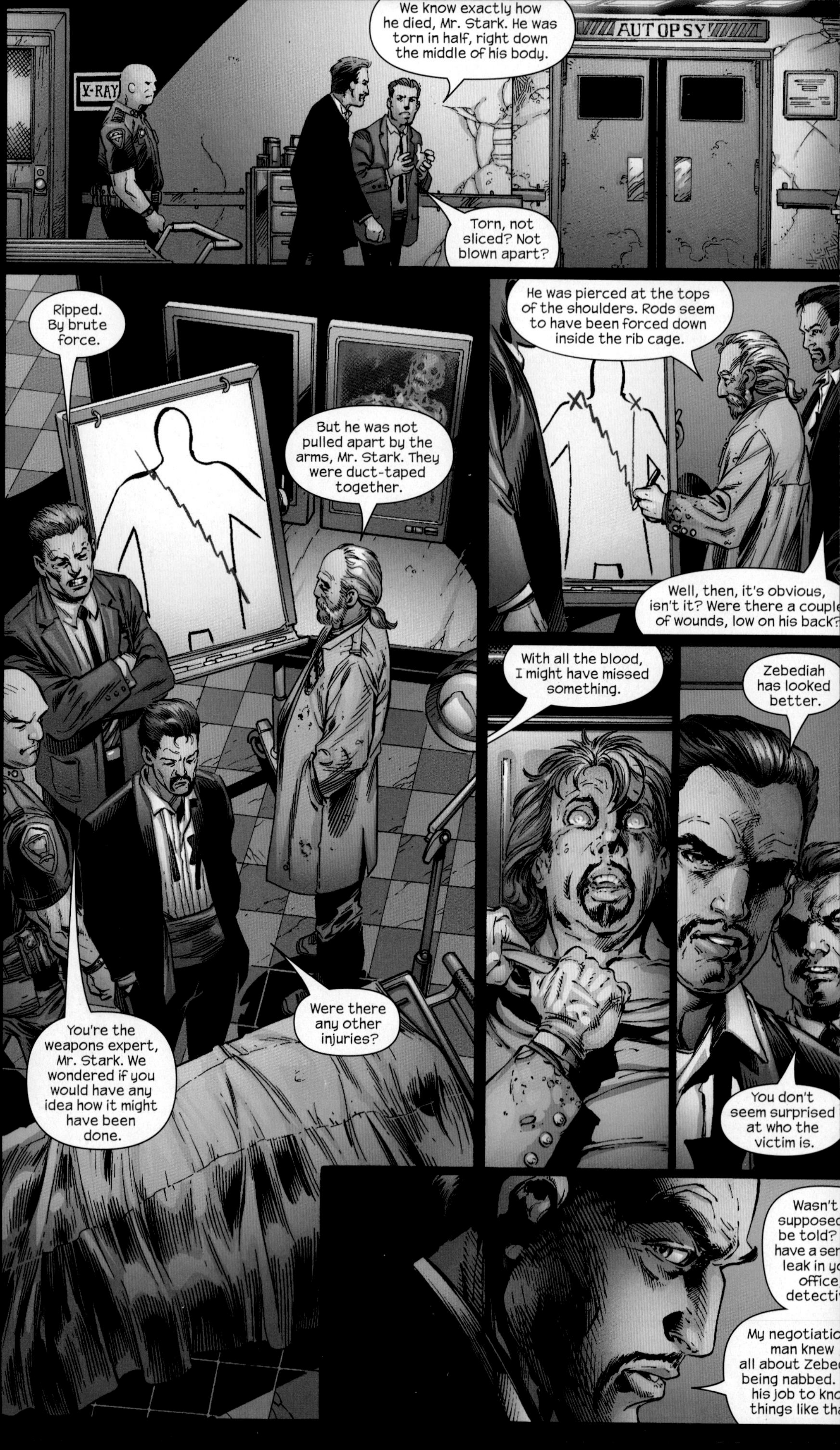
X-RAY
We know exactly how he died, Mr. Stark. He was torn in half, right down the middle of his body.
AUTOPSY
Torn, not sliced? Not blown apart?
Ripped. By brute force.
But he was not pulled apart by the arms, Mr. Stark. They were duct-taped together.
Were there any other injuries?
You're the weapons expert, Mr. Stark. We wondered if you would have any idea how it might have been done.
He was pierced at the tops of the shoulders. Rods seem to have been forced down inside the rib cage.
Well, then, it's obvious, isn't it? Were there a couple of wounds, low on his back?
With all the blood, I might have missed something.
Zebediah has looked better.
You don't seem surprised at who the victim is.

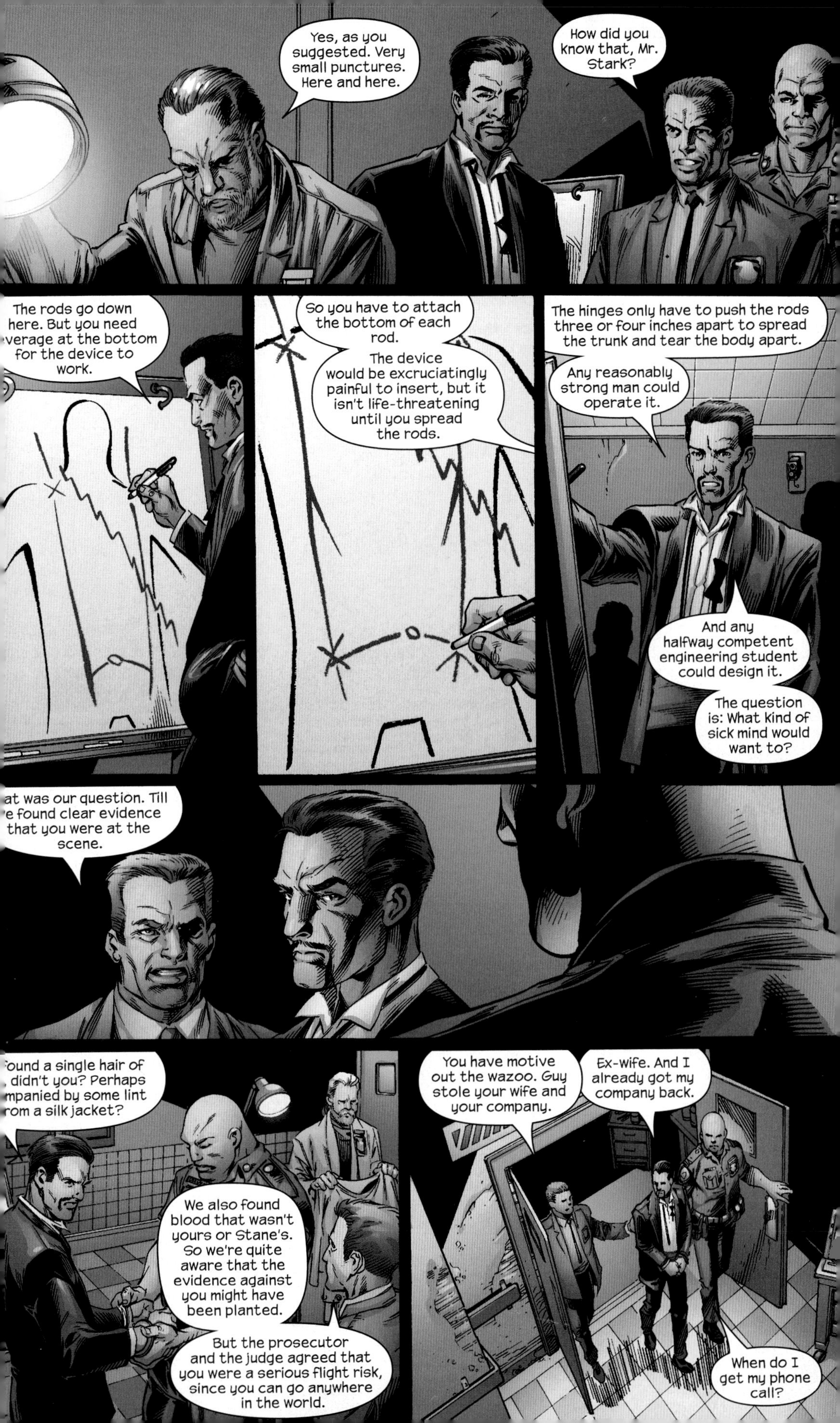
Yes, as you suggested. Very small punctures. Here and here.
How did you know that, Mr. Stark?
The rods go down here. But you need
everage at the bottom for the device to work.
So you have to attach the bottom of each rod.
The device would be excruciatingly painful to insert, but it isn't life-threatening until you spread the rods.
The hinges only have to push the rods three or four inches apart to spread the trunk and tear the body apart.
Any reasonably strong man could operate it.
And any halfway competent engineering student could design it.
The question is: What kind of sick mind would want to?
at was our question. Till
e found clear evidence that you were at the scene.
ound a single hair of
didn't you? Perhaps
mpanied by some lint
rom a silk jacket?
We also found blood that wasn't yours or Stane's. So we're quite aware that the evidence against you might have been planted.
But the prosecutor and the judge agreed that you were a serious flight risk, since you can go anywhere in the world.
You have motive out the wazoo. Guy stole your wife and your company.
Ex-wife. And I already got my company back.
When do I get my phone call?

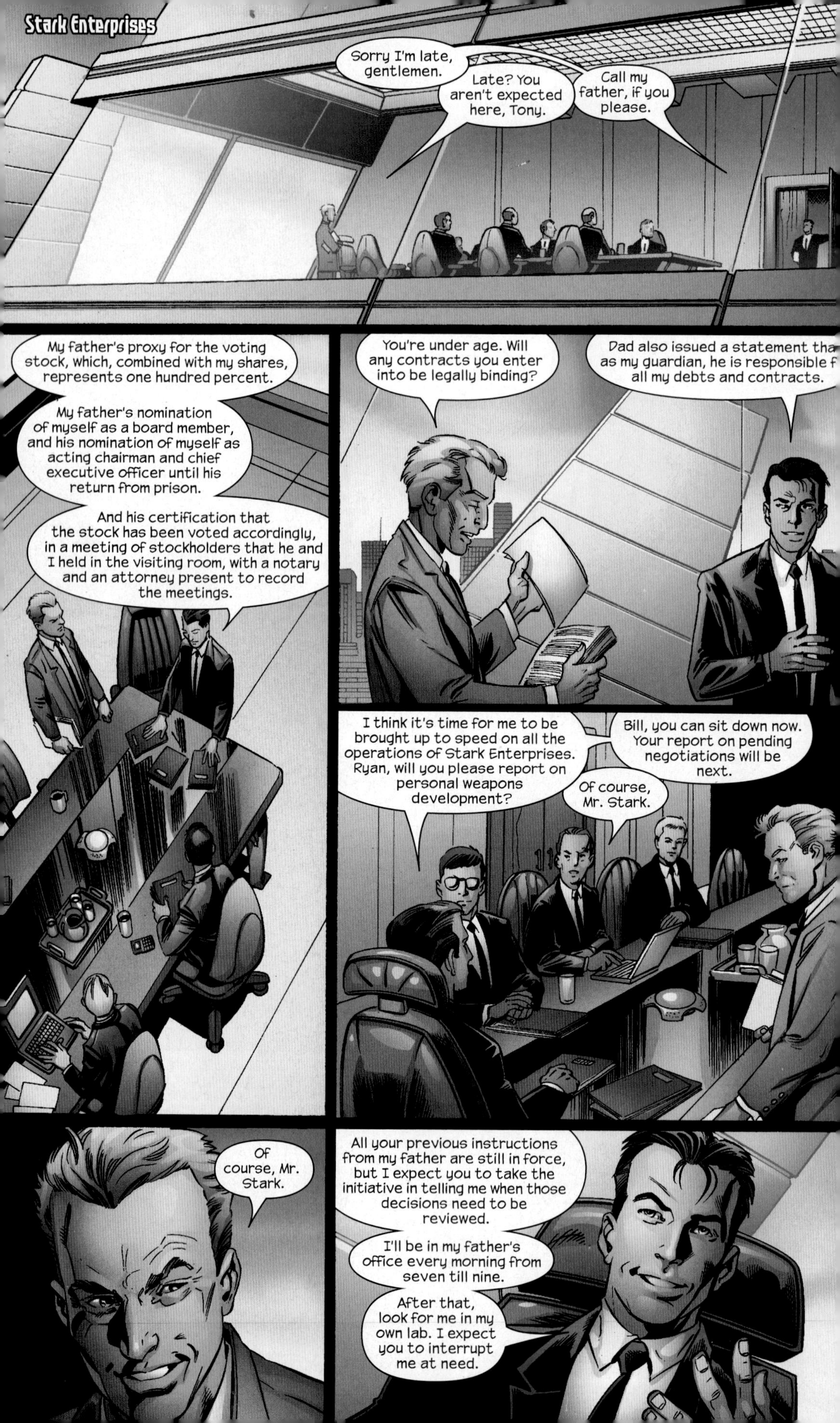
Stark Enterprises
Sorry I'm late, gentlemen.
Late? You aren't expected here, Tony.
Call my father, if you please.
My father's proxy for the voting stock, which, combined with my shares, represents one hundred percent.
My father's nomination of myself as a board member, and his nomination of myself as acting chairman and chief executive officer until his return from prison.
And his certification that the stock has been voted accordingly, in a meeting of stockholders that he and I held in the visiting room, with a notary and an attorney present to record the meetings.
You're under age. Will any contracts you enter into be legally binding?
Dad also issued a statement tha as my guardian, he is responsible f all my debts and contracts.
I think it's time for me to be brought up to speed on all the operations of Stark Enterprises. Ryan, will you please report on personal weapons development?
Bill, you can sit down now. Your report on pending negotiations will be next.
Of course, Mr. Stark.
Of course, Mr. Stark.
All your previous instructions from my father are still in force, but I expect you to take the initiative in telling me when those decisions need to be reviewed.
I'll be in my father's office every morning from seven till nine.
After that, look for me in my own lab. I expect you to interrupt me at need.

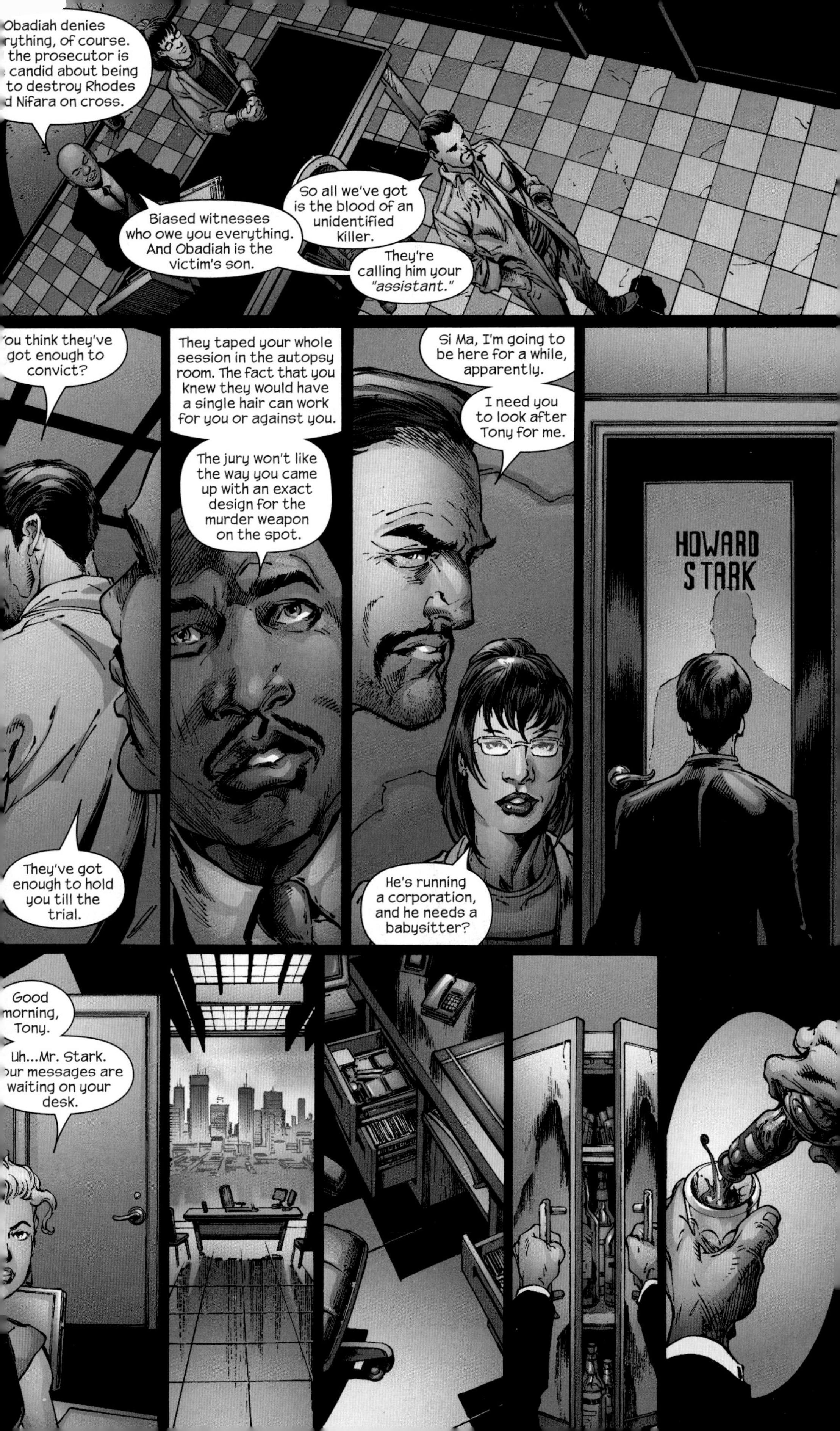
Obadiah denies rything, of course. the prosecutor is candid about being to destroy Rhodes d Nifara on cross.
Biased witnesses who owe you everything. And Obadiah is the victim's son.
So all we've got is the blood of an unidentified killer.
They're calling him your "assistant."
ou think they've got enough to convict?
They've got enough to hold you till the trial.
They taped your whole session in the autopsy room. The fact that you knew they would have a single hair can work for you or against you.
The jury won't like the way you came up with an exact design for the murder weapon on the spot.
Si Ma, I'm going to be here for a while, apparently.
I need you to look after Tony for me.
He's running a corporation, and he needs a babysitter?
HOWARD STARK
Good morning, Tony.
Uh...Mr. Stark. our messages are waiting on your desk.

SI MA. You don't knock?

So you've started drinking?

No. I saw you.

I just *finished* drinking. Till next time.

Your father trusts you with everything. Why start drinking now?

He doesn't trust me *that* much. He sent you.

Other people have hours, days, *months* without pain. They can think clearly.

For the first time in my life, I know what it feels like.

Alcohol kills brain cells. It impairs your judgment.

So I only drink a little.

When you'r impaired, y don't know w "a little" is

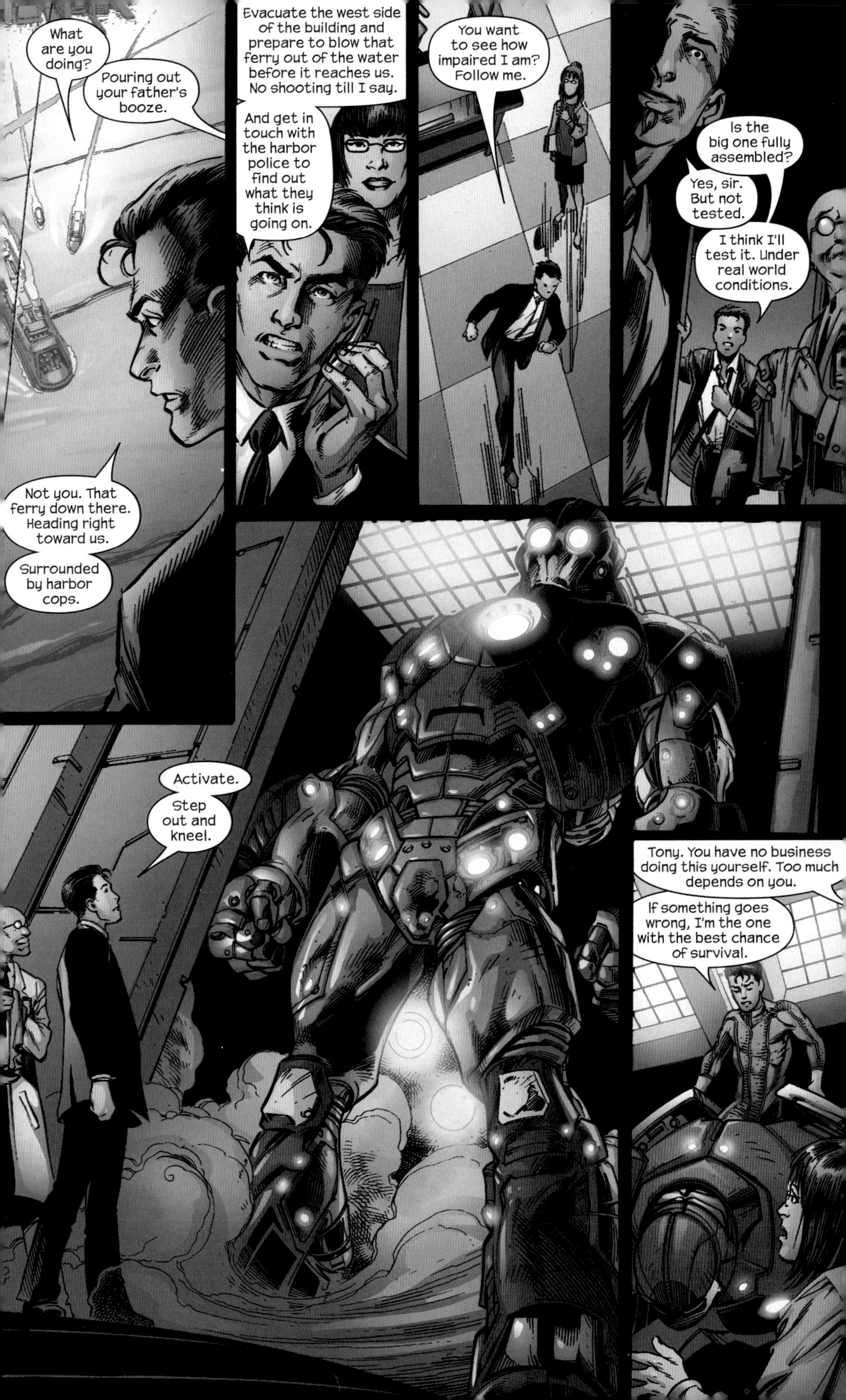
What are you doing?
Pouring out your father's booze.
Not you. That ferry down there. Heading right toward us.
Surrounded by harbor cops.
Evacuate the west side of the building and prepare to blow that ferry out of the water before it reaches us. No shooting till I say.
And get in touch with the harbor police to find out what they think is going on.
You want to see how impaired I am? Follow me.
Is the big one fully assembled?
Yes, sir. But not tested.
I think I'll test it. Under real world conditions.
Activate.
Step out and kneel.
Tony. You have no business doing this yourself. Too much depends on you.
If something goes wrong, I'm the one with the best chance of survival.

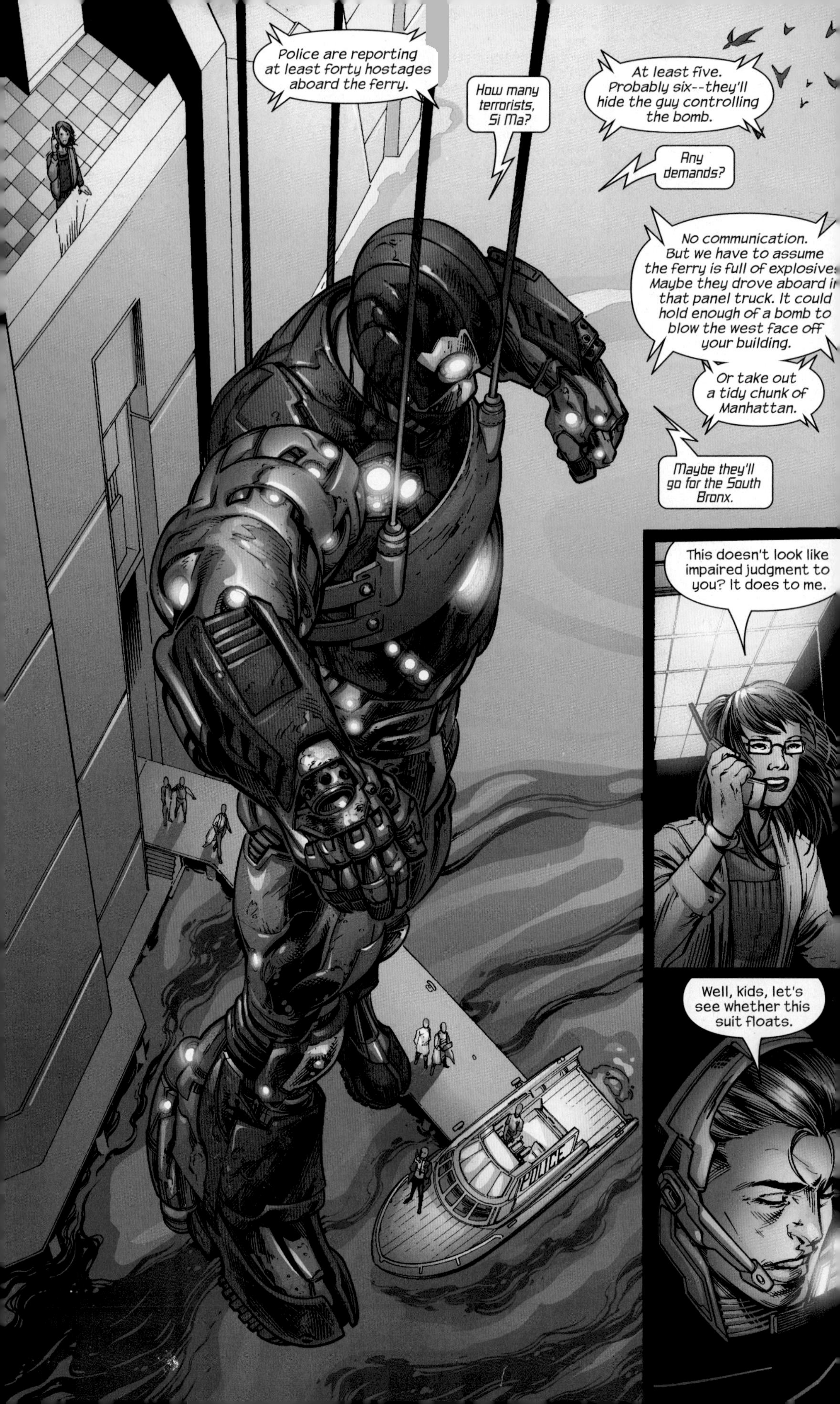
Police are reporting at least forty hostages aboard the ferry.
How many terrorists, Si Ma?
At least five. Probably six--they'll hide the guy controlling the bomb.
Any demands?
No communication. But we have to assume the ferry is full of explosive Maybe they drove aboard in that panel truck. It could hold enough of a bomb to blow the west face off your building.
Or take out a tidy chunk of Manhattan.
Maybe they'll go for the South Bronx.
This doesn't look like impaired judgment to you? It does to me.
Well, kids, let's see whether this suit floats.
POLICE

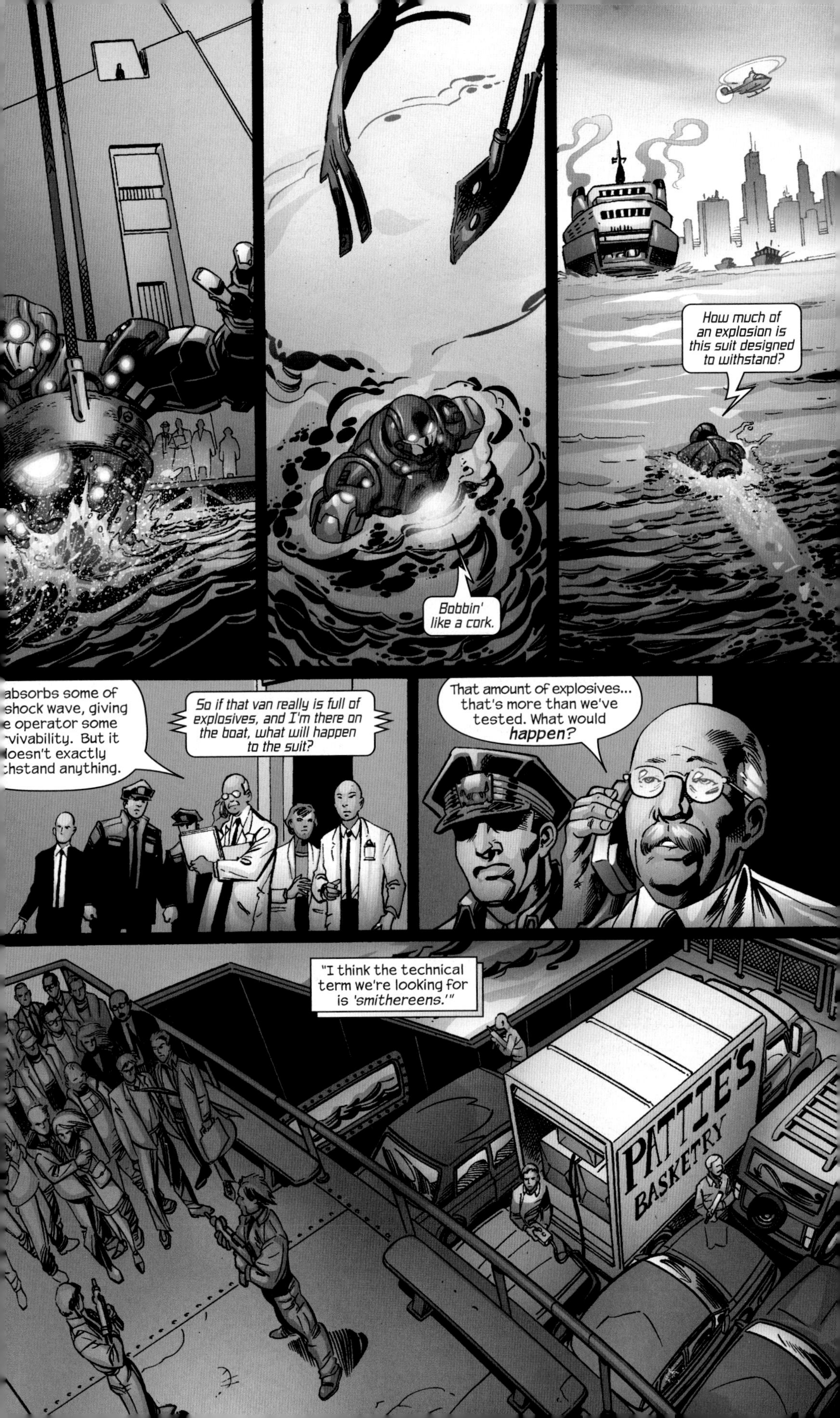
Bobbin' like a cork.
How much of an explosion is this suit designed to withstand?
absorbs some of shock wave, giving e operator some rvivability. But it loesn't exactly chstand anything.
So if that van really is full of explosives, and I'm there on the boat, what will happen to the suit?
That amount of explosives... that's more than we've tested. What would happen?
"I think the technical term we're looking for is 'smithereens.'"
PATTIE'S BASKETRY

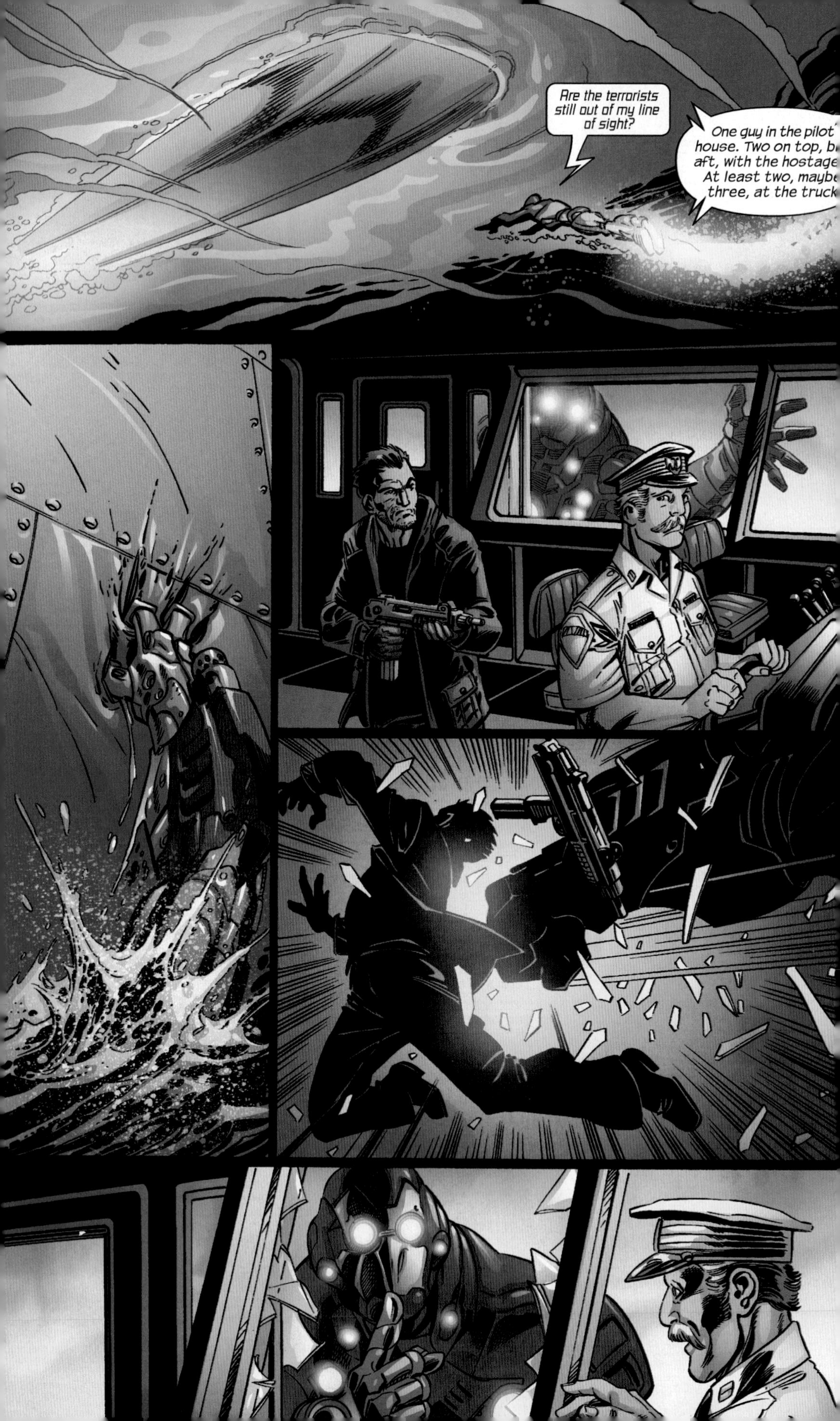
Are the terrorists still out of my line of sight?
One guy in the pilot house. Two on top, b aft, with the hostage At least two, mayb three, at the truck

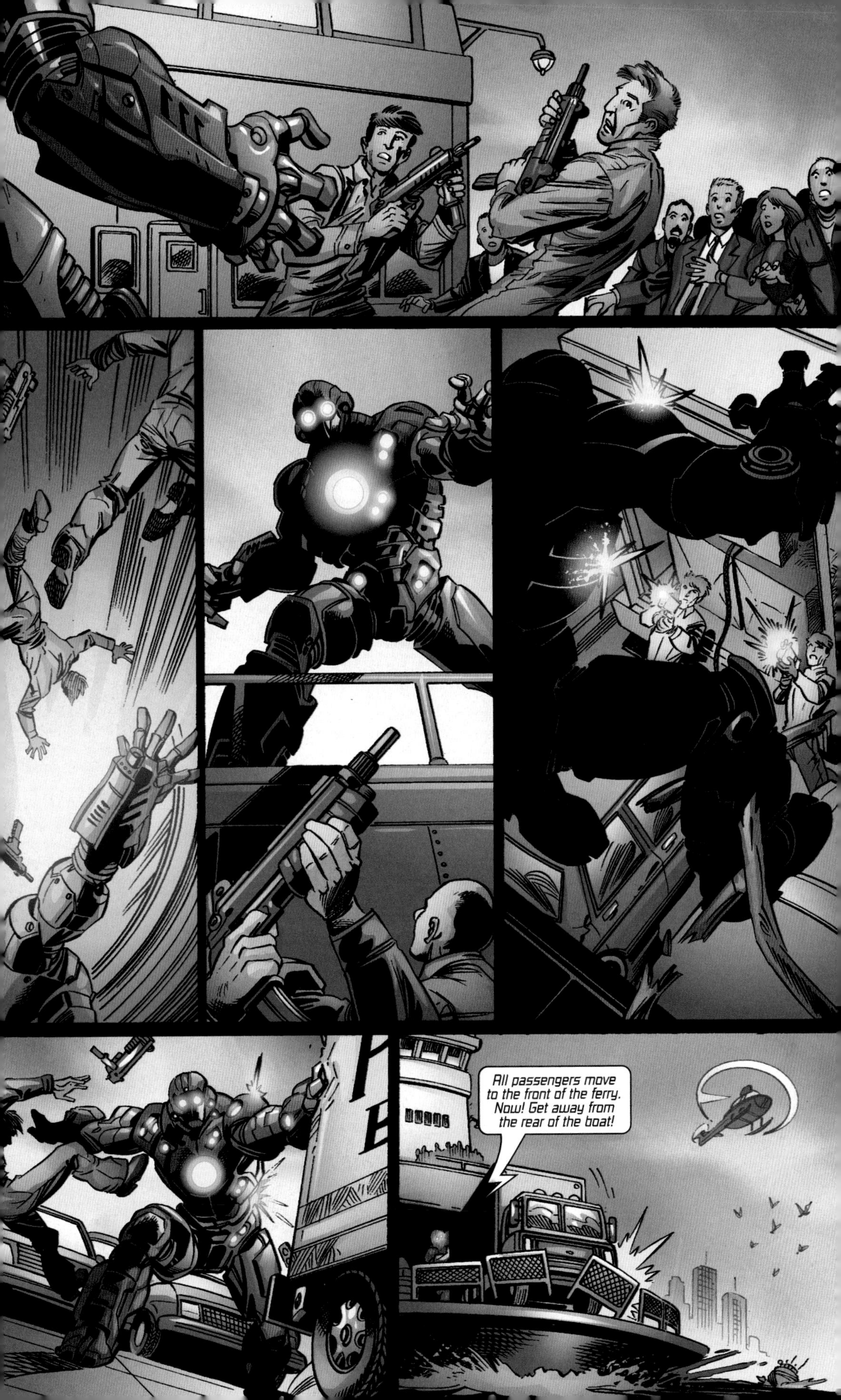
All passengers move to the front of the ferry. Now! Get away from the rear of the boat!

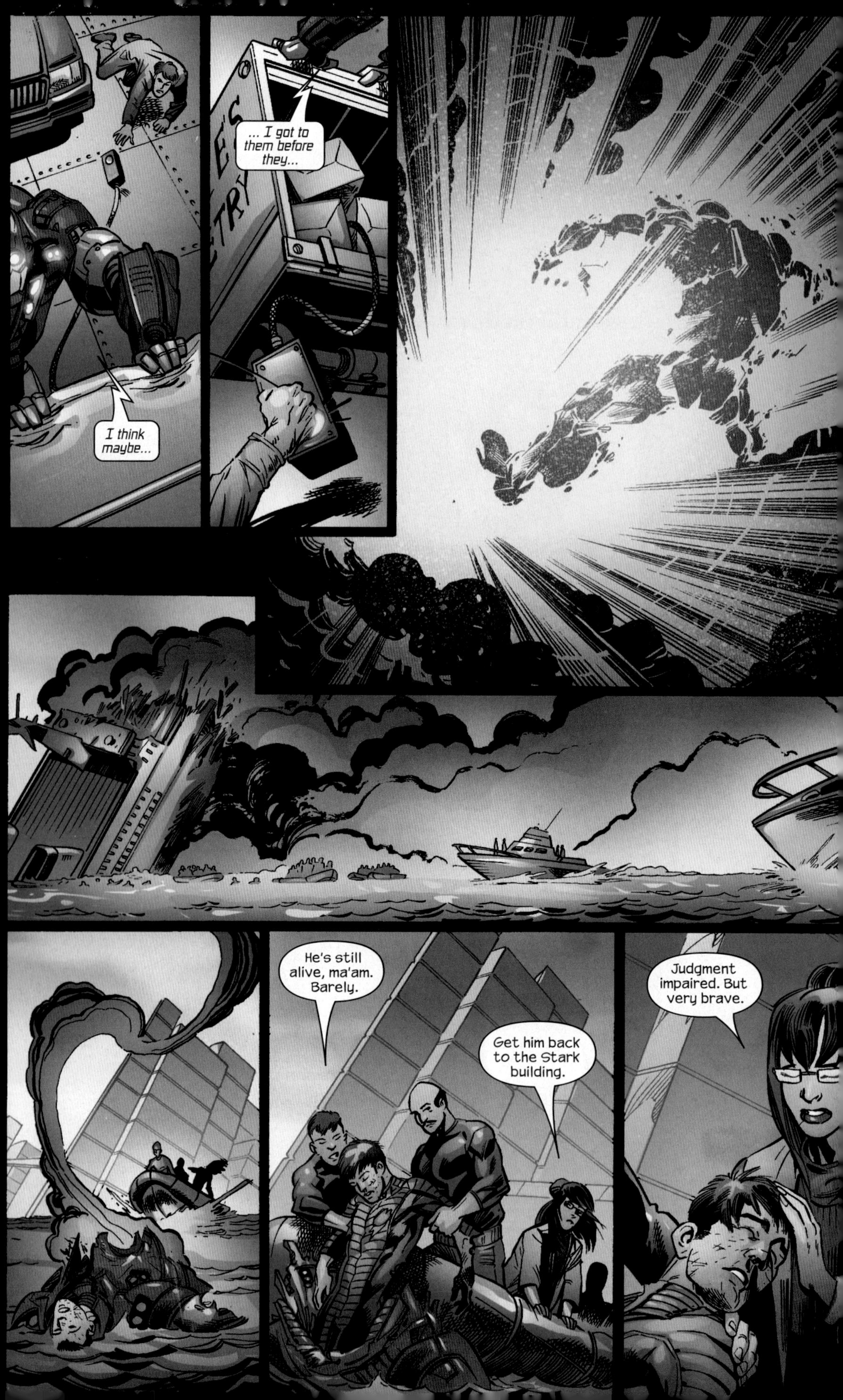
I think maybe...
... I got to them before they...
He's still alive, ma'am. Barely.
Get him back to the Stark building.
Judgment impaired. But very brave.

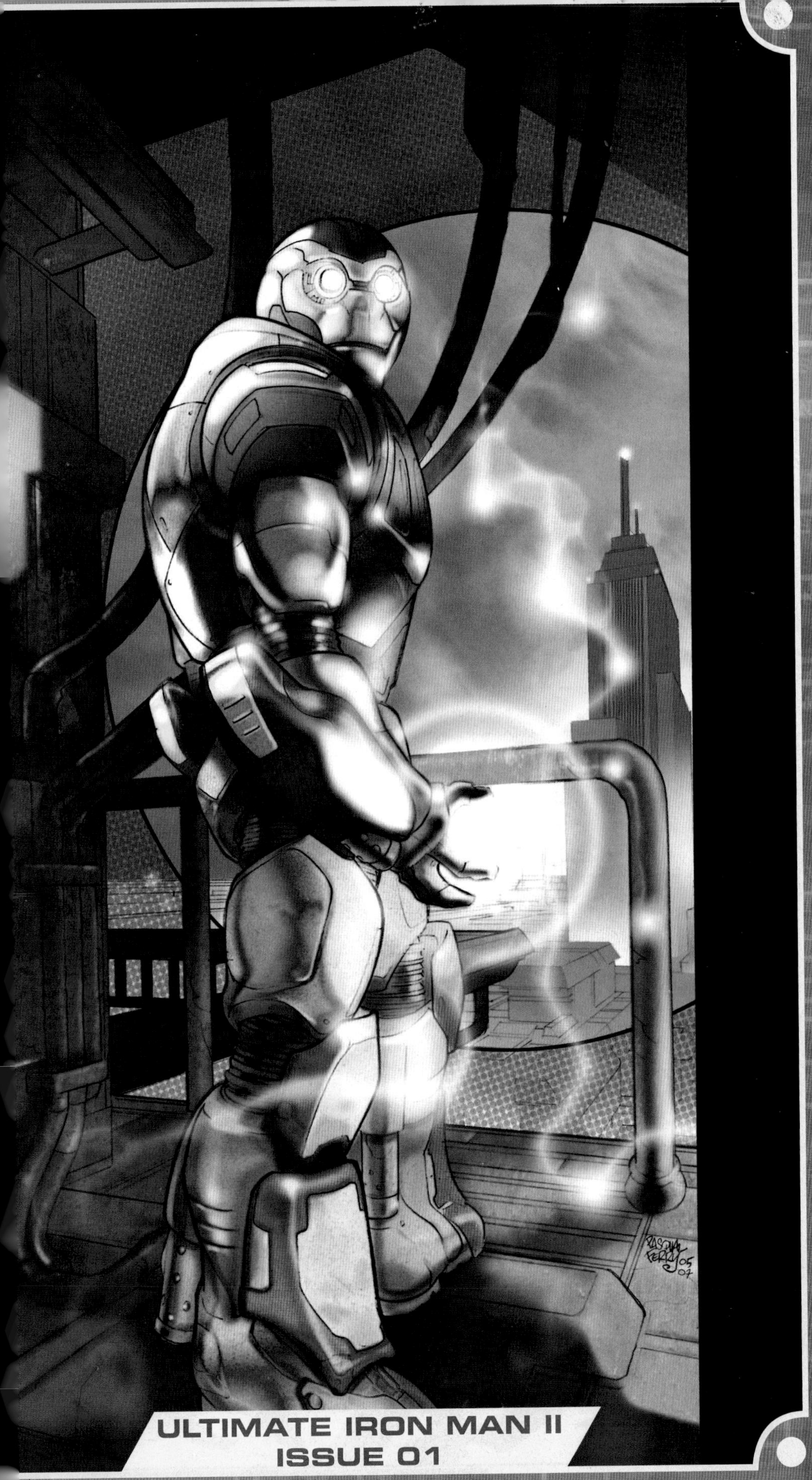
ULTIMATE IRON MAN II
ISSUE 01

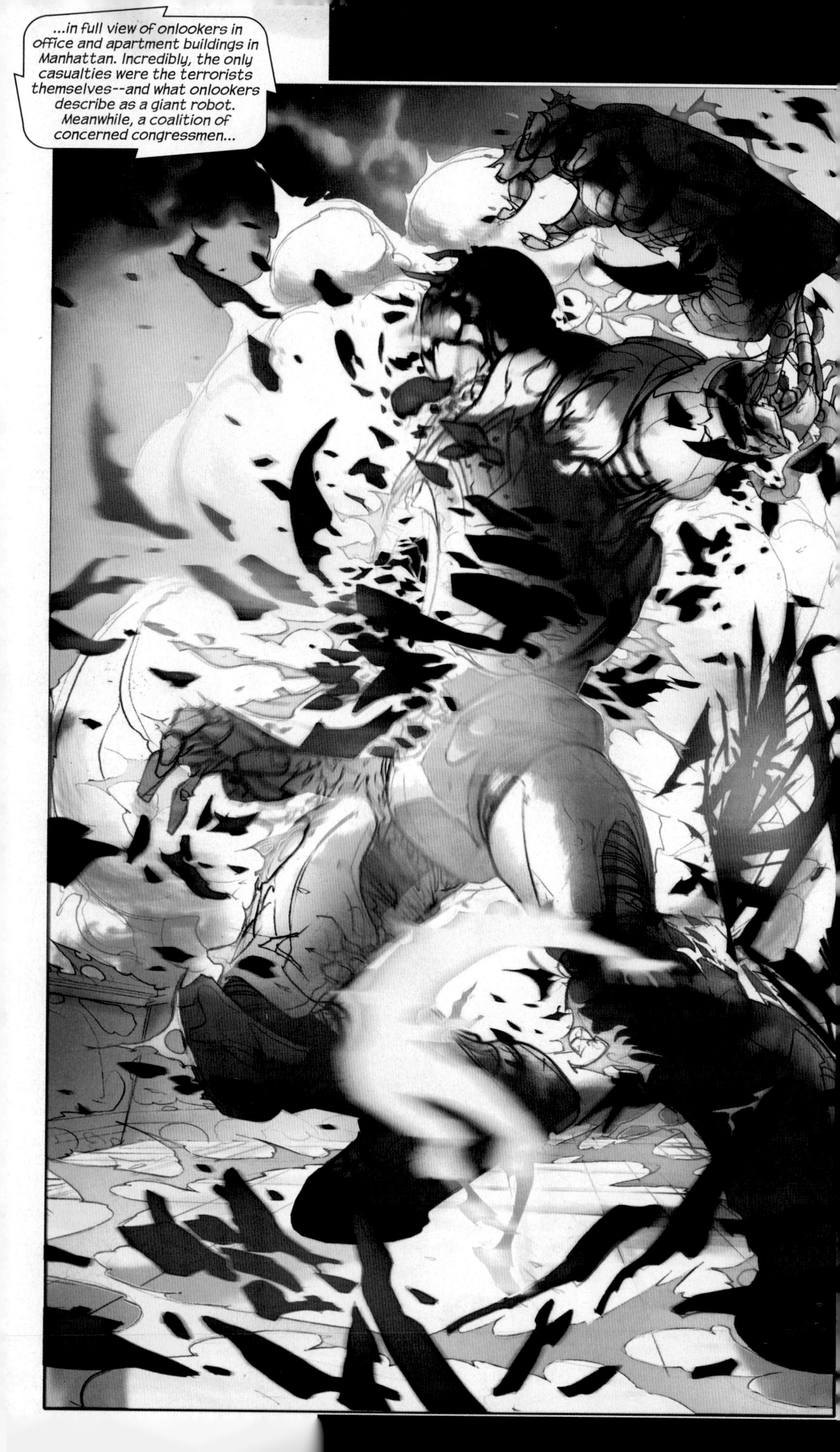
...in full view of onlookers in office and apartment buildings in Manhattan. Incredibly, the only casualties were the terrorists themselves--and what onlookers describe as a giant robot. Meanwhile, a coalition of concerned congressmen...

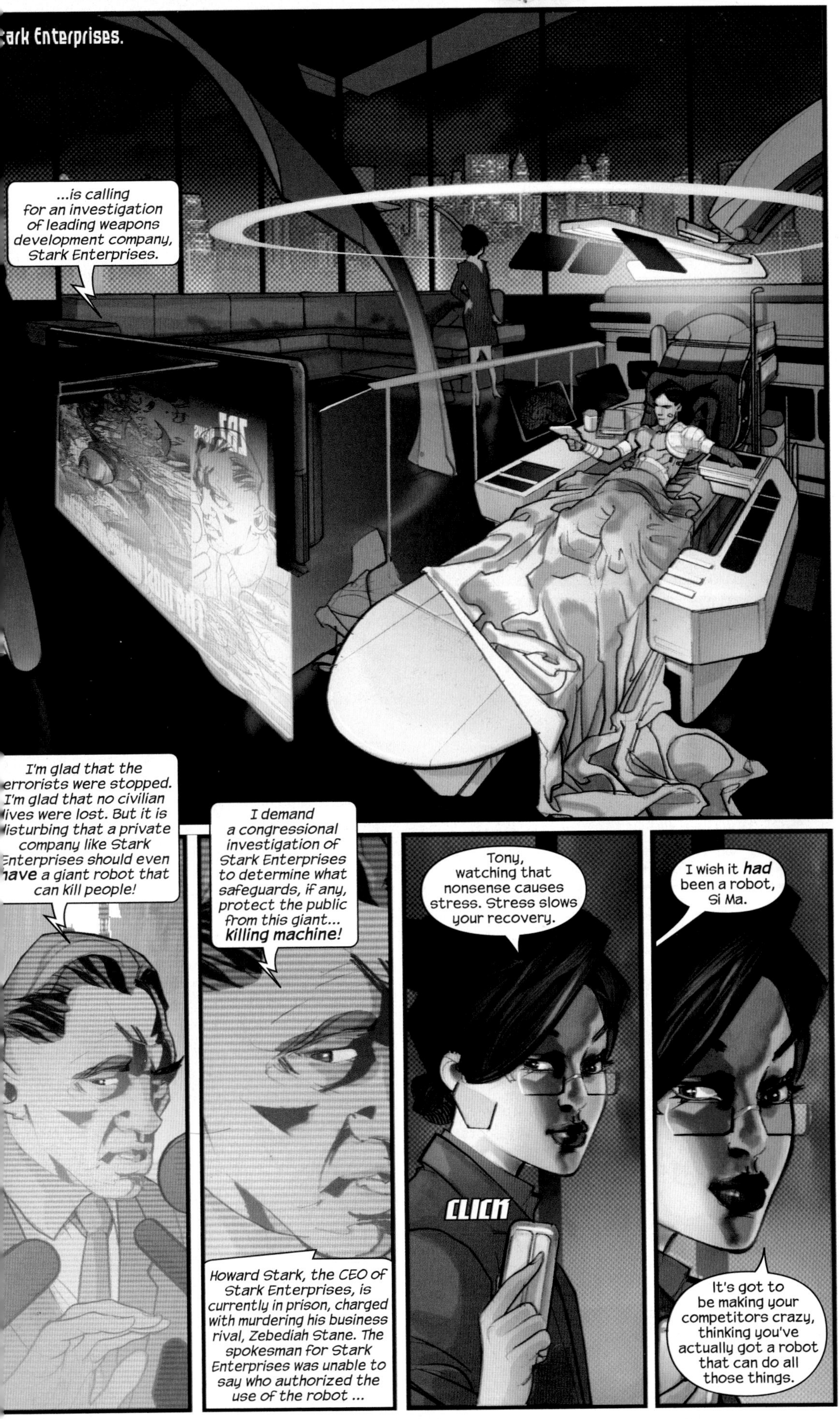
Stark Enterprises.
...is calling for an investigation of leading weapons development company, Stark Enterprises.
I'm glad that the terrorists were stopped. I'm glad that no civilian lives were lost. But it is disturbing that a private company like Stark Enterprises should even *have* a giant robot that can kill people!
I demand a congressional investigation of Stark Enterprises to determine what safeguards, if any, protect the public from this giant... *killing machine!*
Howard Stark, the CEO of Stark Enterprises, is currently in prison, charged with murdering his business rival, Zebediah Stane. The spokesman for Stark Enterprises was unable to say who authorized the use of the robot ...
Tony, watching that nonsense causes stress. Stress slows your recovery.
CLICK
I wish it *had* been a robot, Si Ma.
It's got to be making your competitors crazy, thinking you've actually got a robot that can do all those things.

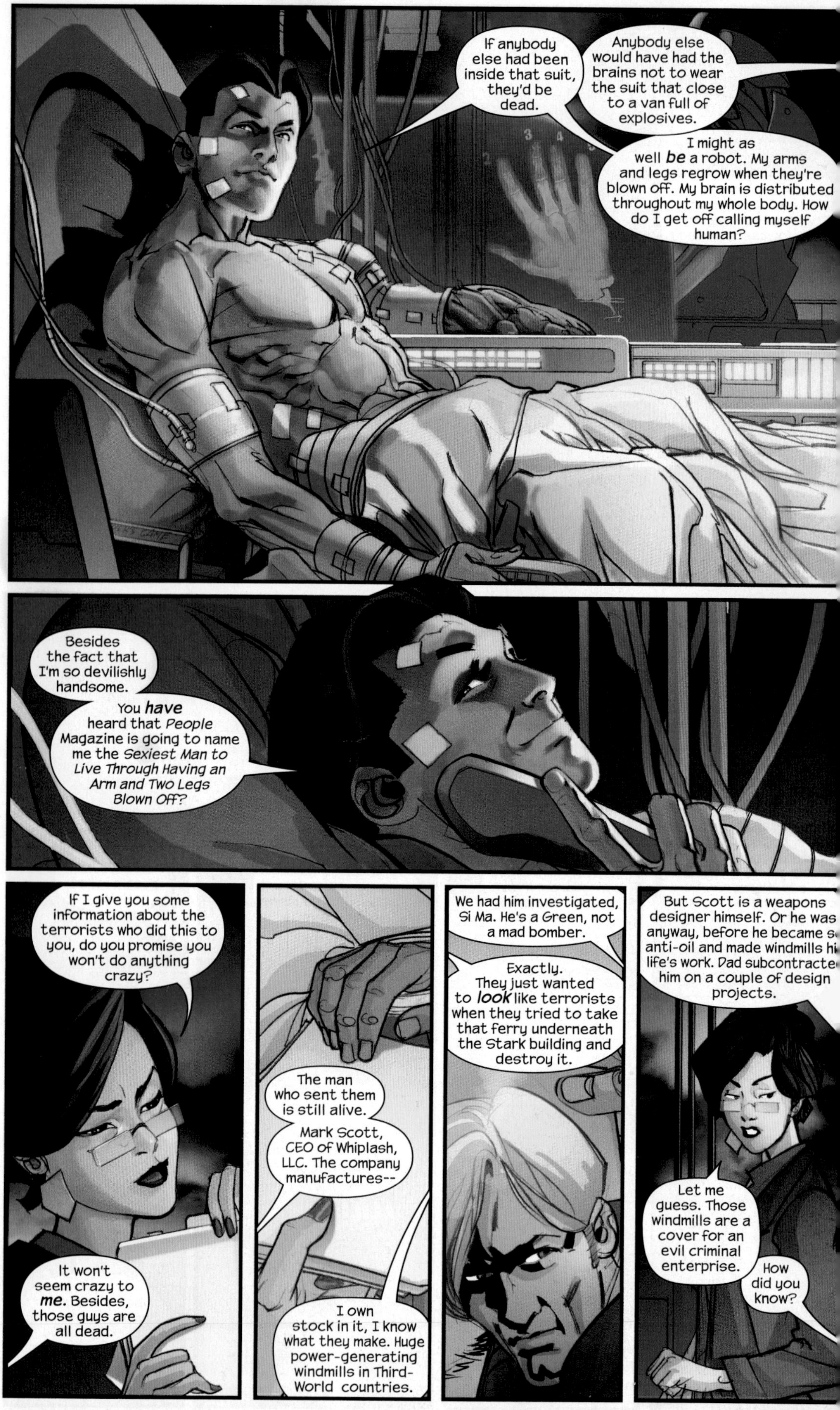
If anybody else had been inside that suit, they'd be dead.
Anybody else would have had the brains not to wear the suit that close to a van full of explosives.
I might as well *be* a robot. My arms and legs regrow when they're blown off. My brain is distributed throughout my whole body. How do I get off calling myself human?
Besides the fact that I'm so devilishly handsome.
You **have** heard that *People Magazine* is going to name me the *Sexiest Man to Live Through Having an Arm and Two Legs Blown Off?*
If I give you some information about the terrorists who did this to you, do you promise you won't do anything crazy?
It won't seem crazy to **me.** Besides, those guys are all dead.
The man who sent them is still alive.
Mark Scott, CEO of Whiplash, LLC. The company manufactures--
I own stock in it, I know what they make. Huge power-generating windmills in Third-World countries.
We had him investigated, Si Ma. He's a Green, not a mad bomber.
Exactly. They just wanted to **look** like terrorists when they tried to take that ferry underneath the Stark building and destroy it.
But Scott is a weapons designer himself. Or he was anyway, before he became s anti-oil and made windmills hi life's work. Dad subcontracte him on a couple of design projects.
Let me guess. Those windmills are a cover for an evil criminal enterprise.
How did you know?

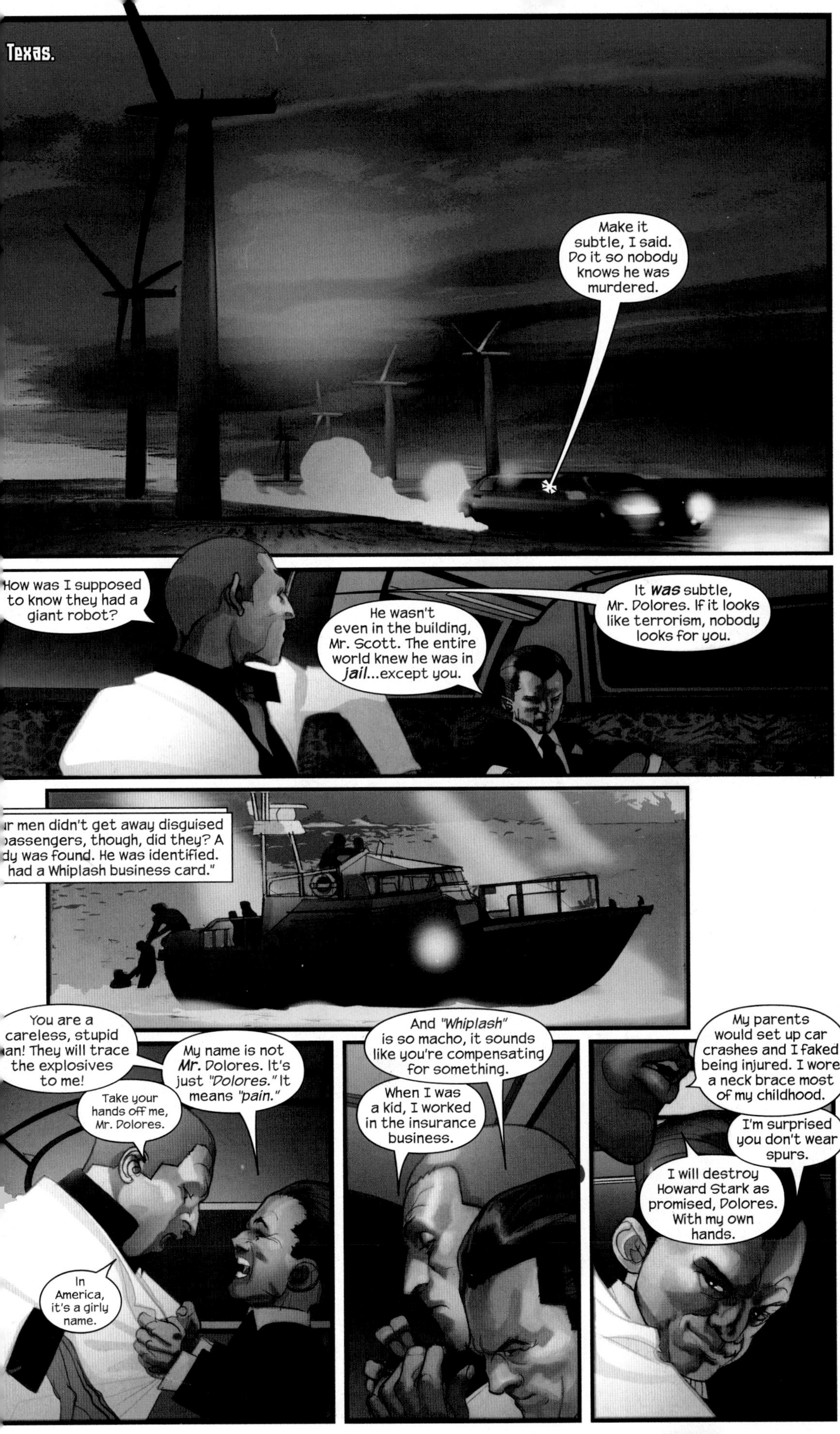

Texas.
Make it subtle, I said. Do it so nobody knows he was murdered.
How was I supposed to know they had a giant robot?
It **was** subtle, Mr. Dolores. If it looks like terrorism, nobody looks for you.
He wasn't even in the building, Mr. Scott. The entire world knew he was in ***jail***...except you.
r men didn't get away disguised
assengers, though, did they? A
dy was found. He was identified.
had a Whiplash business card."
You are a careless, stupid an! They will trace the explosives to me!
My name is not ***Mr.*** Dolores. It's just *"Dolores."* It means *"pain."*
Take your hands off me, Mr. Dolores.
In America, it's a girly name.
And *"Whiplash"* is so macho, it sounds like you're compensating for something.
When I was a kid, I worked in the insurance business.
My parents would set up car crashes and I faked being injured. I wore a neck brace most of my childhood.
I'm surprised you don't wear spurs.
I will destroy Howard Stark as promised, Dolores. With my own hands.

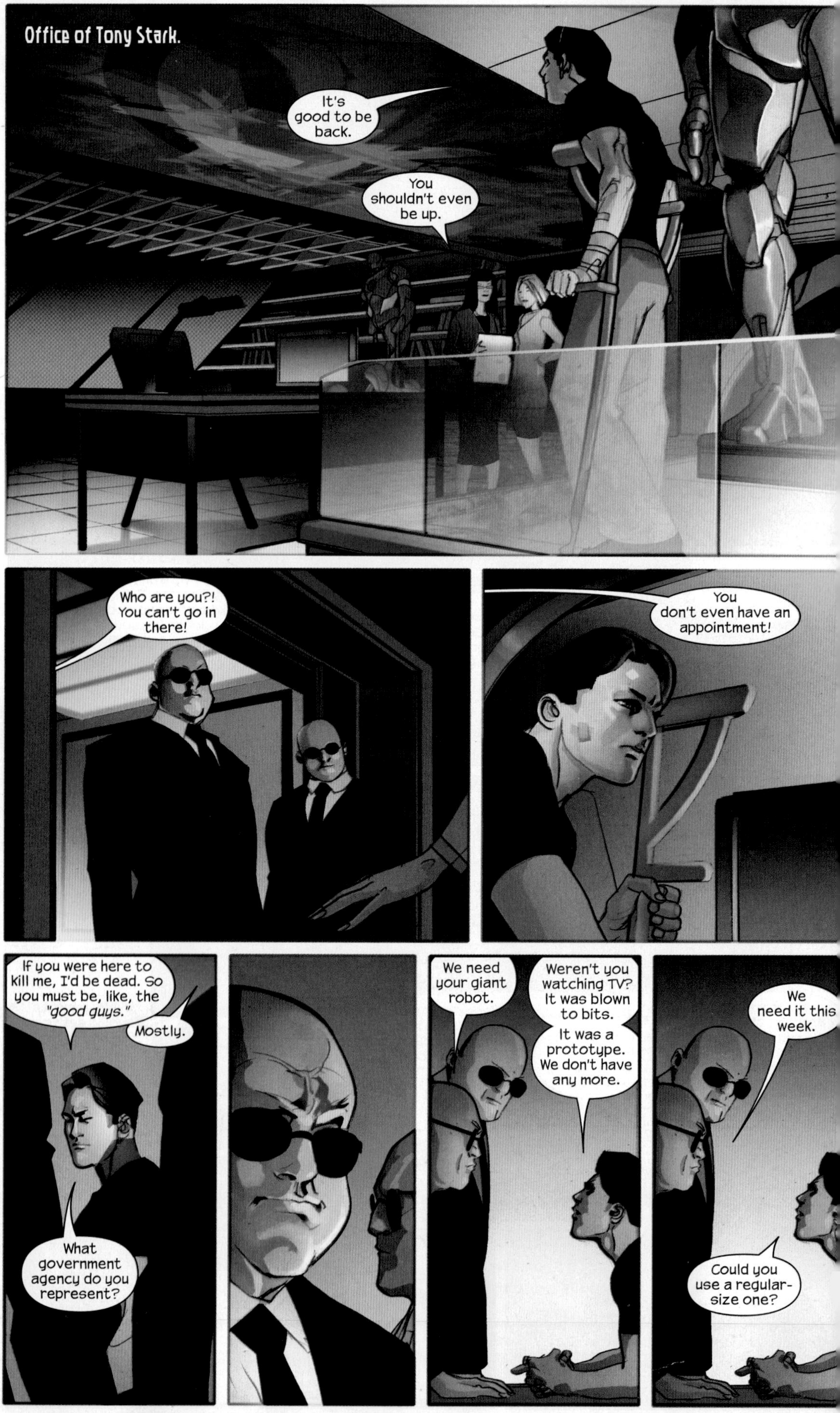
Office of Tony Stark.
It's good to be back.
You shouldn't even be up.
Who are you?! You can't go in there!
You don't even have an appointment!
If you were here to kill me, I'd be dead. So you must be, like, the "good guys."
Mostly.
What government agency do you represent?
We need your giant robot.
Weren't you watching TV? It was blown to bits.
It was a prototype. We don't have any more.
We need it this week.
Could you use a regular-size one?

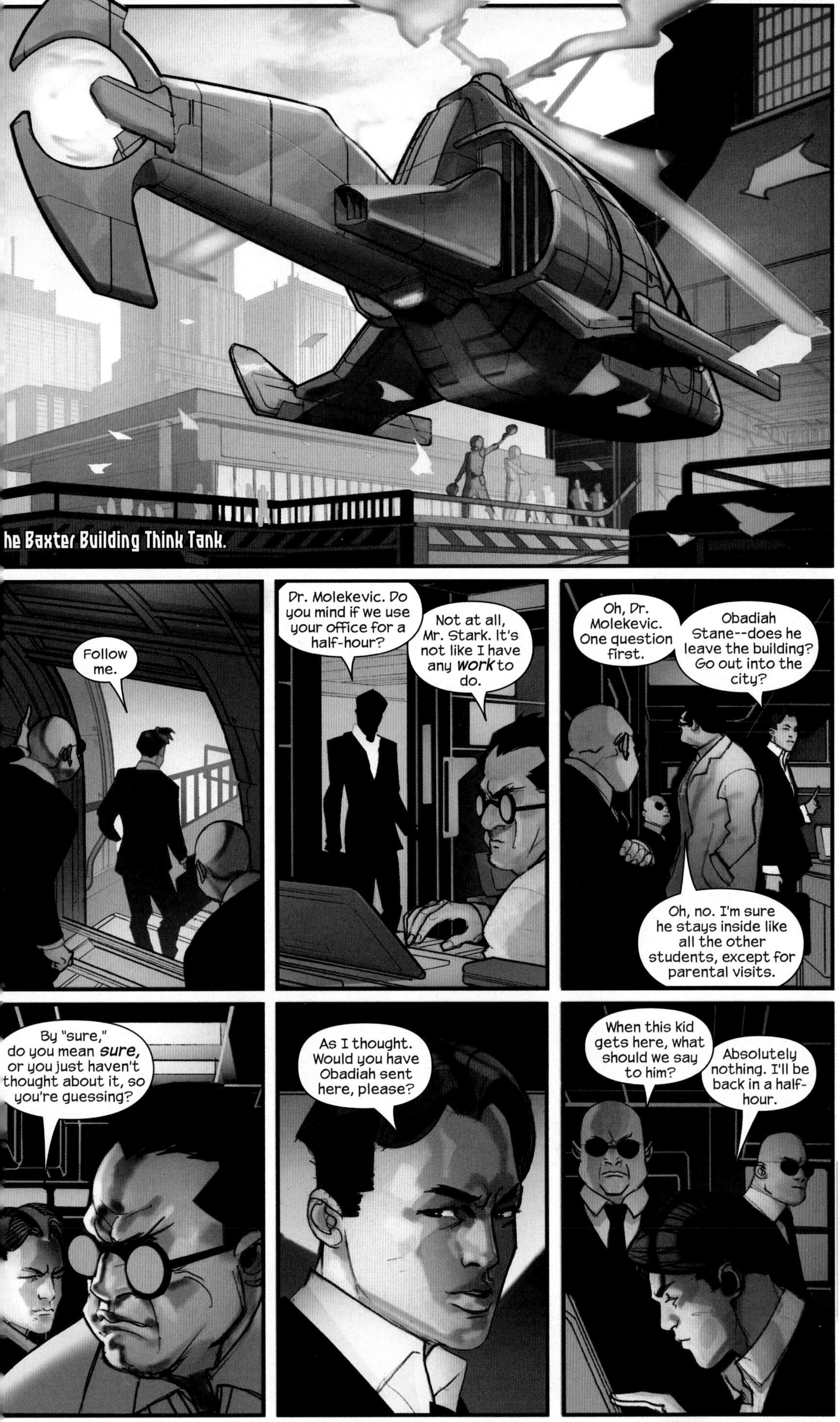
he Baxter Building Think Tank.
Follow me.
Dr. Molekevic. Do you mind if we use your office for a half-hour?
Not at all, Mr. Stark. It's not like I have any *work* to do.
Oh, Dr. Molekevic. One question first.
Obadiah Stane--does he leave the building? Go out into the city?
Oh, no. I'm sure he stays inside like all the other students, except for parental visits.
By "sure," do you mean *sure,* or you just haven't thought about it, so you're guessing?
As I thought. Would you have Obadiah sent here, please?
When this kid gets here, what should we say to him?
Absolutely nothing. I'll be back in a half-hour.

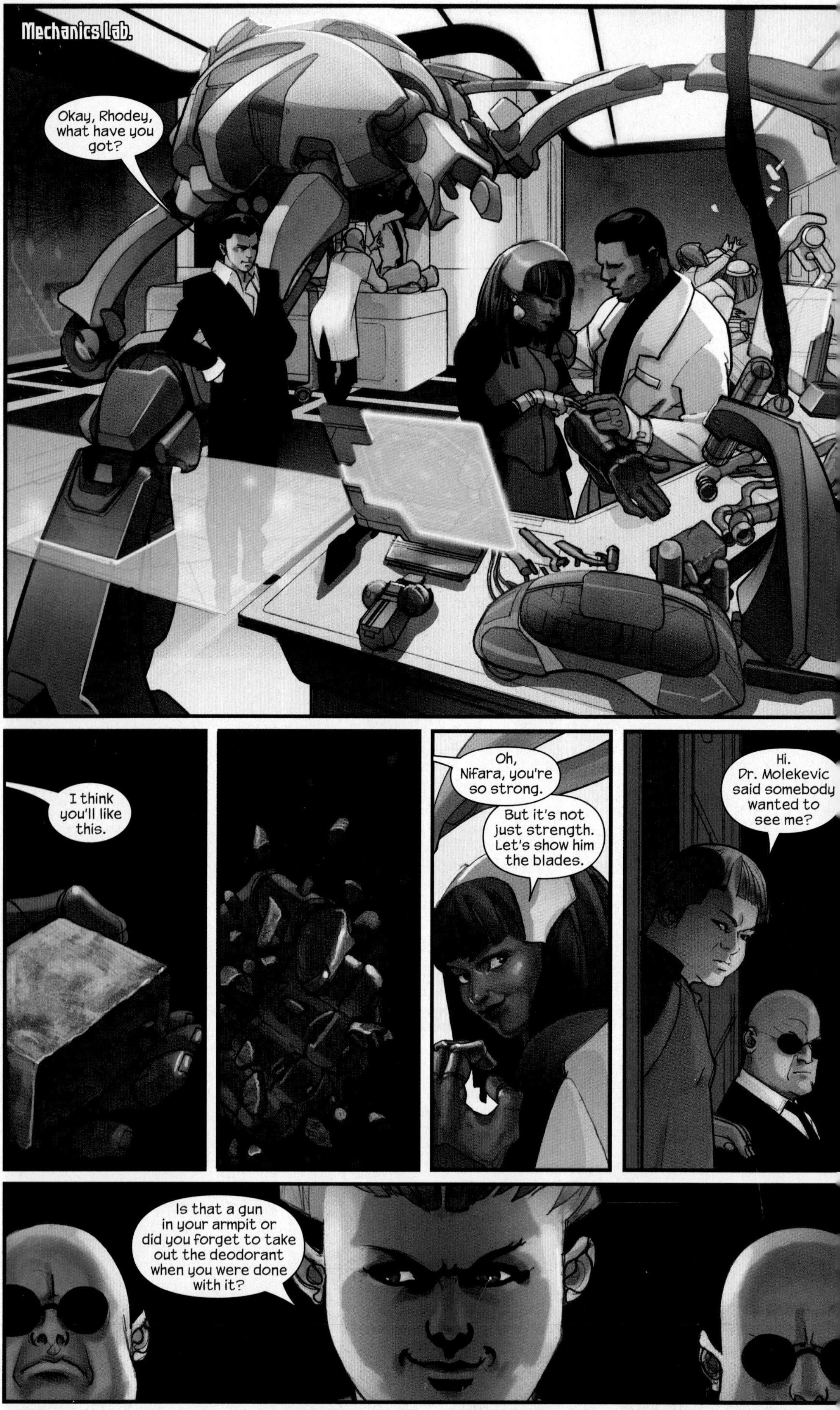
Mechanics Lab.
Okay, Rhodey, what have you got?
I think you'll like this.
Oh, Nifara, you're so strong.
But it's not just strength. Let's show him the blades.
Hi. Dr. Molekevic said somebody wanted to see me?
Is that a gun in your armpit or did you forget to take out the deodorant when you were done with it?

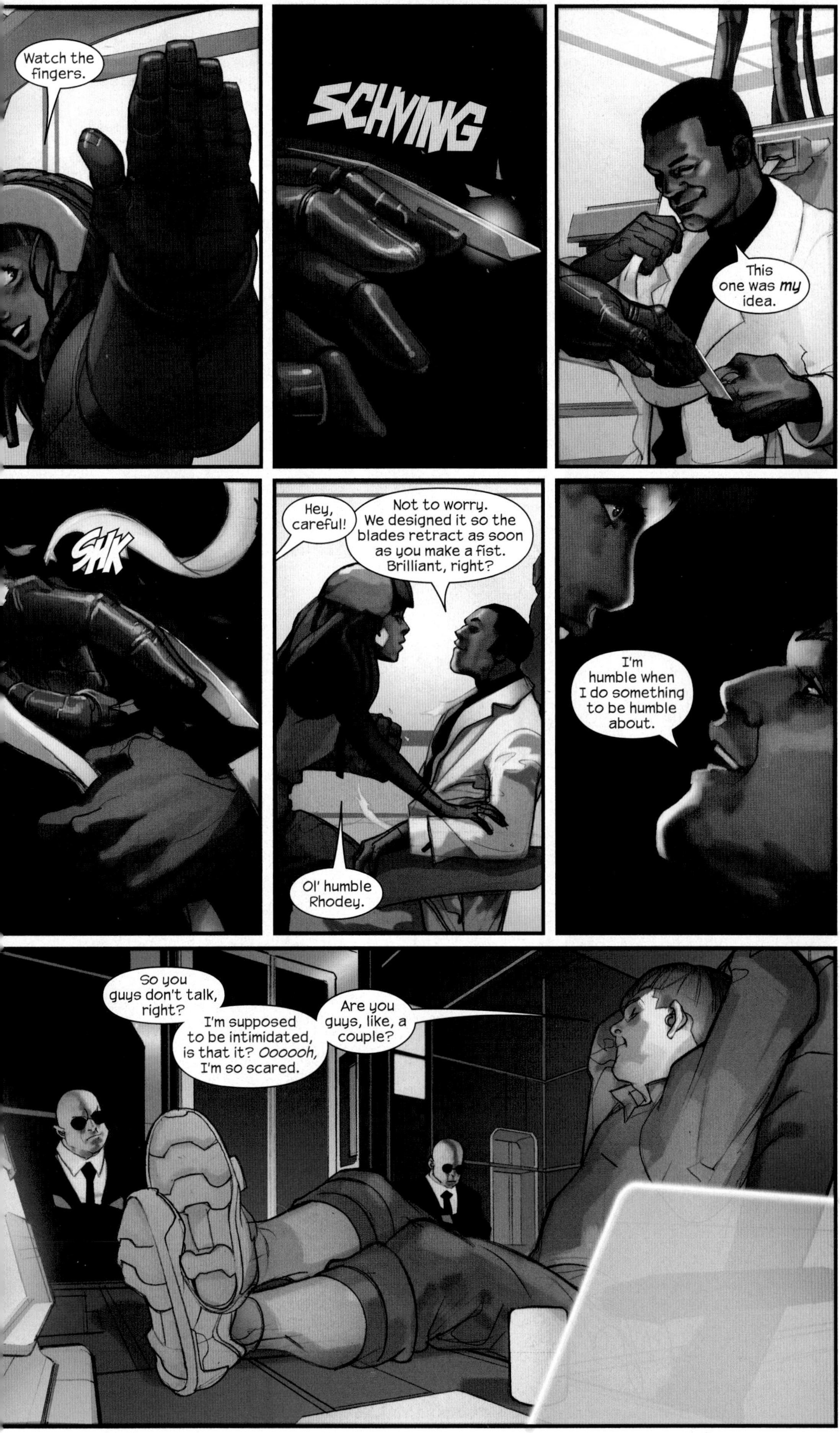

Watch the fingers.
SCHVING
This one was *my* idea.
SHK
Hey, careful!
Not to worry. We designed it so the blades retract as soon as you make a fist. Brilliant, right?
Ol' humble Rhodey.
I'm humble when I do something to be humble about.
So you guys don't talk, right?
I'm supposed to be intimidated, is that it? *Oooooh*, I'm so scared.
Are you guys, like, a couple?

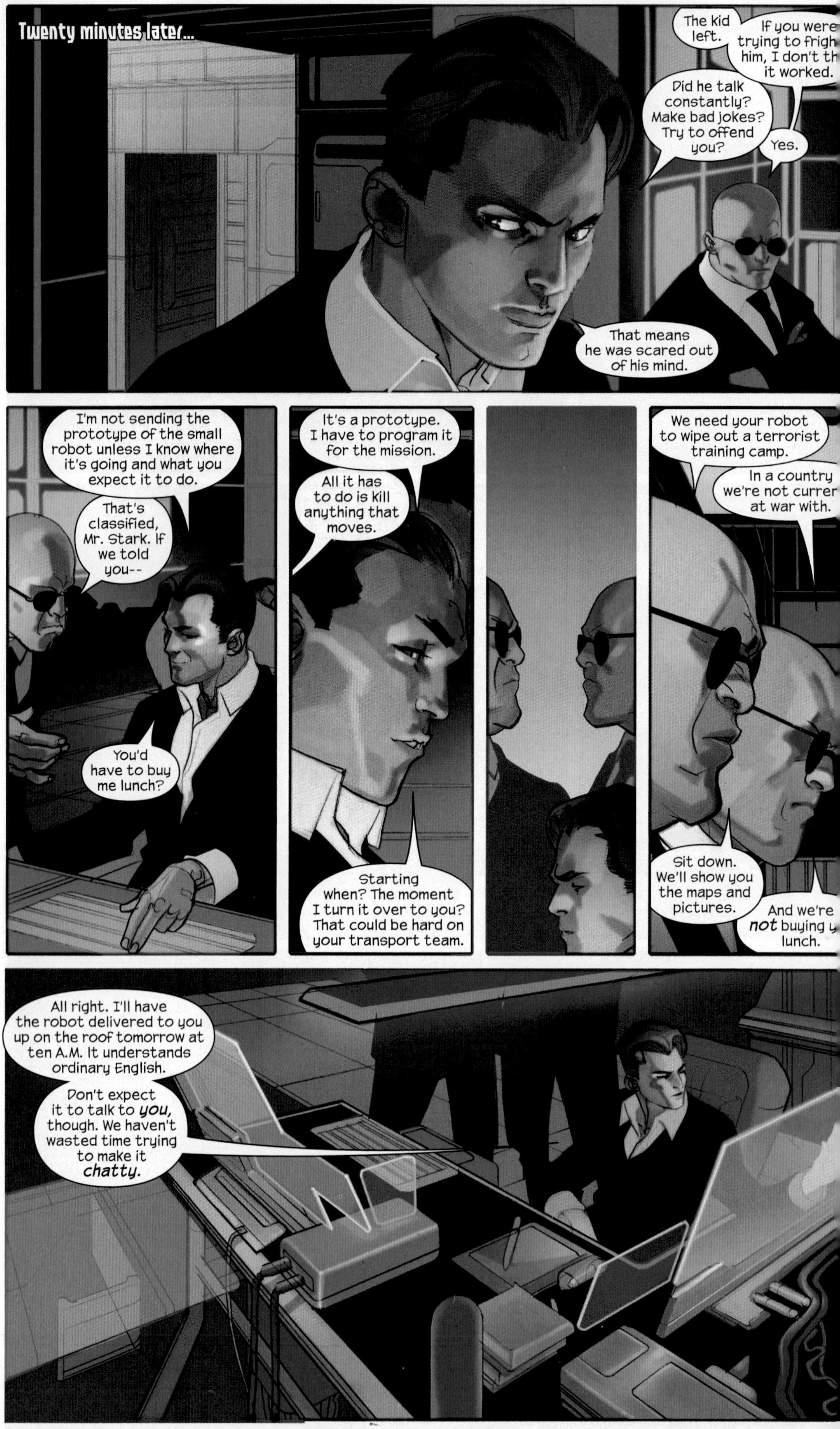
Twenty minutes later...
The kid left.
If you were trying to frigh him, I don't th it worked.
Did he talk constantly? Make bad jokes? Try to offend you?
Yes.
That means he was scared out of his mind.
I'm not sending the prototype of the small robot unless I know where it's going and what you expect it to do.
That's classified, Mr. Stark. If we told you--
You'd have to buy me lunch?
It's a prototype. I have to program it for the mission.
All it has to do is kill anything that moves.
Starting when? The moment I turn it over to you? That could be hard on your transport team.
We need your robot to wipe out a terrorist training camp.
In a country we're not curren at war with.
Sit down. We'll show you the maps and pictures.
And we're *not* buying y lunch.
All right. I'll have the robot delivered to you up on the roof tomorrow at ten A.M. It understands ordinary English.
Don't expect it to talk to *you,* though. We haven't wasted time trying to make it *chatty.*

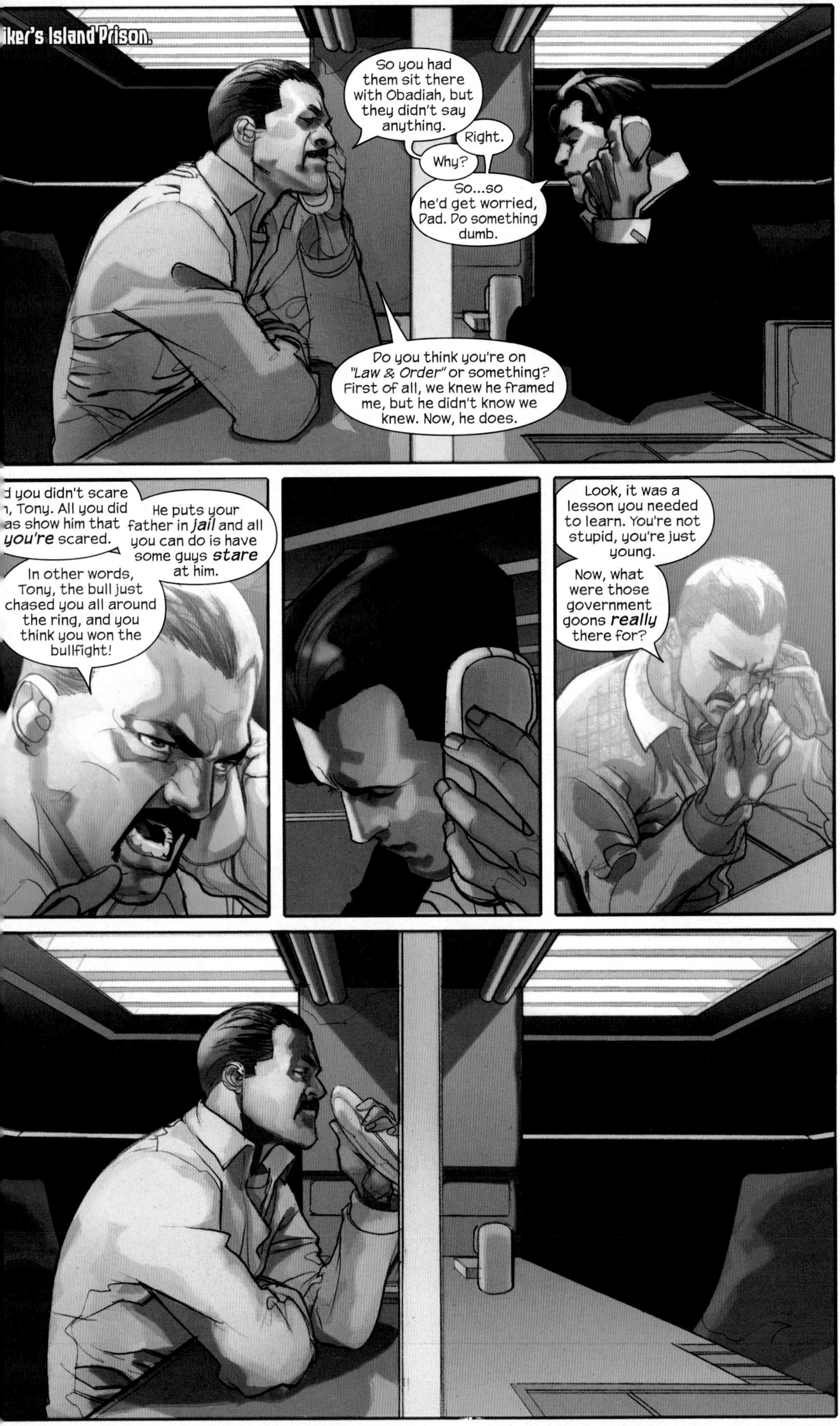

iker's Island Prison.
So you had them sit there with Obadiah, but they didn't say anything.
Right.
Why?
So...so he'd get worried, Dad. Do something dumb.
Do you think you're on "Law & Order" or something? First of all, we knew he framed me, but he didn't know we knew. Now, he does.
d you didn't scare n, Tony. All you did as show him that *you're* scared.
He puts your father in *jail* and all you can do is have some guys *stare* at him.
In other words, Tony, the bull just chased you all around the ring, and you think you won the bullfight!
Look, it was a lesson you needed to learn. You're not stupid, you're just young.
Now, what were those government goons *really* there for?

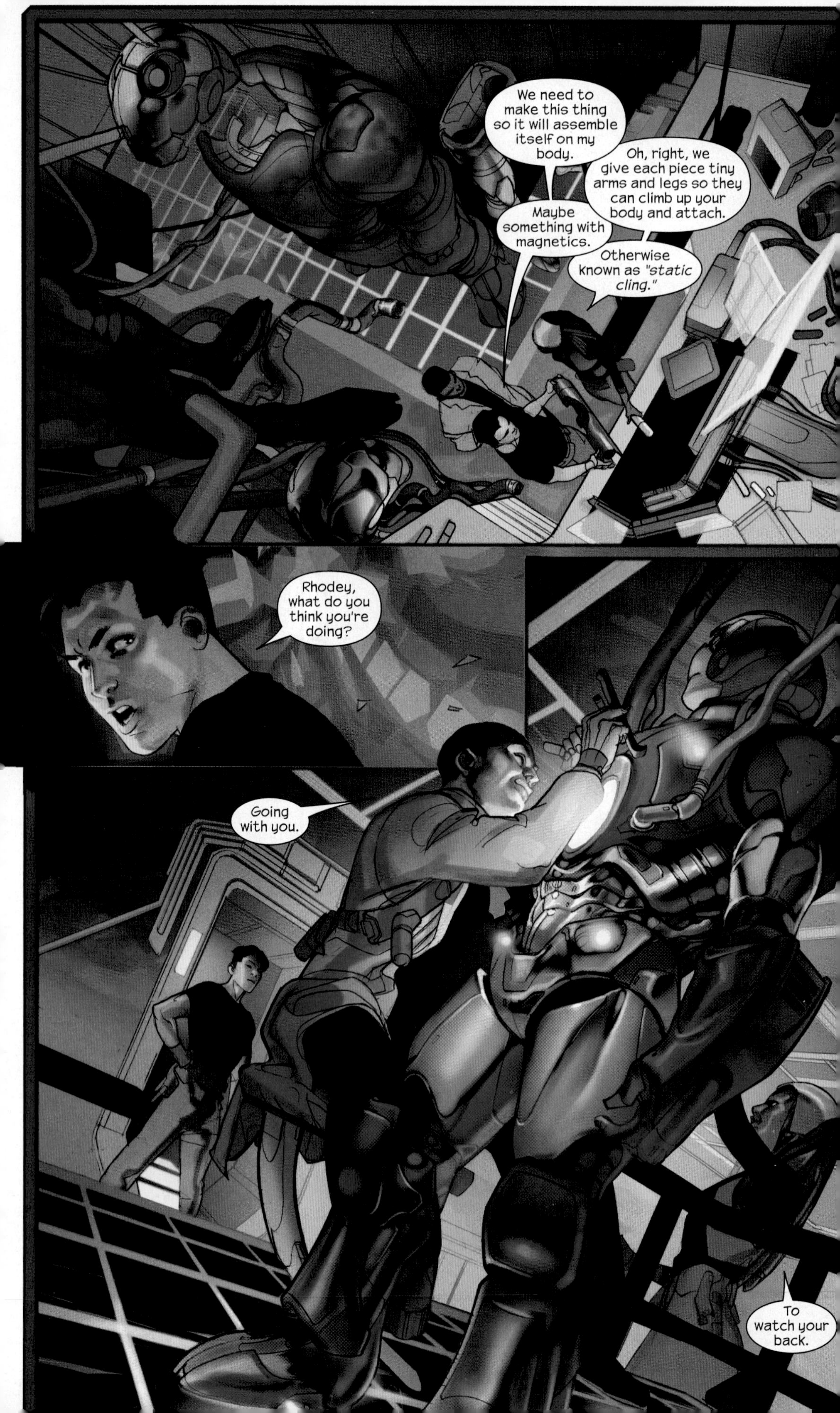
We need to make this thing so it will assemble itself on my body.
Maybe something with magnetics.
Oh, right, we give each piece tiny arms and legs so they can climb up your body and attach.
Otherwise known as "static cling."
Rhodey, what do you think you're doing?
Going with you.
To watch your back.

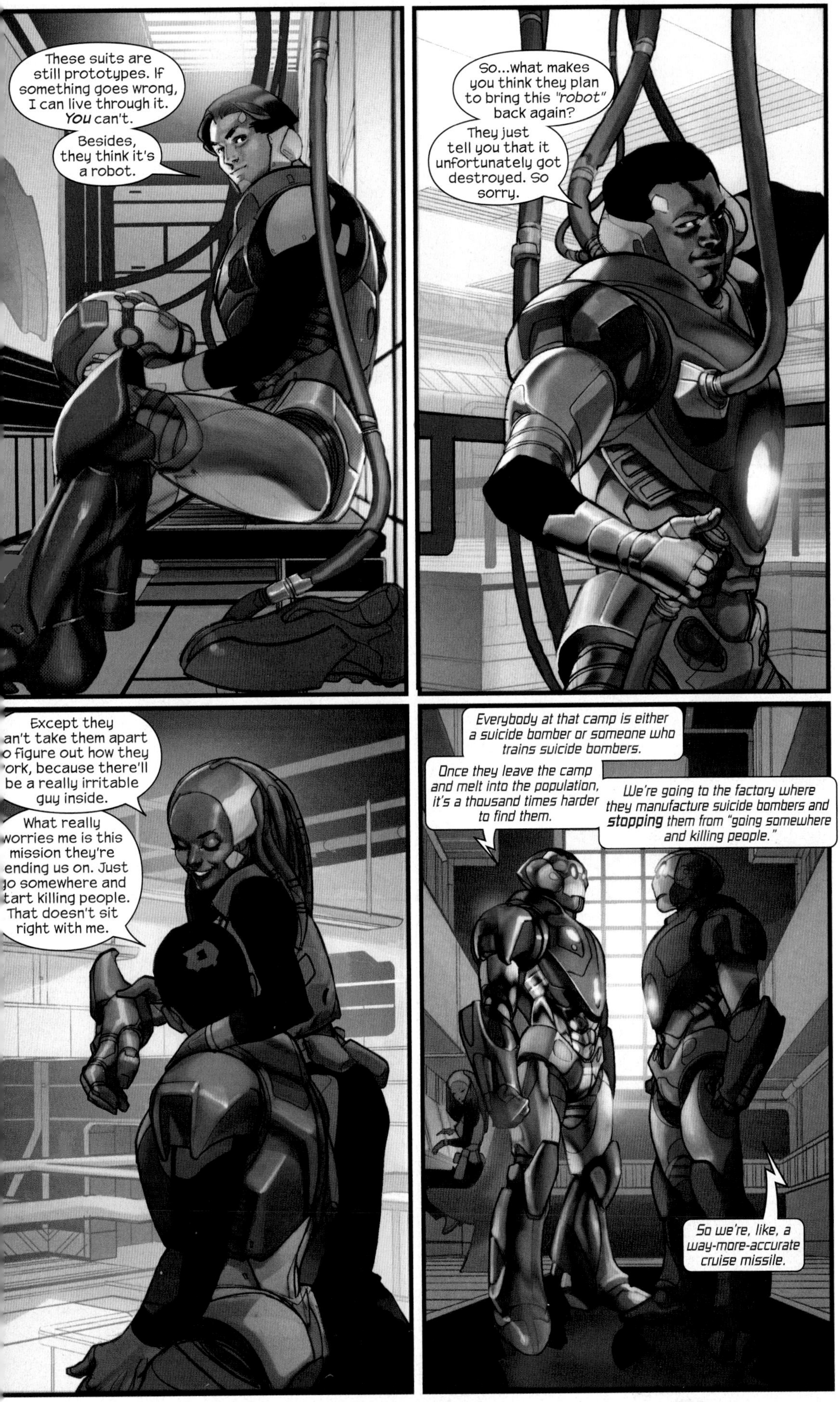
These suits are still prototypes. If something goes wrong, I can live through it. YOU can't.
Besides, they think it's a robot.
So...what makes you think they plan to bring this "robot" back again?
They just tell you that it unfortunately got destroyed. So sorry.
Except they an't take them apart o figure out how they ork, because there'll be a really irritable guy inside.
What really worries me is this mission they're ending us on. Just go somewhere and tart killing people. That doesn't sit right with me.
Everybody at that camp is either a suicide bomber or someone who trains suicide bombers.
Once they leave the camp and melt into the population, it's a thousand times harder to find them.
We're going to the factory where they manufacture suicide bombers and stopping them from "going somewhere and killing people."
So we're, like, a way-more-accurate cruise missile.

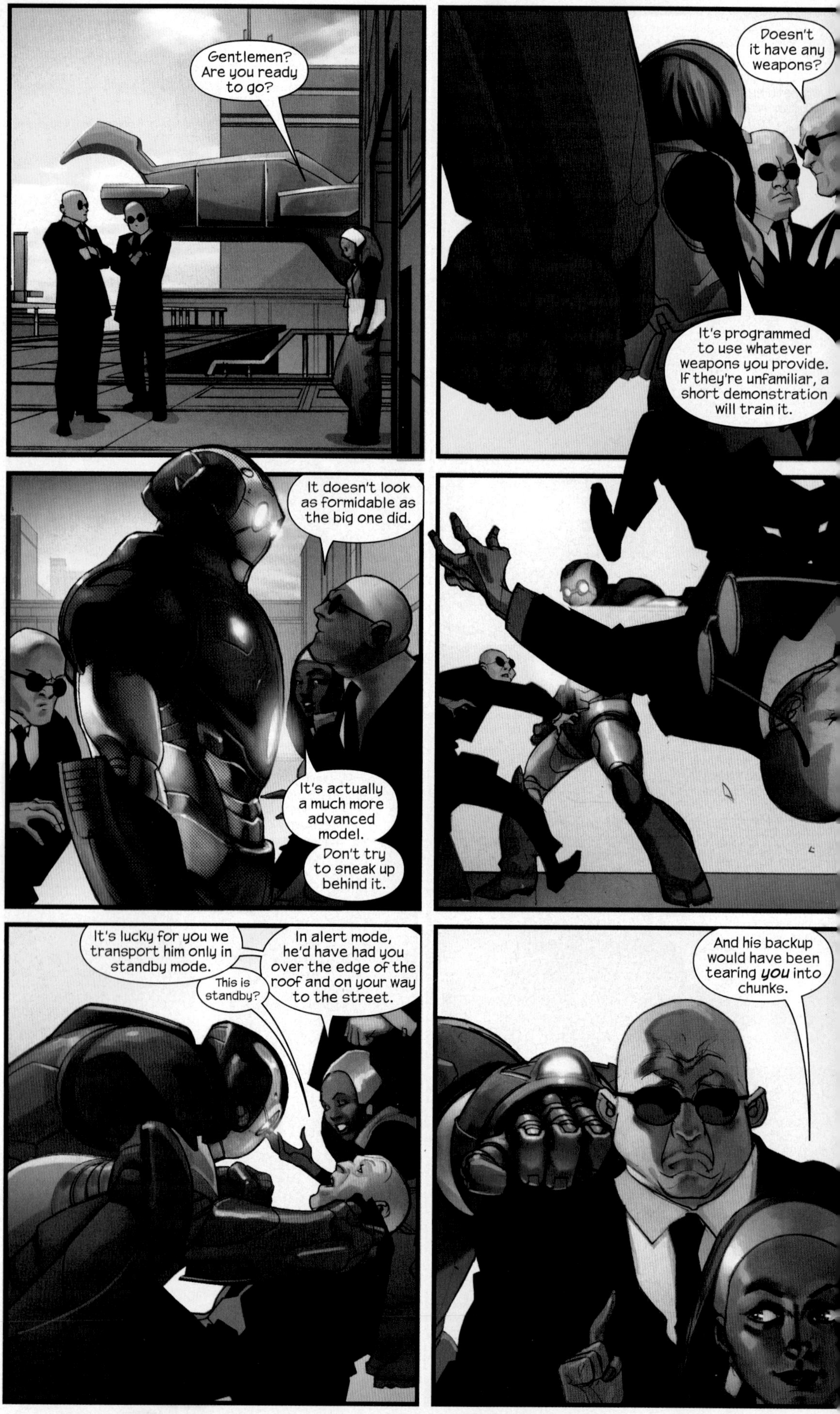
Gentlemen? Are you ready to go?
Doesn't it have any weapons?
It's programmed to use whatever weapons you provide. If they're unfamiliar, a short demonstration will train it.
It doesn't look as formidable as the big one did.
It's actually a much more advanced model.
Don't try to sneak up behind it.
It's lucky for you we transport him only in standby mode.
This is standby?
In alert mode, he'd have had you over the edge of the roof and on your way to the street.
And his backup would have been tearing *you* into chunks.

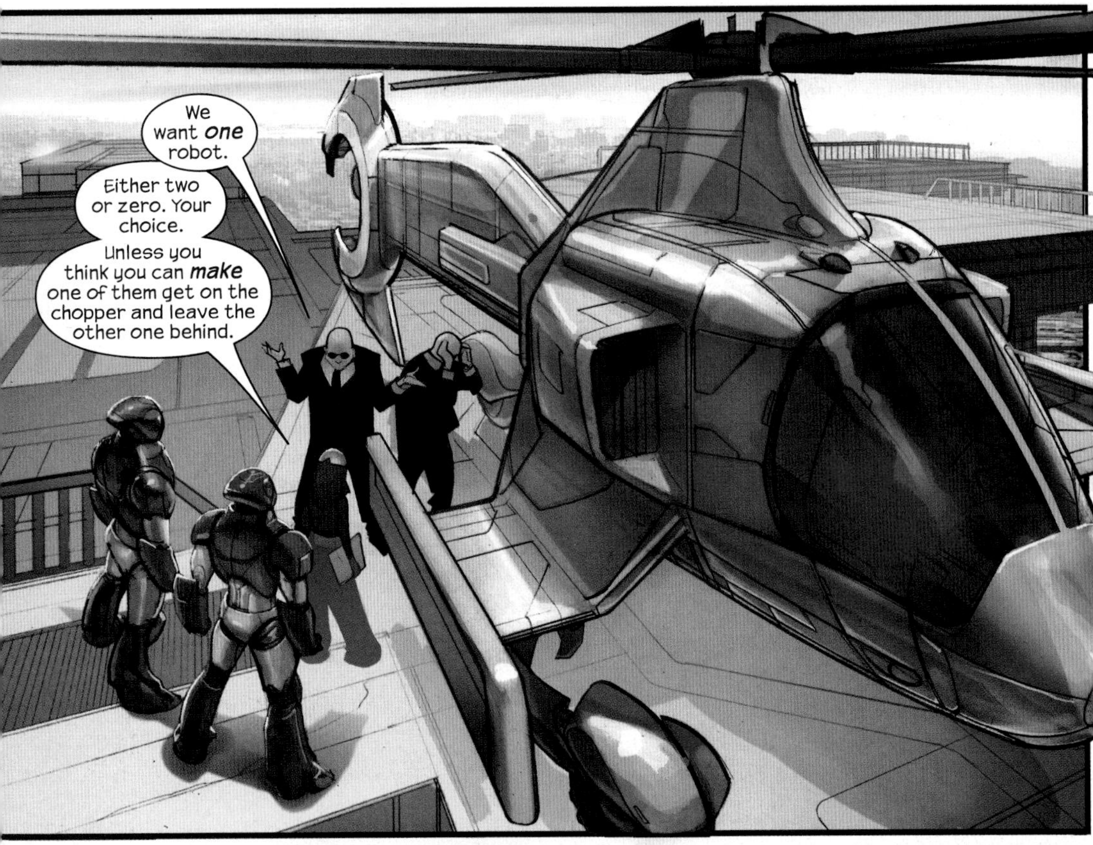
We want *one* robot.
Either two or zero. Your choice.
Unless you think you can *make* one of them get on the chopper and leave the other one behind.

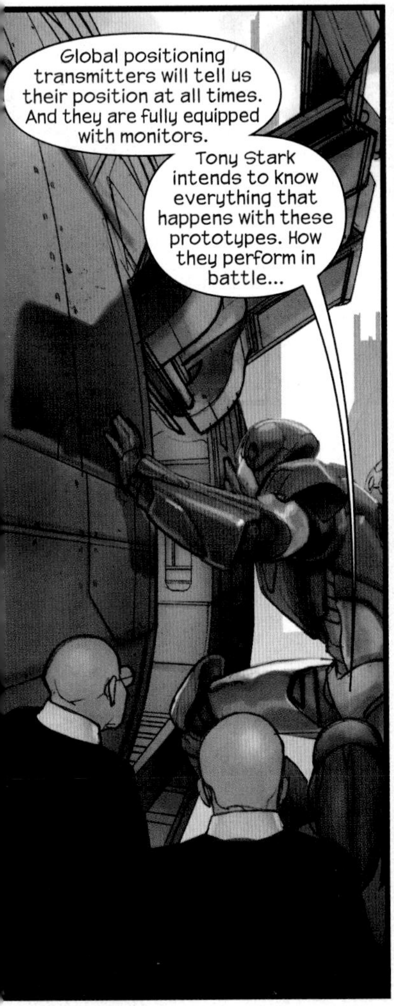
Global positioning transmitters will tell us their position at all times. And they are fully equipped with monitors.
Tony Stark intends to know everything that happens with these prototypes. How they perform in battle...

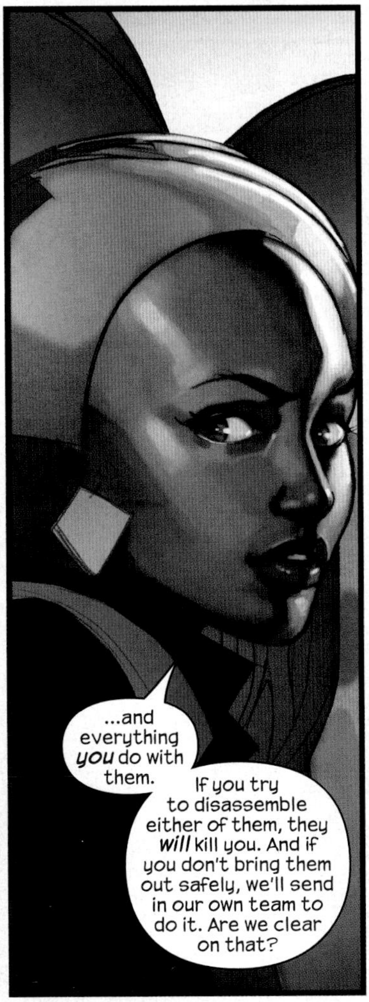
...and everything *you* do with them.
If you try to disassemble either of them, they *will* kill you. And if you don't bring them out safely, we'll send in our own team to do it. Are we clear on that?

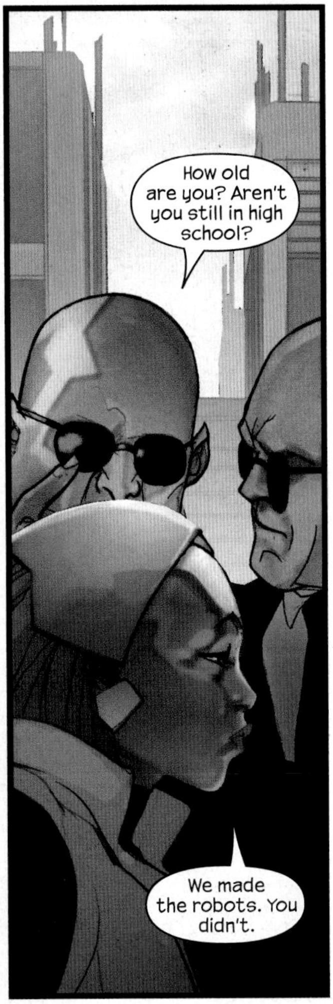
How old are you? Aren't you still in high school?
We made the robots. You didn't.

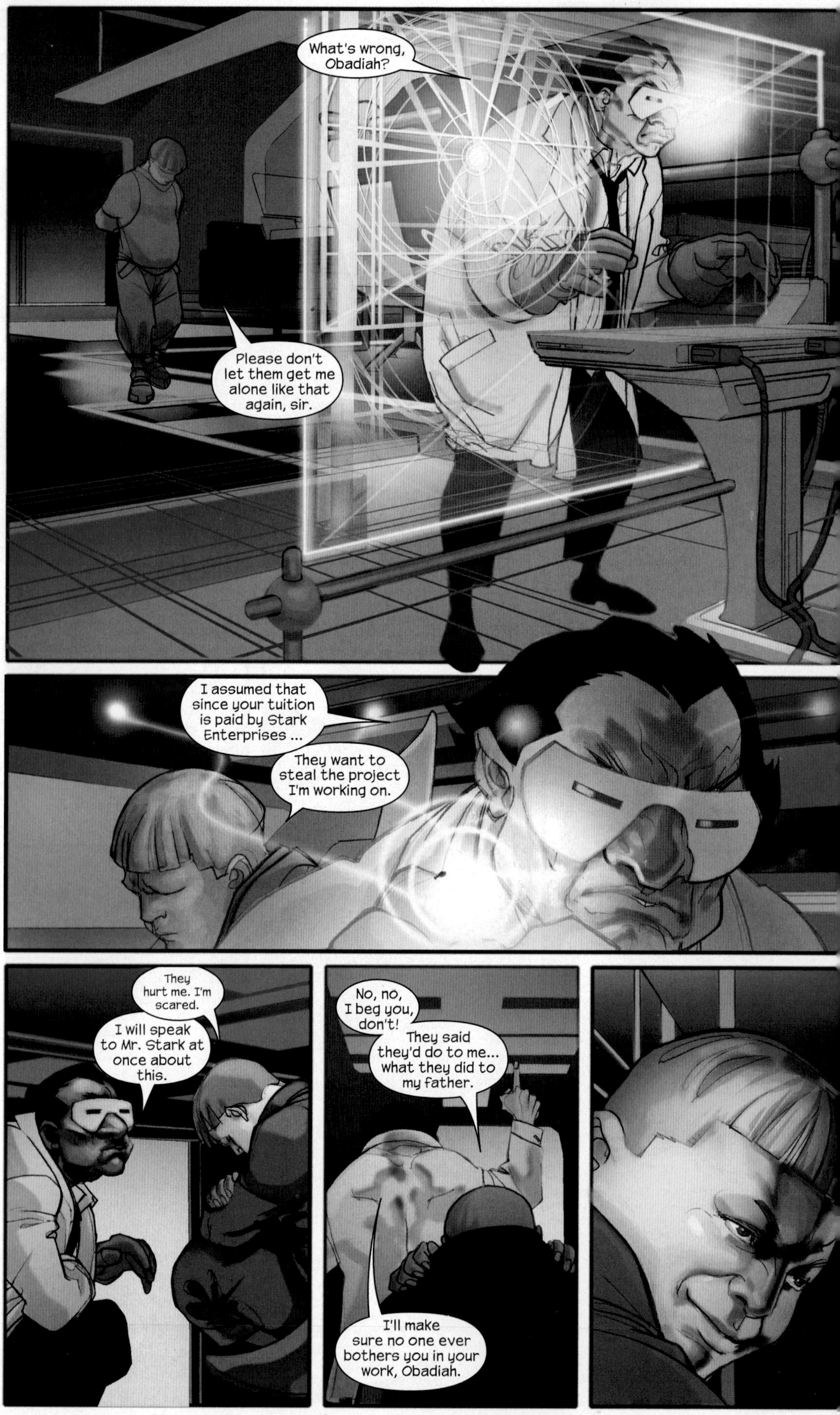
What's wrong, Obadiah?
Please don't let them get me alone like that again, sir.
I assumed that since your tuition is paid by Stark Enterprises ...
They want to steal the project I'm working on.
They hurt me. I'm scared.
I will speak to Mr. Stark at once about this.
No, no, I beg you, don't!
They said they'd do to me... what they did to my father.
I'll make sure no one ever bothers you in your work, Obadiah.

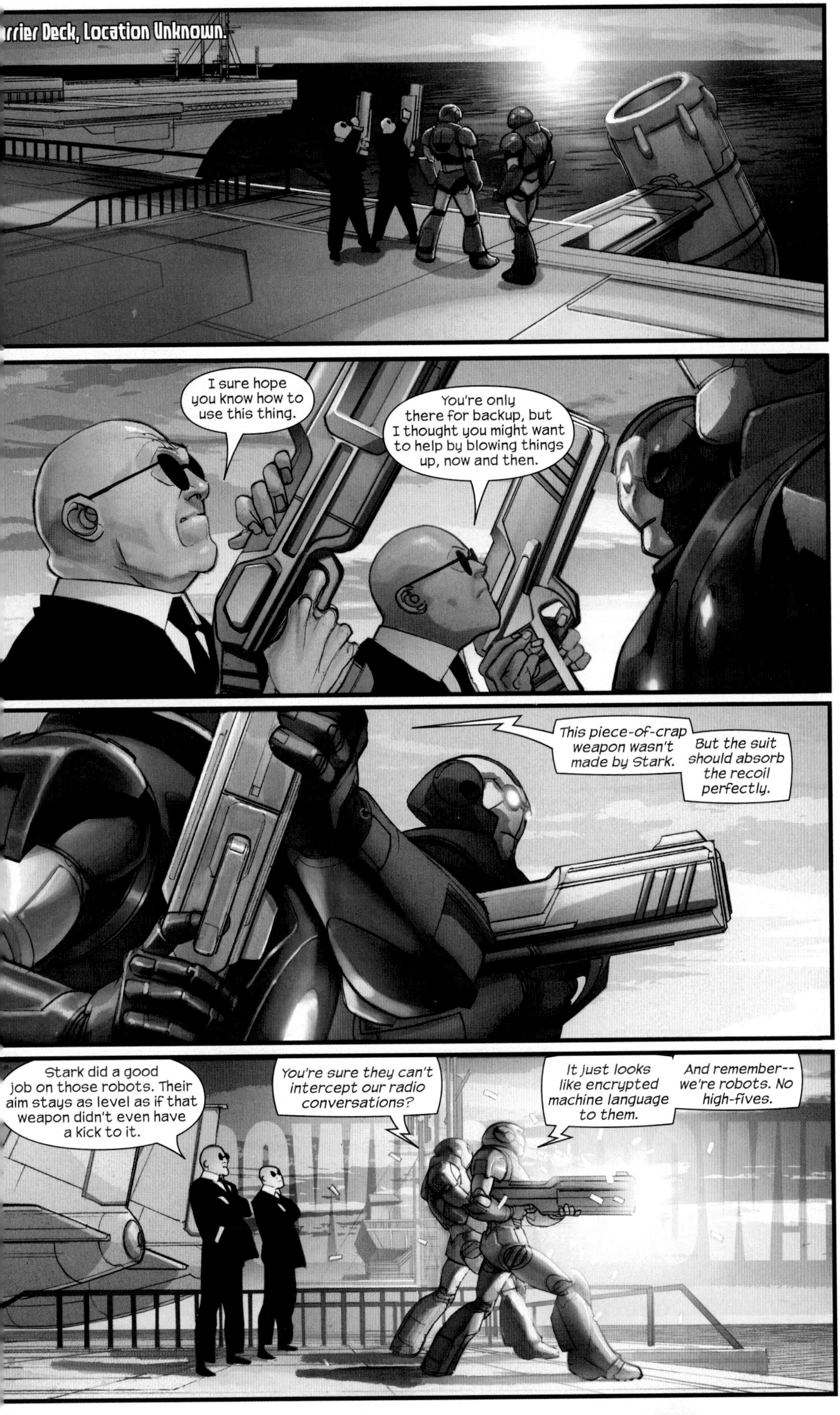

rrier Deck, Location Unknown.
I sure hope you know how to use this thing.
You're only there for backup, but I thought you might want to help by blowing things up, now and then.
This piece-of-crap weapon wasn't made by Stark.
But the suit should absorb the recoil perfectly.
Stark did a good job on those robots. Their aim stays as level as if that weapon didn't even have a kick to it.
You're sure they can't intercept our radio conversations?
It just looks like encrypted machine language to them.
And remember-- we're robots. No high-fives.

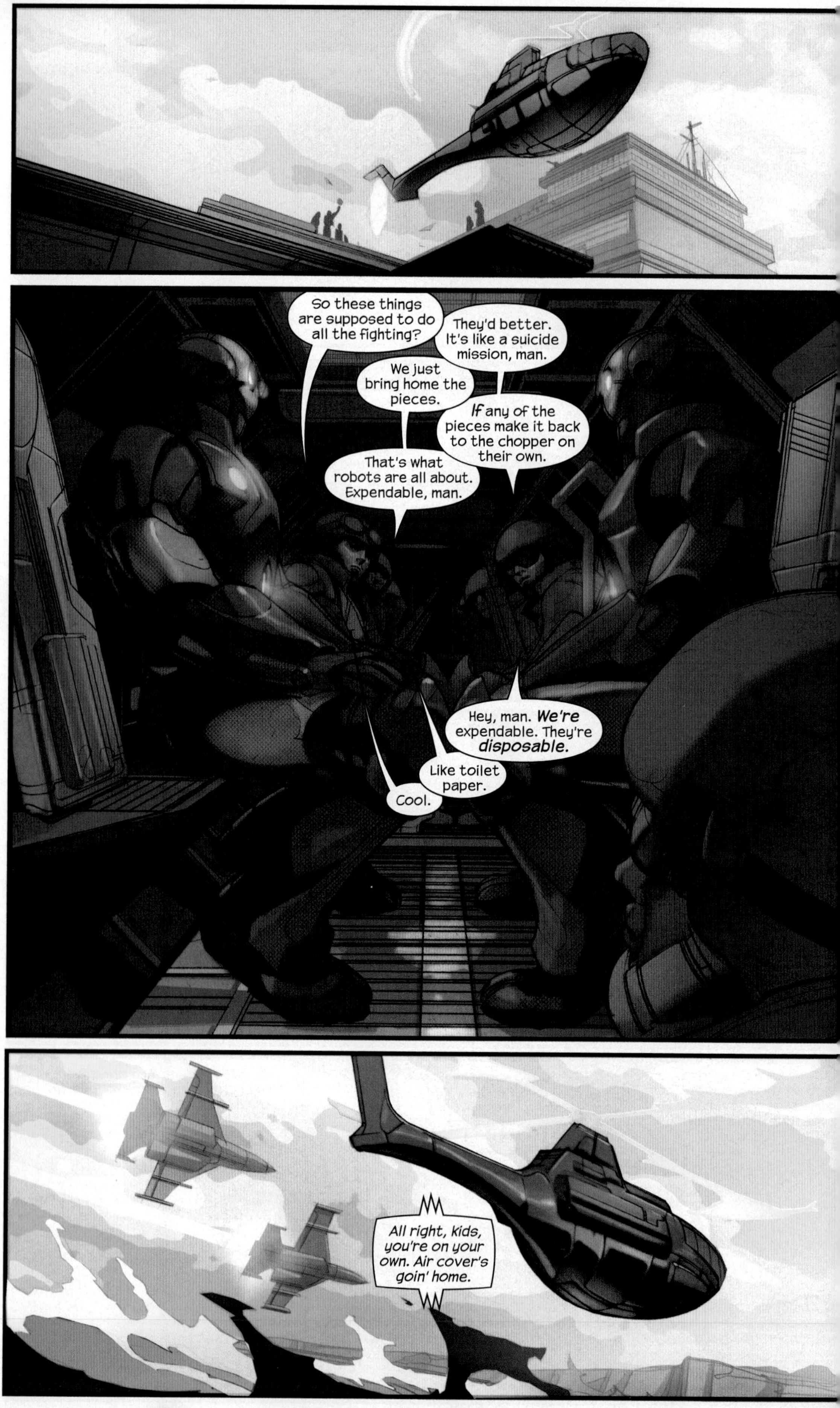
So these things are supposed to do all the fighting?
They'd better. It's like a suicide mission, man.
We just bring home the pieces.
If any of the pieces make it back to the chopper on their own.
That's what robots are all about. Expendable, man.
Hey, man. ***We're*** expendable. They're ***disposable.***
Like toilet paper.
Cool.
All right, kids, you're on your own. Air cover's goin' home.

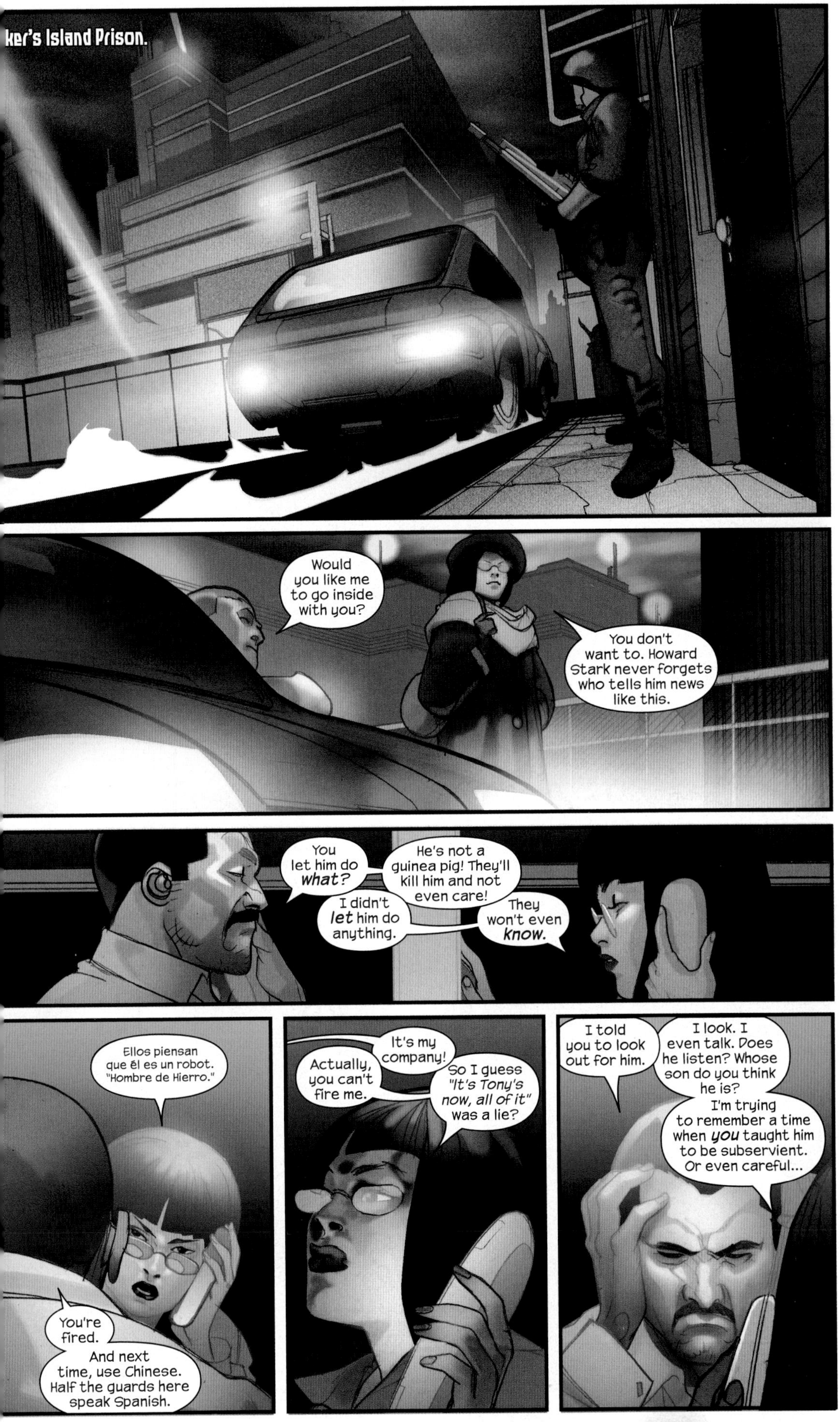
ker's Island Prison.
Would you like me to go inside with you?
You don't want to. Howard Stark never forgets who tells him news like this.
You let him do *what?*
He's not a guinea pig! They'll kill him and not even care!
I didn't *let* him do anything.
They won't even *know.*
Ellos piensan que él es un robot. "Hombre de Hierro."
You're fired.
And next time, use Chinese. Half the guards here speak Spanish.
Actually, you can't fire me.
It's my company!
So I guess *"It's Tony's now, all of it"* was a lie?
I told you to look out for him.
I look. I even talk. Does he listen? Whose son do you think he is?
I'm trying to remember a time when *you* taught him to be subservient. Or even careful...

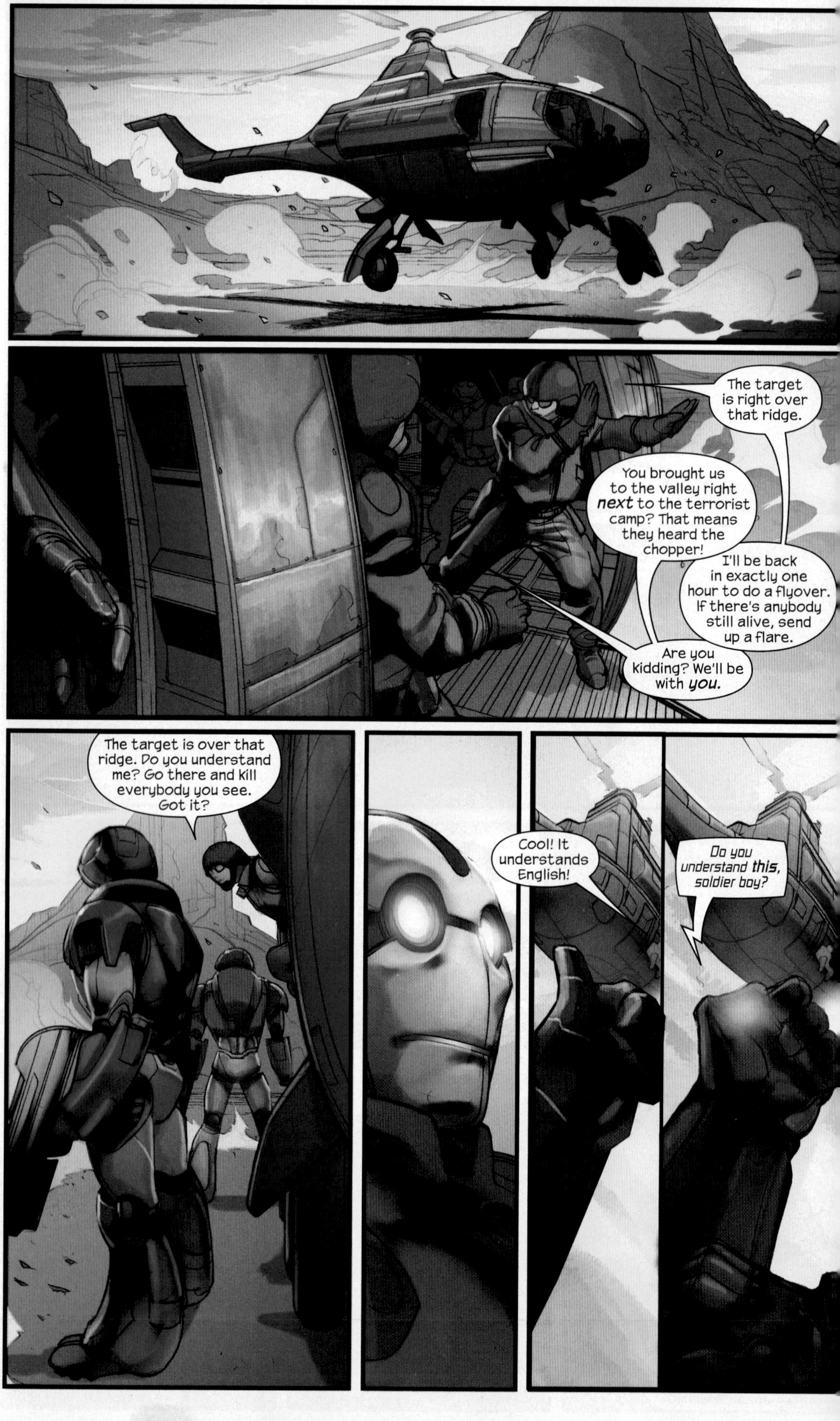
The target is right over that ridge.
You brought us to the valley right *next* to the terrorist camp? That means they heard the chopper!
I'll be back in exactly one hour to do a flyover. If there's anybody still alive, send up a flare.
Are you kidding? We'll be with *you.*
The target is over that ridge. Do you understand me? Go there and kill everybody you see. Got it?
Cool! It understands English!
Do you understand ***this,*** *soldier boy?*

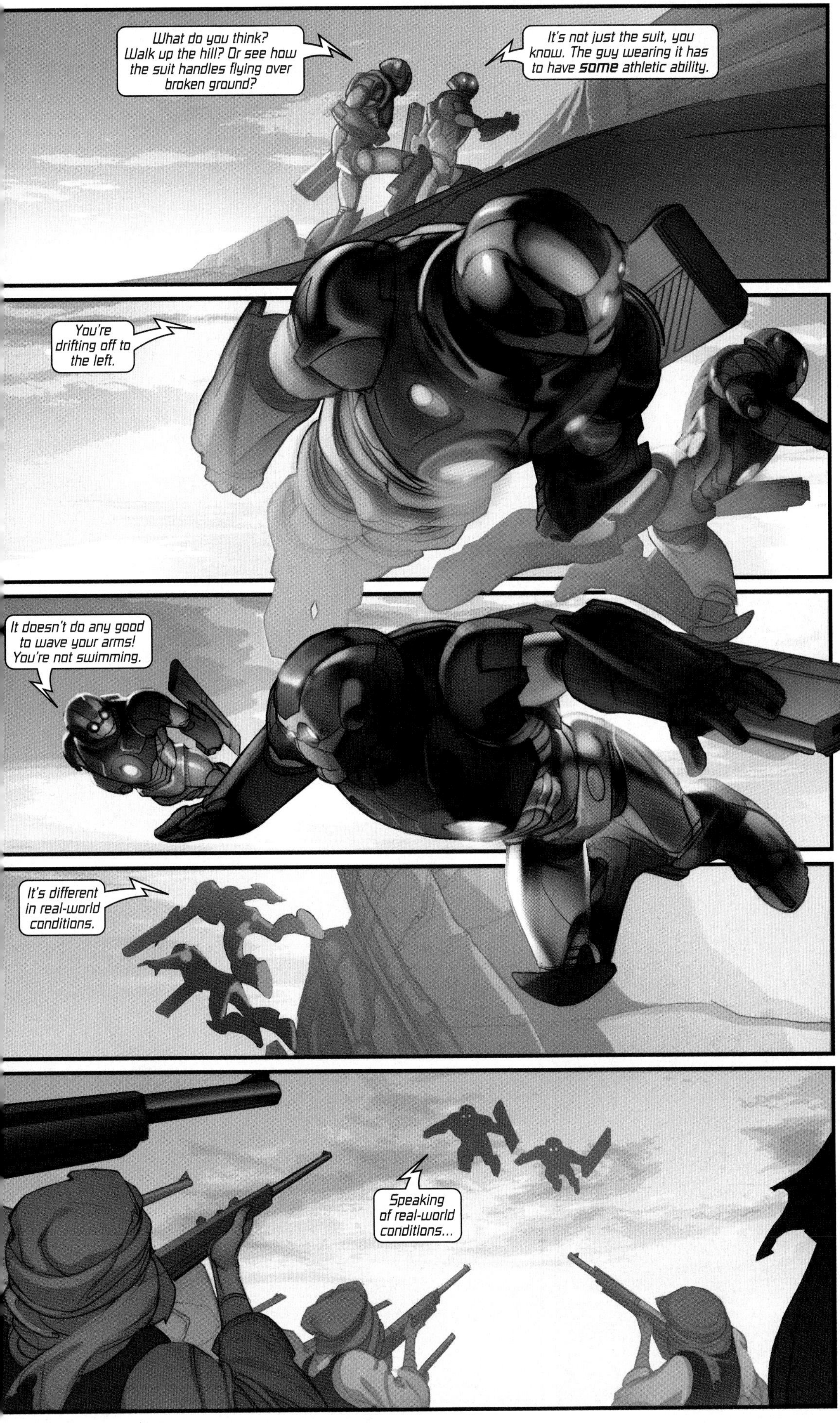
What do you think? Walk up the hill? Or see how the suit handles flying over broken ground?
It's not just the suit, you know. The guy wearing it has to have **some** athletic ability.
You're drifting off to the left.
It doesn't do any good to wave your arms! You're not swimming.
It's different in real-world conditions.
Speaking of real-world conditions...

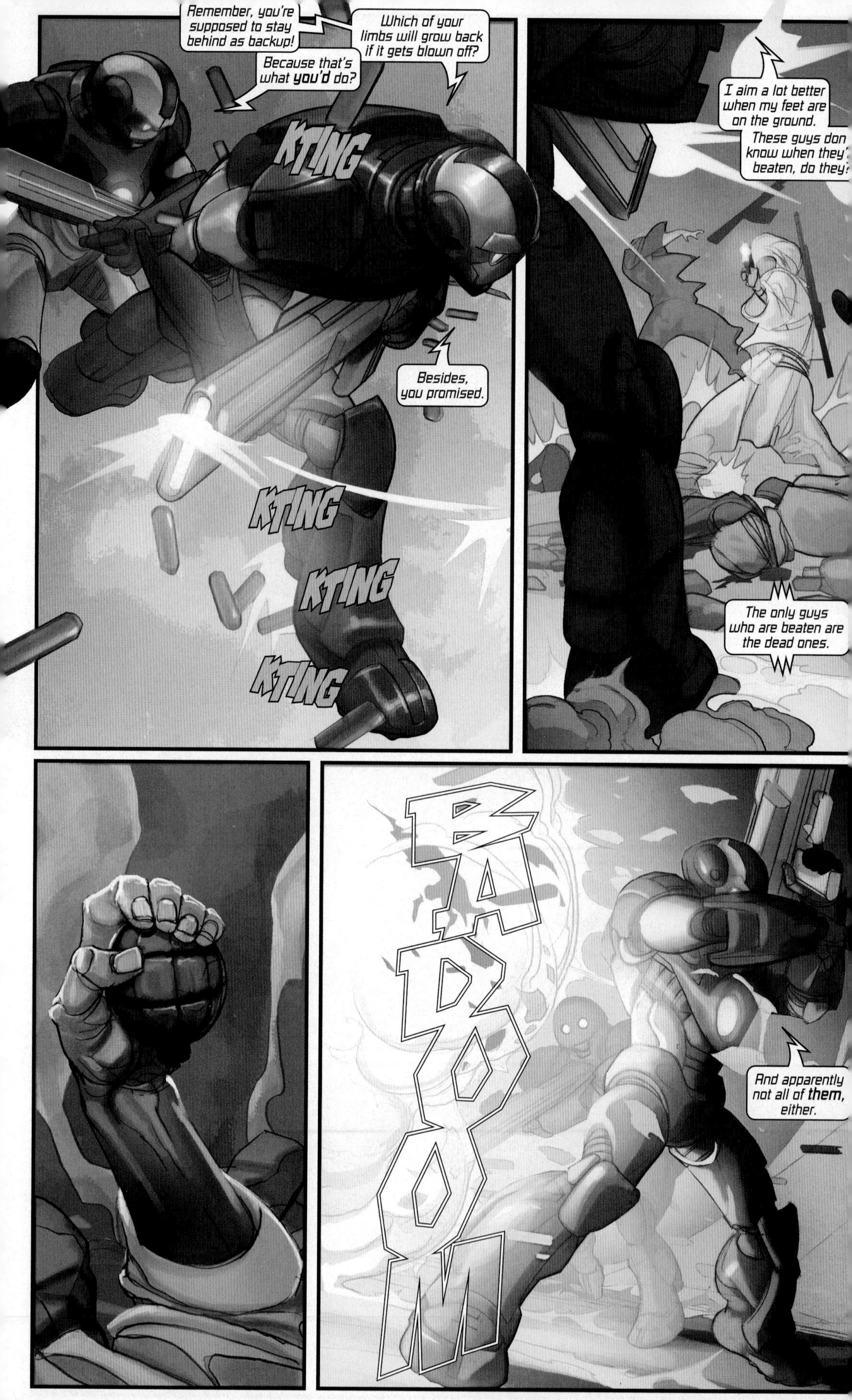
Remember, you're supposed to stay behind as backup!
Which of your limbs will grow back if it gets blown off?
Because that's what **you'd** do?
KTING
Besides, you promised.
KTING
KTING
KTING
I aim a lot better when my feet are on the ground.
These guys don know when they' beaten, do they?
The only guys who are beaten are the dead ones.
BADOOM
And apparently not all of **them**, either.

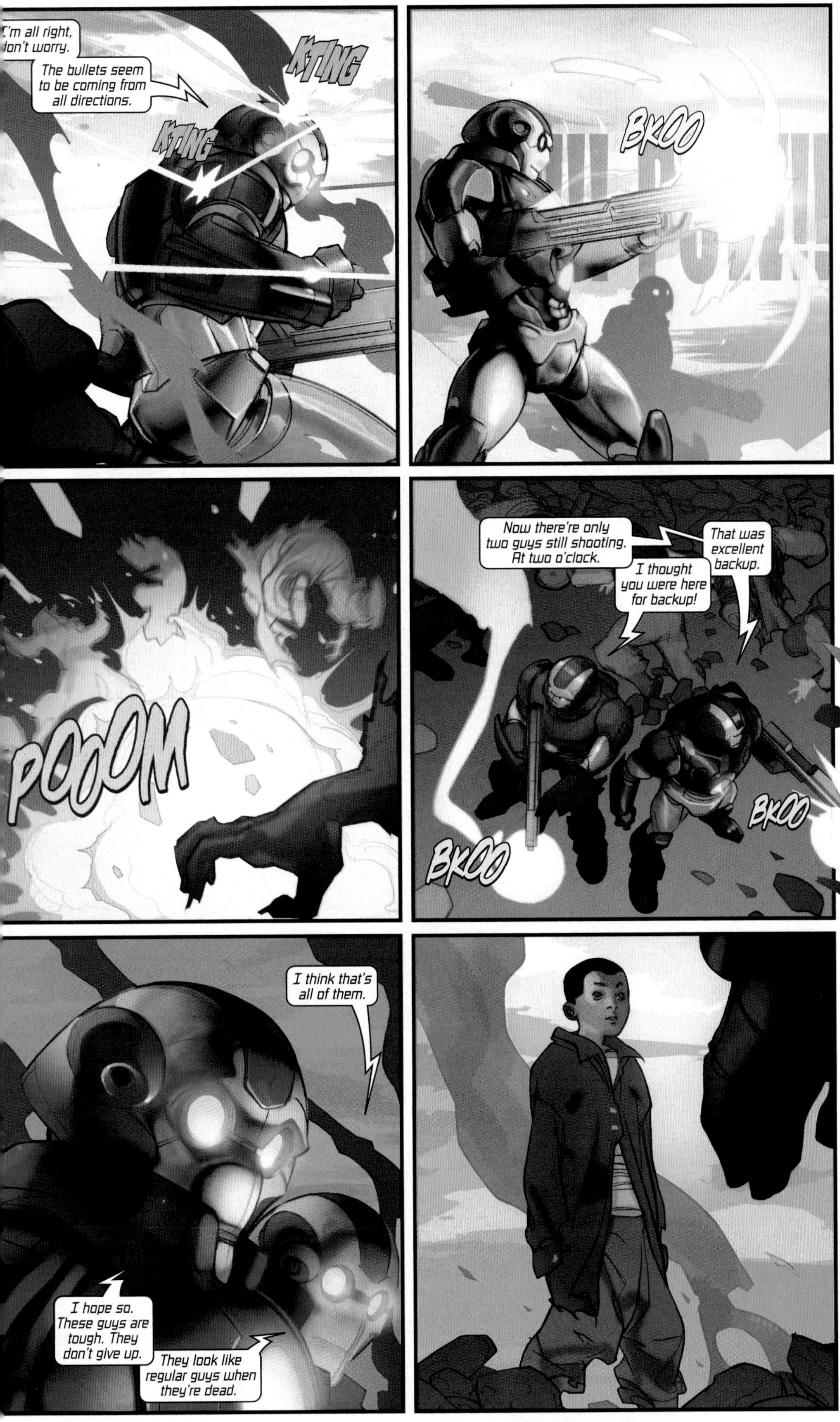
I'm all right, don't worry.
The bullets seem to be coming from all directions.
KTING
KTING
BKOO
POOOM
Now there're only two guys still shooting. At two o'clock.
That was excellent backup.
I thought you were here for backup!
BKOO
BKOO
I think that's all of them.
I hope so. These guys are tough. They don't give up.
They look like regular guys when they're dead.

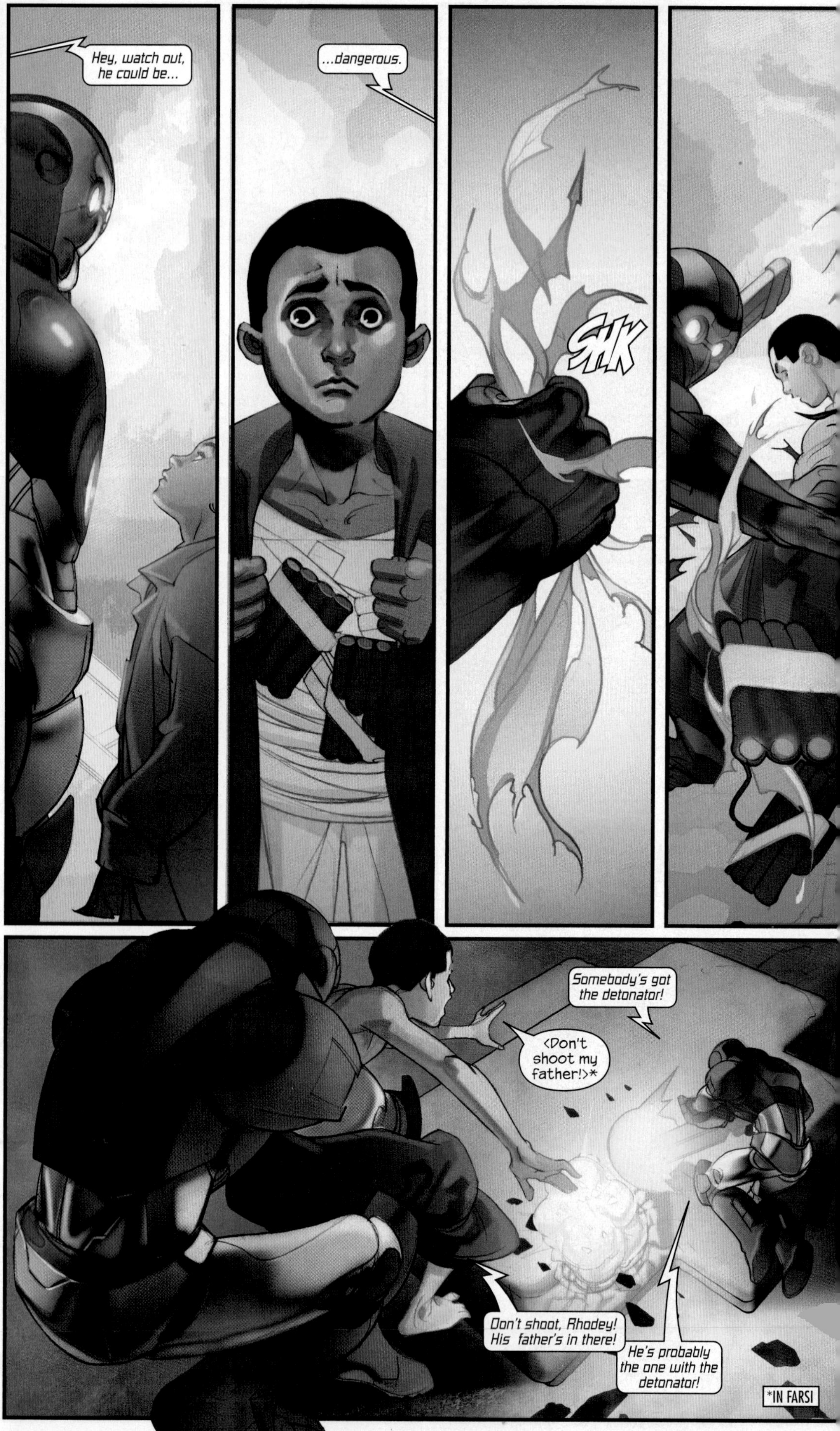

Hey, watch out, he could be...
...dangerous.
SHK
Somebody's got the detonator!
<Don't shoot my father!>*
Don't shoot, Rhodey! His father's in there!
He's probably the one with the detonator!
*IN FARSI

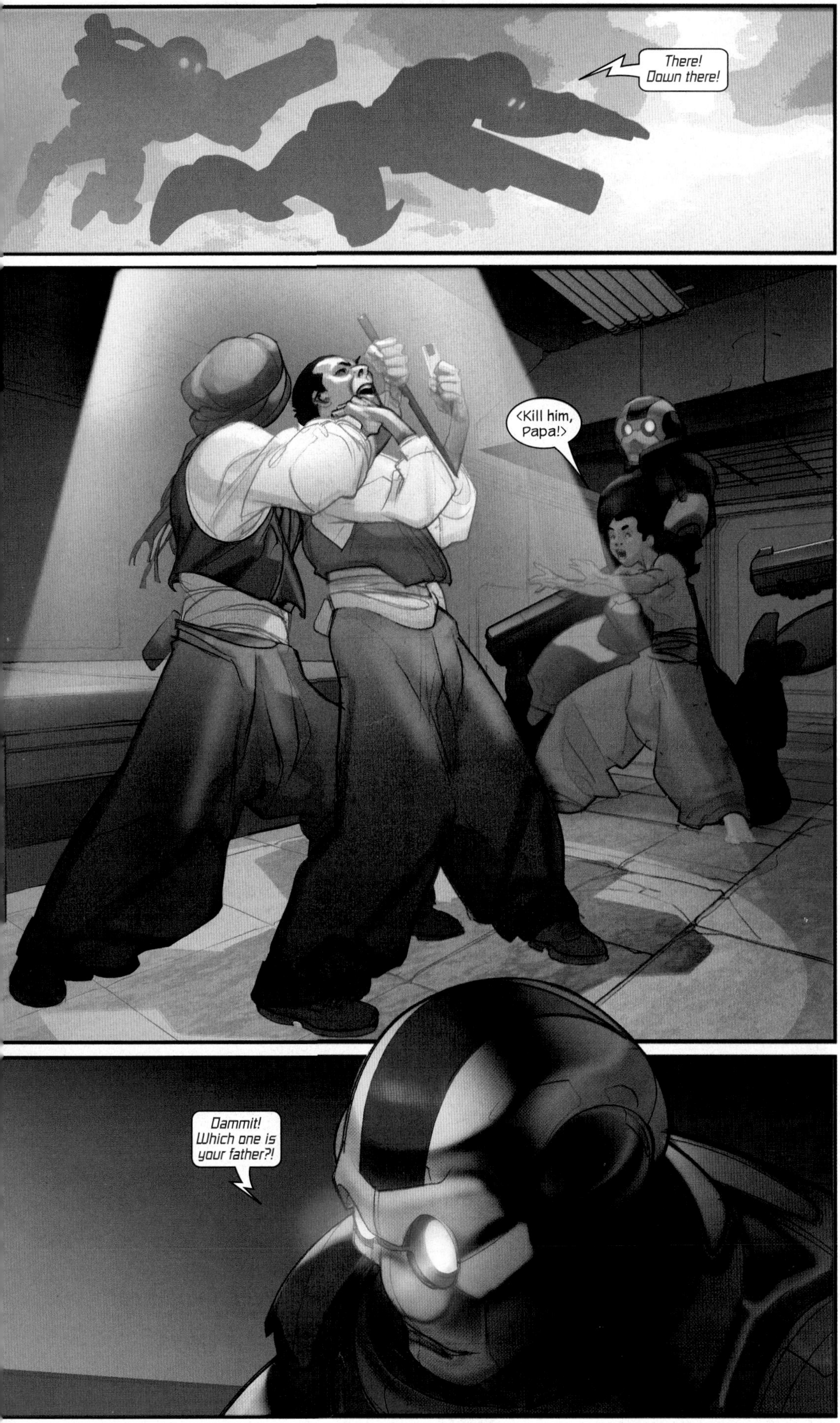
There! Down there!
<Kill him, Papa!>
Dammit! Which one is your father?!

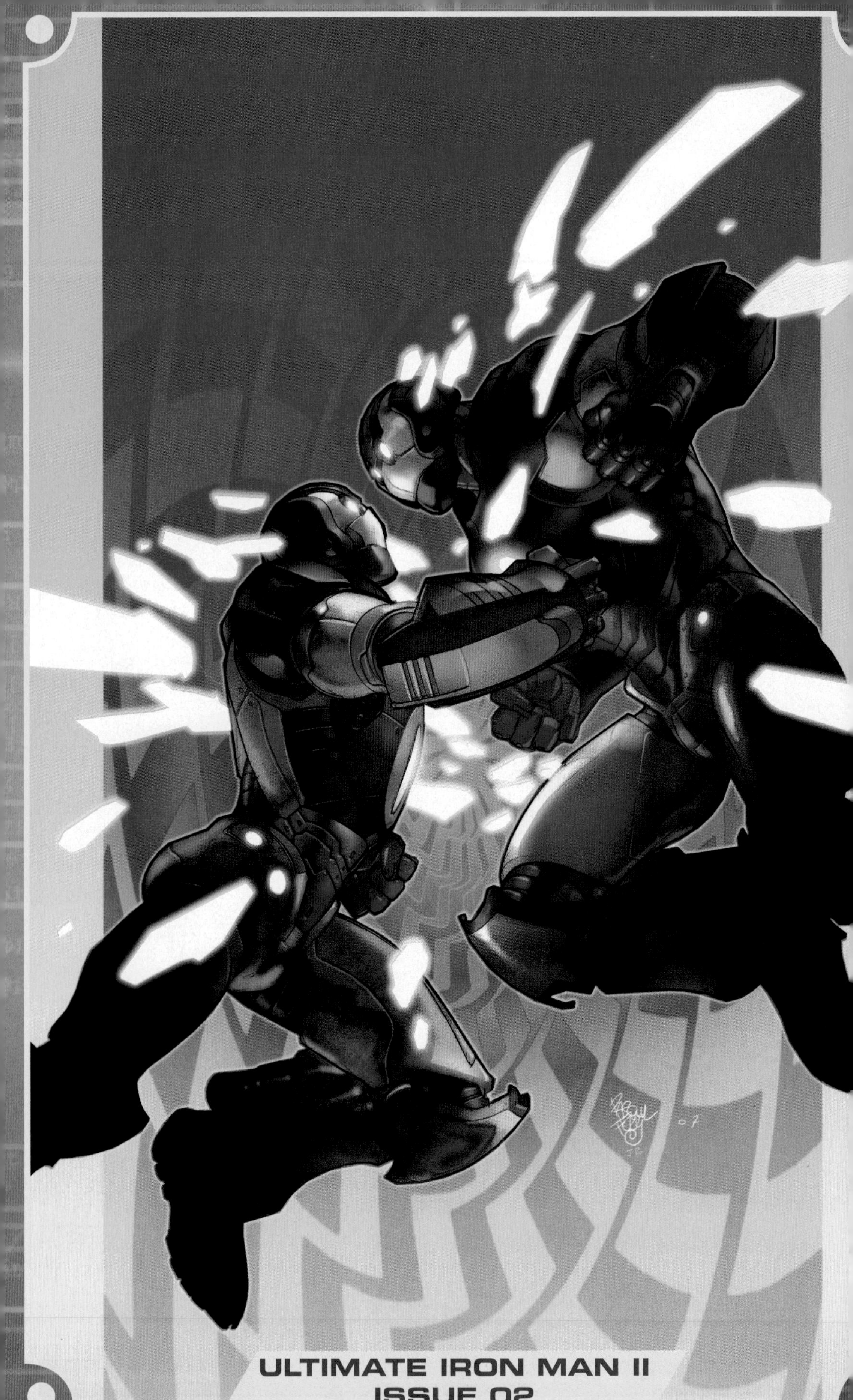

ULTIMATE IRON MAN II
ISSUE 02

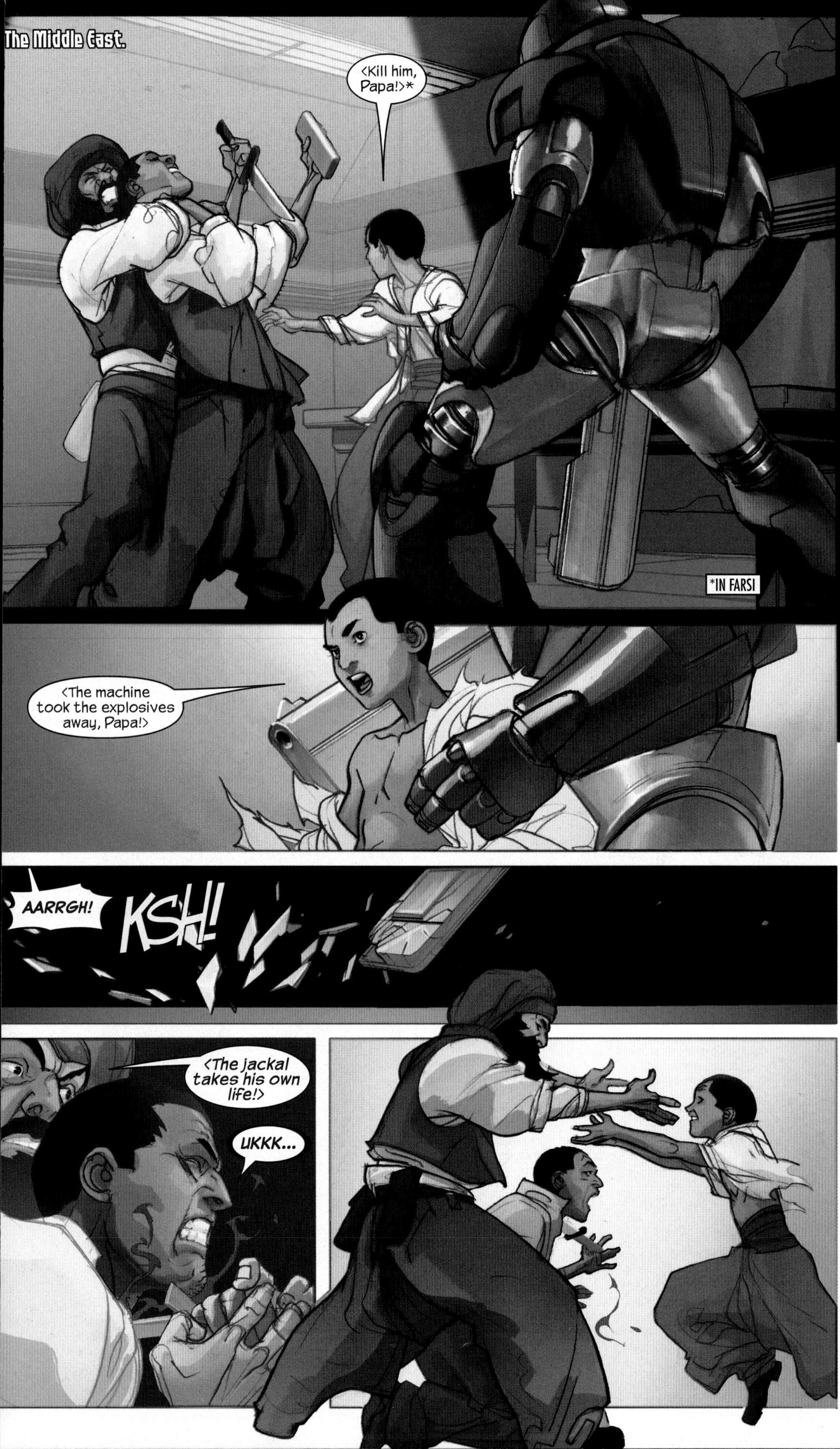

The Middle East.
<Kill him, Papa!>*
*IN FARSI
<The machine took the explosives away, Papa!>
AARRGH!
KSHL!
<The jackal takes his own life!>
UKKK...

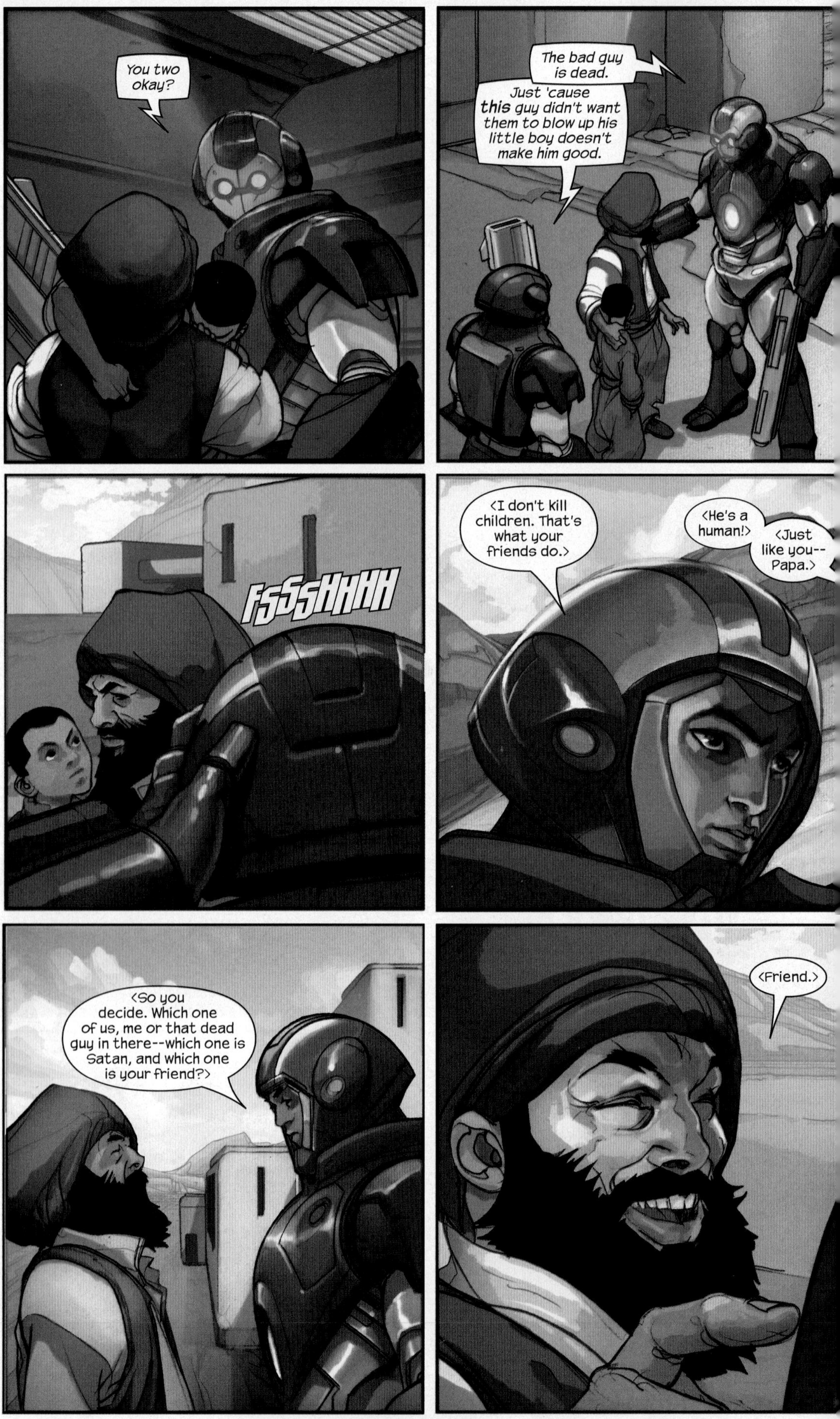
You two okay?
The bad guy is dead.
Just 'cause **this** guy didn't want them to blow up his little boy doesn't make him good.
FSSSHHHH
<I don't kill children. That's what your friends do.>
<He's a human!>
<Just like you-- Papa.>
<So you decide. Which one of us, me or that dead guy in there--which one is Satan, and which one is your friend?>
<Friend.>

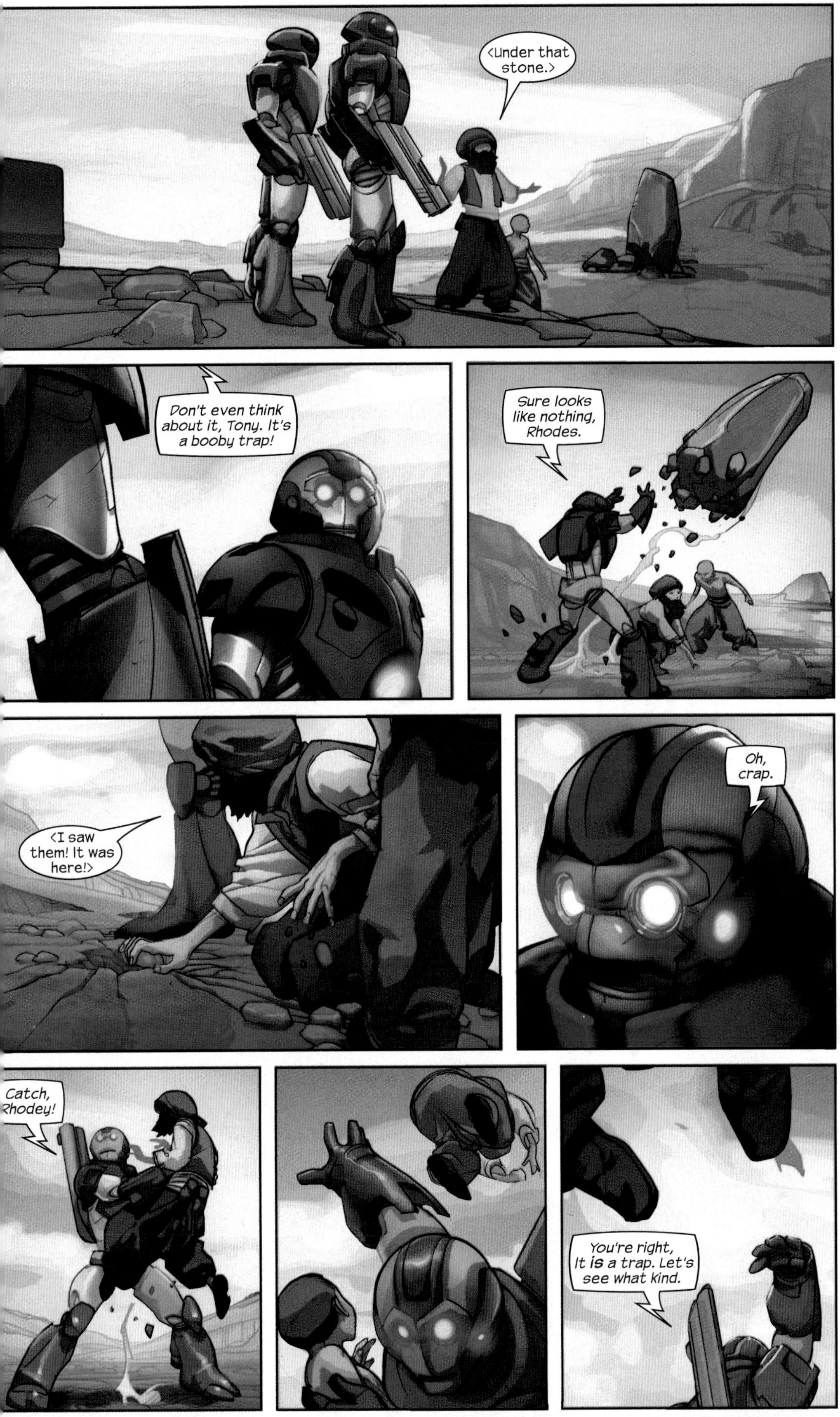
<Under that stone.>
Don't even think about it, Tony. It's a booby trap!
Sure looks like nothing, Rhodes.
<I saw them! It was here!>
Oh, crap.
Catch, Rhodey!
You're right, It **is** a trap. Let's see what kind.

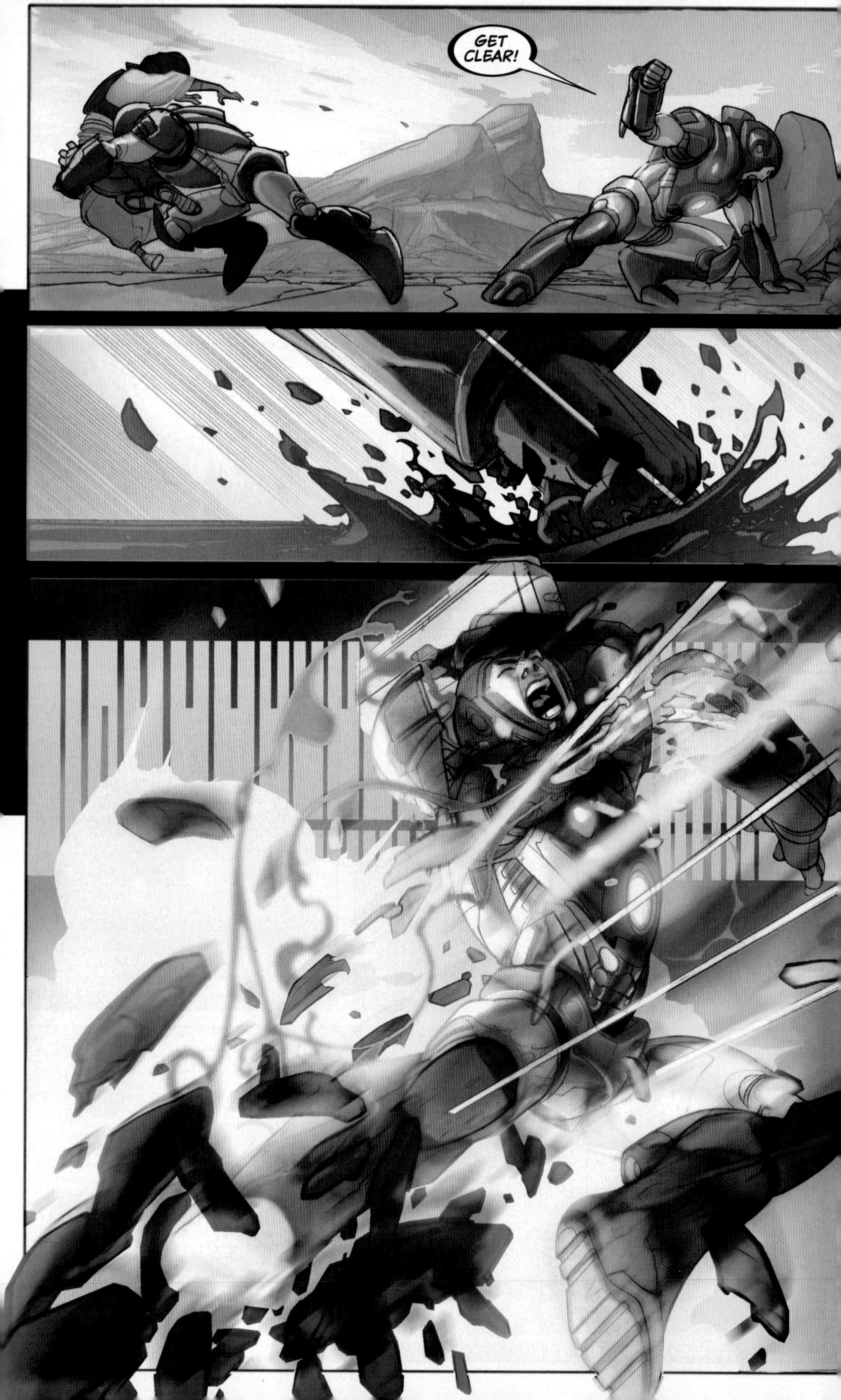
GET CLEAR!

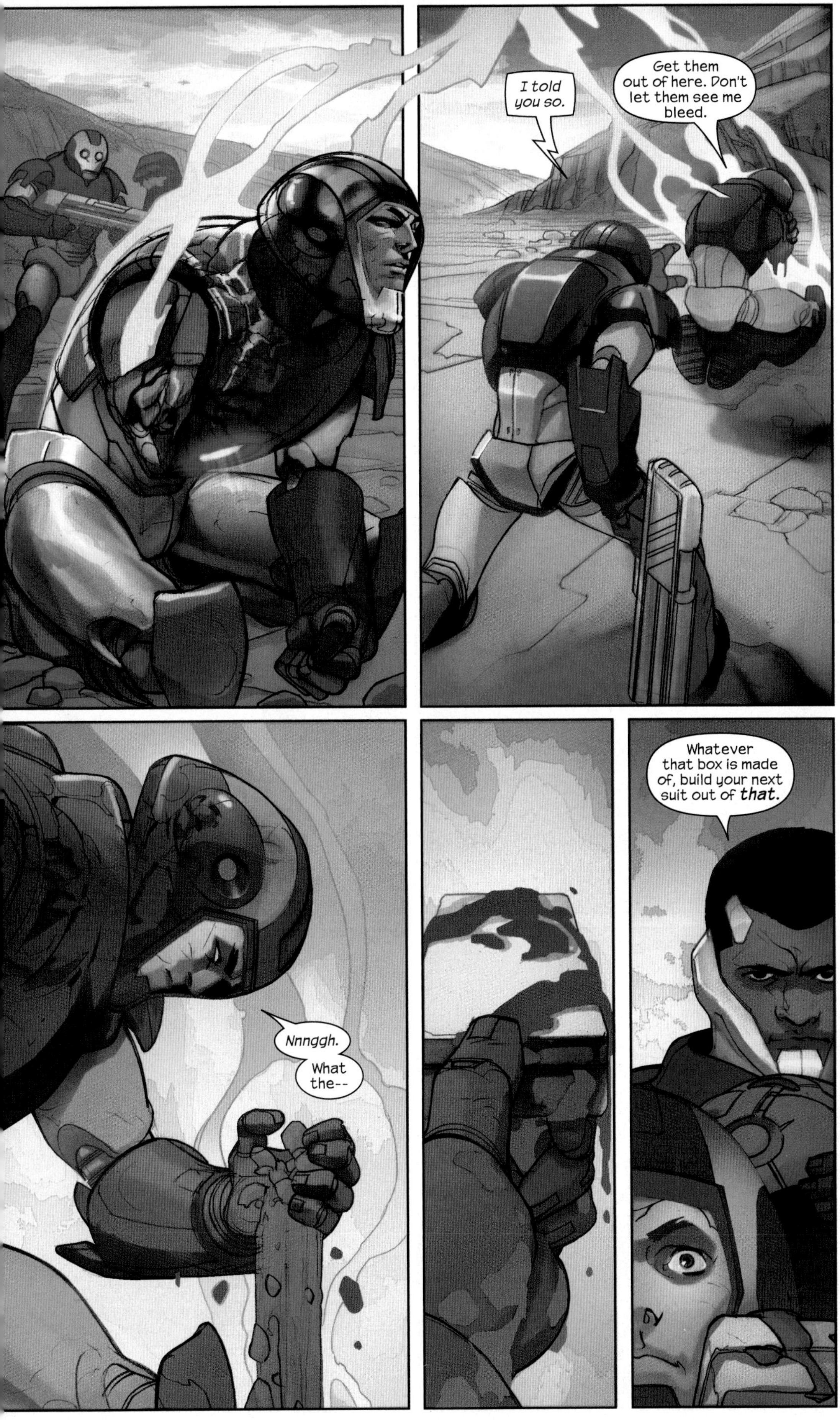
I told you so.
Get them out of here. Don't let them see me bleed.
Nnnggh.
What the--
Whatever that box is made of, build your next suit out of *that.*

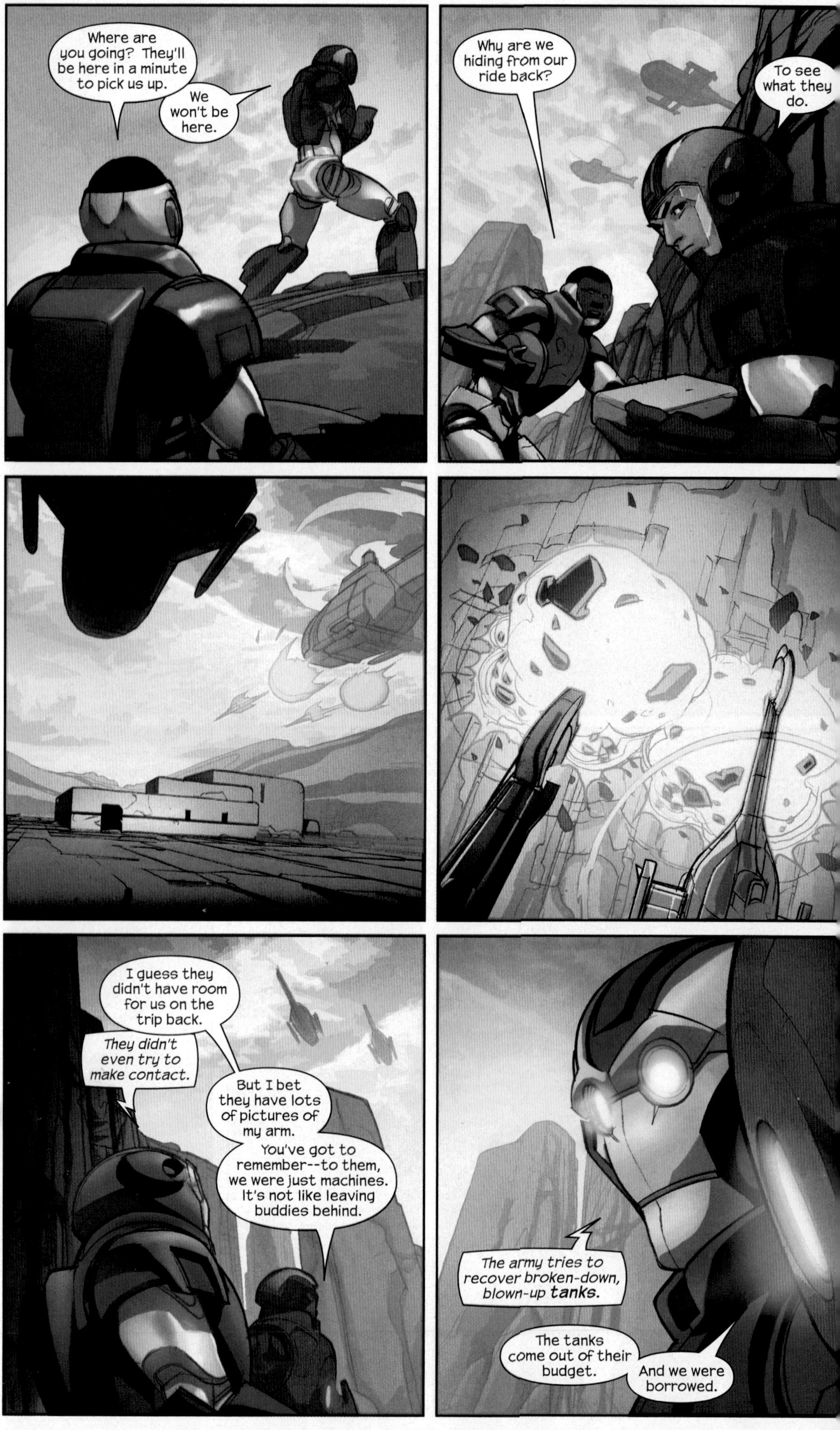
Where are you going? They'll be here in a minute to pick us up.
We won't be here.
Why are we hiding from our ride back?
To see what they do.
I guess they didn't have room for us on the trip back.
They didn't even try to make contact.
But I bet they have lots of pictures of my arm.
You've got to remember--to them, we were just machines. It's not like leaving buddies behind.
*The army tries to recover broken-down, blown-up **tanks.***
The tanks come out of their budget.
And we were borrowed.

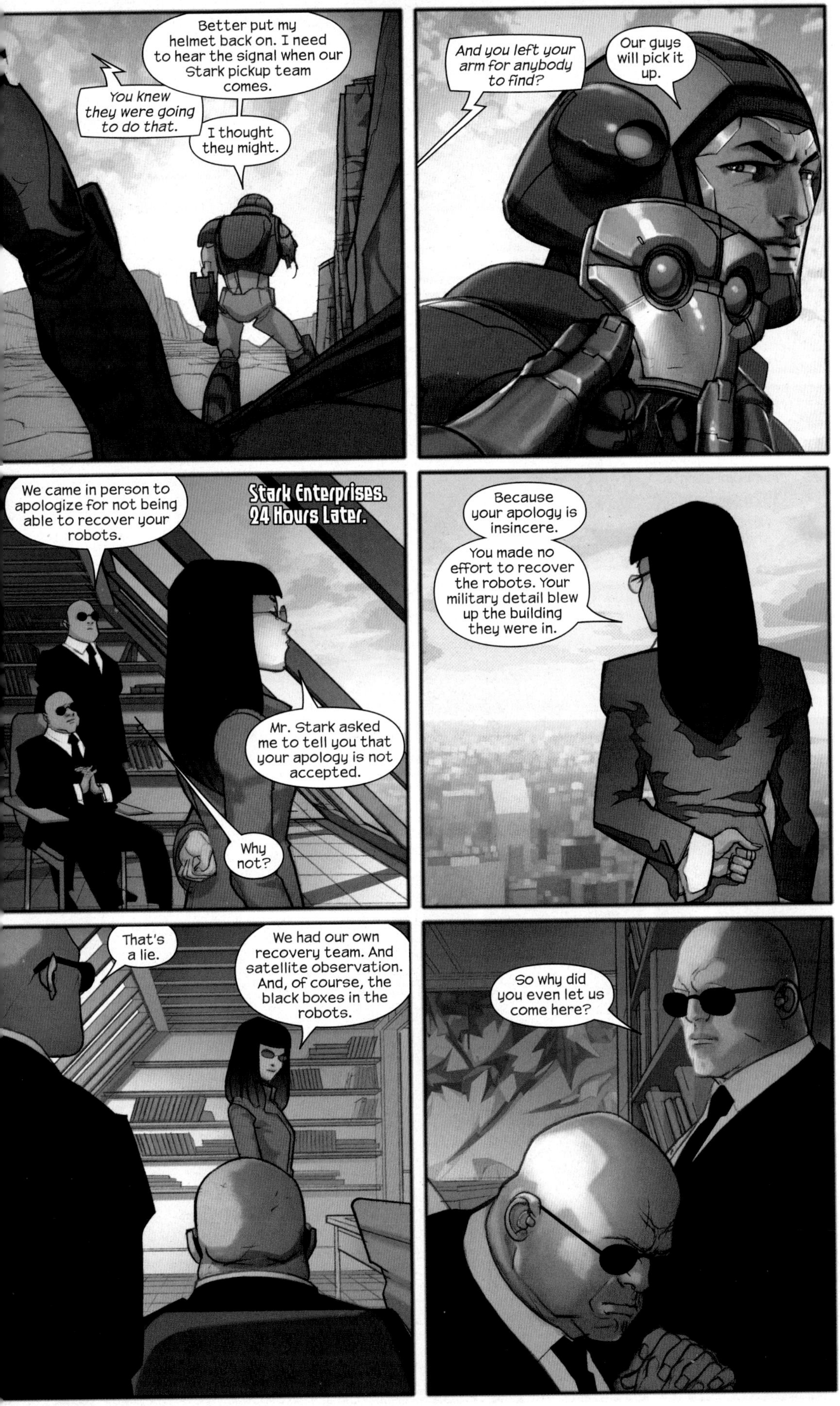
Better put my helmet back on. I need to hear the signal when our Stark pickup team comes.
You knew they were going to do that.
I thought they might.
And you left your arm for anybody to find?
Our guys will pick it up.
Stark Enterprises. 24 Hours Later.
We came in person to apologize for not being able to recover your robots.
Mr. Stark asked me to tell you that your apology is not accepted.
Why not?
Because your apology is insincere.
You made no effort to recover the robots. Your military detail blew up the building they were in.
That's a lie.
We had our own recovery team. And satellite observation. And, of course, the black boxes in the robots.
So why did you even let us come here?

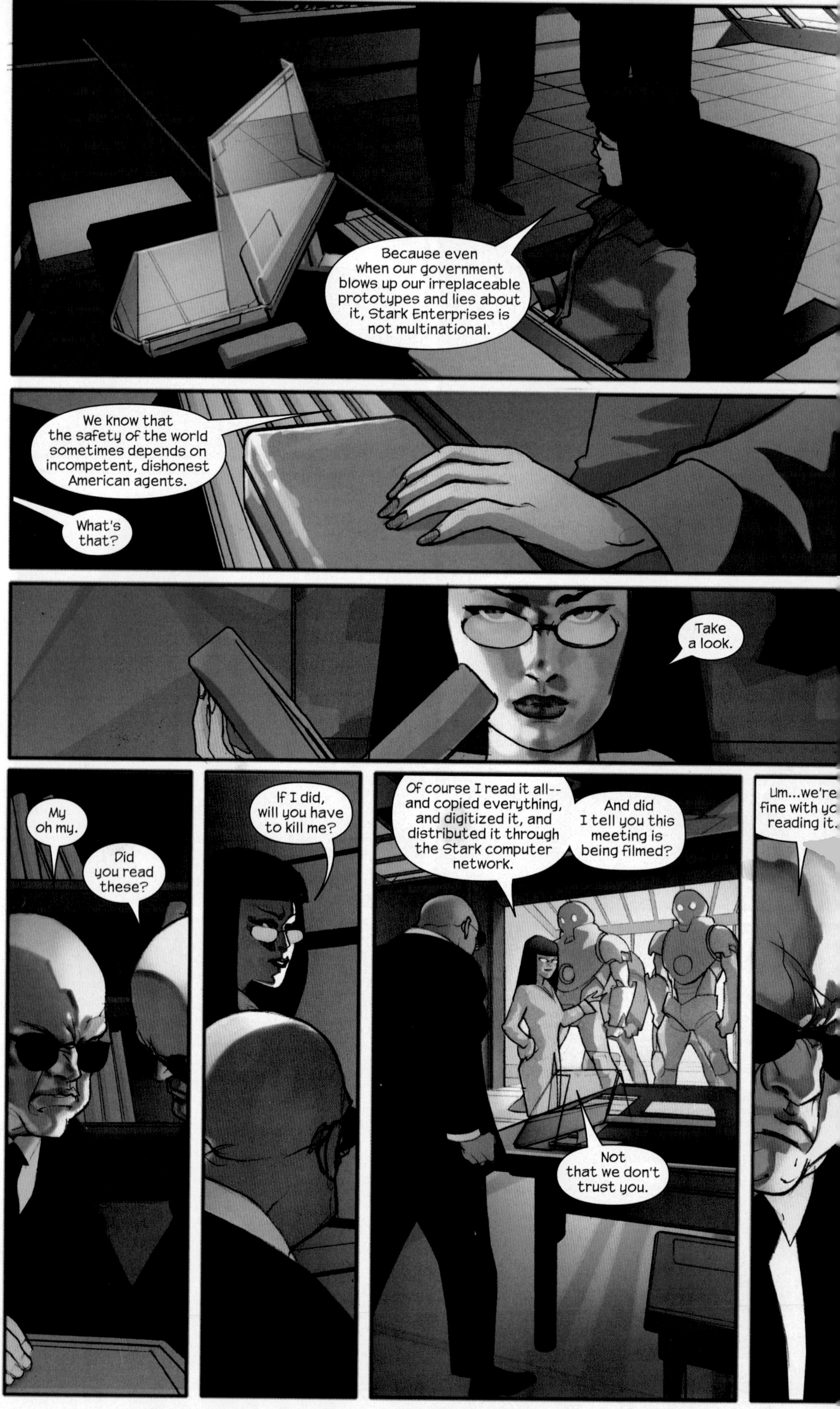

Because even when our government blows up our irreplaceable prototypes and lies about it, Stark Enterprises is not multinational.
We know that the safety of the world sometimes depends on incompetent, dishonest American agents.
What's that?
Take a look.
My oh my.
Did you read these?
If I did, will you have to kill me?
Of course I read it all--and copied everything, and digitized it, and distributed it through the Stark computer network.
And did I tell you this meeting is being filmed?
Not that we don't trust you.

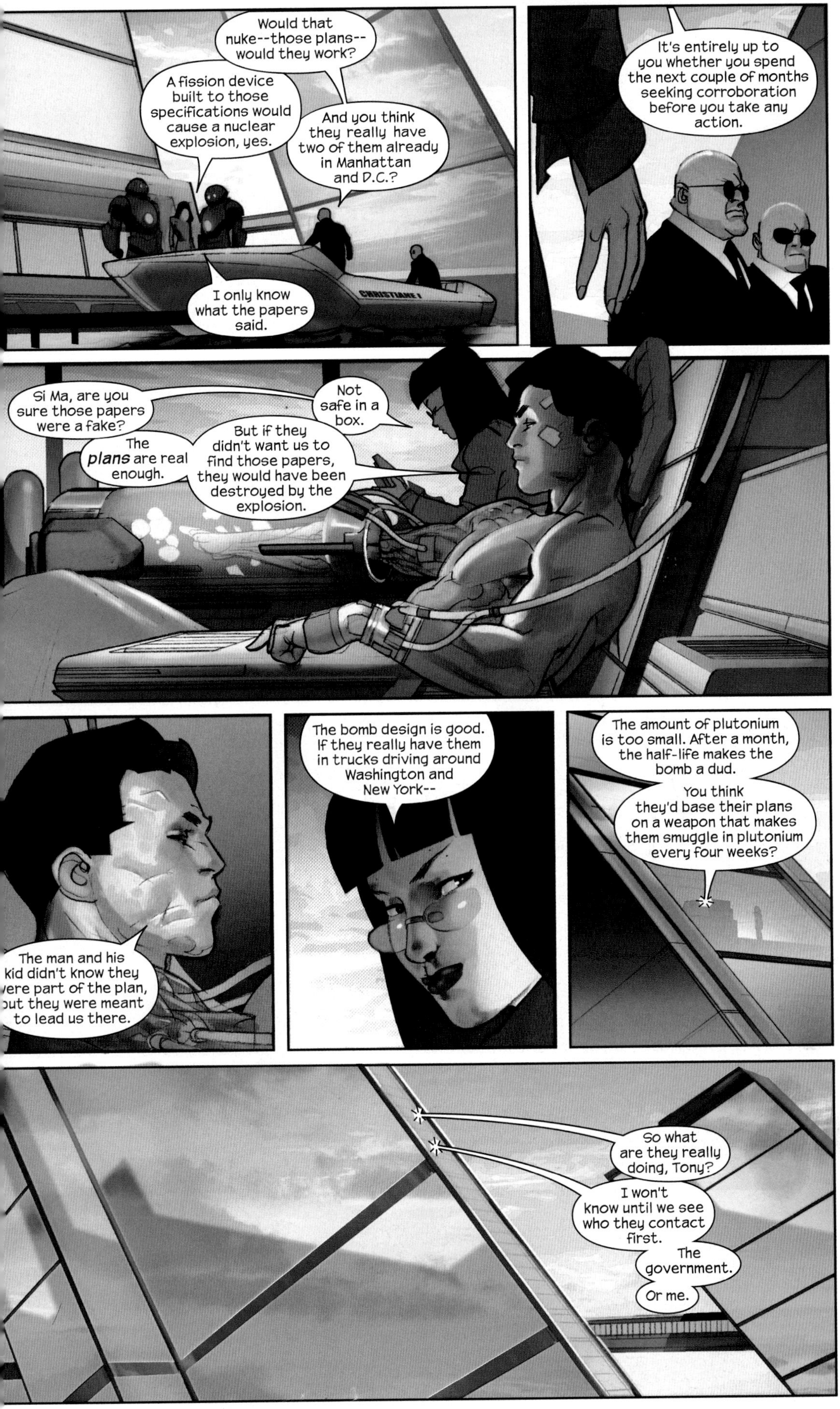
Would that nuke--those plans--would they work?
A fission device built to those specifications would cause a nuclear explosion, yes.
And you think they really have two of them already in Manhattan and D.C.?
I only know what the papers said.
CHRISTINE I
It's entirely up to you whether you spend the next couple of months seeking corroboration before you take any action.
Si Ma, are you sure those papers were a fake?
The *plans* are real enough.
Not safe in a box.
But if they didn't want us to find those papers, they would have been destroyed by the explosion.
The man and his kid didn't know they were part of the plan, but they were meant to lead us there.
The bomb design is good. If they really have them in trucks driving around Washington and New York--
The amount of plutonium is too small. After a month, the half-life makes the bomb a dud.
You think they'd base their plans on a weapon that makes them smuggle in plutonium every four weeks?
So what are they really doing, Tony?
I won't know until we see who they contact first.
The government.
Or me.

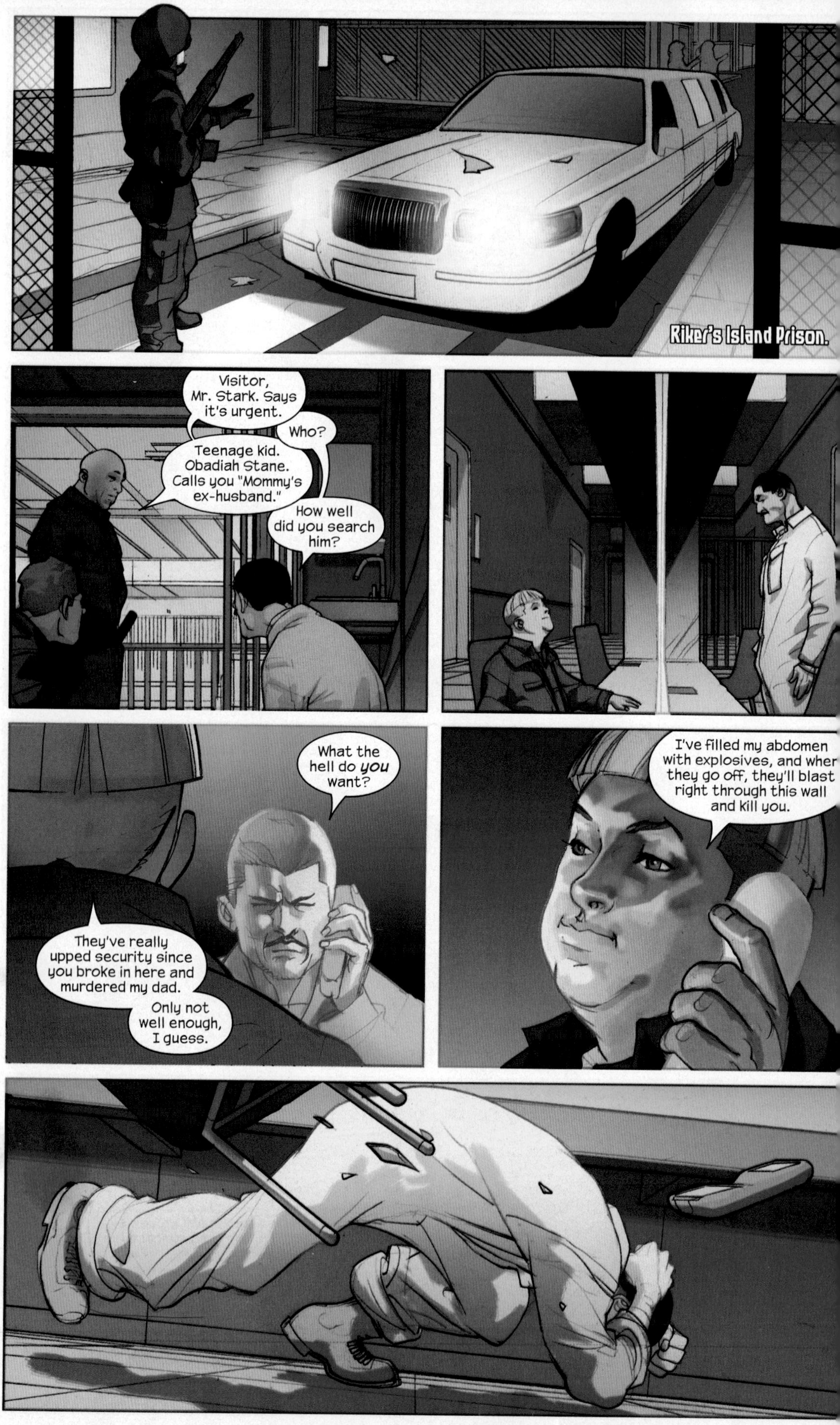
Riker's Island Prison.
Visitor, Mr. Stark. Says it's urgent.
Who?
Teenage kid. Obadiah Stane. Calls you "Mommy's ex-husband."
How well did you search him?
What the hell do *you* want?
They've really upped security since you broke in here and murdered my dad.
Only not well enough, I guess.
I've filled my abdomen with explosives, and wher they go off, they'll blast right through this wall and kill you.

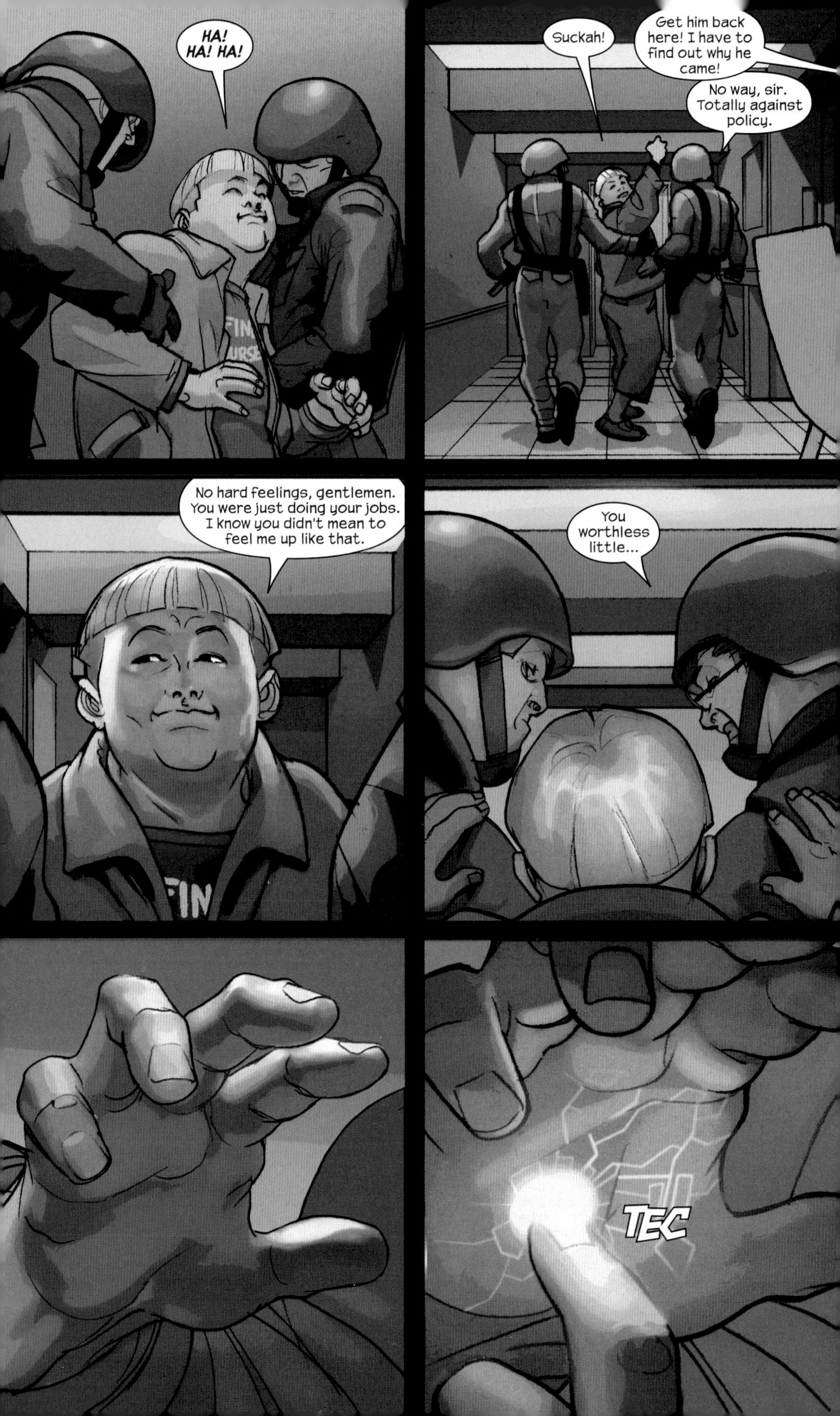
HA! HA! HA!
Suckah!
Get him back here! I have to find out why he came!
No way, sir. Totally against policy.
No hard feelings, gentlemen. You were just doing your jobs. I know you didn't mean to feel me up like that.
You worthless little...
TEC

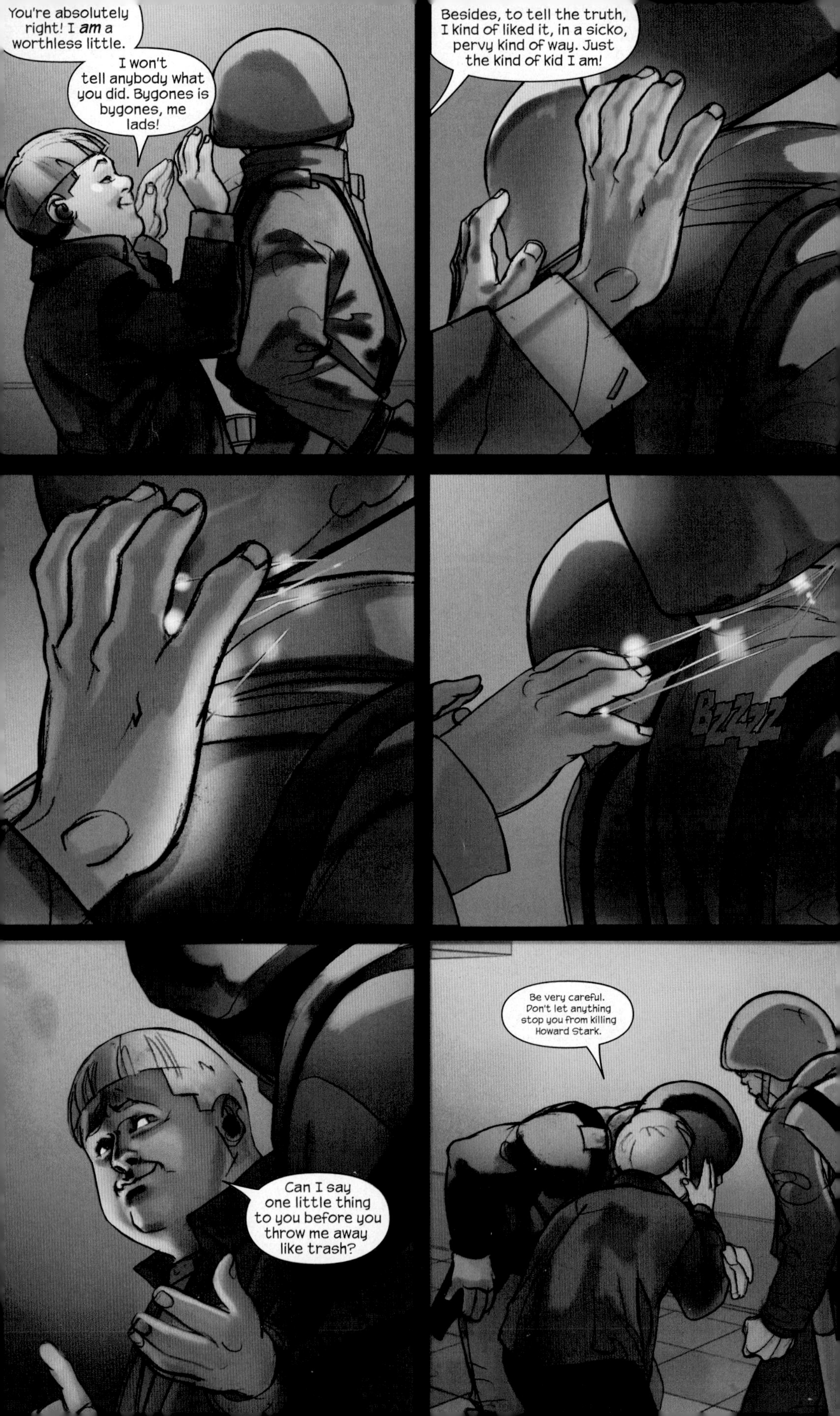
You're absolutely right! I *am* a worthless little.
I won't tell anybody what you did. Bygones is bygones, me lads!
Besides, to tell the truth, I kind of liked it, in a sicko, pervy kind of way. Just the kind of kid I am!
BZZZZ
Can I say one little thing to you before you throw me away like trash?
Be very careful. Don't let anything stop you from killing Howard Stark.

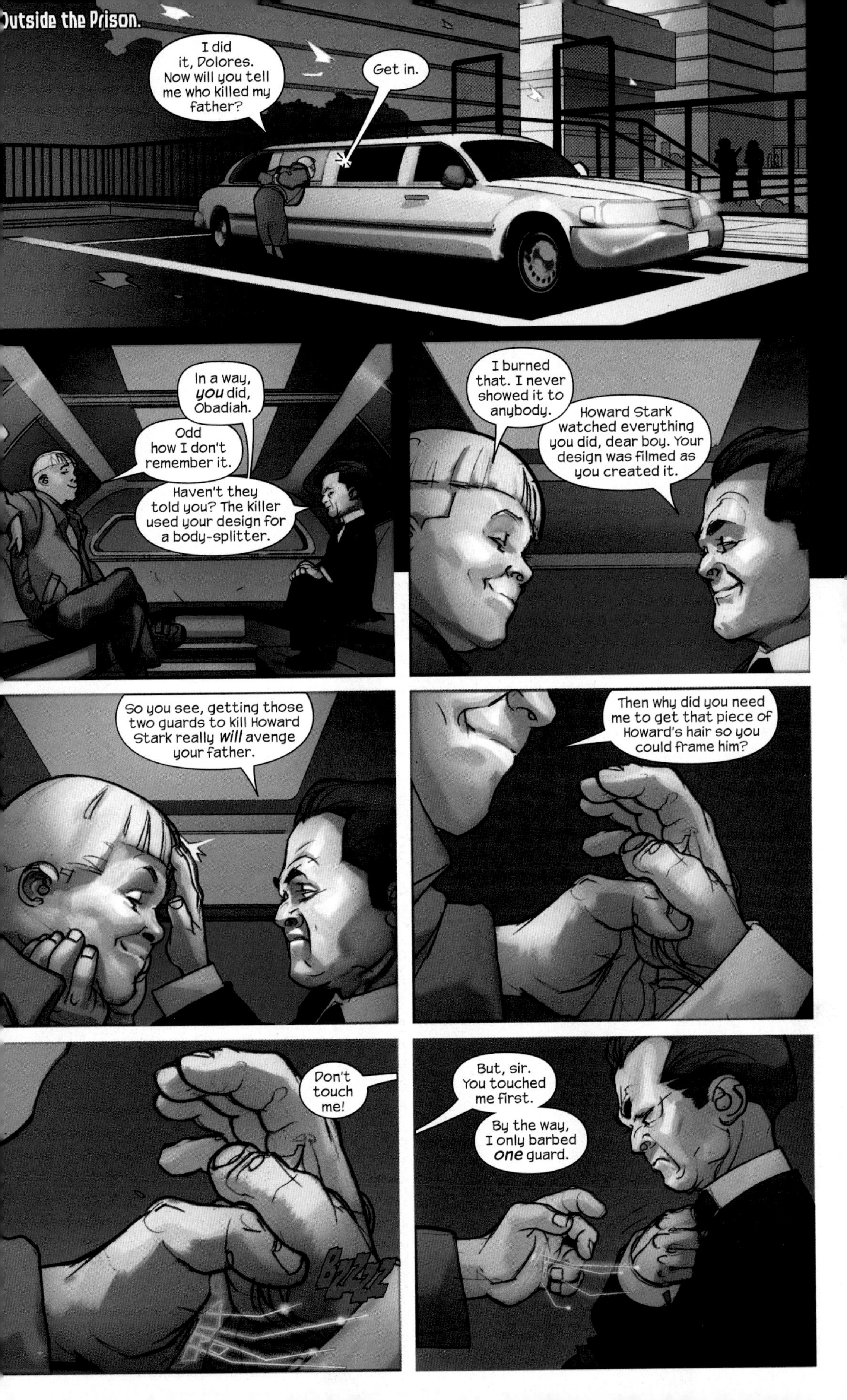
Outside the Prison.
I did it, Dolores. Now will you tell me who killed my father?
Get in.
In a way, you did, Obadiah.
Odd how I don't remember it.
Haven't they told you? The killer used your design for a body-splitter.
I burned that. I never showed it to anybody.
Howard Stark watched everything you did, dear boy. Your design was filmed as you created it.
So you see, getting those two guards to kill Howard Stark really will avenge your father.
Then why did you need me to get that piece of Howard's hair so you could frame him?
Don't touch me!
BZZZZ
But, sir. You touched me first.
By the way, I only barbed one guard.

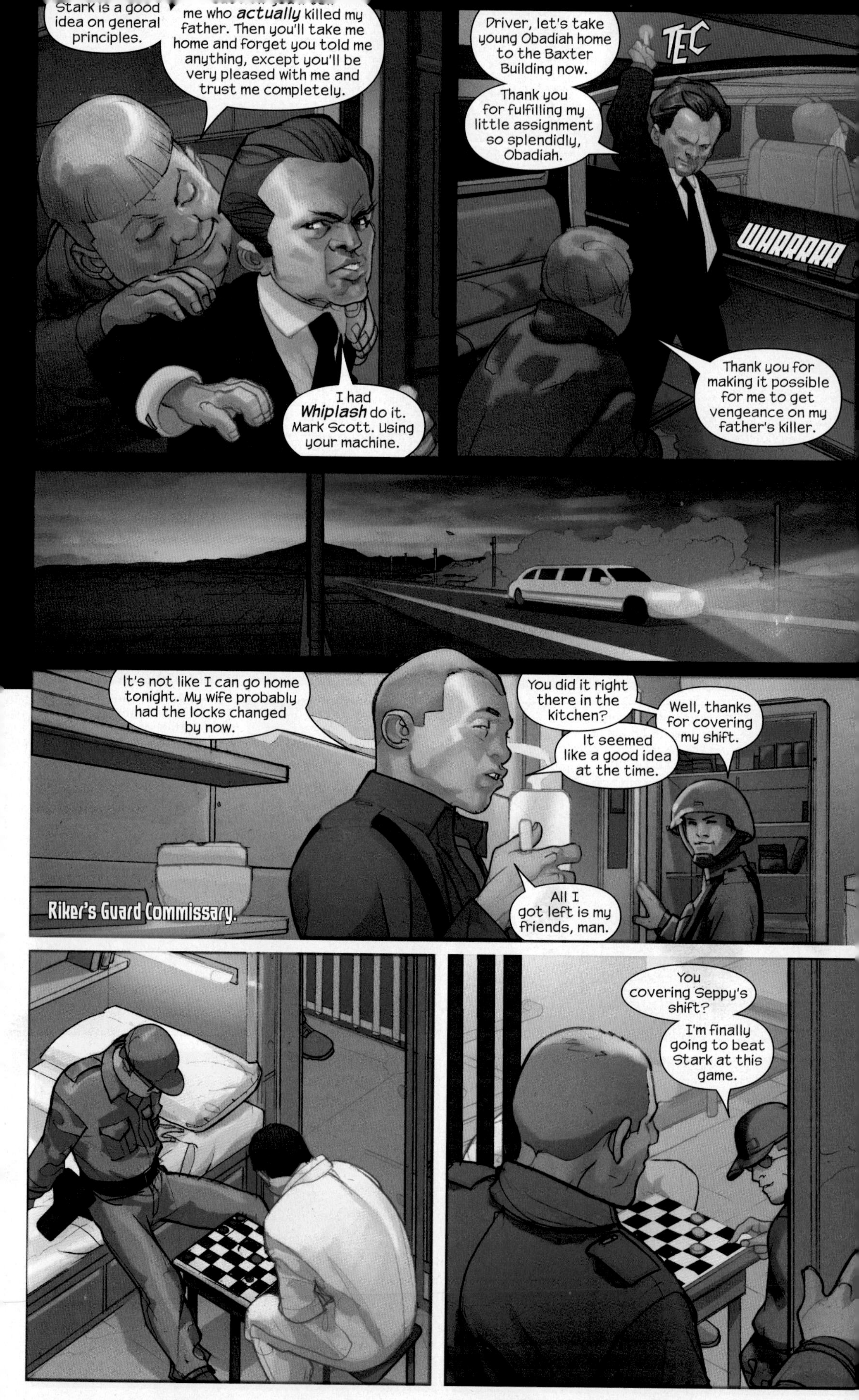
Stark is a good idea on general principles.
me who actually killed my father. Then you'll take me home and forget you told me anything, except you'll be very pleased with me and trust me completely.
I had Whiplash do it. Mark Scott. Using your machine.
Driver, let's take young Obadiah home to the Baxter Building now.
TEC
Thank you for fulfilling my little assignment so splendidly, Obadiah.
WHRRRRR
Thank you for making it possible for me to get vengeance on my father's killer.
Riker's Guard Commissary.
It's not like I can go home tonight. My wife probably had the locks changed by now.
You did it right there in the kitchen?
It seemed like a good idea at the time.
Well, thanks for covering my shift.
All I got left is my friends, man.
You covering Seppy's shift?
I'm finally going to beat Stark at this game.

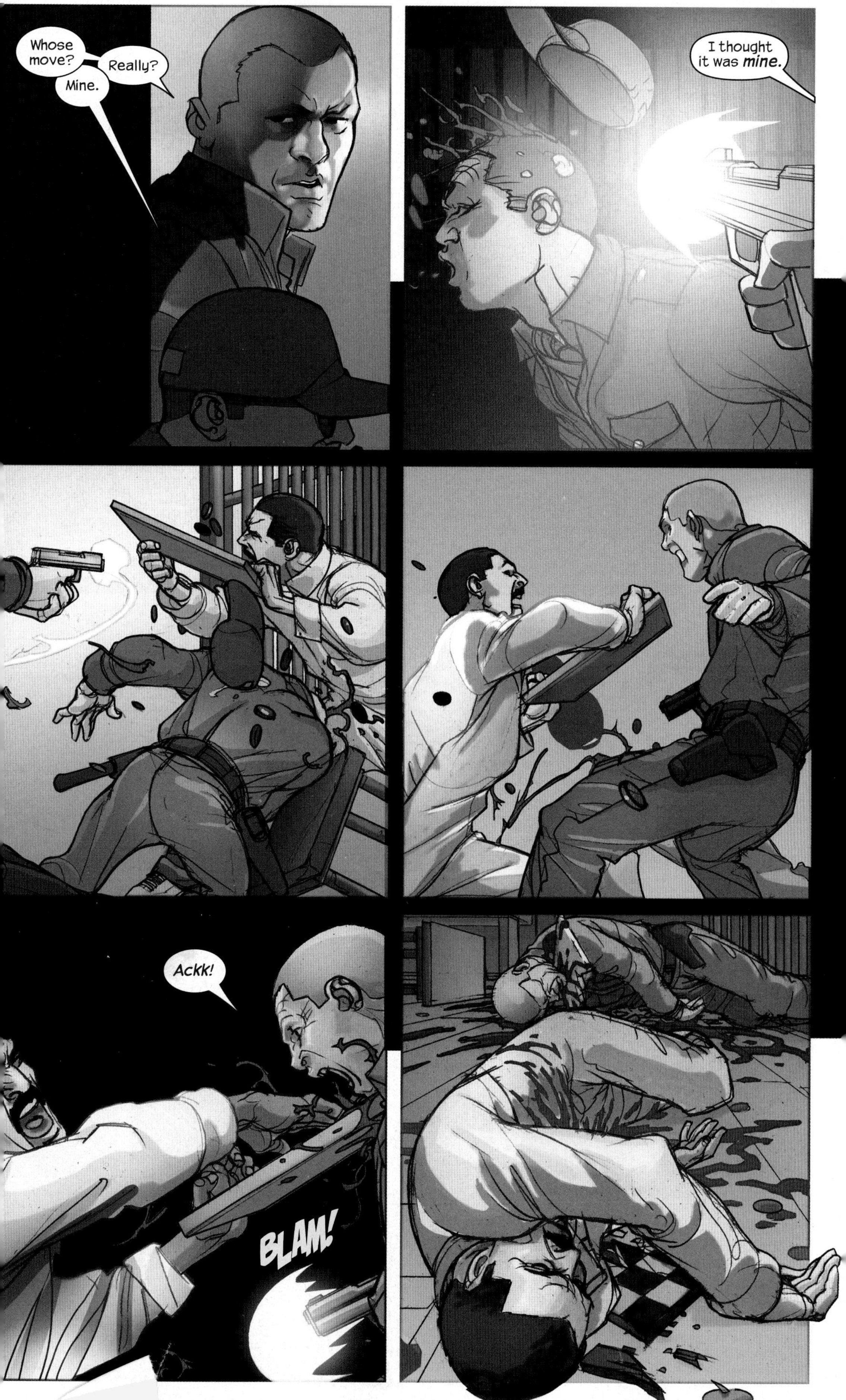
Whose move?
Mine.
Really?
I thought it was *mine.*
Ackk!
BLAM!

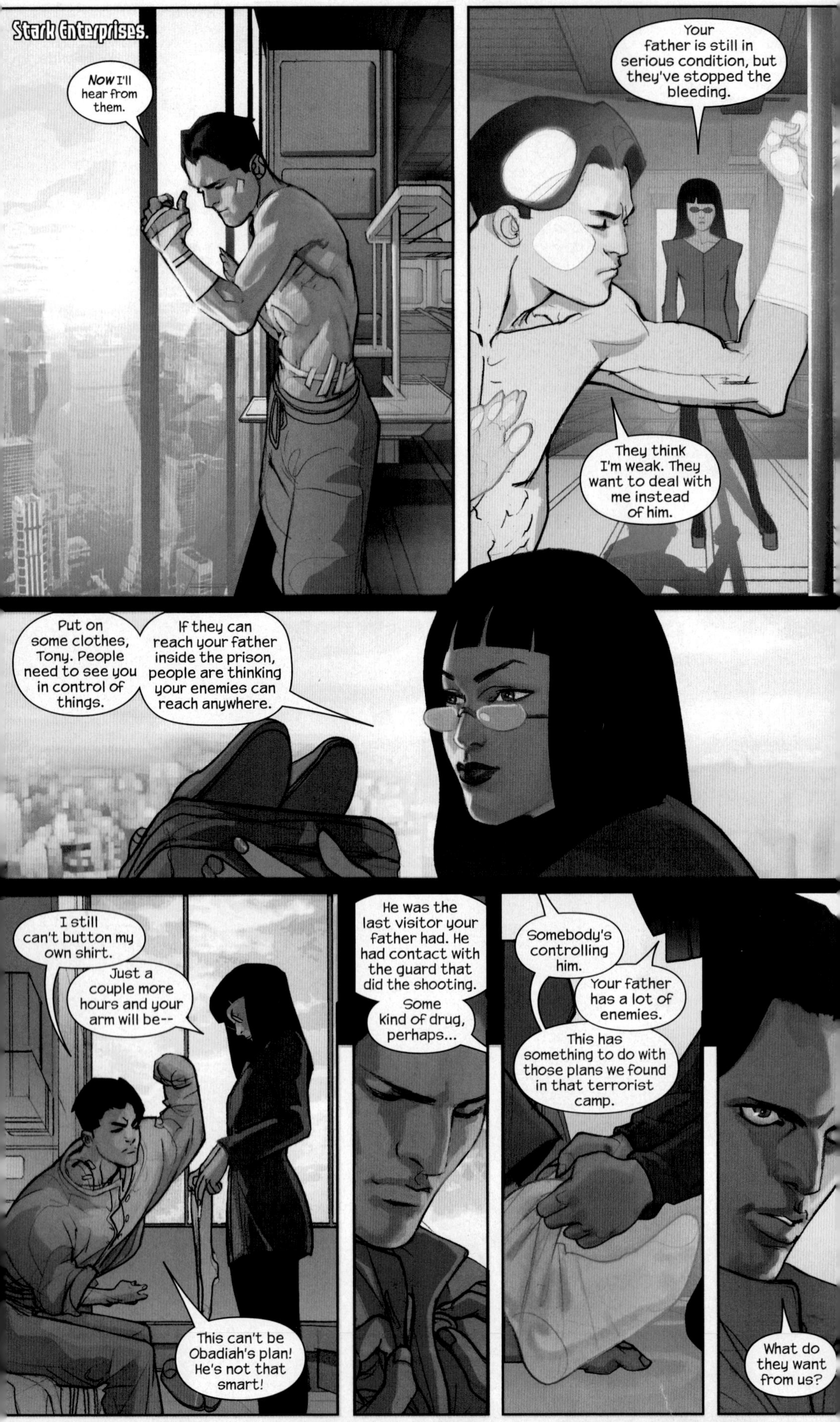
Stark Enterprises.
NOW I'll hear from them.
Your father is still in serious condition, but they've stopped the bleeding.
They think I'm weak. They want to deal with me instead of him.
Put on some clothes, Tony. People need to see you in control of things.
If they can reach your father inside the prison, people are thinking your enemies can reach anywhere.
I still can't button my own shirt.
Just a couple more hours and your arm will be--
This can't be Obadiah's plan! He's not that smart!
He was the last visitor your father had. He had contact with the guard that did the shooting.
Some kind of drug, perhaps...
Somebody's controlling him.
Your father has a lot of enemies.
This has something to do with those plans we found in that terrorist camp.
What do they want from us?

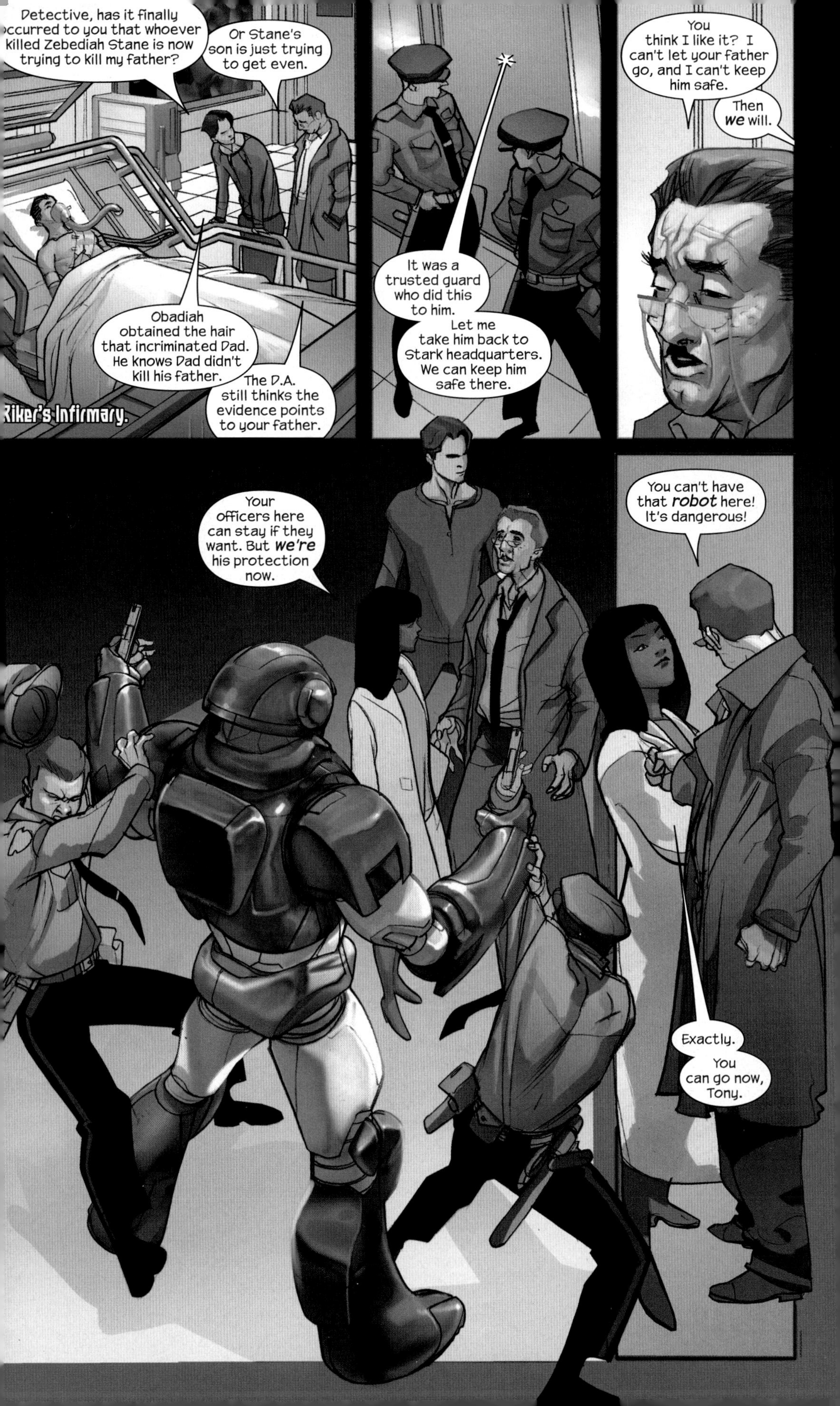
Riker's Infirmary.
Detective, has it finally occurred to you that whoever killed Zebediah Stane is now trying to kill my father?
Or Stane's son is just trying to get even.
Obadiah obtained the hair that incriminated Dad. He knows Dad didn't kill his father.
The D.A. still thinks the evidence points to your father.
It was a trusted guard who did this to him.
Let me take him back to Stark headquarters. We can keep him safe there.
You think I like it? I can't let your father go, and I can't keep him safe.
Then *we* will.
Your officers here can stay if they want. But *we're* his protection now.
You can't have that *robot* here! It's dangerous!
Exactly.
You can go now, Tony.

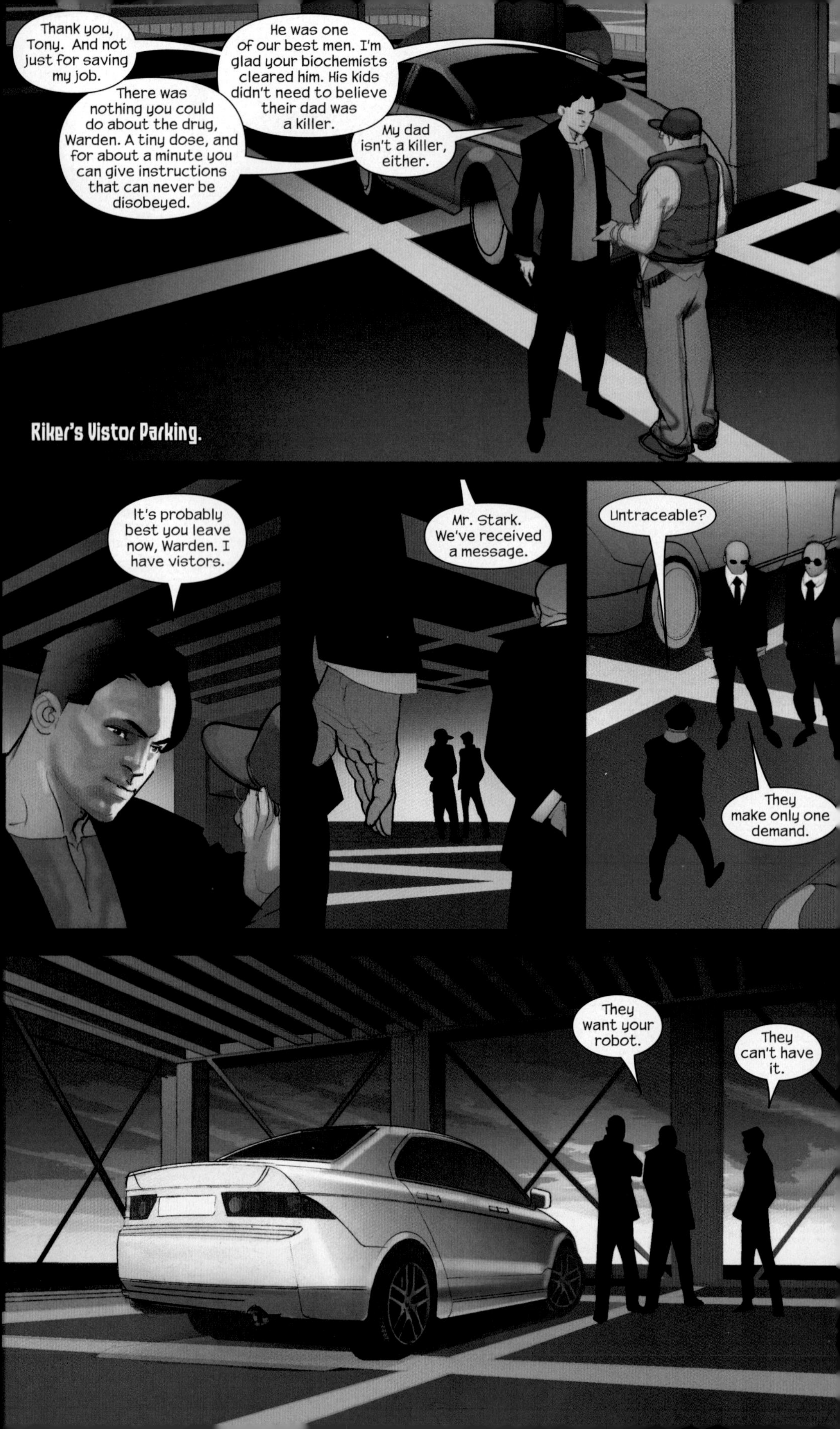
Thank you, Tony. And not just for saving my job.
He was one of our best men. I'm glad your biochemists cleared him. His kids didn't need to believe their dad was a killer.
There was nothing you could do about the drug, Warden. A tiny dose, and for about a minute you can give instructions that can never be disobeyed.
My dad isn't a killer, either.
Riker's Vistor Parking.
It's probably best you leave now, Warden. I have vistors.
Mr. Stark. We've received a message.
Untraceable?
They make only one demand.
They want your robot.
They can't have it.

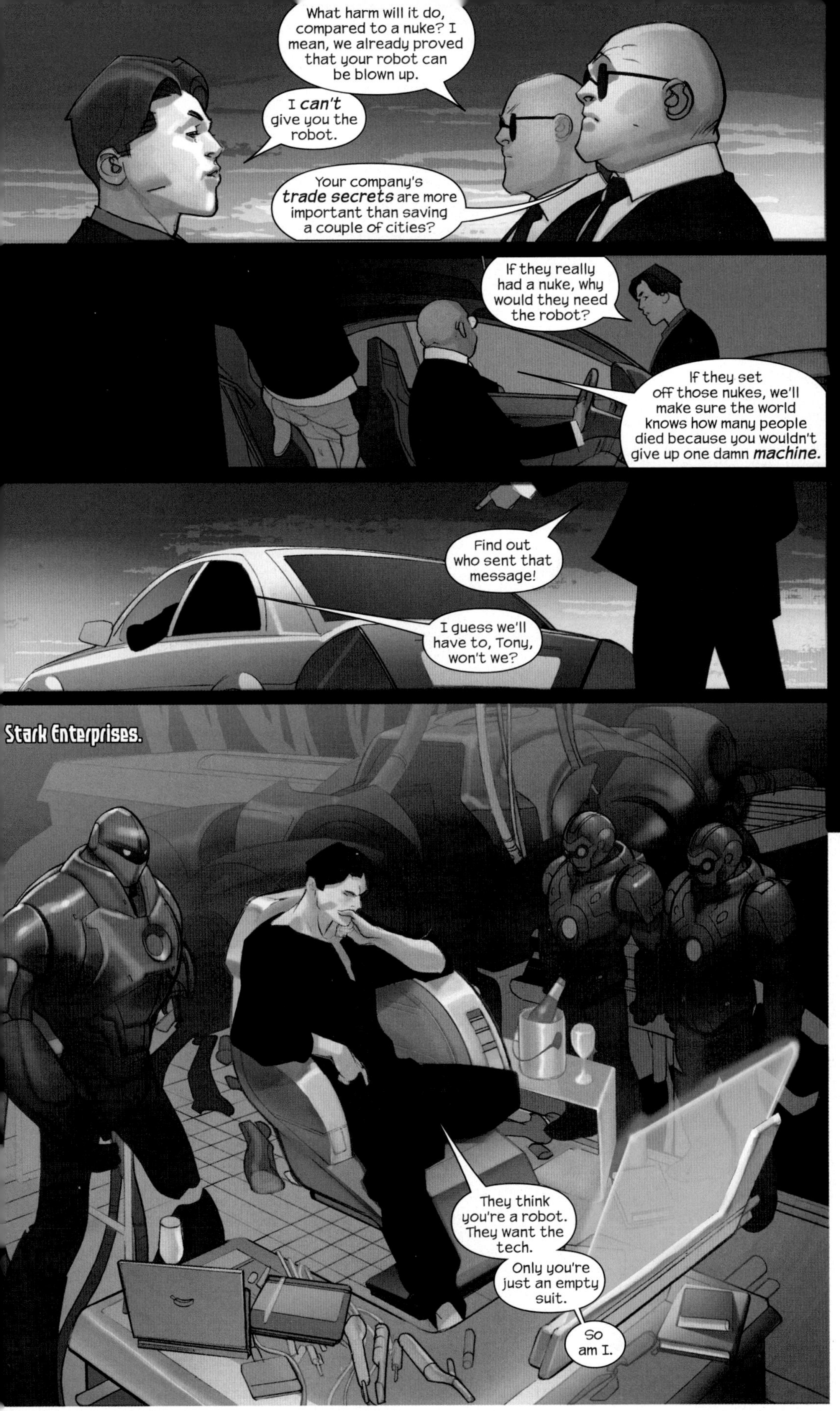
What harm will it do, compared to a nuke? I mean, we already proved that your robot can be blown up.
I *can't* give you the robot.
Your company's *trade secrets* are more important than saving a couple of cities?
If they really had a nuke, why would they need the robot?
If they set off those nukes, we'll make sure the world knows how many people died because you wouldn't give up one damn *machine.*
Find out who sent that message!
I guess we'll have to, Tony, won't we?
Stark Enterprises.
They think you're a robot. They want the tech.
Only you're just an empty suit.
So am I.

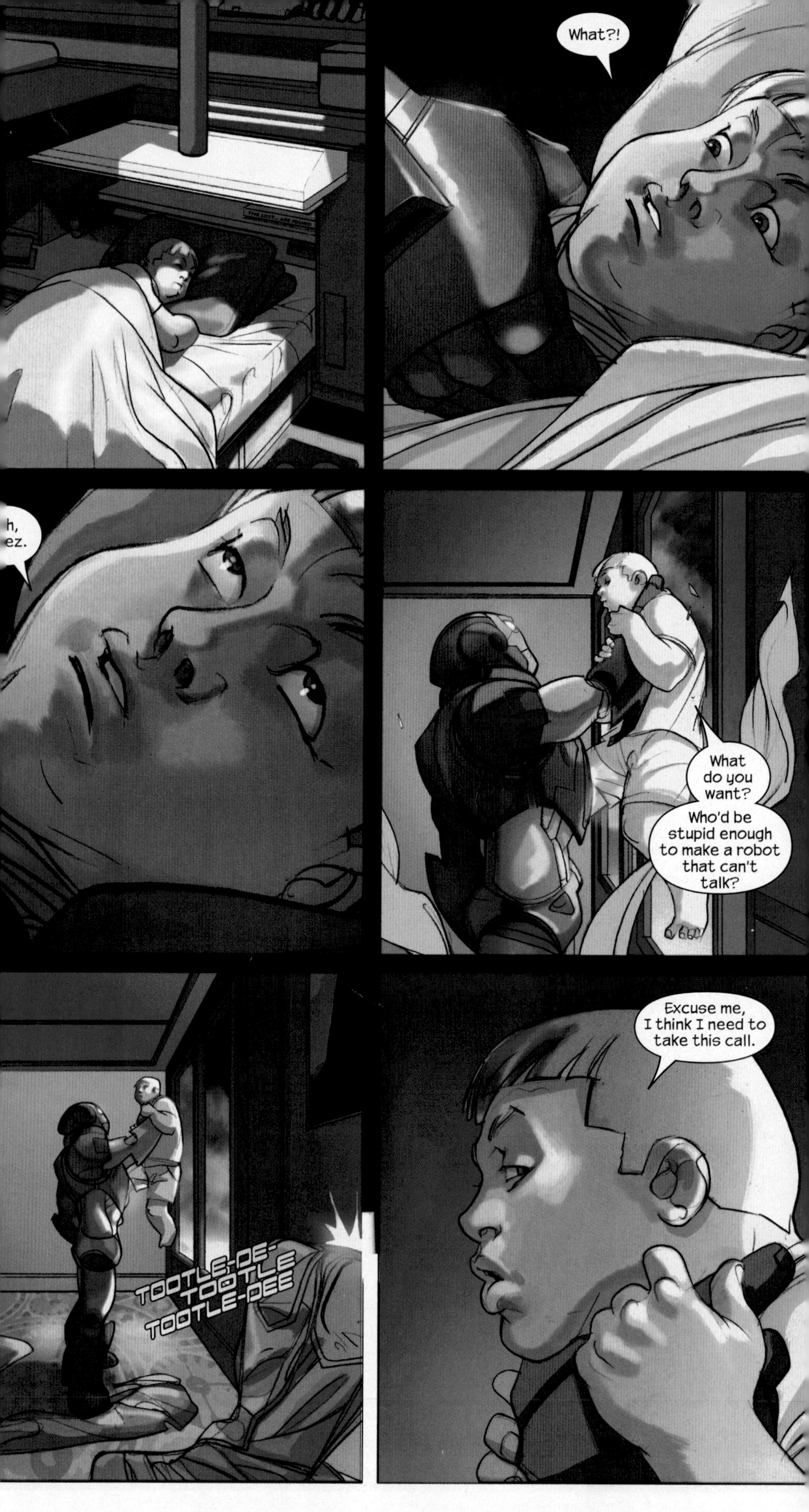

What?!
h,
ez.
What do you want?
Who'd be stupid enough to make a robot that can't talk?
TOOTLE-DE-TOOTLE TOOTLE-DEE
Excuse me, I think I need to take this call.

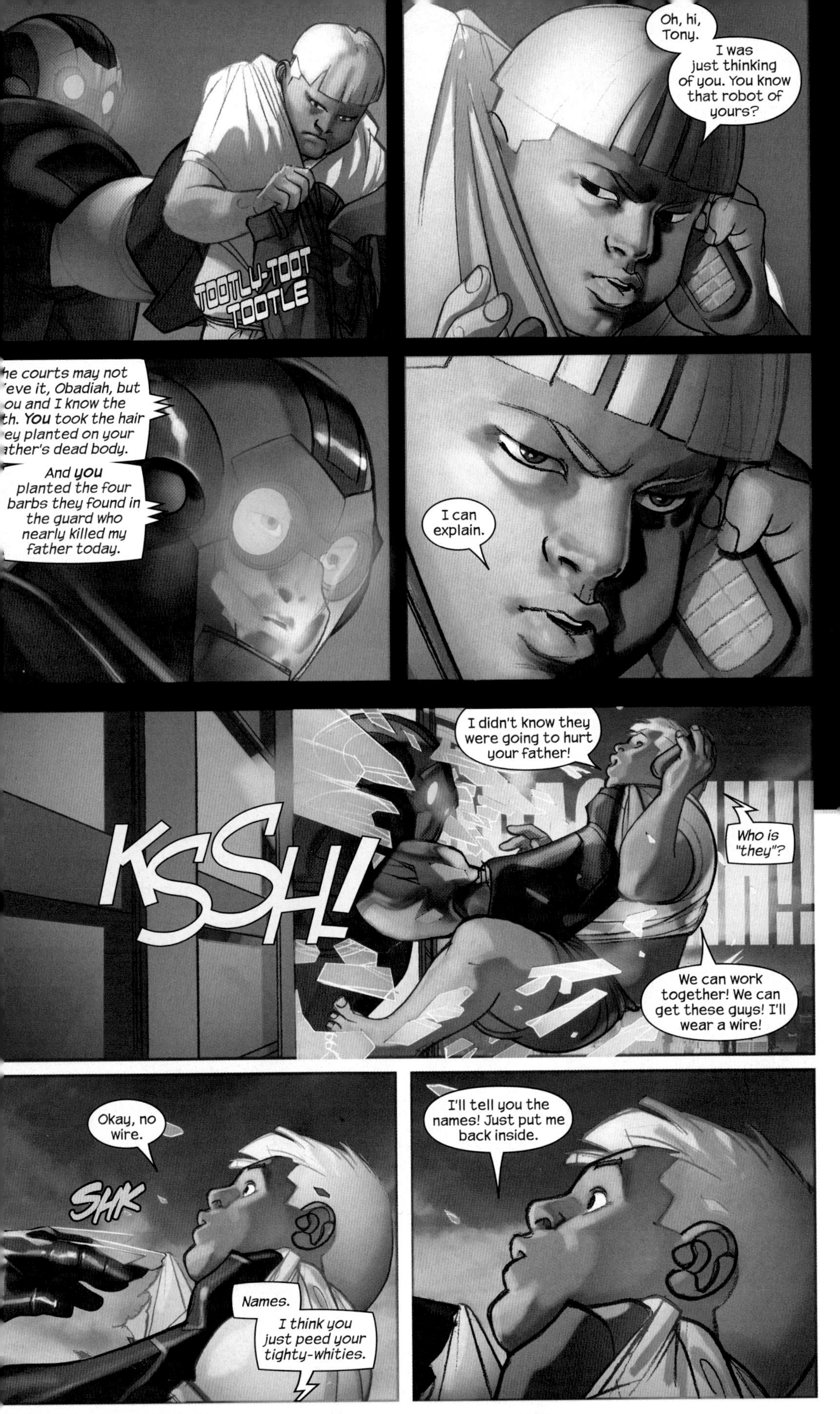
TOOTLY-TOOT TOOTLE
Oh, hi, Tony.
I was just thinking of you. You know that robot of yours?
he courts may not 'eve it, Obadiah, but ou and I know the th. YOU took the hair ey planted on your ather's dead body.
And YOU planted the four barbs they found in the guard who nearly killed my father today.
I can explain.
KSSH!
I didn't know they were going to hurt your father!
Who is "they"?
We can work together! We can get these guys! I'll wear a wire!
Okay, no wire.
SHK
Names.
I think you just peed your tighty-whities.
I'll tell you the names! Just put me back inside.

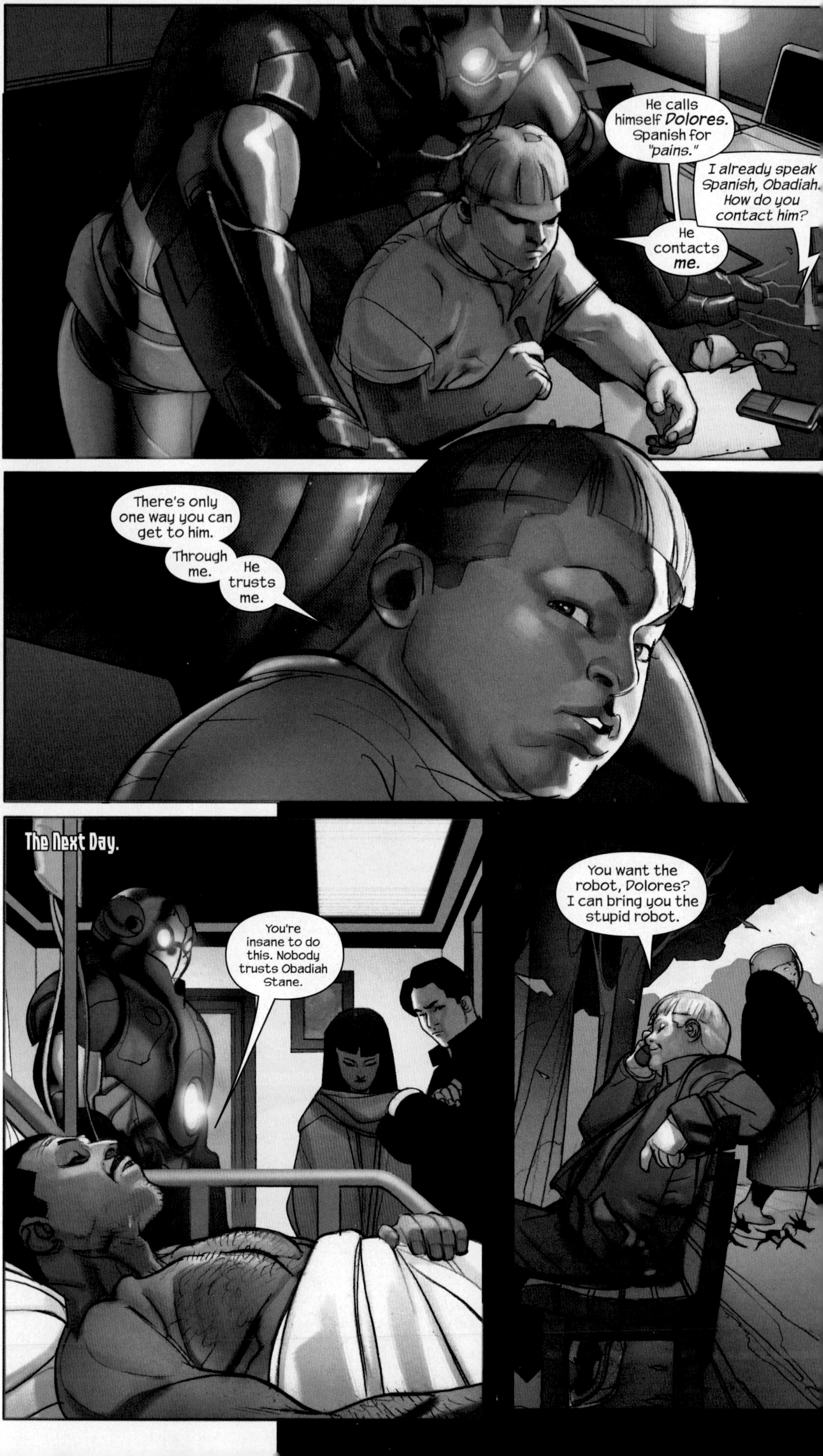

He calls himself Dolores. Spanish for "pains."
I already speak Spanish, Obadiah. How do you contact him?
He contacts me.
There's only one way you can get to him.
Through me.
He trusts me.
The Next Day.
You're insane to do this. Nobody trusts Obadiah Stane.
You want the robot, Dolores? I can bring you the stupid robot.

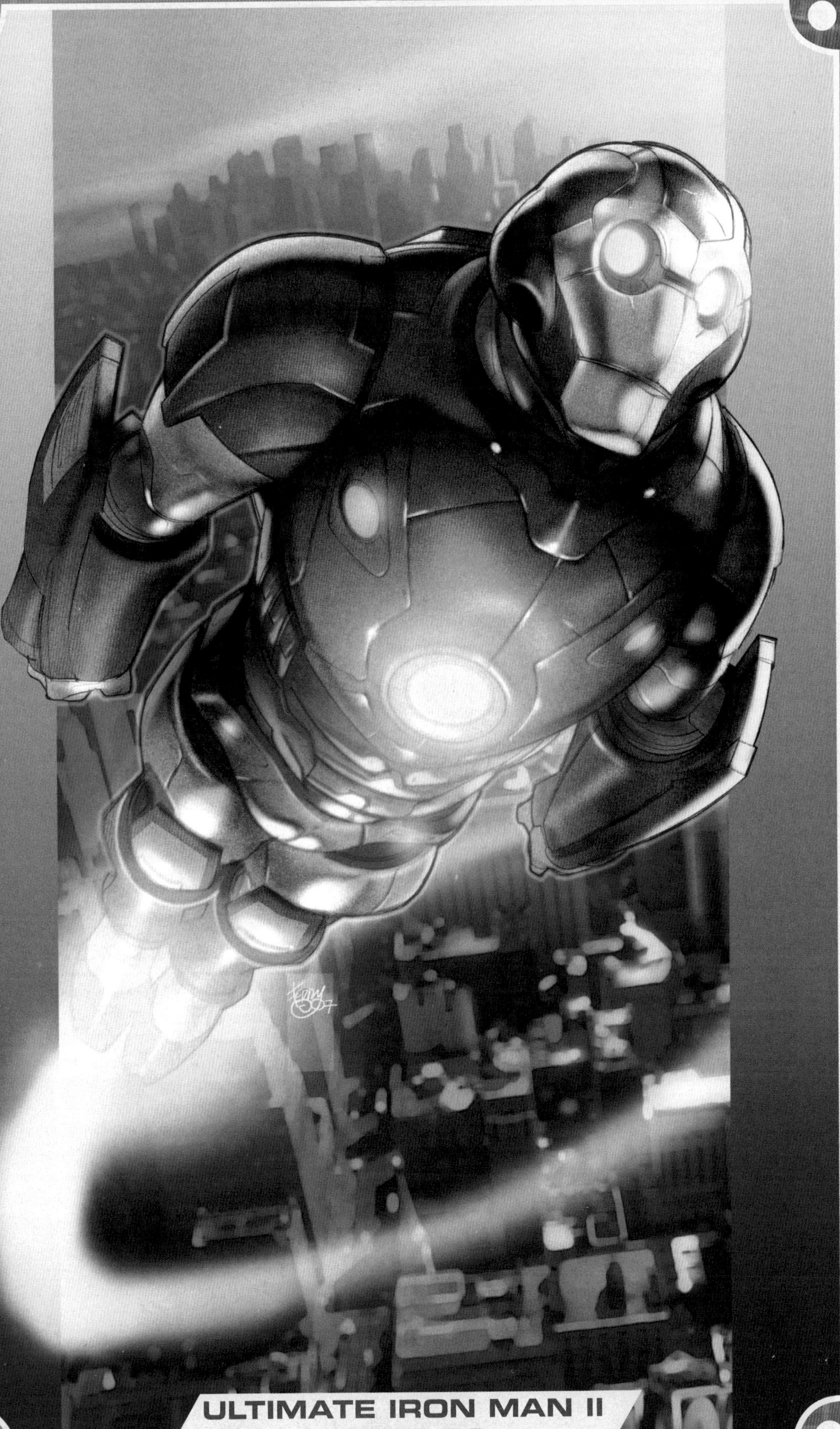

ULTIMATE IRON MAN II
ISSUE 03

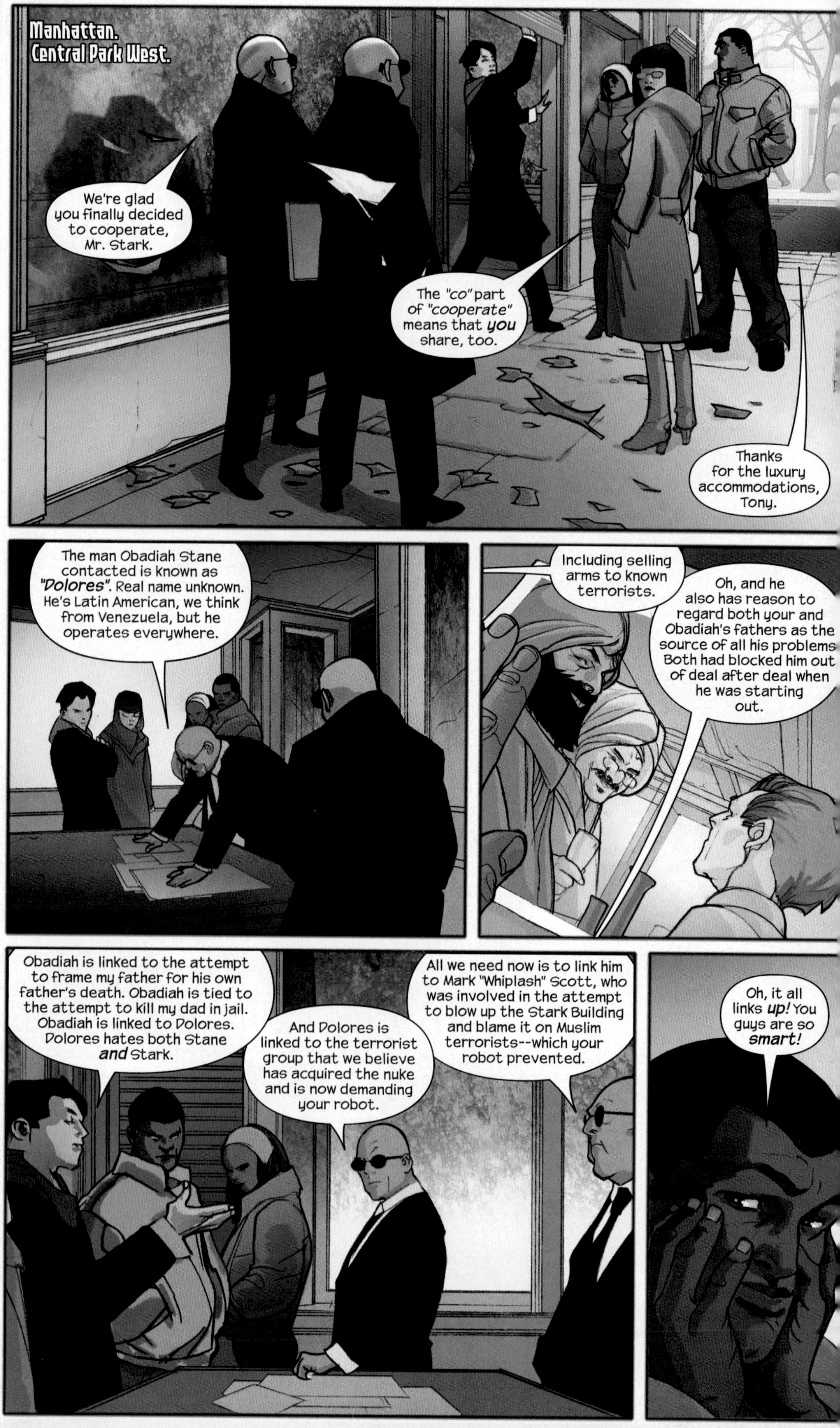

Manhattan. Central Park West.
We're glad you finally decided to cooperate, Mr. Stark.
The "co" part of "cooperate" means that you share, too.
Thanks for the luxury accommodations, Tony.
The man Obadiah Stane contacted is known as "Dolores". Real name unknown. He's Latin American, we think from Venezuela, but he operates everywhere.
Including selling arms to known terrorists.
Oh, and he also has reason to regard both your and Obadiah's fathers as the source of all his problems Both had blocked him out of deal after deal when he was starting out.
Obadiah is linked to the attempt to frame my father for his own father's death. Obadiah is tied to the attempt to kill my dad in jail. Obadiah is linked to Dolores. Dolores hates both Stane and Stark.
And Dolores is linked to the terrorist group that we believe has acquired the nuke and is now demanding your robot.
All we need now is to link him to Mark "Whiplash" Scott, who was involved in the attempt to blow up the Stark Building and blame it on Muslim terrorists--which your robot prevented.
Oh, it all links up! You guys are so smart!

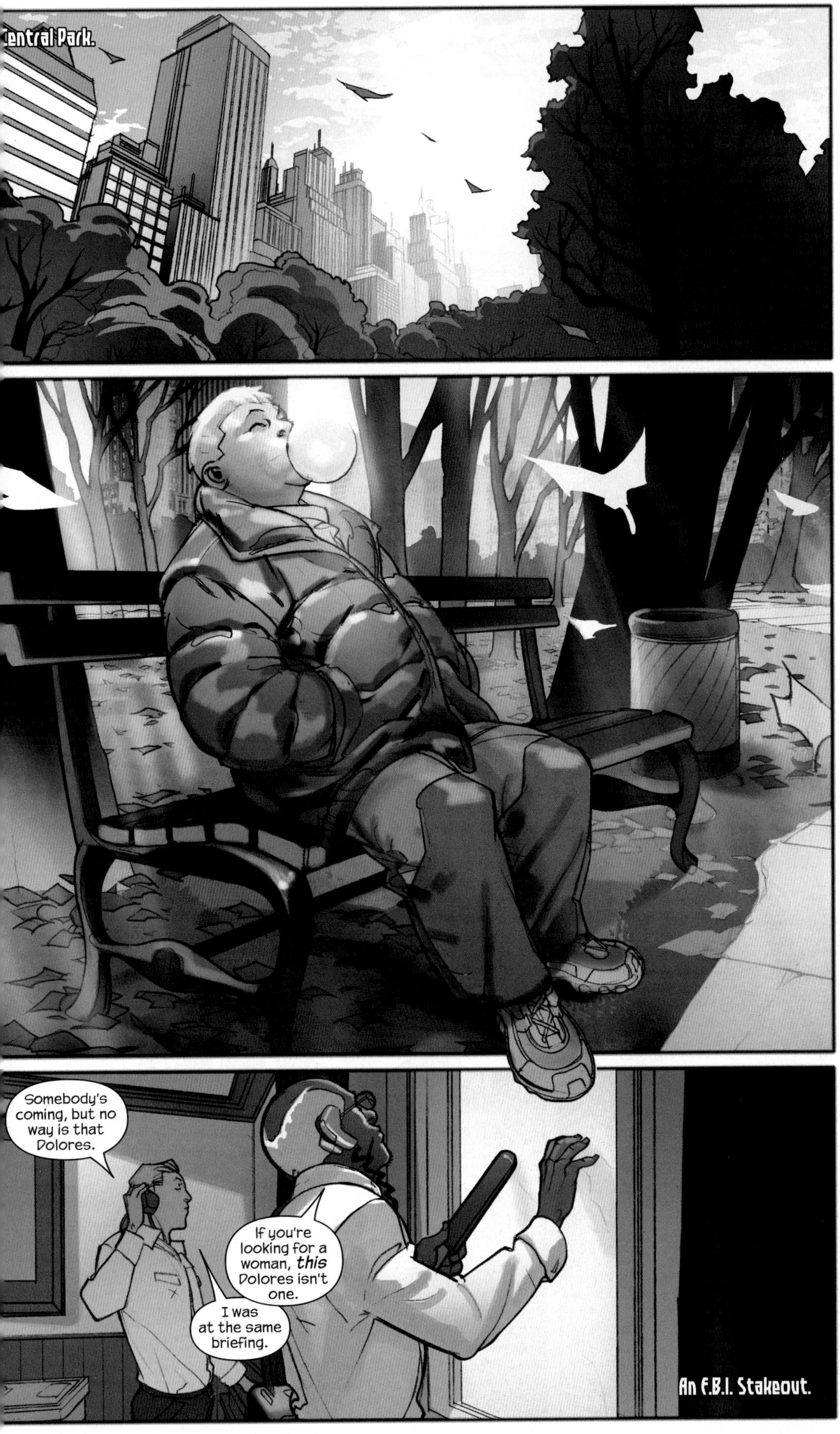
Central Park.
Somebody's coming, but no way is that Dolores.
If you're looking for a woman, *this* Dolores isn't one.
I was at the same briefing.
An F.B.I. Stakeout.

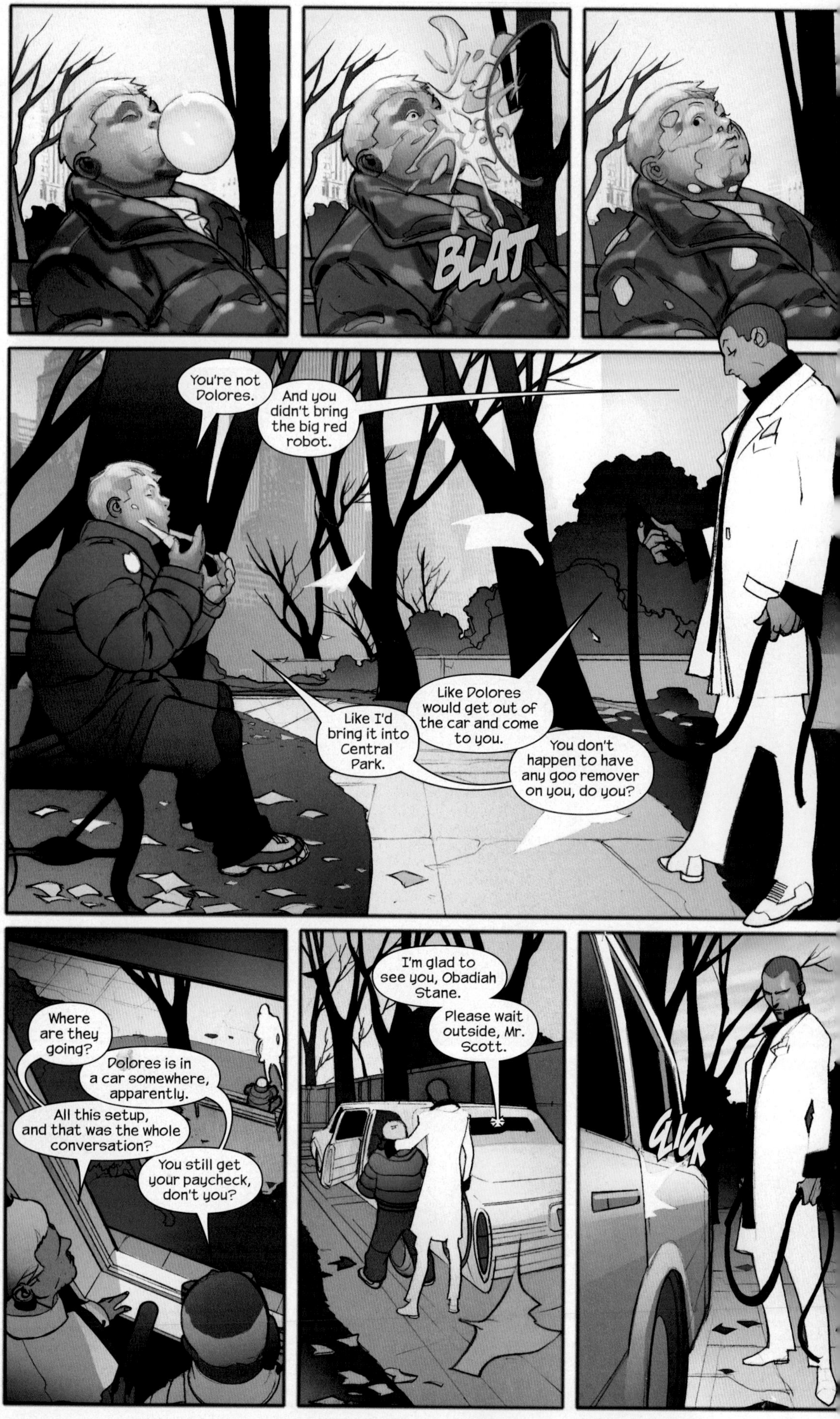
BLAT
You're not Dolores.
And you didn't bring the big red robot.
Like Dolores would get out of the car and come to you.
Like I'd bring it into Central Park.
You don't happen to have any goo remover on you, do you?
Where are they going?
Dolores is in a car somewhere, apparently.
All this setup, and that was the whole conversation?
You still get your paycheck, don't you?
I'm glad to see you, Obadiah Stane.
Please wait outside, Mr. Scott.
CLICK

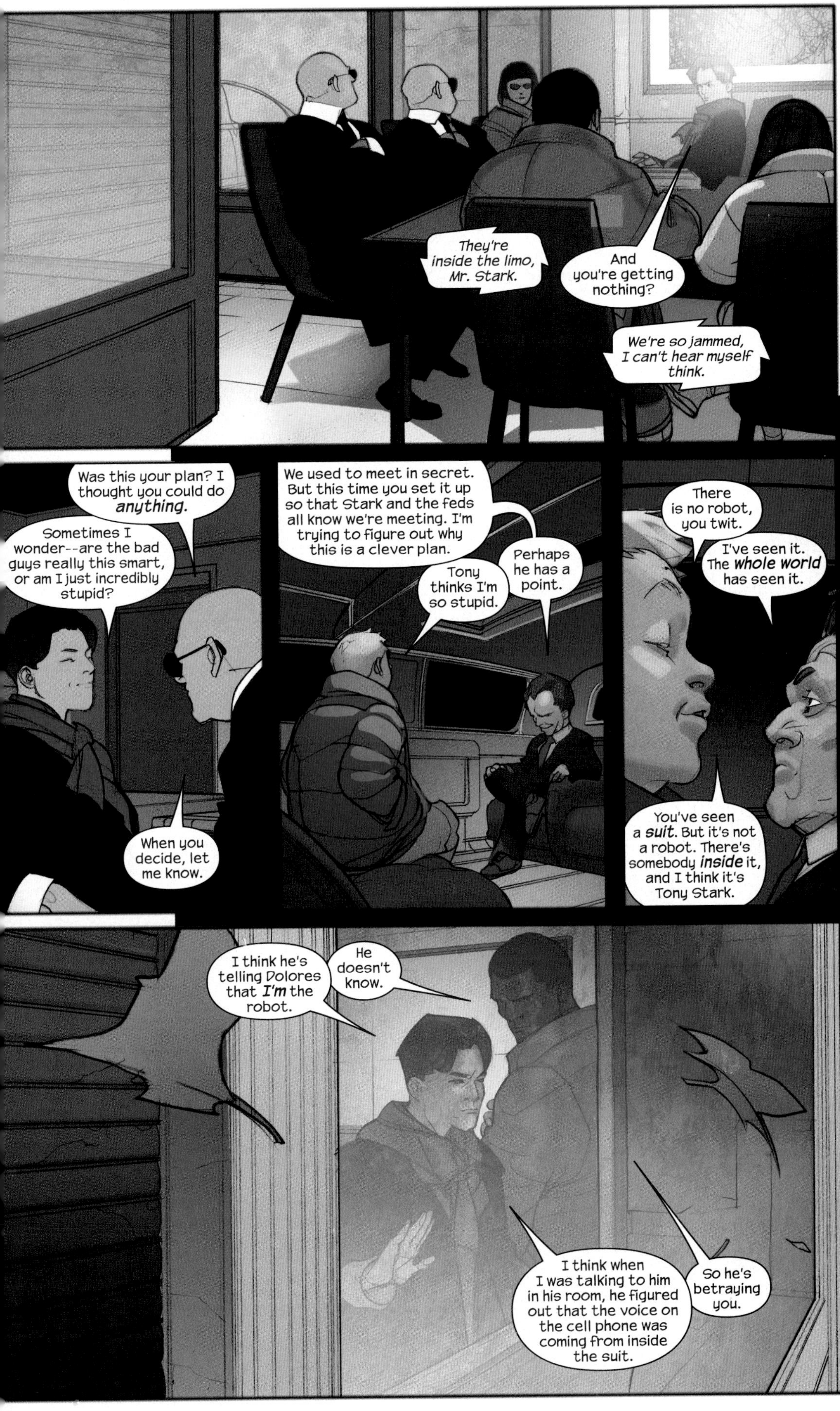

They're inside the limo, Mr. Stark.
And you're getting nothing?
We're so jammed, I can't hear myself think.
Was this your plan? I thought you could do *anything*.
Sometimes I wonder--are the bad guys really this smart, or am I just incredibly stupid?
When you decide, let me know.
We used to meet in secret. But this time you set it up so that Stark and the feds all know we're meeting. I'm trying to figure out why this is a clever plan.
Tony thinks I'm so stupid.
Perhaps he has a point.
There is no robot, you twit.
I've seen it. The **whole world** has seen it.
You've seen a **suit**. But it's not a robot. There's somebody ***inside*** it, and I think it's Tony Stark.
I think he's telling Dolores that ***I'm*** the robot.
He doesn't know.
I think when I was talking to him in his room, he figured out that the voice on the cell phone was coming from inside the suit.
So he's betraying you.

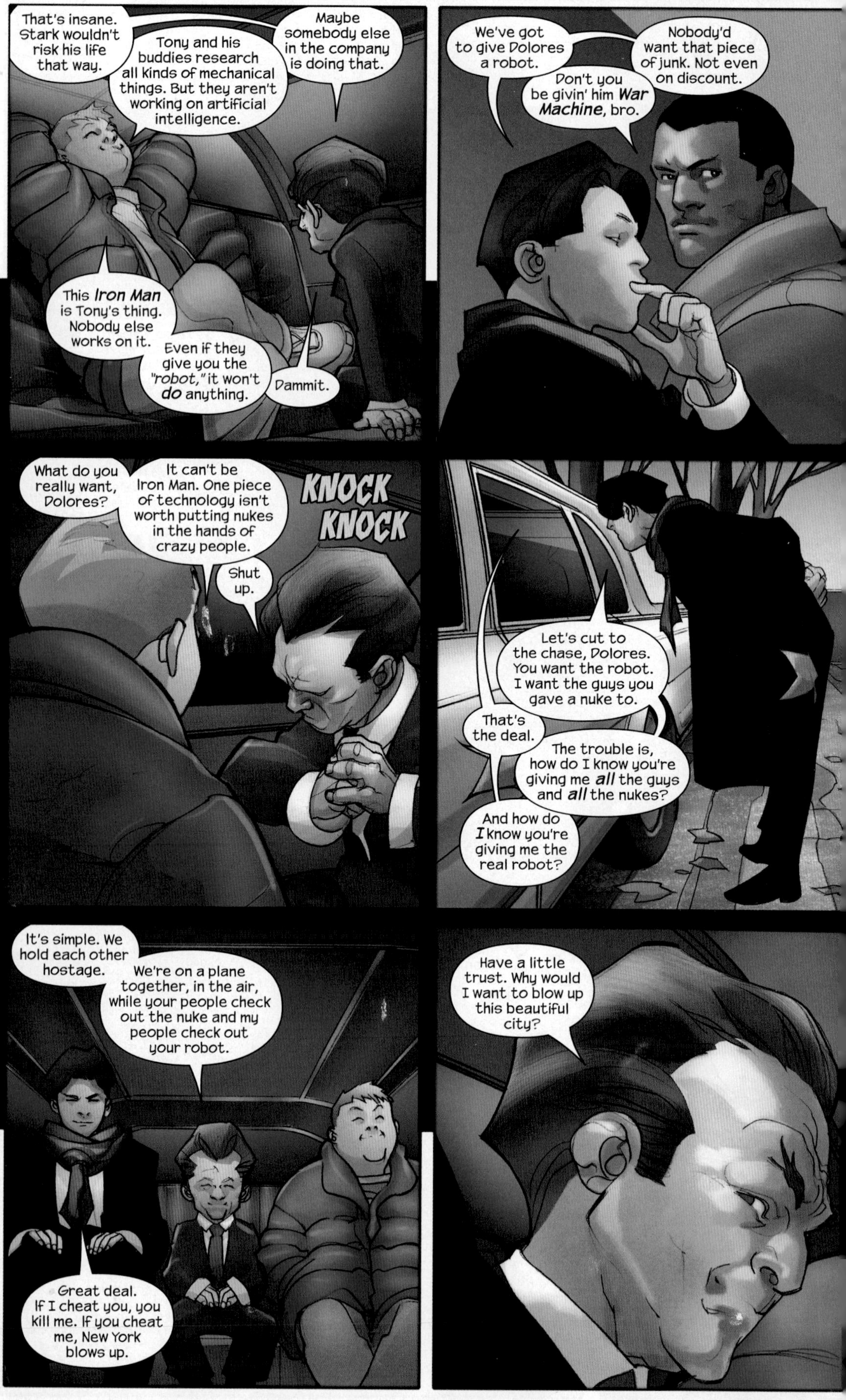
That's insane. Stark wouldn't risk his life that way.
Maybe somebody else in the company is doing that.
Tony and his buddies research all kinds of mechanical things. But they aren't working on artificial intelligence.
This *Iron Man* is Tony's thing. Nobody else works on it.
Even if they give you the *"robot,"* it won't **do** anything.
Dammit.
We've got to give Dolores a robot.
Nobody'd want that piece of junk. Not even on discount.
Don't you be givin' him *War Machine*, bro.
What do you really want, Dolores?
It can't be Iron Man. One piece of technology isn't worth putting nukes in the hands of crazy people.
KNOCK KNOCK
Shut up.
Let's cut to the chase, Dolores. You want the robot. I want the guys you gave a nuke to.
That's the deal.
The trouble is, how do I know you're giving me *all* the guys and *all* the nukes?
And how do *I* know you're giving me the real robot?
It's simple. We hold each other hostage.
We're on a plane together, in the air, while your people check out the nuke and my people check out your robot.
Great deal. If I cheat you, you kill me. If you cheat me, New York blows up.
Have a little trust. Why would I want to blow up this beautiful city?

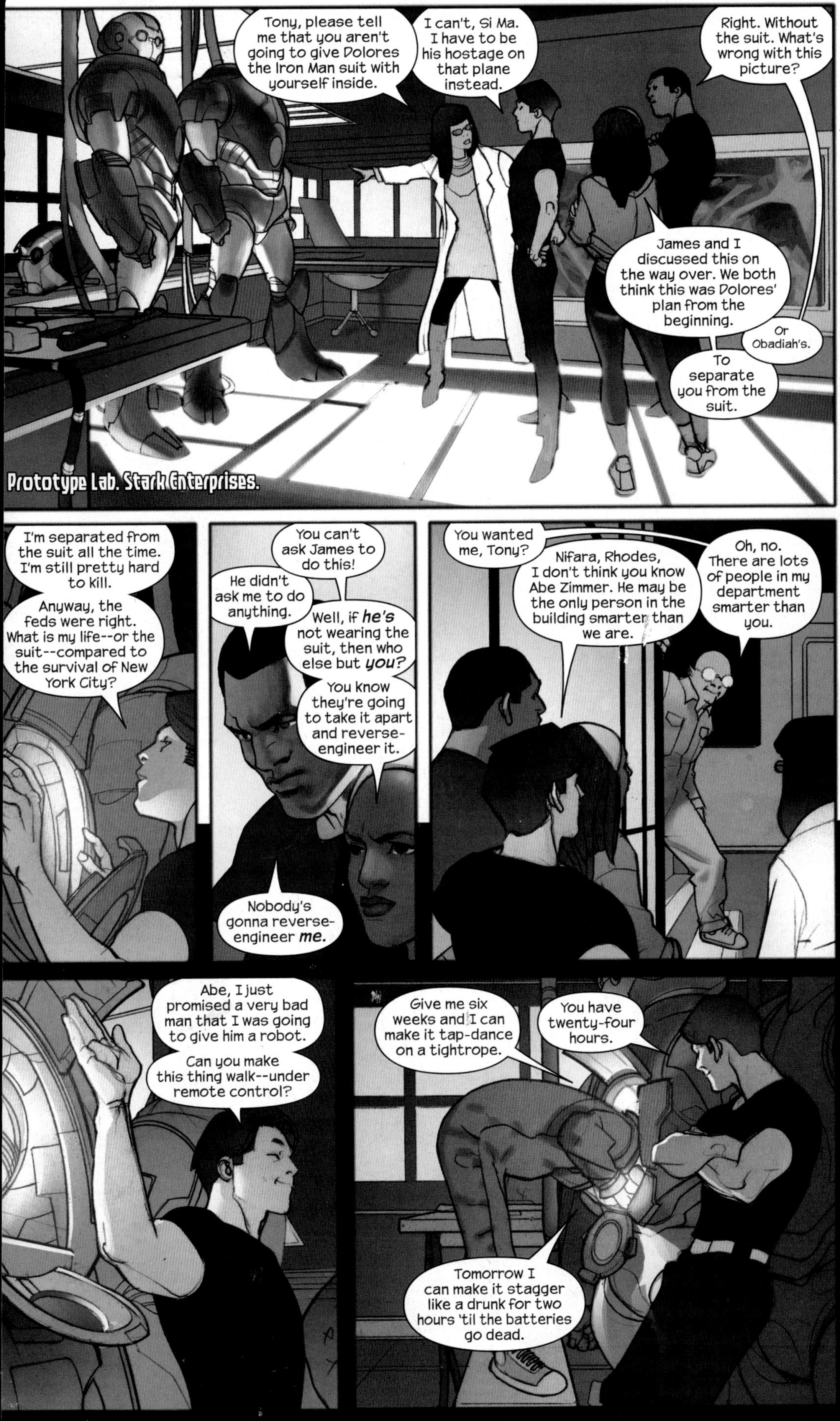
Tony, please tell me that you aren't going to give Dolores the Iron Man suit with yourself inside.
I can't, Si Ma. I have to be his hostage on that plane instead.
Right. Without the suit. What's wrong with this picture?
James and I discussed this on the way over. We both think this was Dolores' plan from the beginning.
Or Obadiah's.
To separate you from the suit.
Prototype Lab. Stark Enterprises.
I'm separated from the suit all the time. I'm still pretty hard to kill.
Anyway, the feds were right. What is my life--or the suit--compared to the survival of New York City?
You can't ask James to do this!
He didn't ask me to do anything.
Well, if *he's* not wearing the suit, then who else but *you?*
You know they're going to take it apart and reverse-engineer it.
Nobody's gonna reverse-engineer *me.*
You wanted me, Tony?
Nifara, Rhodes, I don't think you know Abe Zimmer. He may be the only person in the building smarter than we are.
Oh, no. There are lots of people in my department smarter than you.
Abe, I just promised a very bad man that I was going to give him a robot.
Can you make this thing walk--under remote control?
Give me six weeks and I can make it tap-dance on a tightrope.
You have twenty-four hours.
Tomorrow I can make it stagger like a drunk for two hours 'til the batteries go dead.

I think I saw this robot before. In a movie. From 1955.

It's not a robot. It's a remote-control device.

I asked Abe a year ago to work on creating a disposable man. A cheap machine we could send out by remote control to draw enemy fire.

So far it's not cheap and it doesn't look like a man.

But it can keep its balance, climb stairs, go over obstacles, and make semi-natural hand gestures.

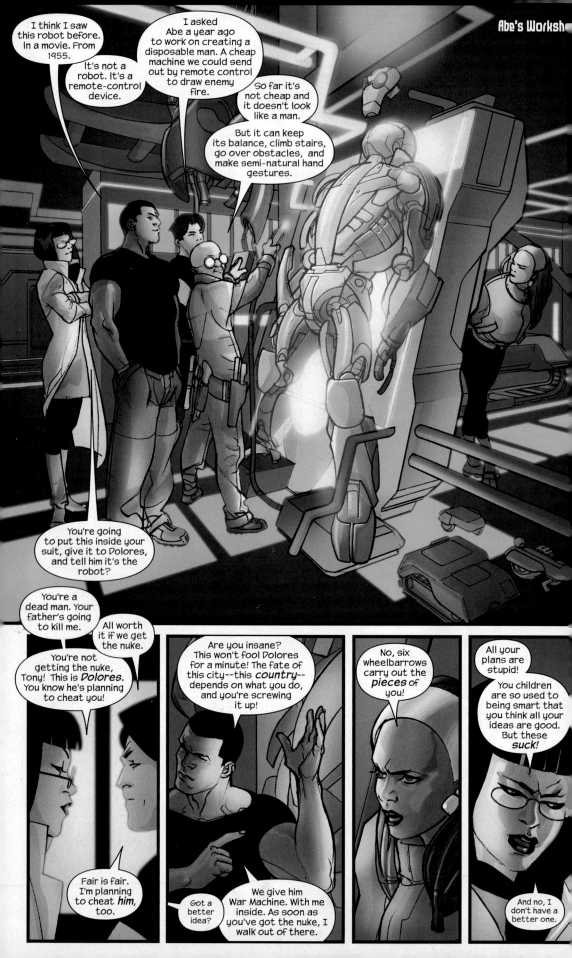

You're going to put this inside your suit, give it to Dolores, and tell him it's the robot?

You're a dead man. Your father's going to kill me.

All worth it if we get the nuke.

You're not getting the nuke, Tony! This is Dolores. You know he's planning to cheat you!

Fair is fair. I'm planning to cheat him, too.

Are you insane? This won't fool Dolores for a minute! The fate of this city--this country-- depends on what you do, and you're screwing it up!

Got a better idea?

We give him War Machine. With me inside. As soon as you've got the nuke, I walk out of there.

No, six wheelbarrows carry out the pieces of you!

All your plans are stupid! You children are so used to being smart that you think all your ideas are good. But these suck!

And no, I don't have a better one.

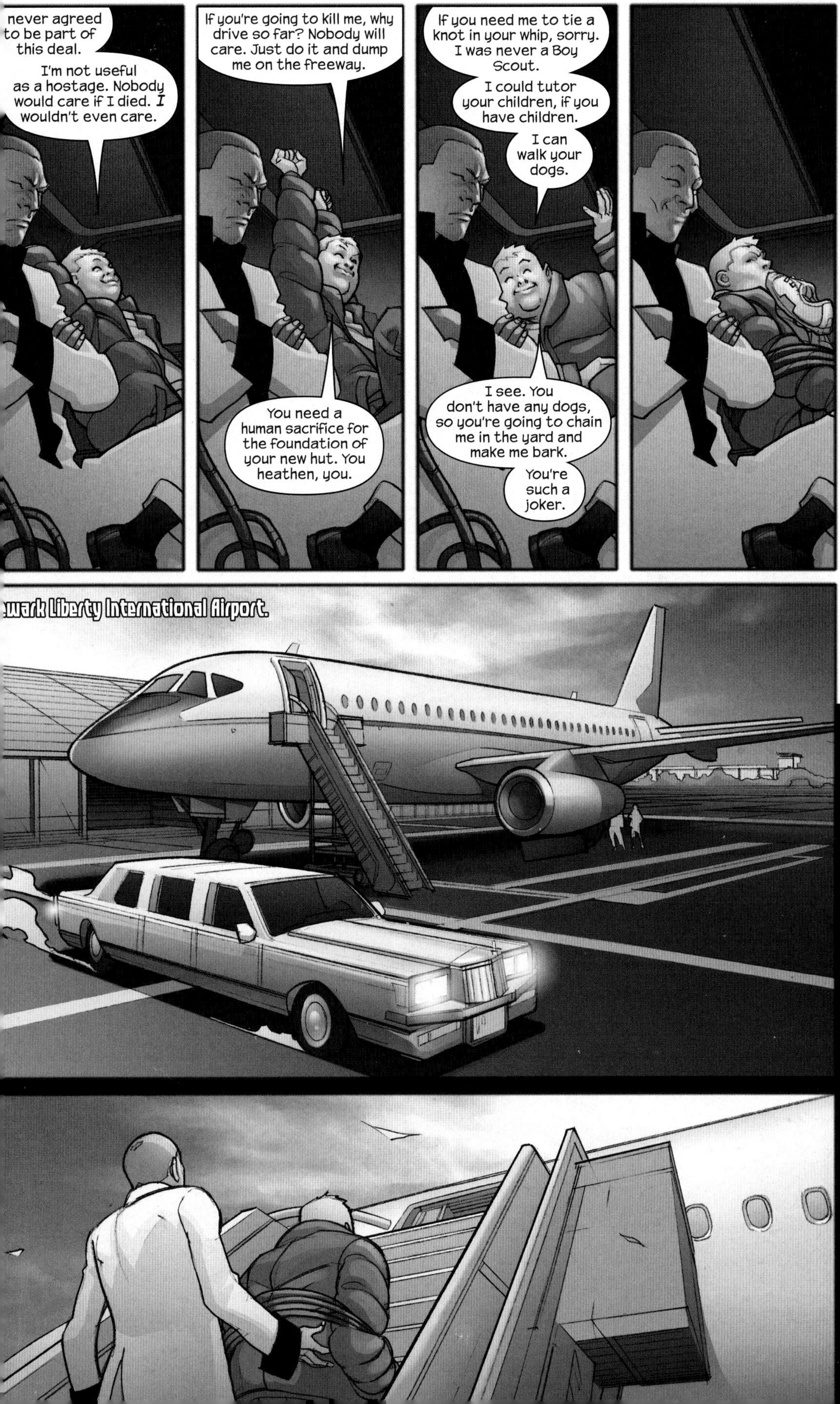

never agreed to be part of this deal.
I'm not useful as a hostage. Nobody would care if I died. *I* wouldn't even care.
If you're going to kill me, why drive so far? Nobody will care. Just do it and dump me on the freeway.
You need a human sacrifice for the foundation of your new hut. You heathen, you.
If you need me to tie a knot in your whip, sorry. I was never a Boy Scout.
I could tutor your children, if you have children.
I can walk your dogs.
I see. You don't have any dogs, so you're going to chain me in the yard and make me bark.
You're such a joker.
wark Liberty International Airport.

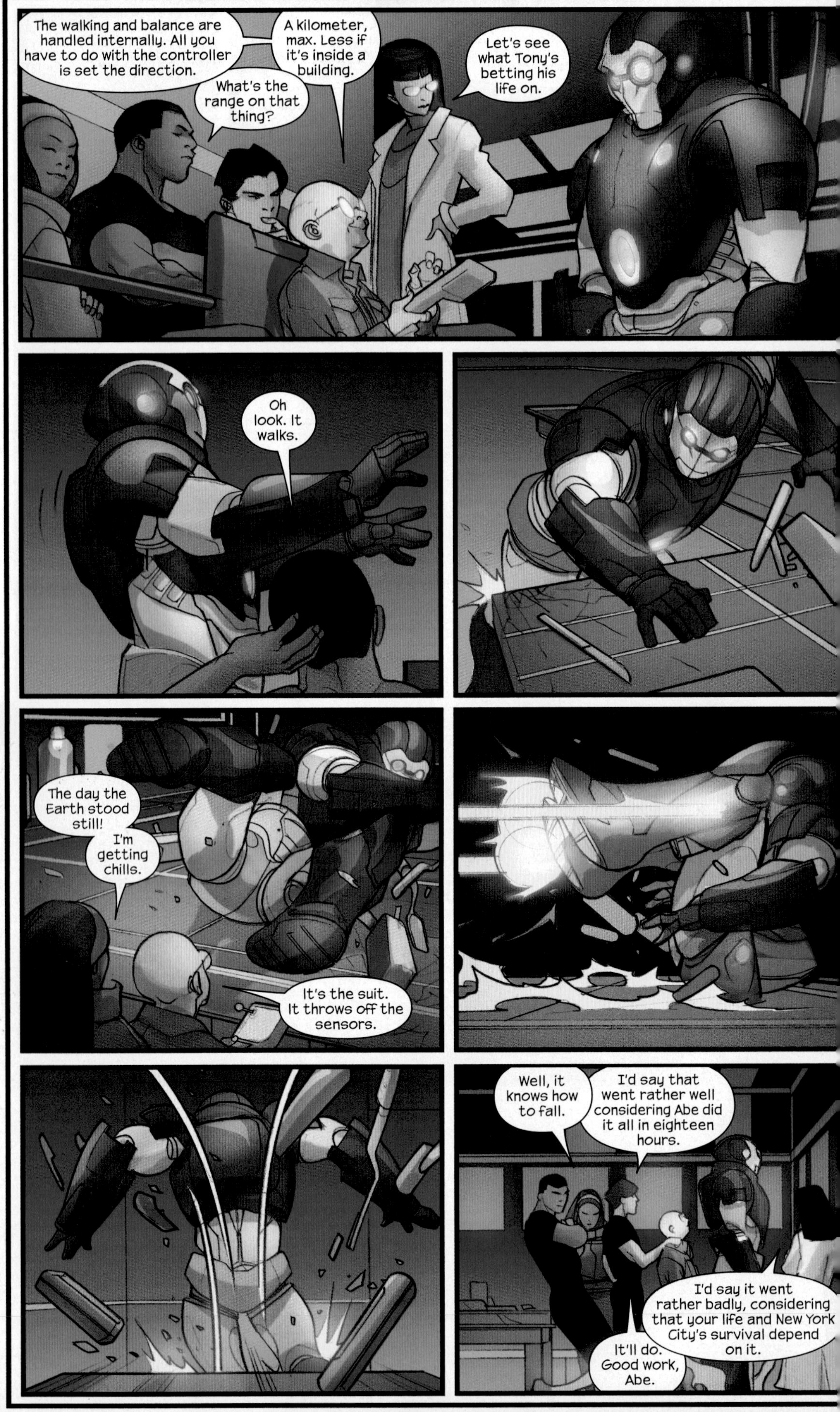

The walking and balance are handled internally. All you have to do with the controller is set the direction.
What's the range on that thing?
A kilometer, max. Less if it's inside a building.
Let's see what Tony's betting his life on.
Oh look. It walks.
The day the Earth stood still!
I'm getting chills.
It's the suit. It throws off the sensors.
Well, it knows how to fall.
I'd say that went rather well considering Abe did it all in eighteen hours.
I'd say it went rather badly, considering that your life and New York City's survival depend on it.
It'll do. Good work, Abe.

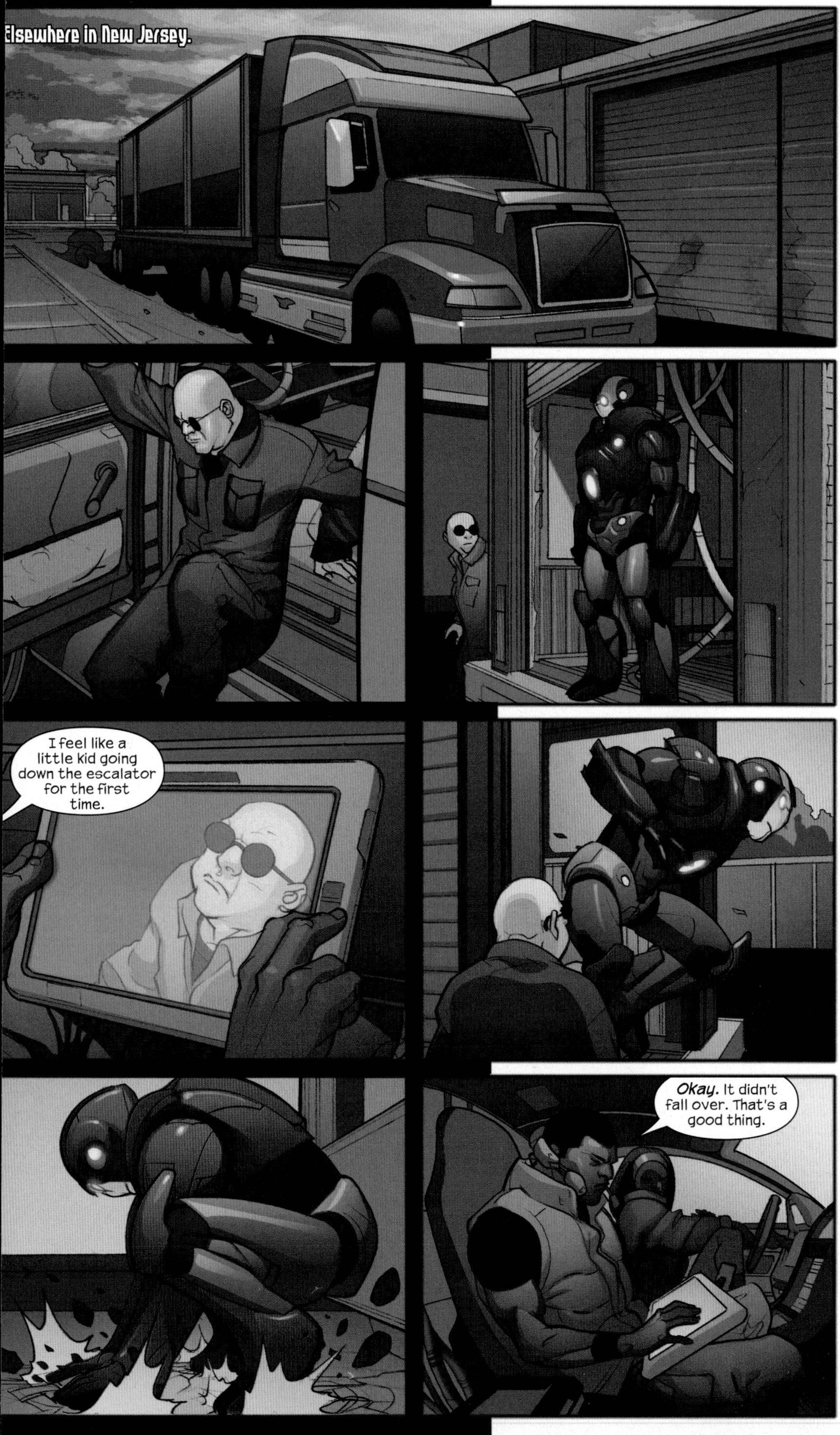
Elsewhere in New Jersey.
I feel like a little kid going down the escalator for the first time.
Okay. It didn't fall over. That's a good thing.

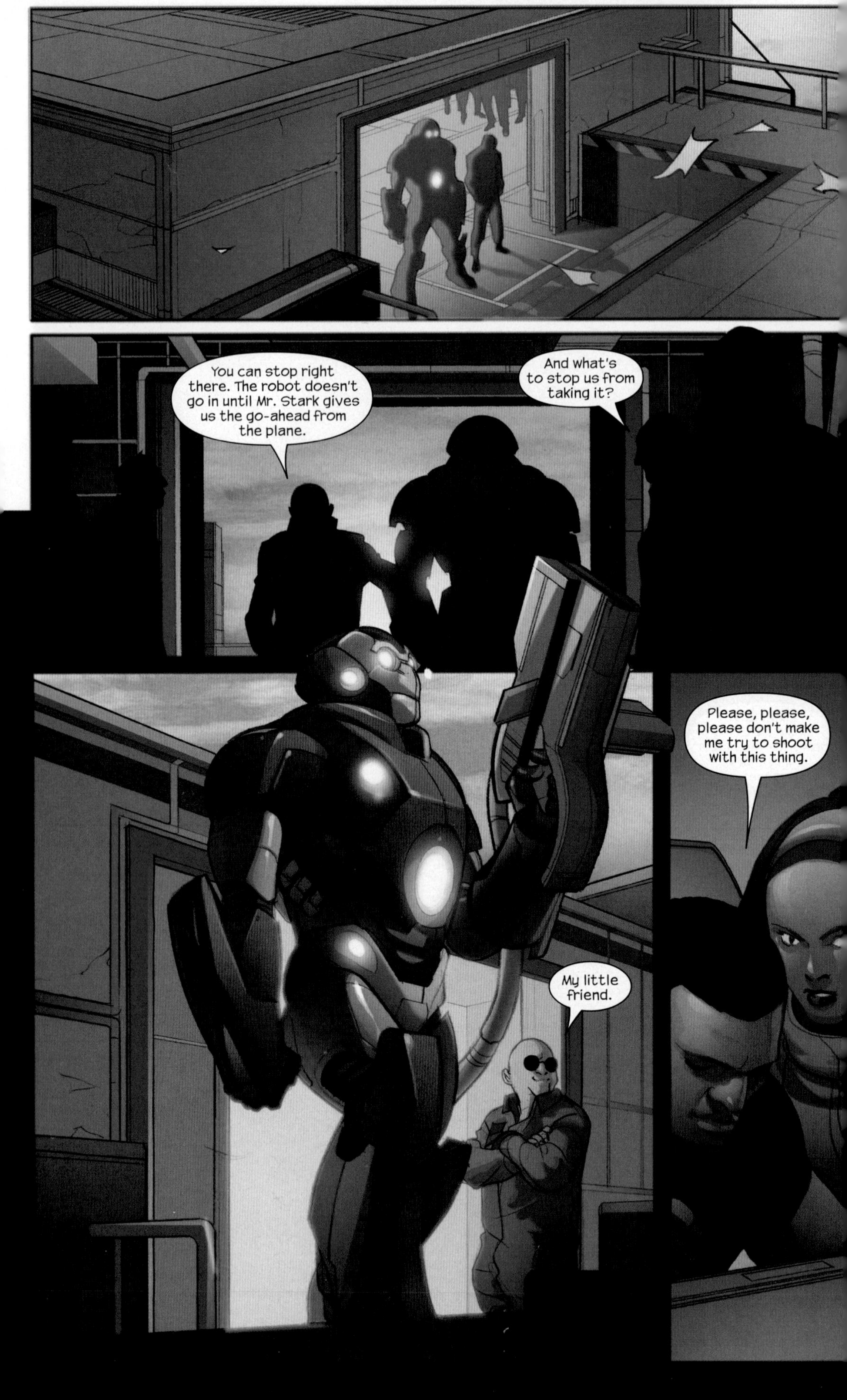

You can stop right there. The robot doesn't go in until Mr. Stark gives us the go-ahead from the plane.
And what's to stop us from taking it?
Please, please, please don't make me try to shoot with this thing.
My little friend.

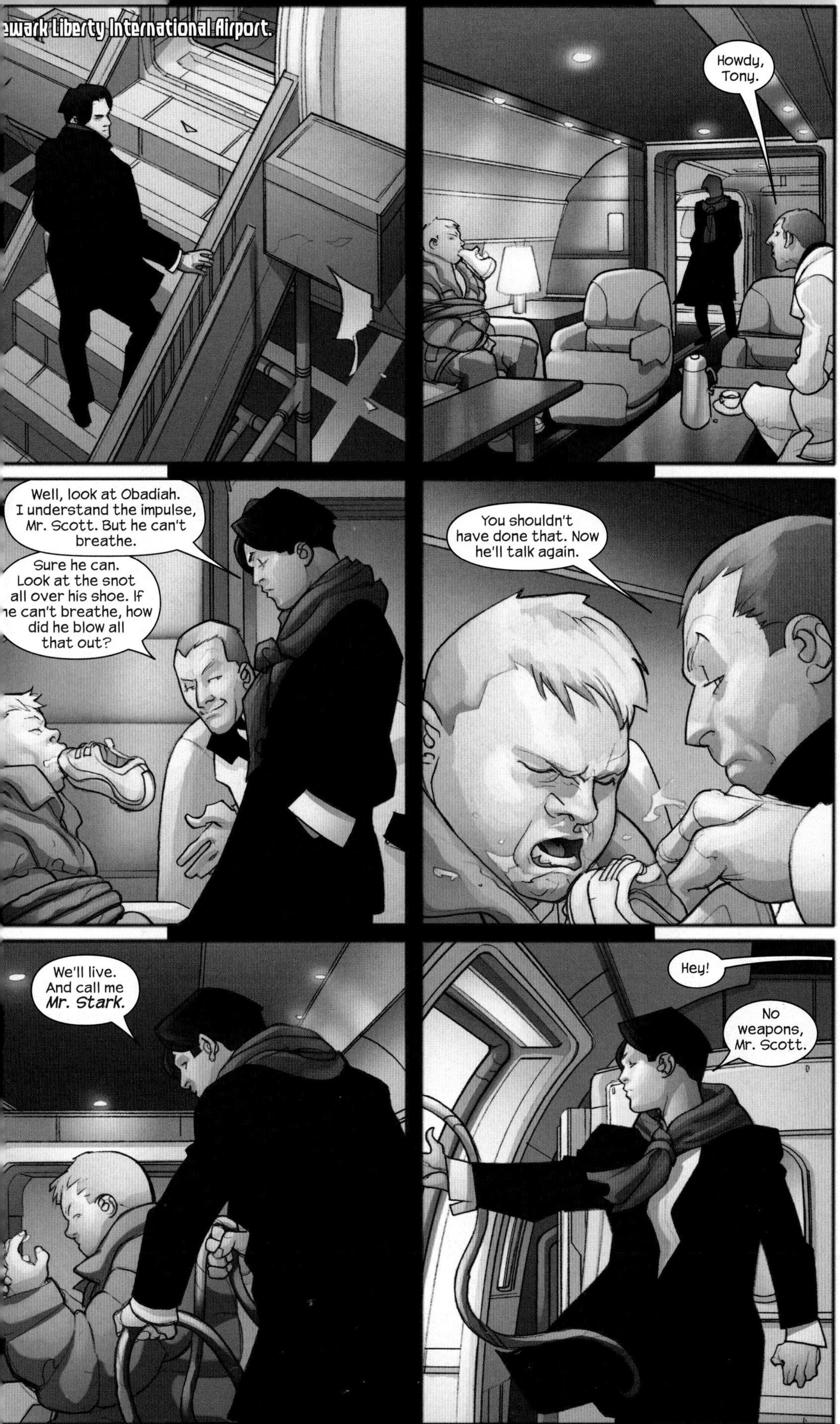

ewark Liberty International Airport.
Howdy, Tony.
Well, look at Obadiah. I understand the impulse, Mr. Scott. But he can't breathe.
Sure he can. Look at the snot all over his shoe. If he can't breathe, how did he blow all that out?
You shouldn't have done that. Now he'll talk again.
We'll live. And call me *Mr. Stark.*
Hey!
No weapons, Mr. Scott.

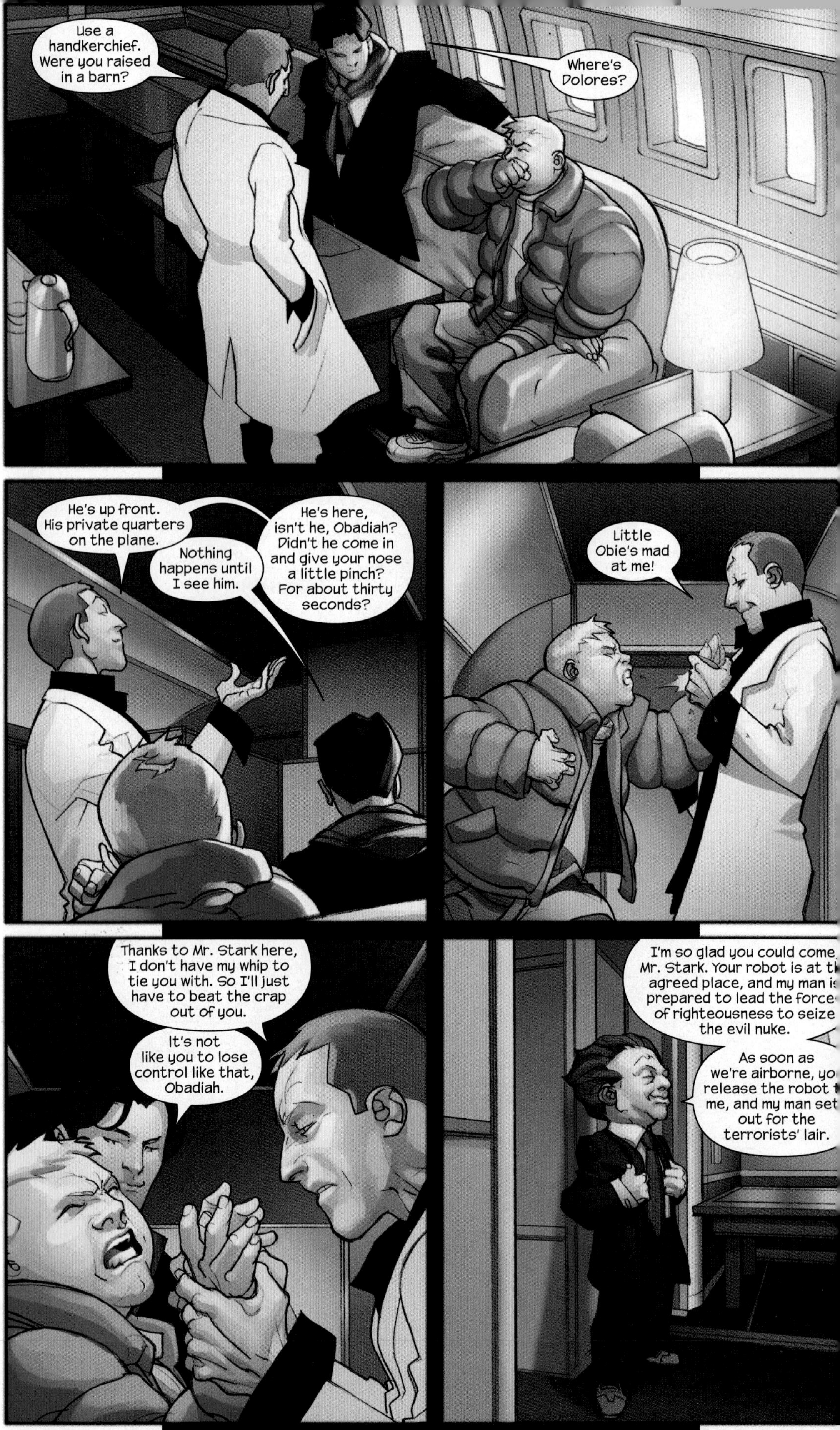
Use a handkerchief. Were you raised in a barn?
Where's Dolores?
He's up front. His private quarters on the plane.
Nothing happens until I see him.
He's here, isn't he, Obadiah? Didn't he come in and give your nose a little pinch? For about thirty seconds?
Little Obie's mad at me!
Thanks to Mr. Stark here, I don't have my whip to tie you with. So I'll just have to beat the crap out of you.
It's not like you to lose control like that, Obadiah.
I'm so glad you could come Mr. Stark. Your robot is at t agreed place, and my man is prepared to lead the force of righteousness to seize the evil nuke.
As soon as we're airborne, yo release the robot me, and my man set out for the terrorists' lair.

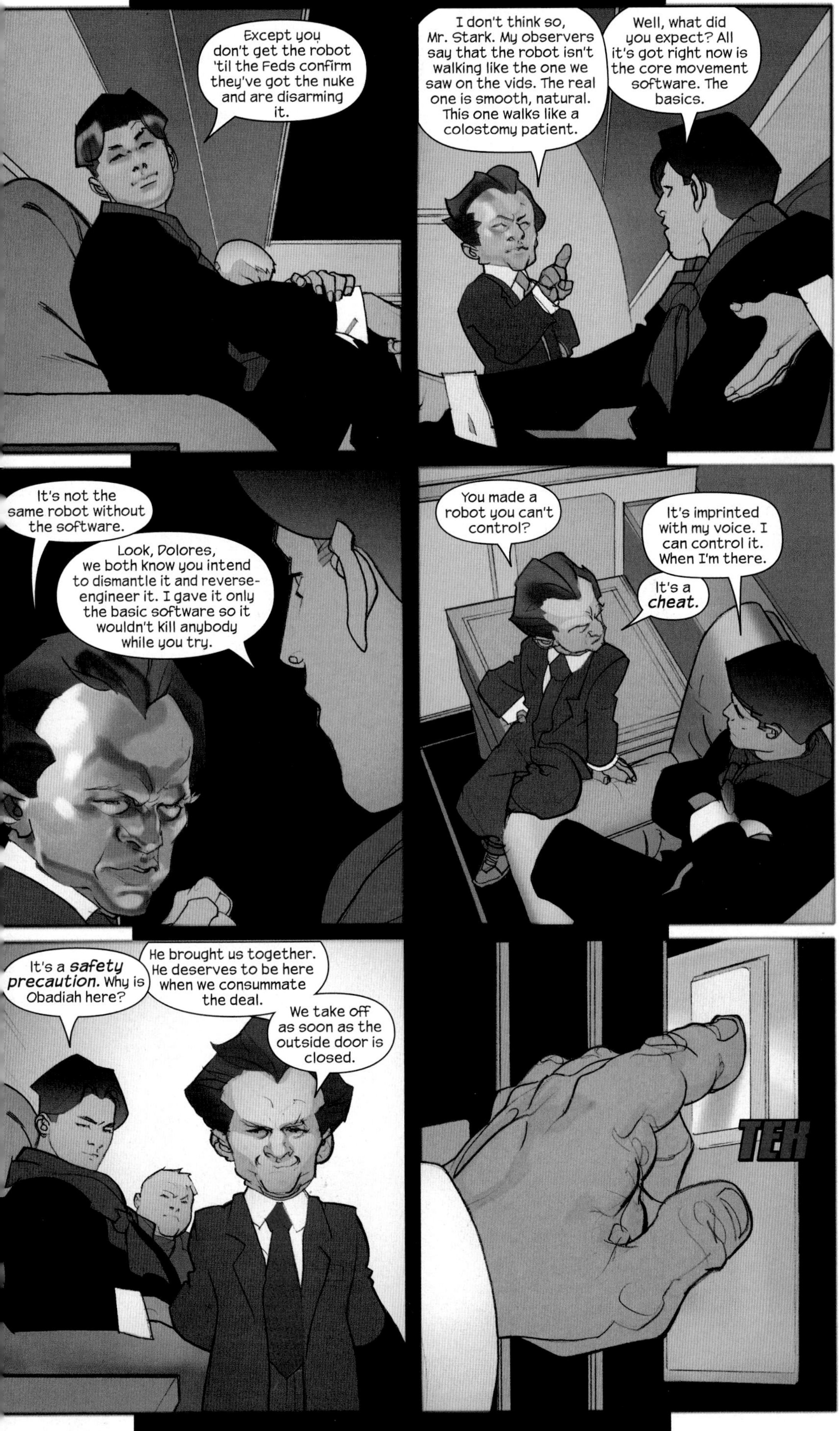
Except you don't get the robot 'til the Feds confirm they've got the nuke and are disarming it.
I don't think so, Mr. Stark. My observers say that the robot isn't walking like the one we saw on the vids. The real one is smooth, natural. This one walks like a colostomy patient.
Well, what did you expect? All it's got right now is the core movement software. The basics.
It's not the same robot without the software.
Look, Dolores, we both know you intend to dismantle it and reverse-engineer it. I gave it only the basic software so it wouldn't kill anybody while you try.
You made a robot you can't control?
It's imprinted with my voice. I can control it. When I'm there.
It's a *cheat.*
It's a *safety precaution.* Why is Obadiah here?
He brought us together. He deserves to be here when we consummate the deal.
We take off as soon as the outside door is closed.
TEK

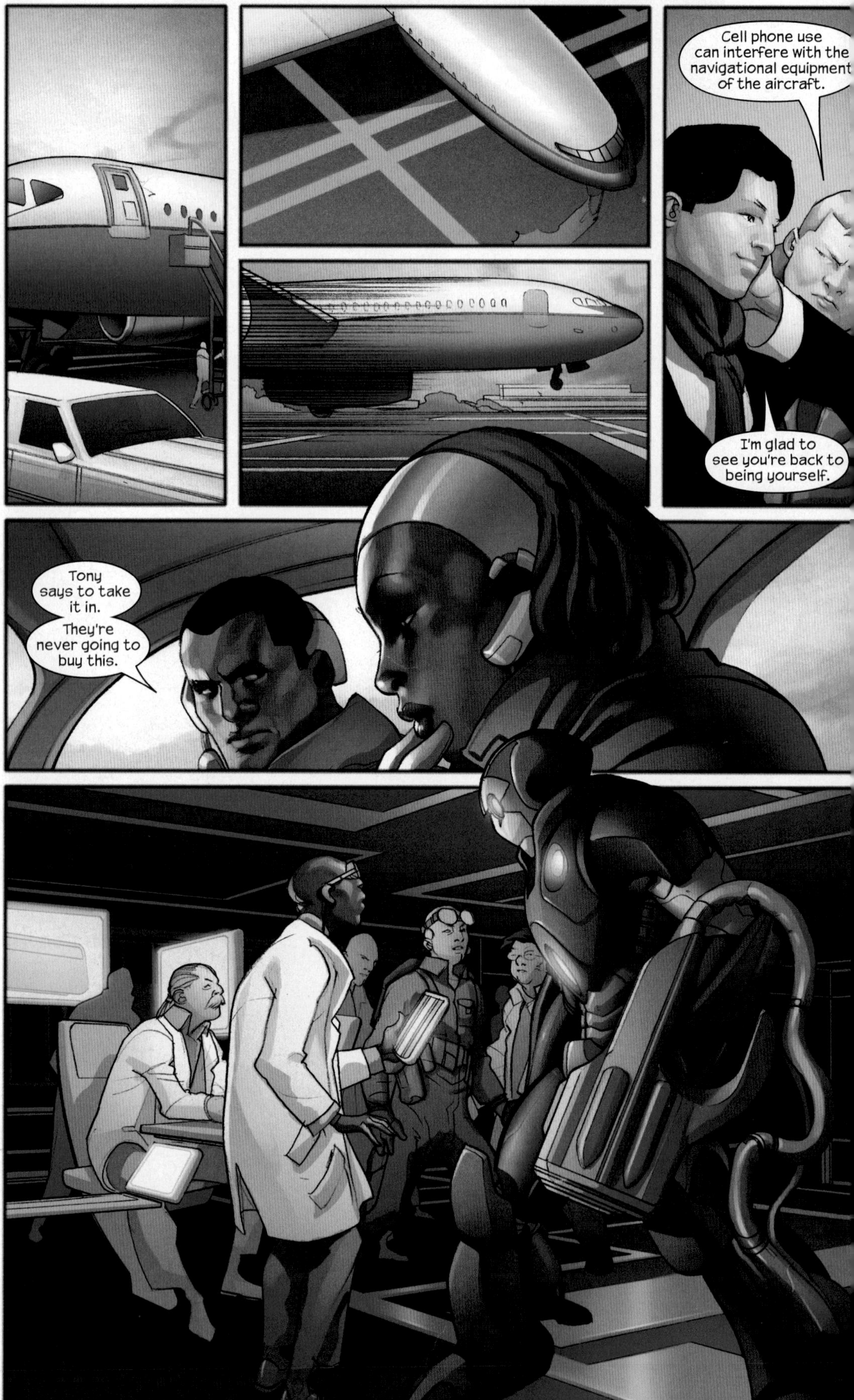
Cell phone use can interfere with the navigational equipment of the aircraft.
I'm glad to see you're back to being yourself.
Tony says to take it in.
They're never going to buy this.

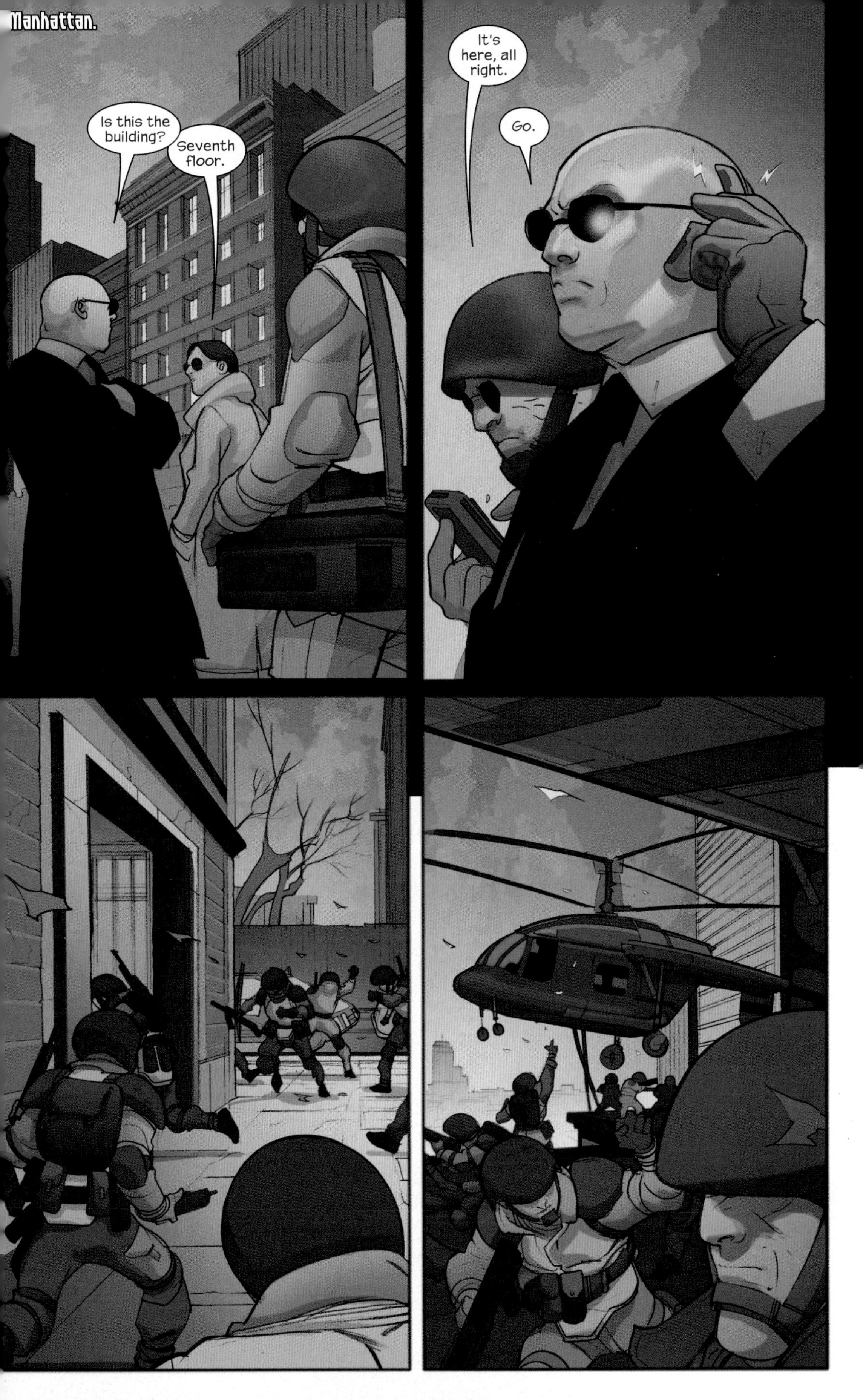
Manhattan.
Is this the building?
Seventh floor.
It's here, all right.
Go.

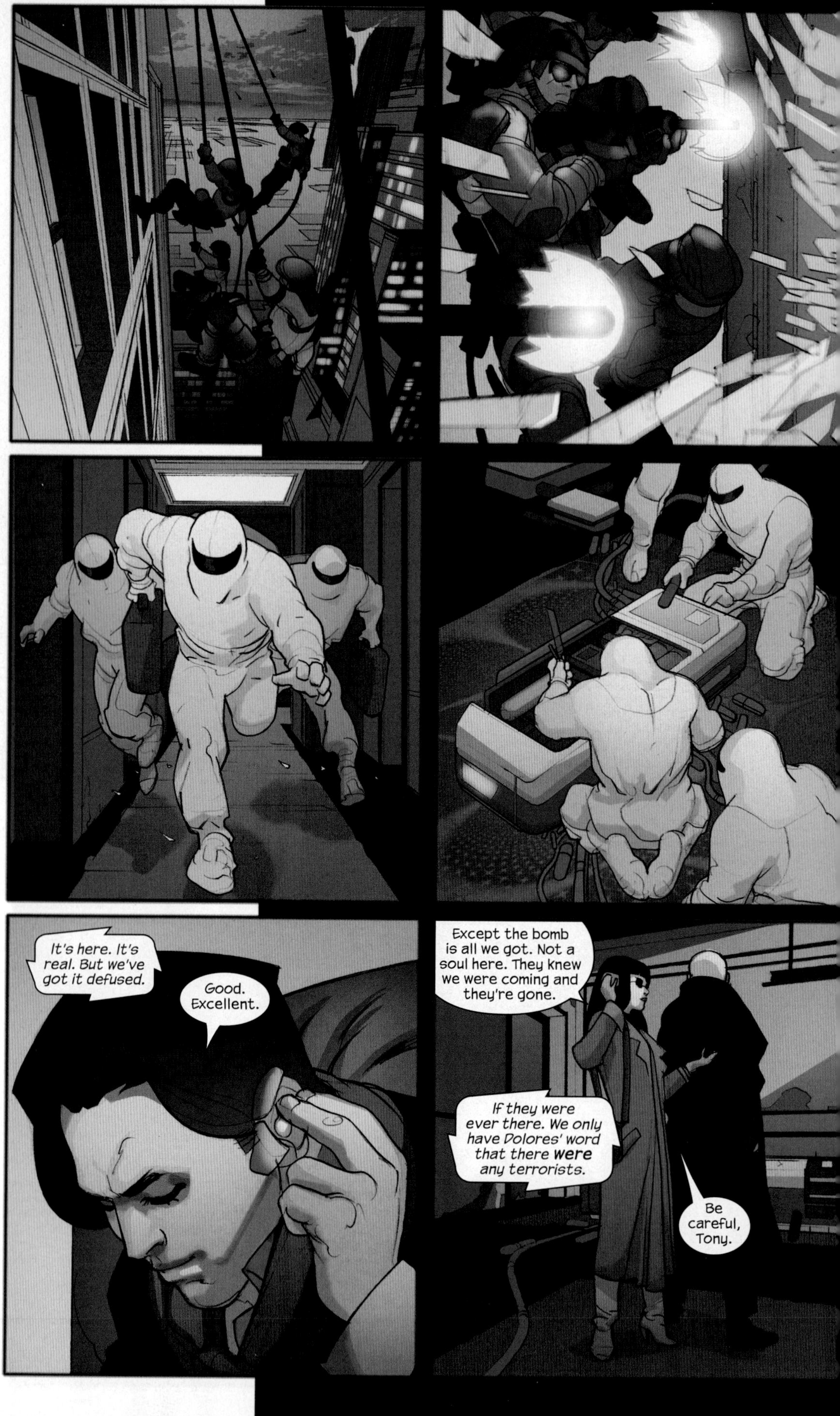
It's here. It's real. But we've got it defused.
Good. Excellent.
Except the bomb is all we got. Not a soul here. They knew we were coming and they're gone.
If they were ever there. We only have Dolores' word that there **were** any terrorists.
Be careful, Tony.

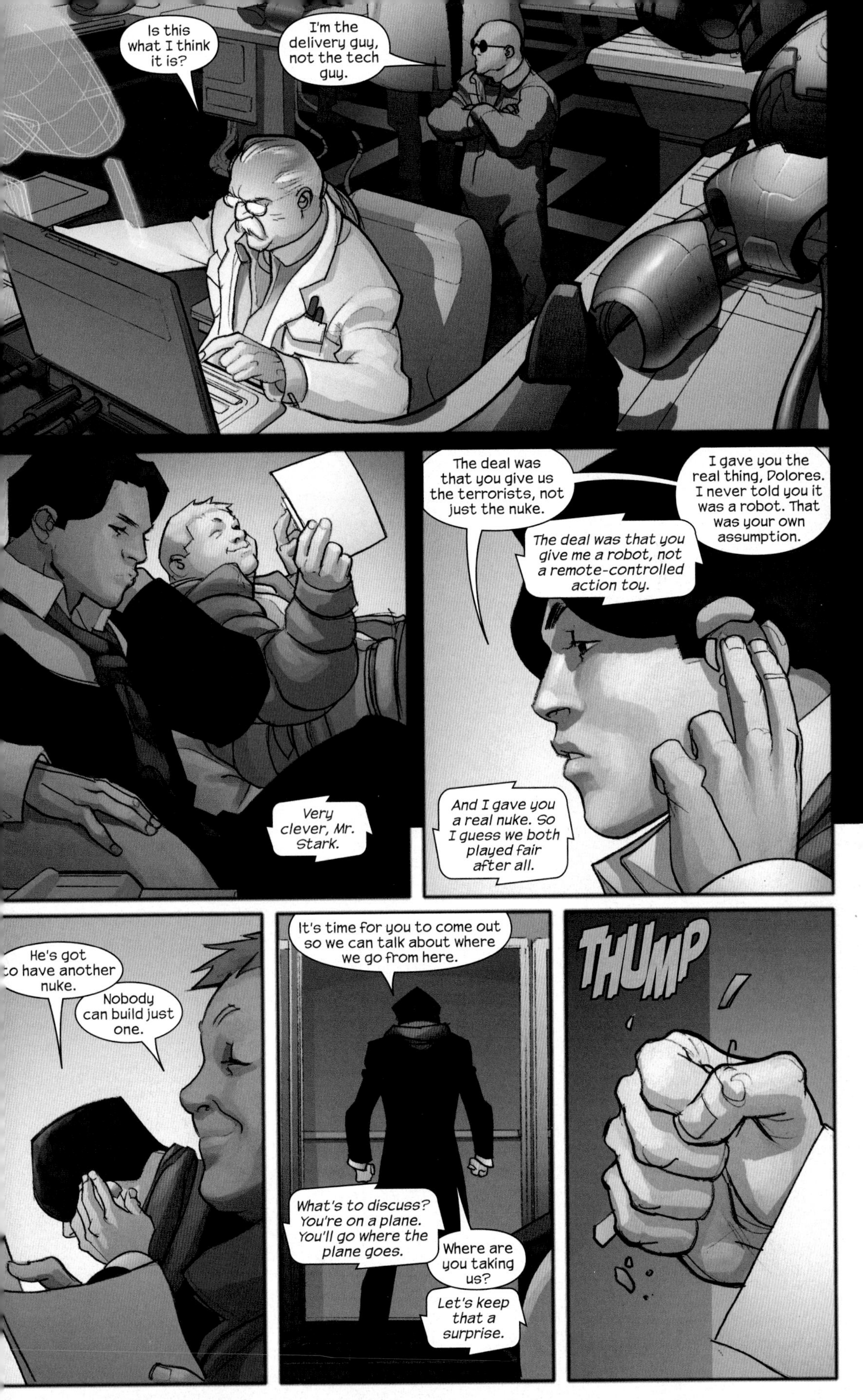
Is this what I think it is?
I'm the delivery guy, not the tech guy.
The deal was that you give us the terrorists, not just the nuke.
I gave you the real thing, Dolores. I never told you it was a robot. That was your own assumption.
The deal was that you give me a robot, not a remote-controlled action toy.
Very clever, Mr. Stark.
And I gave you a real nuke. So I guess we both played fair after all.
He's got to have another nuke.
Nobody can build just one.
It's time for you to come out so we can talk about where we go from here.
What's to discuss? You're on a plane. You'll go where the plane goes.
Where are you taking us?
Let's keep that a surprise.
THUMP

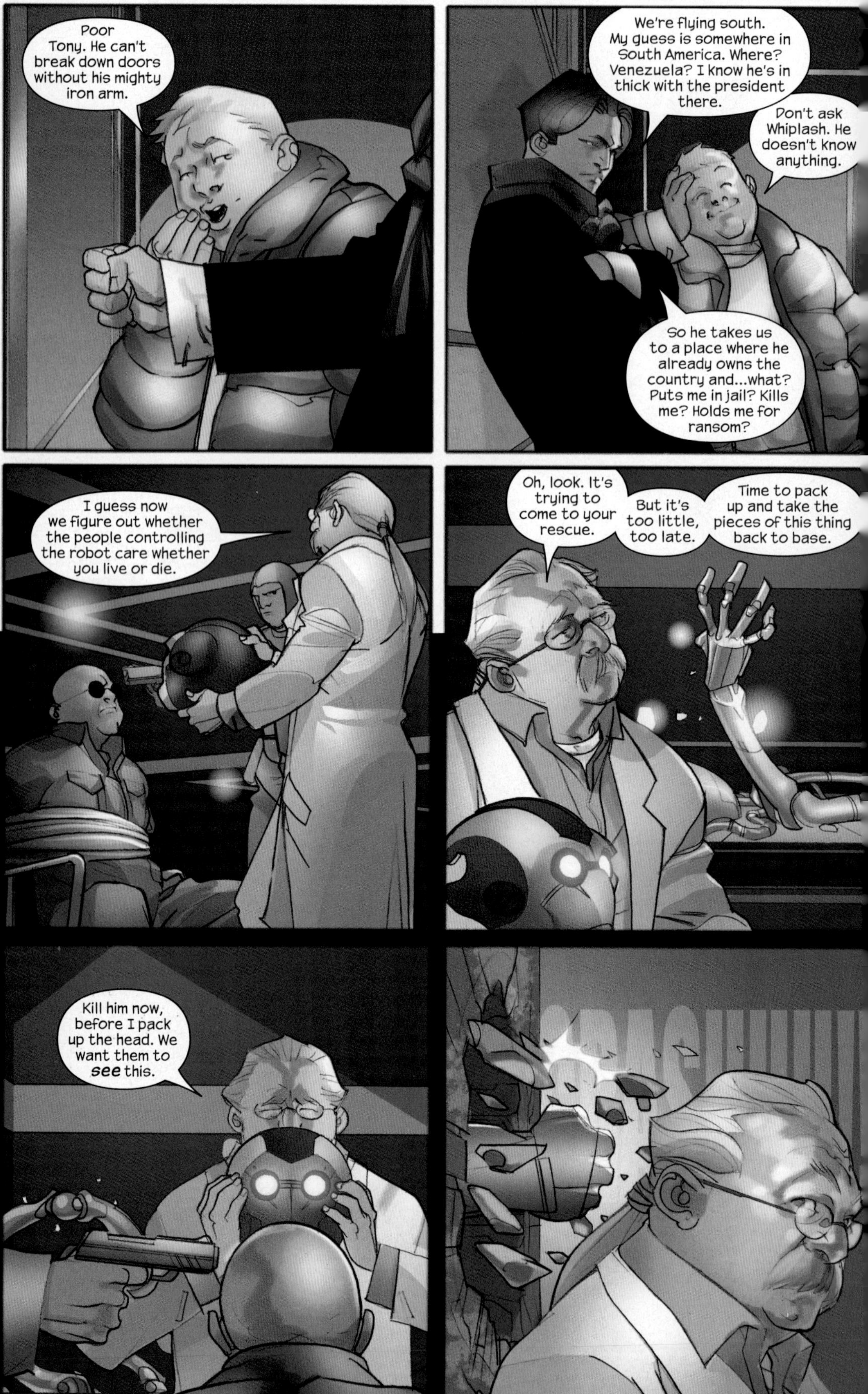
Poor Tony. He can't break down doors without his mighty iron arm.
We're flying south. My guess is somewhere in South America. Where? Venezuela? I know he's in thick with the president there.
Don't ask Whiplash. He doesn't know anything.
So he takes us to a place where he already owns the country and...what? Puts me in jail? Kills me? Holds me for ransom?
I guess now we figure out whether the people controlling the robot care whether you live or die.
Oh, look. It's trying to come to your rescue.
But it's too little, too late.
Time to pack up and take the pieces of this thing back to base.
Kill him now, before I pack up the head. We want them to *see* this.

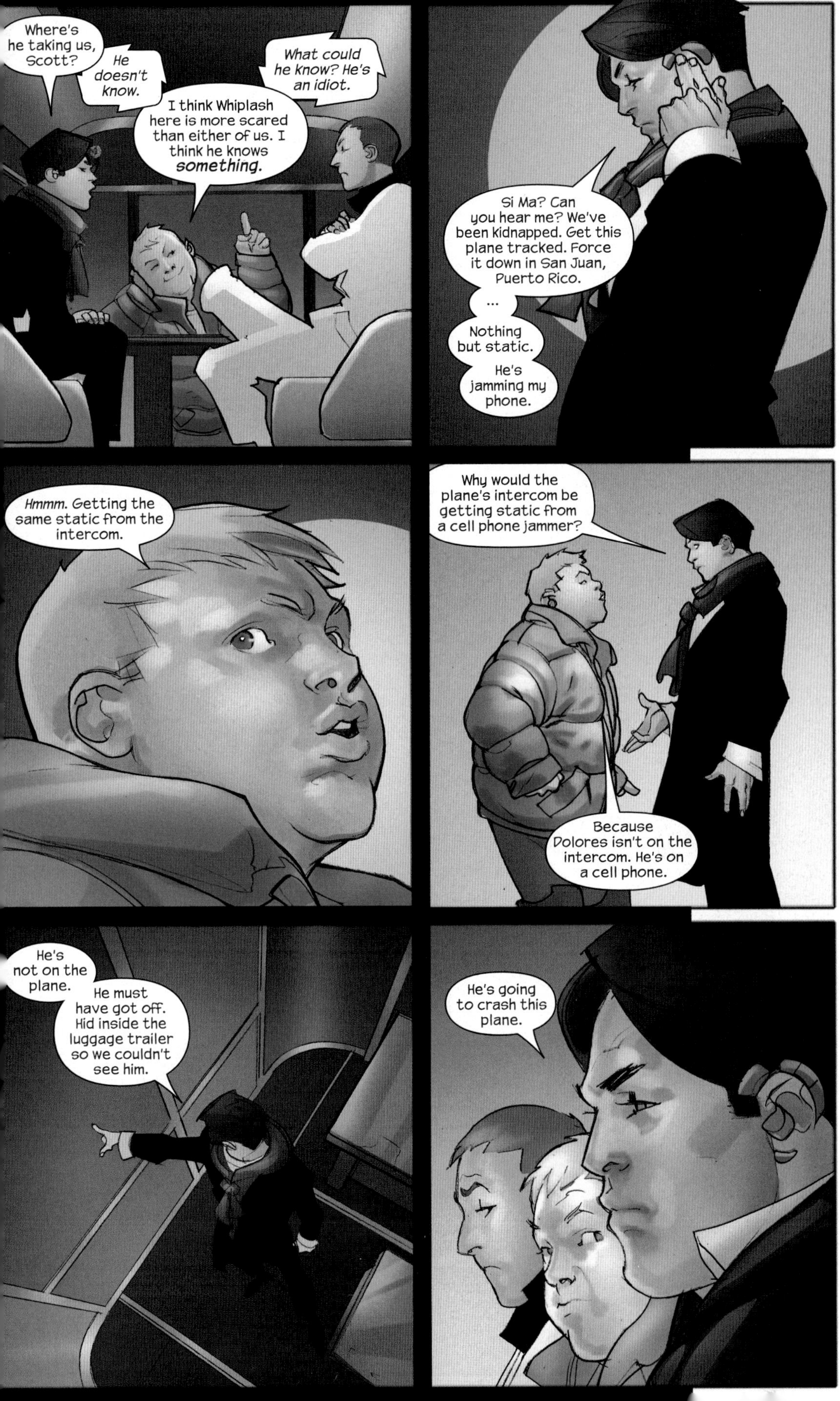

Where's he taking us, Scott?
He doesn't know.
What could he know? He's an idiot.
I think Whiplash here is more scared than either of us. I think he knows *something.*
Si Ma? Can you hear me? We've been kidnapped. Get this plane tracked. Force it down in San Juan, Puerto Rico.
...
Nothing but static.
He's jamming my phone.
Hmmm. Getting the same static from the intercom.
Why would the plane's intercom be getting static from a cell phone jammer?
Because Dolores isn't on the intercom. He's on a cell phone.
He's not on the plane.
He must have got off. Hid inside the luggage trailer so we couldn't see him.
He's going to crash this plane.

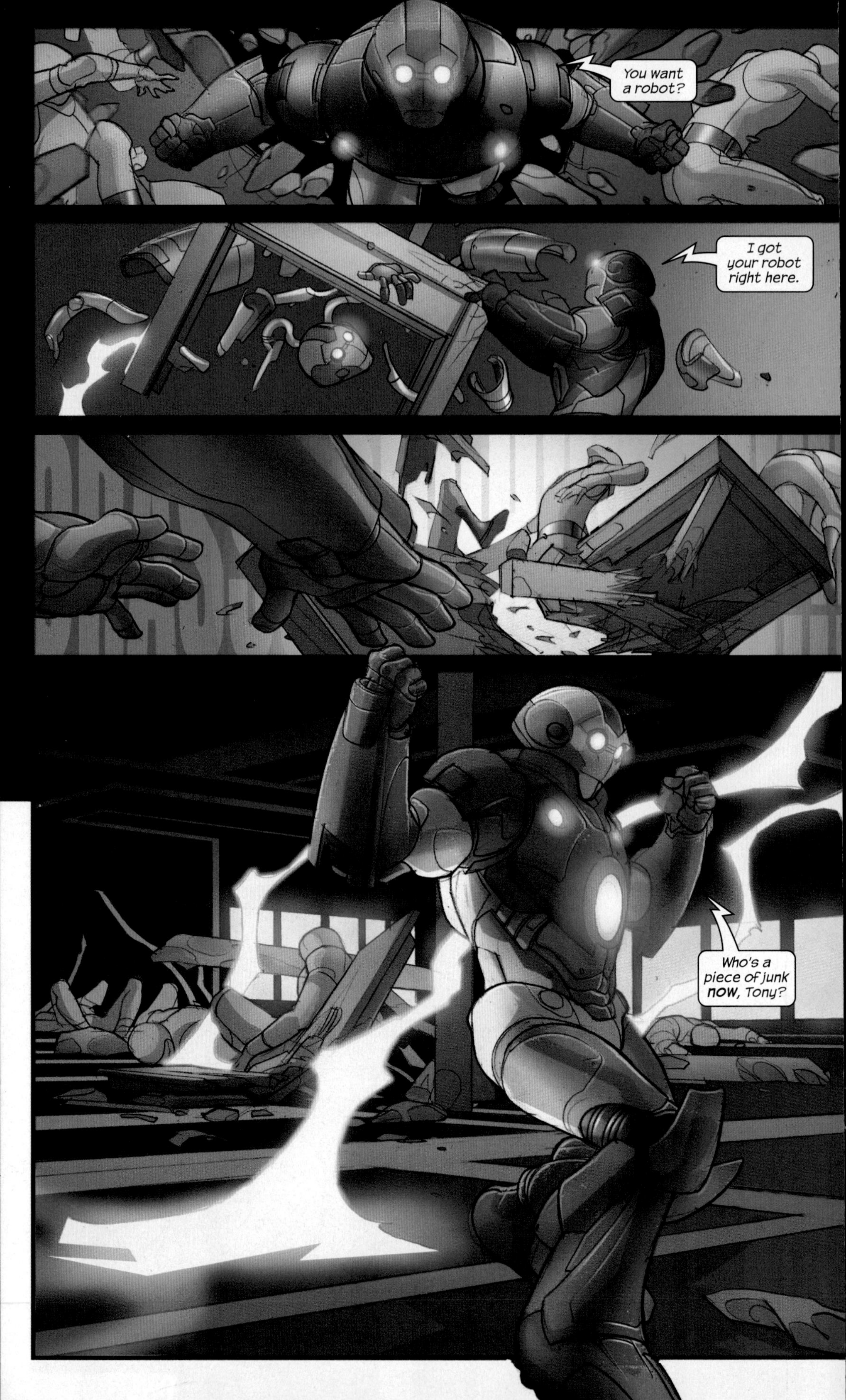
You want a robot?
I got your robot right here.
Who's a piece of junk **NOW**, Tony?

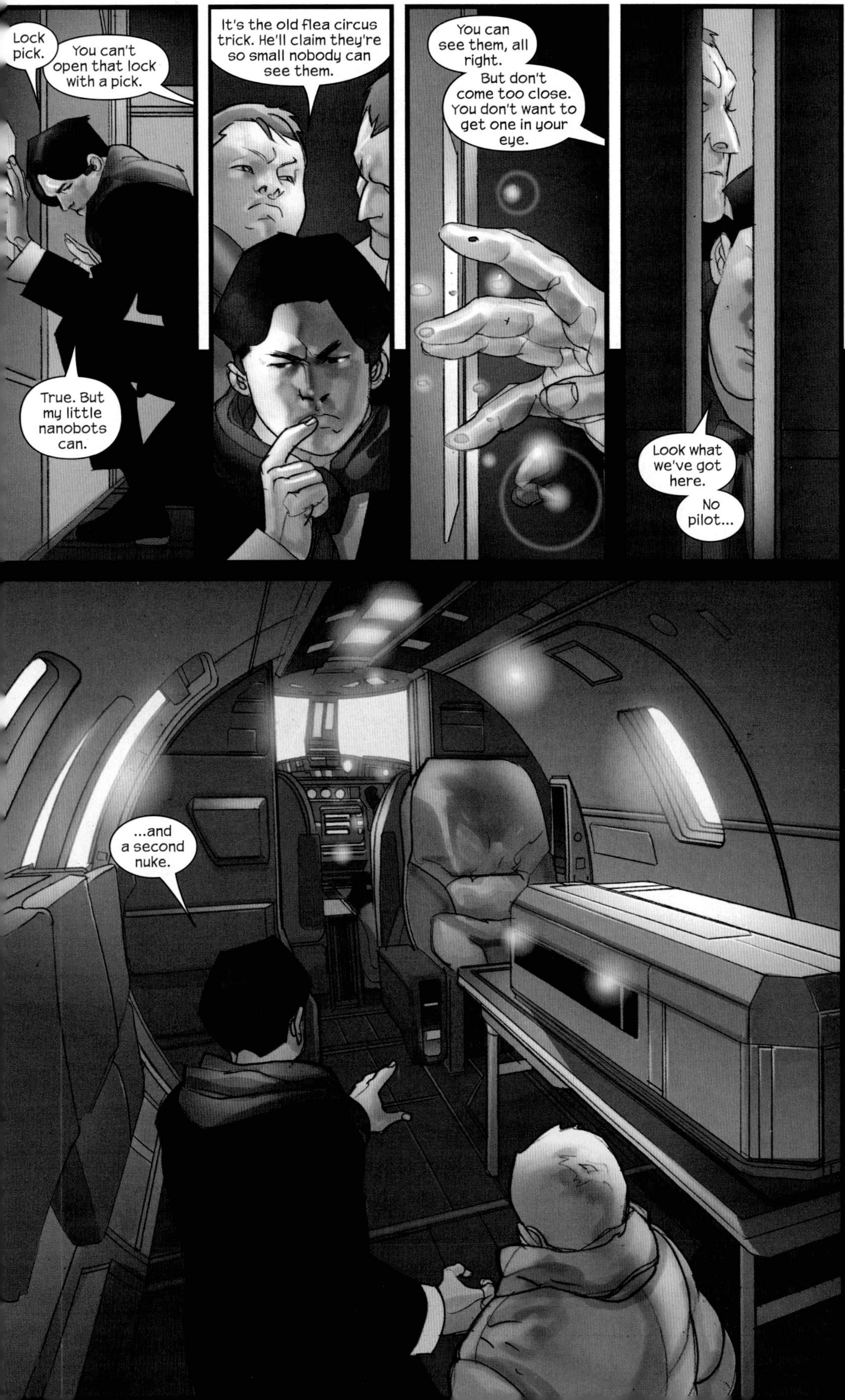
Lock pick.
You can't open that lock with a pick.
True. But my little nanobots can.
It's the old flea circus trick. He'll claim they're so small nobody can see them.
You can see them, all right.
But don't come too close. You don't want to get one in your eye.
Look what we've got here.
No pilot...
...and a second nuke.

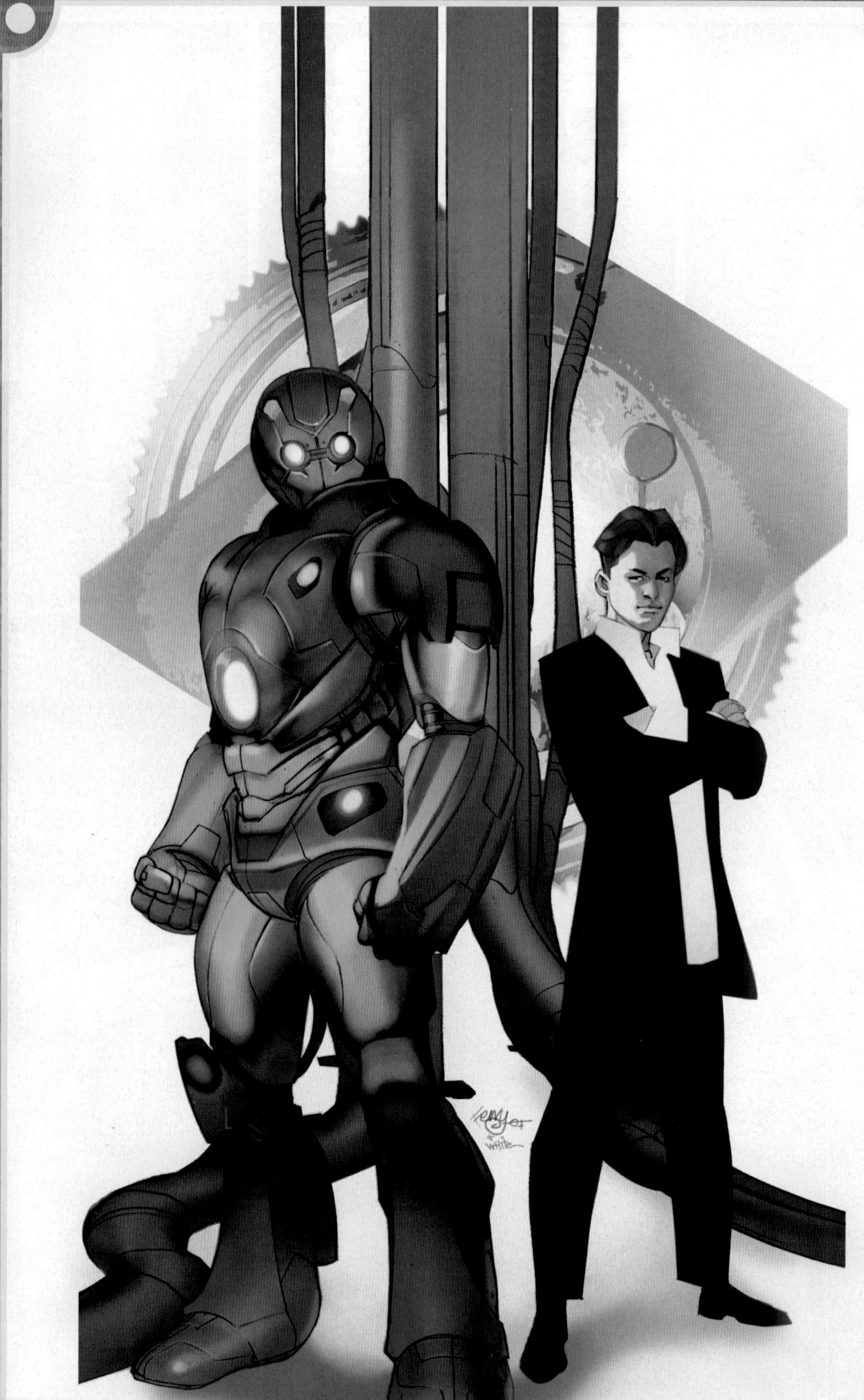

ULTIMATE IRON MAN II
ISSUE 04

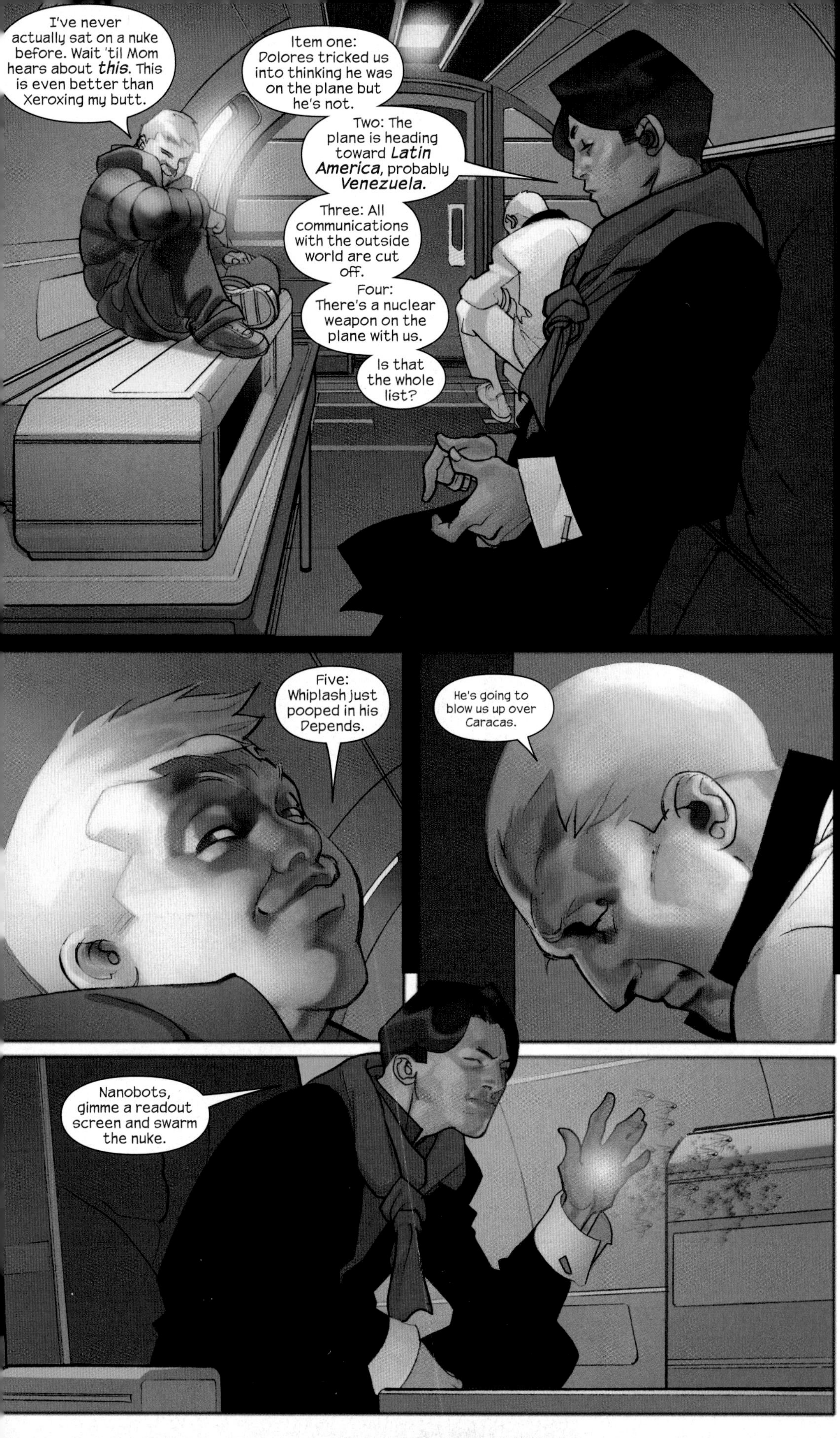

I've never actually sat on a nuke before. Wait 'til Mom hears about *this*. This is even better than Xeroxing my butt.
Item one: Dolores tricked us into thinking he was on the plane but he's not.
Two: The plane is heading toward *Latin America*, probably *Venezuela.*
Three: All communications with the outside world are cut off.
Four: There's a nuclear weapon on the plane with us.
Is that the whole list?
Five: Whiplash just pooped in his Depends.
He's going to blow us up over Caracas.
Nanobots, gimme a readout screen and swarm the nuke.

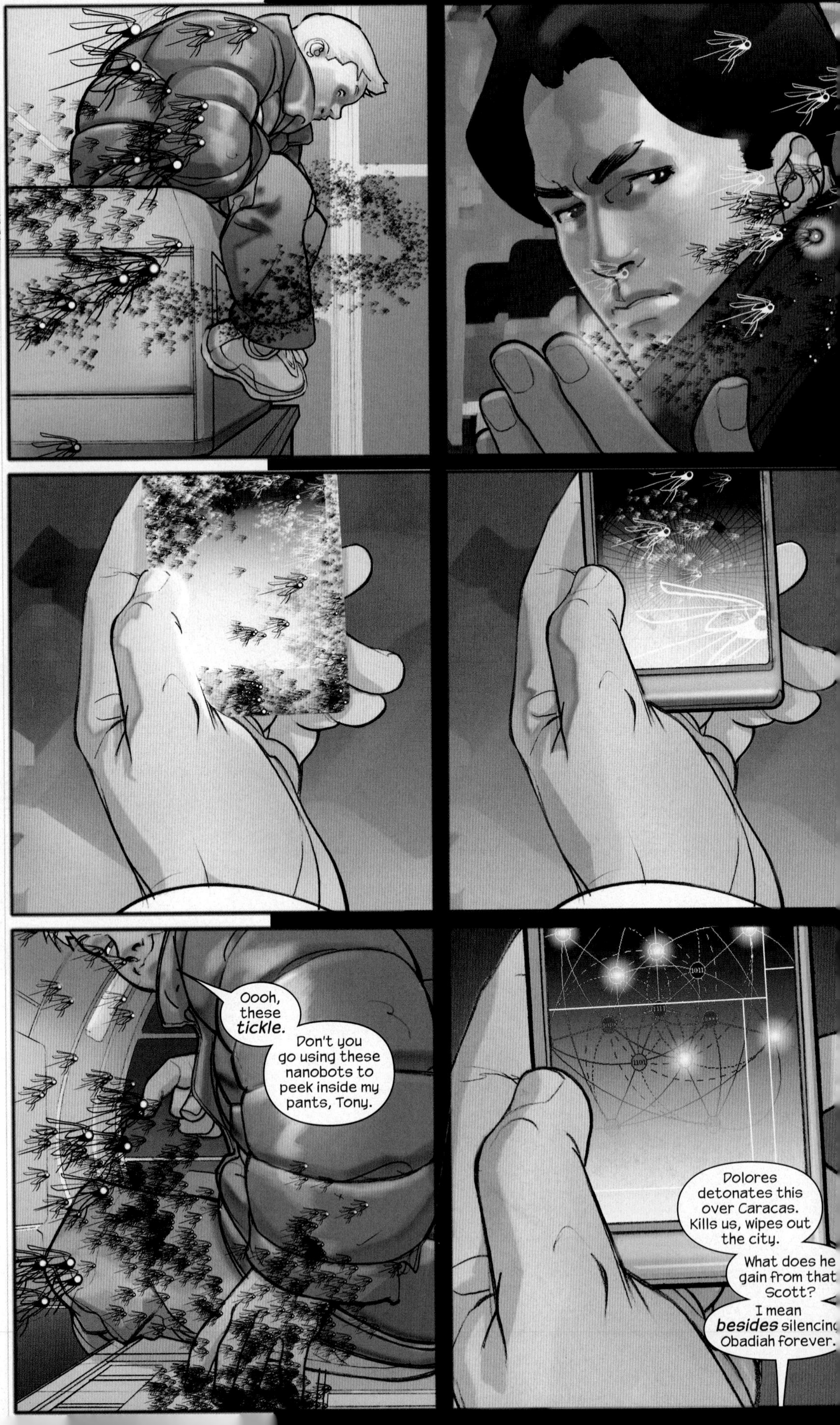
Oooh, these *tickle.*
Don't you go using these nanobots to peek inside my pants, Tony.
Dolores detonates this over Caracas. Kills us, wipes out the city.
What does he gain from that Scott?
I mean *besides* silencing Obadiah forever.

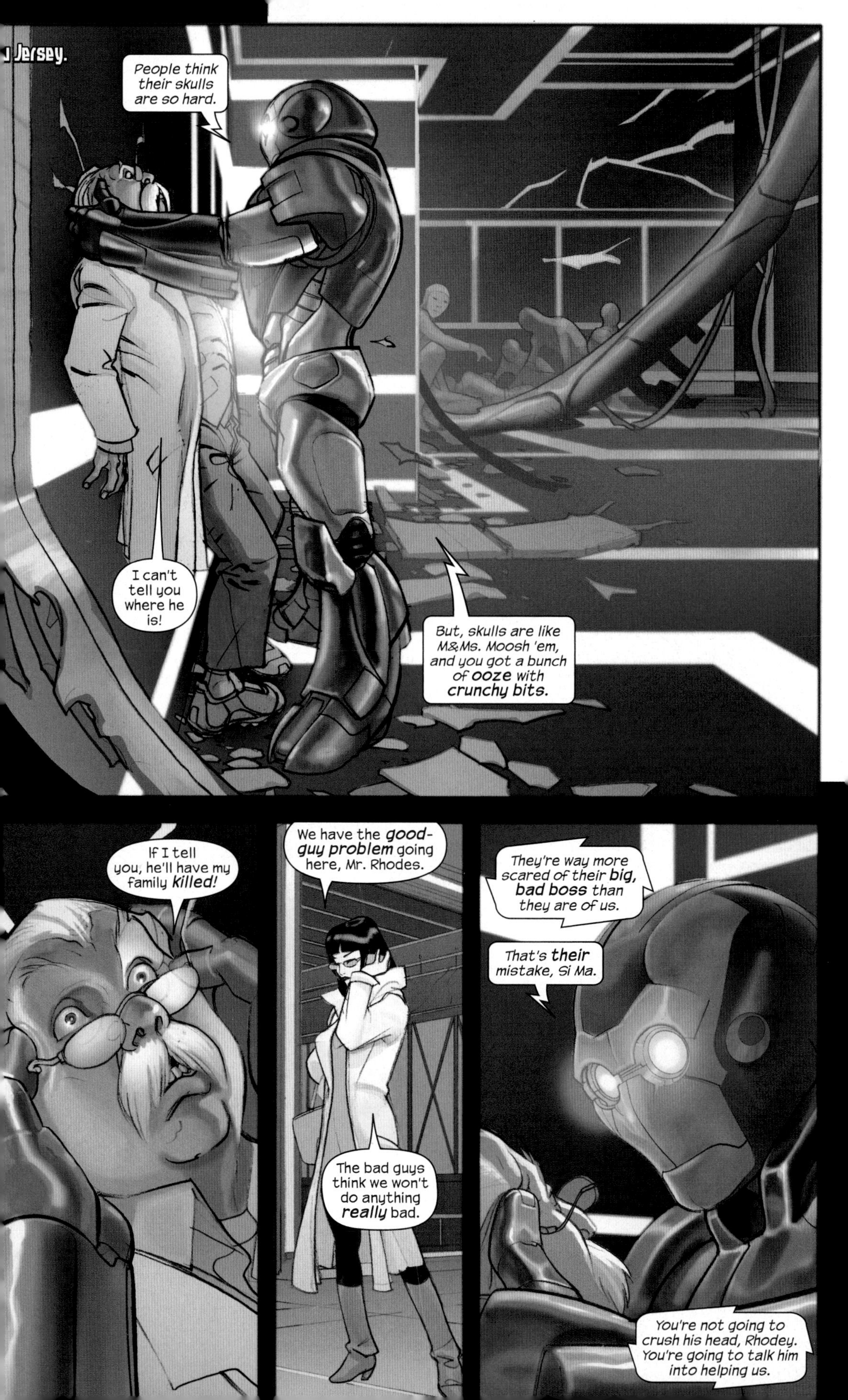

Jersey.
People think their skulls are so hard.
I can't tell you where he is!
But, skulls are like M&Ms. Moosh 'em, and you got a bunch of ooze with crunchy bits.
If I tell you, he'll have my family killed!
We have the good-guy problem going here, Mr. Rhodes.
The bad guys think we won't do anything really bad.
They're way more scared of their big, bad boss than they are of us.
That's their mistake, Si Ma.
You're not going to crush his head, Rhodey. You're going to talk him into helping us.

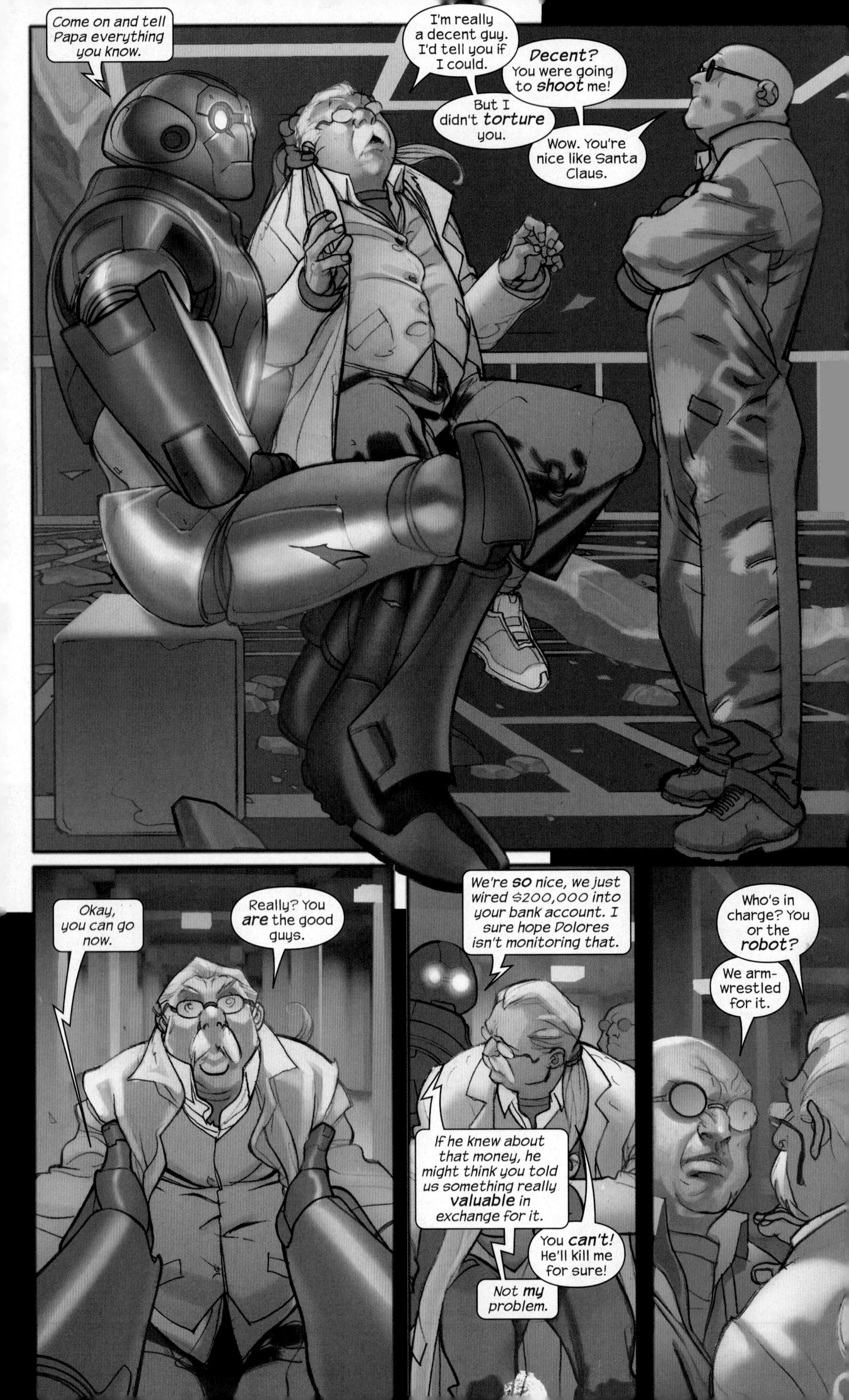
Come on and tell Papa everything you know.
I'm really a decent guy. I'd tell you if I could.
But I didn't torture you.
Decent? You were going to shoot me!
Wow. You're nice like Santa Claus.
Okay, you can go now.
Really? You are the good guys.
We're SO nice, we just wired $200,000 into your bank account. I sure hope Dolores isn't monitoring that.
If he knew about that money, he might think you told us something really valuable in exchange for it.
You can't! He'll kill me for sure!
Not my problem.
Who's in charge? You or the robot?
We arm-wrestled for it.

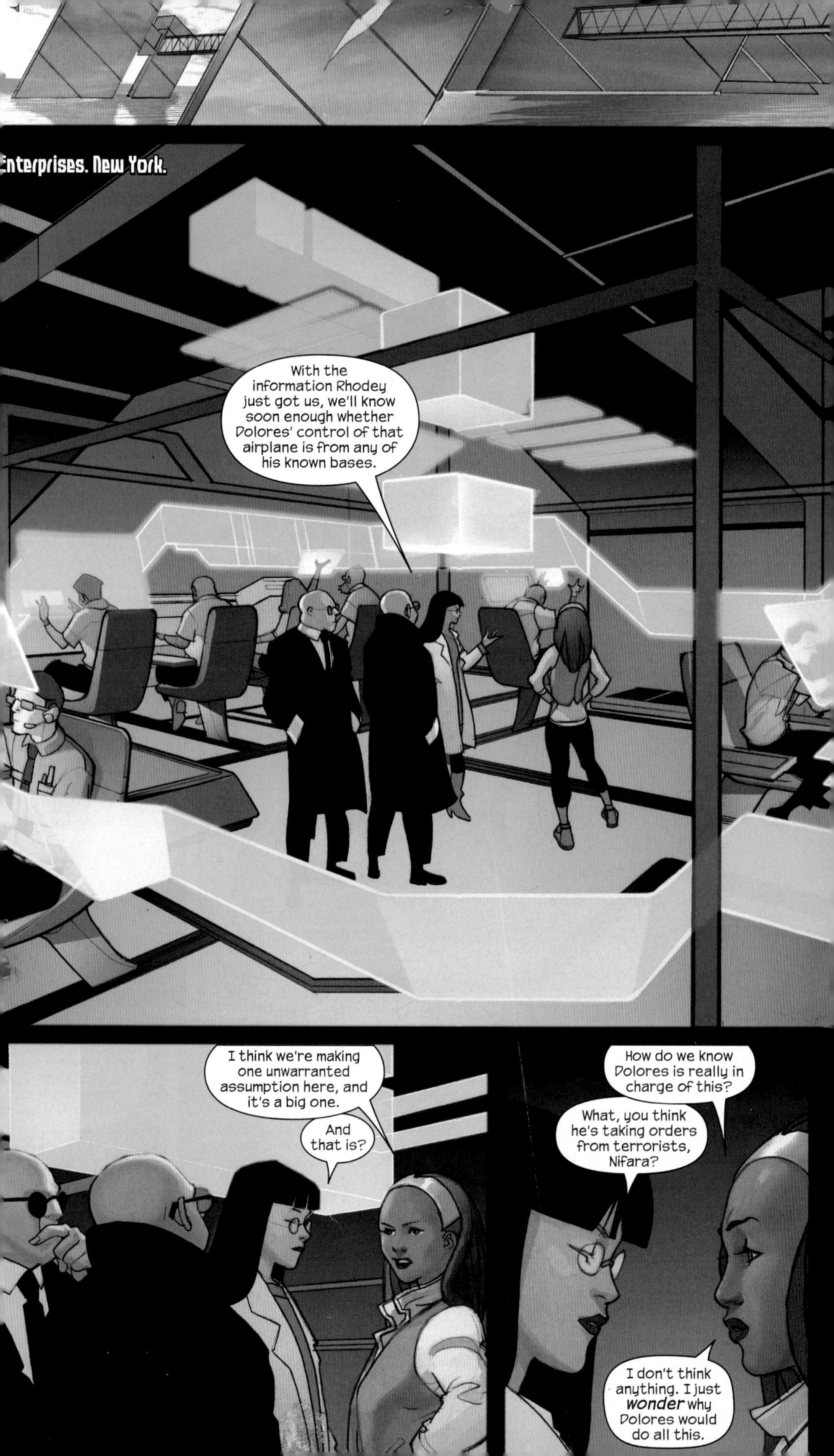

Enterprises. New York.
With the information Rhodey just got us, we'll know soon enough whether Dolores' control of that airplane is from any of his known bases.
I think we're making one unwarranted assumption here, and it's a big one.
And that is?
How do we know Dolores is really in charge of this?
What, you think he's taking orders from terrorists, Nifara?
I don't think anything. I just *wonder* why Dolores would do all this.

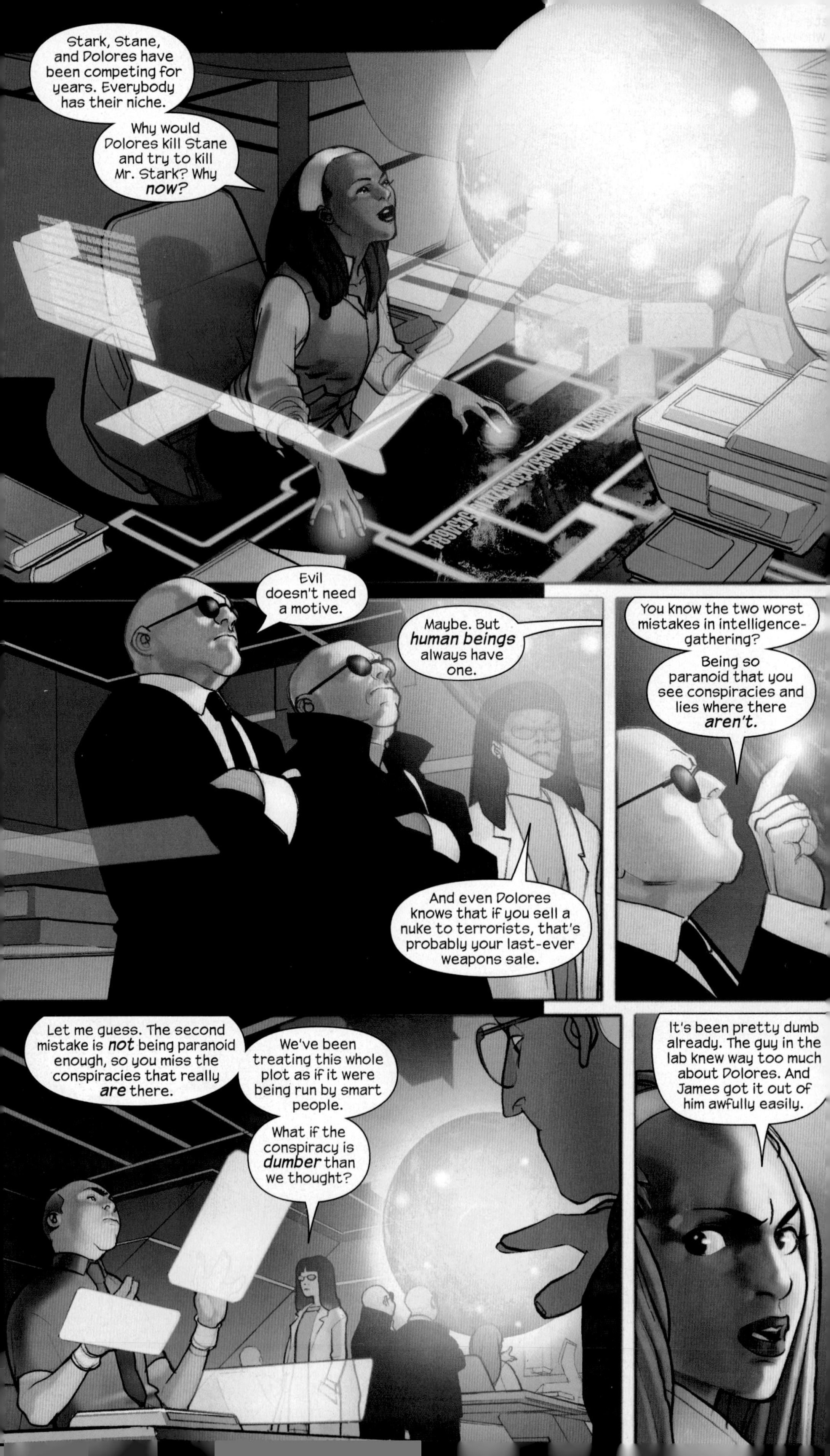
Stark, Stane, and Dolores have been competing for years. Everybody has their niche.
Why would Dolores kill Stane and try to kill Mr. Stark? Why *now?*
Evil doesn't need a motive.
Maybe. But *human beings* always have one.
And even Dolores knows that if you sell a nuke to terrorists, that's probably your last-ever weapons sale.
You know the two worst mistakes in intelligence-gathering?
Being so paranoid that you see conspiracies and lies where there *aren't.*
Let me guess. The second mistake is *not* being paranoid enough, so you miss the conspiracies that really *are* there.
We've been treating this whole plot as if it were being run by smart people.
What if the conspiracy is *dumber* than we thought?
It's been pretty dumb already. The guy in the lab knew way too much about Dolores. And James got it out of him awfully easily.

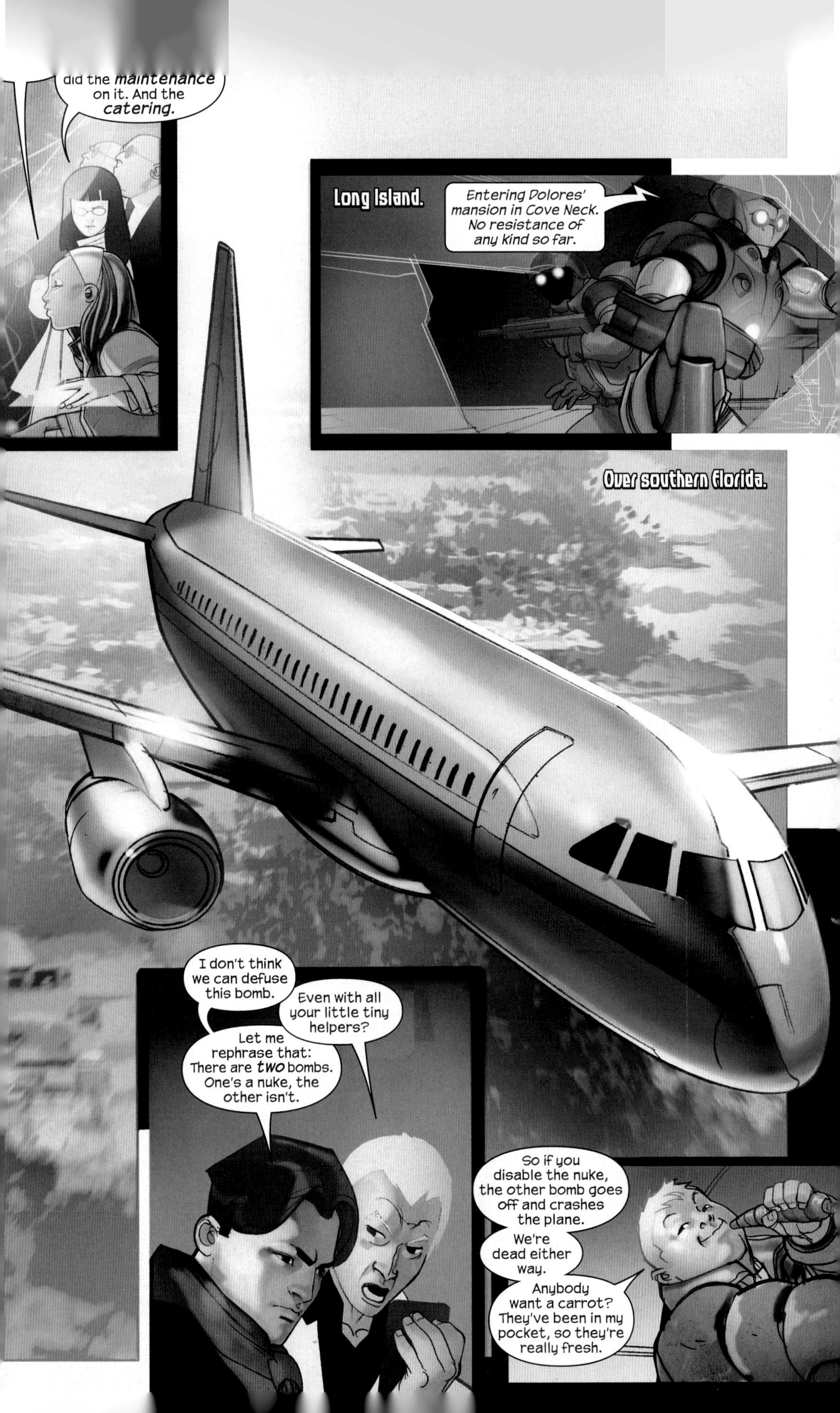
did the maintenance on it. And the catering.
Long Island.
Entering Dolores' mansion in Cove Neck. No resistance of any kind so far.
Over southern Florida.
I don't think we can defuse this bomb.
Even with all your little tiny helpers?
Let me rephrase that: There are two bombs. One's a nuke, the other isn't.
So if you disable the nuke, the other bomb goes off and crashes the plane.
We're dead either way.
Anybody want a carrot? They've been in my pocket, so they're really fresh.

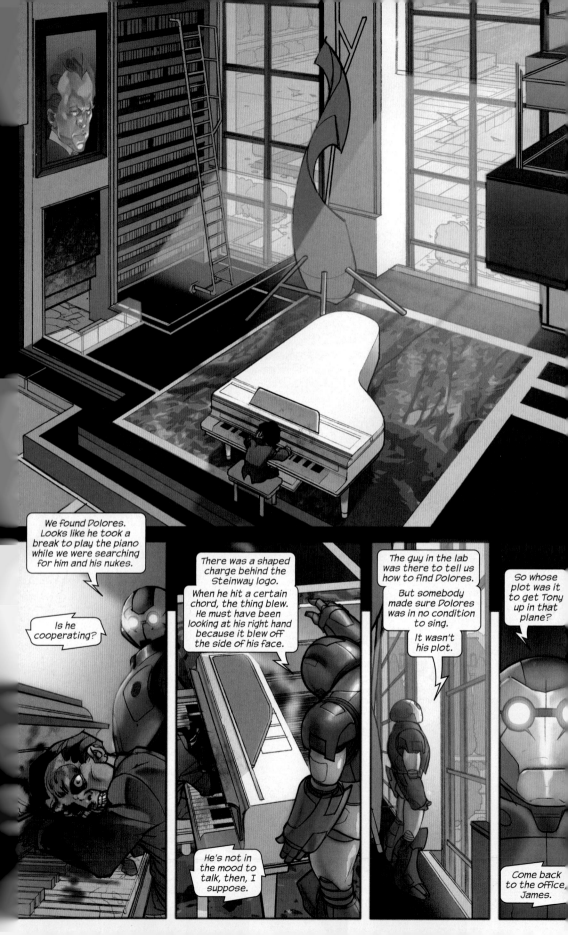

We found Dolores. Looks like he took a break to play the piano while we were searching for him and his nukes.

Is he cooperating?

There was a shaped charge behind the Steinway logo. When he hit a certain chord, the thing blew. He must have been looking at his right hand because it blew off the side of his face.

He's not in the mood to talk, then, I suppose.

The guy in the lab was there to tell us how to find Dolores. But somebody made sure Dolores was in no condition to sing.

It wasn't his plot.

So whose plot was it to get Tony up in that plane?

Come back to the office, James.

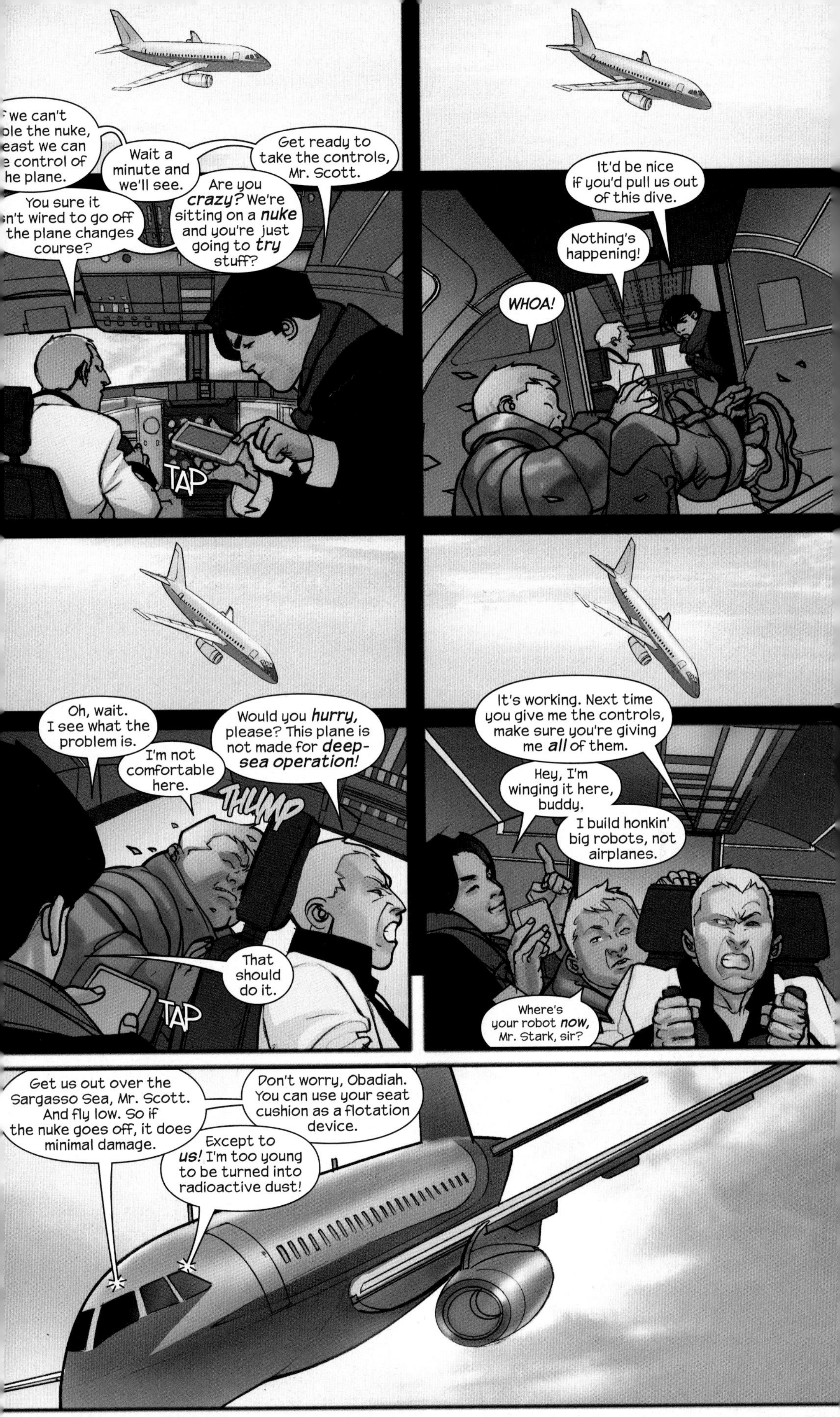

we can't
ole the nuke,
east we can
control of
he plane.
Wait a minute and we'll see.
Get ready to take the controls, Mr. Scott.
You sure it n't wired to go off the plane changes course?
Are you crazy? We're sitting on a nuke and you're just going to try stuff?
TAP
It'd be nice if you'd pull us out of this dive.
Nothing's happening!
WHOA!
Oh, wait. I see what the problem is.
I'm not comfortable here.
Would you hurry, please? This plane is not made for deep-sea operation!
THUMP
That should do it.
TAP
It's working. Next time you give me the controls, make sure you're giving me all of them.
Hey, I'm winging it here, buddy.
I build honkin' big robots, not airplanes.
Where's your robot now, Mr. Stark, sir?
Get us out over the Sargasso Sea, Mr. Scott. And fly low. So if the nuke goes off, it does minimal damage.
Don't worry, Obadiah. You can use your seat cushion as a flotation device.
Except to us! I'm too young to be turned into radioactive dust!

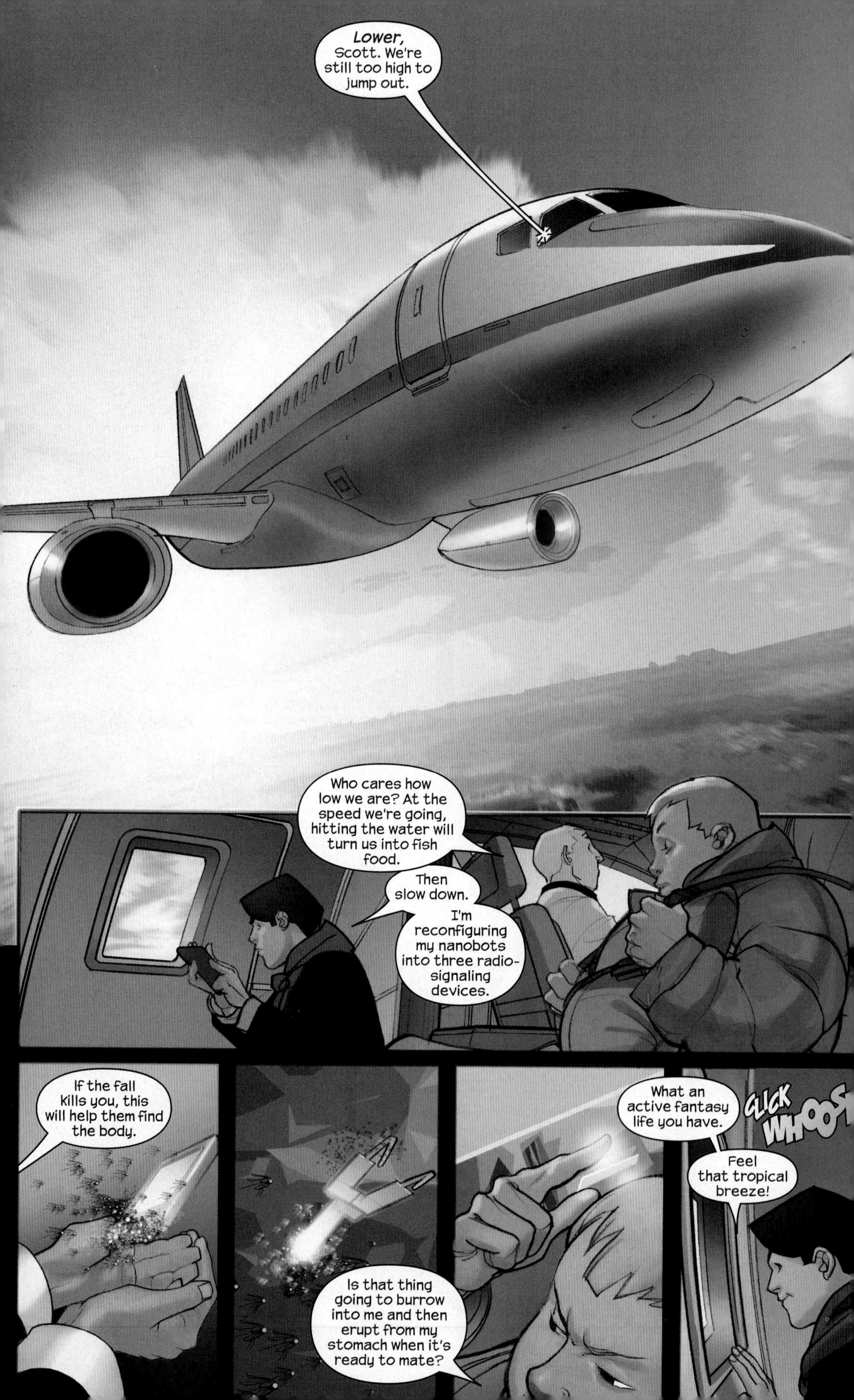
Lower, Scott. We're still too high to jump out.
Who cares how low we are? At the speed we're going, hitting the water will turn us into fish food.
Then slow down.
I'm reconfiguring my nanobots into three radio-signaling devices.
If the fall kills you, this will help them find the body.
Is that thing going to burrow into me and then erupt from my stomach when it's ready to mate?
What an active fantasy life you have.
CLICK
WHOOSH
Feel that tropical breeze!

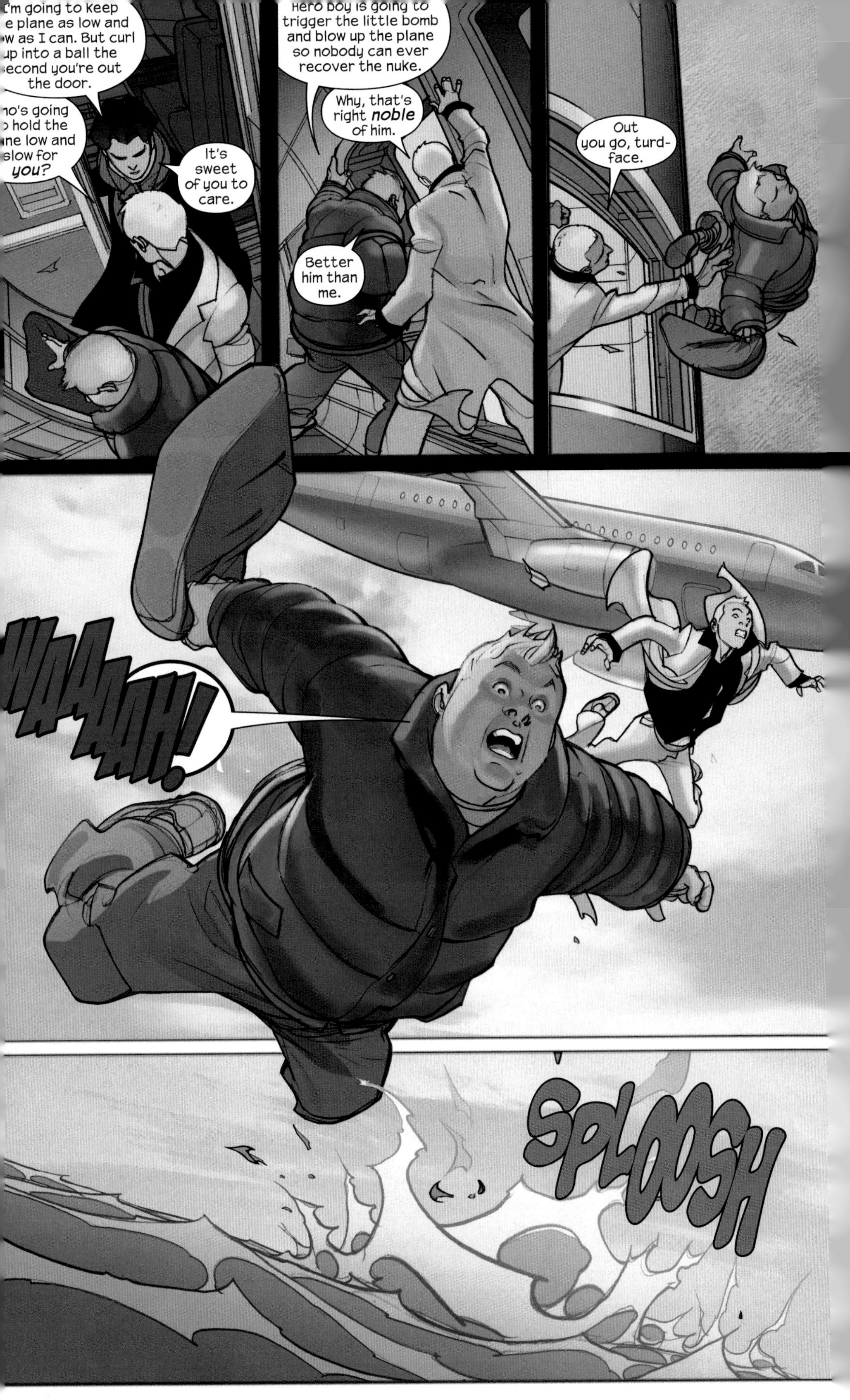
I'm going to keep the plane as low and slow as I can. But curl up into a ball the second you're out the door.
Who's going to hold the plane low and slow for you?
It's sweet of you to care.
Hero boy is going to trigger the little bomb and blow up the plane so nobody can ever recover the nuke.
Why, that's right noble of him.
Better him than me.
Out you go, turd-face.
WAAAAH!
SPLOOSH

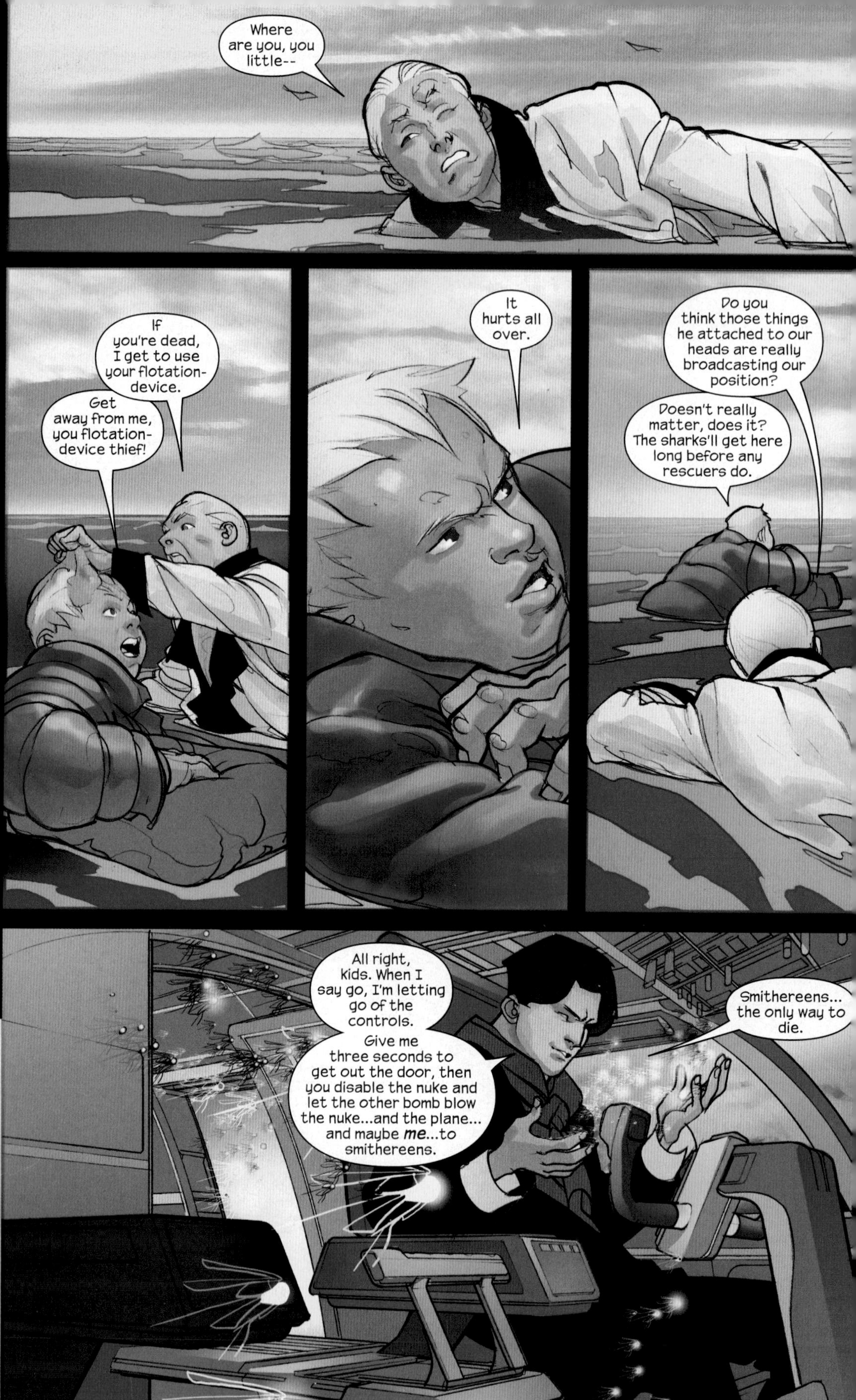

Where are you, you little--
If you're dead, I get to use your flotation-device.
Get away from me, you flotation-device thief!
It hurts all over.
Do you think those things he attached to our heads are really broadcasting our position?
Doesn't really matter, does it? The sharks'll get here long before any rescuers do.
All right, kids. When I say go, I'm letting go of the controls.
Give me three seconds to get out the door, then you disable the nuke and let the other bomb blow the nuke...and the plane... and maybe *me*...to smithereens.
Smithereens... the only way to die.

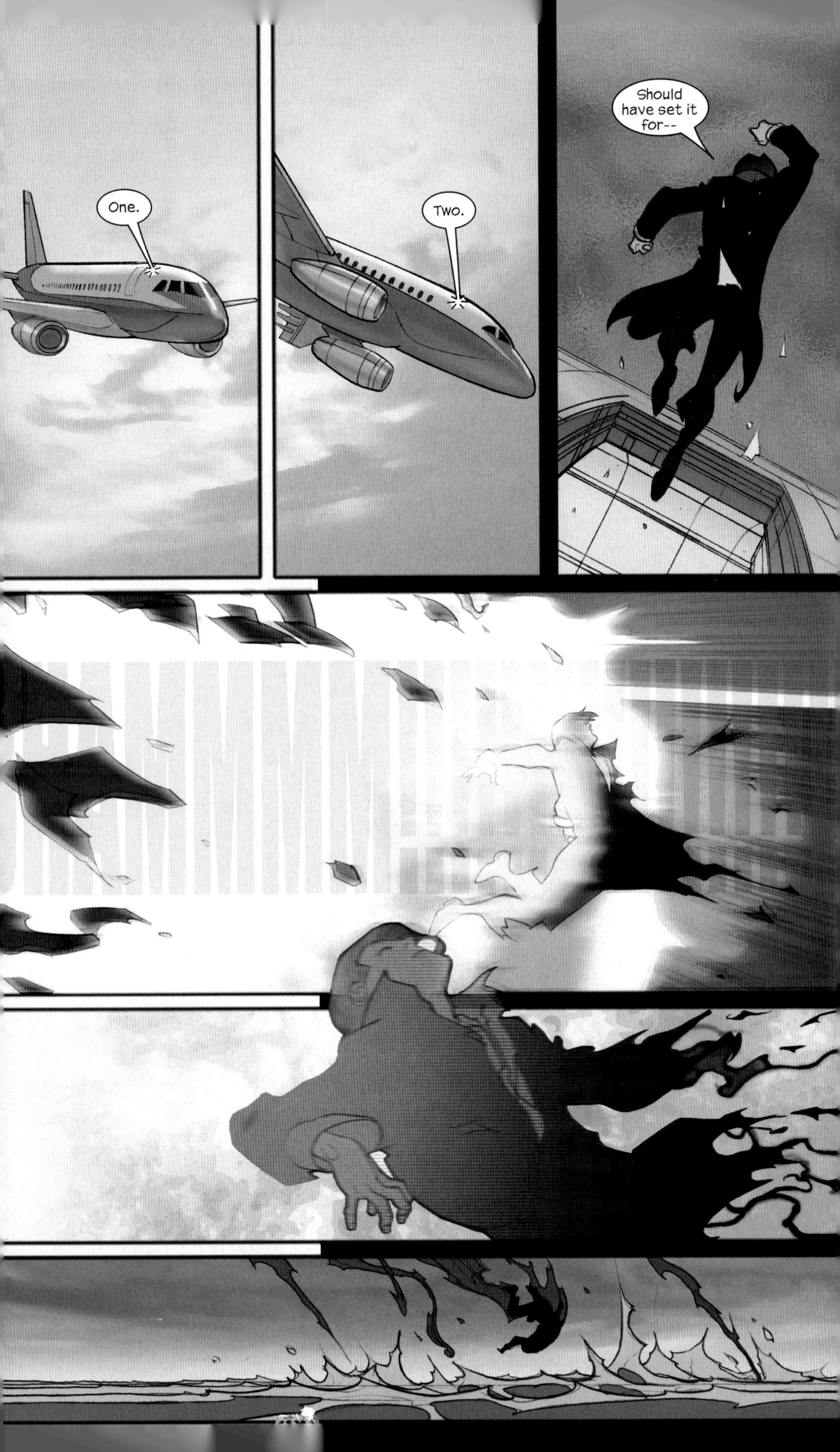

One.
Two.
Should have set it for--

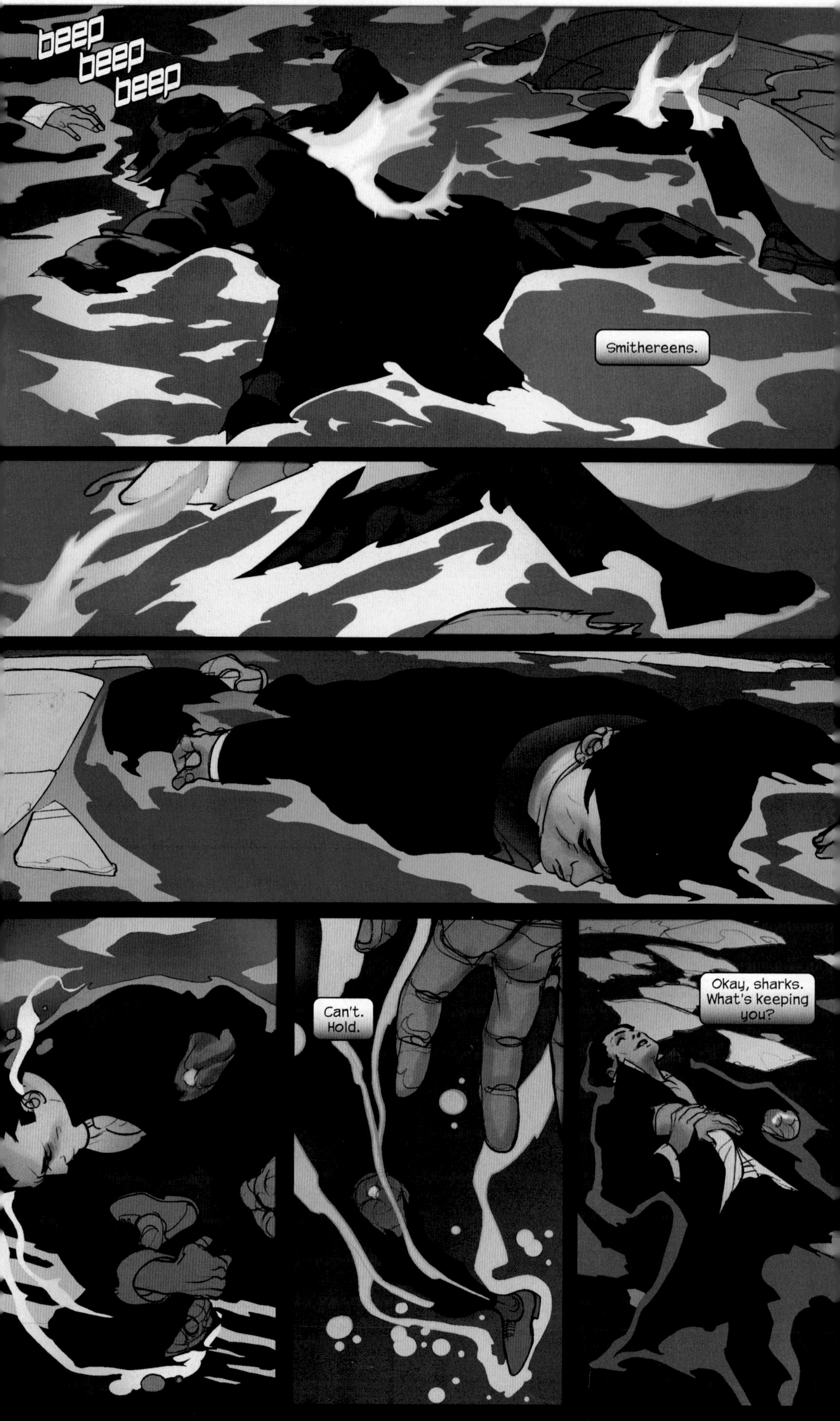
beep
beep
beep
Smithereens.
Can't.
Hold.
Okay, sharks.
What's keeping
you?

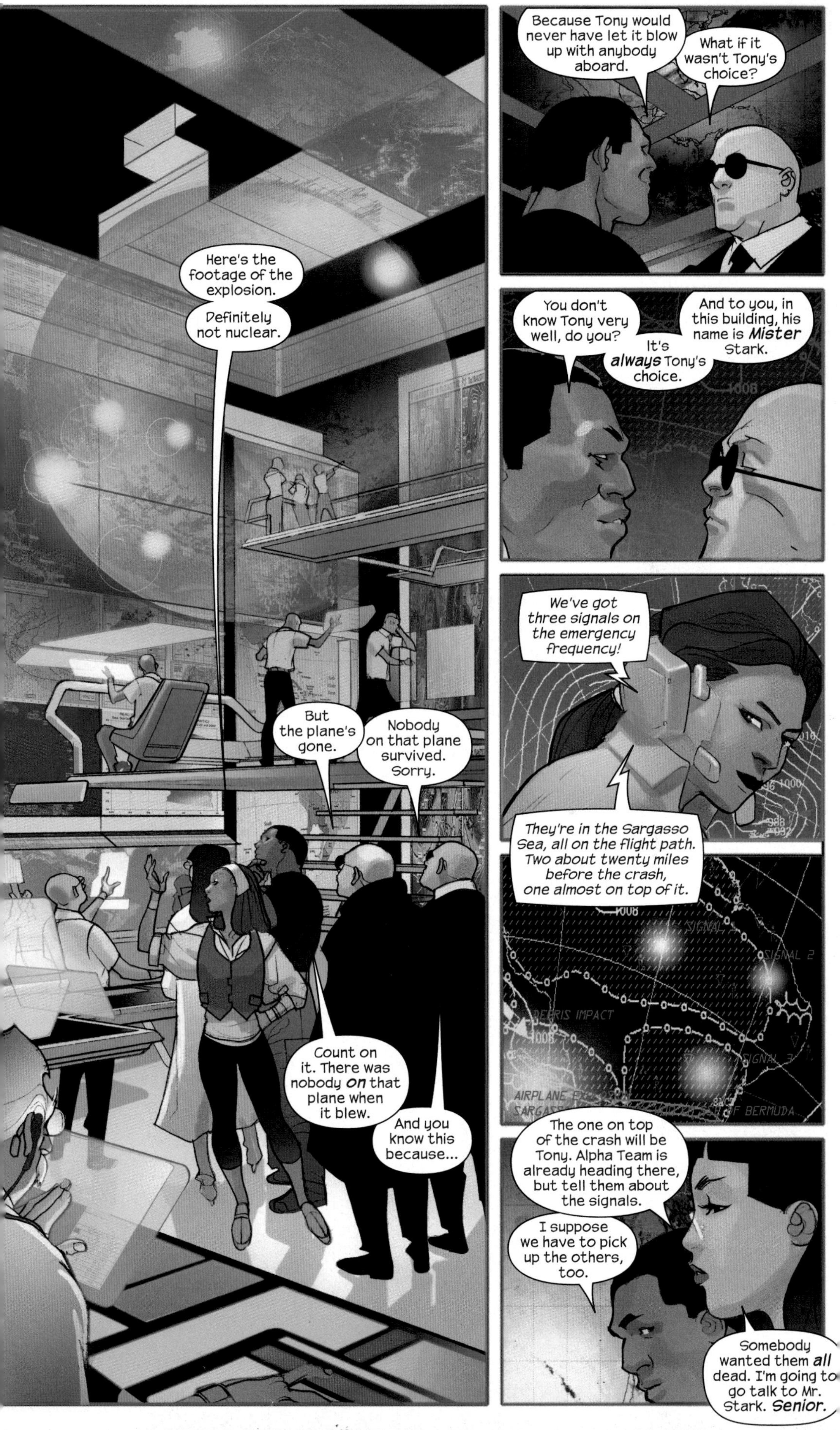
Here's the footage of the explosion.
Definitely not nuclear.
But the plane's gone.
Nobody on that plane survived. Sorry.
Count on it. There was nobody *on* that plane when it blew.
And you know this because...
Because Tony would never have let it blow up with anybody aboard.
What if it wasn't Tony's choice?
You don't know Tony very well, do you?
It's *always* Tony's choice.
And to you, in this building, his name is *Mister* Stark.
We've got three signals on the emergency frequency!
They're in the Sargasso Sea, all on the flight path. Two about twenty miles before the crash, one almost on top of it.
SIGNAL 2
DEBRIS IMPACT
The one on top of the crash will be Tony. Alpha Team is already heading there, but tell them about the signals.
I suppose we have to pick up the others, too.
Somebody wanted them *all* dead. I'm going to go talk to Mr. Stark. *Senior.*

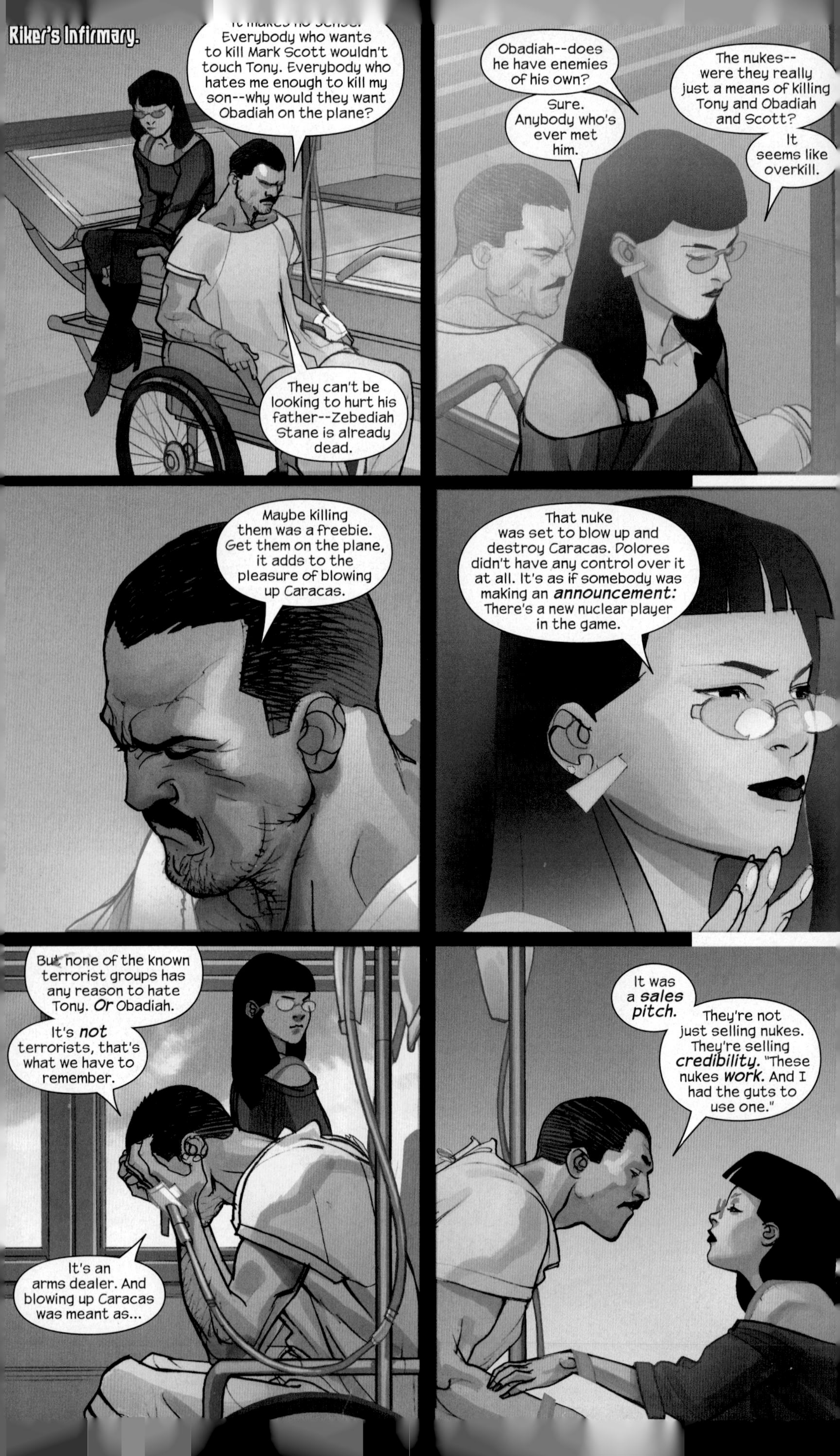
Riker's Infirmary.
Everybody who wants to kill Mark Scott wouldn't touch Tony. Everybody who hates me enough to kill my son--why would they want Obadiah on the plane?
They can't be looking to hurt his father--Zebediah Stane is already dead.
Obadiah--does he have enemies of his own?
Sure. Anybody who's ever met him.
The nukes--were they really just a means of killing Tony and Obadiah and Scott?
It seems like overkill.
Maybe killing them was a freebie. Get them on the plane, it adds to the pleasure of blowing up Caracas.
That nuke was set to blow up and destroy Caracas. Dolores didn't have any control over it at all. It's as if somebody was making an *announcement:* There's a new nuclear player in the game.
But none of the known terrorist groups has any reason to hate Tony. *Or* Obadiah.
It's *not* terrorists, that's what we have to remember.
It's an arms dealer. And blowing up Caracas was meant as...
It was a *sales pitch.*
They're not just selling nukes. They're selling *credibility.* "These nukes *work.* And I had the guts to use one."

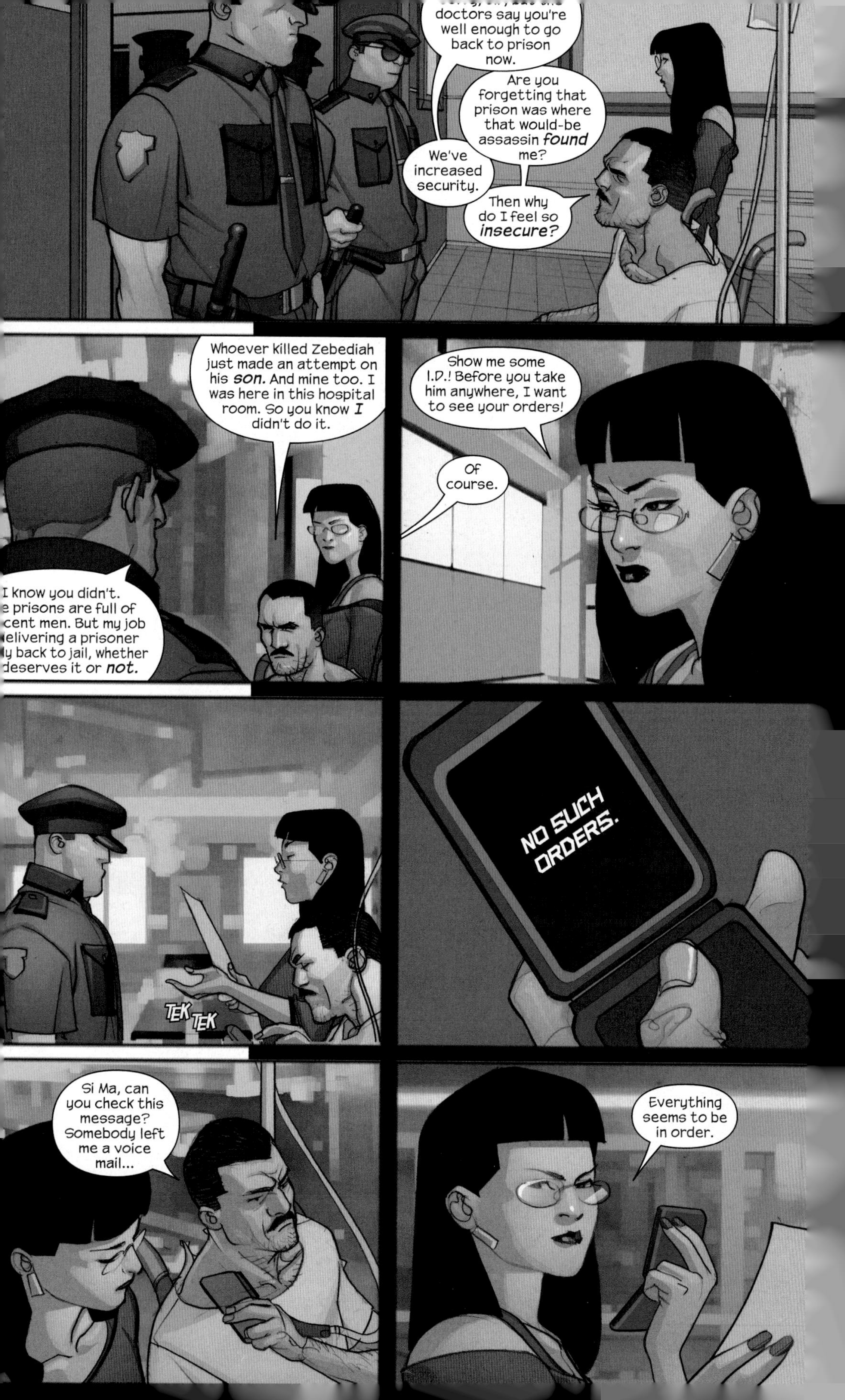
doctors say you're well enough to go back to prison now.
Are you forgetting that prison was where that would-be assassin *found* me?
We've increased security.
Then why do I feel so *insecure?*
Whoever killed Zebediah just made an attempt on his *son.* And mine too. I was here in this hospital room. So you know *I* didn't do it.
I know you didn't. e prisons are full of cent men. But my job elivering a prisoner y back to jail, whether deserves it or *not.*
Show me some I.D.! Before you take him anywhere, I want to see your orders!
Of course.
TEK TEK
NO SUCH ORDERS.
Si Ma, can you check this message? Somebody left me a voice mail...
Everything seems to be in order.

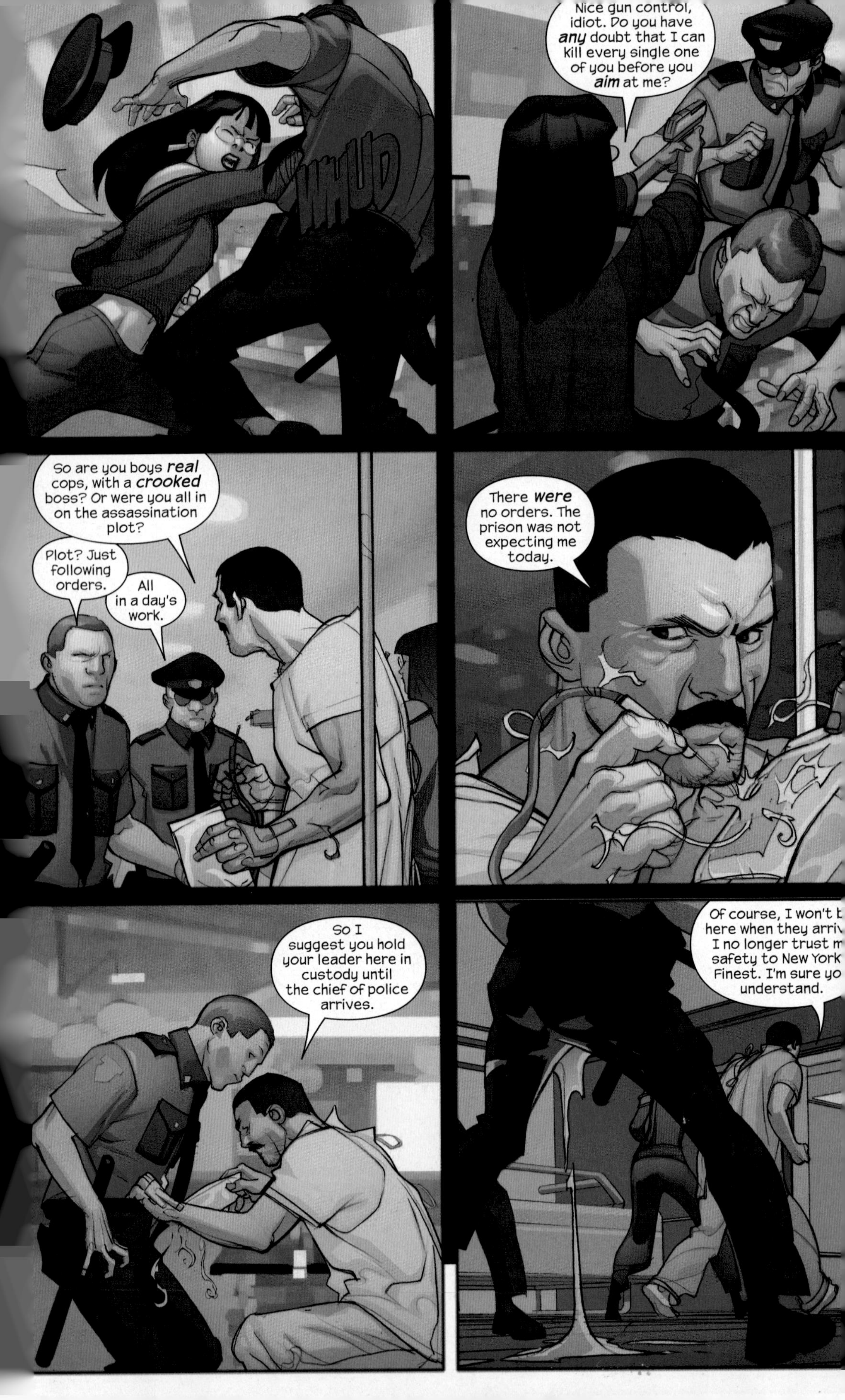
WHUD
Nice gun control, idiot. Do you have any doubt that I can kill every single one of you before you aim at me?
So are you boys real cops, with a crooked boss? Or were you all in on the assassination plot?
Plot? Just following orders.
All in a day's work.
There were no orders. The prison was not expecting me today.
So I suggest you hold your leader here in custody until the chief of police arrives.
Of course, I won't b here when they arriv I no longer trust m safety to New York Finest. I'm sure yo understand.

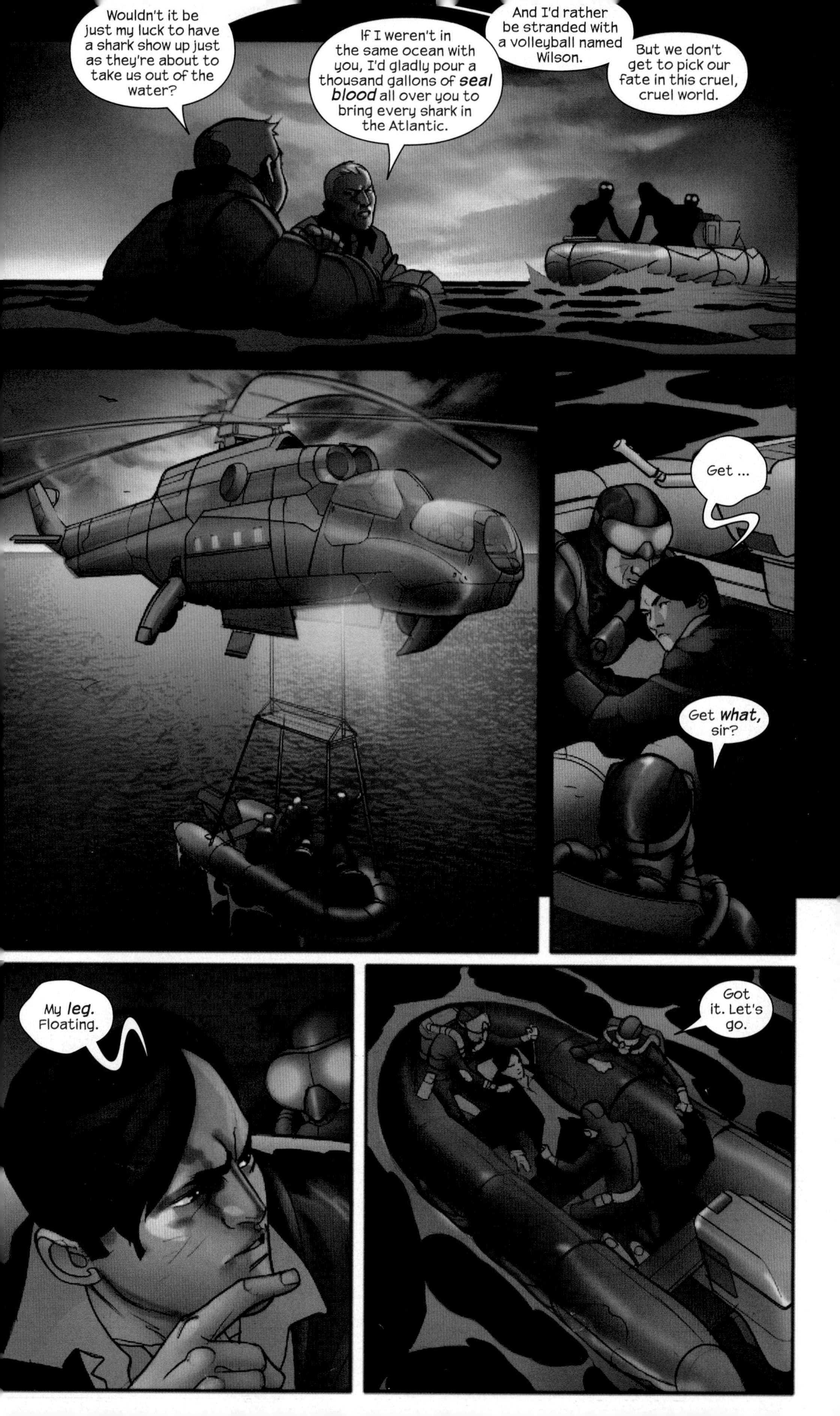
Wouldn't it be just my luck to have a shark show up just as they're about to take us out of the water?
If I weren't in the same ocean with you, I'd gladly pour a thousand gallons of seal blood all over you to bring every shark in the Atlantic.
And I'd rather be stranded with a volleyball named Wilson.
But we don't get to pick our fate in this cruel, cruel world.
Get ...
Get what, sir?
My leg. Floating.
Got it. Let's go.

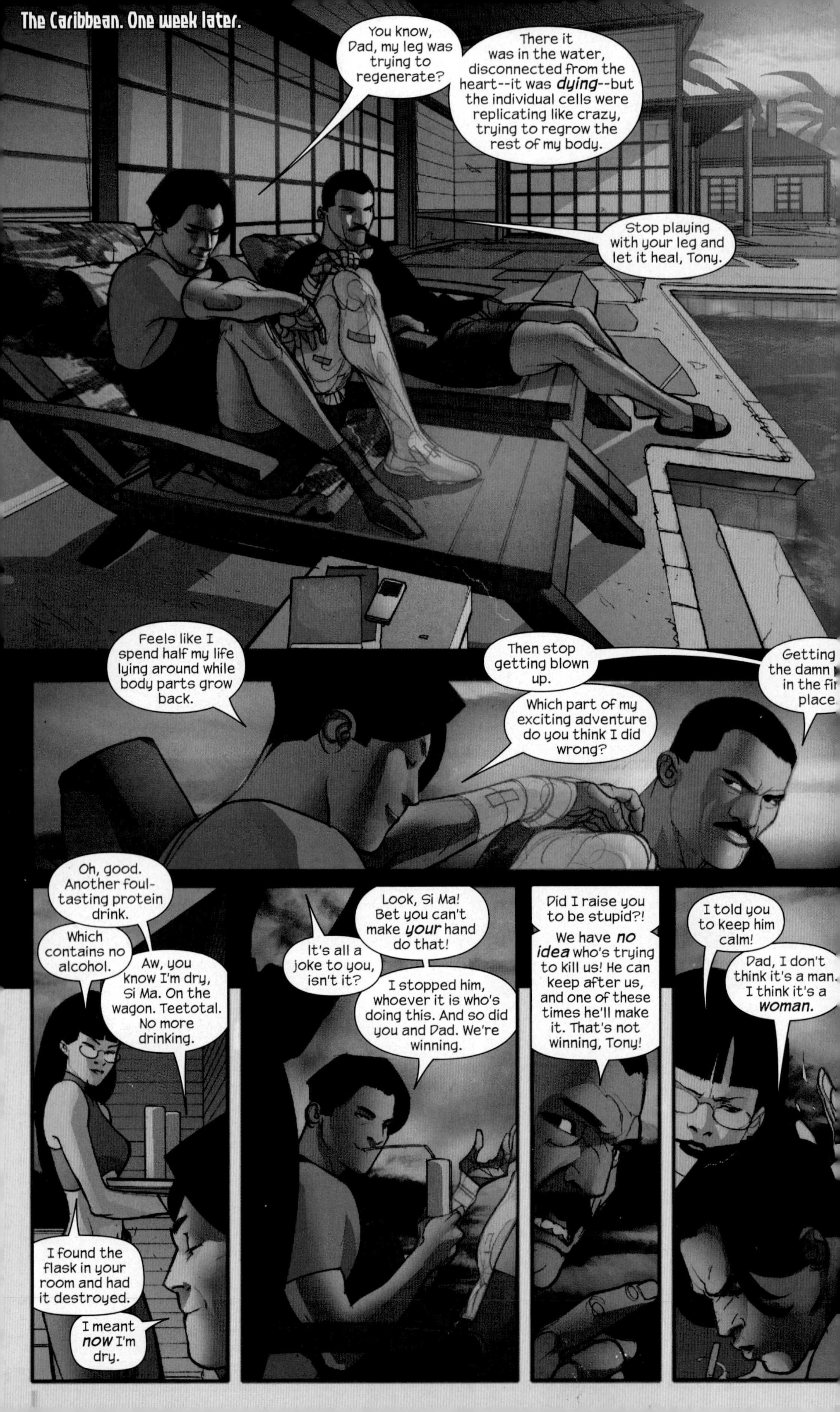
The Caribbean. One week later.
You know, Dad, my leg was trying to regenerate?
There it was in the water, disconnected from the heart--it was dying--but the individual cells were replicating like crazy, trying to regrow the rest of my body.
Stop playing with your leg and let it heal, Tony.
Feels like I spend half my life lying around while body parts grow back.
Then stop getting blown up.
Which part of my exciting adventure do you think I did wrong?
Getting the damn in the fi place
Oh, good. Another foul-tasting protein drink.
Which contains no alcohol.
Aw, you know I'm dry, Si Ma. On the wagon. Teetotal. No more drinking.
I found the flask in your room and had it destroyed.
I meant NOW I'm dry.
It's all a joke to you, isn't it?
Look, Si Ma! Bet you can't make YOUR hand do that!
I stopped him, whoever it is who's doing this. And so did you and Dad. We're winning.
Did I raise you to be stupid?!
We have NO IDEA who's trying to kill us! He can keep after us, and one of these times he'll make it. That's not winning, Tony!
I told you to keep him calm!
Dad, I don't think it's a man. I think it's a WOMAN.

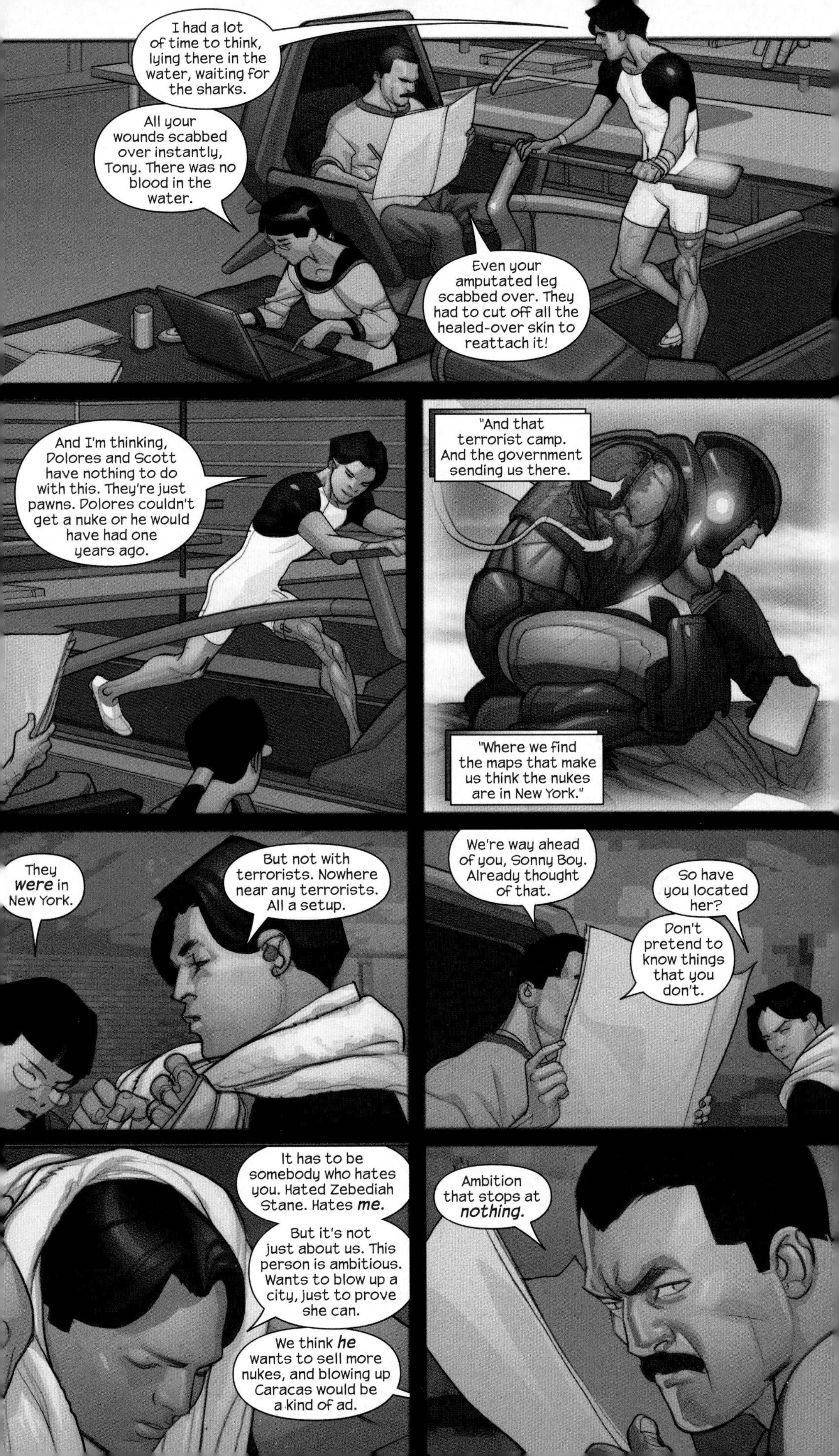

I had a lot of time to think, lying there in the water, waiting for the sharks.
All your wounds scabbed over instantly, Tony. There was no blood in the water.
Even your amputated leg scabbed over. They had to cut off all the healed-over skin to reattach it!
And I'm thinking, Dolores and Scott have nothing to do with this. They're just pawns. Dolores couldn't get a nuke or he would have had one years ago.
"And that terrorist camp. And the government sending us there.
"Where we find the maps that make us think the nukes are in New York."
They *were* in New York.
But not with terrorists. Nowhere near any terrorists. All a setup.
We're way ahead of you, Sonny Boy. Already thought of that.
So have you located her?
Don't pretend to know things that you don't.
It has to be somebody who hates you. Hated Zebediah Stane. Hates *me.*
But it's not just about us. This person is ambitious. Wants to blow up a city, just to prove she can.
We think *he* wants to sell more nukes, and blowing up Caracas would be a kind of ad.
Ambition that stops at *nothing.*

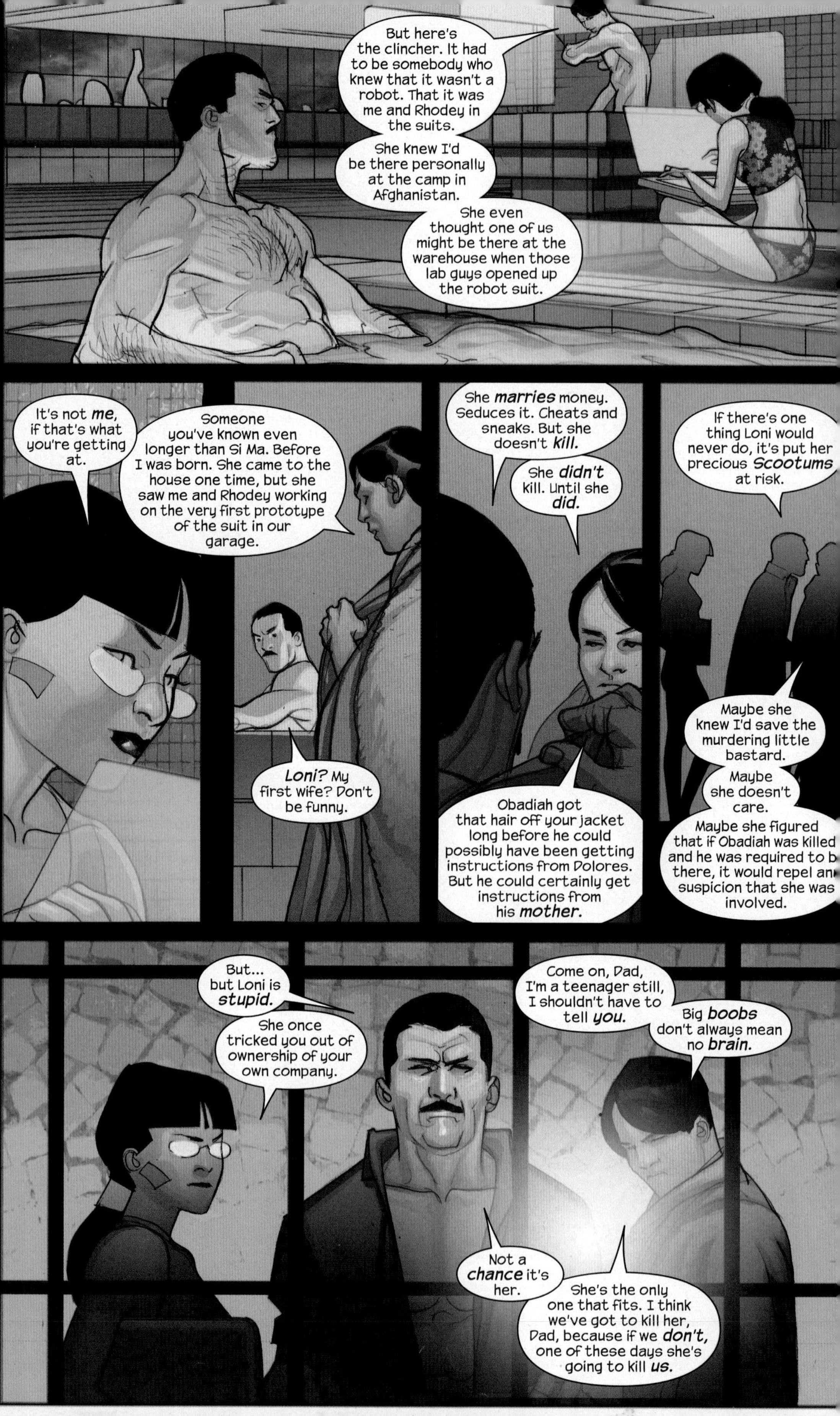

But here's the clincher. It had to be somebody who knew that it wasn't a robot. That it was me and Rhodey in the suits.
She knew I'd be there personally at the camp in Afghanistan.
She even thought one of us might be there at the warehouse when those lab guys opened up the robot suit.
It's not *me*, if that's what you're getting at.
Someone you've known even longer than Si Ma. Before I was born. She came to the house one time, but she saw me and Rhodey working on the very first prototype of the suit in our garage.
Loni? My first wife? Don't be funny.
She *marries* money. Seduces it. Cheats and sneaks. But she doesn't *kill.*
She *didn't* kill. Until she *did.*
Obadiah got that hair off your jacket long before he could possibly have been getting instructions from Dolores. But he could certainly get instructions from his *mother.*
If there's one thing Loni would never do, it's put her precious *Scootums* at risk.
Maybe she knew I'd save the murdering little bastard.
Maybe she doesn't care.
Maybe she figured that if Obadiah was killed and he was required to b there, it would repel an suspicion that she was involved.
But... but Loni is *stupid.*
She once tricked you out of ownership of your own company.
Come on, Dad, I'm a teenager still, I shouldn't have to tell *you.*
Big *boobs* don't always mean no *brain.*
Not a *chance* it's her.
She's the only one that fits. I think we've got to kill her, Dad, because if we *don't,* one of these days she's going to kill *us.*

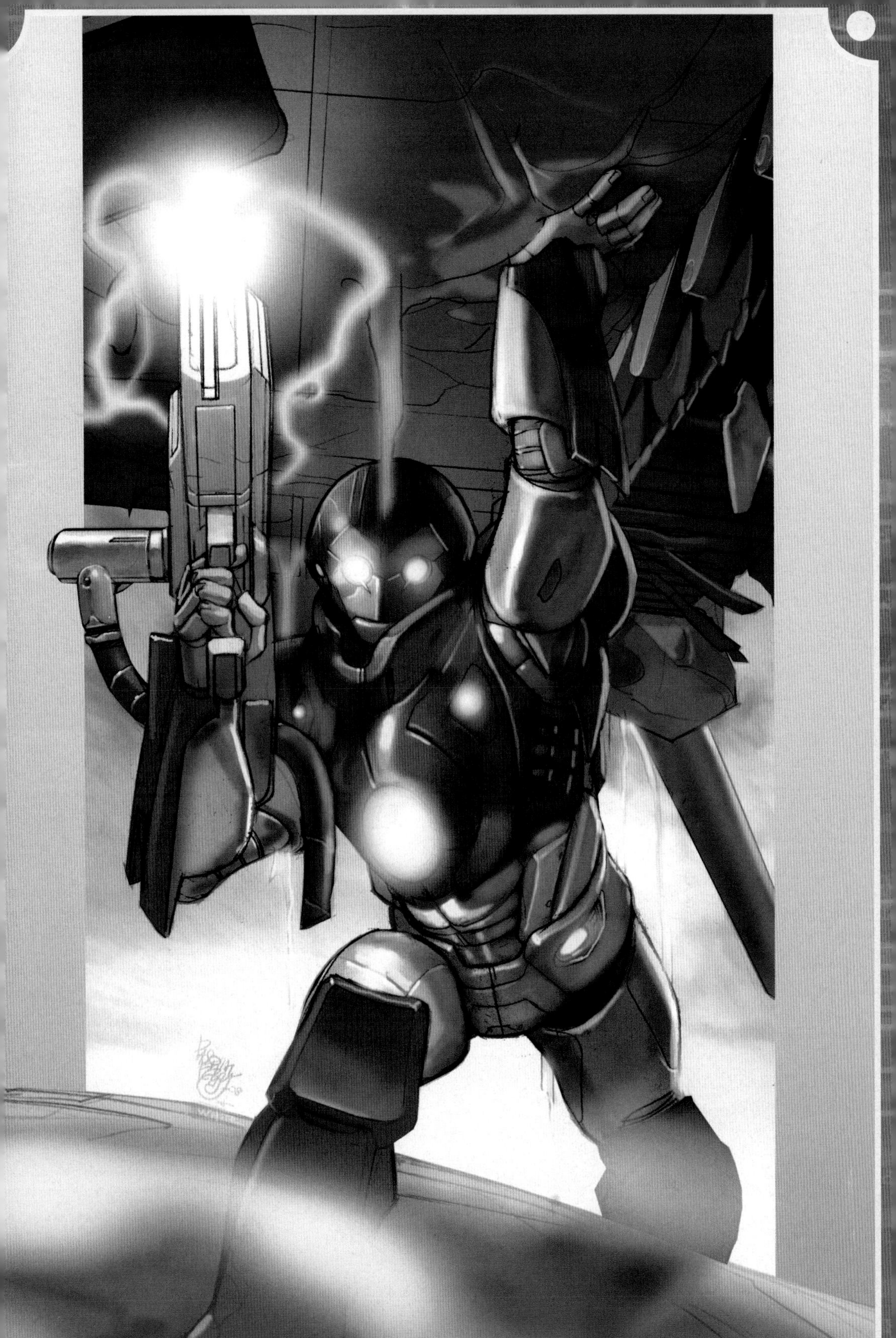

ULTIMATE IRON MAN II
ISSUE 05

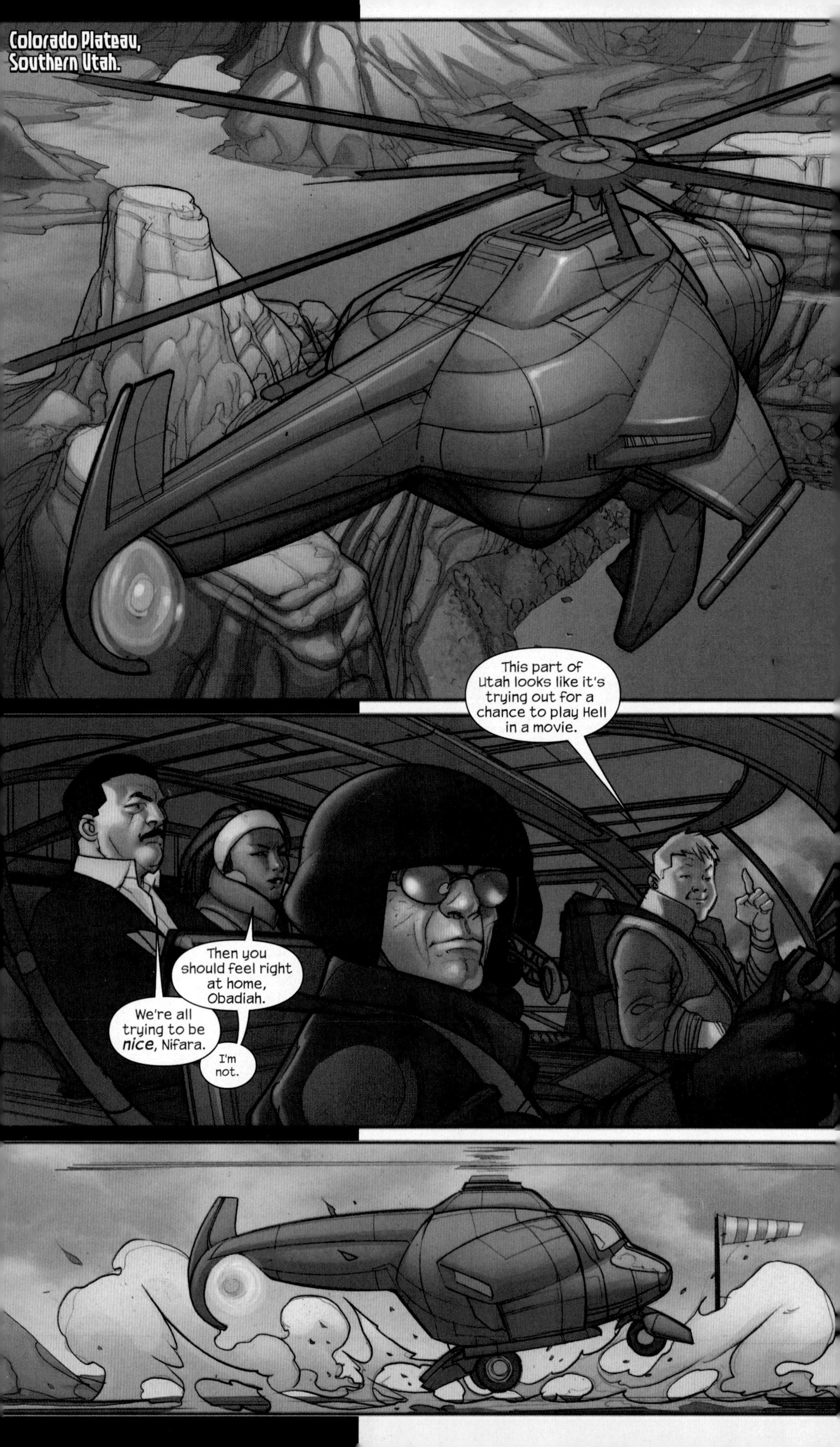
Colorado Plateau, Southern Utah.
This part of Utah looks like it's trying out for a chance to play Hell in a movie.
Then you should feel right at home, Obadiah.
We're all trying to be *nice*, Nifara.
I'm not.

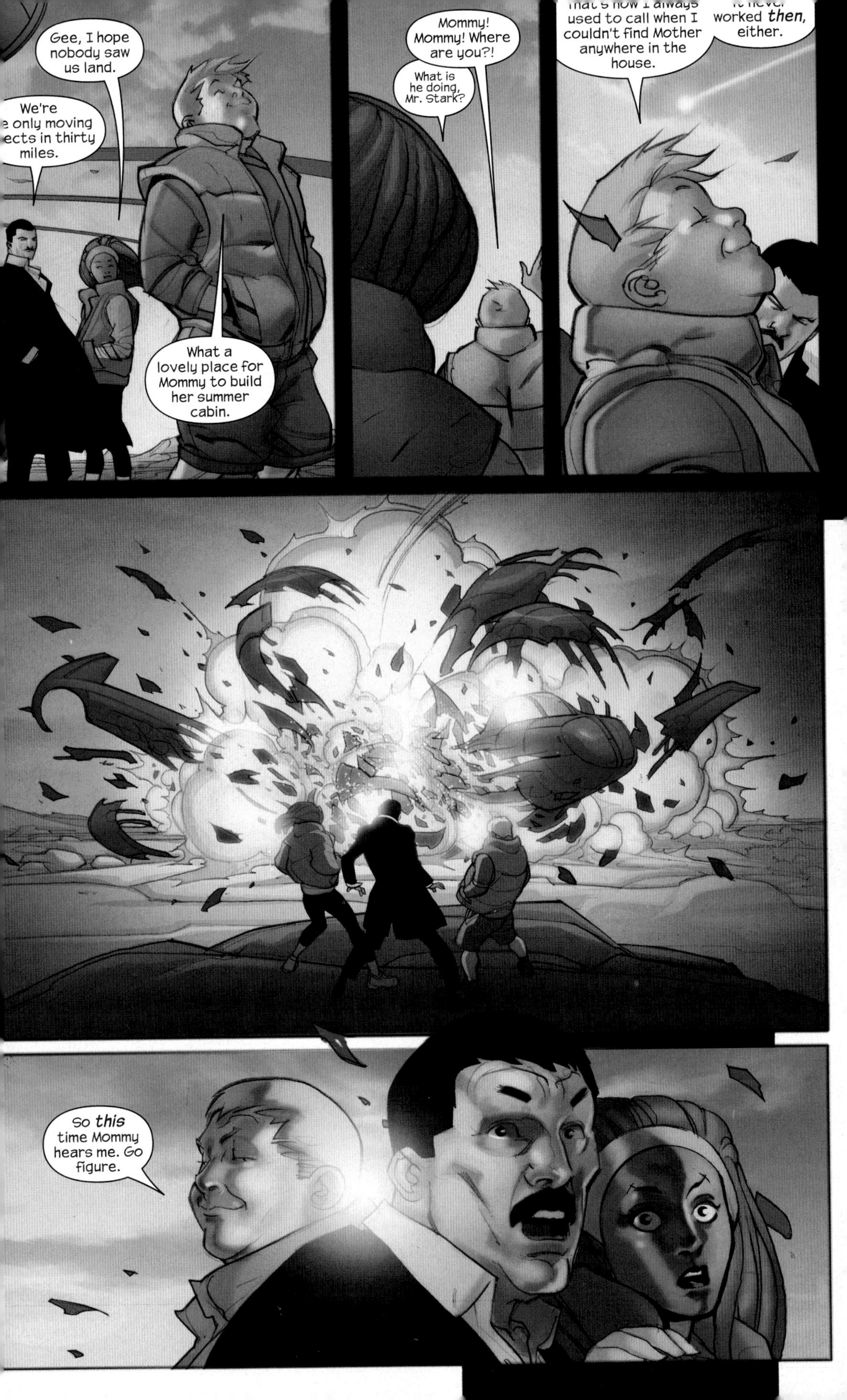
Gee, I hope nobody saw us land.
We're e only moving ects in thirty miles.
What a lovely place for Mommy to build her summer cabin.
Mommy! Mommy! Where are you?!
What is he doing, Mr. Stark?
used to call when I couldn't find Mother anywhere in the house.
worked *then*, either.
So *this* time Mommy hears me. Go figure.

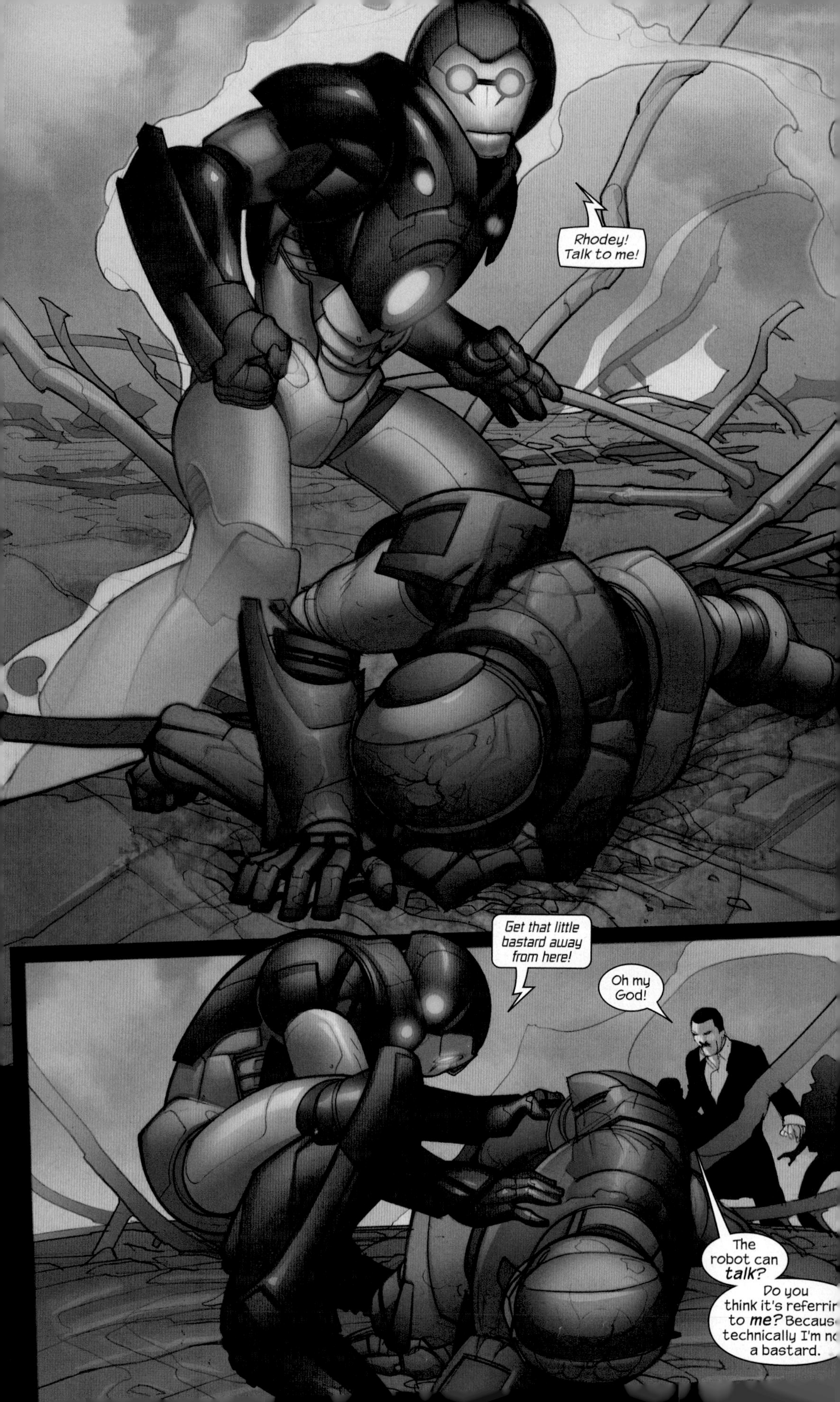
Rhodey! Talk to me!
Get that little bastard away from here!
Oh my God!
The robot can talk?
Do you think it's referrin
to me? Becaus
technically I'm no
a bastard.

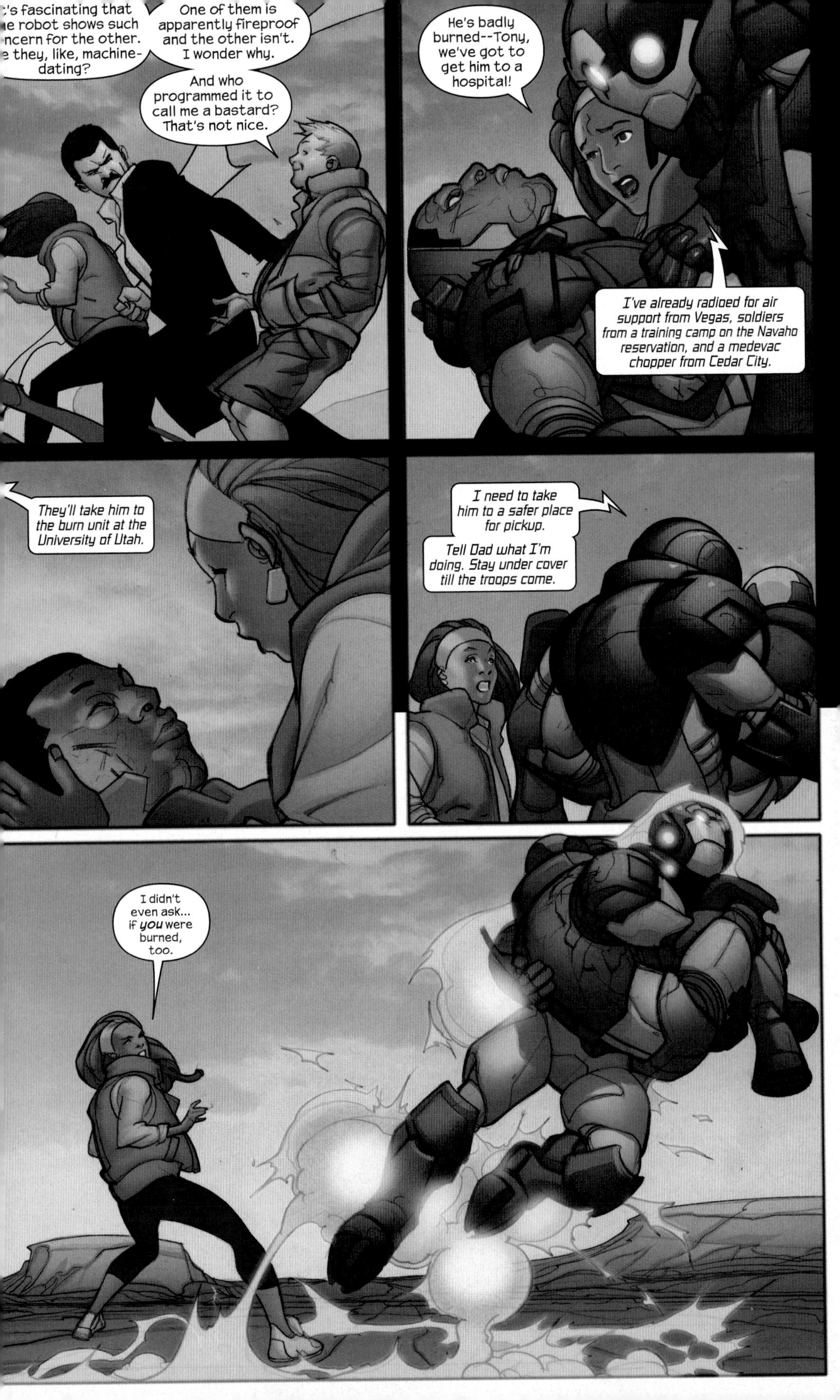

's fascinating that e robot shows such ncern for the other. e they, like, machine-dating?
One of them is apparently fireproof and the other isn't. I wonder why.
And who programmed it to call me a bastard? That's not nice.
He's badly burned--Tony, we've got to get him to a hospital!
I've already radioed for air support from Vegas, soldiers from a training camp on the Navaho reservation, and a medevac chopper from Cedar City.
They'll take him to the burn unit at the University of Utah.
I need to take him to a safer place for pickup.
Tell Dad what I'm doing. Stay under cover till the troops come.
I didn't even ask... if *you* were burned, too.

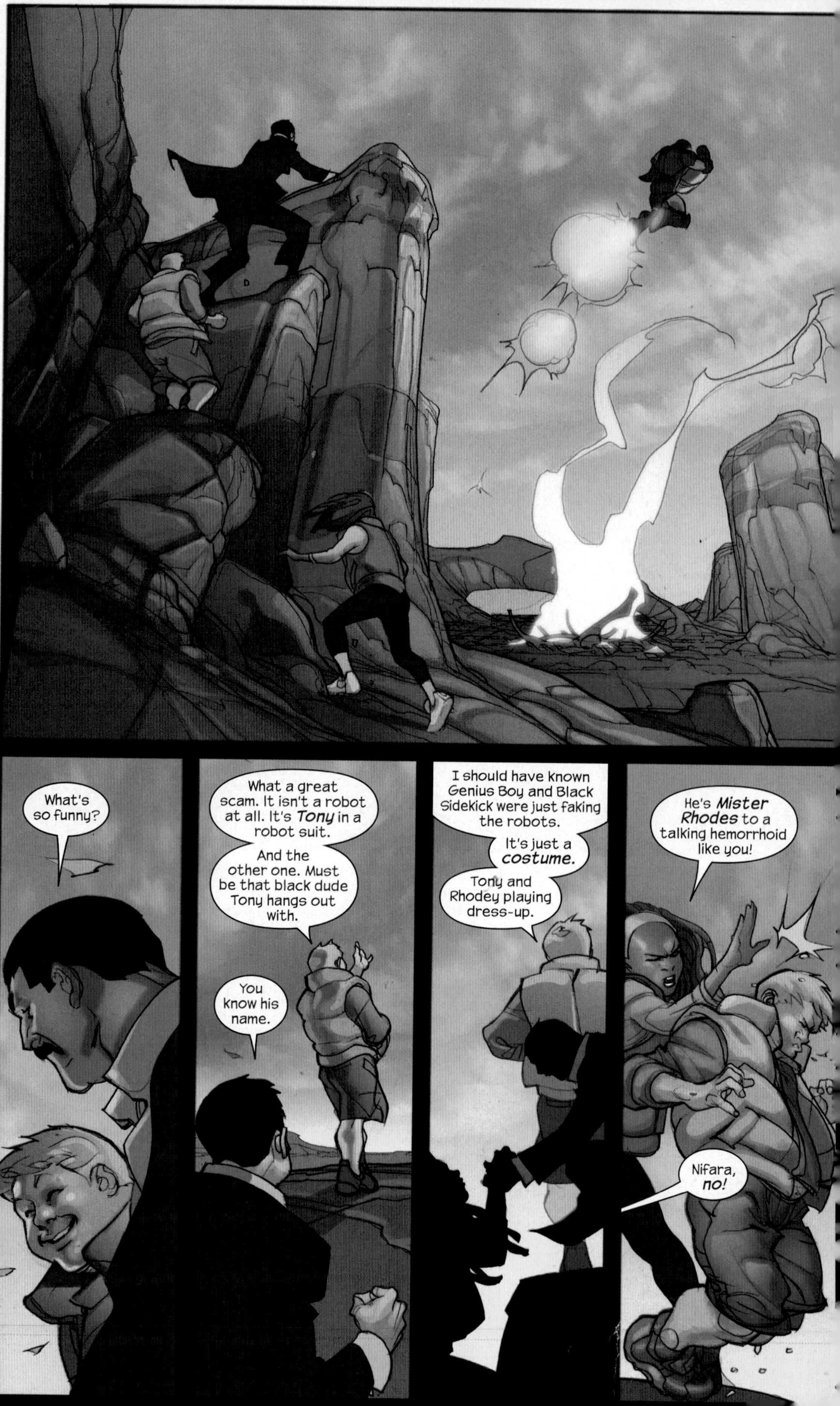
What's so funny?
What a great scam. It isn't a robot at all. It's *Tony* in a robot suit.
And the other one. Must be that black dude Tony hangs out with.
You know his name.
I should have known Genius Boy and Black Sidekick were just faking the robots.
It's just a **costume.**
Tony and Rhodey playing dress-up.
He's ***Mister Rhodes*** to a talking hemorrhoid like you!
Nifara, ***no!***

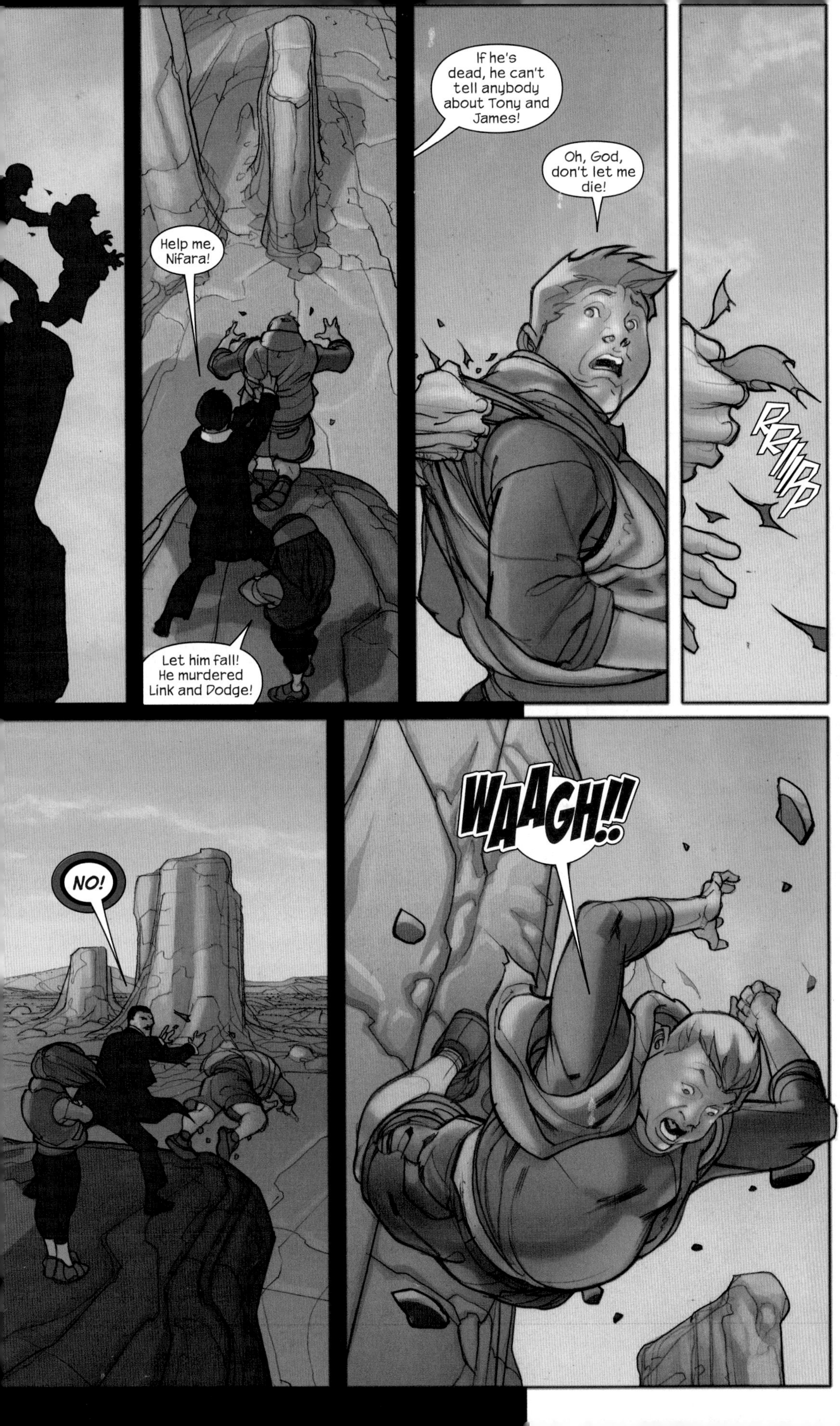
Help me, Nifara!
Let him fall! He murdered Link and Dodge!
If he's dead, he can't tell anybody about Tony and James!
Oh, God, don't let me die!
RRIIPP
NO!
WAAGH!!

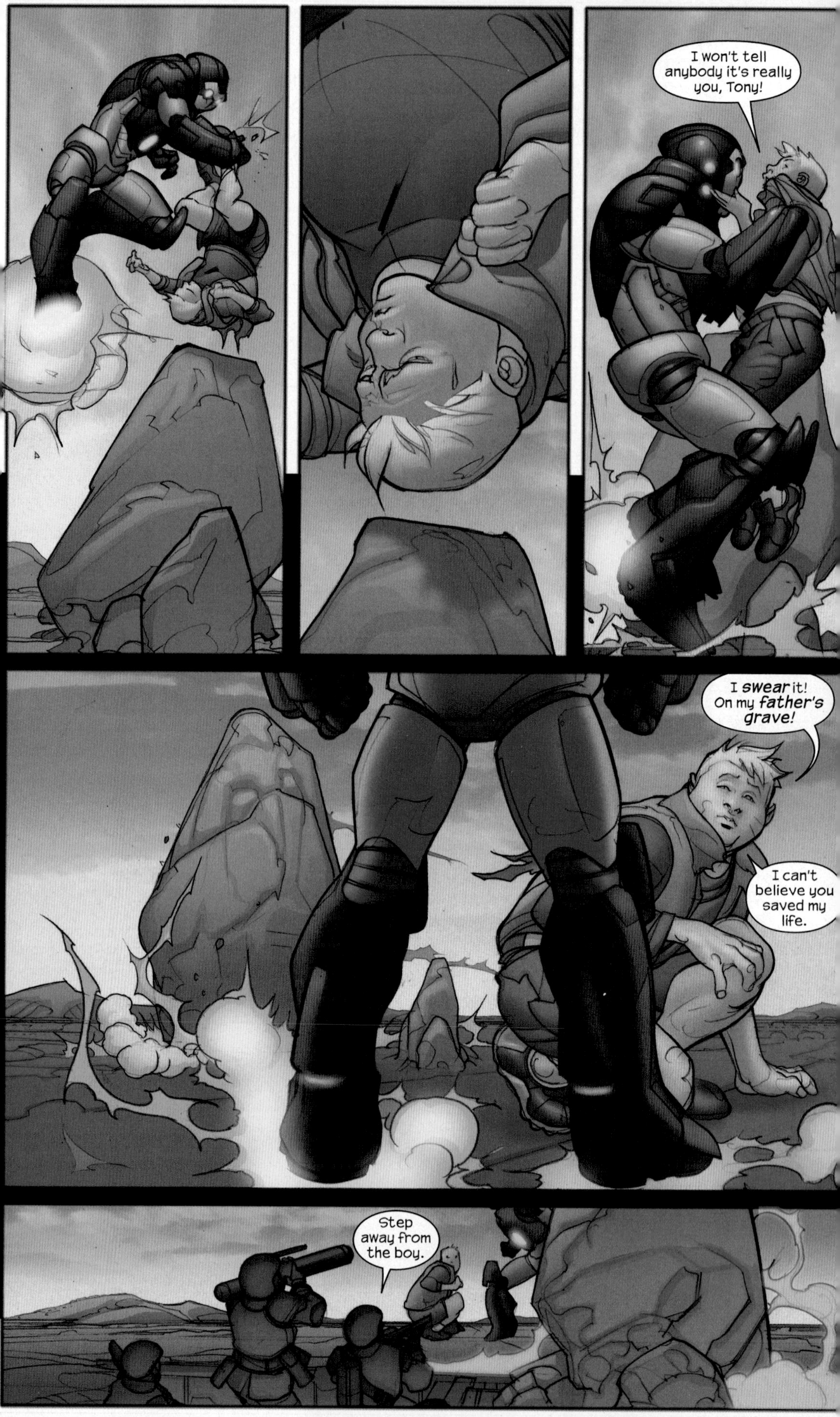
I won't tell anybody it's really you, Tony!
I *swear* it! On my *father's grave!*
I can't believe you saved my life.
Step away from the boy.

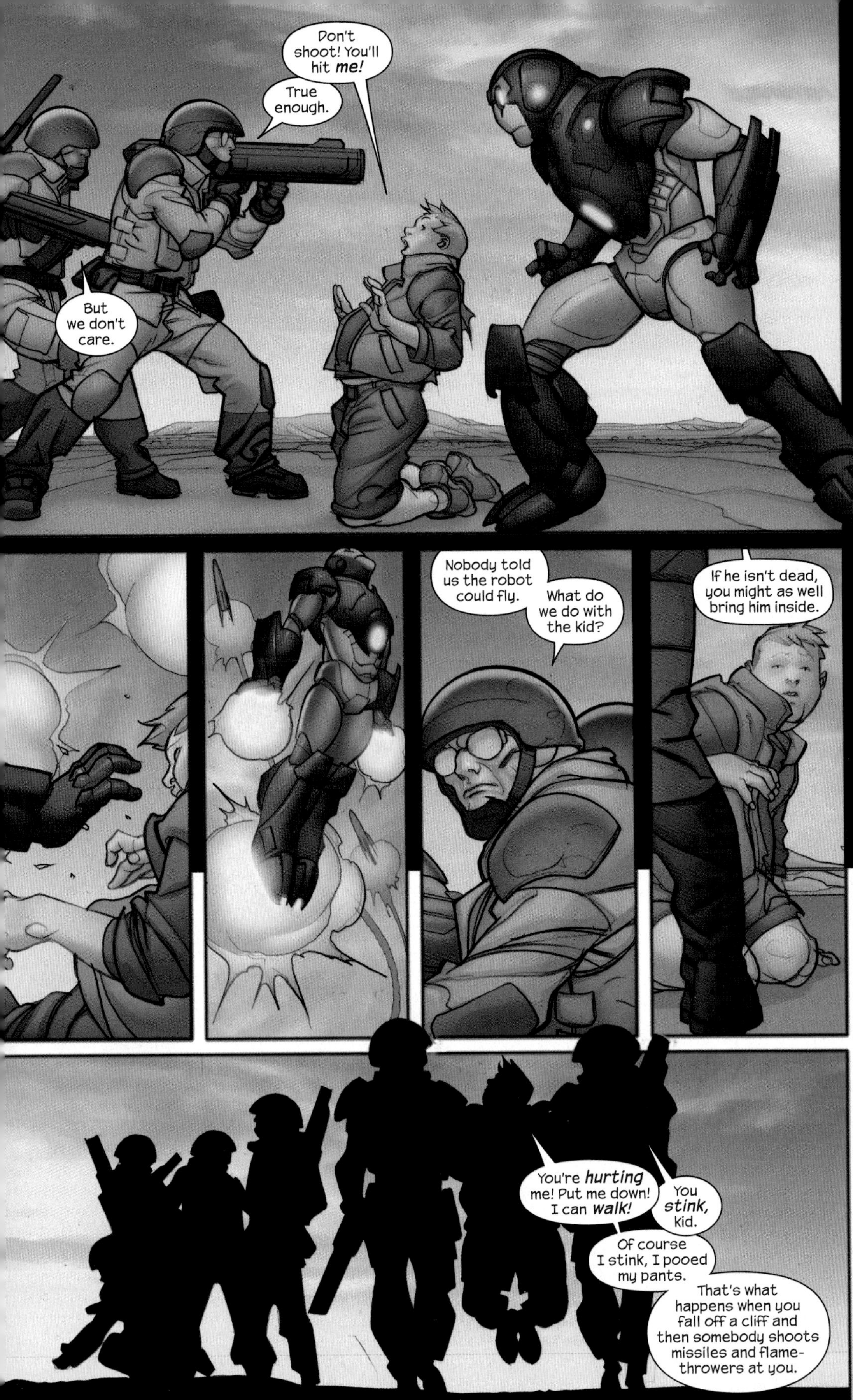
Don't shoot! You'll hit *me!*
True enough.
But we don't care.
Nobody told us the robot could fly.
What do we do with the kid?
If he isn't dead, you might as well bring him inside.
You're *hurting* me! Put me down! I can *walk!*
You *stink,* kid.
Of course I stink, I pooed my pants.
That's what happens when you fall off a cliff and then somebody shoots missiles and flame-throwers at you.

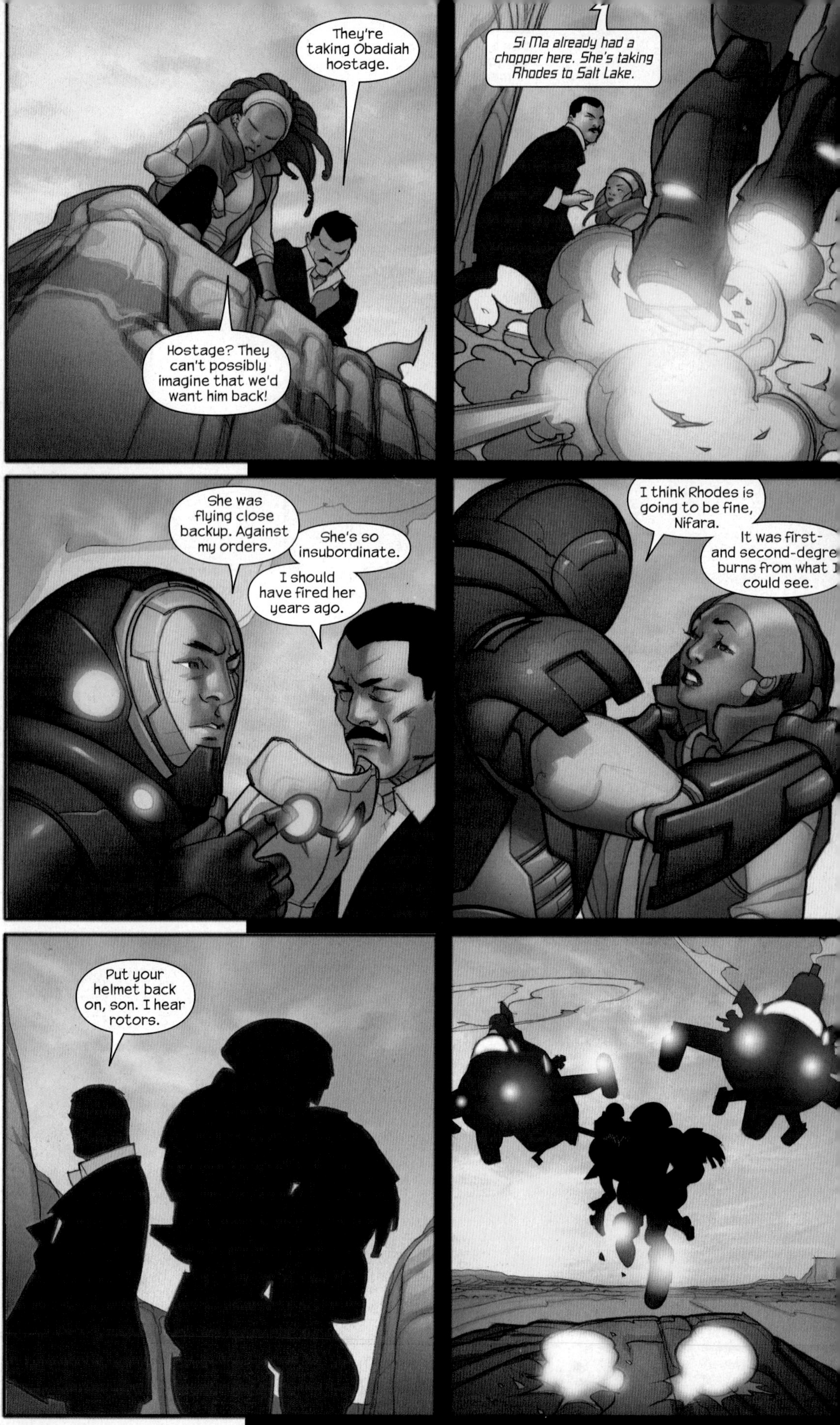
They're taking Obadiah hostage.
Hostage? They can't possibly imagine that we'd want him back!
Si Ma already had a chopper here. She's taking Rhodes to Salt Lake.
She was flying close backup. Against my orders.
She's so insubordinate.
I should have fired her years ago.
I think Rhodes is going to be fine, Nifara.
It was first- and second-degre burns from what I could see.
Put your helmet back on, son. I hear rotors.

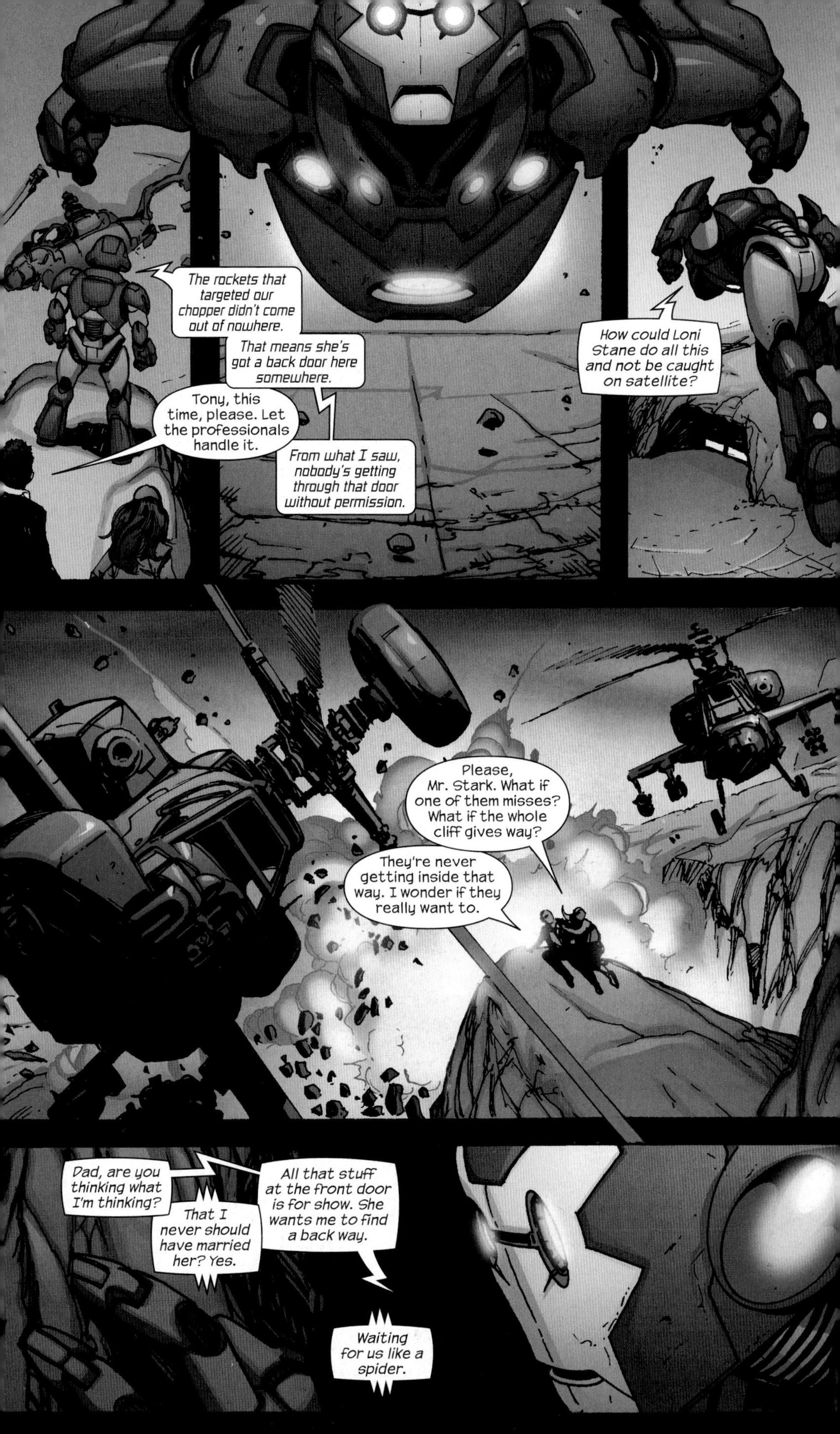
The rockets that targeted our chopper didn't come out of nowhere.
That means she's got a back door here somewhere.
Tony, this time, please. Let the professionals handle it.
From what I saw, nobody's getting through that door without permission.
How could Loni Stane do all this and not be caught on satellite?
Please, Mr. Stark. What if one of them misses? What if the whole cliff gives way?
They're never getting inside that way. I wonder if they really want to.
Dad, are you thinking what I'm thinking?
That I never should have married her? Yes.
All that stuff at the front door is for show. She wants me to find a back way.
Waiting for us like a spider.

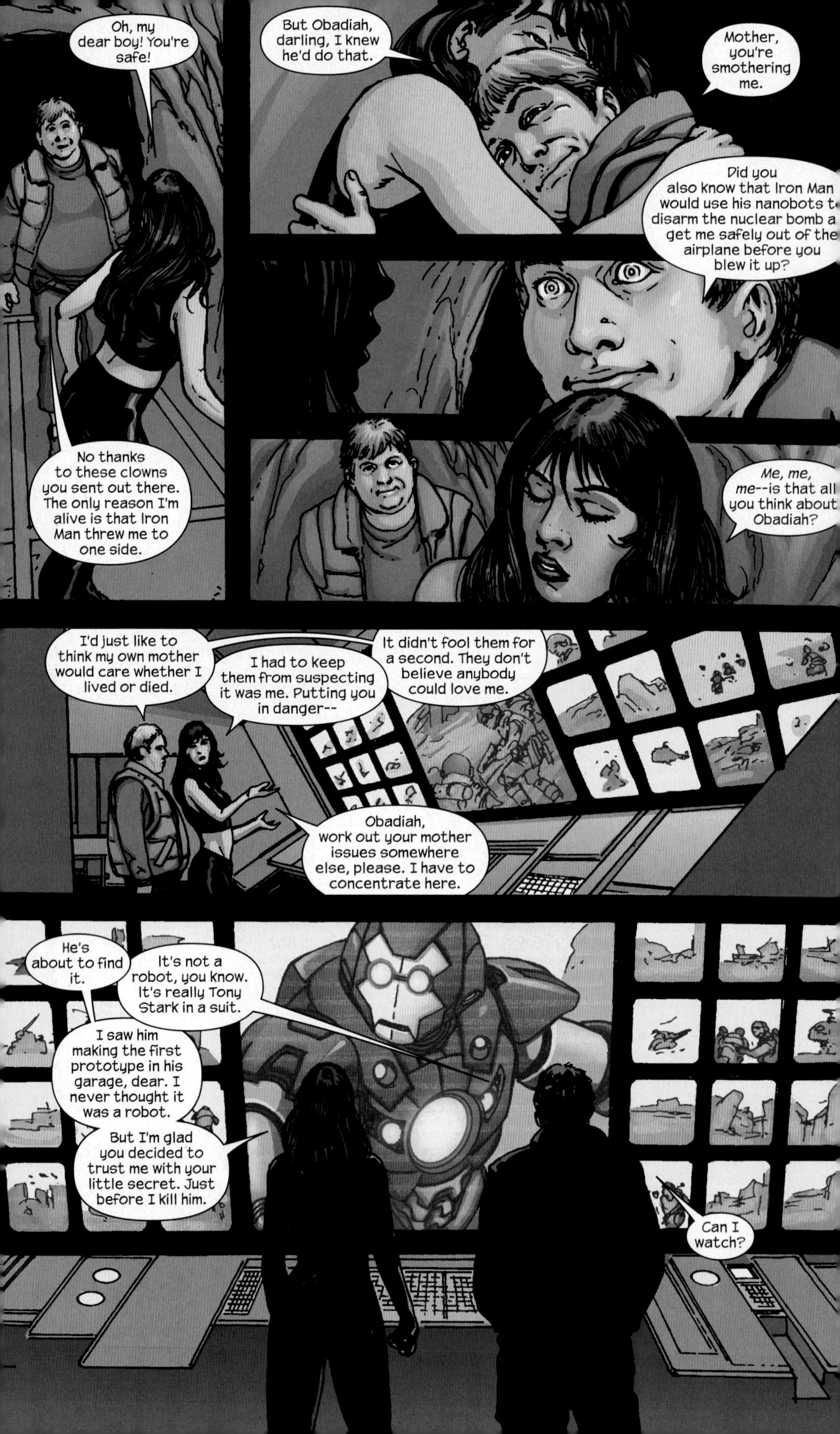
Oh, my dear boy! You're safe!
No thanks to these clowns you sent out there. The only reason I'm alive is that Iron Man threw me to one side.
But Obadiah, darling, I knew he'd do that.
Mother, you're smothering me.
Did you also know that Iron Man would use his nanobots to disarm the nuclear bomb and get me safely out of the airplane before you blew it up?
Me, me, me--is that all you think about Obadiah?
I'd just like to think my own mother would care whether I lived or died.
I had to keep them from suspecting it was me. Putting you in danger--
It didn't fool them for a second. They don't believe anybody could love me.
Obadiah, work out your mother issues somewhere else, please. I have to concentrate here.
He's about to find it.
It's not a robot, you know. It's really Tony Stark in a suit.
I saw him making the first prototype in his garage, dear. I never thought it was a robot.
But I'm glad you decided to trust me with your little secret. Just before I kill him.
Can I watch?

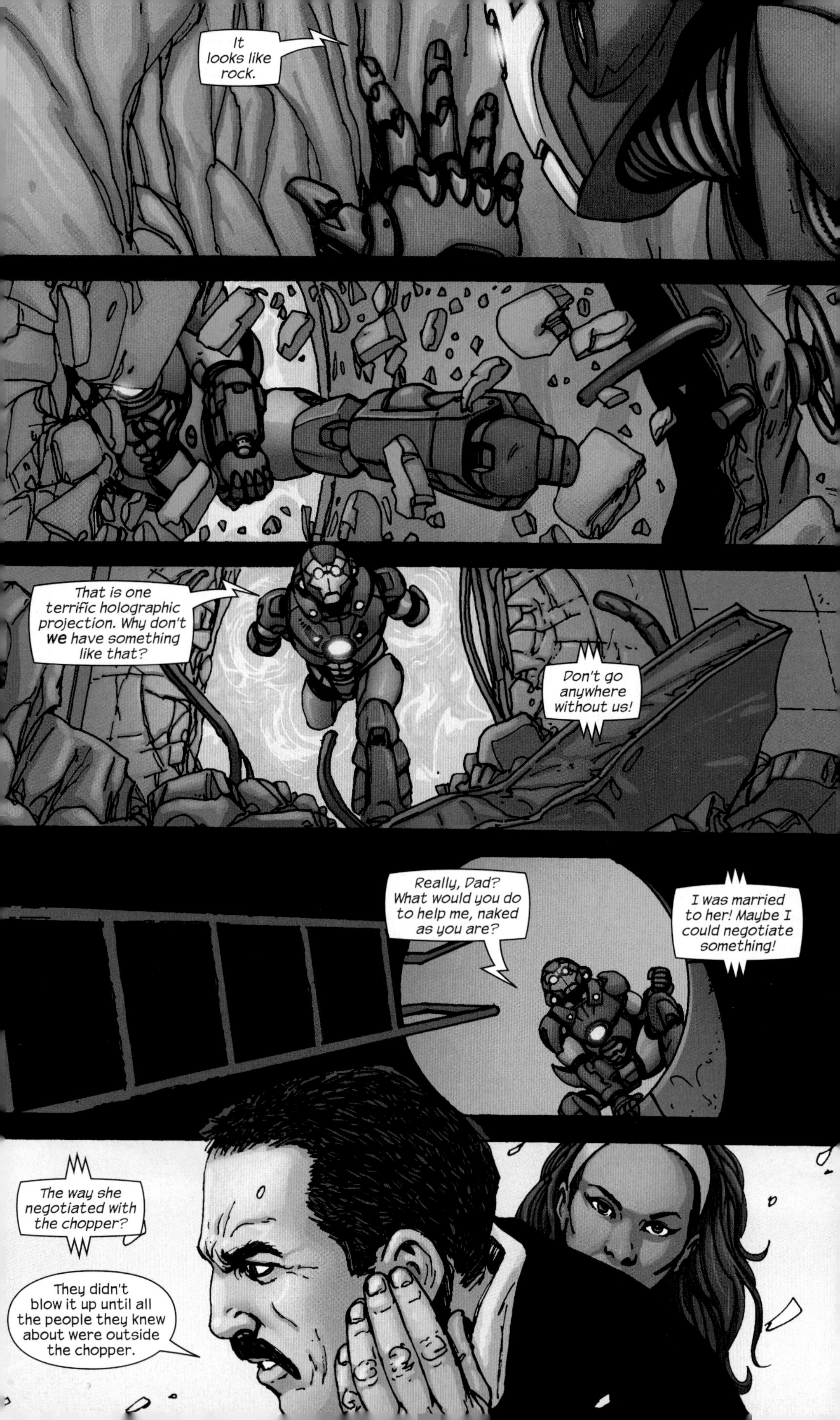
It looks like rock.
That is one terrific holographic projection. Why don't **we** have something like that?
Don't go anywhere without us!
Really, Dad? What would you do to help me, naked as you are?
I was married to her! Maybe I could negotiate something!
The way she negotiated with the chopper?
They didn't blow it up until all the people they knew about were outside the chopper.

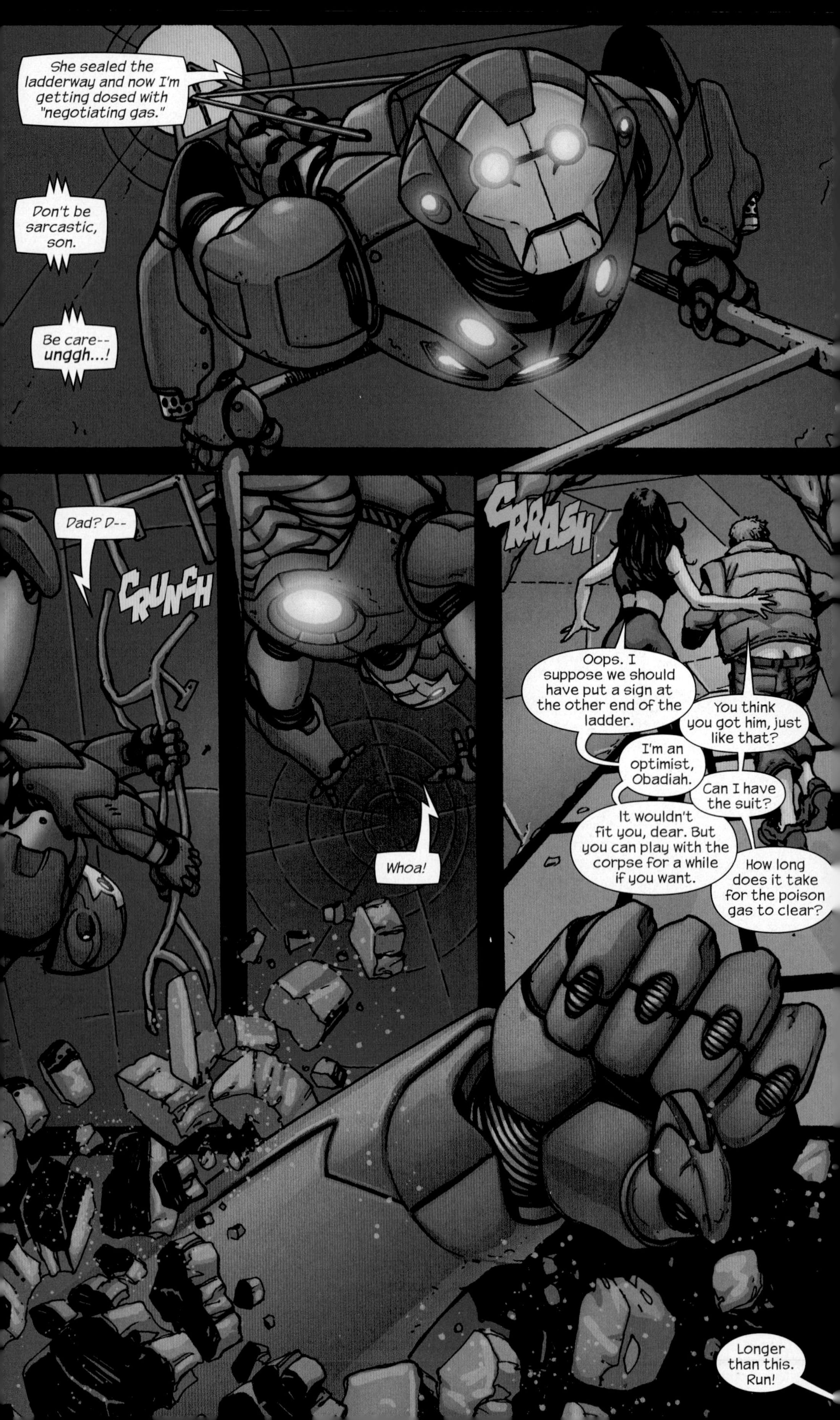
She sealed the ladderway and now I'm getting dosed with "negotiating gas."
Don't be sarcastic, son.
Be care-- unggh...!
Dad? D--
CRUNCH
Whoa!
CRRASH
Oops. I suppose we should have put a sign at the other end of the ladder.
You think you got him, just like that?
I'm an optimist, Obadiah.
Can I have the suit?
It wouldn't fit you, dear. But you can play with the corpse for a while if you want.
How long does it take for the poison gas to clear?
Longer than this. Run!

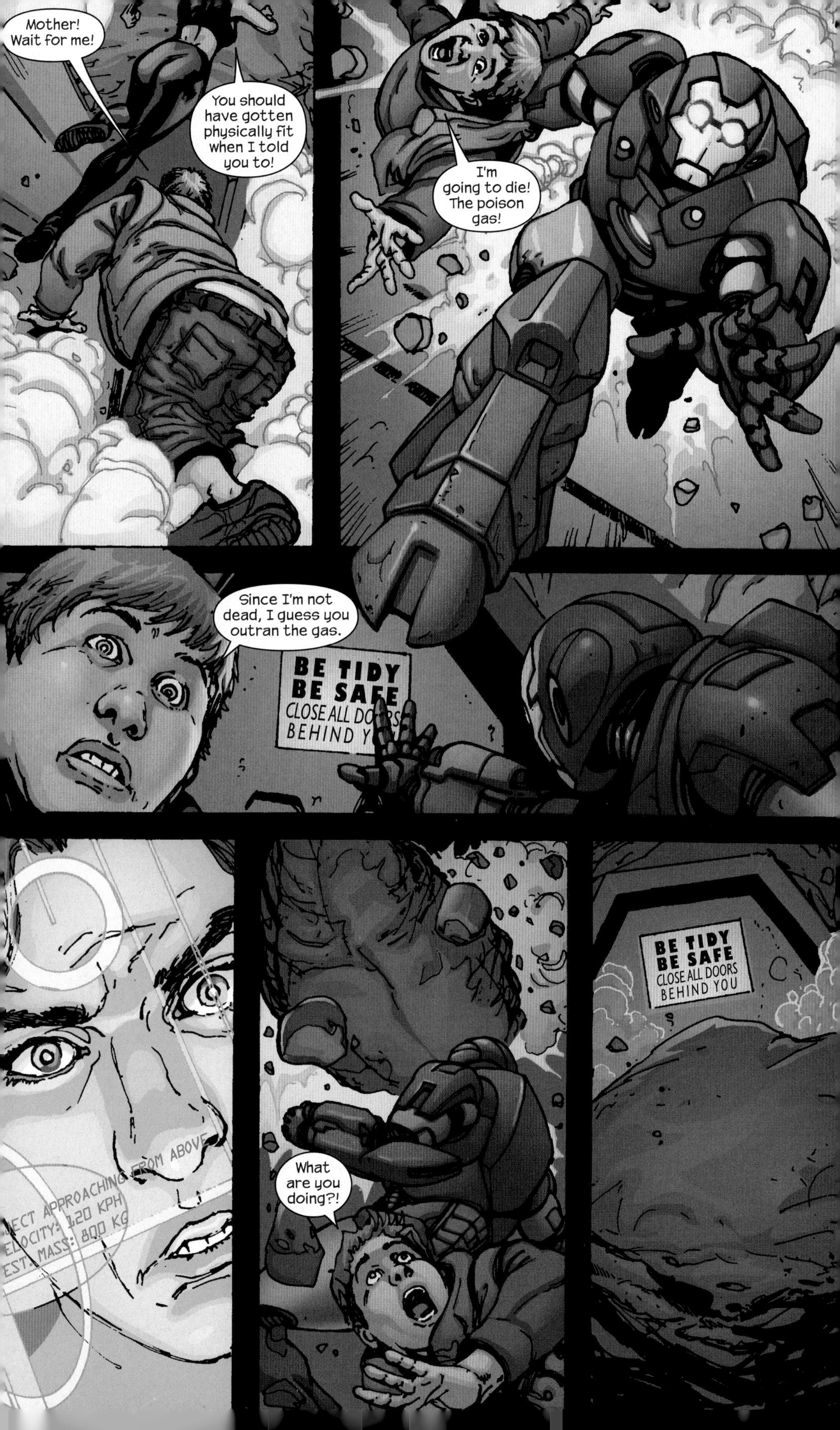
Mother! Wait for me!
You should have gotten physically fit when I told you to!
I'm going to die! The poison gas!
Since I'm not dead, I guess you outran the gas.
BE TIDY
BE SAFE
CLOSE ALL DOORS
BEHIND Y
APPROACHING FROM ABOVE
ELOCITY: 120 KPH
EST. MASS: 800 KG
What are you doing?!
BE TIDY
BE SAFE
CLOSE ALL DOORS
BEHIND YOU

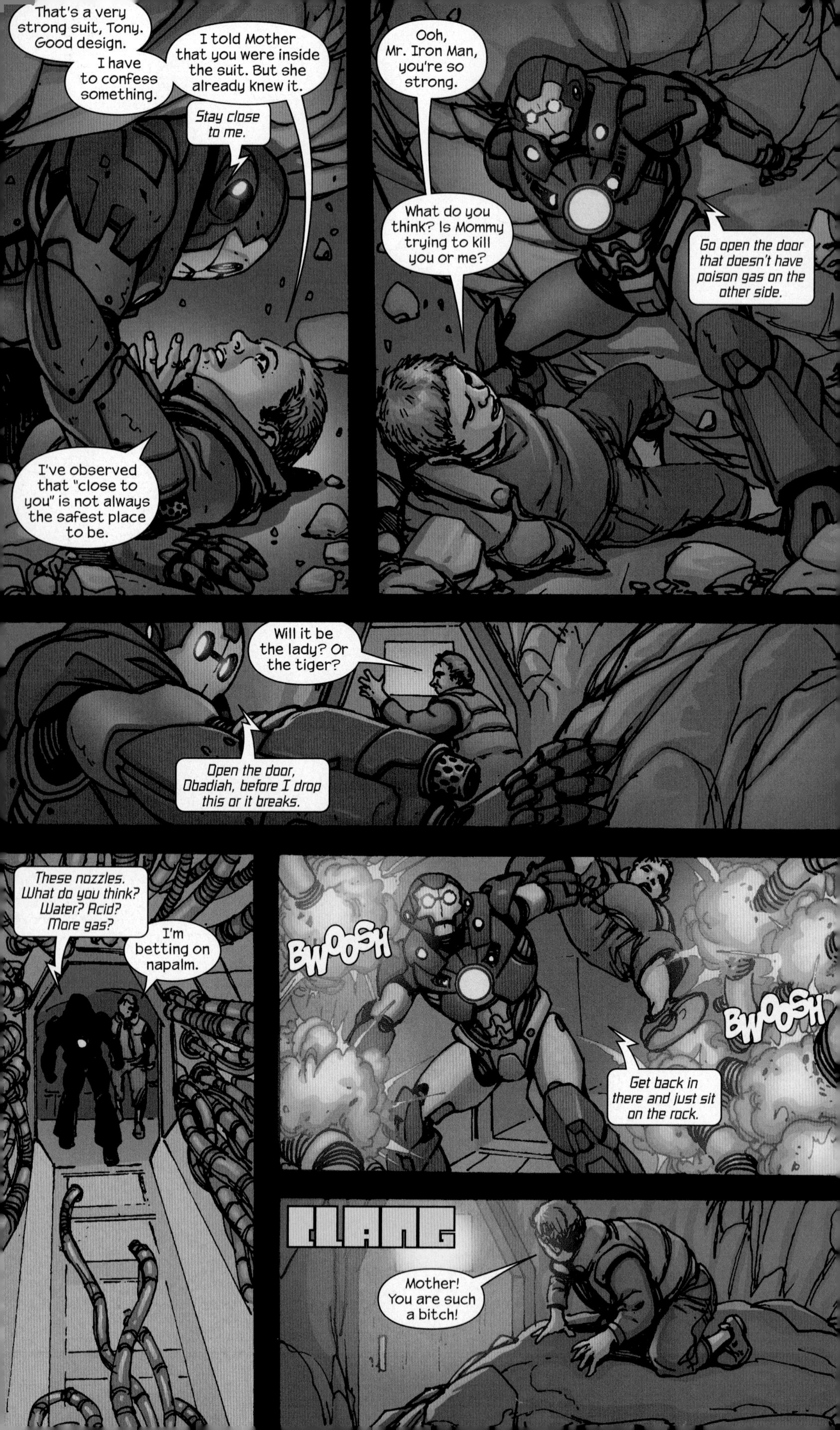
That's a very strong suit, Tony. Good design.
I have to confess something.
I told Mother that you were inside the suit. But she already knew it.
Stay close to me.
I've observed that "close to you" is not always the safest place to be.
Ooh, Mr. Iron Man, you're so strong.
What do you think? Is Mommy trying to kill you or me?
Go open the door that doesn't have poison gas on the other side.
Will it be the lady? Or the tiger?
Open the door, Obadiah, before I drop this or it breaks.
These nozzles. What do you think? Water? Acid? More gas?
I'm betting on napalm.
BWOOSH
BWOOSH
Get back in there and just sit on the rock.
CLANG
Mother! You are such a bitch!

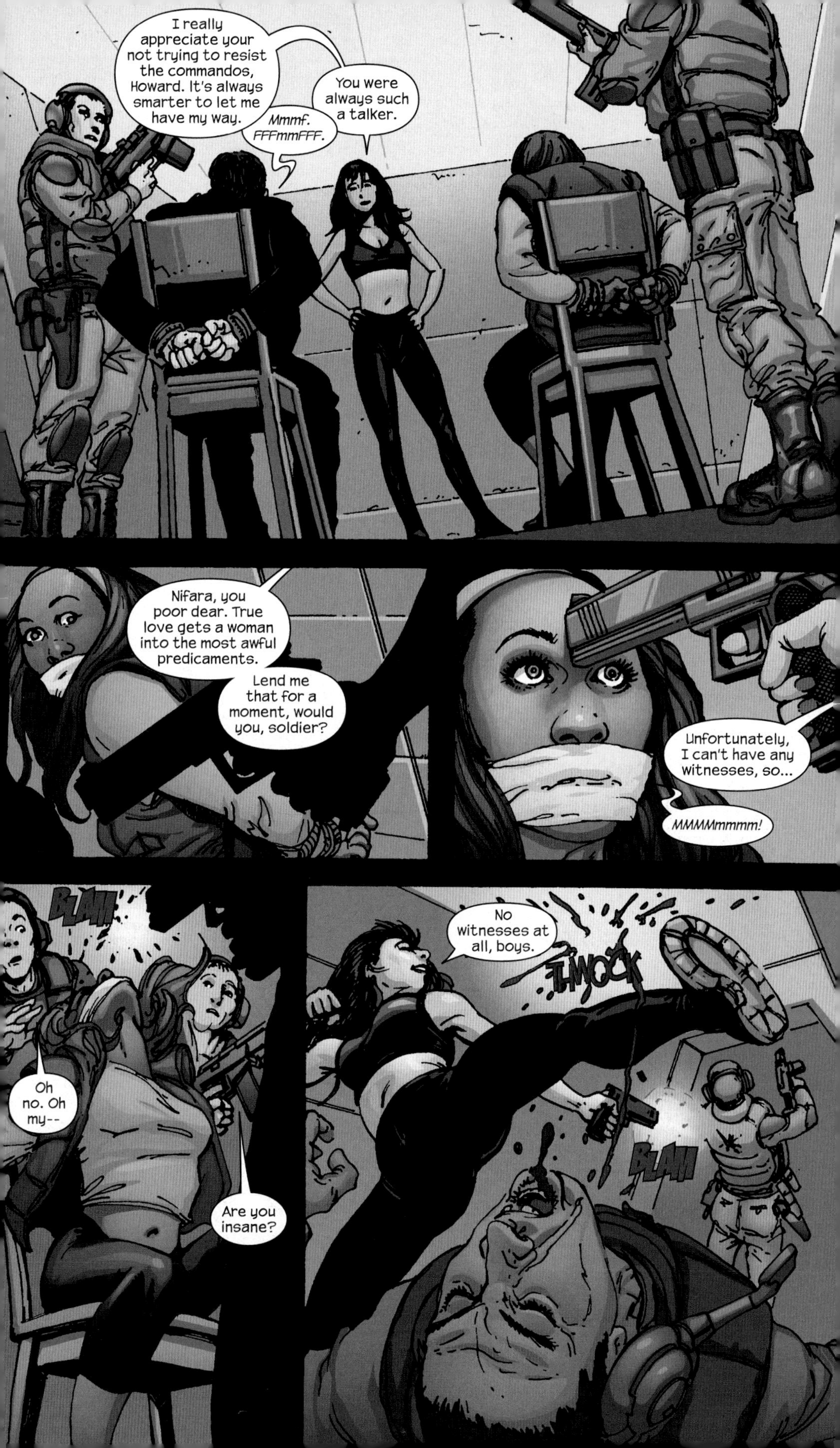
I really appreciate your not trying to resist the commandos, Howard. It's always smarter to let me have my way.
Mmmf. FFFmmFFF.
You were always such a talker.
Nifara, you poor dear. True love gets a woman into the most awful predicaments.
Lend me that for a moment, would you, soldier?
Unfortunately, I can't have any witnesses, so...
MMMMmmmm!
BLAM
Oh no. Oh my--
Are you insane?
No witnesses at all, boys.
THWOCK
BLAM

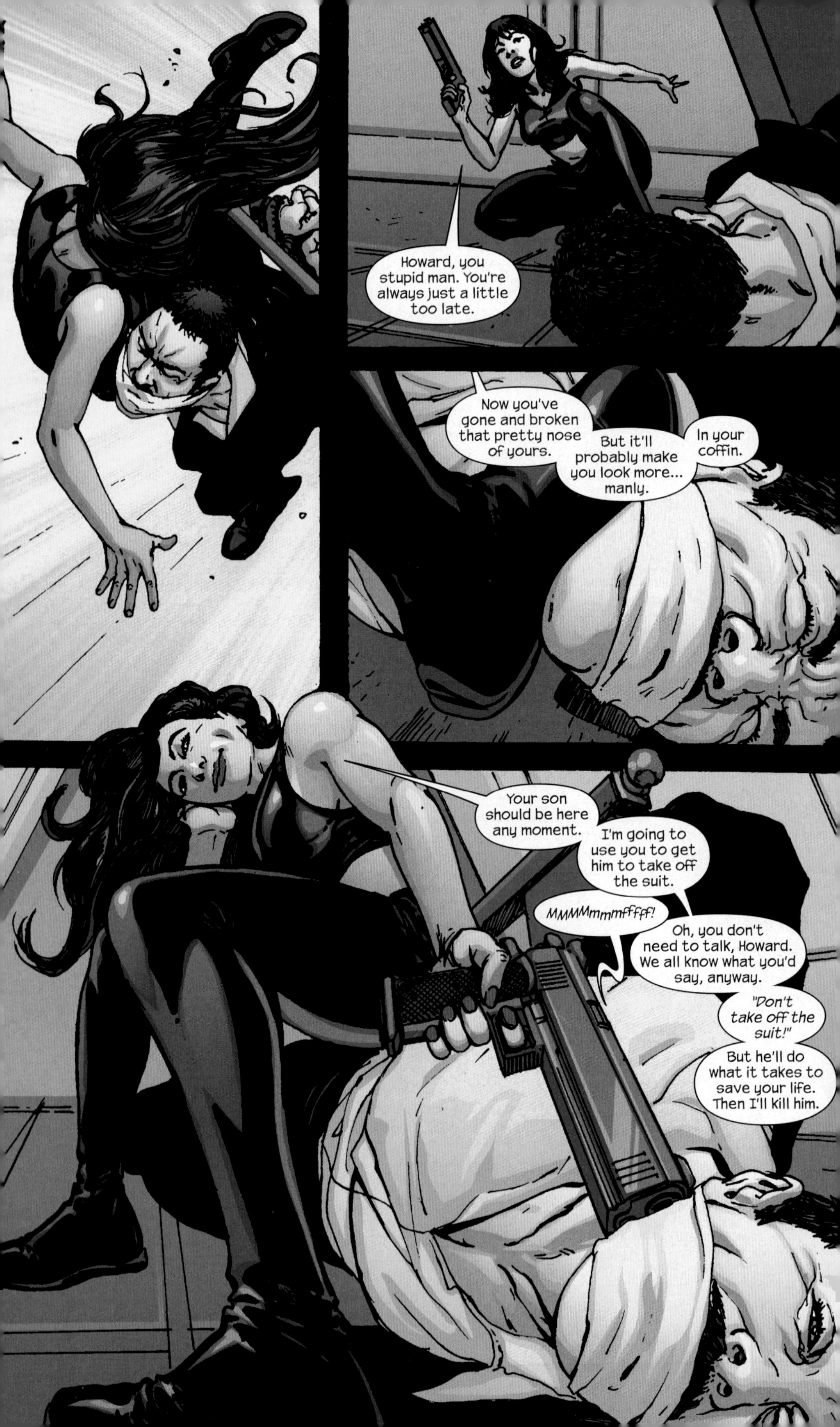
Howard, you stupid man. You're always just a little too late.
Now you've gone and broken that pretty nose of yours.
But it'll probably make you look more... manly.
In your coffin.
Your son should be here any moment.
I'm going to use you to get him to take off the suit.
MMMMmmmffff!
Oh, you don't need to talk, Howard. We all know what you'd say, anyway.
"Don't take off the suit!"
But he'll do what it takes to save your life. Then I'll kill him.

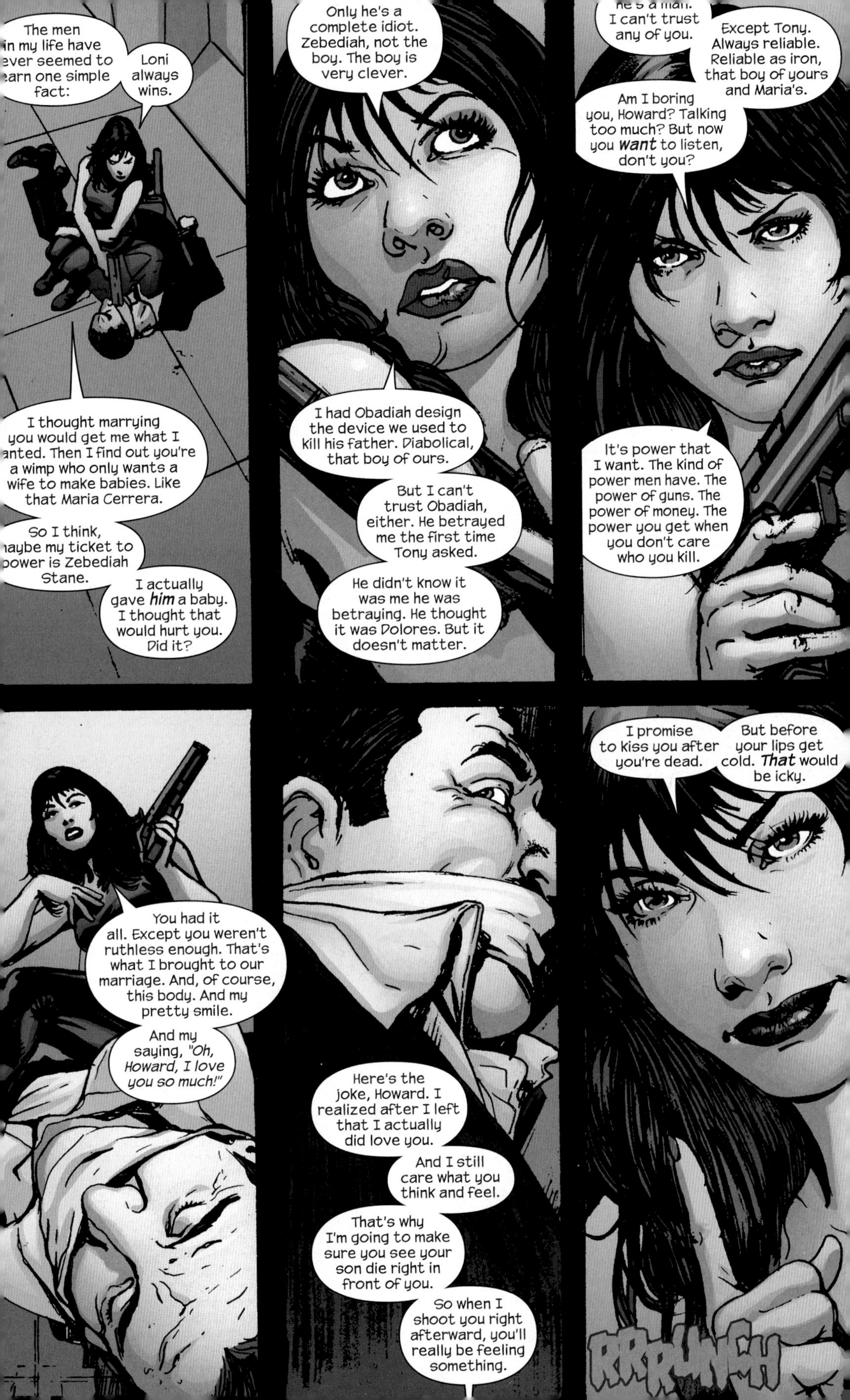

The men in my life have ever seemed to earn one simple fact:
Loni always wins.
I thought marrying you would get me what I anted. Then I find out you're a wimp who only wants a wife to make babies. Like that Maria Cerrera.
So I think, aybe my ticket to ower is Zebediah Stane.
I actually gave *him* a baby. I thought that would hurt you. Did it?
Only he's a complete idiot. Zebediah, not the boy. The boy is very clever.
I had Obadiah design the device we used to kill his father. Diabolical, that boy of ours.
But I can't trust Obadiah, either. He betrayed me the first time Tony asked.
He didn't know it was me he was betraying. He thought it was Dolores. But it doesn't matter.
I can't trust any of you.
Except Tony. Always reliable. Reliable as iron, that boy of yours and Maria's.
Am I boring you, Howard? Talking too much? But now you *want* to listen, don't you?
It's power that I want. The kind of power men have. The power of guns. The power of money. The power you get when you don't care who you kill.
You had it all. Except you weren't ruthless enough. That's what I brought to our marriage. And, of course, this body. And my pretty smile.
And my saying, *"Oh, Howard, I love you so much!"*
Here's the joke, Howard. I realized after I left that I actually did love you.
And I still care what you think and feel.
That's why I'm going to make sure you see your son die right in front of you.
So when I shoot you right afterward, you'll really be feeling something.
I promise to kiss you after you're dead.
But before your lips get cold. *That* would be icky.
RRRUNCH

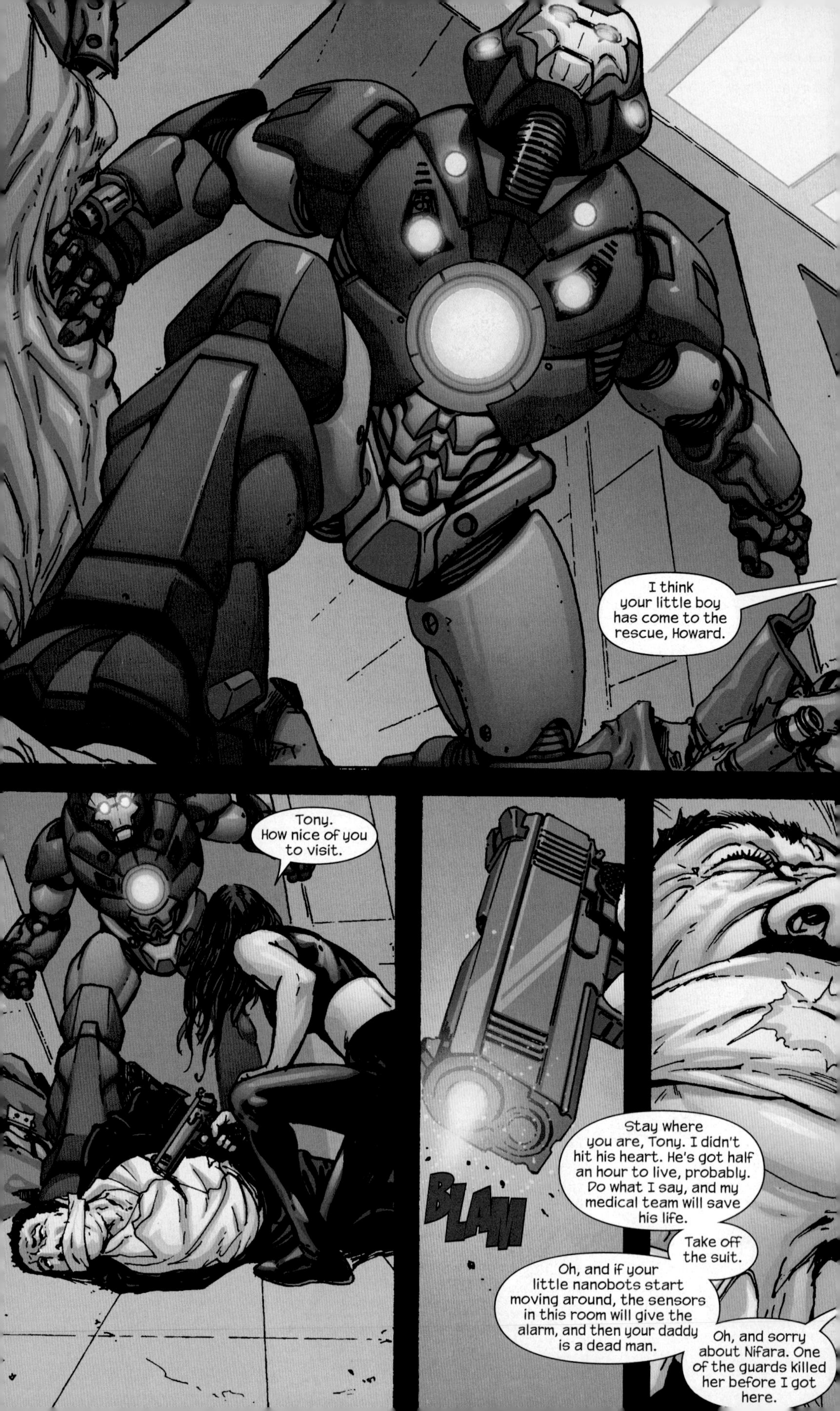
I think your little boy has come to the rescue, Howard.
Tony. How nice of you to visit.
BLAM
Stay where you are, Tony. I didn't hit his heart. He's got half an hour to live, probably. Do what I say, and my medical team will save his life.
Take off the suit.
Oh, and if your little nanobots start moving around, the sensors in this room will give the alarm, and then your daddy is a dead man.
Oh, and sorry about Nifara. One of the guards killed her before I got here.

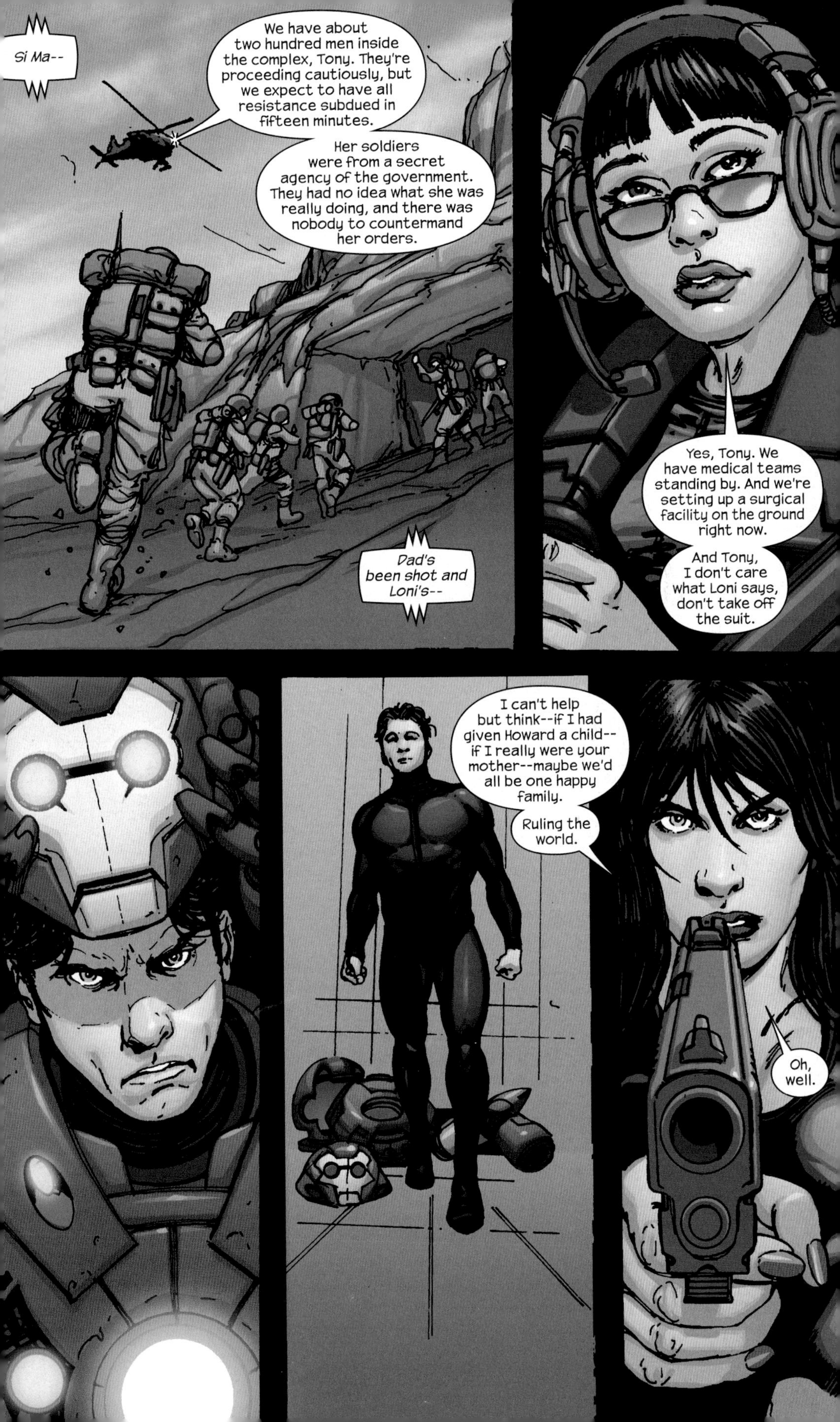
Si Ma--
We have about two hundred men inside the complex, Tony. They're proceeding cautiously, but we expect to have all resistance subdued in fifteen minutes.
Her soldiers were from a secret agency of the government. They had no idea what she was really doing, and there was nobody to countermand her orders.
Dad's been shot and Loni's--
Yes, Tony. We have medical teams standing by. And we're setting up a surgical facility on the ground right now.
And Tony, I don't care what Loni says, don't take off the suit.
I can't help but think--if I had given Howard a child--if I really were your mother--maybe we'd all be one happy family.
Ruling the world.
Oh, well.

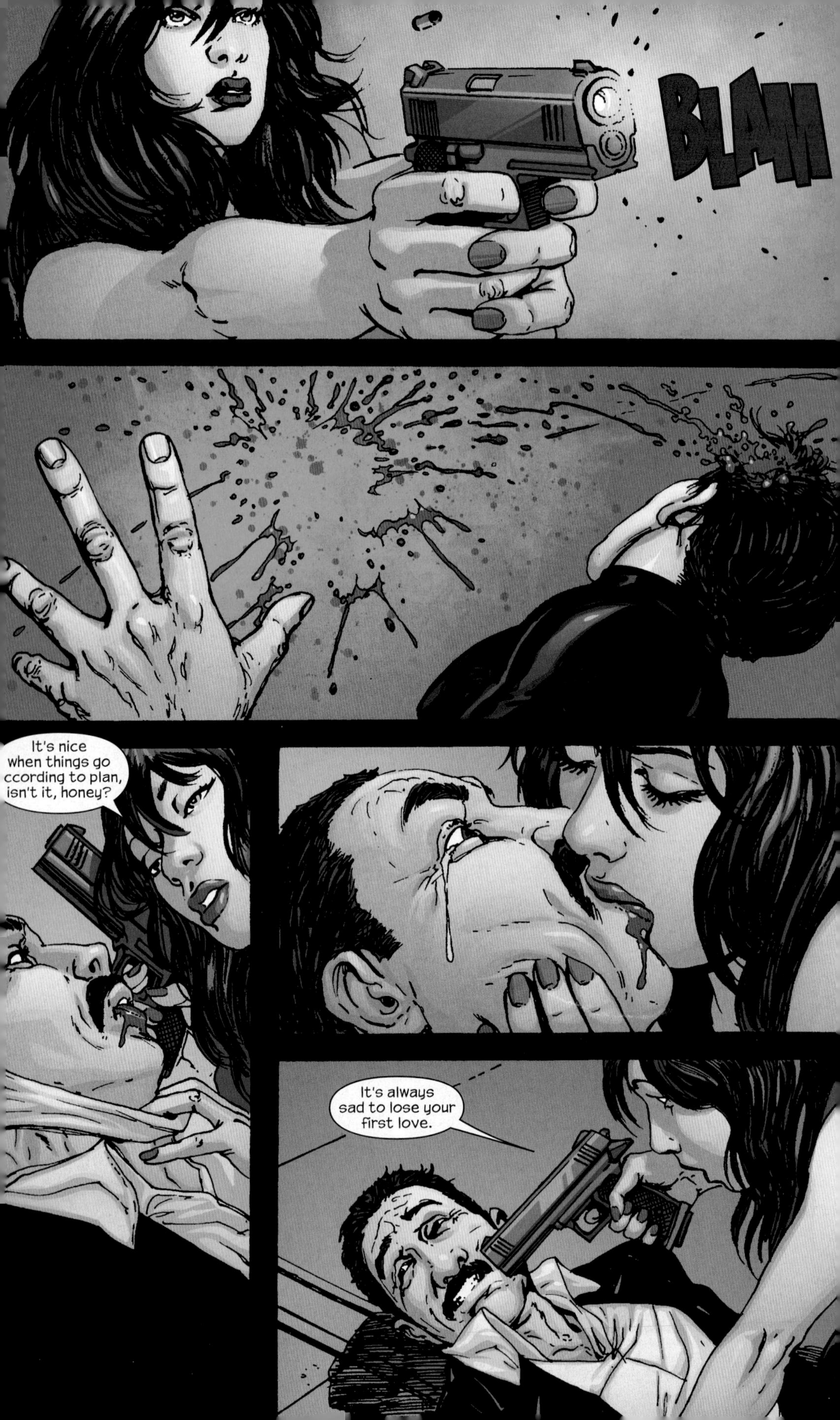
BLAM
It's nice when things go ccording to plan, isn't it, honey?
It's always sad to lose your first love.

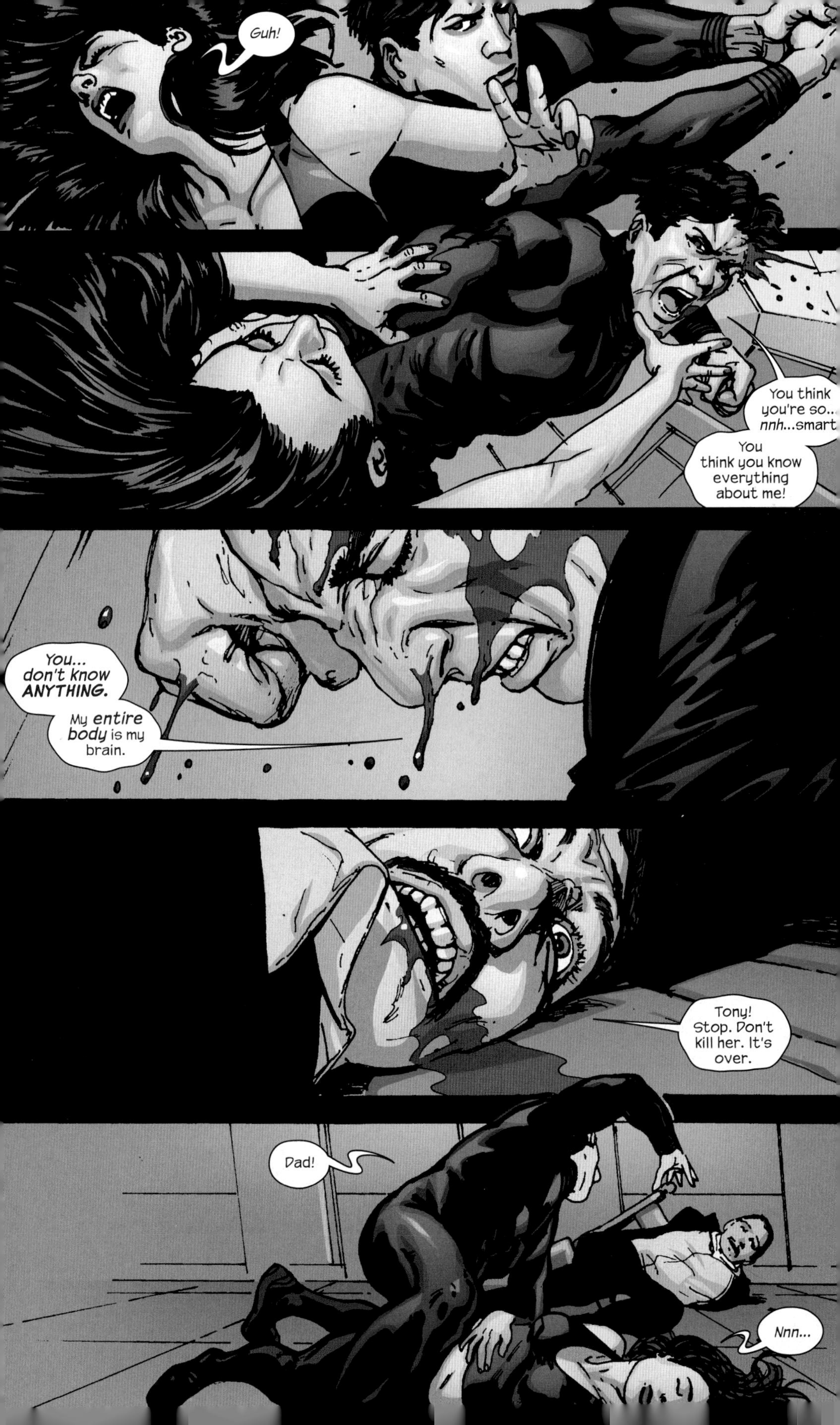
Guh!
You think you're so.. nnh...smart
You think you know everything about me!
You... don't know ANYTHING.
My entire body is my brain.
Tony! Stop. Don't kill her. It's over.
Dad!
Nnn...

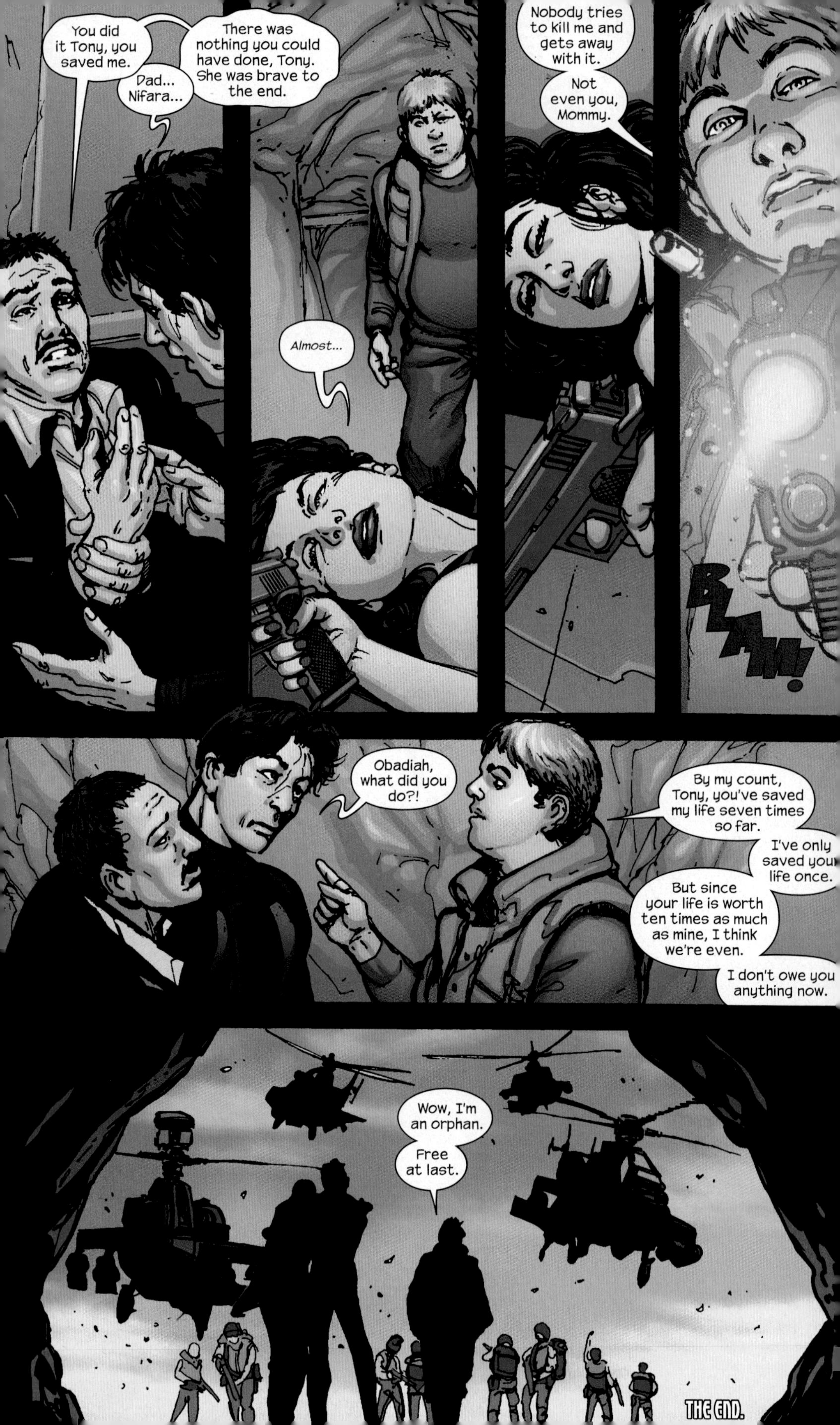
You did it Tony, you saved me.
Dad... Nifara...
There was nothing you could have done, Tony. She was brave to the end.
Almost...
Nobody tries to kill me and gets away with it.
Not even you, Mommy.
BLAM!
Obadiah, what did you do?!
By my count, Tony, you've saved my life seven times so far.
I've only saved you life once.
But since your life is worth ten times as much as mine, I think we're even.
I don't owe you anything now.
Wow, I'm an orphan.
Free at last.
THE END.

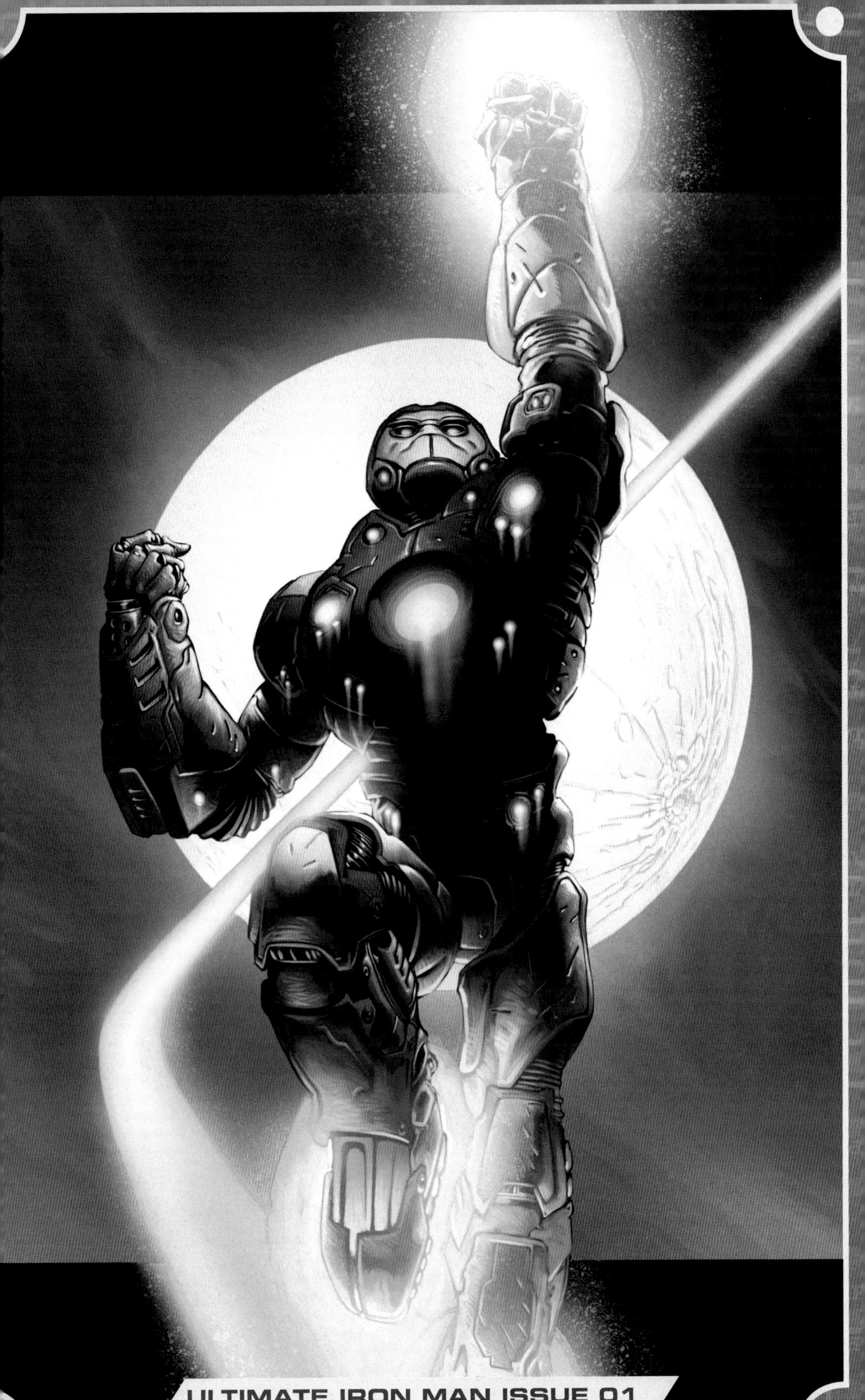

ULTIMATE IRON MAN ISSUE 01
VARIANT BY ANDY KUBERT

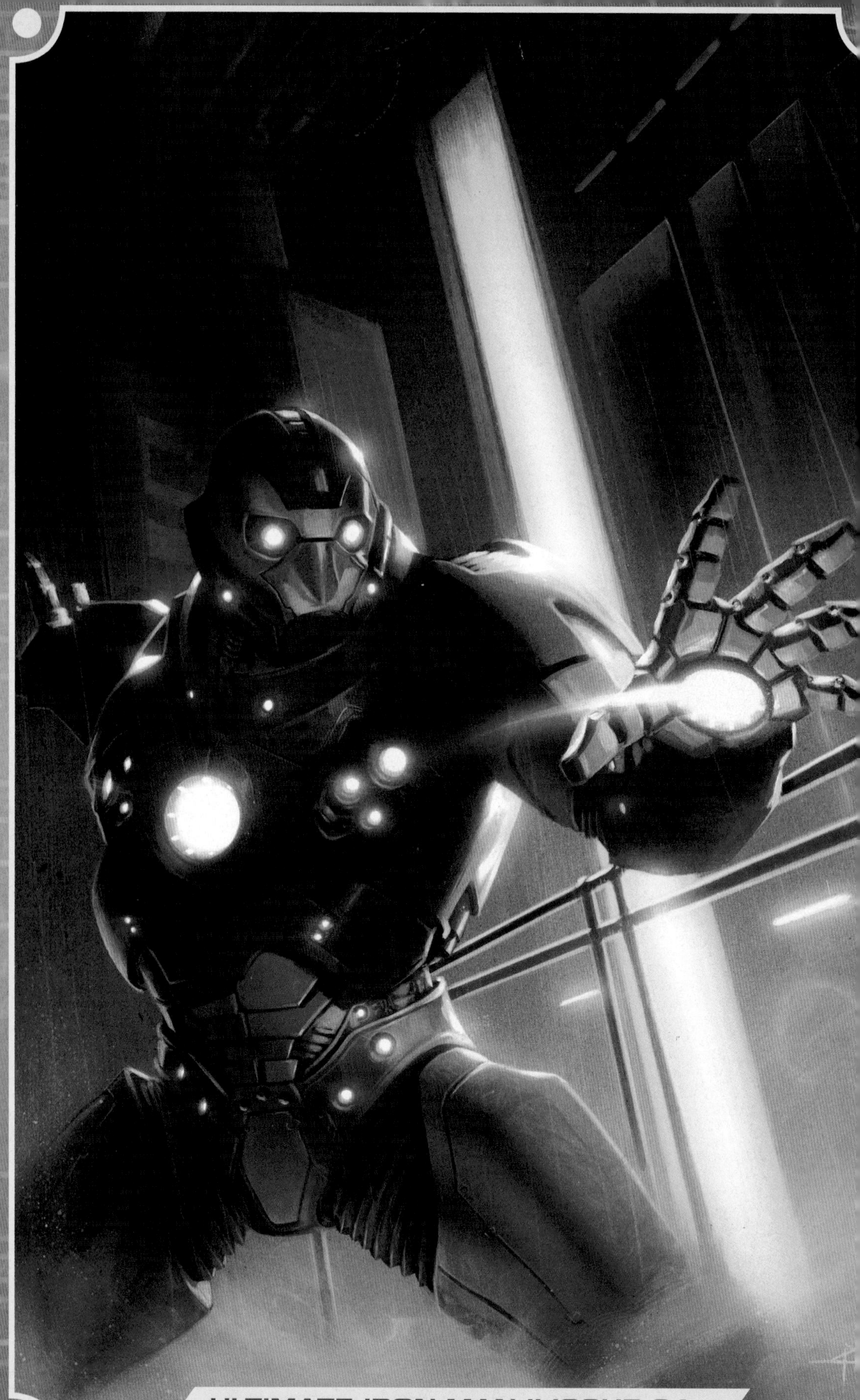

ULTIMATE IRON MAN II ISSUE 01
VARIANT BY GABRIELE DELL'OTTO

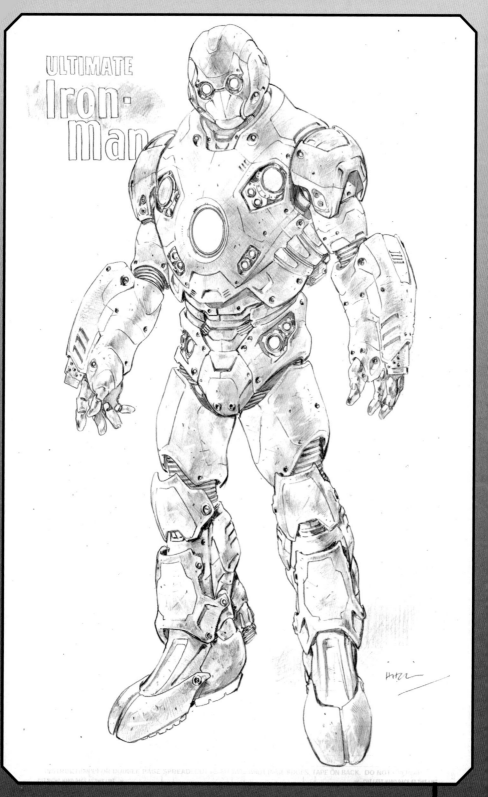

ULTIMATE
Iron-
Man

IRON MAN
ARMOR CONCEPT
BY BRYAN HITCH

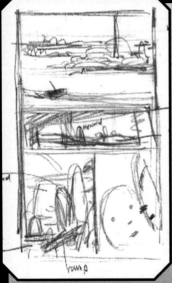
pg.1 thumbnail

ROUGH CUT:
ULTIMATE IRON MAN
ISSUE 01
SCENE ONE

PAGE ONE

Pic 1; AERIAL VIEW: Long Island Sound between the Bronx and Queens. Rising out of the water is the Stark Defense Corporation plant. Domes on stilts, like tied-down bubbles. The domes are hardened for explosion containment, so there are no windows except in a single spire-like office tower in the middle. A fast launch is cutting across the water from Stark Pier in Queens to the plant.

CAPTION: Stark Defense Corporation Headquarters New York City

CAPTION 2:   Years Ago...

Pic 2; The launch is at a landing platform among the stilts. HOWARD STARK, a tall wiry man in his forties, wearing a 1980s suit, reaches out to help MARIA CERRERA, a frail-looking Latina woman of thirty, make the leap onto the dock.

HOWARD: Dr. Cerrera, welcome to Stark Defense Corp.

Pic 3; She stands a little too close to him, so that, tall as he is, she has her head thrown back to look up at him, and he's looking way down at her.

HOWARD: I'm Howard Stark.

MARIA: On TV you looked taller.

HOWARD: I've been losing height.

Pic 4; HOWARD'S POV: Maria gazes up at him. She may be wearing a business suit, but it doesn't hide that she's a woman.

MARIA: You had something to show me?

PAGE TWO

Pic 1; Inside a testing lab. A bare-chested young man is being sprayed by a female lab technician, Si Ma, with what looks like sky-blue paint. Howard and Maria are watching.

Pic 2; Howard is holding up an ice pick.

HOWARD: Here. Stick him with this.

Pic 3; Maria takes the ice pick, frowning.

MARIA: Stick him where?

HOWARD: Wherever.

Pic 4; Maria pushes it against the blue-painted man's arm.

HOWARD (OFF): Come on, put some weight behind it.

Pic 5; The ice pick goes part way in, the skin dimpling under the pressure.

HOWARD (OFF): Harder.

Pic 6; The ice pick is in his arm up to the handle. Maria looks at Blue Man.

MARIA: Doesn't that hurt?

Pic 7; Blue-painted man looks at her blandly.

BLUE MAN: Ouch.

Pic 8; Blue Man grins.

pg.2 thumbnail

PAGE THREE

Pic 1; Maria pulls out the ice pick. Only there's no shaft anymore. The metal looks more like a Brillo pad or a pom-pom — wiry twists of very thin metal going every which way.

Pic 2; Maria holds up the ice pick to show Howard.

MARIA: That blue stuff — it can do this to metal, and it doesn't hurt his skin?

HOWARD: Not for the first fifteen minutes.

Pic 3; Howard picks up a wooden baseball bat.

Pic 4; He rares back to let fly at Blue Man's chest.

BLUE MAN: I hate this part.

Pic 5; The bat connects with his chest.

Pic 6; Blue man flies backward.

HOWARD: Lift off!

pg.3 thumbnail

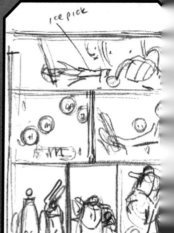

PAGE FOUR

Pic 1; Blue Man is sprawled on the floor.

Pic 2; The lab technician dips a sponge into a pan and wipes off the blue stuff, baring the skin on Blue Man's chest.

Pic 3; Maria kneels by him, examining him.

MARIA: Not even a bruise. What is that stuff?

BLUE MAN: Armor.

Pic 4; Howard helps Blue Man to his feet.

HOWARD: Go wash that off before it eats too much of your skin.

pg.4 thumbnail

Pic 5; As Blue Man and the lab technician leave, Maria and Howard watch.

MARIA: So that blue paste — it's alive?

PAGE FIVE

Pic 1; Howard inserts a cassette into a Betamax.

Pic 2; In a conference room, Howard and Maria watch a picture of swirling sky-blue microbes on the TV screen.

HOWARD: Bacteria. They live on the surface of the skin.

MARIA: Eating skin cells?

HOWARD: Only when they're hungry.

Pic 3; CLOSEUP of the microbes. Little tendrils link them together.

pg.5 thumbnail

HOWARD: Here's what happens when something hits them.

Pic 4; CLOSEUP of the microbes. They suddenly reorient and reshape themselves, long and thin now, and radiating outward from a center point.

HOWARD: They spread the shock of impact outward. The guy still flies across the room, but it's as if the bat were a big soft hand pushing him.

Pic 5; Maria gazes at the brillo-ended ice pick.

> **MARIA:** That still doesn't explain this.

Pic 6; Closeup of a single bacterium. Now we see that the tendrils are covered with tiny globules.

> **HOWARD:** Our bacterium has a parasite. Those little globules are like piranha, only instead of flesh, they eat metal.

> **MARIA:** Any metal?

> **HOWARD:** Not gold. But any metal that can oxidize.

PAGE SIX

Pic 1; Howard turns off the projector.

> **MARIA:** So you've reinvented armor.

> **HOWARD:** Still have a few problems.

Pic 2; Howard leads the way out of the conference room.

> **HOWARD:** It won't stop a bullet. Moving too fast.

Pic 3; Howard leads the way along an outside corridor, only a railing between them and the Long Island Sound far below.

> **HOWARD:** And after about three hours, it eats away all your skin.

Pic 4; Howard leans on the railing, looking out toward New York City in the distance, to the southwest. Maria is looking at Howard.

pg.6 thumbnail

> **MARIA:** So if you're attacked with ice picks and baseball bats...

> **HOWARD:** You're invulnerable. As long as you have soap and water close by.

Pic 5; Maria grins at him.

> **MARIA:** And it's such a lovely color.

> **HOWARD:** Sky blue. Goes with everything.

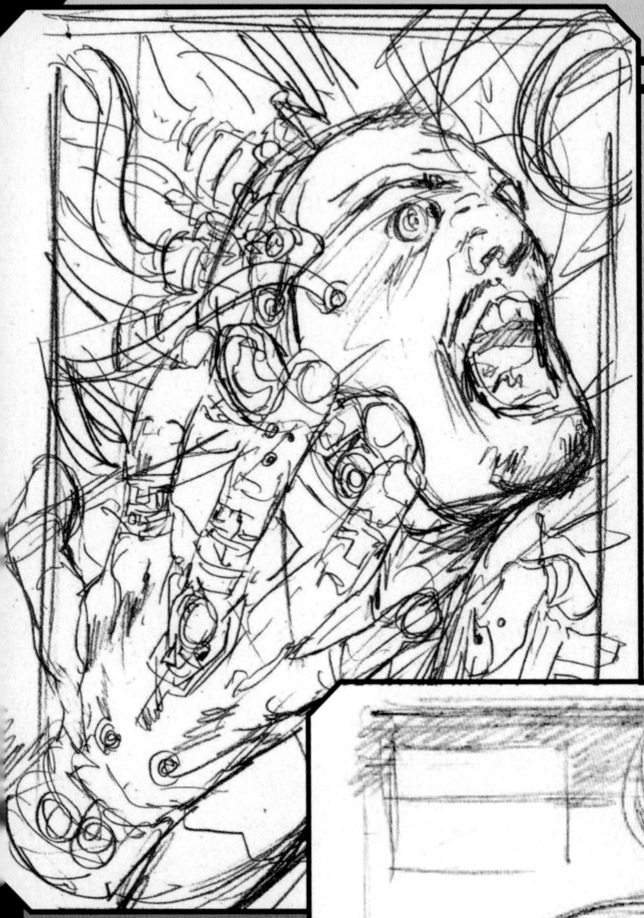

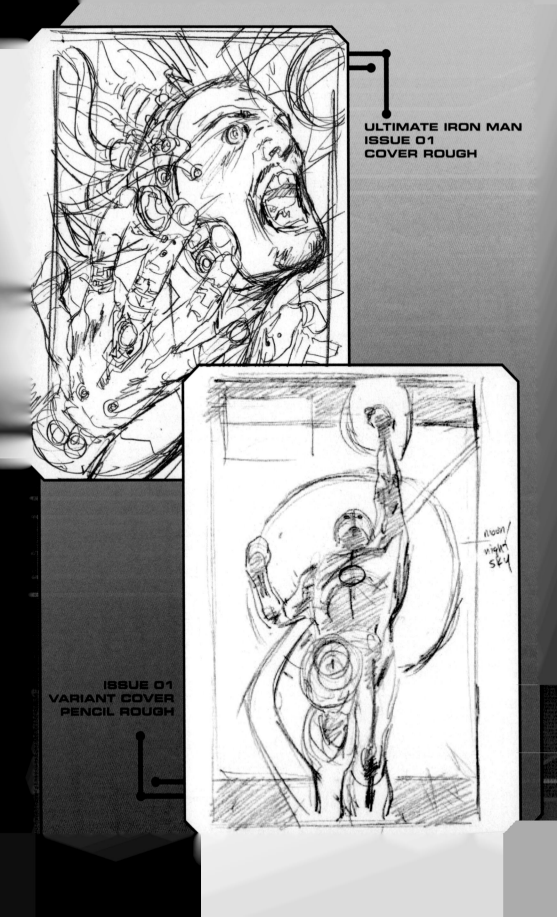

ULTIMATE IRON MAN
ISSUE 01
COVER ROUGH

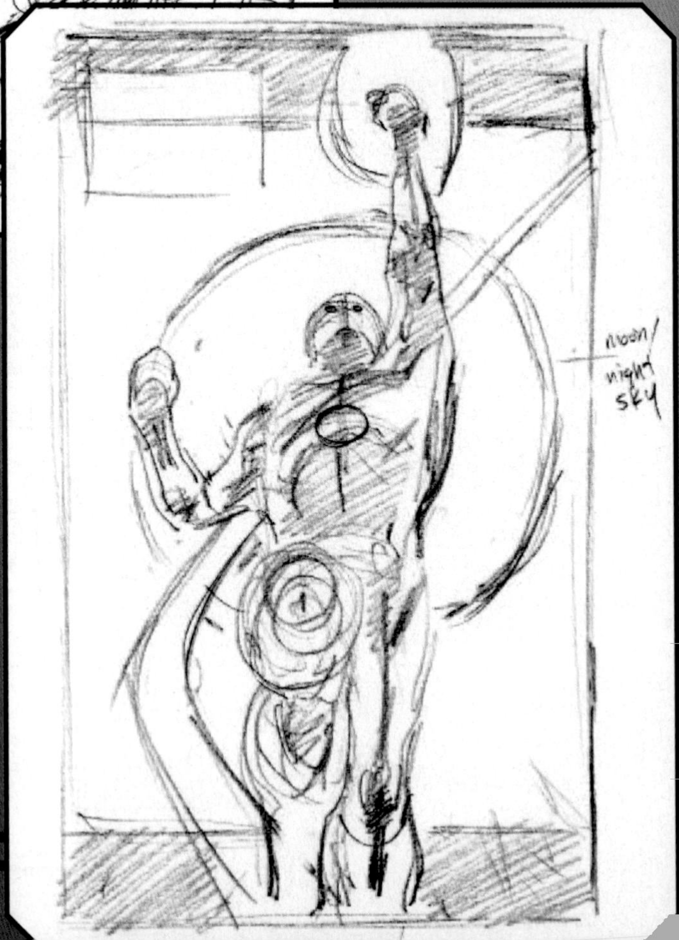
moon/
night
sky

ISSUE 01
VARIANT COVER
PENCIL ROUGH

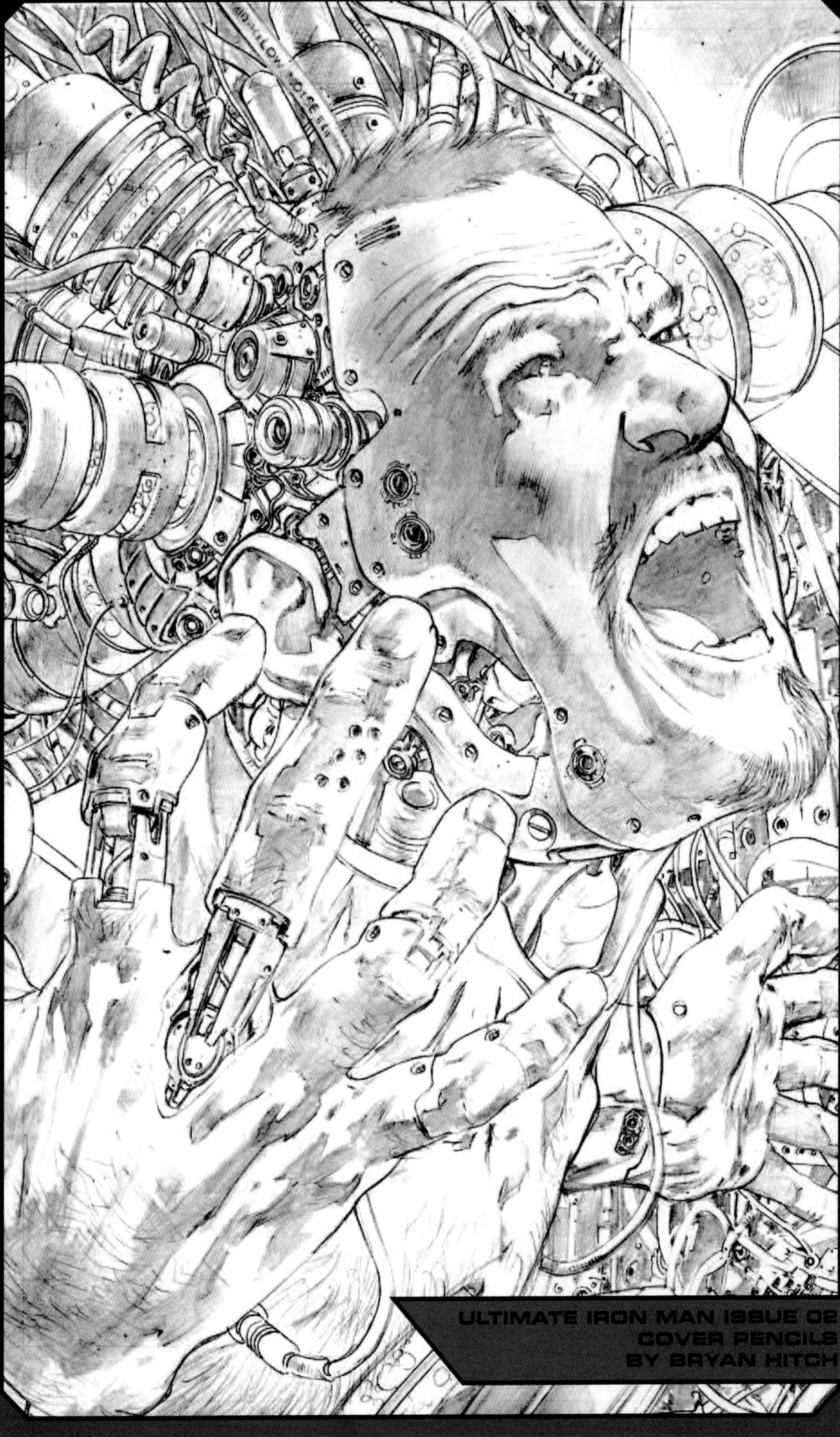

ULTIMATE IRON MAN ISSUE 02
COVER PENCILS
BY BRYAN HITCH

ULTIMATE IRON MAN
ISSUE 02
COVER PROCESS

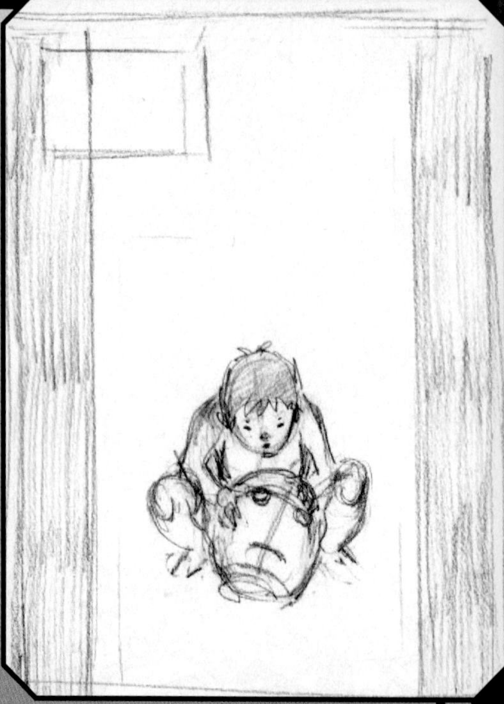

ORIGINAL THUMBNAIL

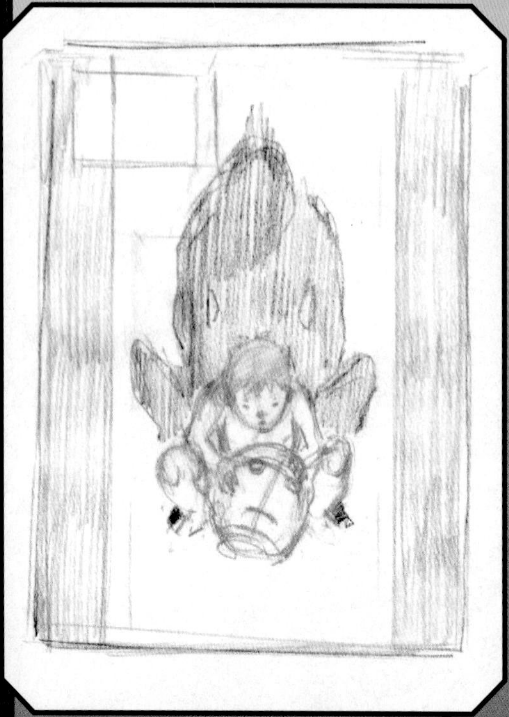

ORIGINAL THUMBNAIL

FINAL LAYOUT

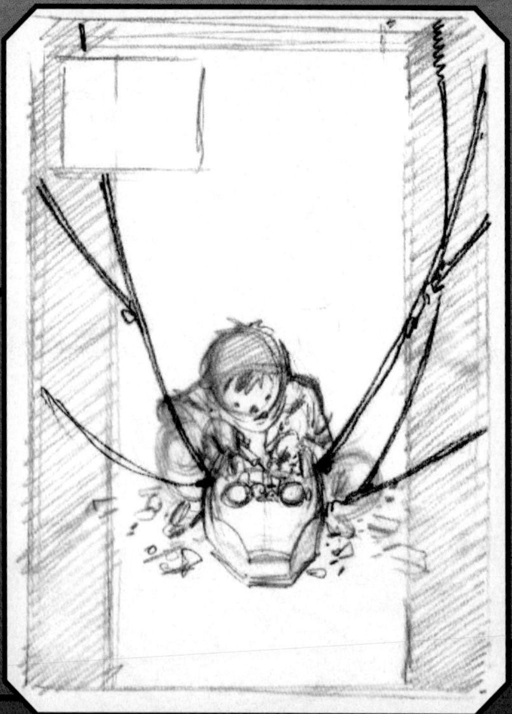

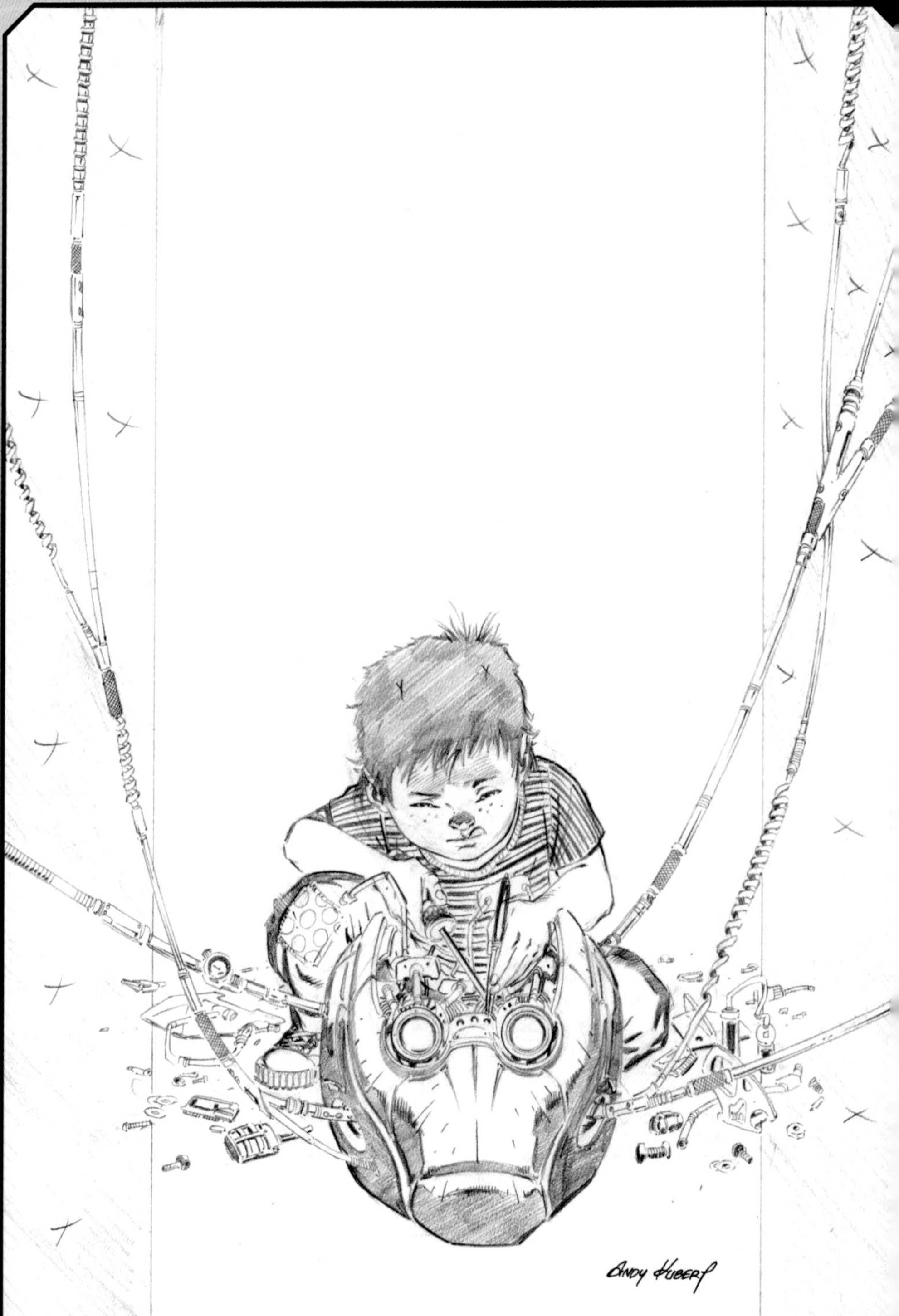
ANDY KUBERT

FINAL PENCILS
BY ANDY KUBERT

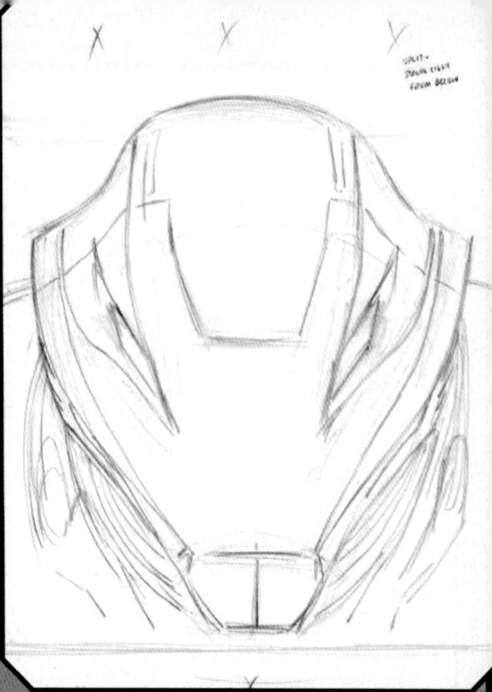

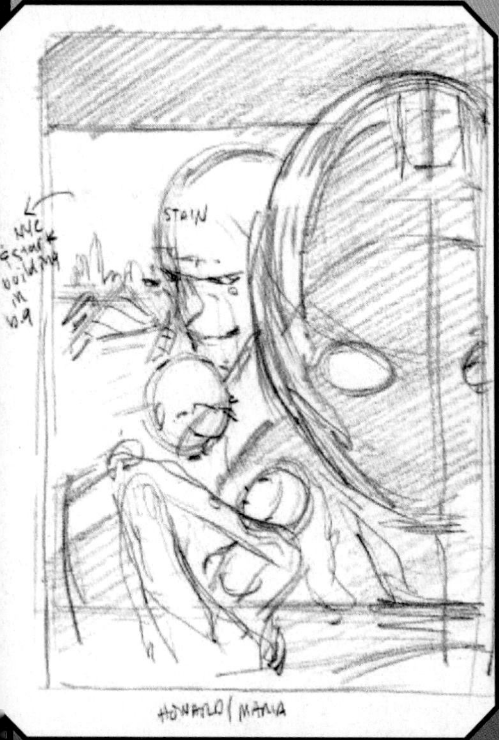
STAIN
HOWARD/MARIA

UNUSED COVER LAYOUTS BY ANDY KUBERT

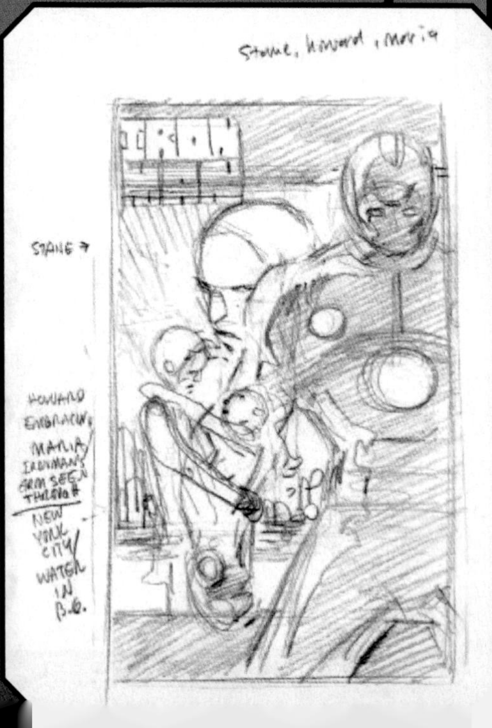
Stane, howard, maria
STANE
HOWARD
NEW
YORK
CITY
WATER
IN
B.G.

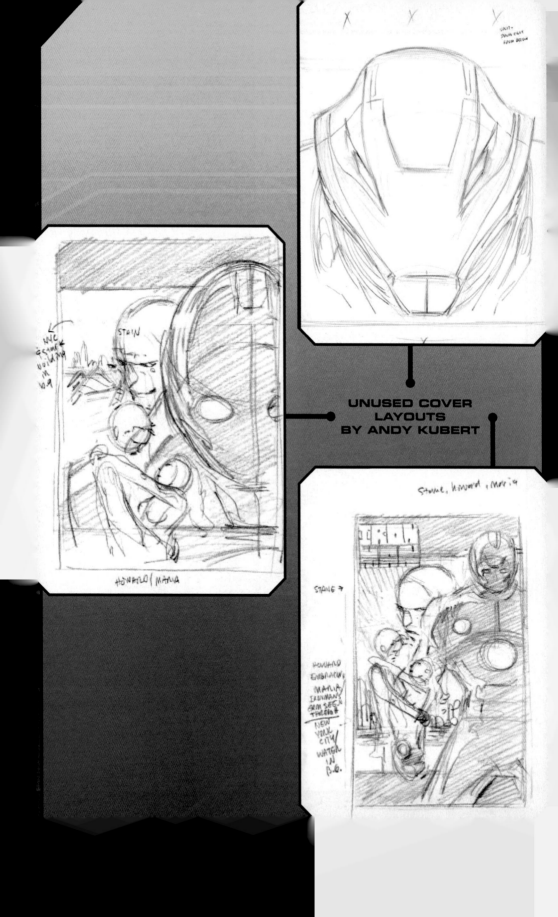

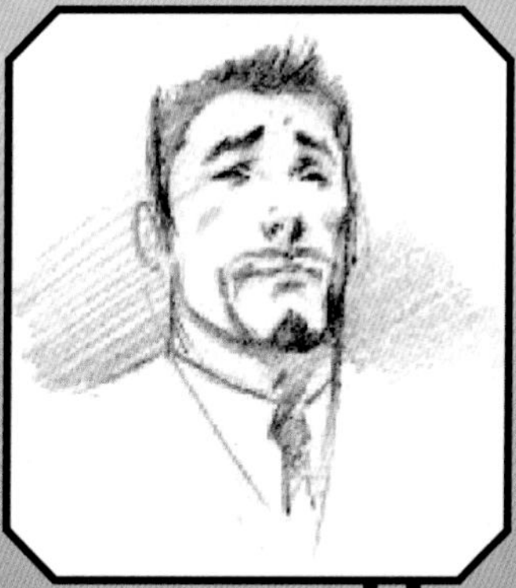

HOWARD
STARK

ORIGINAL
CONCEPT ART
BY ANDY KUBERT

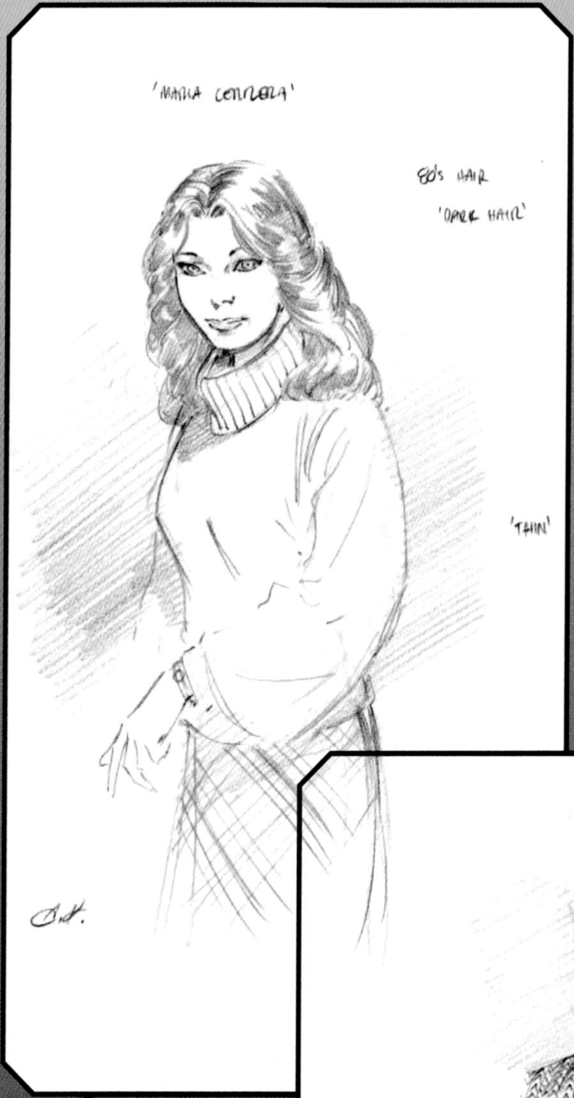
80's HAIR
'DARK HAIR'
'THIN'

MARIA
STARK

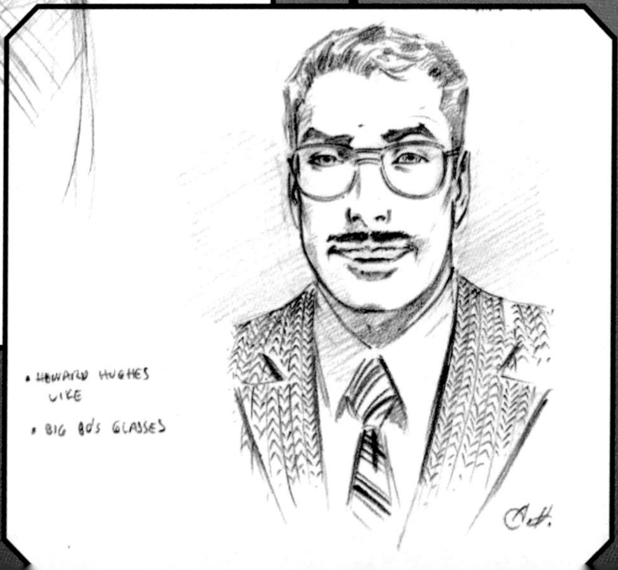
• HOWARD HUGHES
LIKE
• BIG 80's GLASSES

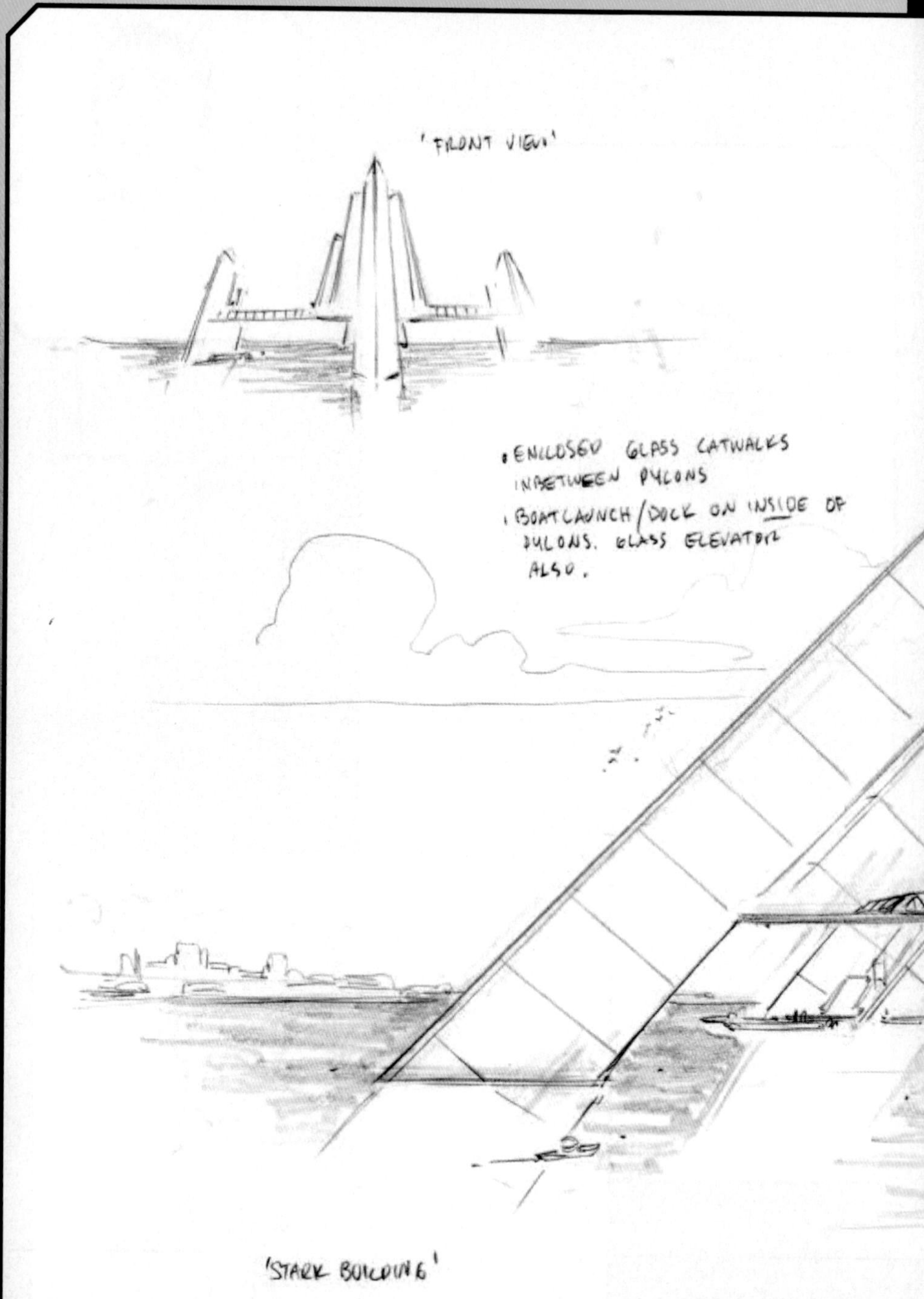
'FRONT VIEW'
• ENCLOSED GLASS CATWALKS INBETWEEN PYLONS
• BOATLAUNCH/DOCK ON INSIDE OF PYLONS. GLASS ELEVATOR ALSO.
'STARK BUILDING'

STARK BUILDING DESIGN
BY ANDY KUBERT

³/₄ view

. VERY SHINY / YET OUTER CASING CAN WITHSTAND
              BLASTS.   AK. 11/11/04

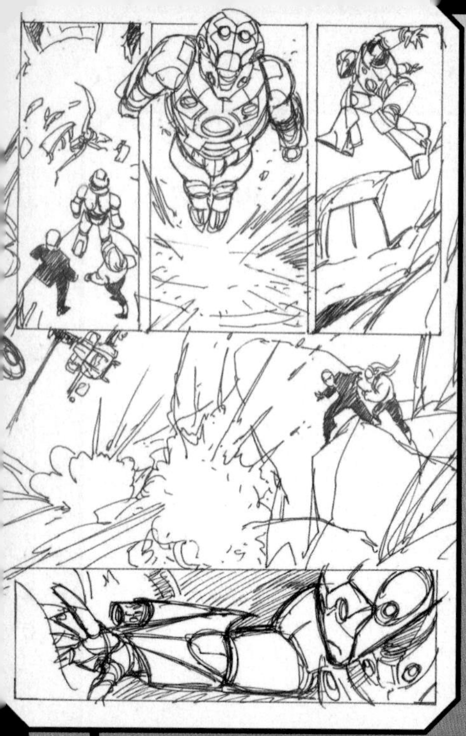

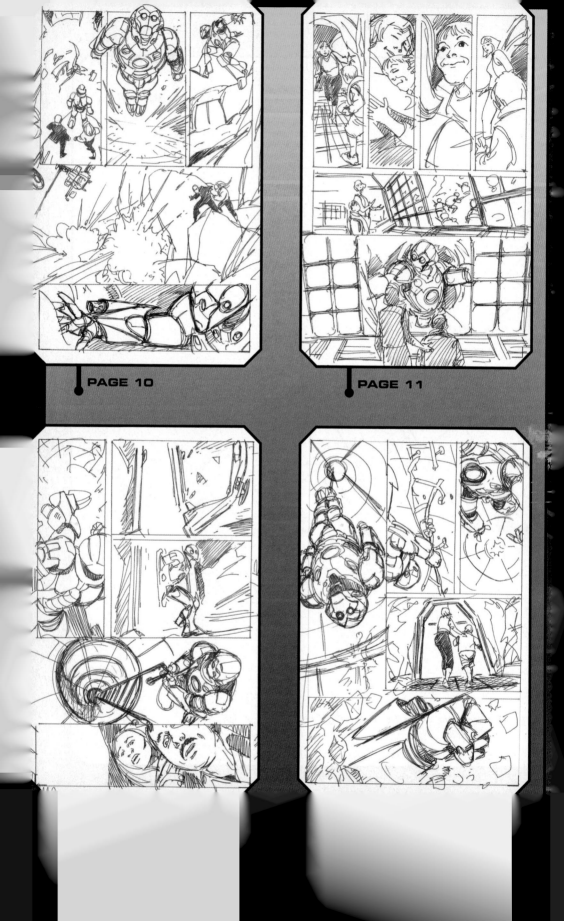

PAGE 10

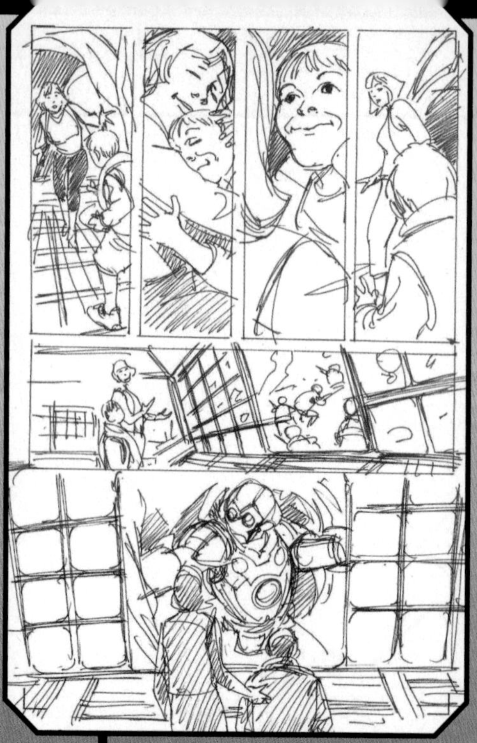

PAGE 11

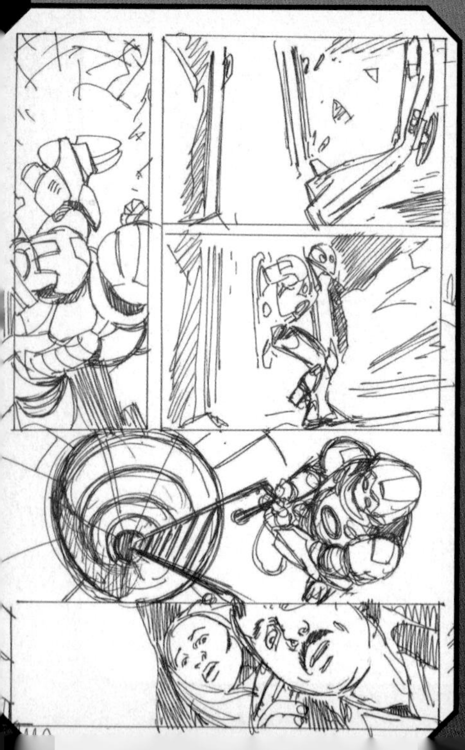

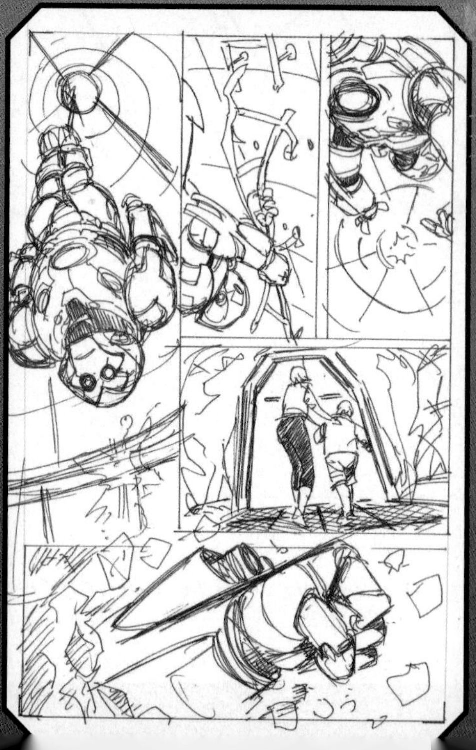

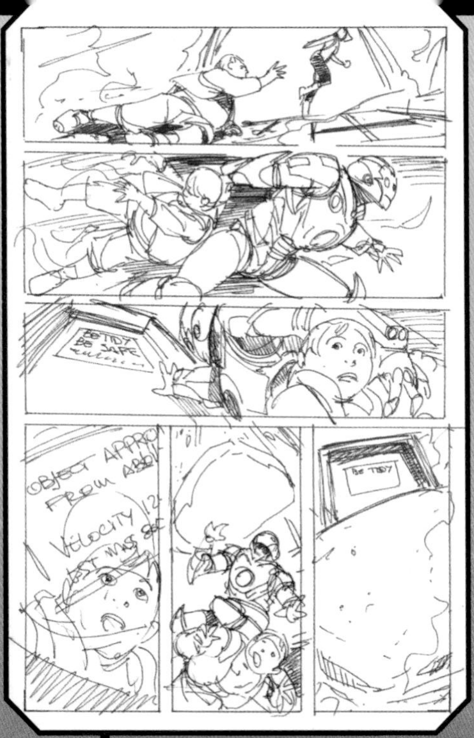
BE TIDY
BE SAFE
OBJECT APPRO
FROM ABO
VELOCITY 12
BE TIDY

PAGE 14

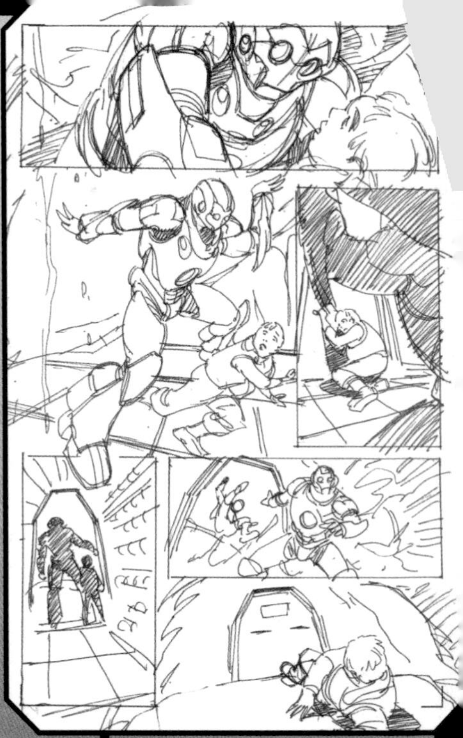

PAGE 15

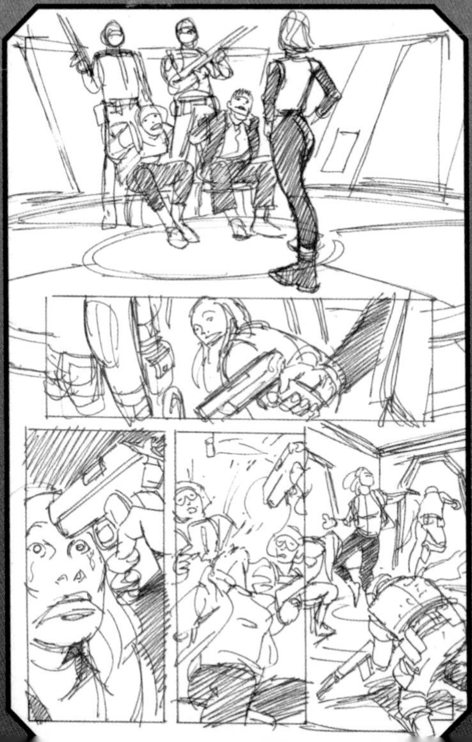

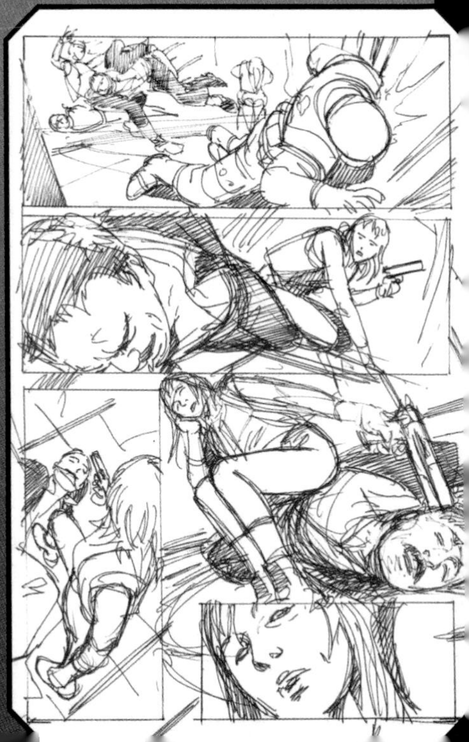

PAGE 18

PAGE 19

PAGE 20

PAGE 21

8010020

3 1191 00937 7573

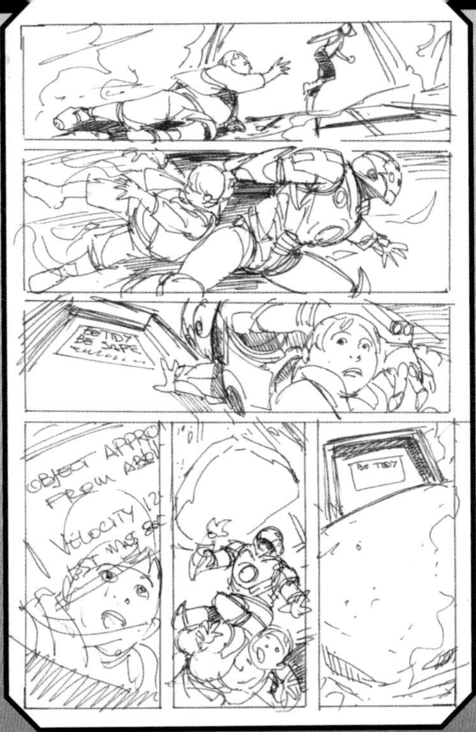
BE TIDY BE SAFE
BE TIDY

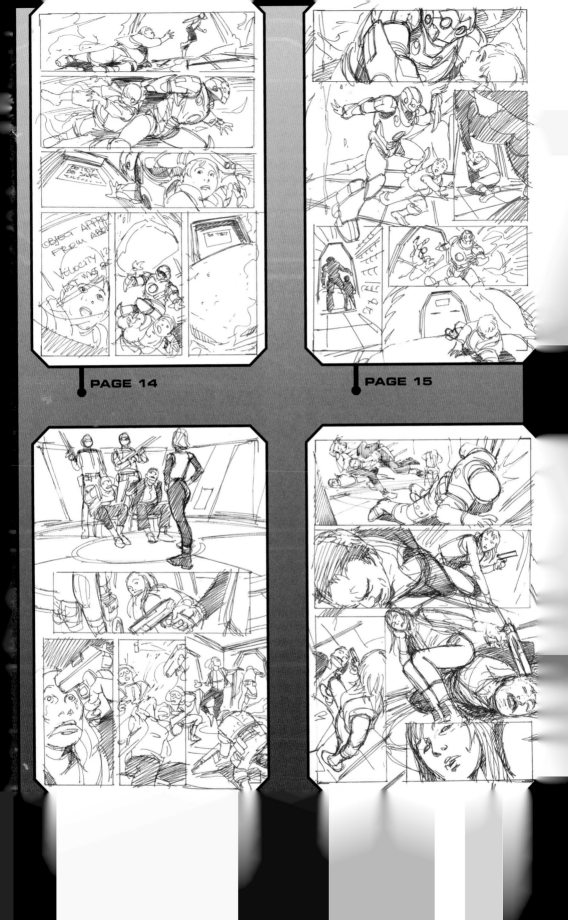

PAGE 14

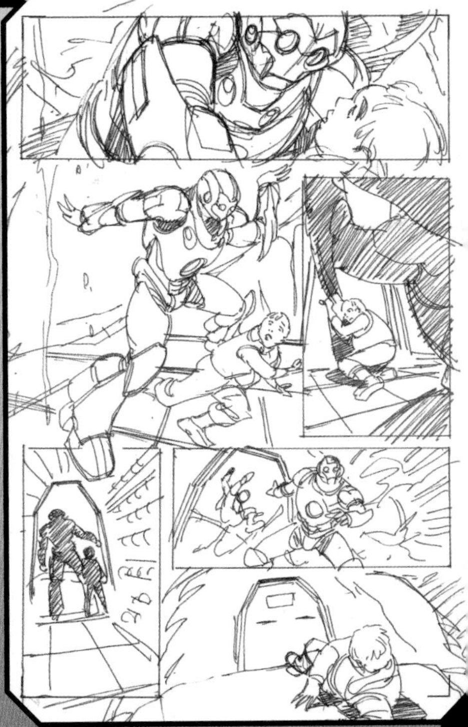

PAGE 15

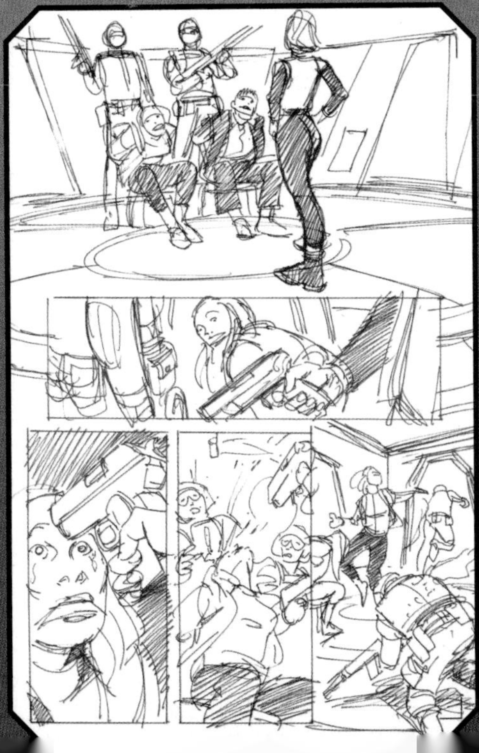

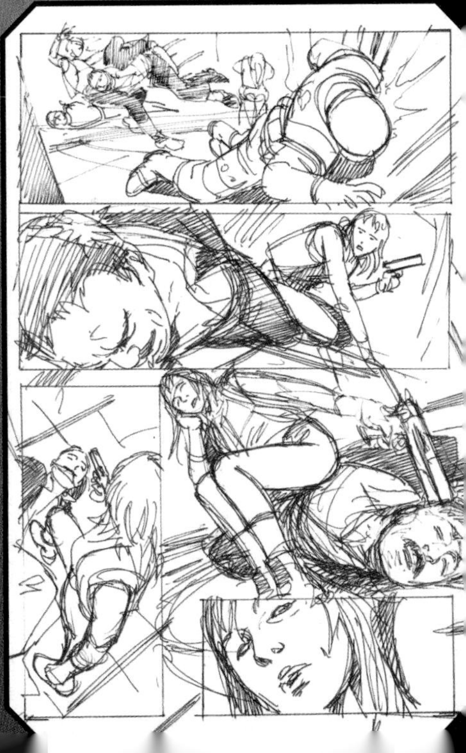

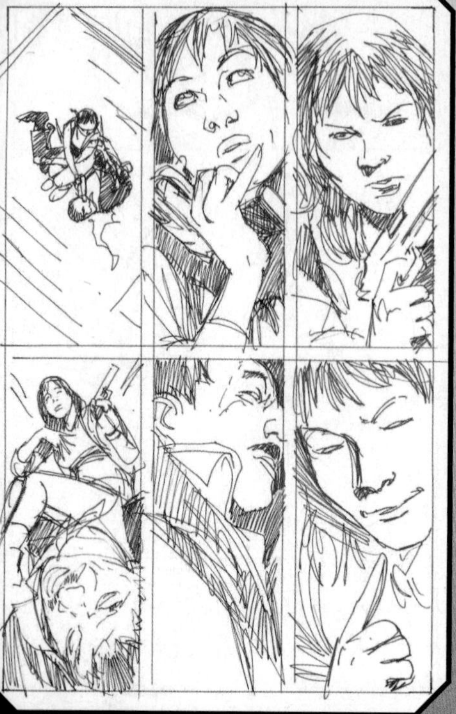

PAGE 18

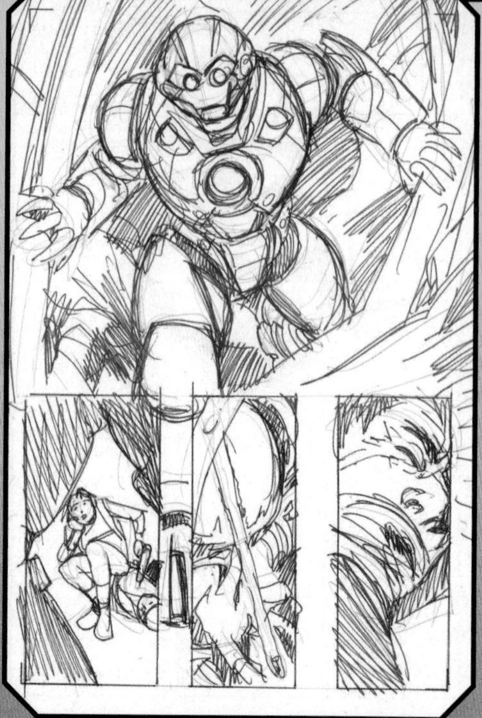

PAGE 19

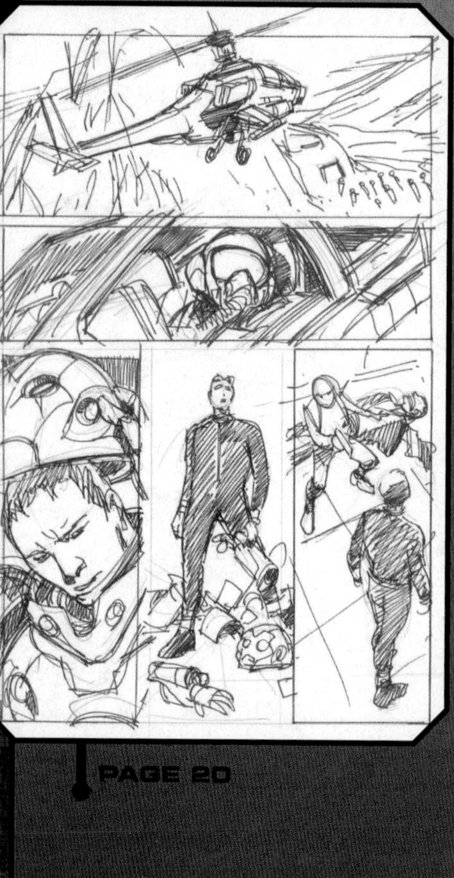

PAGE 20

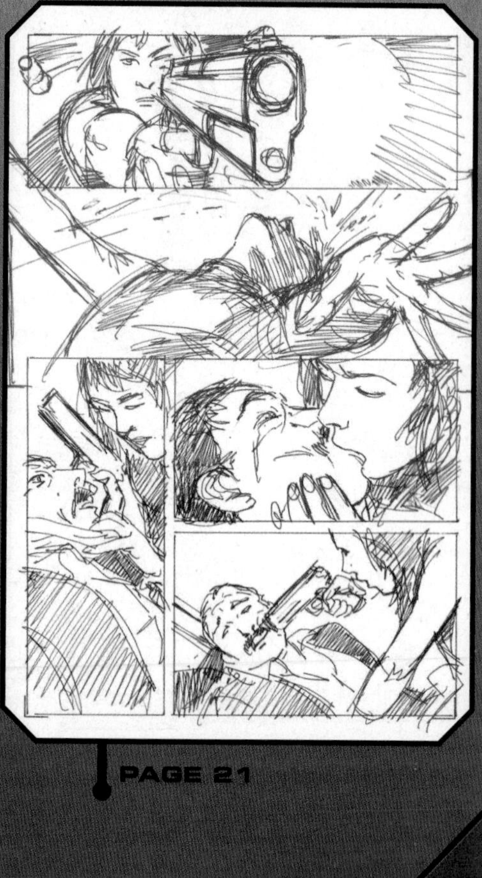

PAGE 21